THE BIBLE AS BOOK

THE HEBREW BIBLE AND THE
JUDAEAN DESERT DISCOVERIES

THE BIBLE AS BOOK
THE HEBREW BIBLE AND THE JUDAEAN DESERT DISCOVERIES

Edited by

EDWARD D. HERBERT & EMANUEL TOV

THE BRITISH LIBRARY
& OAK KNOLL PRESS
in association with The Scriptorium:
Center for Christian Antiquities
2002

DEDICATED TO PROF. BASTIAAN VAN ELDEREN
IN RECOGNITION OF HIS ERUDITION AND
UNTIRING ORGANISATIONAL EFFORTS
ON BEHALF OF SCHOLARSHIP

AND

IN MEMORY OF
DR. MARLIN VAN ELDEREN (1949-2000)

First published 2002 by
The British Library
96 Euston Road
London NW1 2DB

Published exclusively in North and South America by
Oak Knoll Press
310 Delaware Street
New Castle
DE 19720

In association with
The Scriptorium: Center for Christian Antiquities
PO Box 770
Grand Haven
Michigan 49417-0770

© 2002 The Contributors

Cataloguing-in-Publication Data
A CIP record for this book is available from
both The British Library and The Library of Congress

ISBN 1-58456-083-5 (Oak Knoll)
ISBN 0-7123-4726-7 (British Library)

Designed by John Trevitt
Typeset in England by The Skriptorium, Bristol
Printed in England by St Edmundsbury Press, Bury St Edmunds

CONTENTS

Contents

CONTRIBUTORS

Martin G. Abegg Jr, *Trinity Western University*

Philip S. Alexander, *University of Manchester*

George J. Brooke, *University of Manchester*

Sidnie White Crawford, *University of Nebraska-Lincoln*

Stephen C. Daley, *Wycliffe Bible Translators*

Peter W. Flint, *Trinity Western University*

Edward D. Herbert, *International Christian College, Glasgow*

Jesper Høgenhaven, *University of Copenhagen*

Armin Lange, *University of North Carolina at Chapel Hill*

Timothy H. Lim, *University of Edinburgh*

Sarianna Metso, *Albion College*

Orlaith O'Sullivan, *formerly The Scriptorium: Center for Christian Antiquities*

Donald W. Parry, *Brigham Young University*

Harold P. Scanlin, *United Bible Societies*

Shemaryahu Talmon, *Hebrew University, Jerusalem*

Eibert Tigchelaar, *Groningen University*

Emanuel Tov, *Hebrew University, Jerusalem*

Eugene Ulrich, *University of Notre Dame*

James C. VanderKam, *University of Notre Dame*

Arie van der Kooij, *Leiden University*

LIST OF ILLUSTRATIONS

(reproduced between pages 166 and 167)

PREFACE

IT ALL BEGAN at Masada, and in the nearby Scriptorium, on a cold day in the autumn of 1998. It was here that the decision was made to dedicate a special conference in the year 2000 to the texts found in the Judaean Desert. There was no better place to decide upon such a special conference than on the heights of Masada and at a rectangular table in the nearby Scriptorium. At this point, the reader must be wondering whether a scriptorium was discovered at all close to Masada, and also whether there are ever any cold days at that location in the autumn. In fact, the Masada being referred to is not a barren location overlooking the Dead Sea, but rather a luxurious mansion in Grand Haven, USA, overlooking the beautiful Lake Michigan. This Scriptorium is not the famed location in which, according to modern myth, the Qumran 'monks' penned their scrolls or a hitherto unknown scriptorium at Masada, but rather a nearby building housing the Van Kampen Collection of biblical manuscripts and early printed books. These buildings were so named by the late Robert D. Van Kampen, the founder and spiritual father of The Scriptorium: Center for Christian Antiquities. The idea for the conference was also his, and the general concept was worked out in 1998 by Robert Van Kampen and Emanuel Tov. The venue was to be Hampton Court in Herefordshire, England, a place where five similar conferences had been held previously on related topics.

The setting could not have been more beautiful; a fifteenth-century Herefordshire manor house in which the air was filled with the sounds of fine music, and beautiful flower arrangements graced the rooms. At this location, surrounded by woods and farms and far from major universities, the congress attendees discussed the enigma of many a Qumran scroll while walking in the man-made labyrinth of shrubs in the castle gardens, in the woods, or in the fields among the cows.

The spirit behind the meeting was the Executive Director of The Scriptorium, Prof. Bastiaan Van Elderen, a retired Professor of Calvin College, Michigan. Bastiaan's many activities – including his yearly excavations in Wadi Natrun, Egypt, the meetings he organises at the annual Society of Biblical Literature conferences, and the two-year preparations for this conference – belie his status as a retiree. He worked out the framework of the meeting, together with Emanuel Tov and Dr Orlaith O'Sullivan, Curator of the Van Kampen Foundation, and dealt with all the details pertaining to the invitation of twenty scholars from eight countries, together with other specialists who did not read papers. Over the course of time, hundreds of email messages travelled through cyberspace, often on a daily basis, from Grand Haven to Jerusalem and other places. The week before the meeting, when everything was already arranged, Bas shared with us the news of the sudden and tragic death on 12th June of his son, Marlin. Bas was of course unable to attend the conference, and our thoughts were with him throughout.

Edward D. Herbert and Emanuel Tov

This volume is dedicated to Bas in recognition of his untiring efforts in the preparations, both scholarly and organisational, for this and preceding conferences. Bas is a true scholar with vision and an open mind, a man of many interests, and a fine chairman. The volume is also dedicated to the memory of his son, the late Dr. Marlin Van Elderen, who worked tirelessly on the development of ecumenical literature for almost twenty years with the World Council of Churches.

Unfortunately, Mr. Robert Van Kampen did not live to see this conference realised at Hampton Court. Having been ill for some time, he passed away on 29th October 1999 from heart failure. Having graciously supported the publication of the Dead Sea Scrolls, the Introduction volume to that series, vol. XXXIX (Oxford: Clarendon Press, 2002) was dedicated to him.

His place was taken at the conference in 2000 by his wife, Judy Van Kampen, and their daughter and son-in-law, Karla Van Kampen-Pierre and Scott Pierre. They represented the family and the Foundation with dignity, and as the Lady of the Castle, Judy graciously hosted the scholars in *her* house.

It is easy to imagine that scholarship flourished in such a beautiful setting, with ample time being provided for interaction after the presentation of each paper. The opening paper was read by Shemaryahu Talmon, and Emanuel Tov delivered the closing address. At the fireside chat one evening, veteran scholar Geza Vermes reminisced about the early days of the Qumran discoveries and scroll research.

The sessions were skilfully introduced by Dr Orlaith O'Sullivan, who was involved in every stage of the organisation of the conference, from the very beginning to the preparation of the papers appearing in this volume. We want to thank Orlaith for a job well done, with so much grace. Without her involvement, this volume would not have seen the light of day.

We would like to thank all those who worked 'behind the scenes' at the conference, including special thanks to: Bonnie de Nardo, Kayleen Bobbitt, Pat Santucci, Dr Brian Webster, Herb and Kiko Zimmermann, and Bruce O'Connor.

We would also like to thank the staff at the British Library, especially Tony Warshaw and David Way, for their helpfulness and efficiency in seeing the manuscript through to press. We are also grateful to George Mihov of The Skriptorium who undertook the typesetting, Dr Alicia Correa who prepared the indices and Dr. Ian Wilson who undertook much checking of bibliographical entries.

Last, but not least, we want to thank the authors for their fine pieces of research. Without them there would have been neither a conference nor a volume.

Edward D. Herbert and Emanuel Tov
Glasgow – Jerusalem
Easter – Passover 2002

INTRODUCTION

Edward D. Herbert and Emanuel Tov

THE CHANCE DISCOVERY in 1947 of a cave containing scrolls from the period around the turn of the Common Era inaugurated a process of searching that has led to the discovery of fragments of some 900 scrolls from a variety of locations in the vicinity of the Dead Sea. These comprise a wide variety of biblical and non-biblical compositions, which have spawned a burgeoning field of scholarship for more than fifty years. These scrolls have transformed our understanding of the variety of Judaisms which existed in the late Second Temple period - the formative period which gave rise to both Christianity and Rabbinic Judaism. In addition, they have shed considerable light on the history of the biblical text in the period prior to its stabilisation around the end of the first century CE.

The study of these two developing fields of study have remained surprisingly separate – the 'non-biblical' scrolls contributing primarily to the former, and the biblical scrolls to the latter – although an increasing degree of interaction between them has been apparent in recent years. The conference held at Hampton Court, Hereford, in June 2000 sought to encourage the cross-fertilisation between these two fields. It did so, not merely by placing side by side papers which relate respectively to each of the fields, but by examining the scriptural texts and traditions at Qumran in the light of the study of the rewritten scriptural texts and non-biblical compositions, as well as the biblical scrolls.

The focus during the first fifty years of the study of the biblical Dead Sea Scrolls has tended to be on the publication of these texts, the exploration of the textual diversity that characterises them, and the implications of this diversity for understanding the history of the biblical text. A number of papers at the conference further contribute to these important issues. In the last few years, some of the more creative developments have tended to relate to canonical development. This includes how one identifies a biblical text, the degree to which 'biblical' is an inappropriate (anachronistic) term (since a Bible, in terms of a fixed corpus of authoritative writings, does not appear to have existed at the time), and how scriptural authority was perceived and was developing around the turn of the Era. A number of studies at the conference addressed such issues. In particular, study of rewritten scriptural compositions and the usage of Scriptures in non-biblical compositions has provided a rich and creative seam which has been mined by many of the papers.

The conference was well timed at a point when the publication of the Dead Sea Scrolls was almost complete. Indeed, of the biblical and parabiblical scrolls, only the scrolls of Samuel in Cave 4 remained unpublished at the time of the conference. The conference represented the gathering of an international team of key scholars in their fields from eight countries on three continents. Addressing the Scriptures at Qumran on a wide canvas, coupled with the collective expertise represented at Hereford, has resulted in a particularly stimulating conference. The nineteen papers which were presented and the scholarly interaction at that conference have given rise to the current volume.

The first two articles focus on the development of a body of authoritative Scriptures. Shemaryahu Talmon argues that a closed canon of Scriptures arose particularly in response to the fall of Judah to the Romans and the destruction of the Temple. The Qumran Covenanters therefore did not have a fixed canon of Scriptures, but saw themselves as still within the biblical age with a not yet closed corpus of biblical writings in not yet stabilised forms. Armin Lange determines writings that were viewed by the Qumran community as authoritative scripture by identifying which texts were interpreted, quoted or referred to in Essene writings as having religious authority. He then concludes that the different text-types of scrolls relating to certain biblical books were regarded as having equal religious authority.

Three studies of rewritten scriptural texts have implications for our understanding of the nature and development of scriptural authority at Qumran. George Brooke's study on rewritten scriptural texts emphasises the ongoing process of development of scriptural texts and the progressive acceptance of their authority in faith communities, especially during the Second Temple period. He argues that rewritten scriptural texts within the Bible (such as Deuteronomy and Chronicles) and outside the Bible (such as the Temple Scroll and Jubilees) are integral to, and provide evidence of, this process. James VanderKam shows that some of the primary rewritten scriptural texts that are based on the Pentateuch have affinities with the readings of the Samaritan Pentateuch, and argues that such rewritten scriptural texts represent an important component of the evidence relating to the so-called biblical texts. Philip Alexander explores the intertextuality between the developing Enochic and biblical traditions, concluding that the Enochic writers viewed Genesis as in some sense authoritative Scripture as early as the fourth century BCE. Alexander then proposes a possible tradition history for the Enochic literature.

Five articles focus on the Bible as used and quoted in the non-biblical texts from Qumran. Timothy Lim explores the development of better methodology for distinguishing between variants that arise from the source text used by the writer and those that were made by the writer to conform the text to his exegetical purposes. Sarianna Metso explores the biblical quotations in the Community Rule, noting that the quotations generally follow reasonably closely the form of the Masoretic or Septuagint text. She concludes that the quotations were added secondarily to the Rule, with the aim of justifying the rules already in effect in the community, and likens this process to the New Testament's (especially Paul's) use of the Old Testament. Eibert Tigchelaar compares the biblical quotations in the medieval and Cave 4 versions of the Damascus Document. He notes that these quotations had been variously corrupted in both traditions, and comments on possible implications for the growth of the Damascus Document tradition. Jesper Høgenhaven presents a critical text of 4QApocryphal Lamentations (4Q179) and explores the use of biblical quotations and illusions in this composition. Sidnie White Crawford provides a transcription and critical apparatus for 4QTales of the Persian Court (4Q550^{a-c}). She argues that this Qumran text, which was

Introduction

originally styled as 4QprotoEsther araméen, is not evidence that the book of Esther was known at Qumran. Rather it is a royal courtier tale, unrelated to the Book of Esther, which seeks to illustrate the correct behaviour of a Jew in the court of a foreign king.

Seven articles focus on the biblical text or textual criticism in the light of the Qumran discoveries. Emanuel Tov provides an overview of the external characteristics of the biblical manuscripts discovered in the Judaean Desert, and assesses the textual character of these texts, drawing not only on biblical texts but also on the use of biblical texts in non-biblical compositions. Arie van der Kooij compares the practice of textual criticism before the discovery of the Dead Sea Scrolls with the subsequent developments which have occurred in the discipline. Eugene Ulrich notes the almost complete absence of 'sectarian variants' within the biblical Dead Sea Scrolls and offers criteria for distinguishing whether a given variant may be deemed 'sectarian'. Edward Herbert and Donald Parry present studies on the text of 4QSam[a]. Herbert examines, in the light of his work on 4QSam[a], the kaige recension of Samuel in relation to other Samuel witnesses. This leads to a redefinition of the extent of the kaige recension in Samuel and its relationship to the various Greek traditions. Parry lists and reflects on those readings that are unique to 4QSam[a]. Peter Flint and Martin Abegg analyse various aspects of the text of Isaiah. Flint records key data on each of the twenty-two extant Isaiah scrolls and makes several observations regarding the text of Isaiah in the scrolls and regarding the interpretation of Isaiah at Qumran. Abegg's study compares the text of 1QIsa[a] and 1QIsa[b] with that of the Masoretic text of Isaiah. He concludes that 1QIsa[b] is unlikely to be a direct descendant or ancestor of the Masoretic text, but rather represents a parallel stream of tradition, evidencing its own distinct scribal character.

The last two studies relate to the Qumran biblical texts as they are perceived and used today, and represent a further widening of the approaches to the study of biblical texts at Qumran. Stephen Daley examines the influence of the Qumran scrolls on the text-critical decisions exercised in thirteen modern English translations of the Bible by focusing on selected parts of the text of Isaiah and Samuel. Harold Scanlin explores the public's view of the textual fixity of the biblical text, modern translators' use of text-critical data from the Dead Sea Scrolls, and the interplay between these.

It is our hope that these studies together make a significant contribution to the study of the Scriptures at Qumran, and will stimulate further creative thinking in this important field of study.

Easter/Passover 2002
Glasgow/Jerusalem

THE CRYSTALLIZATION OF THE 'CANON OF HEBREW SCRIPTURES' IN THE LIGHT OF BIBLICAL SCROLLS FROM QUMRAN

Shemaryahu Talmon

INTRODUCTION

TACKLING ONCE AGAIN the question of the crystallization of the biblical canon of Hebrew Scripture may be likened to carrying coals to Newcastle, because the issue was researched at length and in depth in the late nineteenth and the early twentieth century. Several major publications, monographs, and numerous articles had set the seal, as it were, on whatever results could be attained on the matter.[1] However, in spite of these investigative efforts, Max Margolis still remarked skeptically in the early twenties, 'whatever we may know about the closing of the canon, it takes our text-books hundreds of pages to say how little we know when the process of canonization[2] began.'[3] Because of this impasse, 'canon' research came to a standstill in the first half of the twentieth century, as A. Jepsen somewhat plaintively pointed out in the late sixties:

Synoptic descriptions of the history of the Old Testament canon, a fair number of which had been available at the end of the last century and still in the first decades of the present one, have not been published for a long time. The material seems to be exhausted, because the available sources, examined from all perspectives, do not provide more information. Only new sources could help solve the many, still open questions.[4]

Such new sources were actually available when Jepsen published his essays, namely the scrolls and scroll fragments of books of the Hebrew Bible which issued from the Qumran caves since the late fifties.[5] Scholars again and again claim that the pre-Christian manuscripts from Qumran, and non-biblical writings which have some pertinence to the issue,[6] have revolutionized scholarly conceptions of the 'canonical process,' and of the transmission history of the biblical text, which is intertwined with it.[7] 'The discovery', says James Sanders, 'has caused a review of nearly every aspect of biblical study including that of questions relating to the canons of Judaism and Christianity and denominations and groups within them.'[8] All theories propounded in the past, were by necessity based on arguments deduced from medieval sources, whereas the new finds contain first-hand evidence, which precedes by more than a thousand years the findings distilled from the earliest 'classical' witnesses to the biblical text. Therefore, a new investigation of these questions is in order.[9] However, it still needs be shown that previously unknown information relating to the evolution and final establishment of the Hebrew Bible canon can indeed be extracted from the scrolls, and that this presumed information requires a radical reassessment of the diverse and conflicting theories put forward in 'pre-Qumran' stages of research. Or, to the contrary, that some hypotheses propounded in the past are not jeopardized by new data.

I fully concur with the opinion that the Qumran finds of (mostly fragmentary) biblical and Bible-related manuscripts have added an important dimension to the investigation of the early stages in the gradual transformation of a corpus of ancient Hebrew writings into what ultimately was accepted as the traditional, fixed and closed Hebrew canon of Scripture, and likewise to the history of their textual transmission. However, at the same time, we must note G. W. Anderson's cautious remark that:

> although the documentary discoveries made in the Judaean Desert since the end of the Second World War have provided abundant materials for the study of the history of the Old Testament text, it is difficult to elicit from them specific evidence of the extent of the canonical corpus which the sect recognized.[10]

I intend in fact to prove that the new evidence does not invalidate conclusions reached by some scholars before the discovery of the Qumran scrolls on the basis of the then available evidence, but rather underpins them.[11]

To put it in a nutshell: I am not concerned with identifying 'pre-canonical', 'proto-canonical,' or 'quasi-canonical' stages of development, nor with a putative 'canonical process'[12] to which the corpus of Hebrew writings presumably was subjected before it was hammered into the definitive Hebrew canon of Scripture.[13] The above imprecise terms can only obfuscate the pivotal issue under consideration by watering down the essentially hard and fast signification of *canon*.[14] In the present context, I solely relate to the specific question of whether the Qumran finds indeed shed light on the crystallization of a *closed* canon of Hebrew Scripture, and on the societal and religious significance and function of that canon.

THE SOCIO-RELIGIOUS FUNCTION OF THE HEBREW BIBLE CANON[15]

I propose to concentrate on the attempt to offer an answer to two pivotal questions:

1. Can we yet identify the stimuli which set in motion the process of conjoining a cluster of ancient Hebrew writings into a compendium, which ultimately was to become the *canon of Hebrew Scripture*?

2. Can we define the *function* of the biblical canon in the historical experience, and the religious thought of Israel in the early post-biblical period?

The following comments and theses will serve as guidelines in my investigation of these questions:

a) The transmission of history- and faith-laden texts, handed down in a community or a nation over generations, is a societal phenomenon of the first magnitude, irrespective of their religious or inspirational significance. In reference to ancient Mesopotamia, William Hallo's category 'canonical texts'[16] parallels the collocation 'stream of tradition', by which Franz Oppenheim defines what 'can be loosely termed the corpus of literary texts, maintained, controlled, and carefully kept alive by a tradition served by successive generations of learned and well-trained scribes.'[17] This definition can be applied to the biblical society only with qualification, because the existence of such a scribal elite in ancient Israel cannot be ascertained beyond doubt, and because non-professional oral transmission supported by public acclaim is not taken into account. It may be said that before the Israelites became the proverbial 'People of the Book', the corpus of literary traditions, in part transmitted orally, and in part handed down in writing, was the 'Book of the People',[18] which constituted the corporate biography of biblical Israel, from Creation to the height of the Second Temple period.[19] The close linkage of literature and life caused, from the outset, the transmission process of these traditions, which culminated in their enclosure in the Hebrew canon of Scripture,[20] to be deeply affected by historical events and religious developments that shaped the profile of the ancient Israelite society.

b) The life of the 'Community of the Renewed Covenant'[21] in history was stressed between the biblical era and the profoundly different mishnaic age. The spiritual universe of its members was strained between their pronounced 'biblical ethos' and an indomitable opposition to the emphatic non-biblical stance of the rabbinic Sages. They conceived of their community as the youngest link in the restored chain of biblical generations, which had snapped with the destruction of the Temple in 586 BCE. Living in the historical reality of the late Second Temple period, the Covenanters nevertheless integrated themselves conceptually into the world of biblical Israel.[22] Therefore, information culled from Qumran sources, which relates or appears to relate to the crystallization of a Hebrew canon of Scripture, on the one hand may be expected to differ substantially from relevant reports in rabbinic sources, and on the other hand to dovetail with facts and attitudes pertaining to the issue which are reflected in the biblical literature.[23]

THE ETYMOLOGY AND THE SIGNIFICATION OF *CANON* IN REFERENCE TO THE HEBREW BIBLE

At this juncture of the discussion, some thought must be given to a clarification of the term *canon* and its conceptual content with reference to the Hebrew Bible. The philological derivations and explanations of the term are adequately reviewed in various pertinent publications.[24] Therefore, it will suffice to bring to mind the evident etymological connection of the Greek term κανων, Latin *canna*, which signifies 'staff' of any kind, with Akkadian *qanû;* Sumerian *qin*, Ugaritc *qn*, Hebrew קנה and Aramaic קני/קניא which severally denote 'reed', 'Schilfrohr', 'roseau', and also 'measuring rod' (especially in Ezekiel 40-42).

Also in the present instance the saying holds true that the tracing of the etymological root of a term does not yet lead to the uncovering of its meaning in specific literary or conceptual contexts. From the above basic meanings derives the use of *canon* as the designation of 'what is exact' or 'marked by straightness', with the further development of the conceptual connotation of 'guideline for human conduct'. In the tradition of the Christian Church, *canon* is synonymous with *rule*, *table of rules*, *regula fidei*, by which the faithful are to be guided in their conduct of life. At the Council of Nicea, the term came to designate the comprehensive corpus of the 'Holy Writ' when the highest ecclesiastical authorities officially legislated the inclusion of the books of the Old and New Testaments in the closed canon of Scripture. The books included were declared to have been written under 'divine inspiration', and the canon in its entirety was invested with normative binding authority, *norma normata*. In the Eastern Church, this status was also conferred upon various Apocrypha and Pseudepigrapha.

7

However, a biblical canon is never universal. The decision of the ecclesiastical authorities did not affect other communities that embraced the Hebrew Bible as the 'Foundation Document' of their respective faiths. Therefore, in an investigation of the crystallization of the phenomenon *Bible Canon*, we are always confronted with a diversity of canons, as James Sanders has recurrently emphasized:[25] Roman Catholic, Protestant, Eastern Orthodox, Samaritan or Jewish.[26] The Jewish Bible canon comprises only the twenty-four books, which in the Christian tradition are part of the Old Testament.[27] Flavius Josephus details twenty-two books which constitute the 'Bible':[28] five books of Moses, thirteen prophetic writings, and four more, which contain hymns and ethical instructions.[29] The Samaritans recognize only the five books of the Pentateuch as their Bible, and the existence of a Covenanters' Bible and its composition remains open to question.[30] In any case, from the last centuries BCE onwards, the varying composition of the biblical canon became signposts of the diverse communities that embraced the Hebrew Bible as a foundation document of their discrete faiths.

It cannot go unnoticed that the Hebrew language does not have any expression which equals *canon*.[31] There is no special term in the Hebrew Bible, or in mishnaic or medieval Hebrew, which comprehensively designates the assemblage of books contained in the biblical compendium. The lack of a technical term does not necessarily prove the absence of a concept. However, in the present instance, the absence of a term gives reason for assuming that the concept of 'canon' is late. Scholars indeed have reasoned that the second and third parts of the traditional canon, viz. the prophetic books, נביאים, and the collection of Hagiographa, כתובים, were combined with the older first part, the Pentateuch, תורה, only in a rather late stage of development.[32]

Rabbinic tradition refers to the closed biblical canon as תורה, (the) 'Law',[33] in an 'expanded' application of the term which mostly denotes the five books of the Pentateuch, or else by כתבי הקדש, 'sacred writings'. In some pertinent instances in which כתב is employed as a denominative verb derived from the compound כתבי הקדש, it does not define the act of writing, viz. the authoring a book, but rather denotes the inclusion of a book in the biblical corpus.[34] Following upon a statement in which the canonical books are itemized (*b. Baba Batra* 14b-15a), the question is raised 'who wrote them, ומי כתבן?', and is answered as follows:[35]

Moses wrote his book [ספרו] and the section(s) [פרשה] of Balaam[36] and Job.[37] Joshua wrote his book, and eight verses in the Torah.[38] Samuel wrote his book[39] and the books of Judges and Ruth. David wrote the Book of Psalms with (the assistance of) ten elders, the first man (viz. Adam), Melchizedek and Abraham, and Moses (Ps 90), and Heman (Ps 88), and Jeduthun (Ps 39; 62; 77), and Asaph (Ps 50; 61; 73-83; cf. Neh 12:46; 2 Chron 29:30; *et al.*), and the three sons of Korah (Ps 42-44; 47-49). Jeremiah wrote his book, and the book of Kings and Lamentations. Hezekiah and his (council or) company (cf. Prov 25:1) wrote [כתבו] Isaiah, Proverbs, Song of Songs, and Ecclesiastes. The men of the Great Synagogue [אנשי כנסת הגדולה] wrote [כתבו] Ezekiel, and the Twelve, Daniel, and the Scroll of Esther. Ezra wrote his book, and the genealogies in Chronicles down to his time (עד לו, or: up to the word לו, 2 Chron 21:12).

This response to the question ומי כתבן in reference to the books of the Bible shows that the Sages were as nescient of the actual facts as we are. In some instances, כתב signifies 'authorship'. In others, it surely indicates the inclusion of a book in the *canon*, presumably effected by a committee, because committees, like '(King) Hezekiah's Council' or the 'Men of the (spurious) Great Synagogue', certainly cannot be accredited with the authoring of a book.

The Crystallization of the 'Canon of Hebrew Scriptures'

Rabbinic tradition also refers to the biblical *canon* by the simplistic and rather indistinct collocations ספרים, 'books,' or כ"ד ספרים, 'twenty-four (books)',[40] which in no way disclose the 'inspired' character of the works in question. What is evidently decisive in the last count is the function of the corpus as a touchstone for identifying as bona fide members of the community all those who adhere by it, and all others as excluded outsiders.

THE PERTINENCE OF 'LOST BOOKS' CITED IN HEBREW SCRIPTURES AND IN THE COVENANTERS' LITERATURE TO THE ISSUE OF *CANON*

We can now turn to a consideration of the questions whether (a) any information relating to the crystallization of a biblical canon can be elicited from the Hebrew Scriptures, and (b) to what degree such information, if found, dovetails with or differs substantially from evidence distilled from the Covenanters' literature.

a) It can be said from the outset that there is no explicit or implicit statement in the Hebrew Scriptures which can give reason to think that in the biblical period a council of any kind, at any time, ever debated the establishment of a corpus of authoritative writings, or enacted the inclusion of a book in such a corpus. It is exactly the absence of any supervising agency or agencies which may explain the exceeding diversity of literary genres, linguistic competence, and religious significance, which marks the books accumulated in the compendium. This fact alone engenders the conclusion that these writings had gained public acclaim, and because of their popularity at first were orally transmitted from generation to generation, and later handed down in writing. In the words of Franz Rosenzweig, 'the Hebrew Bible was born out of the whole span of life of a people, and the whole compass of a national literature.'[41] Therefore, hero tales like *inter alia* the reports on the feats of Jephthah, Samson, or David's Warriors (2 Samuel 23) found acceptance in the corpus next to works of an evident 'inspirational' character, like the Torah, and the books of the Prophets and Psalms. The *vox populi*, rather than formal decisions of authoritative institutions, assured their inclusion in Israel's cultural legacy.

At this juncture of the discussion, another important fact must be brought under review. The twenty-four books contained in the Hebrew biblical canon are only a part of a much larger *fundus* of literary compositions which were current in the biblical age. Various authors, compilers, and redactors of the books included in the canon severally refer by their title to another twenty-four works which are no longer preserved, and in some instances also provide quotations from their texts.[42]

These 'lost' writings are mostly mentioned in the historiographies Kings and Chronicles. With some exceptions, they fall into two main literary categories, which are prominently present in the biblical canon:

1) Historiographical accounts, such as ספר דברי הימים למלכי ישראל, 'Chronicles of the Kings of Israel' (1 Kings 14:19; 15:31 *et al.*), and דברי עזיהו, 'Acts of (King) Uzziah' (2 Chronicles 26:22).

2) Works of the prophetic genre, some of which are ascribed to prophets who also authored books contained in the biblical canon, e.g., דברי שמואל הנביא, 'Words (pronouncements?) of the prophet Samuel' (1 Chronicles 29:29; 2 Chronicles 2:29);

9

דברי שמעיה הנביא, 'Words of Shemaiah the Prophet' (2 Chronicles 12:15); and מדרש הנביא עדו, 'Midrash (work?) of the Prophet Iddo' (2 Chronicles 13:22), which may be identical with חזות עדו החזה, 'Vision of Iddo the Seer'[43] (2 Chronicles 9:29), and דברי עדו החזה, 'Words of Iddo the Seer' (2 Chronicles 12:15).

Only a few 'lost' works are cited in other books: ספר מלחמות יהוה, the 'Book of the Wars of YHWH' (Numbers 21:14); ספר הישר, the 'Book of Yashar' (Joshua 10:13 and 1 Samuel 10:25), which may be identical with ספר השיר (1 Kings 8:13), and similar in character to the 'Book of the Wars of YHWH'.[44] Another two 'records' which relate only indirectly to the history of Israel are adduced in the book of Esther: ספר הזכרנות דברי הימים, the 'Chronicle of Annals' (Esther 6:1), and ספר דברי הימים למלכי מדי ופרס, the 'Chronicles of the Kings of Media and Persia' (Esther 10:2).[45]

The biblical sources do not explicate the criteria on the strength of which twenty-four books were allowed to enter the compendium of sanctified compositions, whereas another twenty-four known and cited works were not included. In any case, nothing indicates that the inclusion or non-inclusion was legislated by an official authority. It would seem rather that, as already noted, public acclaim was the decisive factor:

canon (is) a logical development, but also determined by fortuitous circumstances [...] canon only reflects sanctity which a given era chanced to assign to a given number of books. The books themselves are in part much more important, and in part much less important than the act of canonization.[46]

Compositions which earned popular acclaim were transmitted from father to son, and from teacher to disciple, and thus were preserved, whereas the above mentioned works, still known to biblical authors who quoted them, and probably also to their audiences, were not handed down, and as a result were ultimately lost. Only books and records which were continuously tradited could find a place in the canon of Scripture.

It appears that in a later rabbinic source the attempt was made to explain the non-inclusion of the lost works, ascribed to manifestly legitimate prophets, in the corpus of the 'twenty-four':

Many prophets arose in Israel....but only a prophecy which had validity for generations (viz. did not only pertain to specific historical circumstances) was written (viz. was included in the biblical corpus),[47] a prophecy which did not have validity for generations was not written (included), הרבה נביאים עמדו להם לישראל [...] נבואה שהוצרכה לדורות נכתבה, נבואה שלא הוצרכה לדורות לא נכתבה (b. Meg. 14a).

b) In view of the Covenanters' insistent and ostentatious identification of their community as the youngest link in the generation chain of biblical Israel, it cannot cause any surprise that in reference to the crystallization of a biblical canon, their writings mirror the very same circumstances and attitudes which can be observed in the Hebrew Bible. No discussion or even a hint of the reasons which put on foot the inclusion or non-inclusion of a work among the biblical books can be found in a yaḥad document, nor a mention of an authoritative committee or council that ever legislated in these matters.

Like biblical authors, the authors of yaḥad compositions cite works of manifest significance which are not preserved among the Qumran finds. A prominent example is the ספר ההגו/י, which probably contained essential Covenant rules, יסודי הברית (CD X, 6, cf. 1QSa I, 5-7), and was studied by members of the community from their youth, ומן נעוריו לל[מ]דהו בספר ההגו/י (1QSa I, 6-7). Priests were expected to be especially knowledgeable of its contents. Whenever ten members congregated, a priest well versed in the teachings of this book, כהן מבונן בספר ההגו/י, should be present to address juridical and cultic problems which may arise (CD XIII, 2; cf. XIV, 6-7; cf. 4Q270 7 i 15-16; 4Q266 11).

Furthermore, we find references in Qumran documents to no longer extant historiographical works of *yahad* vintage, which resemble the mentions of such records in Kings and Chronicles. Of special interest is a book, מספר, which appears to have been an account in the style of a chronicle (cf. 2 Chronicles 24:27). In this work major events in the Covenanters' history were recorded, from their putative 'Exodus' or 'deportation' from the Land, after the destruction of the temple of Jerusalem in 586 BCE, and their experiences in 'exile,' to their 'Return', winding up with a mention of the yet uncharted future age termed אחרית הימים:

the returners (and/or repenters) of Israel [...] who had left the land of Judah, they are the elect of Israel, the men of renown, who (will) arise באחרית הימים. Here is the roster of their names according to their families, and the appointed time of their constitution (as a community), the account of their afflictions during the years of their sojourn, שני מגוריהם (in exile or 'abroad').[48] Here is the exposition of their affairs (CD IV, 2-6).[49]

I suggest that this historiographical compilation may have resembled the equally 'lost' biblical 'Book of Genealogy(ies)' ספר היחש (Nehemiah 7:5). Both works to a degree paralleled biblical reports in the books of Haggai, Zechariah, Malachi, and Ezra-Nehemiah relating to the post-exilic Age of Restoration, and like them recorded rosters of the names of returnees, according to their families (Ezra 2 = Nehemiah 7; Ezra 8:1-14; 10:16-43; Nehemiah 3:1-32; 10:1-28 *et sim.*), intertwined with itemized records of events which befell them. The comprehensive biblical report culminates in an unmistakeable reference to 'the great and terrible day of Yahweh' (Malachi 3:4-6), which in the Qumran text is designated אחרית הימים.

The postulation that the Covenanters did not consider their assemblage of biblical writings a closed canon of Holy Writ can be supported by the following considerations. The proposed identification of a 'Qumran Bible canon' consisting of two complete and closed parts – ספר מושה and [דברי הנביאים], Pentateuch and Prophets; and a third part, presumably designated in 4QMMT בדויד, under which were subsumed the Hagiographa,[50] does not stand up to scrutiny.[51] The undefined status of the כתובים,[52] the third component of the Bible canon in the Covenanters' tradition shows in the pesher-like extrapolation of the verse: ונשאתם את סכות מלככם ואת כיון צלמיכם כוכב אלהיכם אשר עשיתם לכם (Amos 5:26) in CD VII, 14-18. The collocation סכות מלככם is taken to refer to the Pentateuch, ספרי התורה הם סוכת המלך; and כיון צלמיכם is understood to represent the books of the Prophets, וכיון הצלמים הם ספרי הנביאים. However, there is no mention at all of the כתובים, the third major component of the canon, although the Amos passage offers another expression which could have been used for the purpose, namely כוכב אלהיכם. Surprisingly, to this term a pesher is appended, which is totally unrelated to the matter of *canon*: והכוכב הוא דורש התורה, 'the star is (refers to) the interpreter of the Torah.'

Qumran literature evinces not only an 'open-ended biblical canon', as is argued, but rather gives witness to what I have termed a 'Living Bible',[53] still in *status nascendi*. This proposition can be substantiated *inter alia* by the variant wording and the different order of 'canonical' psalms in the Psalms Scroll of Cave 11 (11QPs^a).[54] The apparent rearrangement resembles the 'disorderly' consecution of the psalms ascribed to David in the biblical Psalter. The *finis* notation appended to Psalm 72:20: כלו תפלות דוד בן ישי,

'(here) ends the (collection of) prayers of David son of Jesse', which, like in a ring composition, serves as a counterpart to the superscription in which this song is related to his son Solomon, לשלמה (72:1), evidently was meant to indicate that David's songs were assembled in the first 'two books' of the Psalter (Psalms 1-72). However, in actual fact, more compositions with a 'davidic' superscription are interspersed in the latter part of the Psalter (Psalms 101; 103, and possibly 104; 108; 109; 138-142; 145).

Further, eight (or possibly nine)[55] additional compositions, are intromitted in 11QPs[a] between 'canonical' psalms.[56] In one of the added pieces, 'David's Songs' (11QPs[a] XXVII), the king is credited with having written altogether 4050 (liturgical) compositions. Some of these in fact may be contained in other Qumran fragments of Psalms scrolls.[57] The precise division of the sum total of David's songs into discrete categories, which were to be severally recited every day, every Sabbath, and every festival throughout the year, implies that their 'standing' most probably equalled that of the 150 (Masoretic Text) or 151 (Septuagint) Psalms preserved in the biblical Psalter. However, nothing is said to explain their non-inclusion in the biblical book.[58]

Numerous more examples of variances between Qumran manuscripts and the MT and Versions substantiate my thesis that the Covenanters conceived of themselves as living in the biblical age and in the conceptual universe of biblical man. Like the Chronicler and other biblical authors, *yahad* authors approached the not yet closed corpus of biblical writings and their not yet stabilized textual form 'from within', with some not circumscribed leeway for legitimate variation, which now escapes definition.

The efforts to find references to a biblical canon in the Covenanters' literature make light of major traits which characterize the term and concept of 'canon,' which *per definitionem* designates a clearly demarcated and precisely defined closed corpus of textually fixed or at least stable literary works, to which nothing can be added, and from which nothing can be detracted.

THE CRYSTALLIZATION OF A CANON OF SCRIPTURES IN POST-BIBLICAL JUDAISM

An analysis of information in early rabbinic sources, which directly or indirectly pertains to the crystallization of a canon of Scripture, on the one hand (a) reveals similarities with the biblical and the Qumran evidence, and on the other hand (b) discloses telling differences.

a) No proof can be adduced from sources of mainstream Judaism to underpin the assumption that in the Second Temple era, or in the period immediately after the Roman capture of Jerusalem, an official agency ever legislated the inclusion of a book in a canon of Scripture. Equally, neither in the Apocrypha, nor in Hellenistic writings can statements be found which speak of 'academies', 'synods' or any other official body that decided on the *inclusion* of a book among the 'holy writings' or decreed the 'canonization' of the corpus. Moreover, as has been noted, neither the Samaritans' nor the Covenanters' literature preserve evidence that any such institution ever had been active in these separatist communities.

b) Even more striking is the absence of any statement relevant to the issue in the voluminous rabbinic literature. The often publicized hypothesis that at the 'Synod of

The Crystallization of the 'Canon of Hebrew Scriptures'

Jabneh-Jamnia', which convened close to the end of the first century CE, the (pharisaic) rabbis formally decided which books were to be included in the Jewish canon and enacted its closure, is absolutely untenable.[59] D. E. Aune has convincingly demonstrated[60] that the 'Myth of the Jabneh Synod' was introduced into modern scholarship by H. E. Ryle and F. Buhl,[61] who seemingly elaborated an argument by H. Graetz, who on his part had developed a reference to this effect, which he had found in Spinoza's *Tractatus Theologico-Politicus*.[62] However, although the hypothesis has no leg to stand upon it is still propagated in some contemporary scholarly publications.[63]

c) The concept of *canon* has a retrospective thrust; *canon* is the *kerygma* of the past. It defines a fixed corpus of literature to which nothing can be added, and from which nothing can be removed: 'A "canon" is thus by definition a way of setting limits to the books recognized as holy.'[64] The closing of the Bible canon reveals the Sages' conviction that the biblical era had come to an end. They 'sensed that their time was different from the biblical period.'[65] A new era had begun, and with it a process of accumulation of their own literary products which would culminate in the establishment of a canon of rabbinic writings, foremost in the form of the Mishnah.[66]

d) The incompatibility of the world of the Sages and the world of the Bible is encapsulated in the pithy saying 'the language of Torah (viz. the Bible) is one matter, the language of the Sages another', לשון תורה לעצמו לשון חכמים לעצמו (*b. Abod. Zar.* 58b; *b. Men.* 65a): the distinction pertains not to evident linguistic characteristics, but rather aims at highlighting the fundamental and all-embracing heterogeneity which set off the post-Great Divide world of the Sages from the contrastive pre-Great Divide world of biblical Israel.[67]

e) From here arose the insistence on a clear-cut differentiation between the closed Bible canon, תורה שבכתב, literally 'the written law', but in fact a term which defines 'the law' incorporated in the כתבי הקדש,[68] and תורה שבעל פה, the 'oral law', viz. the teaching of the Sages,[69] who never attempted to integrate any of their own literary creations into the Bible canon. There was no crossing of the lines.

f) Reports in the rabbinic literature concerning the composition of the closed Jewish Bible canon, show that 'exclusion rather than inclusion marked the closing of the collection.'[70]

These reports pertain foremost, almost exclusively to two categories of books:[71]

1) Extraneous works, termed חיצונים, were to be prevented from entering the canon, such as various writings, which in the Bible of the Church constitute the Apocrypha, among them also the Proverbs of Ben Sira, although this work is severally quoted in rabbinic literature.[72] The Hagiographa, the least defined of the three major divisions of the canon, was especially in danger of being infiltrated by writings of popular appeal, some of which were contaminated by heretical beliefs.

2) Books already fully integrated into the established canon of Scripture, whose *exclusion* seemingly is brought under consideration.

The discussions on these matters are marked by two technical terms:

a) בקשו לגנוז, 'it was (variously) suggested to withdraw from circulation' the books of Ezekiel, Proverbs, Song of Songs, and Esther;

b) any book שאינו מטמא את הידים, literally 'which does not make the hands unclean', namely Ecclesiastes and Esther, should also be excluded.[73]

All debates on these issues, however, turned out to be scholastic exercises which had no effect whatsoever on the already fixed composition of the canon. All biblical books that were brought under scrutiny under one, or in some instances under both of the above headings, have remained constituent parts of the biblical canon to this day: Ezekiel, Ecclesiastes, Proverbs, Song of Songs, and Esther.

In any case, the above rabbinic statements postdate the 'Great Divide,' viz. the first century CE. Therefore, they cannot give witness to the constitution of the biblical corpus of books, nor to the presumed emergence of a Hebrew biblical canon in mainstream Judaism at the height of the Second Temple period or in the community of the pre-Christian Covenanters.

THE 'GREAT DIVIDE'

We lack means for dating with confidence the waning of the biblical epoch, and the onset of the 'Age of the Sages'. However, with respect to the question of the canon, it may be considered *communis opinio* that the 'Great Divide' between the two eras should probably be located in the late first or in the second century CE. At that time, Judaism was subjected to various political, societal and religious upheavals: the wars against Rome and the Roman conquest of the land, the capture of Jerusalem and the destruction of the temple, and the deportation and/or emigration of large contingents of the Judaean population. The political vicissitudes caused by external forces in part coincided with an internal socio-religious disintegration, which resulted in the emergence of diverse separatist communities and sects.[74] This mesh of centrifugal challenges threatened the unity of Judaism and demanded centripetal responses, which at first were intuitive, and ensuingly determinate. The more deeply disruptive the factors which impacted the socio-political and religious structure of Judaism, the stronger was the will to counter the negative effects by cultivating stabilizing values.

I propose to single out two factors which played a decisive role in this development:

1. The fall of Judah to the Romans, the ensuing dispersion of large contingents of Judaeans through deportation and/or emigration, and the establishment of independent or semi-independent Diaspora communities necessitated the promulgation of unifying commonly shared values, by which all constituent branches of Jewry would abide. Among the responses to this challenge, pride of place was accorded to a textually standardized, clearly demarcated, precisely defined, and *closed Hebrew canon of Scripture*, invested with exclusive authority (see below).

2. The destruction of the Temple and the cessation of the sacrificial service brought about their substitution by Synagogue and devotional prayer service, together with the introduction of readings from Scripture.[75] Lections from the Torah and the Prophets (Haftaroth) became part of the synagogal service on Sabbaths, and on two weekdays (Mondays and Thursdays). Books of the Hagiographa were read on festival days, foremost the Five Megilloth (which for this reason are conjoined in the canon): Song of Songs on Passover, Ruth on Pentecost, Ecclesiastes on Tabernacles, Lamentations on the Ninth of Ab (in commemoration of the destruction of the First, and later also of the Second Temple), and on Purim the Book of Esther, which is altogether absent from the Qumran finds.[76] These practical necessities furthered the crystallization of a clearly circumscribed and fixed canon of Scripture.[77]

None of these events and developments affected the Covenanters' community:[78]

1. The existence of the community in history ended before the fall of Judah and Jerusalem to the Romans, and the destruction of the Temple in 70 CE. These cataclysmic events have left no trace in their writings.

2. The *yaḥad* seemingly conferred the status of 'holy writ' upon the Book of Jubilees, which in matters calendrical was seen to be as authoritative as was the Torah of Moses with respect to the rules pertaining to the general conduct of life (CD XVI, 1-4). The same status was possibly also bestowed upon the ספר ההגו/י and the Temple Scroll. The readiness to widen the corpus of 'holy writings' contrasts sharply with the Sages' refusal to accord to any but the twenty-four books of the biblical canon the status of binding authority.

3. The Covenanters abstained from the sacrificial service in the Temple while it was still functioning. They did indeed institutionalize a synagogue-type devotional worship, probably before it took root in mainstream (pharisaic) Judaism after the destruction of the Temple. However, all references in the Covenanters' literature which are germane to the issue indicate that their devotional service consisted exclusively of 'prayer texts', without any mention of readings from Scripture as a constitutive element.[79] Thus, their pattern of worship did not require the establishment of a definitely closed 'canon of biblical books', nor a standardized transmission of their text.

In sum, the Qumran biblical scrolls and documents do not offer any decisive new evidence pertaining to the crystallization of a closed canon of Hebrew Scriptures, worded in a fixed or essentially standardized text.

NOTES

1 It will suffice to put on record the following works: J. Fürst, *Der Kanon des Alten Testaments nach den Überlieferungen in Talmud und Midrasch* (Leipzig: Dörffling & Franke, 1868); Heinrich Graetz, 'Der Abschluss des Kanons des Alten Testament und die Differenz von kanonischen und extrakanonischen Büchern nach Josephus und Talmud', *Monatschrift für Geschichte und Wissenschaft des Judentums*, 35 (1886), 281-98; G. Wildeboer, *Die Entstehung des Alttestamentlichen Kanons*, trans. by F. Risch (Gotha: Perthes, 1891); Frants Buhl, *Canon and Text of the Old Testament*, trans. by John Macpherson (Edinburgh: T. & T. Clark, 1892); Karl Budde, *Der Kanon des Alten Testaments* (Giessen: Ricker, 1900); Herbert Edward Ryle, *The Canon of the Old Testament* (London: Macmillan, 1892). A comprehensive bibliography is provided *int. al.* by Sid Z. Leiman, *The Canonization of Hebrew Scripture: The Talmudic and Midrashic Evidence*, Transactions of the Conneticut Academy of Arts and Sciences, 47 (Hamden, CT: Archon Books, 1976), and in *The Canon and Masorah of the Hebrew Bible*, ed. by Sid Z. Leiman (New York: Ktav, 1974). See further Brevard S. Childs, *Introduction to the Old Testament as Scripture* (Philadelphia: Fortress Press, 1979), pp. 46-99, and other standard introductions to the Old Testament, foremost Otto Eissfeldt, *Einleitung in das Alte Testament*. 3. neubearbeitete Auflage (Tübingen: Mohr-Siebeck, 1964), pp. 757-81, = *The Old Testament: An Introduction* trans. by Peter R. Ackroyd (Oxford: Blackwell, 1964; repr. 1974), pp. 560-76.

2 For the notion and the term 'process of canonization', see the informative discussion by James A. Sanders, 'The Scrolls and the Canonical Process', in *DSSAFY*, II, pp. 1-23.

3 See Max L. Margolis, 'How the Song of Songs Entered the Canon', in *The Song of Songs: A Symposium*, ed. by W. H. Schoff (Philadelphia: JPS, 1924), pp. 9-17.

4 A. Jepsen, 'Zur Kanongeschichte des Alten Testaments', *ZAW*, 71 (1959), 114-36 (p. 114): 'Zusammenfassende Darstellungen der alttestamentlichen Kanongeschichte, deren es am Ende des vorigen Jahrhunderts und noch in den ersten Jahrzehnten des gegenwärtigen mehrere gab, sind lange nicht erschienen. Der Stoff scheint erschöpft zu sein, da die vorhandenen Quellen nicht mehr hergeben

und allen Seiten hin befragt sind. Nur neue Quellen können weiterhelfen, um die noch offenen Fragen, und deren sind nicht wenige, zu lösen'.

5 Jepsen did not take these finds into consideration, because in his view the Hebrew Bible canon attained its final form only in the third or fourth century CE (Jepsen, 'Kanongeschichte', p. 132): 'Der jüdische Kanon war bis in das 3. und 4. Jh. hinein nocht nicht abgegrenzt; die rabbinischen Entscheidungen des 1. Jh.s sind also nicht sofort überall durchgedrungen.' (a reference to the 'myth' that the Jewish canon presumably was closed at the Synod of Jabneh-Jamnia (see below, 8-9 and notes 50-53).

6 One often neglects to bring into play biblical fragments discovered at other sites in the Judaean Desert (Masada, Murabba'at, Wadi Seiyal and Naḥal Ḥever), which are relevant to the matter under review. See my comments in Shemaryahu Talmon, 'The Old Testament Text', in *The Cambridge History of the Bible*, vol. I, ed. by P. R. Ackroyd and C. F. Evans (Cambridge: Cambridge University Press, 1970), pp. 159-99 (pp. 182-92); repr. in *QHBT*, pp. 1-41 (pp. 24-34).

7 James A. Sanders highlighted the interconnection in numerous publications. See among others James A. Sanders, *From Sacred Story to Sacred Text* (Philadelphia: Fortress Press, 1987) and James A. Sanders, 'Text and Canon: Concepts and Method', *JBL*, 98 (1979), 5-29.

8 James A. Sanders, 'Canon', in *ABD*, I, p. 841.

9 See I. H. Eybers, 'Some Light on the Canon of the Qumran Sect', in *Papers Read at 5th Meeting of Die Ou Testamentiese Werkgemeenskap in Suid-Afrika* (1961), pp. 1-9; republished in Leiman, *Canon and Masorah*, pp. 23-36.

10 G. W. Anderson, 'Canonical and Non-Canonical', in *Cambridge History*, pp. 113-59 (p. 149).

11 See my recent discussion of the issues involved in Shemaryahu Talmon, 'Textual Criticism: The Ancient Versions', in *Text in Context: Essays by Members of the Society for Old Testament Study*, ed. by Andrew D. H. Mayes (Oxford: Oxford University Press, 2000), pp. 141-70.

12 Eissfeldt, *Einleitung* speaks of 'Kanonbildung', 'Hergang der Kanonbildung', 'Werdegang des Kanons' etc., and has been credited with thus introducing into the discussion the concept of 'canonical process'. However, see J. S. Bloch, *Studien zur Geschichte der althebräischen Literatur* (Leipzig: Leiner, 1875), p. 15.

13 I have tried to trace these developmental stages in Shemaryahu Talmon, 'Heiliges Schrifttum und Kanonische Bücher aus jüdischer Sicht – Überlegungen zur Ausbildung der Grösse "Die Schrift" im Judentum', in *Mitte der Schrift? Ein jüdisch-christliches Gespräch: Texte des Berner Symposions vom 6.-12. Januar 1985*, ed. by Martin Klopfenstein and others (Bern: Peter Lang, 1987), pp. 45-79; cf. Hartmut Gese, 'Die dreifache Gestaltwerdung des Alten Testaments', in *jüdisch-christliches Gespräch*, pp. 299-328.

14 The identification of 'pre-', 'proto-', and 'quasi-masoretic' stages in the development of the Masoretic Text cannot be applied to the investigation of the phenomenon 'Canon'.

15 My use of the term 'function' differs somewhat from its employment by J. A. Sanders, 'Adaptable for Life: The Nature and Function of Canon', in *Magnalia Dei: The Mighty Acts of God. Essays on the Bible and Archaeology in Memory of G. Ernest Wright*, ed. by Frank Moore Cross, Werner E. Lemke, and Patrick D. Miller, Jr. (New York: Doubleday, 1976), pp. 531-60.

16 William W. Hallo, 'The Concept of Canonicity in Cuneiform and Biblical Literature: A Comparative Appraisal', in *The Biblical Canon in Comparative Perspective. Scripture in Context 4*, ed. by K. Lawson Younger, Jr., William W. Hallo and Bernard Frank Batto, Ancient Near Eastern Texts and Studies, 11 (Lewiston, NY: Mellen Press, 1991), pp. 1-19 (p. 12).

17 A. Leo Oppenheim, *Ancient Mesopotamia: Portrait of a Dead Civilization*, rev. 2nd edition (Chicago: University of Chicago Press, 1977), p. 13.

18 The present framework does not allow for bringing under consideration the later written transmission of individual and composite oral traditions and their ensuing 'inlibration,' the proliferation of the medium of 'writing' in the Second Temple period, and the impact of these processes on the crystallization of the *Canon of Scripture*. See my comments pertaining to this issue in Talmon, 'Heiliges Schrifttum', esp. pp. 54-65.

19 Cf. Josephus, *Contra Apionem* I, pp. 39-41.

20 See Annemarie Ohler, *Studying the Old Testament from Tradition to Canon*, trans. by David Cairns (Edinburgh: T&T Clark, 1985).

21 For this designation, see Shemaryahu Talmon, 'The Community of the Renewed Covenant: Between Judaism and Christianity', in *CRC*, pp. 3-24 (pp. 7-8).

22 See Shemaryahu Talmon, 'Between the Bible and the Mishnah', in *The World of Qumran from Within: Collected Studies* (Jerusalem: Magnes Press; Leiden: Brill, 1989), pp. 11-52.

23 In respect to the transmission of the biblical texts it can be said that the rather restricted textual divergence between diverse copies of a biblical book found at Qumran approximates the types of variants between diverging versions of a text preserved in the Masoretic Text. See Talmon, 'The Old Testament Text', pp. 184-90.

24 For a concise and informative survey with ample documentation, see among others Eugene Ulrich, 'The Canonical Process, Textual Criticism, and Latter Stages in the Composition of the Bible', in *Shaᶜarei Talmon, Studies in the Bible, Qumran, and the Ancient Near East presented to Shemaryahu Talmon,* ed. by Michael Fishbane and Emanuel Tov, with the assistance of Weston W. Fields (Winona Lake, IN: Eisenbrauns, 1992), pp. 267-91 (pp. 267-76); Eugene Ulrich, 'Canon', *EDSS,* I, pp. 117-20; S. Talmon, 'Heiliges Schrifttum', pp. 45-79; Sanders, 'Canon'.

25 See among others James A. Sanders, *Canon and Community* (Philadelphia: Fortress Press, 1984).

26 Jon D. Levenson, *The Hebrew Bible, the Old Testament, and Historical Criticism* (Louisville: Westminster/John Knox Press, 1993), p. 122.

27 See among others Harry M. Orlinsky, 'The Canonization of the Bible and the Exclusion of the Apocrypha', in *Essays in Biblical Culture and Translation,* ed. by Harry M. Orlinsky (New York: Ktav, 1974), pp. 257-86.

28 *Contra Apionem,* I, 38-42.

29 Only if one assumes that in this roster Ruth was tacitly conjoined with Judges and Lamentations with Jeremiah would that tradition equal the Jewish Bible of twenty-four books. It should, though, be noted that Josephus never quotes Daniel or Esther.

30 The conjectural restitution of a specific 'Qumran Bible', which supposedly was constituted of the twenty-four books of the Hebrew Bible (although no fragment of the Book of Esther was found at Qumran) together with 1 Enoch, Ben Sira (Sirach) and Tobit, is highly implausible. See *DSSB,* p. 199.

31 To quote Max L. Margolis, *The Hebrew Scriptures in the Making* (Philadelphia: JPS, 1922), p. 86, 'The term canon is Christian [...] the word Semitic [...] the thing itself Jewish'.

32 I believe that the first to propagate this notion was Bloch, *Studien,* p. 15: 'Der Mangel aber einer hebräischen Gesamtbezeichnung (for *canon*) lehrt unwiderleglich, dass die Sammlung der letzten Theile (Prophets and Hagiographa), nicht mit den älteren (Pentateuch) zu einem Corpus vereinigt, sondern dass diese Vereinigung erst in einer sehr späten Zeit erfolgte. Der hebräische Kanon besteht demnach aus drei verschiedenen Büchersammlungen die ursprünglich nicht vereinigt, erst wegen ihres späteren, langjährigen, gleichmässigen Gebrauches, sowie ihres innerlich verwandten, theokratischen Charakters vom Volke als zusammengehörig betrachtet und unmittelbar deswegen zu einem Ganzen vereinigt wurden. Ursprünglich hat jede einzelne Sammlung für sich besonders cirkuliert, und es war im Lehrhause lange kontrovers ob man die drei Sammlungen in einem Volumen vereinigen dürfte. R. Jehuda erklärte sich entschieden dagegen' (*b. B.Bath.* 13b). Bloch's argument finds an echo in Sanders' 'hermeneutical triangle: repetition, adaptation, monotheizing hermeneutic'. See Sanders, 'Scrolls and Canonical Process', p. 8, p. 10.

33 See e.g. *b. Pes.* 92a; *b. Sanh.* 91b; *b. B.Bath.* 14b; *b. Jeb.* 7b; *Mek. Beshallah,* ed. by Meir Friedman (repr. New York: OM, 1948) 40b; *Mechilta d'Rabbi Ismael cum variis lectionibus et adnotationibus,* ed. by Haim S. Horowitz and Israel A. Rabin (Jerusalem: Bamberger & Wahrman, 1960), p. 139.

34 In the rabbinic literature, כתב is altogether used in a variety of connotations, and covers practically all activities pertaining to the preparation of a book: original conception, composition, editing, text correction etc. (*Soferim* 1:8; *j. Meg.* 1:9; *b. Meg.* 9a; *Mek. d'Rabbi Ishmael* 14:1), even 'canonization' (*b. Yoma* 29a; *b. Meg.* 7a).

35 Cf. *b. Meg.* 14a.

36 Numbers 22-24.

37 Probably Genesis 36 or 36:31-39. Tradition identified the Edomite king Jobab (36:33-34) with Job who on his part was seen as a contemporary of Moses.

38 Viz. the pericope Deuteronomy 34:5-12 in which Moses' death and burial are reported. However, in the ascription of the Book of Joshua to Joshua no note is taken of the fact that the short section at the end of the book (Joshua 24:29-31) speaks of Joshua's death and burial.

39 Notwithstanding the fact that his death and burial are reported in 1 Samuel 25:1.

40 Only once in the Babylonian Talmud (b. Ta‘an. 8a), more often in the Jerusalem Talmud and in Midrashim.

41 Franz Rosenzweig, 'Weltgeschichtliche Bedeutung der Bibel', in Kleinere Schriften (Berlin: Schocken, 1937), p. 125.

42 A full and detailed roster of these 'non-canonical' writings is provided by Leiman, Canonization, pp. 17-18.

43 Samuel is designated by the synonymous term הראה (1 Samuel 9:9, 11, 18, 19; 1 Chronicles 9:22; 26:28; 29:29; cf. 2 Chronicles 16:7, 10; and Isaiah 28:7; 30:10.

44 See Shemaryahu Talmon, 'Did There Exist a Biblical National Epic?', in Literary Studies in the Hebrew Bible: Form and Content: Collected Studies (Jerusalem: Magnes; Leiden: Brill, 1993), pp. 91-111 (pp. 93-95).

45 I venture to propose that 'the table of the descendants of Esau, that is Edom' (Genesis 36:1) reflects an Edomite chronicle (Genesis 36), yet known to the author or the editor of the Book of Genesis. Similarly, the anti-Moabite song of the 'Bards' (Numbers 21:27-30) probably was quoted by the biblical author from an Amorite source (21:25-26).

46 Samuel Sandmel, 'On Canon', CBQ, 28 (1966), 203-7 (p. 206).

47 For this connotation of כתב cf. above, the compressed analysis of the relevant passage in b. B. Bath (14b-15a).

48 The collocation alludes to a temporary, often enforced sojourn in a foreign territory (e.g. Genesis 19:9; Judges 17:8-9) or country. Egypt predominates as the foreign country, like in the explanation of the reasons of their coming to Egypt for (only) a season which Jacob's sons give the Pharaoh: לגמר בארץ באנו [...] כי כבד הרעב בארץ כנען (Genesis 47:4; cf. 12:10; Jeremiah 42:25, 17; 44:14 and others).

49 I have proposed that the entire 'Exile-Diaspora-Return' terminology does not reflect actual events in the history of the community. Rather, it is meant to invest the Covenanters' retreat into the desert at Qumran with ideas which were inherent in the biblical 'Exodus-Wanderings in the Desert-Landnahme' tradition. See Shemaryahu Talmon, 'The Desert Motif in the Bible and in Qumran Literature', in Talmon, Literary Studies, pp. 216-54 (pp. 245-54).

50 Presumably with the exception of the book of Esther.

51 See DJD X, pp. 58-59; 4QMMT[C], 10 : ובדויד הנביאים ו[ב]ספרי בספר מושה שתבין אליכה כתבנו]. 'In this context דויד probably refers not only to the Psalms of David, but rather to the Hagiographa. This is a significant piece of evidence for the tripartite division of the Canon.' However, in their summary comments on part B of 4QMMT, 'דויד as Part of the Description of a Tripartite Canon', the authors strike a more cautious tone: 'the title of the third section, whatever it contained, is "David" [...]. It is not clear whether "David" refers just to the Psalter, or denotes a Ketubim collection, either one that was open-ended, or one that was closed' (DJD X, pp. 11-12).

52 Likewise, in the early Christian tradition, we do not have as yet a 'clear stabilization of anything beyond Pentateuch and Prophets', Albert C. Sundberg, Jr., The Old Testament of the Early Church. Harvard Theological Studies, 20 (Cambridge, MA: Harvard University Press; London: Oxford University Press, 1964), p. 28.

53 Talmon, 'Between the Bible and the Mishnah', pp. 32-48.

54 DJD IV.

55 If the lines תחלת נבוןורה ל[ד]ויד משמשחו נביא אלהים אזי ראיתי פלשתי מחרף ממ[ן]ערכות פלשתים] (Psalm 151 B) open a separate composition, rather than constitute the continuation of Psalm 151 A.

56 The fact that 11QPs[a] can be a manuscript of the biblical book of Psalms, as claimed by the editor, James A. Sanders, and accepted by other scholars, foremost by Peter W. Flint, The Dead Sea Psalms Scrolls and the Book of Psalms, STDJ, 17 (Leiden: Brill, 1997), does not invalidate the proposition that this text served as a liturgical collection in the Covenanters' prayer service, as argued by Moshe H. Goshen-Gottstein, 'The Psalms Scroll (11QPs[a]): A Problem of Canon and Text', Textus, 5 (1966), 22-33; Shemaryahu Talmon, 'Pisqah Be'emṣa‘ Pasuq and 11QPs[a]', Textus, 5 (1966), pp. 11-21; and others.

57 See Eileen M. Schuller, *Non-Canonical Psalms from Qumran: A Pseudepigraphic Collection*, HSS, 28 (Atlanta, GA: Scholars Press, 1986); Eileen M. Schuller, 'The Psalm of 4Q372 1 Within the Context of Second Temple Prayer', *CBQ*, 54 (1992), 67-79.

58 Flint, *Dead Sea Psalms Scrolls*, competently addresses the pertinent issues arising from an analysis of the Qumran materials in relation to the biblical Psalter.

59 See among others Jack P. Lewis, 'What Do We Mean By Jabneh?', *Journal of Bible and Religion*, 32 (1964), 125-32; Peter Schäfer, 'Die sogenannte Synode von Jabne. Zur Trennung von Juden und Christen im ersten/zweiten Jh. n. Chr. II. Der Abschluss des Kanons', *Judaica*, 31 (1975), 116-24; Sanders, *From Sacred Story*; James A. Sanders, 'Spinning the Bible', *BR*, 14/3 (1998), pp. 22-29, 44-45 (p. 29); Leiman, *Canonization*, pp. 120-24; Roger Beckwith, *The Old Testament Canon of the New Testament Church and its Background in Early Judaism* (Grand Rapids, MI: Eerdmans, 1985), pp. 4-7; Frank Moore Cross, *From Epic to Canon: History and Literature in Ancient Israel* (Baltimore: Johns Hopkins University Press, 1998), p. 221.

60 David E. Aune, 'On the Origins of the "Council of Javneh" Myth', *JBL*, 110 (1991), 491-93.

61 See above, n. 1.

62 C. Gebhard, ed., *Spinozae Opera: Im Auftrag der Heidelberger Akademie der Wissenschaften* (Heidelberg: Carl Winters Universitätsbuchhandlung, 1925), pp. 3, 150.

63 See e.g. Joseph T. Milik, 'Textes hébreux et araméens', in DJD II, 75, who still states that the *Textus Receptus* was established 'vers la fin du 1e siècle de notre ère à l'Academie de Jamnia.'

64 John Barton, 'The Significance of a Fixed Canon of the Hebrew Bible', in *Hebrew Bible/Old Testament: The History of Its Interpretation*, ed. by Magne Sæbø, vol. 1, part 1 (Göttingen: Vandenhoeck & Ruprecht, 1996), pp. 67-83.

65 Frederick E. Greenspahn, 'Why Prophecy Ceased', *JBL*, 108 (1989), 37-49 (p. 43).

66 Jacob Neusner, 'Mishnah and Messiah', in *Judaisms and Their Messiahs at the Turn of the Christian Era*, ed. by Jacob Neusner, William Scott Green and Ernest S. Frerichs (Cambridge: Cambridge University Press, 1987), pp. 265-82 (p. 268): 'The Mishnah and the Mishnah alone, defines the original boundaries of the canon of Judaism as the rabbinic system.' Cf. David Kraemer, 'The Formation of Rabbinic Canon: Authority and Boundaries', *JBL*, 110 (1991), 613-30.

67 Neusner, 'Mishnah and Messiah', p. 267: 'The framers of the (Mishnah) code barely refer to Scripture, rarely produce proof texts for their own propositions, never imitate the modes of speech of ancient Hebrew, as do the writers of the Dead Sea Scrolls at Qumran.'

68 For this connotation of כתב see above, pp. 10-11.

69 See Ephraim E. Urbach, 'The Written Law and the Oral Law', in *The Sages - Their Concepts and Beliefs*, trans. by Israel Abraham, 2 vols (Jerusalem: Magnes, 1975), pp. 287-314; Birger Gerhardsson, *Memory and Manuscript: Oral Tradition and Written Transmission in Rabbinic Judaism and Early Christianity*, Acta Seminarii Neotestamentici Upsaliensis, 22, trans. by Eric J. Sharp (Lund: Gleerup; Copenhagen: Munksgaard, 1961; republished with *Tradition and Transmission in Early Christianity*, Coniectanea Neotestamentica, 20, trans. by Eric J. Sharp (Grand Rapids, MI: Eerdmans; Livonia, MI: Dove, 1998)); Jacob Neusner, 'The Meaning of the Oral Torah', in *Early Rabbinic Judaism: Historical Studies in Religion, Literature and Art*, Studies in Judaism in Late Antiquity, 13 (Leiden: Brill, 1975), pp. 1-33; Jacob Neusner, 'Accommodating Mishnah to Scripture in Judaism: The Uneasy Union and its Offspring', *Michigan Quarterly Review*, 22 (1983), 465-79; Jacob Neusner, *Oral Tradition in Judaism: The Case of the Mishnah*, The Albert Bates Lord Studies in Oral Tradition, 1, Garland Reference Library of the Humanities, 764 (New York: Garland, 1987); Shemaryahu Talmon, 'Oral Tradition and Written Transmission, or the Heard and the Seen Word in Judaism of the Second Temple Period', in *Jesus and the Oral Gospel Tradition*, ed. by Henry Wansbrough, JSNTSup, 64 (Sheffield: Sheffield Academic Press, 1991), pp. 121-58 (pp. 142-58).

70 Margolis, *Hebrew Scriptures*, p. 63.

71 The issue cannot be examined here in detail. Adequate discussions are provided among others in publications recorded above, in notes 1, 3, 22, 25, 27.

72 Solomon Schechter, 'The Quotations from Ecclesiasticus in Rabbinic Literature', *Jewish Quarterly Review, Old Series*, 3 (1891), 682-706.

73 I have dealt in some detail with these matters in Talmon, 'Oral Tradition', pp. 132-39.

74 The roots of this intense process of socio-religious diversification can be traced in the early post-exilic historiographies (Ezra-Nehemiah), and prophetic literature (Haggai, Zechariah and Malachi, esp. ch. 3). See Shemaryahu Talmon, 'The Emergence of Jewish Sectarianism in the Early Second Temple Period', in *King, Cult and Calendar in Ancient Israel: Collected Studies* (Jerusalem: Magnes, 1986), pp. 165-201.

75 Cf. Eissfeldt, *Einleitung*, p. 767.

76 It appears, however, that Covenanters authors knew the book in its present form. See Shemaryahu Talmon, 'Was the Book of Esther Known at Qumran?', *DSD*, 2 (1995), 249-67; Jonathan Ben-Dov, 'A Presumed Citation of Esther 3:7 in 4QD[b]', *DSD*, 6 (1999), 282-84.

77 I fully concur with Schäfer's summary comment ('Synode', above n. 59), p. 122: 'Der Kanon wurde überhaupt nicht festgelegt [...] sondern er kristallisierte sich allmählich heraus (wahrscheinlich vorwiegend den praktischen Bedürfnissen des Synagogengottesdienstes; <kanonisch> bedeutete dann soviel wie "im Gottesdienst verwendbar").'

78 Sanders, 'Scrolls and Canonical Process', pp. 13-14 realizes that 'stabilization and closure of the formative canonical process occurred most likely because historical and cultural facts demanded it.' However, he fails to note that the *yaḥad* was not affected by the critical events, to which mainstream Judaism was subjected. Therefore, the need and urge to establish a fixed and closed canon of Scripture did not arise in the Covenanters' community.

79 See Shemaryahu Talmon, 'The Emergence of Institutionalized Prayer in Israel in the Light of the Qumrân Literature', in *Qumrân: sa piété, sa théologie et son milieu*, ed. by Mathias Delcor, Bibliotheca Ephemeridum Theologicarum Lovaniensium, 46 (Leuven: Leuven University Press, 1978), pp. 265-84; enlarged version repr. in Shemaryahu Talmon, *The World of Qumran From Within*, (Jerusalem: Magnes; Leiden: Brill, 1989), pp. 200-43.

THE STATUS OF THE BIBLICAL TEXTS IN THE QUMRAN CORPUS AND THE CANONICAL PROCESS

Armin Lange

THE ANCIENT COLLECTION of manuscripts which comprise the Qumran corpus consists of around one thousand manuscripts of varying types.[1] An analysis of the status of the biblical texts in this corpus requires several questions to be considered. What exactly is the Qumran corpus? What is meant by the term 'biblical'? Which texts should be categorised as biblical texts? What is their status within the Qumran corpus? Did the Essenes prefer any particular text type?

WHAT IS THE QUMRAN CORPUS?

Since the Madrid conference in 1991,[2] it has become an *opinio communis* among Dead Sea Scrolls scholars that the library of Qumran consisted not only of biblical texts, other texts already known before the discovery of the Dead Sea Scrolls, and texts written by the Qumran Covenanters, but also of unknown texts from other groups within Ancient Judaism. In particular, the group of texts unknown to us before the Qumran discoveries comprise a range of literary works which sometimes even reflect differing views. A good example is the practice of brontology in the omen list of 4Q318, and its rejection in 1 Enoch 8:3 (4QEn[a] 1 IV, 1-5; par 4QEn[b] 1 III, 1-5). The Qumran library should therefore be understood to provide us with a collection of literary works from different groups within ancient Judaism from the third century BCE to the first century CE.[3] It thus consists of a non-representative mix of Jewish literature of the late Second Temple period.

An analysis of the status of the biblical texts in the Qumran corpus would therefore require an evaluation of their status in late Second Temple Judaism in general – a topic far too large for the present contribution. For this reason, I will restrict myself to the question of the status of the biblical texts in the literary life of the Qumran Covenanters who are to be identified as Essenes.[4]

WHAT IS BIBLICAL?

The words biblical and Bible might seem to be anachronistic when applied to a time when neither the canon of the Hebrew nor the Greek Bible had yet finished developing. However, texts like the pesharim or the Midrash Sepher Moshe (4Q249) and references to scriptural authority in 4QMMT demonstrate beyond any doubt that at least some books were understood in the second and first centuries BCE to have had a religious authority which is designated today as biblical.

Just as today in Judaism and in the different Christian denominations there are different canons of Holy Scriptures, so the different religious groups of Second Temple Judaism adhered to different collections of scriptures.[5] The Samaritans and the Sadducees, for example, restricted themselves to the Torah (cf. the Samaritan Pentateuch and Josephus' The Antiquities of the Jews XIII, 297; XVIII, 17). It should therefore be asked which literary works were viewed by the Essene community as Scripture with religious authority.

First indications can be found in the lists of authoritative scriptures provided by 4QMMT and the Community Rule. While 1QS I, 2-3 and its parallels in the 4QS manuscripts advocate behaviour 'according to what he [viz. God] had commanded through Moses and through all his servants, the prophets' (כאשר צוה ביד מושה וביד כול עבדיו הנביאים; cf. also 1QS VIII, 15 and parallels),[6] 4QMMT C 10 names, in addition to 'the Book of Moses' (מושה ספר) and the 'book[s of the] prophets' (ספרי הנביאים), 'David' (דוד). Such a tripartite structure is also attested in the Midrash on Eschatology which, according to the work of Annette Steudel, interprets quotations from Deuteronomy 33 as representative of the Torah in its first section, from 2 Samuel 7:10-14 as a representative of the Prophets in its second section, and from the Davidic Psalter in its third section.[7]

This leads us to ask which scriptures were recognized by the Qumran Covenanters as comprising Moses, the Prophets and David? To ascribe scriptural authority to literary works that are attested by a large number of manuscripts from the Qumran library clearly does not answer this question, since then the Damascus Document and the Community Rule would also be biblical texts. One has to ask, therefore, which books were interpreted, quoted or referred to in the Essene writings as having a high religious authority. To do this, at the moment one is restricted to the list of quotations in the Qumran corpus published by Johann Maier,[8] because a comprehensive list of quotations has still not been compiled. To distinguish for this purpose between explicit quotations introduced by a quotation formula (e.g. כאשר כתוב) and implicit ones without such an introduction does not seem to be advisable.[9] While a quotation formula like כאשר כתוב may identify the quoted texts without any doubt as scriptures, the fact that some of the Essene texts, for example the Hodayot, are constructed substantially out of implicit quotations and allusions, demonstrates the high scriptural authority of these works as well.

According to Maier's list, the following books regarded as biblical today are quoted, alluded to or referred to in the Essene writings:

1. Torah: Genesis, Exodus, Leviticus, Numbers, Deuteronomy.
2. Former and Later Prophets: Joshua,[10] 1-2 Samuel, 1-2 Kings, Isaiah, Jeremiah, Ezekiel, Dodekapropheton[11] (Hosea, Joel, Amos, Micah, Nahum, Habakkuk, Zechariah and Malachi are quoted, alluded or referred to).
3. Writings: Psalms, Proverbs, Job, Lamentations, Daniel.

In the part of the collection which was later to be called Writings, the allusions to Job and Lamentations in the Hodayot[12] might be argued, but the quotations of Proverbs and Daniel in the Damascus Document, the Midrash on Eschatology, and in 11QMelchizedek are quite certain. Interestingly, even Proverbs, Job, and Lamentations are already quoted, alluded or referred to in the earlier Essene writings such as the Damascus Document (CD XI, 20) and the Hodayot (1QH^a XI, 20 [Sukenik III, 19]; 1QH^a XII, 14 [Sukenik IV, 13]; 1QH^a XIII, 13 [Sukenik V, 11]; 1QH^a XIII, 32 [Sukenik V, 30]; 1QH^a XV, 5 [Sukenik VII, 2]; 1QH^a XVI, 34 [Sukenik VIII, 33]; 1QH^a XIX, 22 [Sukenik XI, 19]), whereas Daniel is quoted only in somewhat later texts, i.e. 4QMidrEschat^a (4Q174) IV 3-4 quotes Daniel 12:10 and 11QMelch (11Q13) ii 18-19 quotes Daniel 9:25.

In addition to scriptures quoted, alluded or referred to, continuous pesharim exist for the books of Isaiah (4QpIsa^{c,e}; 4Q163 + 515[13]; 4Q165; 4QpIsa$^{a-b,d}$; 4Q161-2; 4Q164)[14], Hosea (4QpHos^{a-b}; 4Q166-7), Micah (1QpMic; 1Q14), Nahum (4QpNah; 4Q169), Habakkuk (1QpHab), Zephaniah (1QpZeph; 4QpZeph; 1Q15; 4Q170) and Psalms (1QpPs; 4QpPs^{a-b}; 1Q16; 4Q171; 4Q173). Other Commentaries have been found for the books of Genesis (4QCommGen A-D; 4Q252-4; 4Q254a), Isaiah (4QTanḥ; 4Q176, parts of Isaiah, mainly Isaiah 40ff.) and Malachi (4QCommMal; 4Q253a). Furthermore, the Midrash Sepher Moshe (4Q249) published by Stephen Pfann seems to be a halakhic interpretation of selected passages from the pentateuchal laws.

On the other hand, no quotations or exegetical writings have been located so far for the books of Judges, Jonah, Obadiah, Haggai, Canticles, Qohelet, Ruth, Esther,[15] Ezra, Nehemiah and 1-2 Chronicles.

However, at least four literary works that are not canonical today either in Judaism or the major Christian churches are quoted, alluded, or referred to as having high religious authority in the Essene writings:

1. The Book of Jubilees is once alluded to in the Damascus Document (CD X, 9-10 = Jub. 23:1) and once the same text mentions its title (CD XVI, 2-4).[16]

2. 4QTestimonia contains quotations not only of Exodus 20:21b (SP = MT Deut 5:28b-29, 18:18-19), Numbers 24:15-17, and Deuteronomy 33:8-11, but also of the Apocryphon of Joshua (4QTest 21-23 = 4Q379 22 7-15).[17]

3. In 4Q247 (4QPesher on the Apocalypse of Weeks), we find remnants of a commentary on the Apocalypse of Weeks (1 Enoch 93, 91:12-17), whose genre can no longer be identified, and whose Essene origin remains uncertain due to text deterioration.

    In addition, the Damascus Document deals with the myth of the fallen Watchers and their offspring, the Giants, and alludes thus to the Book of Watchers (CD II, 17-9).[18]

4. CD IV, 12-19 interprets Isaiah 24:17 by reference to the three nets of Belial concerning which Levi son of Jacob had said, 'the first is fornication, the second wealth, the third defilement of the temple'. By emending ההין of line 17, not to ההון as it is usually done,[19] but rather to הפחז, Jonas Greenfield was able to identify it as a quotation of the Aramaic Levi Document which reads in the Bodleian manuscript Bodl. b. 14-16 'keep yourself pure of all fornication and uncleanness and of all harlotry.'[20]

5. In 1QSa I, 6-7; CD X, 6; XIII, 2-3; and XVI, 6-8 a halakhic work with the title ספר ההגו is mentioned which, according to my interpretation of 4Q417 1 i 16, claims to be a vision of Enosh with halakhic content.[21]

Thus, the Qumran Covenanters recognized, in addition to the Pentateuch, the Former and the Latter Prophets, the Psalter, Proverbs, Job, Lamentations and Daniel, the following compositions as authoritative: Enochic writings, the Aramaic Levi Document, the Book of Jubilees, the Apocryphon of Joshua, and the Book of Hago.

Canticles, Qohelet, Ruth, Esther, Ezra, Nehemiah and 1-2 Chronicles were probably not viewed by the Essenes as authoritative scriptures. The fact that the Book of Judges is neither quoted nor alluded to may have been due to chance. This conclusion is likely, since the Midrash on Eschatology demonstrates beyond any doubt that the Essenes already understood the books of the Former Prophets to be part of the prophetic collection of Scriptures.

In the case of the missing smaller prophetic books, chance might again account for the absence of quotations of or allusions to them, because all three are in evidence in several copies of the Dodekapropheton in the Qumran library.

Job,[22] the Book of Jubilees and perhaps even the Aramaic Levi Document might have been understood as being a part of 'Moses'; the Enochic writings and Daniel were probably recognized as prophets; and Lamentations and Proverbs were probably extensions added to the Psalter after MMT's list of authoritative scriptures had been written.

The quotation of the Apocryphon of Joshua in 4QTestimonia might suggest that the Apocryphon was understood either as an authoritative text form of the book of Joshua or as a second book of Joshua which was also viewed as belonging to the prophetic collection.

Concerning the ספר ההגו, nothing can be said firmly as such a composition has not been identified among the fragmentary manuscripts of the Qumran library.[23]

It should be noted in this context that the Essene collection of authoritative scriptures as described above comes very close to the scriptures that Ben Sira names in Sir 39:1-3 and to those which his grandson lists in his prologue to the Greek translation of Ecclesiasticus.[24]

THE STATUS OF THE TEXTS REGARDED BY THE ESSENES AS SCRIPTURE IN THE ESSENE COMMUNITY

At first sight, the 200 or so manuscripts of texts regarded as Scripture by the Qumran covenanters are not the largest group in the Qumran library. However, when the manuscripts alluding to Scripture, in the Essene opinion, are taken into consideration, about 120 further manuscripts from Qumran of a parabiblical or exegetical nature are added to the total. In addition, the community rules were understood by the Essenes as expositions of the Torah. This is evident both from the title of the Damascus Document, מדרש התורה האחרון ('the final interpretation of the Torah'; 4QD^a 11 20-1 par 4QD^e 7 II, 15; see also CD XX, 6), and from the superscriptions preserved in 4QS^b and 4QS^d, which designate the text of 1QS V ff. as a 'midrash' (4QS^b IX, 1 par 4QS^d I, 1). Another halakhic text from Qumran written in a cryptic script, the Midrash Sefer Moshe (4Q249), seems to have contained a collection of abbreviated Torah quotations and their halakhic evaluation.[25] When it is further recognized that texts like the Hodayot are composed substantially from biblical quotations and allusions and are written in a biblical language, the dominating influence exercised by the scriptural texts in the Qumran corpus becomes even more evident than implied by the 320 manuscripts attesting to the compositions mentioned above.

The Status of the Biblical Texts

That Scripture and its interpretation was the major source of revelation and guidance for the Qumran Covenanters is also confirmed by the Essene writings themselves:

1. CD VI, 3-11 describes the Torah, in an interpretation of Numbers 21:18, as a well which was dug by the Essenes using the instrument of the interpreter of the law. Without this interpretation of the law they would not have been able to obtain instruction nor to live according to it in the time of wickedness.

2. 1QS VI, 6-8 prescribes that in an assembly of ten people at least one person should interpret the Torah day and night. Lines 7-8 advise that one third of all nights should be spent by the many reading and studying the book and the law. This reminds one of Philo's remark that the Essenes are 'constantly utilizing the ancestral law', χρώμενοι τοῖς πατρίοις νόμοις (Quod omnis probus liber sit, § 80).

3. 1QS VIII, 14-5 interprets the presence of the Qumran covenanters in the Judaean Desert in light of the admonition of Isaiah 40:3, 'Prepare a road for the Lord through the wilderness, clear a highway across the desert for our God' as היאה מדרש התורה ('it is the interpretation of the Torah').[26]

4. 1QpHab II, 7-8 and VII, 1-8 emphasize the central revelatory authority of the prophetic scriptures. From them, the teacher of righteousness and his followers, guided by his hermeneutical authority, were able to decode the mysteries of their eschatologically-interpreted present time.

Thus, according to the Essene writings themselves and according to the dominant role they have in the entire Qumran corpus, the scriptural texts are without any doubt the central group of literature in the Qumran library and the central focus of Essene life and thought.

DID THE ESSENES PREFER A PARTICULAR TEXT TYPE?

What remains to be answered is the question of whether a specific text type of the biblical books, such as the proto-Masoretic text for example, was preferred by the Qumran Covenanters. A recent revision of Emanuel Tov's statistics concerning the distribution of the different types of biblical texts in the Qumran library suggests the need for caution concerning such an approach. Tov is now of the opinion that in the Torah fifty-two per cent of the biblical manuscripts are of proto-Masoretic character, with 6.5 per cent related to the pre-Samaritan version of the Pentateuch, 4.5 per cent to the Hebrew *Vorlage* of several books of the LXX, thirty-seven per cent of non-aligned character. In the other books of Scripture similar statistics are suggested.[27] But in the case of several biblical books, such as the Book of Isaiah, no different text types can be distinguished, with the result that the manuscripts of these books are counted as proto-Masoretic. Therefore, no statistical dominance of any text type should be assumed.

More precise answers to the question of whether a given biblical text type was preferred by the Essenes might be expected from an analysis of the biblical quotations in the Essenes writings. Currently, neither a comprehensive list of biblical quotations nor an analysis of their textual character exists, and because of this, one is restricted here to preliminary observations. Furthermore, such an analysis is only possible for those books which allow a clear distinction between different text types. I will therefore restrict myself to some observations concerning the Pentateuch, Joshua, 1-2 Samuel, Jeremiah, Ezekiel, and the biblical quotations in pesharim. In addition, only those biblical references can be taken into consideration for which textual deviation is attested between the witnesses.

1. The Pentateuch.[28] In addition to quotations agreeing with the proto-Masoretic text of the Pentateuch elsewhere in the Essene writings, 4QTestimonia 1-8 quotes Exodus 20:21b (= MT Deut 5:28b-29 + 18:18-19) according to its pre-Samaritan text type.[29] In addition, lines 14-20 utilize a non-aligned text type of Deuteronomy 33:8-11 that is close to 4QDeut[h].[30] However, lines 9-13 quote Numbers 24:15-17 in a text form close to that attested by MT.[31] Aside from orthographic differences, the textual deviations from MT can mostly be explained as interpretative corrections of forms and terms by the author of 4QTestimonia, which were difficult to understand for the readers of the text, e.g. בנבעור (4QTest 9) instead of בנו בער (Num 24:15)[32], שהתם (4QTest 10) instead of שתם (Num 24:15), and ויקום (4QTest 12) instead of וקם (Num 24:17). ונלו in line 11 is clearly a scribal error. Only אשר (line 10; a plus in Num 24:16), עין (line 11; Num 24:16: עינים), and את (line 13; a plus in Num 24:17) may be variant readings, which were copied by the scribe from his *Vorlage*.

2. Joshua. CD V, 3-4 argues that David 'had not read the sealed book of the law which was in the ark, for it had not been opened in Israel since the day of the death of Eleazar and of Jehoshua, and of Joshua and the elders who worshipped Ashtaroth.' Because the Ark, the deaths of Eleazar and Joshua, the elders, and the worship of Ashtaroth are mentioned nowhere else in this combination than in the longer text of the end of the Book of Joshua attested by LXX (Josh 24:33, 33a-b), the Damascus Document must have relied, as Alexander Rofé has pointed out, in this case on the Hebrew *Vorlage* of the LXX of Joshua.[33]

3. 1-2 Samuel. 2 Samuel 7:11b-14 is quoted in 4Q174 iii 10-11 from a non-aligned shorter text type in which *inter alia* verse 13a is missing.[34]

4. Jeremiah. MT reads in Jeremiah 30:8 ולא יעבדו בו עוד זרים, while LXX has καὶ οὐκ ἐργῶνται αὐτοὶ ἔτι ἀλλοτρίοις and 4QOrd[a] (4Q159) 2-4 2 attests to לוא יעבודו הגויים בזרנים. Either the author of 4QOrdinances altered the LXX's Hebrew *Vorlage*, which might have been בם, to הגויים or was already dependent upon a different version of Jeremiah.

5. Ezekiel. The reading לשבט in 1QSb (1Q28b) V (frgs 27+25), 27 instead of אל שבטי in MT of Ezekiel 19:11 seems to be based on a text of the Book of Ezekiel as attested by the Septuagint. On the other hand, Ezekiel 37:23 is quoted in 4Q174 iii 16f. with only a slight deviation from MT.[35] CD III, 21-4:2 quotes a shorter version of Ezekiel 44:15 which runs otherwise according to MT (יקרבו אלי לשרתני ועמדו לפני is missing, and, instead of להקריב, CD reads in IV, 2 ינישו). Finally, CD III, 18 alludes to Ezekiel 11:15 according to the text attested by MT.

6. The biblical quotations in the pesharim. Concerning the question of an Essene preference for a given biblical text type, the prophetic pesharim are not as helpful as one might hope since, both in the Minor Prophets and the book of Isaiah, all textual witnesses basically attest to a proto-Masoretic text. However, based on a suggestion by Krister Stendahl, William H. Brownlee has already worked out in his detailed study of the biblical lemmas of 1QpHab that this pesher, in the case of his sixty-three variants from MT,[36] seems to collect consciously different readings from different

textual witnesses in order to create in its lemmas a new biblical text, which might well be described as eclectic. The same might be true for the biblical lemmas of 4QpNah which combines twelve proto-Masoretic readings with eight variants attested also by the Septuagint and eighteen non-aligned readings.

Thus, in my opinion, no Essene preference for one text type can be detected at the moment. The different text types of biblical books were regarded and used in the Essene community as of equal religious authority. This is also supported by the fact that no sectarian readings introducing Essene thought into biblical manuscripts have been identified so far.[37]

CONCLUSION

Scripture was of central importance for the literary and religious life and thought of the Qumran Covenanters. Their collection of authoritative scriptures differed distinctively from the canon of the later Hebrew Bible. This gives evidence to the fact, that the different Jewish parties in the years 150 BCE to 70 CE adhered to different collections of authoritative scriptures. It seems to be a strong possibility that, in the time after the destruction of the Herodian Temple in 70 CE, the Pharisaic collection of scriptures developed by default into a canon adhered to by all Jews. For the Essenes the different text types and redactions of the later biblical books were of equal authority. That text types, which differed in the case of several biblical books substantially from each other, have been of equal religious authority for one of the main groups of late Second Temple Judaism, raises the question, as to whether the concept of an 'Urtext' with special religious dignity existed at all in this time. More probably, even biblical texts like the so-called Reworked Pentateuch (4QRP$^{a\text{-}e}$ [4Q158; 4Q364-7]) have been regarded as the word of God which he spoke 'through Moses and through all his servants, the prophets' (1QS I, 3).

NOTES

1   I am obliged to Edward Herbert for improving the English of this article. The article has benefited from several valuable suggestions by Edward Herbert and Emanuel Tov regarding both basic ideas and details.

2   See the conference proceedings: *MQC*.

3   That only some of the texts found in Qumran and not known to us from other sources are of Essene origin was first recognized by Claus-Hunno Hunzinger, 'Fragmente einer älteren Fassung des Buches Milḥamā aus Höhle 4 von Qumrân', *ZAW*, 69 (1957), 131-51 (pp. 149-50). However, with the exception of a few remarks, the idea was not given serious consideration until decades later. For the discussion concerning criteria for the identification of Essene and non-Essene texts, see Hermann Lichtenberger, *Studien zum Menschenbild in Texten der Qumrangemeinde*, Studien zur Umwelt des Neuen Testaments, 15 (Göttingen: Vandenhoeck & Ruprecht, 1980), pp. 15-17; Carol A. Newsom, '"Sectually Explicit" Literature from Qumran', in *The Hebrew Bible and its Interpreters*, ed. by William Henry Propp, Baruch Halpern, and David Noel Freedman, Biblical and Judaic Studies from The University of California, San Diego, 1 (Winona Lake, IN: Eisenbrauns, 1990), pp. 167-87 (pp. 173-79); Devorah Dimant, 'The Qumran Manuscripts: Contents and Significance', in *Time to Prepare the Way in the Wilderness: Papers on the Qumran Scrolls by Fellows of the Institute for Advanced Studies of the Hebrew University, Jerusalem 1989-1990*, ed. by Devorah Dimant and Lawrence H. Schiffman, STDJ, 16 (Leiden: Brill, 1995), pp. 23-58 (pp. 27-36); Armin Lange, 'Kriterien essenischer Texte' in *Brennpunkte gegenwärtiger Qumranforschung*, ed. by Jörg Frey and Hartmut Stegemann,

Armin Lange

(Paderborn: Bonifazius, forthcoming); Charlotte Hempel, 'Methodologische Beobachtungen zur Frage der Kriterien zur Bestimmung "essenischer Verfasserschaft" von Qumrantexten', in *Brennpunkte gegenwärtiger Qumranforschung.*

4   For the Qumran Covenanters' identification as Essenes, see among others Geza Vermes and Martin D. Goodman, *The Essenes: According to the Classical Sources*, Oxford Centre Textbooks, 1 (Sheffield, JSOT Press, 1989), pp. 2-14; Hartmut Stegemann, 'The Qumran Essenes – Local Members of the Main Jewish Union in Late Second Temple Times', in *MQC*, pp. 83-166 (pp. 107-138); James C. VanderKam, *The Dead Sea Scrolls Today* (Grand Rapids: Eerdmans, 1994), pp. 71-98.

5   See Odil Hannes Steck, 'Der Kanon des hebräischen Alten Testaments: Historische Materialien für eine ökumenische Perspektive', in *Vernunft des Glaubens: Wissenschaftliche Theologie und kirchliche Lehre*, Festschrift zum 60. Geburtstag von Wolfhart Pannenberg, ed. by Jan Rohls and Gunther Wenz (Göttingen: Vandenhoeck & Ruprecht, 1988), pp. 231-52 (pp. 240-44); Heinz-Josef Fabry, 'Die Qumrantexte und das biblische Kanonproblem', in *Recht und Ethos im Alten Testament – Gestalt und Wirkung*, Festschrift for H. Seebass, ed. by Stefan Beyerle, Günter Mayer, and Hans Strauß (Neukirchen-Vluyn: Neukirchner Verlag, 1999), pp. 251-71; James A. Sanders, 'The Scrolls and the Canonical Process', in *DSSAFY*, II, pp. 1-23 (pp. 2-7).

6   For a reference to 'Moses and your servants, the prophets', see also 4QDibHam[a] (4Q504) 1-2 III, 12-13 which on paleographical evidence is judged to be a pre-Essene manuscript.

7   For the structure of the Midrash on Eschatology, see Annette Steudel, *Der Midrasch zur Eschatologie aus der Qumrangemeinde (4QMidrEschat[a.b])*, STDJ, 13 (Leiden: Brill, 1994), pp. 129-34.

8   Johann Maier, *Die Qumran-Essener: Die Texte vom Toten Meer*, 3 vols (Uni-Taschenbücher, 1916; repr. München and Basel: Ernst Reinhardt, 1996), III: Einführung, Zeitrechnung, Register und Bibliographie, pp. 161-78.

9   For such an approach, see for example James C. VanderKam, 'Authoritative Literature in the Dead Sea Scrolls', *DSD*, 5 (1998), 382-402 (pp. 389-96).

10   The allusion to Joshua 24:33, 33a-b in CD V, 3-4 is missing in Maier's list, but has been identified by Alexander Rofé beyond any doubt (Alexander Rofé, 'The End of the Book of Joshua According to the Septuagint', *Henoch*, 4 (1982), 17-36).

11   According to the evidence of the 4QXII-manuscripts, the Dodekapropheton was already understood as one book by its Essene readers (cf. also Sirach 49:10). Therefore, it is treated above as one entity, although not all Minor Prophets quotations are still preserved in the Essene writings.

12   Job 3:10: 1QH[a] XIX, 22 [Sukenik XI, 19], Job 31:22: 1QH[a] XV, 5 [Sukenik VII, 2] and XVI, 34 [Sukenik VIII, 33], Job 33:28: 1QH[a] XI, 20 [Sukenik III, 19], Lam 1:3: 1QH[a] XIII, 32 [Sukenik V, 30], Lam 2:16 and 3:46: 1QH[a] XIII, 13 [Sukenik V, 11]. References to 1QH[a] are given according to the edition of Hartmut Stegemann, '*Rekonstruktion der Hodajot: Ursprüngliche Gestalt und kritisch bearbeiteter Text der Hymnenrolle aus Höhle 1 von Qumran*' (unpublished doctoral dissertation, University of Heidelberg, 1963); the designations of E. L. Sukenik (ed.), *The Dead Sea Scrolls of the Hebrew University* (Jerusalem: Magnes, 1955), are given in square brackets.

13   For 4Q515 as part of 4Qpap pIsa[c] (4Q163), see Johann Maier, *Die Qumran-Essener: Die Texte vom Toten Meer*, 2 vols (Uni-Taschenbücher, 1916; repr. München and Basel: Ernst Reinhardt, 1996), III: Einführung, Zeitrechnung, Register und Bibliographie, pp. 72, 679.

14   For the difficulties in identifying 3QpIsa (3Q4) as a pesher, see Maurya Horgan, *Pesharim: Qumran Interpretations of Biblical Books*, CBQ Monograph Series, 8 (Washington: Catholic Biblical Association of America, 1979), p. 260.

15   Contra Shemaryahu Talmon, 'Was the Book of Esther Known at Qumran', *DSD*, 2 (1995), p. 249-67, and Jonathan Ben-Dov, 'A Presumed Citation of Esther 3:7 in 4QD[b]', *DSD*, 6 (1999), p. 282-84, who propose a linguistic influence of the Book of Esther on Sectarian texts.

16   Against Hartmut Stegemann, 'Die "Mitte der Schrift" aus der Sicht der Gemeinde von Qumran', in *Mitte der Schrift? Ein jüdisch-christliches Gespräch: Texte des Berner Symposiums vom 6.-12. Januar 1985*, ed. by Martin Klopfenstein and others, Judaica et Christiana, 11 (Bern: Peter Lang, 1987), pp. 149-84 (pp. 173-74). For the authoritative character of the Book of Jubilees at Qumran, see VanderKam, *Dead Sea Scrolls Today*, pp. 153-55; VanderKam, 'Authoritative Literature', pp. 399-400. The Book of Jubilees is also quoted in 4Q228 1 I (see J. VanderKam and J. T. Milik,

'228. 4QText with a Citation of Jubilees', in DJD XIII, pp. 177-85 (pp. 178, 181-83)), but due to the manuscript's deterioration the Essene character of this text remains doubtful.

17 See Carol Newsom, 'The "Psalms of Joshua" from Qumran Cave 4', *JJS*, 39 (1988), 56-73 (pp. 56, 59-60, 69-73); Carol A. Newsom, '4Q378 and 4Q379: An Apocryphon of Joshua', in *Qumranstudien: Vorträge und Beiträge der Teilnehmer des Qumranseminars auf dem internationalen Treffen der Society of Biblical Literature, Münster, 25.-26. Juli 1993*, ed. by Heinz-Josef Fabry, Armin Lange and Hermann Lichtenberger, Schriften des Institutum Judaicum Delitzschianum, 4 (Göttingen: Vandenhoeck & Ruprecht, 1996), pp. 35-85 (pp. 35-36, 74-78), and the literature quoted there. For a critique of Hanan Eshel's position that the apocrJosh quotes 4QTest (H. Eshel, 'The Historical Background of the Pesher Interpreting Joshua's Curse On the Rebuilder of Jericho', *RevQ*, 15 (1992), pp. 409-20 (pp. 411-12)), see Newsom, '4Q378 and 4Q379', pp. 76-77.

18 For the authoritative character of 1 Enoch at Qumran, see VanderKam, *Dead Sea Scrolls Today*, pp. 155-56; VanderKam, 'Authoritative Literature', p. 398.

19 Thus, originally, Solomon Schechter, *Fragments of a Zadokite Work: Edited from Hebrew Manuscripts in the Cairo Genizah Collection Now in the Possession of the University Library, Cambridge, and Provided with an English Translation, Introduction and Notes* (Cambridge: Cambridge University Press, 1910), p. xxxvi n. 19.

20 Jonas C. Greenfield, 'The Words of Levi son of Jacob in Damascus Document IV, 15-19', *RevQ*, 13 (1988), 319-22. The mention of 'Yaḥanah and his brother' in CD V, 17-9 should not be understood as an allusion to the Book of Jannes and Jambres, but as a midrashic interpretation of the Egyptian magicians mentioned in Exodus 7-9 (see Albert Pietersma, *The Apocryphon of Jannes and Jambres the Magicians*, Religions in the Graeco-Roman World, 119 (Leiden: Brill, 1994), pp. 12-23).

21 Armin Lange, *Weisheit und Prädestination: Weisheitliche Urordnung und Prädestination in den Textfunden von Qumran*, STDJ, 18 (Leiden: Brill, 1995), pp. 84-89.

22 For Job being written by Moses, see b. Baba Batra 14b-15a (see Emanuel Tov, 'Die biblischen Handschriften aus der Wüste Juda – Eine neue Synthese', in *Die Textfunde vom Toten Meer und der Text der Hebräischen Bibel*, ed. by Ulrich Dahmen, Armin Lange and Hermann Lichtenberger (Neukirchen-Vluyn: Neukirchner Verlag, 2000), pp. 1-34 (p. 13)).

23 For the discussion about the Book of Hago, see Heinz-Josef Fabry, 'Der Umgang mit der kanonisierten Tora in Qumran', in *Die Tora als Kanon für Juden und Christen*, ed. by Erich Zenger, Herders Biblische Studien, 10 (Freiburg: Herder, 1996), pp. 293-327 (pp. 318-19).

24 See Fabry, 'Qumrantexte', pp. 266-67. Hartmut Stegemann's idea of a twofold Essene canon consisting of Moses and the Prophets as they are attested in the later Hebrew Bible (Stegemann, 'Mitte der Schrift', pp. 157-68) is based only on texts which were published before 1985. In addition, he ignores the importance of biblical quotations for the question of which texts were of religious authority for the Essenes.

25 See S. Pfann, '249. 4Qpap cryptA Midrash Sefer Moshe', in DJD XXXV, pp. 1-24 (pp. 3-4).

26 See George J. Brooke, 'Isaiah 40:3 and the Wilderness Community', in *NQTS*, pp. 117-32.

27 Emanuel Tov, 'Handschriften', pp. 15-23; see also Tov's contribution in this volume. For the textual variety evident in the biblical manuscripts form Qumran, see also Shemaryahu Talmon, 'Aspects of the Textual Transmission of the Bible in the Light of Qumran Manuscripts', in *QHBT*, pp. 226-63; Shemaryahu Talmon, 'The Textual Study of the Bible – A New Outlook', in *QHBT*, pp. 321-400; Eugene Ulrich, *The Dead Sea Scrolls and the Origin of the Bible* (Grand Rapids: Eerdmans; Leiden: Brill, 1999), pp. 3-120; Eugene Ulrich, 'The Qumran Biblical Scrolls – the Scriptures of Late Second Temple Judaism', in *DSSTHC*, pp. 67-87.

28 Since a comprehensive analysis of the textual character of the pentateuchal quotations in the Essene writings would go far beyond the limits of what can be achieved in one article, only the evidence of 4QTestimonia is analyzed above.

29 See for example Patrick W. Skehan, 'The period of the biblical texts from Khirbet Qumrân', *CBQ*, 19 (1957), 435-40, (p. 435) and DJD V, 57. For further quotations following the pre-Samaritan text of the Pentateuch see for example Deuteronomy 33:8 in 4QMidrEschat[a] I, 9 and Exodus 15:17b, 18 in 4QMidrEschat[a] III, 3 (see Steudel, *Midrasch zur Eschatologie*, pp. 33-34, 42).

30 See Emanuel Tov, 'The Contribution of the Qumran Scrolls to the Understanding of the LXX', in *SSCW*, pp. 11-47 (pp. 31-35); Tov, 'biblischen Handschriften', p. 9.

31 See Annette Steudel, 'Testimonia', in *EDSS II*, 936-38 (p. 936). Further quotations of Numbers 24:17 can be found in CD VII, 19-20 and 1QM XI, 6 (see also the allusion in 1QSb V, 27-28) but only CD VII, 19-20 follows MT exactly.

32 See George J. Brooke, '*E Pluribus Unum*: Textual Variety and Definitive Interpretation in the Qumran Scrolls', in *DSSTHC*, pp. 107-19 (p. 114): 'One suspects that in minor ways the text of Numbers 24 was adjusted to fit syntactically the particular contemporary idiomatic usage of verbal sequences by the various interpreters [viz. in the various Essene quotations of Numbers 24:17] and that their exegetical contexts also played a part in how they variously represented the scriptural text'.

33 Rofé, 'End'.

34 For further details, see Steudel, *Midrasch zur Eschatologie*, p. 45, n. 3, and the literature quoted there. For 2 Samuel 7:10 in 4Q174 iii 1; see Steudel, *Midrasch zur Eschatologie*, p. 42.

35 See Steudel, *Midrasch zur Eschatologie*, p. 47, esp. n. 2.

36 See Krister Stendahl, *The School of St. Matthew and Its Use of the Old Testament*, Acta Seminarii Neotestamentici Upsaliensis, 20 (Lund: Gleerup, 1954), p. 190; William H. Brownlee, *The Text of Habakkuk in the Ancient Commentary from Qumran*, JBL Monograph Series, 11 (Philadelphia: Society of Biblical Literature and Exegesis, 1959), pp. 113-118; L. Vegas Montaner, 'Computer-Assisted Study of the Relation between *1QpHab* and the Ancient (mainly Greek) Biblical Versions', *RevQ*, 14 (1989-1990), p. 307-323 (p. 318). For a discussion about the biblical lemmas of the pesharim, see also Timothy H. Lim, *Holy Scriptures in the Qumran Commentaries and Pauline Letters* (Oxford: Clarendon Press, 1997), pp. 69ff.

37 For the debate about the absence of sectarian readings in the Qumran biblical manuscripts, see recently Brooke, '*E Pluribus Unum*', pp. 107-110, and the literature discussed there.

THE REWRITTEN LAW, PROPHETS AND PSALMS: ISSUES FOR UNDERSTANDING THE TEXT OF THE BIBLE

George J. Brooke

I. INTRODUCTION

A. GENERAL

THE PURPOSE of this short presentation is to attempt to make some common-sense remarks[1] on what the so-called Rewritten Bible[2] compositions may contribute to the modern understanding of the text of the Bible itself, particularly as it was passed on in the late Second Temple period. There are some excellent introductory studies on various aspects of the Rewritten Bible compositions,[3] but very few that try to draw out the lessons that can be learnt for the better understanding of the Bible from an overall consideration of those compositions that variously rewrite the Law, the Prophets and the Psalms.[4]

The attention in this study to the Law, Prophets and Psalms is deliberate, because, amongst other things, I wish to argue briefly that the Rewritten Bible compositions are not just to be found as narratives;[5] these compositions from the Second Temple period are a major indicator of the emergence of an authoritative body of Jewish literature after the exile, but especially from the third century BCE onwards. Furthermore, there has been a tendency in recent studies to focus almost exclusively on the Law (Torah). This is unsurprising, given the relatively recent publication of multiple manuscript copies of the Book of Jubilees in Hebrew,[6] the in-depth analytical edition of the principal extant copy of the Temple Scroll,[7] which can readily be conceived as a rewritten form of Exodus 34 to Deuteronomy 22, and the very extensive remains of the Reworked Pentateuch.[8] However, other compositions seem to share many of the characteristics of the pentateuchal Rewritten Bible compositions and so need to be taken into account as an overall picture of the significance of all this rewriting activity is drawn together.

B. WHAT IS A REWRITTEN TEXT?

To begin with, the term 'Rewritten Bible' is somewhat inappropriate for the texts discussed in this study, because the label Bible, in the sense of a fixed collection of books in a particular textual form, can only be applied to the texts of the late Second Temple period anachronistically,[9] and because the term implies something which is obviously secondary in authority. For the purposes of this study I will refer to the works that might belong to this literary corpus as rewritten scriptural texts. A rewritten scriptural text is essentially a composition which shows clear dependence on a scriptural text. It must be clearly recognised at the outset that, by virtue of its being dependent on an authoritative scriptural text, a rewritten text is not necessarily thereby non-authoritative, or in anachronistic terms non-canonical. There are plenty of examples of rewritten texts in what came to be the scriptural canon, most obviously in the dependence that some parts of Deuteronomy have on some passages in Exodus and in the dependence that some parts of 1 and 2 Chronicles have on the Books of Samuel and Kings. There are other less obvious examples too, such as the dependence one way or the other of 2 Samuel 22:2-51 on Psalm 18, or the dependence one way or the other of 1 Chronicles 16:8-36 on Psalm 105:1-15, 96:1-13, and 106:1 and 47-48,[10] or the need to explain the parallels between Isaiah 36-39 and 2 Kings 18-20.[11] The general characteristic of dependence can be focused in at least four additional ways so that the definition of the category can become slightly clearer.

Firstly, the dependence of a rewritten scriptural text on its source is such that the source is thoroughly embedded in its rewritten form not as explicit citation but as a running text. This running text may resemble word for word that which may be deemed to be its source, or it may be more free in its handling of the supposed source –paraphrasing, abbreviating, omitting, glossing and expanding as may be deemed appropriate by its composer.[12] Naturally, textual critics may be most enthusiastic about those passages in rewritten scriptural compositions which are the same or very similar to what may be considered to be the authoritative source; those passages can clearly be used as support for scriptural readings and the minor variants which may be apparent within the scriptural manuscript tradition itself. However, the more paraphrastic forms of rewritten scriptural composition should not be dismissed, since their variations may indicate how some passage in the scriptural source, perhaps considered as problematic for some reason, was understood and interpreted.

Secondly, the dependence of a rewritten scriptural text on its source is also such that the order of the source is followed extensively. In some of the more extensive compositions this is obvious. The Reworked Pentateuch manuscripts represent more or less what may be deemed to be the whole of the Pentateuch, even though that might make any one of its exemplars into a scroll longer than any other that has survived in the Qumran caves. The Book of Jubilees likewise runs from Genesis 1 to Exodus 16:1 with a preface. Columns 53-66 of the Temple Scroll largely follow the order of Deuteronomy 12:15-23:1, but with significant adjustments in the harmonizing of Deuteronomy with other scriptural sources. All this is clear, but the matter is less clear, for example, in relation to the variant that is found in 4QJosh[a]. In this manuscript the building of the first altar in the newly-entered land occurs straight after the crossing of the Jordan at Gilgal, in effect just before the main body of Joshua 5.[13] In the Masoretic Text the altar is built on Mount Ebal and is described in Joshua 8. Though supported by the Greek translation, it appears as if what is now presented in the Masoretic Joshua is in fact a rewritten scriptural form of Joshua with respect to the altar. The Masoretic Text represents a version of Joshua which, in at least this case, gives a substantially reordered text of Joshua.

Thirdly, the dependence of a rewritten scriptural text on its source is also such that the content of the source is followed relatively closely without very many major insertions or omissions. It has been suggested that the order of the texts cited in 4QTestimonia from Exodus 20, Numbers 24, Deuteronomy 33, and Joshua 6 follows that of a notional hexateuch, but this collection of extracts is simply a collection rather than an attempt to summarize the content of all those books from which it quotes: it is not a rewritten scriptural composition. Several other manuscripts found in the Qumran caves and containing excerpted scriptural texts can also be excluded from the category being considered in this study, though, of course the scriptural texts included in them retain their importance for the appreciation of the text of Scripture.[14] However, it is difficult to quantify just how many variations of more than a few words take a composition from being a form of rewritten Scripture towards being something more obviously exegetical. This issue seems to lie behind the editors' hesitations with regard to several manuscript fragments which have now formally been classified as 4Q365a (4QTemple?) rather than being published as integral to 4Q365.[15] Although 4Q365 does indeed contain some significant variations from its supposed source, such as the so-called Song of Miriam (4Q365 6a ii), the fragments containing similarly-sized variations were separated out as probably being from a separate composition.

Fourthly, the dependence of a rewritten scriptural text on its source is such that the original genre or genres stays much the same. Narrative is represented as narrative, law as law, oracle as oracle, and poetry as poetry. In many cases the original source is enhanced in various ways, both major and minor, and so the genre may be refined to a certain degree, but to a large extent the source provides the generic model.

This modelling by the source might also be considered in relation to language. In this respect rewritten scriptural compositions seem to fall into two categories; those which reuse the language of the authoritative source, such as Jubilees which is in Hebrew, or Josephus' The Antiquities of the Jews which echoes its authoritative Greek scriptural source material; and those which are translations of the source, such as the Genesis Apocryphon or the Aramaic Targumim. The question may then arise: is every translation of a scriptural source a rewritten scriptural text? The answer depends on one's stance in relation to all this exciting range of material.

An additional set of features might be described, but they are not so central to the definition as those already outlined. I mention them nevertheless as they raise significant and suggestive parameters. Rewritten scriptural compositions do not seem to have been composed to replace the authoritative sources which they rework, all operate some kind of interpretative strategy (however veiled that might be), they can only offer one interpretation at a time in their re-presentations of the scriptural text, and they tend themselves not to be cited explicitly elsewhere as authoritative (though Jubilees is an obvious exception here – perhaps it may have been known as a rewritten text by some people and thought not to be such by others).

II. THE ISSUES

A. WHAT IS A SCRIPTURAL TEXT?

The introductory remarks above attempt to define what constitutes a rewritten scriptural text in terms of its dependence on an authoritative scriptural source in being implicit representation, in having similar order, content, genre and even language.

However, the question needs also to be put from the other side to highlight one of the major contributions which the rewritten scriptural compositions have made to the better understanding of the text of Scripture. Before the wealth of (so-called) biblical manuscripts from Qumran had come to light, and even since, many textual critics have seemed to work on the assumption that, for the majority – if not all – of the biblical books, there was a relatively stable text form from the time of writing through into the early Rabbinic period and then up to the early Middle Ages. In the light of all the evidence from Qumran, it is now possible to see that authoritative scriptural compositions were often passed from one generation to the next in a variety of text forms or multiple editions.[16] Becoming aware of this diversity, the text critic can no longer hold on to ideas of textual stability and anachronistic understandings of how scribes were faithful to the letter of the text they were copying.

The scrolls from Qumran have, more than anything else, highlighted the problem concerning what might be labelled a biblical or scriptural manuscript. An example will help sharpen the point. In the Hebrew text of Genesis 1:5 which is attested from the Second Temple period onwards, the noun יום, 'day', is used with two different meanings. On the one hand it is used of the twenty-four hour period ('and there was evening and there was morning, the first day'); on the other hand it is used for daytime ('God called the light day'). It seems as if the scribe who copied 4QGen[g] (or a scribe at some point in the chain of transmission) realized this double use might seem odd. The text of Genesis 1:5 in 4QGen[g] differentiates between the two, using יום for the twenty-four hour cycle and יומם, an adverbial form, perhaps best rendered into English as 'daytime', for the period of light. This distinction is also to be found in other witnesses.[17] For several very pertinent reasons the reading of יומם must be deemed to be secondary. The editor of the manuscript, James Davila, in the mould of a good old-fashioned text critic, supposes that the variant arose through a scribal error, an error which was then carried forward through the tradition as it was seen to make some sense.[18] I would strongly suggest, however, that this was an exegetical variant from the outset; it seems to me to be clearly dependent upon a particular understanding of the undifferentiated text of Genesis as received. Whatever the case, the question has to be posed: is 4QGen[g] really a scriptural manuscript? Is it a scriptural manuscript with its scribe operating within the parameters of limited flux which Shemaryahu Talmon has outlined as acceptable,[19] or is it a rewritten scriptural version of Genesis?[20] I suspect that most scholars would readily classify 4QGen[g] as a scriptural or biblical manuscript, and I would be inclined to agree with them, but this example is mentioned to focus our attention on how very difficult it is to be clear quite how each manuscript should be classified.[21]

One matter becomes very clear. The practices of Jewish scribes in the Second Temple period need a fresh comprehensive description. Part of the responsible scribe's role seems to have been what might have been deemed as the steady improvement of the text. This was always recognised in some fashion both for the translators of the various scriptural books into Greek and also for the text which underlies the Samaritan tradition, but often the variant readings in these were viewed as aberrant in some way and clearly of a secondary character (with 'secondary' having a pejorative force). In one sense every copy of an authoritative scriptural book made in the late Second Temple period is a rewritten scriptural manuscript. Drawing attention to this helps to loosen the rigid categories which are often applied somewhat anachronistically to Jewish manuscript materials from this period.

B. THE MATTER OF FUNCTION AND SETTING

Attention to the actual circumstances of the copying of authoritative texts signals that the activity was probably more varied than might be supposed. Scribal practices are often considered by text critics in an abstract way which divorces them from real settings in life. If it is really the case that scribal practices as mentioned in relation to the previous point were more open-ended than is sometimes supposed, then the next set of questions to be asked concerns the purposes which all forms of the authoritative scriptural texts might have served. The rewriting activity must have been motivated by the desire to achieve some aim in a particular situation. Some brief examples of such aims and the way such texts might have been used follow.

In addition to the temple, it can be suitably suggested that the situation closest to the scribal schools where scriptural compositions were copied and passed on was the school system itself. There is very little direct evidence for this in the latter half of the second century BCE, though the newly-published wisdom texts found at Qumran provide us with educational traditions that probably go back into the third century BCE or earlier. Many of the changes in rewritten scriptural compositions could be understood as having been introduced for educative reasons, whether these were formally set in a school or not. The harmonizations of the text type which is visible in the Samaritan Pentateuch, 4QpaleoExod^m and the Reworked Pentateuch compositions are primarily educatively clarificatory.

The attention to several legal traditions in the Torah strongly suggests that the reformulation of Mosaic tradition was driven to provide texts for use in either various court settings or in semi-formal debates amongst the educated concerning the significance of some laws. Such quasi-halakhic rewritings are often ideologically motivated. Parts of the Book of Jubilees and of the Temple Scroll fall readily into this category, but we might even need to include texts such as the Samaritan version of the Decalogue which, in its expanded rewritten form, is non-sectarian in all but a few essentials.

Liturgical use also motivates the adaptation of authoritative texts for certain purposes. For example, it might be that the distinct size of many of the copies from the Qumran caves of the constituent parts of what emerged later as the *Megillot* indicate some special use in this period,[22] and poetic texts also seem to have been variously adapted for new settings.[23] In this light, the whole debate over whether the 11QPs^a scroll represents a scriptural form of the part of the Psalter which it covers or is a liturgical compilation can be seen to be presenting the issue as a false dichotomy.[24] Those who pose the question in this way imply that nothing in Scripture was written for liturgical purposes, an assumption which should surely be challenged.

Scriptural works were written for a variety of purposes, and manuscript copies of them were made for use in a variety of settings. Use outside a scribal school does not automatically disqualify a composition from being an authoritative scriptural work, just as copying within a scribal school does not thereby automatically endow a composition with scriptural authority. The rewritten scriptural compositions belong to a variety of settings just like their scriptural counterparts: function and setting cannot be used exclusively to distinguish scriptural from non-scriptural works.

C. A SLIDING SCALE

What emerges from a consideration of the scriptural and rewritten scriptural compositions in this overall manner is that there is no neat separation of the two classes of works. It is certainly not the case that the emerging authoritative collection contained no rewritten works. The categorization into canonical and non-canonical does not serve our purposes suitably. Rather, it seems as if there is a sliding scale of affinity or dependence and that function needs to be considered in a qualified way too. This sliding scale approach prevents us from applying the anachronistic labels of scriptural or non-scriptural too quickly to manuscript evidence which is so obviously replete with variety, pluralism, multiple editions of books and a range of secondary compositions.

D. THE ABANDONED QUEST

Open any guide to the text criticism of the Hebrew Bible and you will be told that the sole or principal aim of text criticism is the quest for the original form of the biblical text. Emanuel Tov, who knows the scriptural and rewritten scriptural manuscripts from Qumran better than anyone, has modified the aim somewhat, but still has written as follows: 'textual criticism deals with the origin and nature of all forms of a text, in our case the biblical text. This involves a discussion of its putative original form(s) and an analysis of the various representatives of the changing biblical text'.[25] This puts it neatly, but perhaps it is time to shift the emphasis. Text critics may indeed still make suggestions about the original form or, rather, forms of a scriptural text, but the wealth of information both in what seem to be the scriptural manuscripts and also in their rewritten forms provides us with an enormous descriptive task in which the original forms of a text become significant not so much in themselves but because of the way in which they might provide explanations for the variety of witnesses that exist. The text critic's quest should be for a greater understanding of the 'changing biblical text', to borrow Tov's phrase, and less for what any putative author, whether an Isaiah or even a Moses in earlier centuries may have written.[26] The rewritten forms of the scriptural books mentioned briefly in this study show that the suitable analysis of the transmission of authoritative compositions, broadly conceived, in the second half of the Second Temple period should become a major focus of pre-Masoretic studies.

E. THE FLUIDITY OF THE TEXT

Since the discovery of the biblical scrolls in the Qumran caves and before they have all been fully published, it has been widely appreciated that textual pluralism was characteristic of late Second Temple Palestinian Judaism. Various suggestions have been made over the years to explain the textual diversity, and the names of Frank Moore Cross, Shemaryahu Talmon, Emanuel Tov and Eugene Ulrich have joined the text critics' hall of fame. As yet, there has been virtually no consideration of what part the rewritten scriptural compositions might play in the better understanding of that textual diversity, either as a socio-religious or as a historical phenomenon.

The Rewritten Law, Prophets and Psalms

An example to ponder is that of the so-called Reworked Pentateuch. Here is a rewritten scriptural composition which predominantly reflects the readings which are suitably labelled as of the pre-Samaritan type. Tov's work in assessing the affinities of the text of 4Q364 in particular are seminal and, in the principal edition of the manuscripts by Emanuel Tov and Sidnie White, we have the important observation that

it seems natural to conclude that the biblical text used by the author of 4QRP (especially 4Q364 and 4Q158) can be characterized as belonging to a group of texts recognized previously in research, namely, the so-called pre-Samaritan group [...] As for the editorial changes (omissions and transpositions) not shared by 4QRP and Sam, the evidence adduced here suggests that while most of them were probably inserted by the author of 4QRP, some have been introduced by Sam in non-sectarian issues. If this assumption is correct, 4QRP provides further information on the different layers of Sam.[27]

This is an exemplary statement and we now need similar in-depth analysis of the scriptural texts which may lie behind other rewritten scriptural compositions such as the Book of Jubilees and the Temple Scroll. The fluidity of the text of most scriptural books in the late Second Temple period can only be understood when all the evidence, including that of the rewritten scriptural compositions, is considered in detail.

F. REWRITTEN TEXTS AND THE DEFINITION OF AUTHORITY

A further issue concerns the place of the rewritten scriptural compositions in the analysis of the emergence of collections of authoritative books in Second Temple Judaism. If the over-arching defining characteristic of rewritten scriptural compositions is that they are dependent on a text which is deemed authoritative in some way, then their very existence is an assertion of the authority of the texts which they rewrite. Some scholars have suggested that some rewritten scriptural compositions were designed to replace the biblical books upon which they were dependent, but the majority opinion would side with Philip Alexander, who has stated that 'despite the superficial independence of form, these texts are not intended to replace, or to supersede the Bible.'[28] Indeed the reverse is often the case. It is commonly argued, for example, that the author of the Book of Jubilees clearly assumes that the Law which is available to everybody stands (Jubilees 6:2: 'I [the angel of the presence] have written in the book of the first law which I have written for you'); the Law in some form may need supplementing or adjusting, it may need a particular halakhic spin, but it cannot be done away with.

In a neatly interactive way, just as the existence of the rewritten scriptural texts shows that some works were of increasing scriptural authority, so the inclusion of some rewritten scriptural texts amongst those with authority in their own right gave permission for the whole enterprise of rewritten scriptural compositions. Notably the existence of Deuteronomy encourages the constant reformulation of legal tradition, whether in rewritten scriptural form before the fall of the Temple or in catalogued rabbinic opinion from the Mishnah onwards. The rewritten scriptural forms of the Law are thus given some authority themselves as the appropriate way for at least some Jews to read their authoritative sources, just as later and even to the present day in many quarters it is impossible to read the Law and the Prophets without the Talmudim and the great medieval commentators.[29] The rewritten scriptural compositions thus both give authority and receive it.

G. COMMUNITY INSPIRATION

So what do the manuscripts of the rewritten scriptural compositions tell us about the Bible? They remind us forcefully that what we have now in front of us in this wealth of manuscripts from the Second Temple period is the prehistory of the Bible, the pre-biblical Bible. The rabbinic Bible is a fixed collection of books in a particular text form imbued with authority by particular religious communities. Although, apart from the Law, there is no evidence that there were fixed lists of authoritative works in the late Second Temple period, delimited collections may have existed amongst some groups of Jews in Second Temple times, but that seems to be more accurate in relation to the Hebrew text for rabbinic times and later. The inspiration of the text rests more in the working practices of particular faith communities which have inherited traditions in various forms than in the work of individual authors whose words may be subsequently changed in both minor and major ways over many generations before becoming more or less fixed. The rewritten scriptural texts thus show how the authority given to a scriptural text is the responsibility of the believing community.

In certain ways in the light of its inheritance it is the contemporary community which makes the shift from text to canon. Nevertheless, that shift takes place most acutely in the late Second Temple period and the century afterwards, between about 200 BCE and 200 CE. The shift is best represented by the change from rewritten scripture to explicit running commentary. In a few compositions from that period the shift is visible to see. Most neatly in 4Q252, Commentary on Genesis A, there is both rewritten scripture in the reworked presentation of the flood story according to a particular calendrical system, but there is also explicit quotation of the blessings of Jacob with attached running commentary which relates the text atomistically to the life of the community.

III. CONCLUSION

This brief survey has raised some of the issues which are provoked by the presence in the Qumran literary corpus of a collection of so-called Rewritten Bible texts. We can summarize what I have tried to say in three points. Firstly, the rewritten scriptural texts need to become much more explicitly part of the arsenal of the text critic, playing their full part in the description of the fluid transmission of the texts of the various scriptural books in the late Second Temple period. Secondly, when these fascinating texts take their proper place, then the canons of the practice of text criticism must themselves change: most obviously this is seen in three respects: in the shift away from a sole concern with the quest for the original form of the text; with the adoption of a more neutral set of terms for describing what is attested in the manuscript evidence; and in a move away from seeing every variant principally in terms of scribal error. Thirdly, the rewritten scriptural compositions must not be prevented on the basis of anachronistic reasoning from taking their proper place, not as secondary and therefore second class witnesses to the books of the Bible themselves, but as primary evidence for how authoritative traditions were appropriated and managed in particular communities in the late Second Temple period. From the sensitive appreciation of such appropriation may come lessons for today about how authoritative scriptures should be used rather than abused by those who hold them to be of ongoing importance.

1. 'A man who possesses common sense and the use of reason must not expect to learn from treatises or lectures on textual criticism anything that could not, with leisure and industry, find out for himself. What the lectures and treatises can do for him is to save him time and trouble by presenting to him immediately considerations which would in any case occur to him sooner or later', A. E. Housman, 'The Application of Thought to Textual Criticism', *Proceedings of the Classical Association*, 18 (1922), 67-84 (p. 68).

2. The term Rewritten Bible was coined by G. Vermes to indicate the earliest forms of haggadic interpretation: 'In order to anticipate questions, and to solve problems in advance, the midrashist inserts haggadic development into the biblical narrative - an exegetical process which is probably as ancient as scriptural interpretation itself', Geza Vermes, *Scripture and Tradition in Judaism: Haggadic Studies*, Studia Post-Biblica, 4, 2nd edn (Leiden: Brill, 1973), p. 95.

3. See, for example, George W. E. Nickelsburg, 'The Bible Rewritten and Expanded', in *Jewish Writings of the Second Temple Period: Apocrypha, Pseudepigrapha, Qumran Sectarian Writings, Philo, Josephus*, ed. by Michael E. Stone, Compendia Rerum Iudaicarum ad Novum Testamentum (vol. II pt2) (Assen: Van Gorcum; Philadelphia: Fortress Press, 1984), pp. 89-156; Emil Schürer, *The History of the Jewish People in the Age of Jesus Christ (175 B.C.-A.D.135)*, revised and edited by Geza Vermes, Fergus Millar and Martin Goodman (Edinburgh: T&T Clark, 1986), pp. 308-41; Philip S. Alexander, 'Retelling the Old Testament', in *It is Written: Scripture Citing Scripture: Essays in Honour of Barnabas Lindars, SSF*, ed. by D. A. Carson and H. G. M. Williamson (Cambridge: Cambridge University Press, 1988), pp. 99-121. On these compositions from a specifically Qumran angle see, for example, Sidnie White Crawford, 'The "Rewritten Bible" at Qumran: A Look at Three Texts', *ErIsr*, 26 (Archaeological, Historical and Geographical Studies: Frank Moore Cross Volume, 1999), pp. 1*-8*; George J. Brooke, 'Rewritten Bible', in *EDSS*, II, pp. 777-81.

4. The major exceptions are two studies by Emanuel Tov, 'Biblical Texts as Reworked in Some Qumran Manuscripts with Special Attention to 4QRP and 4QParaGen-Exod', in *CRC*, pp. 111-34; and 'Rewritten Bible Compositions and Biblical Manuscripts, with Special Attention to the Samaritan Pentateuch', *DSD*, 5 (1998), 334-54, and the study by Julio Trebolle Barrera, 'Qumran Evidence for a Biblical Standard Text and for Non-Standard and Parabiblical Texts', in *DSSTHC*, pp. 89-106.

5. In attempting to define the genre of Rewritten Bible, Philip Alexander has written: 'Rewritten Bible texts are narratives, which follow a sequential, chronological order', Alexander, 'Retelling the Old Testament', p. 116.

6. See especially the edition of the Cave 4 copies by J. VanderKam and J. T. Milik, 'Jubilees', in DJD XIII, pp. 1-185.

7. Yigael Yadin (ed.), *The Temple Scroll*, 3 vols (Jerusalem: IES, The Institute of Archaeology of the Hebrew University of Jerusalem, The Shrine of the Book, 1983 [Hebrew, 1977]).

8. E. Tov and S. White, 'Reworked Pentateuch', in DJD XIII, pp. 187-351.

9. See the similar but more detailed and thoroughly pertinent comments in the study by James VanderKam in this volume.

10. On the relationship between Psalms 105 and 106 and I Chronicles 16, see George J. Brooke, 'Psalms 105 and 106 at Qumran', *RevQ*, 14 (1989), 267-92.

11. See Alessandro Catastini, *Isaia ed Ezechia: Studio di storia della tradizione di II Re 18-20 // Is. 36-39*, Studi Semitici Nuova serie, 6 (Rome: Università degli Studi "La Sapienza", 1989).

12. This characteristic is defined somewhat similarly by Philip Alexander in the following terms: 'Rewritten Bible texts follow the Bible serially, in proper order, but they are highly selective in what they represent', Alexander, 'Retelling the Old Testament', p. 117.

13. For the parameters of the interpretative debate see the two studies, Alexander Rofé, 'The Editing of the Book of Joshua in the Light of 4QJosh^a' and Eugene Ulrich, '4QJoshua^a and Joshua's First Altar in the Promised Land', in *NQTS*, pp. 73-80 and pp. 89-104. The principal edition of 4QJosh^a with suitable editorial comments is published by Eugene Ulrich in DJD XIV, pp. 143-52.

14. Emanuel Tov classifies this group as non-authoritative but correctly points out that 'for the purpose of textual analysis these texts have the same value as any other text, except that their exegetical minuses should be disregarded', Tov, 'Rewritten Bible Compositions', pp. 336-37.

15 See the editorial comments in the principal edition of these fragments by E. Tov and S. White, '365a. 4QTemple?', in DJD XIII, pp. 319-20.

16 See the detailed and important statements on this diversity by Emanuel Tov, 'The Significance of the Texts from the Judean Desert for the History of the Text of the Hebrew Bible: A New Synthesis', in *QONT*, pp. 277-309, and by Eugene Ulrich, *The Dead Sea Scrolls and the Origins of the Bible* (Grand Rapids: Eerdmans; Leiden: Brill Academic Publishers, 1999).

17 The Targumim and the Syriac version.

18 James R. Davila, '4QGen^g' in DJD XII, pp. 57-60 (p. 59).

19 Shemaryahu Talmon, 'The Textual Study of the Bible - A New Outlook', in *QHBT*, pp. 321-400 (p. 326).

20 For Emanuel Tov it 'is not the amount of exegesis or deviation from MT which counts, but the purpose of the manuscript under investigation' (Tov, 'Rewritten Bible Compositions', p. 334), but he never defines clearly which purposes give a manuscript authoritative scriptural status and which do not.

21 In a similar way, because of the many similarities between them and the text type which lies behind the Samaritan Pentateuch, several scholars might wish to classify the so-called Reworked Pentateuch manuscripts as authoritative scripture.

22 See the comments made by John Jarick, 'The Bible's "Festival Scrolls" among the Dead Sea Scrolls', in *The Scrolls and the Scriptures: Qumran Fifty Years After*, ed. by Stanley E. Porter and Craig A. Evans, Journal for the Study of the Pseudepigrapha Supplement Series, 26, Roehampton Institute London Papers, 3 (Sheffield: Sheffield Academic Press, 1997), pp. 170-82.

23 See especially the editions of 4Q380 and 4Q381: E. Schuller, 'Non-Canonical Psalms' in DJD XI, pp. 75-172.

24 On 11QPs^a see especially Peter W. Flint, *The Dead Sea Psalms Scrolls and the Book of Psalms*, STDJ, 17 (Leiden: Brill, 1997), pp. 202-27, with an extensive bibliography listed on pp. 202-204.

25 *TCHB*, p. 1.

26 See the contribution by Shemaryahu Talmon to this volume with regard to his denial of the existence of an original form for any scriptural book.

27 Tov and White, 'Reworked Pentateuch', p. 196.

28 Alexander, 'Retelling the Old Testament', p. 116.

29 It is intriguing to note that whereas for the books of Isaiah and the Twelve Minor Prophets there are many sectarian running commentaries in which the scriptural text is quoted explicitly, for Jeremiah and Ezekiel there are only rewritten forms; what this differentiation implies for how the books of Jeremiah and Ezekiel were viewed has yet to be worked out.

THE WORDING OF BIBLICAL CITATIONS IN SOME REWRITTEN SCRIPTURAL WORKS*

James C. VanderKam

INTRODUCTION

MODERN TEXTUAL critics and translators of the Hebrew scriptures have many more sources at their disposal than did their predecessors, primarily but not exclusively because of the Dead Sea Scrolls. While the approximately 200 so-called 'biblical' scrolls from Qumran and several more from other sites in the Judean desert along with works such as targums, *tefillin,* and *mezuzot*[1] have provided the most direct contribution to our knowledge regarding the text of books in the Hebrew Bible, other compositions unearthed in the caves have been or could be beneficial in a text-critical sense. Several of these other works have been examined for their possible contributions to textual criticism of the Hebrew Bible, but their evidence is less frequently cited than are the data from the 'biblical' scrolls.

One example of these other types is the pesharim which have constituted an intriguing field of study all their own. They reproduce the 'biblical' text and thus serve as direct witnesses to what was found in, say, a Hebrew copy of Habakkuk in the late second temple period. William Brownlee assembled and discussed 135 variants from the Masoretic Text (MT) (in addition to the absence of Habakkuk 3 from the Pesher) and he labelled some fifty of them 'principal variants'.[2] Of these he found about one-third to be superior and one-third inferior to the MT; another one-fourth he called qualified and questionable.[3] He also noted that some readings could be called sectarian and said about them:

One may often suspect textual alteration for the sake of interpretation, but where the reading may be explained by a common type of scribal error, or where it is to be found in agreement with the versions, the charge of deliberate alteration is hazardous.[4]

In cases of what appear to be prime candidates for sectarian readings - e.g., הון rather than היין at Habakkuk 2:5 = 1QpHab VII, 3 or מועדיהם rather than מעוריהם at Habakkuk 2:15 = 1QpHab XI, 3 - Brownlee entertained the possibility that 'the sect possessed a manuscript containing precisely the Hab. Text of DSH and that eclecticism and even deliberate alteration influenced the formation of that text.'[5] He concluded that the writer rarely resorted to deliberate alteration:

Many divergent texts were current from which one might well select the reading most advantageous to the purpose at hand. This in no way minimizes the importance of individual readings in the scroll; for where readings were *found* (as attested by the versions) rather than *invented* (i.e., coined), our scroll presents the invaluable proof that such a reading certainly existed in Hebrew by the 1st century B.C.[6]

Brownlee had observed already in his first publication on the Habakkuk Pesher[7] that it contained what he called dual readings, that is, 'the expositions in DSH sometimes attest a reading at variance with the first, or directly cited, one.'[8] He found four of these and thought the author of the Pesher knew from the targum the readings in the commentary agreeing with the MT.[9] Whatever their source, variant readings apparently did not disturb the commentator. He simply exploited the extra information in his exegesis and in this way displayed an almost playful approach to textual variants - something salutary for all textual critics to keep in mind. The pesharim contain subtleties in their citations and interpretations - subtleties that require one to be cautious in using their readings for text-critical purposes - but they are one window on an ancient form of Hebrew scriptural texts.[10]

The sixteen or seventeen fragmentary manuscripts named pesharim are not the only Qumran texts with pesher exegesis. The term is used in other compositions in connection with scriptural material (e.g., CD IV, 14 regarding a citation from Isaiah 24:17) which also belongs to the text-critical fund of the scrolls. Moreover, there are other sorts of texts in which direct quotations from Scripture play a major part. So, for example, there are texts containing what have been called anthologies of excerpts[11] (e.g., 4QFlorilegium [4Q174]; 4QCatena[a] [4Q177]; 4QOrdinances [4Q159, 513-14]; 4QTanḥumim [4Q176]; and 11QMelchizedek [11Q13]). Tov has written about the excerpted or abbreviated texts that 'with the exception of some of the phylacteries and *mezuzot* [...], none of the collections is close to the MT.'[12] There are also a number of places where other texts quote scriptural passages for one reason or another (e.g. Isaiah 40:3 in 1QS VIII, 14; there are many examples in the Damascus Document).[13]

TEXTS OF THE PENTATEUCH IN REWRITTEN SCRIPTURE TEXTS

The focus of the remainder of this article will be on another set of works, at times containing large amounts of textual information that is rarely exploited in text-critical publications. The works in question all have to do with the text of parts of the Pentateuch and all of them allow glimpses into the history of the scriptural texts in the Hebrew language during the late Second Temple period. As it turns out, all of them also present a range of possibilities and challenges. The texts to be surveyed are the Reworked Pentateuch, the Temple Scroll, Pseudo-Philo's Biblical Antiquities, Jubilees, and the Genesis Apocryphon. All of these fall - at least in the opinion of some scholars - under the rubric coined by Geza Vermes - Rewritten Bible.[14]

The works that we often call Rewritten Bible, ones that exhibit both adherence to and yet a certain independence from a scriptural text, by their very nature offer information about the early history of the biblical text. In recent times a number of scholars have turned their attention to the books within this category in order to identify the kinds of 'biblical' text which lie behind them and have drawn conclusions from the data regarding the wording of various scriptural copies in Second Temple times. Several titles of articles in this volume show that this is a lively concern at present. The practice of exploiting such evidence began long before the Qumran scrolls were found and has continued on a somewhat more secure footing now that the scrolls have added substantially to the textual basis for them.

The Wording of Biblical Citations

As we do so often in our fields, we encounter terminological difficulties here. Traditionally, words such as *Apocrypha* and *Pseudepigrapha* have been employed, but they are encumbered with a number of difficulties, not least of which are the biases they embody and the ambiguities they possess. They retain a certain usefulness primarily because they are familiar. Vermes's term *Rewritten Bible* is appealing in that it highlights an important feature of a whole series of texts, but the word *Bible* is anachronistic for the texts we are studying, that is, works from the Second Temple period.[15] Moreover, as we shall see, it turns out to be a rather slippery term in Early Judaism. What exactly is the Bible that is being rewritten? It may be added that some works classified as Rewritten Bible do not present themselves as a rewriting of something else, judging by the claims put forward by their authors and, in some cases, by the receptions they received (e.g., some of the Enoch booklets, Jubilees). Perhaps a more appropriate phrase would be *Rewritten Scripture(s)*. It has in its favour the fact that the term *scripture(s)* is used in our sources. Naturally it would embrace the idea that a book of the Rewritten Scripture(s) could itself be a part of the scriptures for a group.

There are many problems associated with using books in the Rewritten Scriptures for the purpose of establishing the wording of the scriptural copies consulted by their authors. So, for example, because they rewrote older scriptural passages, the authors made changes of their own beyond what they found in their sources. Also, we do not always know whether they worked directly from written texts or from memory; if the latter, then changes could have been introduced through imprecise recollection. Or, as could happen in sectarian texts, scribes may have made deliberate alterations. Of course, it could also happen that the authors who did use written copies of scriptural passages miscopied them into their compositions. Those difficulties are then multiplied when one is dealing with a translation or a translation of a translation. The text of the book under consideration could have been corrupted or altered in various ways and at different points as it was translated and transmitted, at times across religious boundaries. Scriptural citations and allusions could have been altered to fit the form familiar to the translator, whether through the unconscious influence of his own memory or by his consulting copies.

Regarding the issue of the types of readings in such rewritten scriptural works that are likely to preserve ancient variants, the following principles should be noted.

a. Omissions in these texts are not reliable indicators of the wording of an underlying scriptural copy. This is not to say that omissions are not evidence of a variant reading; it is only to emphasize that the level of certainty is lower in such cases because omissions could be triggered by various factors such as paraphrase, purposeful abbreviation, forgetfulness, other scribal lapses, etc.

b. Readings that are present in the text and that agree with one or more of the ancient versions or copies are far more likely to reflect what was present in an author's scriptural base. Naturally, these variants may have arisen in other ways (e.g. from parallel passages, independent interpretations) but they are more likely to be actual readings from a scriptural copy than are omissions.

c. Using readings present in a rewritten scriptural text, the likelihood that one is dealing with readings drawn from 'biblical' manuscripts increases if one can

43

demonstrate a pattern of agreements with a known version or copy of a scriptural text or texts. An example is the chronology for the period leading to the Flood as it appears in Jubilees: here an entire series of numbers agrees precisely with the system found in the Samaritan Pentateuch in every case that can be checked. It is very difficult to attribute such systematic agreement to any source other than dependence on a text with this chronology.

If we keep the difficulties and principles in mind, Jewish works that are in some sense related to older, authoritative texts can serve as sources of information about the wording of those texts, just as citations and allusions in the New Testament and patristic writings can. In doing such research, we should honour the fact that rewritten scriptural texts do not relate to the authoritative text in just one way. D. Dimant has proposed that works which nowadays go under the rubrics *Apocrypha* and *Pseudepigrapha* display two approaches to the older scriptural texts: expositional and compositional. As she explains her terms:

In compositional use biblical elements are interwoven into the work without external formal markers; in expositional use they are presented explicitly as such, with a clear external marker. These two distinctive functions have different aims. In the exposition the divine word is introduced in order to interpret it as such, while the composition [*sic*] is employed when the biblical element is subservient to the independent aim and structure of its new context.[16]

Not surprisingly, her classification 'expositional' is the smaller of the two (although some passages in the Apocrypha and Pseudepigrapha can be so characterized), while the 'compositional' category is the larger one. In her essay Dimant speaks of 'explicit use of Mikra' and 'implicit use of Mikra'. The explicit uses fall into two types - 'explicit quotations' (she isolates nineteen of them in the Apocrypha) and 'explicit mention of persons and circumstances' such as lists of historical examples and isolated references. The category 'explicit quotations' is the one that should make the most direct contributions to textual criticism because in these cases the author indicates that a quotation is forthcoming and then offers the quotation. However, the examples are less numerous than we would like. In her second category 'implicit use of Mikra – composition' she includes three types: implicit quotations, allusions, and models and motifs. The latter two of these are less likely to be helpful in a text-critical sense, but the first - implicit quotations - has the potential to make a contribution. She defines implicit quotations as 'a phrase of at least three words, which stems from a specific recognizable biblical context'. [17] Here, on her view, is where the books of the Rewritten Bible fit, as one of her sub-categories called 'implicit quotations in biblical expansion', that is, narratives that closely follow the sequence and wording of a text.[18] Her examples are Jubilees, Pseudo-Philo's Biblical Antiquities, the Genesis Apocryphon, and 1 Enoch 6-11. Perhaps less manageable from a text-critical standpoint are the books in her category of freer biblical expansions; here the examples are the Life of Adam and Eve and Joseph and Asenath.[19]

As noted above, some texts that may be assigned to the rewritten scriptures and that have the potential to supply text-critical information are the Reworked Pentateuch, the Temple Scroll, Pseudo-Philo's Biblical Antiquities (to use a non-Qumran example), Jubilees, and the Genesis Apocryphon. As it happens, all of these have been examined by scholars in search of the scriptural text that underlies them. In the course of this research, some useful lessons have been learned and valuable evidence has been adduced. These compositions should now be surveyed along with the scholarship that has been devoted to them in order to see what they may have to contribute to our knowledge of Hebrew texts of Scripture in the late Second Temple period. It should be noted that there are several other texts that could have been included in this survey (e.g., 4Q252, 4Q422), but the ones selected give a good impression of the types of questions that arise.

1. Reworked Pentateuch (formerly called Pentateuchal Paraphrase [4Q158, 364-67])

The Reworked Pentateuch is virtually a copy or possibly is a copy of large stretches of the Torah. E. Tov has subjected the work to close analysis for determining its literary type and has concluded that:

this composition contained a running text of the Pentateuch interlaced with exegetical elements. The greater part of the composition follows the biblical text closely, but many small exegetical elements are added, while other elements are changed or omitted and in other cases their sequence is altered.[20]

Though it may indeed contain elements that justify giving the composition a title such as Reworked Pentateuch and excluding it from the list of 'biblical' manuscripts from Qumran, it remains the case that it quotes large amounts of the Torah and is thus another important witness to its Hebrew wording at a relatively early time. A comparison of its readings with those of other ancient witnesses has led Tov to describe its underlying scriptural text as 'belonging to a group of texts recognized previously in research, namely, the so-called pre-Samaritan group.'[21] The specific evidence for the conclusion is that it agrees with the MT in twenty seven cases and disagrees in thirty five, while it agrees with the Samaritan Pentateuch forty times, disagreeing in 17 readings; also it 'agrees exclusively with 𝔐 against 𝓊 in only two instances, while it agrees exclusively with 𝓊 against 𝔐 in seventeen instances.'[22]

Tov assigns Reworked Pentateuch to the category Rewritten Bible,[23] but if that is its proper classification the accent would have to fall on the word *Bible*, not on *Rewritten*. It is not easy to see how the Reworked Pentateuch differs in character from, say, the earlier layer of the Samaritan Pentateuch, and in a number of his comments Tov acknowledges this state of affairs.[24] As he discusses the relation between 4Q158 and 4Q364-67, he notes that 4Q158 and 4Q364 reflect the text of the Samaritan Pentateuch 'in its major harmonizing characteristics in several small details and in its deviating sequence of biblical passages in frg. 6-8.'[25] He attributes these readings to the biblical manuscript being used by the writer. So, for example, in 4Q158 Exodus passages in the Sinai pericope are supplemented with parallels drawn from Deuteronomy; this procedure of combining passages that are separated in other witnesses such as the MT and LXX is, of course, also paralleled in the Samaritan Pentateuch. An interesting example is the pairing of the two passages about the daughters of Zelophehad (Numbers 27 and 36) in 4Q365 frg. 36 because 4QNum[b] may do the same.[26] In the Numbers manuscript, as reconstructed by N. Jastram, the two pericopes are combined but not in exactly the same way: frg. 36 of 4Q365 presents four words from Numbers 27:11 before eight words from Numbers 36:1-2; according to Jastram's reconstruction of the Numbers copy, the order was: Numbers 36:1-2; 27:2'-11'; 36:3-4; 36:1'-2'; 36:5-13.[27]

Reworked Pentateuch, then, raises interesting questions about what is to be designated a text of Scripture and what an example of Rewritten Scripture. It seems to be a borderline case falling at a point close on a continuum with the so-called pre-Samaritan texts (e.g. the earlier stratum in the Samaritan Pentateuch, 4QpaleoExod[m], 4QNum[b], 4QDeut[n], 4QTest) by having the same sorts of traits and readings (e.g. harmonizations, grammatical adjustments). Since we lack the beginning of the work, we must resign ourselves to guessing about its purpose (if a purpose was stated at the beginning) or the setting chosen by the author. It strains the adequacy of our terminology, as the editors may be implying by resorting to an unusual label such as Reworked Pentateuch.[28] What is the dividing line between a text of the 'pre-Samaritan' type and a supposedly rewritten scriptural text such as Reworked Pentateuch? Or, as M. Bernstein puts it more positively: 'The Reworked Pentateuch (4Q364-367) texts stand on the unclearly marked border between biblical text and biblical interpretation.'[29] One could add that 4Q158 and 4Q364-67 may lie at slightly different points on that 'unclearly marked border'.

2. The Temple Scroll (4Q365a?; 4Q524; 11Q19-20; 11Q21?)

This text should be treated next because, in relation to the 'biblical' manuscripts, it often stands at a greater remove than Reworked Pentateuch does and we can detect something of the new setting into which the author/redactor has placed the scriptural sections – a direct revelation to Moses. The Temple Scroll confronts one with interesting problems, but its scriptural material is quite accessible because its numerous citations from pentateuchal texts have been collected and studied in detail by Tov.[30] Tov notes that there are many deviations in the Temple Scroll relative to the MT and that a number of them agree with the LXX, the Samaritan Pentateuch, or both. But there are two fundamentally different ways of assessing these variants: 1) they preserve ancient readings, or 2) they are due to the nature of the scriptural rewriting in the Temple Scroll which must first be considered in evaluating the citations in the scroll. If the latter is the case, the resulting differences from the MT and other witnesses would not be ancient readings but redactional touches.

In his essay Tov tests these two possibilities. First he examines whether variations between the scriptural material in the Temple Scroll and the MT are due to the freedom that the author takes with details of the 'biblical' text, just as he demonstrably took liberties with its content. Tov does find evidence of such freedom: the writer not only changes third-person references to the deity to first-person ones (a procedure carried out incompletely and inconsistently), but in other places enters the same sorts of changes in different passages, leaving the impression that he altered the base text in such cases. Some of these modifications reflect the linguistic situation of the time. Also the writer abbreviated scriptural passages worded awkwardly in the original, and he inserted verses that appear in different places - whether in the same chapter, a different chapter, or another book. Tov adds to such examples cases that may be considered omissions and harmonizations. From all of this he concludes that the better one comes to know the Temple Scroll's system of combining sources and skipping over 'irrelevant' details the more one attributes differences between the Temple Scroll and the MT to this authorial tendency.[31]

As he goes on to explain, however, these types of readings must be balanced by many others in which the Temple Scroll differs from the MT and is supported in this disagreement by one or more of the ancient witnesses. In this category, Tov places some sixty three readings and compares them with the LXX, the Samaritan Pentateuch (SP), the Peshitta, the Vulgate, and targums Onqelos and Pseudo-Jonathan,[32] He is inclined to attribute most of the scroll's differences to the author's method of rewriting, but he does acknowledge that the work preserves some ancient readings. His statistics for agreements with the ancient versions, in those cases where the scroll differs from the MT, are:

Temple Scroll = LXX SP ≠ MT	22
Temple Scroll = LXX ≠ SP ≠ MT	26
Temple Scroll = SP ≠ LXX	2
Temple Scroll = SP = MT	6[33]

The statistics suggest that the 'biblical' material in the Temple Scroll is related most closely to the Hebrew text underlying the LXX and then to the Samaritan Pentateuch.

However, numbers of agreements taken in isolation are, as Tov has consistently maintained, misleading. They must be evaluated in the light of two other types of readings: those where the Temple Scroll disagrees with the LXX and Samaritan Pentateuch and those for which the scroll has unique readings. When the text of the Temple Scroll is scoured for these categories of readings, the following figures result:

Temple Scroll ≠ LXX SP	33 (for these the LXX and SP usually agree)
Temple Scroll ≠ LXX	6
Temple Scroll ≠ SP	11

Moreover, when unique readings (which are difficult to isolate in such a text) are taken into account, it can be seen that the Temple Scroll deviates from more than it agrees with the versions. That is, the Temple Scroll is an independent witness to the text of the Torah. This is in line with Tov's familiar thesis that we should not speak of text types or recensions but simply of texts that are related with one another in a complicated pattern of agreements and disagreements.[34]

After Tov's comprehensive study was published, other treatments of parts of the biblical material in the Temple Scroll appeared. George Brooke analyzed the passages in it that 'correspond in some measure with Exodus 35-40 to discover whether the Hebrew text of Exodus reflected in some parts of 11QT^a can be described as offering an example of what may have been akin to a Hebrew *Vorlage* for the translator of the LXX of these chapters.'[35] Brooke does mention a few cases in which the compiler of the scroll seems to reflect a text like the MT, not the LXX, but he finds considerably more evidence of agreement with the LXX, not with the MT. In cols III-X, which are poorly preserved, he locates and discusses nine passages. From them he concludes:

Whilst the interpretative skills of the Greek translator of Exodus 35-40 should not be denied, nevertheless some of the LXX text's principal characteristics, discernible especially in the order and brevity of its *Vorlage*, are now vaguely recognizable in part of the Temple Scroll, particularly 11QT^a 3 and 10.[36]

Lawrence Schiffman, in the same collection in which Brooke's essay appeared, contributed a study of what he calls 'shared "halakhic" variants' between the Temple Scroll and the LXX. He adduces nine passages in which the two agree on readings that both differ from what is present in the MT and also have legal significance - usually clarifying a law that was left ambiguous in the MT. As he discusses these variants, he consistently raises the possibility that they came from a Hebrew *Vorlage*, not from independent interpretations of the law in question. Naturally, in some cases it is difficult to decide. He writes about these shared exegetical and prescriptive readings:

In these cases, we cannot assume that the scroll has originated the particular reading, especially in passages which deal with halakhic matters known to have been debated in Second Temple times. In general, the examples we have examined are cases in which we must conclude that either the author/redactor of the scroll found these variants in his *Vorlage* or that he knew of the exegesis represented in the LXX and incorporated this interpretation into his scroll. In either case, it seems that the rulings of the shared halakhic variants cannot be considered to be original to the *Temple Scroll*.[37]

Brooke returned to the subject in his 1992 essay containing comparisons of the text of the Temple Scroll with that of the newly published Qumran manuscripts of the Pentateuch, especially 4QpaleoExod[m], 11QpaleoLev[a], tefillin and mezuzot, and 4QtgLev.[38] He notes the readings with mixed textual associations in all these witnesses but concludes that

[t]he treatment of the biblical text in the Temple Scroll and even the very text of the scriptural passages it interprets and supplements stands in the tradition of scribal activity to which these Qumran pentateuchal manuscripts witness in the last two or three centuries B.C.E.[39]

Or, as he says in another place, 'it is no longer so easy to distinguish between exegesis within biblical texts and exegesis of biblical texts.'[40]

These important studies have helped to clarify the nature of the scriptural readings in the Temple Scroll, while at the same time highlighting problems inherent in evaluating their significance for textual criticism. The Temple Scroll poses another difficulty for our terminology because, though it does in fact rework a scriptural base and place it in a different setting, it itself seems to stake a claim that it is authoritative. In other words, it may fall into two categories, Scripture and Rewritten Scripture, just as Deuteronomy and 1-2 Chronicles do. Nevertheless, its readings, when they can be separated from the author's method of rewriting, reveal the wording of a Hebrew text of the Torah in the Second Temple period.

3. *Liber Antiquitatum Biblicarum*

Another work with an underlying scriptural text that raises some additional problems is Pseudo-Philo's Biblical Antiquities (LAB). In 1971 Daniel Harrington published a study in which he argued that the Hebrew biblical text mirrored in the quotations in the work belonged to what Frank Cross called the Palestinian text type.[41] Harrington first showed that the LAB, available only in Latin, does not cite scripture according to a known version of the Old Latin; also, it does not reflect an extant copy of the LXX, though it very likely had been translated from Hebrew into Greek and then from Greek into Latin. That is, the scholars responsible for translating the LAB were not demonstrably influenced by the biblical texts in their own languages:

The biblical text in LAB definitely does not correspond to the MT. LAB appears to preserve witness to what is known as the Palestinian biblical text-type. Particularly important are the many agreements with the Lucianic manuscripts in the Jos-Jgs-1 Sam sections. Equally significant as indicators of Palestinian text are the agreements with the LXX and the Samaritan Pentateuch.[42]

Harrington's conclusions have been challenged by Howard Jacobson in his edition of and commentary on the LAB. In his critique he raises some important methodological issues, although in fairness it should be said that Harrington was quite aware of them and took them into consideration[43]:

But such an attempt, when grounded in a text like LAB, is almost inevitably destined for failure. In principle, the notion of determining LAB's biblical text on the basis of LAB's text is hard to sustain, primarily for two reasons. First, LAB is routinely paraphrase rather than quotation: contractions, expansions, alterations. Second, LAB is often recalling the biblical text from memory and small lapses will produce reasonable, viable readings that look plausibly like alternative textual traditions. Nonetheless, there is evidence that LAB's biblical text did occasionally differ from MT, and that can scarcely be surprising (especially for the books of Joshua and Samuel). But there is no compelling evidence that his text was very different from MT. Nor is there consistency in this regard.[44]

He then goes on to oppose the way in which Harrington explained a number of cases, but his explanations are more asserted than argued and hardly serve as refutations of Harrington's interpretations. So, for example, Harrington noted that in LAB 19:10, a passage related to Deuteronomy 34:1, 4, the land of Egypt is mentioned, just as it is in the Samaritan Pentateuch at Deuteronomy 34:1. Jacobson declares this a non-parallel, but it is not obvious that he is right. A more telling point raised by him has to do with the places in which LAB agrees with the MT against other texts; an account of these too must be given.[45]

4. The Book of Jubilees (1Q17-18; 2Q19-20; 3Q5; 4Q176 frgs 19-21; 4Q216, 218-24; 11Q12)

Jubilees is a work similar to the Temple Scroll in that it is clearly a rewriting of earlier scriptures which places the material in a new setting and one that quotes extensively from the more ancient text. It is at least interesting that Jubilees deals with Genesis 1 to Exodus 24, while the Temple Scroll begins at that point (relying more heavily on Exodus 34 than on the parallel in Exodus 24) and carries through to the end of the Pentateuch. Jubilees was perhaps the first rewritten scriptural text to be exploited by modern scholars for its possible contribution to understanding the early history of the biblical text in Hebrew. A. Dillmann, who presented the first translation and edition of Ethiopic Jubilees, took up the question in his initial publication on the book in 1850-51. At that early stage in his study of the book, he concluded that Jubilees's agreements with the LXX were due to a translator who had altered the original Semitic text toward the Septuagint as he rendered it into Greek.[46] Some thirty years later, when he had a more secure textual basis from which to work, he returned to the question in greater detail. In a weighty article,[47] he adduced eighty nine readings in which Jubilees sided with the MT against the LXX; in a shorter list he specified cases of the reverse kind, that is, ones in which Jubilees supported the LXX against the MT. For this latter set he found three explanations: 1) Most of the readings in agreement with the LXX were due to the person who translated Jubilees into Greek (or the subsequent Latin translator); 2) A smaller number of them were instances in which the author adopted exegetical traditions found in the LXX (especially in explaining rare expressions); and 3) Others were actual variants and were to be traced back to the Hebrew scriptural text that the author used. For him this last category proved that the Hebrew copies of the Pentateuch at the time when Jubilees was composed (he dated the book to the first century CE) by no means agreed fully with the later official text. He thought that the differences relative to that official text were not as numerous as one finds in the LXX and usually concerned only unimportant matters; nevertheless, these readings were often in agreement with the LXX or the Samaritan Pentateuch.[48] It is curious that Dillmann found more cases in which Jubilees agreed with the MT than with the LXX because, as we shall see, the numbers point in the opposite direction.

Dillmann's views were later confirmed by Charles in his 1902 translation of and commentary on Jubilees.[49] He too compiled lists of variant readings and the ancient witnesses that supported them. These led him to the conclusion that 'our book attests an independent form of the Hebrew text of the Pentateuch. Thus it agrees at times with the Sam. or LXX or Syr. or Vul. or even with Onk. against all the rest.'[50] For him the Hebrew scriptural text reflected in Jubilees fell 'midway between the forms presupposed by the LXX and the Syriac'.[51]

I later compiled all of the biblical citations in Jubilees (using Charles' 1895 edition, the most recent one available at the time), compared all of them in detail with the ancient witnesses (MT, Samaritan Pentateuch, Peshitta, LXX, Old Latin, Ethiopic (since Jubilees survives fully only in Ethiopic), the targums, the Genesis Apocryphon, and Josephus).[52] It seemed at the time that a comprehensive listing would be less subject to bias than a selective one, but such a quantitative approach has the disadvantage of including everything, not only what may be important. As a consequence many of the variants recorded could be explained in a variety of ways, not necessarily as ancient readings from a copy of Genesis-Exodus. The overall results were, however, clear. There was no indication that Jubilees' citations from Genesis and Exodus had been altered toward Greek or Ethiopic (or Latin) biblical versions as the book was translated into those languages. Rather, the data favoured the view that the scriptural material reproduced in Ethiopic Jubilees (=EJ) was a reliable reflection of a Hebrew copy of Genesis and Exodus. A comparison of Ethiopic Jubilees with the few Qumran Hebrew fragments of the book then available gave further grounds for considering the Ethiopic text to be a faithful rendition, via Greek, of the Hebrew base.

Several interesting patterns of agreement emerged from the extensive data bank of biblical readings thus acquired:

The most significant relations for determining the basic nature of EJ's biblical text are those where MT ≠ Sam and those where MT ≠ LXX. In those situations the following statistics obtained: where MT ≠ Sam, Jub. agreed with Sam in 71 of 91 cases (78%); where MT ≠ LXX, Jub. opted for the LXX in 283 of 472 readings (67%). This marked adherence to Sam and the LXX brands Jub.'s biblical material as distinctively Palestinian in character.[53]

The overall totals for Jubilees's agreements with the different versions were these:

LXX	742
OL	708
Syriac	705
SP	699
MT	648
Eth	557

From these data it was apparent that, while Ethiopic Jubilees most often agreed with the LXX, the high number of agreements with the Old Latin showed that it tallied with

a very old level of the Greek tradition. The striking number of agreements with Syr and Sam provides incontestable proof of Jub.'s Palestinian rootage; no other explanation for these data is satisfactory. The relatively low total of agreements with the MT demonstrates that one should not look to the MT or proto-

MT as the source of Jub.'s biblical material. Rather, the text was at home in Palestine. Moreover, the significantly higher number of agreements with the LXX than with Sam requires that one characterize its biblical text as an *early* Palestinian type.[54]

The conclusions were, perhaps understandably, drawn within the framework of Frank Cross's theory of local texts. Cross himself had earlier characterized the biblical citations in Jubilees as witnesses to the Palestinian text.[55]

Some years later, at the invitation of Emanuel Tov, I revisited the question in an essay published in *Textus*.[56] By that time I had finished an edition of the Ethiopic version of Jubilees, drawing on a much larger manuscript basis than had been available to Charles in 1895. A check of readings in the new edition (done independently from the earlier lists) against those given in the 1977 study showed few changes for the biblical citations. The result was that the data in *Textual and Historical Studies in the Book of Jubilees* could be retained.

In the second study the patterns of agreement and disagreement were assessed not only in light of Cross's theory of three local texts but also in view of Tov's analyses of the situation with regard to Hebrew copies of the Bible in the Second Temple period. For example, in presenting what he calls 'a modern textual outlook', that is, one not encased in the pre-Qumran straitjacket of a tripartite division of pentateuchal witnesses, he has urged that not only the agreements between witnesses but also their disagreements be drawn into the picture (see above for the implications of this approach for the Temple Scroll).[57] When one does this from the lists compiled in the first study the results are

Jub. = LXX 492 (742)[58]	Jub. ≠ LXX 404
Jub. = SP 449 (699)	Jub. ≠ SP 447
Jub. = MT 398 (648)	Jub. ≠ MT 498

The conclusion suggested by these numbers and patterns was that Jub. manifestly does not agree with any of these versions consistently but charts its own course through the text of Genesis-Exodus. It does indeed side more often with the LXX and Sam than with the MT; and in those relatively few cases where Sam and MT differ it decidedly follows Sam (71-20). Moreover, where Sam and LXX combine to disagree with MT, Jub. supports them at a rate of 54-11. These numbers can in fact be explained by the theory of local texts. But when one adds to the high number of disagreements with each of these three versions the fact that Jub. opposes all three of them in 198 readings [...], it appears likely that Jub's biblical citations were drawn from a text that was rather more independent of the Palestinian family of which Sam and the LXX are, at different stages, supposed to be witnesses.[59]

Ronald Hendel has made use of Jubilees's readings in his book *The Text of Genesis 1-11*. Specifically in the context of describing his 'stemmatic model for Genesis 1-11' he mentions the evidence from texts like Jubilees and LAB. Beneath his Genesis archetype he distinguishes a 'proto-M hyparchetype' and an 'old Palestinian hyparchetype', the latter of which is further subdivided into a 'proto-S hyparchetype' and a 'proto-G hyparchetype'. 'Although we do not at present have evidence for more than two hyparchetypes at this level, texts such as Jub. and LAB suggest the possibility of other branchings and occasions for horizontal transmission.'[60] After mentioning my two studies, he adds: 'I would differ with VanderKam's emphasis on unique readings and his primarily statistical method..., but the picture of many Palestinian texts in circulation in the Second Temple period with varying degrees of affinity to S and G is very plausible.'[61]

5. The Genesis Apocryphon

In 1978 I published a similar study of the scriptural quotations in the Genesis Apocryphon.[62] From comparing the readings in Jubilees with those in the Genesis Apocryphon it had become apparent that the Genesis text presupposed by the cave 1 Aramaic work was nearly identical with the one reflected in Jubilees. The readings in it were compared with those in the MT, LXX, and Samaritan Pentateuch. The results were: in the nine instances where the Genesis Apocryphon had a reading for which the MT and Samaritan Pentateuch differed, it always sided with Samaritan Pentateuch (which is supported by the LXX in six of the nine). These readings were either expansionistic or served to smooth out the text. In eleven cases the Genesis Apocryphon sided with the MT and Samaritan Pentateuch against the LXX; in these cases it is likely that original readings are involved. In nineteen other readings, the Genesis Apocryphon joined the LXX against both the MT and the Samaritan Pentateuch. These were understood to be older Palestinian readings surviving in the LXX but not present in the Samaritan Pentateuch. That is, the frame of reference was again Cross's theory of local texts and the conclusion was that the author of the Genesis Apocryphon 'cited from an older Palestinian type of biblical text'.[63]

CONCLUSIONS

We have glanced at several compositions which are of different literary types and which work with older authoritative texts in one way or another. The Reworked Pentateuch stands so close to known copies of scriptural texts that it may belong among them; the other four works surveyed are members of the category *Rewritten Scriptures* and contain what Dimant labels 'implicit quotations in biblical expansion'. Some conclusions may be drawn from our survey of these works and the research published on them.

1) We should avoid using terms such as *Bible* and *biblical* when we are engaged in the academic study of the Second Temple period and communicating with academic audiences. We lack evidence that there was a Bible - especially one accepted by most Jewish people - and hence are not able to define exactly what was and was not a 'biblical' text in that period. If the Samaritan Pentateuch, whether in its pre-sectarian or sectarian form, is placed in a certain category ('Bible', Scripture, etc.) why should the Reworked Pentateuch not also be assigned to the same set? For Qumran, from which so much of our new evidence comes, the category of 'biblical' manuscripts is anachronistic and unduly limiting.

2) If there was an original text of the Pentateuch or of each book individually, we do not have it and thus do not know what it looked like. There appear to have been different texts of books such as Genesis and Exodus circulating in the late Second Temple period. Some of them have many pre-MT readings, others have more of other kinds. All of the compositions surveyed in this paper show affinities with the readings and types of readings in the Samaritan Pentateuch. The MT does preserve a relatively short text of these books and some other copies show marks of revisions (e.g., harmonizations), but how the pre-MT version arose and whether it is more pristine than the others are questions that our limited evidence may not enable us to answer. I find Ulrich's hypothesis of multiple literary editions to be an appealing one for the

evidence we do have;[64] how far back this process went and the bases for the individual editions are beyond the point to which sources lead us.

3) Not only should we avoid using terms such as *Bible* and *biblical* in our academic discourse about the Second Temple period, but we should also recognize that statistics of the number of 'biblical' copies from Qumran and other places and the ways in which they are classified are probably inaccurate.[65] The fuzzy picture would emerge into better focus if all evidence were adduced, including the Reworked Pentateuch and the scriptural texts underlying compositions such as the Temple Scroll and Jubilees. The more complete picture would have the advantage of showing that the pre-Samaritan kinds of texts were more numerous than they are at times said to be.

4) We have many different texts with limited numbers of groupings of texts. For this reason we should, in producing the pertinent textual evidence, draw upon the range of what is available, not just on the so-called 'biblical' manuscripts. *The Dead Sea Scrolls Bible*[66] (and the Semitic edition to follow) is a wonderful start in accumulating the evidence for a translation of the Bible, but even it, despite its size, is based only on the 'biblical' manuscripts, not on the pesharim or the other sorts of texts surveyed in this essay. Of course, the editors have made a move in the right direction by including Jubilees, 1 Enoch and other works not found in the official Hebrew Bible (though they have not presented translations of the surviving fragments).

With virtually all of the Judean Desert texts now accessible in official editions, the time is ripe for accumulating all of the information regarding the wording of ancient scriptural texts, not just the portion of it that has for too long gone under the label *Bible*.

NOTES

*   I would like to thank Angela Kim for her helpful comments on drafts of this paper and on the subject in general.

1   On these see J. T. Milik, in DJD VI, 39; and *TCHB*, p. 119. As Tov indicates, their readings often differ from the MT. While the variations may be due to scribes writing them from memory, some of them agree with those in other ancient witnesses, including 'biblical' copies from Qumran, and thus probably preserve ancient scriptural variants.

2   William H. Brownlee, *The Text of Habakkuk in the Ancient Commentary from Qumran*, JBL Monograph Series, 11 (Philadelphia: Society of Biblical Literature and Exegesis, 1959).

3   Brownlee, *Text of Habakkuk*, pp. 112-13.

4   Brownlee, *Text of Habakkuk*, p. 115.

5   Brownlee, *Text of Habakkuk*, p. 117.

6   Brownlee, *Text of Habakkuk*, p. 118. In the same place he observed that the scroll often substantiates the antiquity of readings now in the MT, whether those readings are superior or inferior to others.

7   W. H. Brownlee, 'The Jerusalem Habakkuk Scroll', *BASOR*, 112 (1948), 8-18 (see p. 17 n. 21).

8   Brownlee, *Text of Habakkuk*, p. 118.

9   Brownlee, *Text of Habakkuk*, p. 123. In his list on p. 119 he gives five, but on pp. 121-22 he removes one of them.

10   See George J. Brooke, 'The Biblical Texts in the Qumran Commentaries: Scribal Errors or Exegetical Variants?', in *Early Jewish and Christian Exegesis: Studies in Memory of William Hugh Brownlee*, ed. by Craig A. Evans and William F. Stinespring, Homage Series, 10 (Atlanta: Scholars Press, 1987), pp. 85-100.

11   Emanuel Tov, 'Excerpted and Abbreviated Biblical Texts from Qumran', *RevQ*, 16 (1995), 581-600.

12   Tov, 'Excerpted and Abbreviated Biblical Texts', 599.

13   See, for example, Joseph A. Fitzmyer, 'The Use of Explicit Old Testament Quotations in Qumran

James C. VanderKam

Literature and the New Testament', *NTS*, 7 (1960-61), 297-333; Geza Vermes, 'Biblical Proof-Texts in Qumran Literature', *JSS*, 34 (1989), 493-508. Both of these collections were made before the recent wave of publication; it would be very helpful to have a full compilation of all these citations and near citations, however difficult it may be at times to determine what is and is not a quotation.

14   Although he introduced the term, Vermes has, to my knowledge, not given a precise definition for it. In Geza Vermes, *Scripture and Tradition in Judaism: Haggadic Studies*, Studia Post-Biblica, 4, 2nd edn, (Leiden: Brill), p. 73, he writes, after using material from Sefer ha-Yashar at the beginning and end of his study of the life of Abraham: 'this examination of the Yashar story fully illustrates what is meant by the term "rewritten Bible". In order to anticipate questions, and to solve problems in advance, the midrashist inserts haggadic development into the biblical narrative—an exegetical process which is probably as ancient as scriptural interpretation itself.' In the same place he refers to the Palestinian Targum, Jewish Antiquities, Pseudo-Philo, Jubilees, and the Genesis Apocryphon. For other treatments of the topic without objections to the phrase *Rewritten Bible*, see Philip S. Alexander, 'Retelling the Old Testament' in *It is Written: Scripture Citing Scripture: Essays in Honour of Barnabas Lindars, SSF*, ed. by D. A. Carson and H. G. M. Williamson (Cambridge: Cambridge University Press, 1988), pp. 99-121; George J. Brooke, 'Rewritten Bible', in *EDSS*, II, pp. 777-81. Daniel J. Harrington provides a helpful survey of the various terms that have been suggested (midrash, targum, texte continué) in Daniel J. Harrington, 'Palestinian Adaptations of Biblical Narratives and Prophecies', in *Early Judaism and Its Modern Interpreters*, ed. by Robert A. Kraft and George W. E. Nickelsburg, The Bible and Its Modern Interpreters, 2 (Philadelphia: Fortress; Atlanta: Scholars Press, 1986), pp. 239-47, (pp. 242-43). There he reserves the term *The Bible Rewritten* for narratives.

15   On this, see Sidnie White Crawford, 'The "Rewritten Bible" at Qumran: A Look at Three Texts', *ErIsr*, 26 (Archaeological, Historical and Geographical Studies (Frank Moore Cross volume), 1999), pp. 1*-8* (p. 1*).

16   Devorah Dimant, 'Use and Interpretation of Mikra in the Apocrypha and Pseudepigrapha', in *Mikra: Text, Translation, Reading and Interpretation of the Hebrew Bible in Ancient Judaism and Early Christianity*, ed. by Martin Jan Mulder and Harry Sysling, Compendia Rerum Iudaicarum ad Novum Testamentum, II, 1 (Assen: Van Gorcum; Philadelphia: Fortress, 1988), pp. 379-419 (p. 382). It should be said that the same charge of anachronism can be levelled at the use of *Mikra* for this period as for its English equivalent *Bible*.

17   Dimant, p. 401.

18   See Dimant, pp. 402-406.

19   Dimant, 'Mikra', pp. 384-419.

20   Emanuel Tov, 'The Textual Status of 4Q364-367 (4QPP)', *MQC*, pp. 43-82 (p. 49). See also the edition of 4Q364-367 in DJD XIII, 191 for virtually the same sentences. Tov's fellow editor, Sidnie White Crawford, has written a brief account of the work: 'Reworked Pentateuch', in *EDSS*, II, pp. 775-77.

21   DJD XIII, p. 196.

22   DJD XIII, p. 195. The numbers here differ slightly from the earlier formulation in Tov, 'Textual Status', p. 78.

23   Tov, 'Textual Status', pp. 51-52.

24   Crawford distinguishes Reworked Pentateuch from the pre-Samaritan copies in that it *adds* new material not drawn from elsewhere in the Pentateuch (Crawford, 'The "Rewritten" Bible at Qumran', p. 3). But do we know it adds *new* material? And why should this be thought to make it less authoritative? A more important criterion may be whether the older material is placed within a new editorial setting, with the writer in this way signalling a difference from the older text, as the author of Jubilees does. But the case of Jubilees makes plain that the issue of form is a different one than the matter of authority.

25   Tov, 'Textual Status', p. 47.

26   Tov, 'Textual Status', p. 50.

27   Nathan Jastram, '4QNum^b', in DJD XII, pp. 205-67 (pp. 262-64).

28   Tov distinguishes between 'reworking/rewriting which involved a limited intervention in the biblical text, and rephrasing involving a major intervention, often in such a way that the underlying biblical text is hardly recognizable. Adding exegetical comments to the biblical text is a form of rewriting.'

The Wording of Biblical Citations

Emanuel Tov, 'Biblical Texts as Reworked in Some Qumran Manuscripts with Special Attention to 4QRP and 4QParaGen-Exod', in *CRC*, pp. 111-34 (p. 112).

29   Moshe J. Bernstein, 'Pentateuchal Interpretation at Qumran', in *DSSAFY*, I, pp. 128-59 (pp. 134-35). Bernstein doubts that all of the Reworked Pentateuch texts are from the same composition and does not think 4Q158 belongs with 4Q364-67. This point was argued by Michael Segal, 'Biblical Exegesis in 4Q158: Techniques and Genre', *Textus*, 19 (1998), 45-62. Segal has more recently maintained that while 4Q158 is from a different work than 4Q364-67, even these latter four numbers are not copies of one composition: 4Q364-65 are copies of the Pentateuch, the fragmentary 4Q366 is also a copy of the Pentateuch, while the poorly preserved 4Q367 may be an excerpted text of Leviticus: Michael Segal, '4QReworked Pentateuch or 4QPentateuch?', in *The Dead Sea Scrolls: Fifty Years After Their Discovery: Proceedings of the Jerusalem Congress, July 20-25, 1997*, ed. by Lawrence H. Schiffman (Jerusalem: IES, 2000), pp. 391-99. Eugene Ulrich has written: 'it is possible that 4Q364–367 preserve yet a third variant literary edition of the Pentateuch, alongside the MT and the second Jewish variant edition that was at home in Second Temple Judaism and used by the Samaritans as the textual basis for their form of the Pentateuch' (*DSSAFY*, I, pp. 79-100 (p. 89)).

30   'The "Temple Scroll" and Old Testament Textual Criticism', Hebrew with English summary, *ErIsr*, 16 (1982) (Archaeological, Historical and Geographical Studies (Harry M. Orlinsky Volume); Jerusalem: IES), pp. 100-111.

31   'Temple Scroll', pp. 100-103.

32   'Temple Scroll', pp. 104-108.

33   'Temple Scroll', p. 109.

34   'Temple Scroll', p. 110.

35   George J. Brooke, 'The Temple Scroll and LXX Exodus 35-40', in *SSCW*, pp. 81-106 (p. 81).

36   Brooke, 'Temple Scroll and LXX Exodus', pp. 100-101.

37   Lawrence H. Schiffman, 'The Septuagint and the Temple Scroll: Shared "Halakhic" Variants', in *SSCW*, pp. 277-97 (p. 292).

38   George J. Brooke, 'The Textual Tradition of the *Temple Scroll* and Recently Published Manuscripts of the Pentateuch', in *The Dead Sea Scrolls: Forty Years of Research*, ed. by Devorah Dimant and Uriel Rappaport, STDJ, 10 (Leiden: Brill; Jerusalem: Magnes, 1992), pp. 261-82.

39   Brooke, 'Textual Tradition of the *Temple Scroll*', p. 282.

40   Brooke, 'Textual Tradition of the *Temple Scroll*', p. 263.

41   Daniel J. Harrington, 'The Biblical Text of Pseudo-Philo's *Liber Antiquitatum Biblicarum*', *CBQ*, 33 (1971), 1-17.

42   Harrington, 'Biblical Text', 6.

43   Against the charge that the book is a paraphrase, Harrington writes: 'This is indeed an objection to be taken seriously, yet so consistent and patterned are the agreements between LAB and certain known biblical texts that the objection does not really stand', in D. Harrington, 'Biblical Text', 6.

44   Howard Jacobson, *A Commentary on Pseudo-Philo's Liber Antiquitatum Biblicarum with Latin Text and English Translation*, Arbeiten zur Geschichte des antiken Judentums und des Urchristentums, 31, 2 vols (Leiden: Brill, 1996), I, p. 255.

45   Jacobson, *A Commentary*, I, p. 255; Harrington, however, also deals with such cases (Harrington, 'Biblical Text', pp. 10, 16). Perhaps more importantly, he identifies a number of texts as Lucianic in the Pentateuch, but he was operating with an older understanding of which are the Lucianic manuscripts there - a point which does affect his analysis.

46   A. Dillmann, 'Das Buch der Jubiläen oder die kleine Genesis: aus dem Äthiopischen übersezt', *Jahrbücher der Biblischen Wissenschaft*, 3 (1851), 1-96 (pp. 88-90).

47   A. Dillmann, 'Beiträge aus dem Buch der Jubiläen zur Kritik des Pentateuch-Textes', in *Sitzungsberichte der königlichen preussischen Akademie der Wissenschaften zu Berlin*, 1 (Berlin: Verlag der königlichen Akademie der Wissenschaften, 1883), pp. 323-40.

48   Dillmann, 'Beiträge', pp. 324-34.

49   R. H. Charles, *The Book of Jubilees or the Little Genesis* (London: Black, 1902; reprinted Jerusalem: Maqor, 1972), pp. xxxiii-xxxix.

50   Charles, *Book of Jubilees*, p. xxxviii.

51   Charles, *Book of Jubilees*, p. xxxviii.

52 James C. VanderKam, *Textual and Historical Studies in the Book of Jubilees*, HSM, 14 (Missoula, MT: Scholars Press, 1977), pp. 142-98.

53 VanderKam, *Textual and Historical Studies*, p. 136.

54 VanderKam, *Textual and Historical Studies*, p. 137.

55 F. M. Cross, Jr., 'The Contribution of the Qumrân Discoveries to the Study of the Biblical Text', *IEJ*, 16 (1966), 81-95 (p. 89).

56 James C. VanderKam, 'Jubilees and Hebrew Texts of Genesis-Exodus', *Textus*, 14 (1988), 71-85. The article contains a fuller history of the subject than the one offered here.

57 See, for example, Emanuel Tov, 'A Modern Textual Outlook Based on the Qumran Scrolls', *HUCA*, 53 (1982), pp. 11-27.

58 The numbers in parentheses are those to the left of the parenthetical number plus 250; the 250 readings are ones in which Jubilees agrees with all of these versions against the Ethiopic Genesis-Exodus.

59 VanderKam, 'Jubilees and Hebrew Texts of Genesis-Exodus', 83.

60 Ronald S. Hendel, *The Text of Genesis 1-11: Textual Studies and Critical Edition* (New York: Oxford University Press, 1998), p. 100.

61 Hendel, *Text of Genesis 1-11*, p. 100.

62 James C. VanderKam, 'The Textual Affinities of the Biblical Citations in the Genesis Apocryphon', *JBL*, 97 (1978), 45-55.

63 VanderKam, 'Textual Affinities', p. 55.

64 Several of the essays in which he has developed his theory are now collected in Eugene Ulrich, *The Dead Sea Scrolls and the Origins of the Bible* (Grand Rapids: Eerdmans; Leiden: Brill, 1999).

65 Tov divides the 'biblical' manuscripts from Qumran into five categories. One of these, the 'pre-Samaritan', is said to include about 5% of the texts. A percentage such as this would change if the survey included all relevant material, not just the 'biblical' scrolls (see *TCHB*, pp. 114-17); for revised figures given by Tov, see his paper in the present volume.

66 *DSSB*.

THE ENOCHIC LITERATURE AND THE BIBLE: INTERTEXTUALITY AND ITS IMPLICATIONS

Philip S. Alexander

THE PROBLEM OF 'ENOCH' AND THE 'BIBLE'

WHAT LIGHT does the ancient Enochic literature throw on the text of the Bible and on the formation of the biblical canon? In attempting to answer this question we must not assume at the outset that we are dealing with two fully formed and distinct bodies of literature — the Bible and the Books of Enoch — and that one, the Books of Enoch, quoted the other, the Bible, and used it as authoritative Scripture. This was not necessarily the case. The Enochic literature is composite and grew up over a long period of time. When its oldest layers were laid down, the Pentateuch as we know it may still have been in flux. The authors of the Books of Enoch may, therefore, have known the biblical traditions in a rather different form from that which we now have in our Bibles, and, in any case, they may not have regarded those traditions as 'Scripture' in the accepted theological sense of that term. The Enochic and biblical traditions may for a period have grown side by side, and have been, in consequence, intertwined. We must bear this possibility and the dangers of anachronism constantly in mind.

In order to treat this question properly it is necessary first to obtain an overview of the Enochic corpus. Our starting point is the Ethiopic Book of Enoch, known commonly as 1 Enoch, the only more or less complete version of the Enochic writings that we now possess. This is extant in a number of Ethiopic manuscripts.[1] It is evident from even a cursory reading of 1 Enoch that it is a patchwork of different sources of very different dates. Five of these have been distinguished. They are, in probable order of composition: (1) The Book of the Heavenly Luminaries (1 Enoch 72-82); (2) The Book of the Watchers (1 Enoch 1-36); (3) The Book of Dreams (1 Enoch 83-90); (4) The Epistle of Enoch (1 Enoch 91-108); and (5) The Similitudes or Parables of Enoch (1 Enoch 37-71).[2] Each of these so-called 'books' is in itself composite and made up of diverse materials. Ethiopic Enoch was probably translated from a Greek version of Enoch, substantial parts of which have been preserved, but the Greek in its turn was translated from an Aramaic original composed in the Second Temple period.[3] Scholars had come to this conclusion on the basis of internal analysis of the Greek and Ethiopic texts. Their deductions were completely vindicated when fragments of the original Aramaic Enoch were discovered among the Dead Sea Scrolls. The Dead Sea Sect did not write the Books of Enoch, but they clearly held them in high regard. Fragments of four of the five books of the Ethiopic Enoch have been found at Qumran, and they generally confirm that the Ethiopic version is a reasonably accurate representative of the original. The text that was missing was the Similitudes of Enoch. In its place another Enochic work surfaced at Qumran, The Book of Giants. This had partly survived, unrecognized by scholars for what it was, in the Manichaean Book of Giants and in the curious little Hebrew work, which Adolf Jellinek had published in the nineteenth century called *Midrash Shemhazai ve-Aza'el*.[4] This, then, is the Enochic literature from Second Temple times, the relationship of which to Scripture it is our purpose to explore. There are around two hundred parallels to Scripture in 1 Enoch, ranging from verbal echoes to 'quotations', the books of Genesis, Deuteronomy, Job, Psalms, Isaiah, Jeremiah and Daniel being particularly prominent. However, two passages from Scripture are of fundamental importance for our present purposes — the genealogy of Enoch in Gen 5:18-25 and the account of the Sons of God in Genesis 6:1-8. These two texts are all-pervasive in the Enochic corpus and a close analysis of them will serve to illuminate the question of how the Books of Enoch relate to Scripture.

THE GENEALOGY OF ENOCH
AND THE STORY OF THE SONS OF GOD

Before turning to the Books of Enoch we must investigate the biblical text in its own terms to find out what it might mean and what problems and possibilities it throws up. We must look at it, not only with the eyes of the modern critical scholar, but with the eyes of the ancient exegete. First, Genesis 5:18-25:

(18) And Jared lived a hundred and sixty-two years, and begat Enoch: (19) and Jared lived after he begat Enoch eight hundred years, and begat sons and daughters: (20) and all the days of Jared were nine hundred and sixty-two years: and he died. (21) And Enoch lived sixty-five years, and begat Methuselah: (22) and Enoch walked with God after he begat Methuselah three hundred years, and begat sons and daughters: (23) and all the days of Enoch were three hundred and sixty-five years: (24) and Enoch walked with God [ויתהלך חנוך את האלהים], and he was not; for God took him.[5]

At first sight this does not seem to tell us much. It appears to offer nothing more than a dry-as-dust genealogy. Appearances, however, are deceptive. The text uses a number of ambiguous but suggestive phrases, and generally gives the impression that it is alluding to a fuller story, which the reader may be expected to know. What is meant by 'Enoch walked with God'? Is the sense that he lived a godly life and was a righteous man, or is the sense of האלהים here not 'God' but 'gods' or 'angels', in which case what would it mean to say that Enoch walked with the angels? That he consorted with them in some way? That they communed with him and possibly passed on to him secrets? And why are there *two* mentions of 'walking with God', one in verse 22 and the other in verse 24? Is this repetition significant? What is meant by saying, 'and he was not, for God took him'? The obvious sense is that he vanished from human society because God removed him to somewhere else. But how did God remove him, and why and where to? The verb 'to take' is suggestive because it is used elsewhere in Scripture for the removal of Elijah to heaven in the chariot of fire (2 Kings 2:5). Did God remove Enoch without dying to heaven or to paradise? And why is Enoch's lifespan so markedly shorter than that of the other figures in this genealogy? And is there any significance in the fact that it corresponds to the number of days in the solar year? There are two names in the passage which cry out for etymology. The first is 'Enoch': the root of this, חנך, means to 'dedicate', 'train' or 'instruct'. Is this significant? The other is 'Jared' which can be easily explained as a noun meaning 'descent' from the root ירד, 'to descend'. But what descent might be alluded to in the name? Turning to the broader context, it is notable that the regular and predictable pattern of the genealogy in Genesis 5 breaks down with Enoch. Why is he singled out? Can it be significant that he is the seventh member of a ten-member genealogy that spans the history of the world from the creation to the Flood? The passage is a lot more promising exegetically than one might at first reading suppose.

The passage on the Sons of God in Genesis 6:1-8 more obviously raises exegetical and theological problems:

(1) And it came to pass, when men began to multiply on the face of the ground, and daughters were born to them, (2) that the sons of God saw the daughters of men that they were fair; and they took for themselves wives of all that they chose. (3) And the Lord said, My spirit shall not strive with man for ever, since he is also flesh: yet shall his days be one hundred and twenty years. (4) The Nephilim were in the earth in those days, and also after that, when the sons of God came in unto the daughters of men, and they bare children to them: the same were the mighty men that were of old, the men of renown. (5) And the Lord saw that the wickedness of man was great in the earth, and that every imagination of his heart was only evil continually. (6) And it repented the Lord that he had made man on the earth, and it grieved him at his heart. (7) And the Lord said, I will destroy man whom I have created from the face of the ground; both man and beast, and creeping thing, and fowl of the air; for it repents me that I have made them. (8) But Noah found grace in the eyes of the Lord.

Here too, as in the genealogy of Enoch, the story has an air of allusiveness about it. Who are the 'Sons of God': are they righteous human beings or are they angels? If the latter, how can celestial beings couple with human women? Is this not contrary to the natural order established at creation of each procreating 'after its kind'? And who are the גבורים ('mighty men') and the Nephilim mentioned in verse 4. Is it significant that the latter name appears to mean 'fallen ones'? What is the 'fall' alluded to here? And what is the relationship between the wickedness on the earth which provoked God to bring the Flood (Genesis 6:5-8) and the activity of the Sons of God? Were the Sons of God in some sense responsible for the moral condition of the world that provoked the Flood?

THE ENOCHIC LITERATURE AND GENESIS 5:18-25

Let us now consider the parallels in the Enochic literature to these texts. There are three passages which are directly linked with the genealogy in Genesis 5:18-25. The first is 1 Enoch 81:1-10:

(1) And he [Uriel] said to me: 'Look, Enoch, in the book of the heavenly tablets, and read what is written therein, and acquaint yourself with every single fact.' (2) And I looked at everything in the heavenly tablets, and I read everything that was written, and I understood everything. And I read the book, and everything that was written in it, all the deeds of mankind and of all the children of flesh who shall be on the earth, unto the generations of eternity. (3) And at once I blessed the great Lord, the king of glory, for ever, because he has made all the works of the world, and I praised the Lord because of his patience, and I blessed him on account of the sons of Adam. (4) And then I said: 'Blessed is the man who dies righteous and good, about whom no book of unrighteousness has been written, and against whom no sin has been found.' (5) And those seven Holy Ones brought me and placed me on earth before the door of my house, and said to me: 'Make everything known to your son Methuselah, and show all your children that no flesh is righteous in the sight of the Lord, for he created them. (6) For one year we shall leave you with your son until you again have given them your last commandments, so that you may teach your children and record [these things] for them, and testify to all your children. And in the second year you shall be taken from their midst. (7) Let your heart be

strong, for the good shall proclaim righteousness to the good; the righteous shall rejoice with the righteous, and shall wish one another well. (8) But sinner shall die with sinner, and the apostate shall sink with the apostate. (9) And those who practice righteousness shall die because of the deeds of men, and be taken away because of the deeds of the godless.' (10) And in those days they finished speaking with me; and I returned to my people, blessing the Lord of the world.[6]

The text here appears to be truncated from a longer story (note, for example, the unexplained reference to the 'seven Holy Ones' in verse 5), and the link with Genesis 5 is not at first sight obvious. But it is certainly there: it is particularly evident at verse 5, 'And the seven Holy Ones brought me and placed me on earth before the door of my house, and said to me: "Make everything known to your son Methuselah"'. 1 Enoch 81:1-10 can be construed as a close reading of Genesis 5 in which a number of key exegetical decisions have been taken to clarify and supplement the biblical text. The crucial phrase ויתהלך חנוך את האלהים has been taken in a two-fold sense. The primary meaning is that Enoch consorted with the angels, he 'walked' with them, and they showed him secrets, in this case the heavenly tablets, which function both as a record of the righteous and the wicked and as the script for the unfolding drama of history from the creation to the eschaton.

Just how Enoch consorted with the angels is not entirely clear, but an ascent to heaven is hinted at: where else would one see the 'heavenly tablets' if not in heaven? And note the precise wording of verse 5, 'and the seven Holy Ones brought me and placed me *on earth*.' But note also the implicit interpretation of the double use of the phrase ויתהלך חנוך את האלהים in Genesis 5. Enoch consorted with the angels (i.e., ascended to heaven), then descended to earth again to pass on to his son Methuselah the mysteries that he had seen (he, therefore, in keeping with the etymology of his name, 'instructed' his son: he was a revealer of secrets). He performed this function for two years and then was summoned by the angels to walk with them again, to ascend this time permanently to heaven. The second interpretation which our Enochic author has made of ויתהלך חנוך את האלהים is to take it as indicating that Enoch was a godly man. This is an obvious source for his assertion (repeated tirelessly throughout the Enochic literature) that Enoch was righteous. There is a hint that righteous Enoch functions as the prototype or the forerunner of all the righteous, and just as he escaped death (an implicit interpretation of 'and God took him' in verse 24), so too will the righteous (note 1 Enoch 81:9).

Three other passages of 1 Enoch also contain clear allusions to Genesis 5:18-25. The first is 1 Enoch 12:1-2:

(1) Before these things Enoch was taken up,[7] and none of the children of men knew where he had been taken up, or where he was or what had happened to him. (2) But his dealings were with the Watchers, and his days were with the Holy Ones.

At first reading this seems no more than a straightforward paraphrase of Genesis 5:22 and 24, but, short though it is, it contains significant elements of interpretation. The phrase ויתהלך חנוך את האלהים is clearly taken as meaning that Enoch consorted with the angels, but note the spin: the angels are here identified as the Watchers, that is, *in context*, the fallen angels.[8] The emphasis here, then, is not on Enoch's role as a revealer of secrets which the angels showed to him, but on the other great role which he plays in the Enochic literature as an agent of divine judgement. Here he functions specifically as an intermediary between the fallen Watchers on the one hand and God and the good angels on the other. Note too the hint of an ascension to heaven, and the clarification of the words, 'and he was not': 'and none of the children of men knew where he had been taken up, or where he was or what had happened to him.'

The second passage is 1 Enoch 70:1-3:

(1) And it came to pass after this that the name of the Son of Man was raised up to the Lord of the Spirits from those who dwell on earth.[9] (2) And he was lifted up in the chariots of the spirit, and his name vanished from among them. (3) And from that day I was no longer counted among them. And he placed me between two regions, between the north and the west, where the angels took the cords to measure for me the place for the elect and righteous.

Here the element of translation is stressed. In terms of the exegetical tradition, the reference must be to the second and final removal of Enoch from human society. Note, however, the clear allusion to the translation of Elijah: Enoch was taken up 'in the *chariots* of the spirit'. This is exegetically based on the fact, as we noted earlier, that the verb לקח is used in both the translation of Elijah and the translation of Enoch. The place to which Enoch is translated here, however, does not seem to be heaven, but rather the paradise prepared for the righteous which is located in the north-west of the world. The 'earth', therefore, in verse 1, should be taken as the *oikoumene*, and not in the sense of the earth as opposed to the heavens. Once again we find righteous Enoch, who 'walked with God', playing the role of the forerunner of all the righteous who would ultimately follow him into the paradise of righteousness. It is unclear what is implied by the statement that it was 'the *name* of the Son of Man' that was raised up to the Lord of the spirits. There is a debate within the Enochic tradition as to whether Enoch was translated *bodily* or only in spirit. Some of those who held that his translation was into heaven asserted that the translation was only in spirit or in a dream, probably because they could not envisage flesh and blood enduring the physical rigours of the fiery heavenly world. Those who did hold to a bodily ascent into heaven were forced to assume that the material body was transformed into a more spiritual entity that could survive in heaven. The clearest example of this latter line of thought is found in 2 Enoch. Others, however, because they could not accept that human beings could physically survive the rigours of heaven had him *bodily* translated to paradise, which, though not part of the *oikoumene*, existed on the same terrestrial plane and shared, so to speak, the same atmosphere. Here, if 'the name of the Son of Man' is effectively equivalent to his 'spirit', we have a curious mixture of the two lines of thought: Enoch is *spiritually* translated to *paradise*![10]

1 Enoch 71:1-17, the final passage which we shall consider, is one of the richest in allusions to Genesis 5:18-25:

(1) And it came to pass after this that my spirit was translated, and I ascended into the heavens. And I saw the sons of the holy angels, treading on flames of fire. Their garments were white, and their robes and the light of their faces were like snow. [...] (3) And the angel Michael, one of the archangels, seized me by my right hand, and lifted me up and led me forth into all the secrets of mercy, and the secrets of righteousness. (4) And he showed me all the secrets of the ends of the heavens, and all the storehouses of all the stars, and all the luminaries, whence they come out in the presence of the holy ones. (5) And he translated my spirit, and I, Enoch, was in the heaven of heavens, and I saw there, in the midst of the luminaries, a structure built as it were of hailstones, and among those hailstones tongues of living fire. [...] (8) And I saw angels who could not be counted. [...] (10) And with them was the Chief of Days, whose head was white and pure as wool, and his raiment indescribable. [...] (14) And that angel [Michael] came to me and greeted me with his voice

and said to me: 'You are the Son of Man who is born to righteousness, and righteousness abides in you, and the righteousness of the Chief of Days will not forsake you. [...] (16) And all shall walk in your ways, since righteousness never forsakes you. With you shall be their dwelling-places, and with you their lot, and they shall not be separated from you for ever and ever. (17) And so there shall be length of days with that Son of Man, and the righteous shall have peace, and the righteous shall have a straight way, in the name of the Lord of Spirits for ever and ever.

Here ascension into heaven is clearly asserted, but note that the ascension is 'in spirit' (verses 1 and 5). Again there is the double interpretation of ויתהלך חנוך את האלהים, as implying both that Enoch consorted with the angels, here specifically to learn cosmological secrets, and that he was a righteous man who walked piously with God. He is seen here, as elsewhere, as the forerunner of the righteous, who anticipates the bliss that they shall finally enjoy. There are clear internal allusions to the Book of the Heavenly Luminaries (at verse 4) and to the Book of the Watchers (at verse 5), suggesting the comparative lateness of this passage. Also noteworthy is the very clear reference to the vision of the Chief of Days in Daniel 7.

Before proceeding to our second biblical passage let us pause and take stock. We have looked at a number of passages from the Enochic corpus which bear a strong relationship to Genesis 5:18-25. These passages agree in broad outline on their reading of the biblical text, but each has its own particular spin. We are dealing here with a dynamic exegetical tradition, in which later stages of the tradition are aware of the earlier and reacting to them. There is intertextuality not only between these passages and Genesis 5, but between one passage and another. The passages come from widely different strata of the Enochic corpus. 1 Enoch 81 is associated with the oldest layers, the Book of the Heavenly Luminaries, though it belongs to the appendix to that Book and is certainly not as old as the core section contained in chapters 72-99. 1 Enoch 12 is firmly embedded in the Book of the Watchers. It seems to mark a crucial turning point in the development of the tradition whereby Enoch in Genesis 5 was linked into the story of the Fall of the angels in Genesis 6. This link appears to have been effected exegetically through the etymologizing of the name of Enoch's father Jared in Genesis 5 as meaning 'descent'. What descent? The descent of the Watchers from heaven to couple with the daughters of men. 1 Enoch 70 and 71 are from the Similitudes of Enoch, which, as we noted earlier, are among the latest strata of the corpus. Interestingly the allusions here to Scripture are perhaps the clearest. A general pattern is exemplified: the later the stratum of the Enochic corpus, the clearer and fuller the allusions to Scripture.

THE ENOCHIC LITERATURE AND GENESIS 6:1-8

Now let us turn to our second biblical passage, the account of the Sons of God in Genesis 6:1-8. This text too is pervasive in the Enochic literature, but the fullest allusions to it are, not surprisingly, in the Book of the Watchers, of which it forms the bedrock. The most important passages are in chapters 6, 7, 15 and 16 (cf., 4Q201; 4Q202; 4Q204):

(6:1) And it came to pass, when the children of men had multiplied, in those days there were born [to them] fair and beautiful daughters. (2) And the angels, the sons of heaven, saw them and desired them, and lusted after them; and they said one to another: 'Come, let us choose for ourselves wives from the daughters of men, and let us beget for ourselves children. (3) And Shemihazah, who was their leader, said to them: 'I fear you will not be willing to do this deed, and I alone shall pay the penalty for a great sin.' (4) And they all answered him and said: 'Let us all swear an oath, and bind one another with curses, not to abandon this plan till we have completed it and done this deed.' (5) Then they all swore together and bound one another with curses. (6) And there were two hundred who descended in the days of Jared on the summit of Mount Hermon; and they called the mount Hermon, because they swore and bound one another with curses upon it. (7) And these are the names of their leaders ... [a list of twenty names follows] ... (8) These are the leaders who [were each over] ten.

(7:1) And they took for themselves wives. Each of them chose for himself a wife, and they began to cohabit with them and to defile themselves with them; and they taught them charms and spells, and showed them the cutting of roots and herbs. (2) And they became pregnant by them, and bore great Giants three thousand cubits tall. (3) These devoured the fruits of men's labour, until men were unable to sustain them. (4) Then the Giants behaved outrageously towards them and devoured mankind. (5) And they began to sin against the birds and the beasts of the earth, the reptiles and the fish, and to devour each other and drink the blood. (6) Thereupon the earth made accusation against the lawless ones.

(15:8) And now the Giants, who were born from spirits and flesh, shall be called evil spirits upon the earth, and on the earth shall be their dwelling-place. (9) Evil spirits shall come forth from their bodies, for from above have they come, and from the Holy Watchers was the beginning of their creation and the beginning of their foundation. Evil spirits they shall be upon the earth. (10) As for celestial spirits, heaven shall be their dwelling-place; as for terrestrial spirits, born upon the earth, on the earth shall be their dwelling-place. (11) But the vicious spirits [issuing] from the Giants, the Nephilim,[11] inflict harm, destroy, attack, wrestle and dash to the ground, causing injuries; they eat nothing, but fast and thirst and produce hallucinations, and strike down.[12] (12) And these [spirits] will rise against the sons of men and women, because they came forth from them. (16:1) From the day of the time of the slaughter, destruction and death of the Giants, the Nephilim, the mighty ones of the earth, the great, renowned ones, the spirits that have gone out from their souls, as from flesh, will destroy without judgement. Thus they will destroy until the days of the end, until the great judgement, in which the great aeon will be consummated.

Here we find a very clear reading of Genesis 6:1-8 which answers unequivocally all the exegetical questions which we raised earlier. The 'Sons of God' are identified as angels, specifically with an order of angels known as Watchers. They descended to earth on Mount Hermon, the name of which recalls the oath which they swore to bind themselves to go through with their rebellious act of leaving their proper heavenly station and trespassing into a domain where they did not belong. They descended in the days of Jared, Enoch's father, whose name commemorates their fateful arrival. The result of their union with human women — as might be expected from a coupling so contrary to the laws of nature — was monstrous offspring, Giants. This is clearly the Enochic interpretation of the הגבורים of Genesis 6:4. The fallen Watchers, according to the Enochic account were directly and indirectly responsible for the sorry moral state of the world which led directly to the cataclysmic divine judgement of the Flood. They corrupted humankind by introducing them to corrupting knowledge. As the Book of the Watchers makes clear, this knowledge was of three kinds: first, how to make cosmetics and jewellery: the result was an increase in promiscuity and sexual immorality (the Book of the Watchers is strongly puritan in tone); second, a knowledge of how to makes weapons: the result was an increase in war and strife (there is a whiff of technophobia pervading the Book of the Watchers); and third, a knowledge of sorcery, some of which has to do with the healing arts and may be a negative reaction to the introduction to Judaea of Greek medicine — a new-fangled form of knowledge which was, a little later, somewhat to trouble Ben Sira.[13]

The Watchers were also indirectly responsible for the deplorable condition of world. Their monstrous offspring, the Giants, proved to be utterly lawless and oppressed animals and humans alike. The Watchers and their progeny had to be dealt with: the Watchers were incarcerated in a place of punishment awaiting the final judgement at the end of history. The Giants, in ways that echo the Greek *gigantomachia*, had to be killed and the world which they had so comprehensively corrupted cleansed by the waters of the Flood. However, the Giants could not be totally destroyed: their immortal *spirits* survived and continued to attack humankind. These spirits appear to be identified with the Nephilim of Genesis 6:4. What is here proposed is an aetiology of demons, to whom are attributed illness, specifically conditions involving fevers and epilepsies: note 15:11, 'But the vicious spirits [issuing] from the Giants, the Nephilim, inflict harm, destroy, attack, wrestle and dash to the ground, causing injuries' (anyone acquainted with ancient magical texts will immediately detect here the language of amulets); 'they eat nothing, but fast and thirst and produce hallucinations, and strike down.' These spirits, because of their very nature, could not be destroyed by the waters of the Flood. They survived the Flood and are the cause of the continuing corruption in the world. They will only be dealt with finally at the end of time: 'they will destroy until the days of the end, until the great judgement, in which the great aeon will be consummated' (15:8).

This rich elaboration of the story of the Sons of God in Genesis 6:1-8 was to prove to be one of the primal myths of European civilization. It enshrines a number of powerful theological ideas. It bears, within the biblical *Heilsgeschichte*, an interesting relationship with Genesis 2-3. The story of the expulsion of humankind from Eden was clearly known to the authors of the Enochic writings: it provides them with their vision of paradise where the righteous will be rewarded (see, for example, 25:4-6), but for the redactor of the Book of the Watchers it is not the Fall of Adam that is the primary cause of the corruption of the world, but the Fall of the Watchers (1 Enoch 32:6; cf., 9:6, 9, 10; 10:8). There are interesting parallels between the two Falls: both cast women in a baleful role, both have to do with forbidden knowledge, but clearly, for whatever reason, the Enochic writers found the Fall of the Angels a better vehicle for their theological ideas than the story of the Garden of Eden.

THE IMPLICATIONS OF INTERTEXTUALITY

There is a great deal more that could be said about these two immensely rich passages, but we have said enough for our present limited purposes. We have shown that there is an intense, detailed, and highly explicit intertextuality between Genesis 5 and 6 on the one hand and the Enochic literature on the other. But what precisely is the nature of this relationship? I have modelled it as basically exegetical. I have done so, not because I am anachronistically assuming that Enoch and the Bible were two fixed bodies of literature, one of which was 'quoting' the other, but because I can find no other type of relationship which makes as good sense of the data as they stand. To my eye, the Enochic writers are offering a close reading of the biblical text more or less in the form in which we now have it. That reading is exactly of the kind with which I am familiar from my work on later rabbinic Midrash. More precisely, this reading represents a type of Bible exegesis known as 'Rewritten Bible', in which the narrative of Scripture is reworked with explanatory additions. Classic examples of this genre of interpretation are found in the Book of Jubilees, in Josephus, The Antiquities of the Jews and in the Genesis Apocryphon from Qumran.[14]

This might all seem rather obvious were it not for the implications of this model, which may not be all that congenial to current thinking on the development of the canon of Scripture in the Second Temple period. The exegetical model presupposes that the text being exegeted is in some sense authoritative. Are we prepared to accept this, given how *early* some strata of the Enochic corpus are? Our analysis indicates that the explicit allusions to Scripture generally grow stronger the later we come in the Enochic writings, but exegesis seems to be implicit right from the start. Was there, then, some sort of canon of authoritative Scripture for the author of the Book of the Heavenly Luminaries even in the fourth century BCE? This goes rather against the grain of current scholarship, but I can see no plausible alternative. It has been suggested that, at least in the earliest layers of the Enochic literature, the relationship may in fact be the reverse: it is Scripture that is alluding to the Enochic traditions. This proposal has a certain plausibility. The Sethite genealogy in Genesis 5 comes from the so-called P-strand of the Pentateuch which may, according to some scholars, have been finally edited only in the Persian period.[15] In consequence it may not be all that distant in time from the earliest strata of Enoch. The close match between Enoch and Genesis 5-6 is impressive. There is nothing said in the one source which directly contradicts what is said in the other. But the relationship is ambiguous and can, in principle, be read in either direction. It is on the face of it attractive, given the extreme allusiveness of the biblical passages, to postulate that Genesis is abbreviating Enoch, rather than Enoch exegeting and expanding Genesis. The close verbal echoes suggest to me that realistically there are only two alternatives: either Enoch knew Genesis or Genesis knew Enoch. To postulate a shared third source, a common scholarly fudge in such situations, is an unnecessary hypothesis that can be eliminated by a quick shave with Ockham's razor. However, the theory that Genesis is quoting Enoch does not, in my view, stand up to close investigation. In numerous small ways the Enochic literature indicates that it is exegeting Genesis. Note, for example, its *double* interpretation of ויתהלך חנוך את האלהים, taken both in the sense that Enoch walked with the angels and that he was a righteous man. If Genesis is alluding to Enoch we would surely not have expected it to be quite so ambiguous, or to summarize Enoch in precisely the enigmatic phrases which it did. Genesis 6 and even more so Genesis 5 are unquestionably allusive: there is a bigger story here than we are being told, but that story is not necessarily contained in the Enochic corpus. As scholars have long suspected we may get some hints about the bigger story which the author of Genesis 5 has in mind from Babylonian sources, for example from the Babylonian lists of the ten primeval kings.[16] I conclude then from my analysis that the exegetical model is the best available to explain the intertextuality of the Enochic corpus and the Book of Genesis. The Enochic writers knew Genesis in the form in which we now have it; they regarded Genesis in some sense as authoritative Scripture, worthy of the closest of readings and useful for purposes of validation; they stood at some remove from the text of Genesis, and were not privy to the sources on which the redactor of Genesis based his work.

Philip S. Alexander

THE ENOCHIC TRADITIONS IN THE LATE BIBLICAL PERIOD: A PROPOSED TRADITION-HISTORY

To put the above mildly revisionist deduction in a broader framework, I shall conclude by outlining a history of the development of the Enochic literature. The Enochic literature is like an immense and complicated jigsaw, and its complex literary history is almost impossible to untangle. All accounts are bound to be speculative, but the following is offered as a reasonable tradition-history which helps to clarify Enoch's relationship to the Bible.

From the literary remains it is evident that we are dealing with an ongoing and active *tradition*, and this suggests circles of scribes interested in the Enochic lore, passing it on from one generation to another, elaborating and adapting it to suit their own circumstances. The origins of these Enochic circles goes back to the Persian period in the fourth, or even possibly the fifth century BCE. These circles first became interested in Enoch when they were looking for a patron for new scientific knowledge which they were importing into Israel. This knowledge, which was largely astronomical and cosmographical in content, was ultimately Babylonian in origin, but it was transmitted to them through the medium of Aramaic. This is why the Books of Enoch are written in Aramaic and not in Hebrew: the original body of knowledge which started off the tradition was in that language, because it came from abroad. There is good evidence for the transmission of 'Babylonian Wissenschaft' through the medium of Aramaic.[17] The introduction of this new scientific knowledge into Judah marked an intellectual revolution comparable in many ways to that which had taken place a little earlier in Greek-speaking Ionia, possibly (as we are beginning to appreciate from the works of Martin West and Walter Burkert) under the same oriental influences.[18] The knowledge was new in Judah and to domesticate it within Jewish tradition it was attributed to Enoch, an ante-deluvian figure mentioned in native tradition. The choice of Enoch was for one purpose and one purpose only — validation. It was, therefore, from the outset exegetical. Enoch may have had some features which made him particularly useful to the Enochic circles. There may have been a tradition that he was a primeval culture-bringer, like Prometheus. The fact that he lived before the Flood would have been attractive: antiquity gives *cachet*; but there was possibly also the added idea, common in many folklores, that primeval knowledge possessed by humanity had been seriously disrupted by some ancient cataclysm, such as a flood.

Enoch, then, was installed as the patron saint of the new science. But seeds of conflict were sown. Only a little earlier there had been another intellectual revolution in Judah, inaugurated by Ezra with the backing of the Persian court. This had attempted to set the Torah of Moses at the centre of Jewish thought and society.[19] There was a potential clash here: to put it rather simplistically two paradigms of Judaism were emerging together, a Mosaic based on Law and an Enochic based on 'science'. The tension between Enoch and Moses within the tradition is palpable. The Enochic literature proclaims itself as prophecy: it is as large and impressive as the Mosaic literature, and may, as J. T. Milik suggested, have finally been redacted in emulation into a Pentateuch.[20] It shows remarkably little interest in the themes that are central to Mosaic Judaism, such as the Covenant and the giving of the Torah on Sinai. It largely ignores Deuteronomy, which is the touchstone of the Mosaic tradition in the Second Temple period, and such allusions as there are to that book can, in certain cases, be read as polemical. Later tradition certainly sensed a rivalry between Moses and Enoch, and responded to it either by denying the exegetical bases of the Enoch tradition (e.g., Enoch was not a righteous man and his 'taking' was a 'taking' by God in death), or by dressing up Moses in Enoch's clothes.[21]

The struggle to reconcile these two traditions can be traced in the surviving literature. A crucial moment is represented by the Book of Jubilees from around 150 BCE. This clearly knew and deeply respected the Enochic literature, but it effectively integrates it into a Mosaic narrative and subordinates it to a Mosaic paradigm. Enochic circles, however, continued. Their thinking underwent a profound change of emphasis. One can sense their growing marginalization within Jewish intellectual life. They find their scientific knowledge and the solar calendar which it advocated at odds with the views of the increasingly dominant Mosaic group. Their view of the world takes on a darker hue: Enoch, having been originally a culture-bringer, becomes now a preacher of righteousness. They see new knowledge as potentially corrupting. They become puritan and technophobic. They sense a parallelism between their own days and the days before the Flood. The world is manifesting the same signs of radical corruption as provoked the Flood. It stands under the threat of imminent, cataclysmic judgement, just as it did in the days of Noah. Again we can detect in the Enochic literature this revisionism. The crucial move probably came when the story of the Sons of God in Genesis 6 was linked into the Enoch story in Genesis 5. There was a negative re-evaluation of the Sons of God traditions. Originally (as a careful reading of Jubilees shows)[22] the Watchers may have been presented, like Enoch, as culture-bringers, who only later went bad. Even the Giants, if a version of the myth preserved by Alexander Polyhistor is ancient, may have at one time been thought of as culture-bringers.[23] But the dominant view clearly became that much modern knowledge was wicked and corrupting. The outlook of the group became darker and almost totally focused on sin and judgement.

The Enoch circles survived in some shape or form down to the end of the Second Temple period, when, I would suggest, the *Vorlage* of our present Ethiopic Enoch was put together, possibly, in the first century CE, when the Similitudes were composed. There is, I believe, considerable merit in Milik's suggestion that the Similitudes replaced the Book of Giants in this final redaction of the Enochic Pentateuch.[24] The problem may have been the extremely mythological and 'pagan' feel of the Book of Giants. He is probably wrong, however, in supposing that the Similitudes is a Christian work. They were more likely composed by the Jewish Enochic circles to round off the Enochic Pentateuch by emphasizing once again, and in an emphatic manner, the themes of sin and impending judgement. But the story does not end there. The canonisation of an Enochic corpus ensured the transmission of the Enoch traditions to posterity. New Enochic literature continued to be composed and old traditions adapted right down to the Middle Ages, and Enoch found himself reprising again and again his role as counter-cultural hero to the regnant cultural icons of Judaism, Christianity and Islam.

NOTES

1   For the Ethiopic text see Michael A. Knibb, *The Ethiopic Book of Enoch*, 2 vols (Oxford: Clarendon Press, 1978). Translation and commentary: R. H. Charles, *The Book of Enoch or 1 Enoch*, 2nd edn

(Oxford: Clarendon Press, 1912); Matthew Black, *The Book of Enoch or I Enoch*, Studia in Veteris Testamenti Pseudepigrapha, 7 (Leiden: Brill, 1985).

2   See Appendix: Second Temple Period Books of Enoch.

3   Greek text: M. Black, *Apocalypsis Henochi Graece* (Leiden: Brill, 1970); Aramaic fragments from Qumran: J. T. Milik with the collaboration of Matthew Black, *The Books of Enoch: Aramaic Fragments of Qumrân Cave 4* (Oxford: Clarendon Press, 1976).

4   For the Qumran fragments of the Book of Giants see L. Stuckenbruck, in DJD XXXVI, pp. 3-94. Further: John C. Reeves, *Jewish Lore in Manichaean Cosmogony: Studies in the Book of Giants Traditions*, Monographs of the Hebrew Union College, 14 (Cincinnati: Hebrew Union College Press, 1992); Loren T. Stuckenbruck, *The Book of Giants from Qumran* (Tübingen: Mohr Siebeck, 1997). For *Midrash Shemhazai ve-Aza'el* see Adolph Jellinek, *Bet ha-Midrasch*, 6 vols, 2nd edn (Jerusalem: Bamberger & Wahrmann, 1938), IV, 127-28; Milik, *Books of Enoch*, pp. 321-39.

5   Translations are my own based on the Revised Version.

6   The translations are based on Charles but revised against the manuscripts. I have chosen eclectically the readings which seemed to me best, generally preferring the Greek, where available, to the Ethiopic.

7   See the notes of Charles, *Book of Enoch*, p. 27, and Black, *Book of Enoch*, p. 141.

8   Originally this may not have been the sense of the verse.

9   I accept here Black's emendation of a difficult text (p. 250). The reading, however, does not affect the present argument.

10   See further Philip S. Alexander, 'From Son of Adam to Second God: Transformations of the Biblical Enoch', in *Biblical Figures outside the Bible*, ed. by Michael E. Stone and Theodore A. Bergren (Harrisburg, PA: Trinity Press International, 1998), pp. 87-122 (pp. 102-04).

11   Emending the corrupt νεφελας in the Greek to Ναφελειμ.

12   In general I follow here Black's translation.

13   See Ben Sira 37:27-38:15. Further Armin Lange, 'The Essene Position on Magic and Divination', in *Legal Texts and Legal Issues: Proceedings of the Second Meeting of the International Organization for Qumran Studies Cambridge 1995, Published in Honour of Joseph M. Baumgarten*, ed. by Moshe Bernstein, Florentino García Martínez and John Kampen, STDJ, 23 (Leiden: Brill, 1997), p. 377-435 (pp. 383-86).

14   See further Philip S. Alexander, 'Retelling the Old Testament', in *It is Written: Scripture Citing Scripture*, ed. by D. A Carson and H. G. M. Williamson (Cambridge: Cambridge University Press, 1988), pp. 99-121.

15   See Claus Westermann, *Genesis 1-11: A Continental Commentary*, trans. by John J. Scullion (Minneapolis: Fortress Press, 1984), p. 347.

16   Westermann, pp. 348-54.

17   See M. J. Geller, 'The Survival of Babylonian Wissenschaft in Later Tradition', in *The Heirs of Assyria: Proceedings of the Opening Symposium of the Assyrian and Babylonian Intellectual Heritage Prroject Held in Tvärminne, Finland, October 8-11, 1998. Melammu Symposia vol. 1*, ed. by Sanna Aro and R. M. Whiting (Helsinki, 2000), pp. 1-6.

18   M. L. West, *Early Greek Philosophy and the Orient* (Oxford: Clarendon Press, 1971), pp. 111-202; Walter Burkert, *The Orientalizing Revolution: Near Eastern Influence on Greek Culture in the Early Archaic Age*, Revealing Antiquity, 5 (Cambridge, MA: Harvard University Press, 1992).

19   The nature of the reforms of Ezra, and indeed the historicity of his mission, have been much debated (for a judicious survey see Lester L. Grabbe, *Judaism from Cyrus to Hadrian*, 2 vols (London: SCM Press, 1992), I, p. 94-98). The fact is that Moses did become the dominant authority of post-exilic Judaism, and it seems to me that the traditional view that the reforms of Ezra the Scribe had something to do with this, though not without difficulty, is still the most satisfactory hypothesis.

20   Milik, *Books of Enoch*, p. 4.

21   See Alexander, 'From Son of Adam to Second God', pp. 107-10.

22   Jubilees 4:15.

23   See Stuckenbruck, *Book of Giants*, pp. 33-36.

24   Milik, *Books of Enoch*, p. 4.

APPENDIX: THE SECOND TEMPLE PERIOD BOOKS OF ENOCH

Books of Enoch	I Enoch	Dead Sea Scrolls	Content	Date
The Book of the Heavenly Luminaries	I En. 72-82	4Q209; 4Q210; 4Q211 (Qumran text contained more astronomical lore than Ethiopic Enoch)	72-79 Core astronomical book 80:2-82:3 Moralizing additions 82:4-6 Polemical appendix advocating solar calendar	c. 350 BCE
The Book of the Watchers	I En. 1-36	4Q201; 4Q202; 4Q204; 4Q205; 4Q206	1-5 Preamble (impending judgement) 6-11 The Fall of the Watchers (frgs of a Noah Book; cf. 60 and 106-107) 12-16 Enoch's throne vision 17-36 Cosmographical, including 20-21, the 'Nekyia'	c. 250 BCE
The Book of Giants		1Q23; 1Q24; 2Q26; 4Q203; 4Q206; 4Q530; 4Q531; 4Q532; 6Q8	Highly fragmentary reworking of the story of the Fall of the Watchers, but concentrating on the deeds of their giant offspring (Mahawa, Ohyah, Hahyah, Hobabes and Gilgamesh)	c. 200 BCE
The Book of Dreams	I En. 83-90	4Q204; 4Q205; 4Q206; 4Q207	83-84 First Dream Vision (the Deluge) 85-90 Second Dream Vision (the Zoomorphic History of the World — from Adam to the Eschaton: 90:6-15 = the Maccabean Revolt)	c. 160 BCE
The Epistle of Enoch	I En. 91-108	4Q204; 4Q212	Miscellaneous moralizing pieces 93:3-10 + 91:11-17 The Apocalypse of Weeks (from Enoch to the Eschaton) Essene?	c. 130 BCE
The Similitudes of Enoch	I En. 37-71		Theme: the eschatological judgement 37-44 The First Similitude 45-57 The Second Similitude 58-71 The Third Similitude (70-71, Appendix, The Ascension of Enoch = Gen 5:7:14; identifies the Son of Man of 46:1-6 and 48 with Enoch)	c. 75 CE
The Second Book of Enoch			Survives only in Slavonic Long and short recensions 1-68 The Life of Enoch (1-21 Enoch's ascent through the 7/10 heavens; 22-35 Enoch's throne vision; 36-66 Enoch's return to earth and instruction to his children; 67-68 Enoch's final translation to heaven) 68-73 Events from Enoch's disappearance till the death of Noah	c. 100 CE

BIBLICAL QUOTATIONS IN THE PESHARIM AND THE TEXT OF THE BIBLE—METHODOLOGICAL CONSIDERATIONS

Timothy H. Lim

I. INTRODUCTION

IN THE EARLY DAYS of Qumran research, there was intense interest in the study of the Habakkuk text embedded as quotations in the Pesher. Monographs and extensive articles by J. van der Ploeg, Georg Molin, Karl Elliger, Stanislav Segert and William Brownlee, among others, discussed every variant found in the Habakkuk text of 1QpHab.[1] By 1959, Brownlee declared that 'our [i.e. Elliger, Segert and his own] discussion of each variant in turn has made further discussion of most of the textual variants [in the Habakkuk Pesher] unnecessary'[2] Studies of other pesharim were nowhere near as comprehensive or detailed as that of the Habakkuk Pesher.

Between approximately 1960 and 1990, articles and studies continued to be published about the pesharim, but the emphasis shifted away from the characterization of the biblical quotations to how the pesherist creatively altered and interpreted his texts. When scholars did express their views about the characteristics of the biblical texts in the Habakkuk Pesher or other pesharim, these opinions varied from the careful and guarded (e.g. Maurya Horgan)[3] to the bald and blunt (e.g. Raphael Weiss)[4]. Other scholars simply took it for granted that the biblical texts found in the pesharim were proto-Masoretic; this assumption is basic to their discussions of the interpretative techniques. Readings that differed from the Masoretic Text (MT) were explained as exegetical variants generated by the pesherists who were concerned with reading contemporary events into the biblical text. In the apparatuses of critical editions of the Hebrew Bible, the pesherite variants are selectively or comprehensively included, depending upon the editorial policy and date of publication of the editions (compare, for example, *BHS* and *HUBP*).

In the past decade, the characteristics of the biblical texts found in the pesharim have been and are continuing to be re-evaluated in the light of the increased recognition of the plurality of text types in the Second Temple period. Since it is now widely held that there had been a multiplicity of biblical texts prior to AD 100 both in the sectarian Qumran community and Palestinian Judaism generally, revisiting the same issues from this vantage point is a clear desideratum. How should one evaluate the variants in the pesherite quotations? Some are clearly scribal errors, while others are integral to the pesherite interpretation. The latter cases would raise the obvious question: did the pesherist modify the words for the sake of his interpretation or was he moved to an inspired exegesis upon finding this reading in a text that already had the variant? Or, in common parlance: was the interpretative chicken or textual egg first? What criteria can be used to evaluate whether a variant is exegetical or textual? Methodological issues of the kind considered here are indispensable for a proper analysis of pesherite exegesis. It will simply not do to invoke the vague and subjective 'common-sense' argument when there are equally plausible explanations at hand. One has to reflect upon how we know that a variant is exegetical or textual rather than simply assert it.

Before discussing the issues, let me remove possible sources of unclarity by defining my terms and setting my parameters. First, when referring to pesharim and pesheresque texts, there is in view the fifteen texts of the continuous pesher genre (4QIsa[a] [4Q161]; 4QpIsa[b] [4Q162]; 4QpIsa[c] [4Q163]; 4QpIsa[d] [4Q164]; 4QpIsa[e] [4Q165]; 4QpHos[a] [4Q166]; 4QpHos[b] [4Q167]; 1QpMic [1Q14]; 4QpNah [4Q169]; 1QpHab; 1QpZeph [1Q15]; 4QpZeph [4Q170]; 1QpPs [1Q16]; 4QpPs[a] [4Q171]; and 4QpPs[b] [4Q173]), the thematic pesharim (4QOrd[a, b] [4Q519, 4Q513 and perhaps also 4Q514]; 4QFlor [4Q174]; 4QCatena[a] [4Q177][5]; 4QAgesCreat [4Q180]; 11QMelch [11Q13]), and other texts that use the technical term 'pesher' or are related to it (4Q252; 4Q253; 4Q253a; 4Q254; 4Q254a; 4Q464; and CD IV, 14 and possibly in 4Q266 3 i 8-24[6]). Included in this list are 3QpIsa [3Q4] and 4QCommentary on Malachi [4Q253a] as well as other texts that are related to interpretations even if they do not include the technical term 'pesher'.[7] This textual corpus will serve as the framework for the following discussion, since it is well beyond the scope of the present paper to discuss the variants of all the texts. Second, unless stated otherwise, the term 'variant' will be used in the formal sense of a reading that differs from the MT standard. This is not to assume any knowledge of the generative process, if any, of the reading. It is a formal descriptor for heuristic purposes only. Third, rather than provide an overview of the well-known pesherite exegeses, the following will discuss selectively texts that illustrate the methodological issues.

II. EVALUATING A VARIANT

It is surprising just how few scholars have discussed their method of ascertaining whether a variant is textual or exegetical, particularly since there has been such a lot written on pesherite exegetical techniques. One suspects that the casual comparison with MT while reading a pesherite text leads one to assume that the MT reading was the original and the pesherite variant was exegetically created. More recently, there have been some methodological discussions, centring around a variant found in 4Q252.

In 1991, I published an article discussing the chronology of the Flood story in the first two columns of 4Q252,[8] a text renamed by its official editor George Brooke with the innocuous title of 'Commentary on Genesis A'.[9] In the now famous opening lines of the commentary, it reads '[In the] four hundred and eightieth year of Noah's life, their end came to Noah. And God said: 'My Spirit shall not dwell (לא ידור) in man forever' (Genesis 6:3). My brief comment in the notes was: '*Line 2:* ידור (MT: ידון) is a variant attested by the LXX (οὐ μὴ καταμείνῃ τὸ πνεῦμά μου). The '120 year' period is clearly understood to mean the temporary respite from the flood-waters rather than the maximum age of man'.[10] My concern in that article was, of course, on getting the chronology of 4Q252 right, since it is so easy to go wrong with numbers and since the application of the 364-day solar calendar to the Flood story was more complicated than one might have realised, especially when there was no previous study to build on.

Surprisingly, Moshe Bernstein responded to these brief comments with an entire article in *Revue de Qumrân* devoted to this variant in 4Q252.[11] Bernstein states that Lim is alone to date [viz. 1992] among scholars to insist upon ידור as a variant. Eight years later, it seems that Bernstein was premature in his judgement. In his Edinburgh Conference paper, George Brooke suggests that the contentious לא ידור 'may reflect a textual variant, rather than being an interpretative reading'.[12] Ronald Hendel, in his article on 'Scriptures: Translations' in the *Encylopedia on the Dead Sea Scrolls*, also takes ידור in 4Q252 as a textual variant.[13] Apparently, Bernstein's view that לא ידור is an exegetical variant has instead become 'the minority conclusion'.

The arguments and underlying methodological issues need to be unpacked. Bernstein argues that לא ידור ('will not dwell') is a contextual guess of לא ידון by the commentator of 4Q252 and this exegetical move is similar to ones found in LXX, Targum Onqelos, the Vulgate and Jubilees. It is an ancient guess, because the imperfect ידון ('will judge' as is commonly translated)[14] does not seem to fit well into the verse. In what sense will Yahweh's spirit not judge in man forever? The most obvious contextual interpretation is to understand ידון not as 'to judge' but 'to dwell'. Bernstein describes לא ידור in 4Q252 as a 'loose translation' of לא ידון. This however, seems odd, since the latter is also written in Hebrew. In what sense is this a translation? 'Paraphrase' is a better term, and that seems to be what he means.[15]

First, Bernstein argues that the attestation of four (or five) ancient sources – there are, in fact, more – to 'will dwell' does not prove dependence upon the textual variant, ידור, even though we now have this variant in Hebrew. He points out that the Aramaic אתקיים of Targum Onqelos usually represents the Hebrew חיה, and the Ethiopic *nabara* of Jubilees 5:8 normally translates the Hebrew ישב. Moreover, the LXX reading καταμείνει is an exegetical guess at the meaning of ידון, since this Greek verb translates either Hebrew ישב by itself (Numbers 20:1; 22:9) or in an expression with the verb יאל (Joshua 7:7) in the LXX, but never ידור. Conversely, the rare root דור is translated in Psalm 84:11 by οἰκεῖν and not καταμενεῖν. LXX οὐ μὴ καταμείνῃ, therefore, is an interpretation of ידון and not a literal rendering of the variant ידור.

Second, Bernstein maintains that lines 1-2 of column i of 4Q252 do not constitute a quotation, but a paraphrase of selected portions of Genesis, even though the relevant phrase is introduced by 'and God said'. This argument is supported by the omission of בשגם הוא בשר ('for he is flesh') and the rewriting of והיו ימיו מאה ועשרים שנה ('but his days shall be a hundred and twenty years') as ויחתכו ימיהם מאה ועשרים שנה ('now their days shall be determined to be one hundred and twenty years'). Bernstein states: 'the very fact that the second half of 6:3 is 'quoted' in non-Massoretic form by 4Q252 [...] can be said to point in the opposite direction [i.e. to Lim's view], that is towards 4Q252 containing a rewording of 6:3 rather than its citation'.[16] Bernstein's phrase 'in non-Massoretic form' is important for the following discussion.

First, the argument that LXX uses οἰκεῖν and not καταμενεῖν to translate the root דור. This Semitic verb occurs in Aramaic and Hebrew. It is indeed rare, meaning 'to dwell' in the Hebrew Bible only in the infinitive and only at Psalm 84:11: מדור באהלי רשע 'than to dwell in the tents of wickedness'. LXX here reads ἢ οἰκεῖν ἐν σκηνώμασιν ἁμαρτωλῶν ('than to dwell in the tents of sinners'). However, the choice of the verb οἰκεῖν ('to dwell, to inhabit', 'to live') is deliberate since the translator is playing on the divine dwelling mentioned immediately, ἐν τῷ οἴκῳ τοῦ θεοῦ μᾶλλον ('I would rather be a cast off [Heb: stand at the threshold] in the *house* of God [Heb. בבית אלהי 'in the house of my God']). In other words, the LXX translator uses οἰκεῖν not because this Greek word is the only one that could translate the root דור, but because it will allow him to indulge in pun: the Psalmist would rather be a doorkeeper (as in the RSV's translation) in the *oikos* of God than *oikein* in the tents of sinners. The dynamics of the LXX translation account well for the choice of the Greek verb.

On the other hand, the one instance of ידור in the Hebrew Bible does not allow us to draw any far reaching conclusions about how the Septuagint would have translated the Hebrew verb, let alone posit a retroversion as Bernstein has done. The argument that οἰκεῖν is the only translation equivalent of דור is highly questionable. καταμενεῖν is a perfectly good Greek synonym for οἰκεῖν. George Brooke has pointed out in his principal edition of the text, that καταμενεῖν is the verb used by Philo when he cites Genesis 6:3 οὐ καταμενεῖ τὸ πνεῦμά μου (*On the Giants* 5:265).[17]

Second, Bernstein's argument that Genesis 6:3 is not cited but paraphrased in 4Q252 is a case of special pleading. It would be difficult to understand the opening phrase 'and God said' in any other way other than to introduce a direct quotation. The issue is where the quotation ends. For Bernstein, it clearly ends in line 3, 'until the end of the waters of the Flood'. But this understanding of the first three lines is unlikely. The verbatim quotation is: 'My spirit shall not dwell in man forever'. What follows, 'Now their days shall be determined to be one hundred and twenty [ye]ars until the end of the waters of the flood' is a chronological explanation based upon the numerical figures in Genesis 6:3 and 7:6. In 7:6, it tells us that Noah was 600 years old when the flood of waters came upon the earth. This number is subtracted by the 120 years of Genesis 6:3 when God declared that his spirit will not ידון or ידור in man forever and that man's days shall be 120 years. Thus, the commentator of 4Q252 is able to begin the commentary with 'in the 480th year of Noah's life their end came to Noah'. This figure is not biblical, although it could be easily deduced from Genesis in the way that the commentator of 4Q252 has done. Both comments on the 480th year of Noah's life and the 120 years of man's days use biblical language to make chronological points: line 1 is based upon Genesis 6:13 ('the end of all flesh came before me'); and lines 2-3 on Genesis 6:3 ('now their days will be one hundred and twenty years') and 7:6 ('waters of the flood'). In short, Bernstein's view of the paraphrastic nature of Genesis 6:3 is based upon the mistaken understanding of the extent of the verbatim citation.

The argument about the non-Masoretic form of the phrases needs to be underscored. As already discussed, Bernstein appears to be setting up a straw man by arguing against the putative position that 'my Spirit' to 'end of (the) waters of (the) flood' should be taken as a whole, and then to reject it as a quotation because it does not conform to MT. In the 1992 article, the inverted commas were placed around 'My Spirit shall not dwell in man forever'.[18] Brooke, in his DJD edition, likewise limits the verbatim quotation to these words.[19]

Bernstein is clearly working with the assumption that MT is the base text. In his recent article, he states:

Given the fact that the Qumran biblical scrolls manifest a variety of so–called text types, there is no reason to assume that scriptural citations in the nonbiblical material need to conform to the Masoretic Text, the Septuagint, or any other known recension of the Hebrew scriptures. On the other hand, it is probably incorrect to assume that whenever a citation formula introduces a text that varies from the Masoretic Text it represents a variant reading of some sort.[20]

As a statement of principle, I would agree with the first part, but question the way he singles out MT in the latter. The variety of text types that he mentions – the MT, Septuagint or any other known recension – in the statement of principle is dropped when he turns to practice: 'On the other hand, it is probably incorrect to assume that whenever a citation formula introduces a text that varies from the *Masoretic Text* it represents a variant reading of some sort' (my italics). Why just the Masoretic Text? Seen together with his arguments concerning the non-Masoretic form of Genesis 6:3 in 4Q252, it is clear that he considers MT to be the base text, even when other versions, in this case the Septuagint, supports the variant reading in 4Q Commentary on Genesis A.[21]

Is לא ידור, then, a textual variant? As mentioned above, Brooke has recently argued that 'will not dwell' is a textual variant. He believes that this is so because nothing exegetical depends upon it. He points out that 4Q Commentary on Genesis A contains two other variants that are attested in the Septuagint 'your father' (Genesis 28:4 in 4Q252 III, 13) and 'you are unstable' (Genesis 49:4 in 4Q252 IV, 4) and neither seems to be used exegetically. What can be understood by Brooke's reasoning is that nothing *lexically* depends upon 'will dwell'. By contrast to the lexical and grammatical gymnastics exercised by other pesherite and pesheresque texts, 4Q252 does not use the word ידור to any exegetical advantage. True though this may be, it should be qualified by the observation that ידור is semantically significant. The notion that God's spirit will not dwell or abide in man forever inaugurates the destruction of all humanity and created things from the earth by the Deluge. The implication that God's spirit will depart is a common biblical theme for impending judgement. The MT's reading – 'will not judge in man forever' – can be understood as the determination of a time when judgement will cease. Rather than inaugurating the judgement by flood of waters, it implies a present judgement that will cease at some point. In 4Q252 Genesis 6:3 clearly announces the upcoming (120 years later) destruction of the flood rather than its eventual cessation. Nothing lexically depends upon ידור, but chronologically it is significant.

There is a further consideration. If an exegesis depends upon a variant, is then the variant exegetical? This is the converse of Brooke's methodological point. Because 4Q252 uses ידור in its chronological scheme, does it *necessarily* mean that it was exegetically created or, in Bernstein's formulation, contextually interpreted?

Another case to illustrate this methodological issue. In 1QpHab VI, 8-12, the pesherite comment about the *Kittim*, or Romans, laying waste to many 'by the sword' clearly depends upon the variant 'sword' (חרבו) in place of the MT's 'net' (חרמו) in Habakkuk 2:16. In the early part of the last century it had already been noted that this variant in Habakkuk was extant in Bohairic and a marginal reading in one Greek codex (Minuscule 86) of the Lucianic recension. Hypothetically, it might even have been argued that the Coptic and marginal Greek reading were contextual interpretations like the pesherite biblical lemma, since 'sword' is a better fit for the metaphor of the vengeful sword ('mercilessly slaying nations for ever') than of fishing. Moreover, חרבו and חרמו are graphically very similar. The variant חרבו is now found in the minor prophet scroll from Naḥal Ḥever, 8HevXIIgr, a text that is dated to approximately the time of the Habakkuk pesherist, namely 50 BC. In this kaige or proto-Theodotion recension the reading is μαχαιραν αυτου.[22] It is even possible that the Habakkuk pesherist had access to this text found near Qumran as has been argued elsewhere.[23] The point is clear: even if the comment depends upon a variant it is not necessarily exegetical.

The only sure way that we can know something is an exegetical variant, is when the commentator cites the same verse twice in two different ways (Habakkuk 2:17 in 1QpHab XII, 6-10).[24] This method has been described as 'conservative', but is not applicable. Rather, my approach demands stricter criteria of evidence. One should first identify a core group of passages with the highest degree of certainty. Added to this are other passages with varying degrees of probability of also being exegetical. Thus, for example, exegetical modification may also be suggested when there is grammatical incongruity in the biblical quotation as in the case of Habakkuk 1:13b in 1QpHab V, 8-12.

To return to the question, is לא ידור a textual variant? On balance, it would seem so. There is no one decisive evidence, but the cumulative force of wide textual attestation in the versions and the independent reference in Philo would tip the balance in favour of being a textual variant. Philo's rendering seems to be independent because it differs from LXX which uses the emphatic negative and a different tense and mood.

III. BIBLICAL TEXTS IN THE QUOTATIONS

The above discussion of just one variant shows the care that is needed in evaluating the biblical quotations for their textual value. Recently, my approach has been described as 'maximalistic' to the manuscript variation of *all* the pesharim.[25] In my 1997 study of the pesharim, I did indeed collect all the variants embedded in the quotations of the continuous pesharim and compared them to MT, but my intention was strictly practical – to question the procedure by which previous scholarship had ascertained that a variant was exegetical.[26] My attention was trained on exegesis and not textual criticism.

Moreover, I have maintained – and continue to do so – that while the texts belonging to the genre of continuous pesharim share common features (the sequential citation, followed by introductory formula and interpretation of large portions of the biblical texts), many of them have distinctive features. For example, 4QpIsa[c] is close to the thematic pesharim, a conclusion that Moshe Bernstein has arrived at subsequently and independently.[27] Or again, 4QpNah is distinctive because of its relatively more frequent occurrence of atomization and identification.[28] It would, therefore, be inconsistent, not to mention patently naïve and simplistic, to hold a general, all encompassing maximalistic approach.

Are the biblical quotations in the continuous pesharim drawn from a different underlying text? Well, it depends on which pesher. For the Habakkuk Pesher, I follow Brownlee, Elliger and Stendahl in holding to a view of the eclectic nature of the Habakkuk text. William Brownlee first proposed that prior to the composition of the Habakkuk Pesher, peculiar readings 'were discovered in some manuscript (or manuscripts) and were treated as authoritative'.[29] Krister Stendahl developed this and stated that 'The Habakkuk text now in DSH has certainly never existed as 'a text' outside the commentary'.[30] There is much to commend in this eclectic theory, since it is clear that the pesherist did have a choice of readings as evident in a comparison of the lemmas with the comments (העריל) and הרעל of Habakkuk 2:16 in 1QpHab XI being the best known). Stendahl states: 'We must rather presume that DSH was conscious of various possibilities, tried them out, and allowed them to enrich its interpretation of the prophet's message which in all its forms was fulfilled in and through the Teacher of Righteousness.'[31] I should add that the pesherist appears to be much more intrusive in his approach to his Habakkuk text than, say, the commentator of Pesher Isaiah[b] (4Q162) whose comments are little more than one-line comments between large quotations of Isaiah. If I were to hold to a maximalistic position on any of the biblical texts, it probably would be the Isaianic text of 4QpIsa[b], since the pesherist here does not appear to do more than gloss the text in identifying the drunkards with the scoffers who are in Jerusalem. The extant text of Isaiah in 4QpIsa[b] shows that the text is remarkably similar to MT, with fifteen per cent overall difference and just nine per cent variants (and these variants are not very significant).[32] What makes the Isaianic text of 4QIsa[b] particularly interesting is that it is clearly missing Isaiah 5:15-24.[33] Other pesherite texts are also missing large sections of the biblical text: 1QpHab does not have chapter 3; the first part of Hosea 2:9a is absent in 4QpHos[a] (4Q166); Hosea 5:14b is missing in 4QpHos[b] (4Q167); 4QIsa[c] (4Q163) lacks Isaiah 9:12 and 14:9-25; and 4QpPs[a] (4Q171) skips from Psalm 37 to 45 to 60.

Some of these may be due to the incorrect joining of the fragments (e.g. 4QpIsa[c]), while others look like exegetical selections (e.g. 4QpPs[a] skips from Psalm 37 to 45 to 60, leaving a blank line between 37 and 45; the text is mutilated between 45 and 60). The missing chapter 3 of 1QpHab has been explained as the pesherist's loss of interest in his prophetic text, apparently evident already in the dwindling comments at the end of columns XII and XIII. This is one explanation, but lack of exegetical interest can manifest itself in the alternate form of citing large sections with little comment as in the case of 4QpIsa[b]. Moreover, the individual lament of Habakkuk 3 has as its enemy the 'wicked' (רשע), which in Habakkuk 1:4 and 13 are rather important for the pesherist. Habakkuk 3 is included in two versions of the collection of *Odai* or *Cantica* found in Codex Alexandrinus and Codex R (Veronensis), but these appear to be secondary as evident in the addition of the *Magnificat*.[34]

No such exegetical factors can be detected in missing passages of 4QpIsa[b] nor can editorial error or mutilation account for it, since column II, 6 of plate VI of DJD V ends with Isaiah 5:14 and column II, 7 of the same document begins with Isaiah 5:24. It is a pesher, and not a rewritten Bible, as is clear from 'the pesher of the verse with regard to the end of days' in line 1 of column II. William Lane's suggestion that this exegetical comment ('these are the scoffers who are in Jerusalem. They are the ones *who rejected the law of Yahweh* [verse 24c]'[35]) bridges the gap left by 5:15-23 is not persuasive, since the demonstrative and independent pronouns אלה הם 'these are they' and הם 'they' are elsewhere used in place of 'pesher'.[36] There is no obvious error of parablepsis. Moreover, verses 15-24 in MT are suitable as they include four of the six woes of this funeral dirge that condemn the perversion of righteousness, drunkenness, and bribery. As the text stands, the shorter Isaianic text of 4QpIsa[b] would make the drunkards of the first woe who take no notice his work the direct cause of Yahweh's anger.

Timothy H. Lim

IV. CONCLUSIONS

By engaging recent studies on the one variant of 4Q252 and the biblical texts of some of the continuous pesharim, it is hoped that the methodological issues in the study of biblical quotations have been raised. Rather than outlining a series of broad methodological points that may or may not apply to any particular discussion, this paper has intentionally followed a 'case study' approach. Actual arguments by scholars on a contentious variant raise a number of important methodological points. These include: 1) the debatable assumption that the Masoretic Text is the base text of the pesherite quotations; 2) the use of the Septuagint and the dangers of using evidence based on a retroversion from Greek to Hebrew; 3) the limits of the rule of thumb that exegetical variants are determined by the accompanying interpretative comment; 4) the importance of paying careful attention to the distinguishing characteristics of each pesher; and 5) the hitherto little recognized importance of interpretative intervention in the evaluation of pesherite quotations.

The increased recognition of the plurality of text types that was mentioned at the beginning of this paper has not lessened but increased the complexity of evaluating readings that appear to vary from the Masoretic Text. Becoming aware of the methodological issues and assumptions is the first step towards a better understanding of the biblical quotations embedded in the pesharim.[*]

NOTES

1   J. van der Ploeg, 'Le Rouleau d'Habacuc de la grotte de "Ain Fešḥa"', *BO*, 8 (1951), 2-11; Georg Molin, 'Der Habakukkommentar von 'En Fešḥa in der alttestamentlichen Wissenschaft', *Theologische Zeitschrift*, 8 (1952), 340-57; Karl Elliger, *Studien zum Habakuk-Kommentar vom Toten Meer* (Tübingen: Mohr-Siebeck, 1953); Stanislav Segert, 'Zur Habakuk-Rolle aus dem Funde vom Toten Meer I-IV', *Archiv Orientální*, 21 (1953), 218-39; 22 (1954), 99-113; 444-59; 23 (1955), 178-83, 364-73 and 575-619; William H. Brownlee, 'Biblical Interpretation Among the Sectaries of the Dead Sea Scrolls', *BA*, 14 (1951), 54-76; W. H. Brownlee, 'The Habakkuk Midrash and the Targum of Jonathan', *JJS*, 7 (1956), 169-86; and William H. Brownlee., *The Text of Habakkuk in the Ancient Commentary from Qumran*, JBL Monograph Series, 11 (Philadelphia: Society of Biblical Literature and Exegesis, 1959).

2   Brownlee, *Text of Habakkuk*, p. 96.

3   Maurya P. Horgan, 'Palestinian Adaptations of Biblical Narratives and Prophecies II: The Bible Explained (Prophecies)' in *Early Judaism and Its Modern Interpreters*, ed. by Robert A. Kraft and George W. E. Nickelsburg (Philadelphia: Fortress Press; Atlanta, GA: Scholars Press 1986), pp. 247-53 (p. 253), writes that further investigation should include a study of the pesherite biblical quotations.

4   Raphael Weiss, 'A Comparison between the Massoretic and the Qumran Texts of Nahum III, 1-11', *RevQ*, 4 (1963), 433-39 (p. 433) states: 'I shall refer only to the Massoretic Text which is apparent behind the verses quotes in the *Pešer* [...].'

5   See now Annette Steudel, *Der Midrasch zur Eschatologie aus der Qumrangemeinde (4QMidrEschat^{a.b})*, STDJ, 13 (Leiden: Brill, 1994), who argues that the non-overlapping texts of 4Q174 and 4Q177 are two copies of the same eschatological midrash.

6   Badly mutilated in the extant text, see DJD XVIII, 40.

7   George J. Brooke's reconstruction of 4Q253a 1 i 1-5 concerning the Teacher of Righteousness is possible, given the identification of 'the righteous' with *Moreh Ha-tsedeq* elsewhere in the sectarian literature, but the technical term 'pesher' is entirely reconstructed (DJD XXII, pp. 214-15).

8   Timothy H. Lim, 'The Chronology of the Flood Story in a Qumran Text (4Q252)', *JJS*, 43 (1992), 288-98.

9   DJD XXII, pp. 185-207, pls XII-XIII.

10   Lim, 'Chronology of the Flood Story', p. 292.

11   Moshe J. Bernstein, '4Q252 i 2 לא ידור רוחי באדם לעולם: Biblical Text or Biblical Interpretation', *RevQ*, 16 (1994), 421-27.

12   'E Pluribus Unum: Textual Variety and Definitive Interpretation in the Qumran Scrolls', in *DSSTHC*, pp. 107-19 (p. 112).

13   Ronald S. Hendel, 'Scriptures: Translations', in *EDSS*, II, pp. 836-39 (p. 838).

14   Many commentaries and studies have tried to resolve the problems related to this verb. Based on cognate roots and contexts, several meanings have been suggested, including 'to strive', 'to endure', 'to be humble', 'to be strong', 'to judge', 'to govern' and 'to dwell' (A. Dillmann, (ed.), *Genesis: Critically and Exegetically Expounded*, trans. by Wm. B. Stevenson, 2 vols (Edinburgh: T&T Clark, 1897), pp. 236-37), but each in its own way is problematic (Claus Westermann, *Genesis 1-11: A Continental Commentary*, trans. by John J. Scullion (Minneapolis: Fortress Press, 1984), p. 375). The form of ידון is exceptional as the imperfect of דון or דין. Although Umberto Cassuto has argued that the verb comes from דנן meaning 'to abide permanently' (U. Cassuto, *A Commentary on the Book of Genesis*, trans. by Israel Abrahams, 2 vols (Jerusalem: Magnes, 1961), I, pp. 295-96), the meaning 'will judge' is most commonly followed.

15   Moshe J. Bernstein, 'Scriptures: Quotation and Use', *EDSS*, II, pp. 839-42 (p. 842).

16   Bernstein, 'Biblical Text or Biblical Interpretation', p. 426.

17   DJD XXII, p. 197.

18   Lim, 'Chronology of the Flood Story', p. 290.

19   DJD XXII, p. 196.

20   Bernstein, 'Scriptures: Quotation and Use', p. 841.

21   For a recent view that minimizes the text-critical value of the Septuagint of Genesis, see Martin Rösel, 'The Text-Critical Value of Septuagint-Genesis', *BIOSCS*, 31 (1998), 62-70 and the cogent rebuttals by William P. Brown, 'Reassessing the Text-Critical Value of Septuagint Genesis 1: A Response to Martin Rösel', *BIOSCS*, 32 (1999), 35-39 and especially Ronald S. Hendel, 'On the Text-Critical Value of Septuagint Genesis: A Reply to Rösel', *BIOSCS*, 32 (1999), 31-34.

22   See DJD VIII, pp. 53, 152 and plate XI.

23   Timothy H. Lim, 'The Qumran Scrolls, Multilingualism and Biblical Interpretation', in *Religion in the Dead Sea Scrolls*, ed. by John J. Collins and Robert A. Kugler (Grand Rapids, MI: Eerdmans, 2000), pp. 57-73.

24   Timothy H. Lim, *Holy Scripture in the Qumran Commentaries and Pauline Letters* (Oxford: Clarendon Press, 1997), ch. 6.

25   Emanuel Tov, 'The Significance of the Texts from the Judean Desert for the History of the Text of the Hebrew Bible: A New Synthesis', in *QONT*, pp. 277-309; and 'Scriptures: Texts', p. 835.

26   Lim, *Holy Scripture*, p. 72, note 9: 'this is not a textual classification as such, but an examination of the presumed proto-Masoretic Text of the pesherite *Vorlage*'.

27   Ibid, p. 130 and note 30.

28   Ibid, p. 96.

29   Brownlee, *Text of Habakkuk*, p. 115.

30   Krister Stendahl, *The School of Matthew and its Use of the Old Testament*, Acta Seminarii Neotestamentici Upsalensia, 20 (Lund: Gleerup, 1954), p. 194.

31   Ibid, p. 190.

32   Lim, *Holy Scripture*, p. 90.

33   Ibid, p. 93 and notes 30-31.

34   Sidney Jellicoe, *The Septuagint and Modern Study* (Oxford: Clarendon Press, 1968), p. 198 and Henry Barclay Swete, *An Introduction to the Old Testament in Greek* (Cambridge: Cambridge University Press, 1914), pp. 254-55.

35   William R. Lane, 'Pešer style as a reconstruction tool in 4Q Pešer Isaiah *b*', *RevQ*, 2 (1959-60), 281-83.

36   See the convincing arguments by Maurya P. Horgan, *Pesharim: Qumran Interpretations of Biblical Books*, The CBQ Monograph Series, 8 (Washington DC: Catholic Biblical Association of America, 1979), p. 92.

*   I am grateful to Ronald S. Hendel for his comments on a draft of this paper.

BIBLICAL QUOTATIONS IN THE COMMUNITY RULE

Sarianna Metso

THE NUMBER of biblical quotations in the Community Rule is quite small, but this document has much to contribute to our understanding of both the nature of the biblical text available at Qumran and the way in which the Qumran writers made use of it. Some of the major differences between the preserved copies of the Community Rule involve Old Testament quotations, for two of the preserved manuscripts, 4QS[b] and 4QS[d], lack the explicit biblical quotations included in 1QS.[1]

In what follows I shall, firstly, carry out a detailed study of the biblical quotations in the Community Rule and consider their relationship to the Hebrew Bible in its various textual forms. Secondly, I will study the function of these quotations in the Community Rule and discuss the question as to which came first — whether the rules regulating community life were created as a result of biblical exegesis or whether the direction of the process was the reverse, so that the scriptural quotations were added to the text secondarily in order to justify the rules already in effect. Thirdly, I will provide a few examples of a use of the biblical text analogous to that which was probably operative in the Community Rule by comparing the Qumran writers' use of biblical quotations to that of New Testament writers.[2]

This article focuses especially on the manuscripts that most clearly display the differences between the various copies of the Community Rule concerning their use of biblical quotations: 1QS, 4QS[b] and 4QS[d]. 1QS, the best preserved copy of the Community Rule, is written in a Hasmonean hand and has been dated to 100-75 BC. The manuscripts 4QS[b] and 4QS[d], on the other hand, are in a Herodian script and can be dated to 30-1 BC.[3] Both 4QS[b] and 4QS[d] give a form of the text shorter than that of 1QS. Moreover, the text of 4QS[b] is practically identical with that of 4QS[d] except that, whereas 4QS[b] includes part of the text from all sections of the Community Rule, 4QS[d] does not, and presumably did not even in its complete form, contain any parallel to columns 1QS I-IV, i.e., the liturgical and theological sections.[4]

Although the focus of this paper is on the explicit biblical quotations contained in the Community Rule, one should note that the Community Rule is saturated with allusions to the Old Testament. Old Testament words and expressions are used as the basic building blocks to create a new composition. This kind of style is the result of thorough familiarity with and meditation upon the Scriptures,[5] and often the writer may not have been aware of the scriptural context from which the words emanated. Isolated explicit Old Testament citations, however, are introduced by specific formulae, clearly setting them apart from the surrounding text.[6]

Sarianna Metso

OLD TESTAMENT CITATIONS IN THE COMMUNITY RULE

Two Old Testament citations are found in 1QS column V, which begins a collection of rules for community life. The passage commencing in line 7 speaks about the oath to be taken by those desiring to become members of the community. They are to bind themselves to the law of Moses (1QS V, 7b-10a) and to separate themselves from the men of injustice (1QS V, 10b-20a). In 1QS V, 7 the passage has a clear title: 'These are their rules of conduct, according to all these statutes, when they are admitted to the community'[7] (ואלה תכון דרכיהם על כול החוקים האלה בהאספם ליחד), while 4QS[b,d] lacks a title and simply begins with the words 'Everyone who joins the council of the community...' (כול הבא לעצת היחד). A brief glimpse at the two versions in contrast reveals that the text of 1QS is more than twice as long as that of 4QS[b,d]. In the Hebrew text, the parts where the versions clearly differ from each other in content are underlined.

I

1QS V, 13b-16a:

אל יבוא במים לנעת בטהרת אנשי הקודש כיא לוא יטהרו [14] כי אם שבו
מרעתם כיא טמא בכול עוברי דברו ואשר לוא יחד עמו בעבודתו ובהונו
פן ישיאנו [15] עוון אשמה כיא ירחק ממנו בכול דבר כיא כן כתוב מכול
דבר שקר תרחק ואשר לוא ישוב איש מאנש[י] [16] היחד על פיהם לכול תורה
ומשפט

4QS[b] fragment 5, 8b-10a:

[ואשר לוא יגעו לטהרת אנשי] [9] הקודש ואל יוכל אתו בֿ°יחד ואשר ל[וא]
ישוב איש מאנשי היחד על פיהם] [10a] לכול תורה ומשפט

4QS[d] fragment 1 i, 7b-9a:

[7b] וֿאֿשֿר לא יגעו לטהרת אנשי [8] [הקוד]ש ואל יוכל אתו בֿניחד ואשר לא
ישוב א[י]ש מאנשי היחד על פיהם לכל [9a] [תורה] ומשפט

Though the beginning of the passage is roughly similar in the two forms of the text (1QS and 4QS[b,d]), in 1QS V, 13b-15a there is a section which is completely lacking in 4QS[b,d]. If we follow the end of line 7 and the beginning of line 8 in 4QS[d] (which is here better preserved than 4QS[b]), we can see that the words 'They shall not touch the purity of the men of holiness' (ואשר לא יגעו לטהרת אנשי הקודש) provide a loose parallel to 1QS V, 13 'He shall not enter the waters in order to touch the purity of the men of holiness' (אל יבוא במים לנעת בטהרת אנשי הקודש). The sentences begin somewhat differently, but the words לטהרת אנשי הקודש are practically identical. These words occur in 4QS[b,d] followed by the sentence 'He shall not eat with him within the community' (ואל יוכל אתו ביחד), which has no counterpart in 1QS.[8] Instead of the sentence ואל יוכל אתו ביחד, 1QS has a long passage which includes a biblical citation: 'No-one shall join with him (i.e., with a man of injustice) with regard to his work or his wealth lest he burden him with iniquity and guilt. But he shall keep away from him in everything, for thus it is written, "You shall keep away from everything false".' After the citation in 1QS the two forms of the text resume their agreement: 'No one of the men of the community shall answer...' (ואשר לוא ישוב איש מאנשי היחד).

In this passage in 1QS the basic statement of the oath to separate oneself from outsiders is clarified and confirmed with biblical proof-texts — Leviticus 22:16 and Exodus 23:7. The first is cited implicitly (cf. Leviticus 22:(15-)16 ולא... והשיאו אותם עון אשמה), but the second is a direct quotation. An introduction formula announces the quotation from Exodus: כיא כן כתוב, which is followed by the citation מכול דבר שקר תרחק. Interestingly enough, the citation is in a form which corresponds with the Septuagint (LXX) rather than with the Masoretic Text (MT). The word כול is not included in the MT (מדבר שקר תרחק), but has an equivalent in the LXX (ἀπὸ παντὸς ῥήματος ἀδίκου). It is likely that the Hebrew biblical manuscript used by the author contained this little word as a variant reading. Actually Exodus 23:7 has to do with justice in law-suits, but here — typically for Qumran exegesis — it has been disconnected from its original context and applied to an entirely different matter. The catchwords here are רחק and דבר. The latter occurs not only immediately before the citation formula but also earlier in line 14, in the third of five sentences starting with the conjunction כיא (note that this series of five consecutive sentences beginning with כיא is unusual and is a result of redactional development). Thus, in the longer form of the Community Rule attested by 1QS, the scriptural quote exactly follows the form of the Hebrew Scriptures that underlies LXX.

II

1QS V, 16b-19a:

16bואשר לוא יוכל מהונם כול ולוא ישתה ולוא יקח מידם כול מאומה 17אשר

לוא במחיר כאשר כתוב חדלו לכם מן האדם אשר נשמה באפו כיא במה נחשב

הואה כיא 18כול אשר לוא נחשבו בבריתו להבדיל אותם ואת כול אשר להם

ולוא ישען איש הקודש על כול מעשי 19aהבל כי הבל כול אשר לוא ידעו את

בריתו

4QSᵇ fragment 5, 10b-12a:

10bואל יואכל 11איש מא[נ]שי הקודש   ולא ישענו על כול 12aמעשי

ההבל כי הבל כו[ל] אשר לוא [י]דעו את בריתו

4QSᵈ fragment 1 i, 9b-11a⁹:

9bואל יואכל איש מאנשי הקדש 10[ל[   ]   ]°[ולא ישענו על כ]ול מע[ש]י

ההבל כי הבל כל אשר[ן לא ידעו את 11aבריתו

The next direct quotation occurring in 1QS is in lines 16b-18, and again is lacking in 4QSᵇ,ᵈ. As in the previous example, the two forms of the Community Rule have a similar beginning, then 1QS has a passage containing a biblical quotation not in 4QS^{b,d}, and then the two forms resume their common text. In line 9 of 4QS^d the words ואל יואכל ('He shall not eat') correspond to the words ואשר לוא יוכל in 1QS V, 16. In 4QS^d they are followed by the phrase איש מאנשי הקדש ('man among the men of holiness') which is lacking in 1QS. Then there is a gap of about three words in 4QS^d followed by the words ולא ישנעו על ('They shall not rely on'; note the scribal error in the verb, for ישענו) which correspond to the words ולוא ישען איש הקודש על ('No man of holiness shall rely on') in line 18 of 1QS. No matter what the missing words in the gap were, it is clear that the whole of the passage 1QS V, 16b-18a, with the citation from Isaiah 2:22, was not included in the text of 4QS^{b,d}. The missing passage in 1QS beginning with ואשר לוא יוכל reads in full: 'No one shall eat or drink anything of their property, or take anything at all from their hand except for payment, as it is written, "Have no more to do with man in whose nostrils is breath, for what is he worth?" For all those who are not counted in his covenant, they and everything that belongs to them are to be kept separate.'

The passage continues the prohibition of contact with the men of injustice, apparently with the concern to preserve the ritual purity of the community. The formula preceding the citation differs from the one in the previous passage. Instead of כיא כן כתוב, 1QS reads כאשר כתוב. The citation is in a form identical with that of MT except for the longer form of the personal pronoun הואה. 1QIsa^a uses the Masoretic הוא, but opts for the longer form לכמה which, however, in 1QS occurs in the Masoretic form לכם. The quotation is followed by an interpretative comment. Note that, in the context of the previous citation, such an expository element is lacking. Obviously, the writer played with the verb נחשב 'be accounted, be esteemed' and twisted its sense to bear the meaning 'being reckoned in the community' (cf. the occurrence of the same verb in 1QS V, 11). In the text of Isaiah, this verse, which according to many commentators is a gloss (note that it is absent from LXX), counsels the people to cease trusting in the proud man, for in the day of God's judgement human pride will be humbled. The warning of Isaiah has been turned into a sort of precept concerning an entirely different matter. Just as in the previous example, here the longer form of the Community Rule attested by 1QS includes a scriptural quote that, apart from minor spelling, faithfully follows a form of the biblical text that we know.

III

1QS VIII, 12b-16a[10]:

^{12b}ובהיות אלה ליחד בישראל ¹³בתכונים האלה יבדלו מתוך מושבהנשי העול
ללכת למדבר לפנות שם את דרך הואהא ¹⁴כאשר כתוב במדבר פנו
דרך •••• ישרו בערבה מסלה לאלוהינו ¹⁵היאה מדרש התורה [אשר] צוה
ביד מושה לעשות ככול הנגלה עת בעת ^{16a}וכאשר גלו הנביאים ברוח קודשו

4QS^d fragment 2 i, 6b-8a:

^{6b}ובהיות אלהן בישראל]יבדלו מ[תוך מושב] ⁷אנשין העול ללכת למדבר
לפנות שם את דרך האמת(?)]היאה מדרש התורה]ה אשר צוה ביןד מושה לע]שות
כל[הנגלה] ^{8a}ענת בעת וכאשר גלו הנביאים ברוח קודשו

Biblical Quotations in the Community Rule

The third biblical quotation occurring in the Community Rule is found in 1QS VIII, 12b-16a, in a section which contains a threefold occurrence of the clause בהיות אלה בישראל ('When these exist in Israel'). The passage has been the subject of intense scholarly debate. Some see the section 1QS VIII-IX as referring to the time of the founding of the community and argue that it represents a sort of 'manifesto' or 'programme of the community'.[11] Hartmut Stegemann, on the other hand, considers that the whole of columns VIII and IX to be a patchwork of secondary elements.[12] However, on the basis that 4QS^{e}[13] does not have the lengthy passage that constitutes 1QS VIII, 15b-IX, 11, a strong case can be made to see it as a secondary addition.[14] The passage corresponding to 1QS VIII, 1-10, however, is present in 4QS^{e}, and it is perhaps best interpreted as an introductory passage for the following sections with regulations addressed to the wise leader. These regulations for the wise leader may well have originated in an early period in the community's history, but I find it more compelling to speak simply of an introduction which is comparable to two other introductions in 1QS, namely those at the beginning of column I and at the beginning of column V.

Whichever interpretation one chooses, it remains true that the passage returns to the theme of separation from the men of injustice. The fragmentary 4QS^{b} has nothing extant for this passage, but a fragment in 4QS^{d} with the left edge of a column preserves enough text to allow a comparison with the text in 1QS. This column of 4QS^{d} to which the fragment belongs had 15-18 words per line. Leaving out the orthographical differences, the text seems in lines 1-5 to follow 1QS rather closely (the inserted text above the lines in 1QS VIII, 9-11 was apparently included as part of the regular text in 4QS^{d}). In the middle of line 6, however, from the sentence starting with ובהיות אלה בישראל ('When these exist in Israel') onwards, the text begins to differ. The words ליחד ('as a community') and בתכונים האלה ('in accordance with these rules') written above the lines in 1QS VIII, 12-13 are lacking in line 6 in 4QS^{d}, and the gap at the beginning of line 7 has room for only about ten words, while in 1QS there are twenty. Obviously, some of the text of 1QS VIII, 13-15 was not included in 4QS^{d}, and filling up the gap with the rest of the sentence, which begins with ובהיות אלה בישראל, reveals that the missing part was the citation of Isaiah 40:3.

The text of 4QS^{d} thus reads as follows: 'When these exist [in Israel], they shall separate themselves fr[om the settlement] of the men of [injustice and shall go into the wilderness to prepare there the way of truth (?). This is the study of the la]w which he commanded through [Moses, that they should d]o all [that has been revealed] from ti[me to time and in accordance with what the prophets revealed by his holy spirit]'. An alternative reading for דרך הואה ('the way of him') of 1QS is provided by 4QS^{e}, which reads דרך האמת ('the way of truth') instead of the syntactically difficult personal pronoun הואה. It is interesting that both writers avoided the use of the name 'Yahweh' that was included in the original text of Isaiah. The more extensive version of 1QS has the phrases 'as a community' (ליחד) and 'in accordance with these rules' (בתכונים האלה) added above lines 12 and 13 to be read after the words 'When these exist in Israel', and the citation of Isaiah 40:3 follows the words 'to prepare there the way of him'. The text of 1QS reads: 'When these exist as a community in Israel in accordance with these rules, they shall separate themselves from the settlement of the men of injustice and shall go into the wilderness to prepare there the way of him, as it is written: "In the wilderness

85

prepare the way of ••••, make level in the desert a highway for our God." This (way) is the study of the law w[hich] he commanded through Moses, that they should act in accordance with all that has been revealed from time to time and in accordance with what the prophets revealed by his holy spirit.'

The same introductory formula כאשר כתוב that was used previously in 1QS V, 17 is used again in 1QS VIII, 14, while the introductory words קול קורא in MT are left out as unnecessary. With respect to the text of 1QS, the citation reads: במדבר פנו דרך •••• ישרו בערבה מסלה לאלוהינו. The scribe of 1QS has used four dots instead of the tetragrammaton; this phenomenon also occurs elsewhere in the scrolls, sometimes by the scribe of 1QS (4QTest, 4QSam^c), sometimes by other scribes (4QTanḥ, 4Q391). In some cases the name of God is, out of reverence, written in paleo-Hebrew script instead of in the Jewish ('square') script. The manuscript 4QS^d, in fact, provides two examples of the paleo-Hebrew script at 4QS^d 2 iii, 9 and iv, 8 for the parallels to 1QS IX, 25 and X, 9. The manuscript 1QIsa^a has a small variant from MT, adding the copula, thus וישרו (for ישרו MT). In the book of Isaiah, the context for this verse is the introductory call narrative of Second Isaiah, beginning the Book of Consolation. The victorious divine warrior is preparing to lead his people out of exile and into freedom, as he did at the Exodus from Egypt into the Promised Land. A glorious highway is to be prepared through the desert. However, the Qumran writer is not interested in the historical details of the original context, but uses the verse to provide a motive for the community's withdrawal into the desert to live a life of perfection in accordance with the Law. In the New Testament all four evangelists use this same verse with reference to John the Baptist (Matthew 3:3, Mark 1:3, Luke 3:4-6, John 1:23). There the purpose of the verse is to explain John's presence in the desert preparing the way for the coming of Jesus. The exegetical method by which the evangelists have detached the verse from its original context and accommodated it into a new environment is nearly identical to that used in the Community Rule.

In conclusion, the pattern of the use of Scripture is remarkably similar in the three examples of quotations from Scripture. In the third example, 1QS preserves the longer form which incorporates a scriptural quote that follows the traditional text as preserved in MT and in the Hebrew underlying LXX. Thus, while our close reading of the text indicates that the Community Rule underwent considerable editorial work (to be discussed in the following sections), we may already conclude that the citations in 1QS faithfully quote the biblical text as attested in MT and LXX, even though the redactor may interpret them in a revised context.

THE MORE ORIGINAL VERSION

The contrast of the longer form of the text in 1QS and the shorter form in 4QS^{b,d} urges the questions, which of the two is more original, and what was the rationale for shortening or lengthening it to produce the secondary redaction. A more comprehensive comparison of the text of 1QS with its parallels in 4QS^{b,d} reveals not only the absence of the citations in 4QS^{b,d} but also that 4QS^{b,d} lack other passages, individual words, and phrases found in 1QS, and have variant readings at other places. The title at the beginning of 1QS V, for example, is different from that in 4QS^{b,d}; while 4QS^{b,d} uses the technical term הרבים, 1QS V, 2-3 has a long phrase involving the sons of Zadok (i.e. the priests) and the men of the community; in some places 4QS^{b,d} appear to lack words like 'the community' (היחד) and 'the eternal covenant' (ברית עולם). The words and phrases which are present in 1QS but lacking in 4QS^{b,d} have the function of either strengthening the self-understanding of the community or providing a scriptural justification for the community's regulations. In my opinion, the insertion of theologically significant words into the text is natural and to be expected in the developmental process, whereas intentionally omitting them is very difficult to explain. The intentional omission of words or sections from the text happens only in narrowly limited situations, for example, when a text is out of date, or when it contains elements now considered somehow questionable. It seems more logical to me that 4QS^{b,d} present the earlier form of the text and that 1QS shows subsequent expansion and revisions to provide more authority in support of the community's regulations through biblical legitimization.[15]

The alternative hypothesis would posit that the citations were omitted because they were considered self-evident. One must note, however, that in two out of three instances of biblical quotations the writer has assumed that the direct quotation of a biblical passage was insufficient to express the full meaning of Scripture, and therefore he supplied additional explanation in order to bridge the citation with the community's regulation.[16] Even with an interpretative explanation, the connection between a regulation and the supporting citation appears, at least for a modern reader, arbitrary. Furthermore, even if it were plausible that a redactor may have wished to shorten the text by omitting the citations and the supplementary explanations, it remains especially difficult to explain why terms like 'the community' (היחד) and 'the eternal covenant' (ברית עולם) which are important for the self-understanding of the community, were excluded from the text.

An additional argument in support of the view that the shorter version in 4QS^{b,d} is the more original is that the text of 4QS^{b,d} runs smoothly without any breaks in the syntax and line of thought, whereas in 1QS the natural flow of the text is interrupted. In the middle of 1QS V, 13 the third person plural used for the men of injustice changes to the singular, although the theme of separation is maintained. In 1QS V, 15b after the citation of Exod 23:7 plural forms are again used of the wicked. It is difficult to see the passage 1QS V, 13b-15a as referring to a person joining the community. The passage seems rather to speak about one of the men of injustice, or about a person whose conversion is not sincere. Some commentators have suspected that this passage was an interpolation even before the material from Cave 4 was available.[17] The thought which is interrupted at the end of line 13 continues at the end of line 15. The syntax of the passage 1QS V, 13b-15a is also very peculiar, for the particle כיא appears there five times, suggesting an accumulation of clauses. Moreover, the likelihood of interpolation is further supported by the fact that a blank space has been left in the middle of line 13 with an accompanying *paragraphos* mark in the margin. In contrast, there is no problem of plural vs. singular in 4QS^{b,d}; rather, it runs smoothly without the passage in 1QS V, 13b-15a and the preceding passage in the plural form in V, 11b-13a. The second passage containing a citation in 1QS which is lacking in 4QS^{b,d} seems to be better adjusted to its context, but it may be noted that line 18 actually only repeats what is being said before in lines 10b-11a. The third citation in 1QS VIII seems to fit into the context quite well also, but the sentence preceding the citation formula has so many words in common with the text of Isaiah 40:3 that one may speak of an implicit citation. It is logical to assume that the redactor recognized the allusion to the book of Isaiah and added the explicit citation.

BIBLICAL EXEGESIS OR JUSTIFICATION OF RULES ALREADY IN EFFECT?

The evidence indicates that 1QS presents a secondary redaction of an earlier form of the Community Rule. The redaction was designed both to provide legitimization from Scripture for the community's rules and to strengthen the community's self-understanding. A possible motive for adding the proof-texts is that enthusiasm within the community may have begun to decrease and the need for separation may have been questioned. Thus the authoritativeness of the ascetic regulations was justified by appeal to the Torah and the Prophets.

The manuscripts 4QS[b] and 4QS[d] are palaeographically dated to the last third of the last century BC, while 1QS is dated to 100-75 BC. Thus, 4QS[b] and 4QS[d] are paleographically several decades later than IQS. Since the 4QS manuscripts nevertheless represent a more original form of the text, it is clear that 1QS and 4QS[b,d] cannot be directly dependent on each other or even belong to close branches of the same textual family. There must have been a split in the textual tradition at a very early stage, about 100 BC or even earlier. A parallel phenomenon occurs in biblical manuscripts: 4QJer[b], for example, which displays an early edition of the book of Jeremiah, is palaeographically about a half a century later than 4QJer[a] which contains the later, expanded edition of that book.[18]

Inquiry into the more original form of the Community Rule and its redactional development is related to the larger problem of the genesis of the rules that formed the Qumran legal documents, especially the Community Rule and the Damascus Document. Lawrence Schiffman takes as his starting point that the doctrine of the oral transmission of law, and more fundamentally, the concept of oral law, was absent at Qumran. He thinks that the legal traditions in the Qumran texts can originate only from scriptural exegesis.[19]

Both Philip Davies and Moshe Weinfeld have criticized Schiffman's views from different angles. Firstly, Davies distinguishes between the two rules. The regulations in the Damascus Document, according to him, are based on scriptural exegesis, with only one or two exceptions. In contrast, the regulations in the Community Rule are not and were not intended to be understood as derived from scriptural exegesis. Davies thus believes that the Damascus Document and the Community Rule must have originated in two different groups.[20]

Secondly, Weinfeld, differing from Schiffman, offers yet another perspective, studying the parallels in Greco-Roman society. He notes that the Qumran regulations governing the community organization and admission of new members are similar to those found in Hellenistic and Roman religious groups. He distinguishes between rules sanctified by the Torah and those of merely human origin that the community itself devised. The laws based on Torah belong to the realm of the covenant between God and Israel, and are of a different nature from community regulations for social organization, to which the members are bound only by a voluntary commitment. Thus, Weinfeld does not agree with Schiffman that a member of the community was ultimately rejecting a divine commandment if he rejected a communal rule given by a superior.[21]

Insofar as the trajectory of redactional development above be correct, it too would differ from Schiffman's view. It would indicate that the laws regulating 'matter of fact' details of community life emerged first. These did not originate as a result of scriptural exegesis. It was only at a later stage, presumably in a situation where the community's strict rules had been questioned, that the scriptural quotations or allusions were added, arising from need to provide a scriptural legitimization for the rules already in effect.

In fact, a glimpse into a situation where community legislation was being created is provided by 1QS VI, 8-13, which deals with the session of the *rabbim*. In this passage where the rules for judicial procedures are laid out, neither the Torah nor written rules are mentioned at all. Whenever community authority is discussed in the Community Rule, the decisions are said to be made on the basis of the word of the *rabbim* (על פי הרבים) or, as in IX, 7, on the word of the sons of Aaron. The hypothesis, however, that the community would have made a distinction between its own rules and the regulations of the Torah does not seem plausible. The fact that in the redactional process of the Community Rule scriptural quotations were added as proof-texts for the community regulations, speaks rather for the assumption that ultimately the community regarded its own regulations as resting on the Old Testament authority. The formula 'for thus it is written' (כאשר כתוב / כיא כן כתוב) is a clear indication for this. From the point of view of a modern reader, the connection between a regulation and a citation supporting it may be artificial. The community, however, considered its laws to be in accordance with the Torah.

PARALLEL PHENOMENA IN THE NEW TESTAMENT

The New Testament provides already-known examples that parallel the phenomenon we find in the redactional development of the Community Rule. Matthew, in order to point out the emphases he wished to convey to his readers, expanded the text of Mark with quotations from the Scripture (e.g. Mark 1:21/Matthew 4:13-16; Mark 3:7-11/Matthew 12:15-21; Mark 11:7/Matthew 21:4-5). The redactional development of both the Community Rule and the Gospels reveal that the later version contains scriptural quotations for proof while the earlier one lacks them.

Perhaps an even better parallel can be found in some sections of the letters of Paul where Paul discusses issues related to community life. We can see that citations whose context originally had very little to do with the issue in question were used as proof-texts to provide scriptural legitimization for a practice followed by a community.

In 1 Corinthians 10 Paul deals with the question of whether a Christian is allowed to eat marketplace food, even though some of this food may have been offered to idols or slaughtered by a pagan priest. Paul quotes Psalm 24:1 in order to defend his permissive view: 'Eat whatever is sold in the meat market without raising any questions on the ground of conscience, for "the earth and its fullness are the Lord's".'

Commentators on Paul's text have noted that here Paul is reflecting the Jewish usage of this Psalm, for the rabbis used that passage in support of the practice of saying a blessing over every meal.[22] The rabbis interpreted the verse as the reason for giving thanks to God for their pure food, whereas Paul uses the Psalm verse to legitimate eating *all* foods, without regard to questions of purity or impurity. Paul disregards the original context of the passage of Psalm 24 that he quotes; this psalm forms a liturgy on entering the sanctuary and makes no mention of pure or impure food. In addition to disregarding the original biblical context, he surprisingly also twists the traditional rabbinic interpretation of the verse.

A second example where an Old Testament passage is detached from its original context and used as a proof-text in a matter related to a community practice can be found in 1 Corinthians 14:20-25, where Paul discusses women and men's conduct in worship and especially speaking in tongues.

In 1 Corinthians 14:21-22 Paul quotes a passage from Isaiah 28:11-12 and says: 'In the law it is written, "By people of strange tongues and by the lips of foreigners I will speak to this people; yet even then they will not listen to me," says the Lord. Tongues, then, are a sign not for believers but for unbelievers.' According to Hans Conzelmann, here Paul follows neither the Masoretic Text nor the Septuagint, but is closest to the text of Aquila, although the change of pronoun from the third person into the first may be due to Paul's contextualization.[23]

Conzelmann notes that, whereas in Paul's text preceding the quotation the 'argument had been based on the fact that people *cannot* understand speaking with tongues, in the quotation it is based on the fact that they *will* not understand. The application that follows operates once more with the idea of inability. Thus the quotation is made use of only for the *one* thought, that speaking with tongues is a "sign" (namely, for unbelievers, see verse 23).'[24]

The original text of Isaiah deals with the threat of judgement against Israel. They have ignored the words of the prophets, and therefore their enemies will invade the land, flooding it with the foreign tongues of the oppressors. Paul refocuses the idea from the old Israel to the present church. For him, the purpose for speaking in tongues is a sign for those who have not yet become members of the church. Whereas in the prophetic message of Isaiah the foreign tongues functioned as a sign of judgement against the *believing* community of Israel (who were failing at that time), for Paul speaking in tongues is aimed at the *unbelievers* (i.e. those who do not yet believe). Thus, Paul uses the Old Testament proof-text not according to the original meaning in its Isaianic context but adapts it to fit the current practice of his community.

CONCLUSION

I summarize my article as follows:

1. The biblical quotations included in 1QS seem to follow fairly closely the forms of the biblical text that we now know through the Masoretic Text and the Septuagint.

2. The quotations were added into the Community Rule secondarily, during the redactional development, in the need to justify the rules already in effect. This can be seen through the comparison between 4QS[b,d] and 1QS.

3. The way in which the Qumran writers used biblical quotations as a proof and justification for community practices as well as events in the community's history is analogous to the way biblical quotations were used in the New Testament. In the writings of Paul especially, we see how, as in Qumran, Old Testament passages were

detached from their original context and used as a proof-text in a matter related to a community practice.

NOTES

1   For the text of 4QS^b and 4QS^d, see Elisha Qimron and James H. Charlesworth (with an Appendix by F. M. Cross), 'Cave IV Fragments Related to the Rule of the Community (4Q255-264 = 4QS MSS A-J)', in *The Dead Sea Scrolls: Hebrew, Aramaic, and Greek Texts with English Translations*, I: *Rule of the Community and Related Documents*, ed. by James H. Charlesworth and others (Tübingen: Mohr-Siebeck; Louisville: Westminster John Knox, 1994), pp. 53-103 (pp. 60-67, 72-83); Corrado Martone, *La 'Regola della Comunité.' Edizione critica*, Quaderni di Henoch, 8 (Torino: Silvio Zamorani Editore, 1995), pp. 162-64, 166-69; Sarianna Metso, *The Textual Development of the Qumran Community Rule*, STDJ, 21 (Leiden: Brill, 1997) pp. 22-31, 36-47, 74-90; DJD XXVI, pp. 39-64, 83-128.

2   This article is a revised form of an earlier article, Sarianna Metso, 'The Use of Old Testament Quotations in the Qumran Community Rule', in *QONT*, pp. 217-31.

3   On the dating of 1QS, see Frank Moore Cross, Jr., *The Ancient Library of Qumrân and Modern Biblical Studies: The Haskell Lectures 1956-1957* (London: Duckworth, 1958), p. 58; N. Avigad, 'The Palaeography of the Dead Sea Scrolls and Related Documents', in *Aspects of the Dead Sea Scrolls*, ed. by Chaim Rabin and Yigael Yadin, Scripta Hierosolymitana, 4 (Jerusalem: Magnes, 1958), pp. 56-87 (p. 57); G. Bonani, and others, 'Radiocarbon Dating of the Dead Sea Scrolls', '*Atiqot*, 20 (1991), 27-32. The manuscripts 4QS^b and 4QS^d have been dated to the second half or the last third of the first century BC; see J. T. Milik, 'Numérotation des feuilles des rouleaux dans le scriptorium de Qumrân (Planches X et XI)', *Sem*, 27 (1977), 75-81 (pp. 76-78); Frank Moore Cross, 'Paleographical Dates of the Manuscripts', in *The Dead Sea Scrolls* I: *Rule of the Community*, p. 57; A. J. Timothy Jull and others, 'Radiocarbon Dating of Scrolls and Linen Fragments from the Judaean Desert,' *Radiocarbon*, 37 (1995), 11-19.

4   Metso, *Textual Development*, p. 37; DJD XXVI, p. 83.

5   Joseph A. Fitzmyer, 'The Use of Explicit Old Testament Quotations in Qumran Literature and in the New Testament', *NTS*, 7 (1961), 297-333 (pp. 298-99).

6   The introductory formulae occurring in the Dead Sea Scrolls have been discussed, e.g., by Maurya P. Horgan, *Pesharim: Qumran Interpretation of Biblical Books*, CBQ Monograph Series, 8 (Washington, DC: Catholic Biblical Association of America, 1979), pp. 239-44; Moshe J. Bernstein, 'Introductory Formulas for Citation and Re-citation of Biblical Verses in the Qumran Pesharim', *DSD*, 1 (1994), 30-70; James C. VanderKam, 'Authoritative Literature in the Dead Sea Scrolls', *DSD*, 5 (1998), 382-402 (pp. 391-394).

7   The translations of 1QS in this article follow Michael A. Knibb, *The Qumran Community*, Cambridge Commentaries on Writings of the Jewish and Christian World 200 BC to AD 200, 2 (Cambridge: Cambridge University Press, 1987), which I have modified for 4QS^b,d,e.

8   To be quite accurate, a similar kind of sentence does occur a little later in 1QS V, 16, but it appears in 4QS^b,d also. Thus the prohibition to eat with a man of injustice occurs twice in 4QS^b,d, which makes one wonder whether the first occurrence is the result of an error (יוחד - יוכל; the verb יוכל appears in both 4QS^b and 4QS^d, however).

9   Note the scribal error for ישענו in the top line.

10   Note the scribal error for אנשי in the top line.

11   For example, Edmund F. Sutcliffe, 'The First Fifteen Members of the Qumran Community: A Note on 1QS 8:1ff.', *JSS*, 4 (1959), 134-38; A. R. C. Leaney, *The Rule of Qumran and Its Meaning*, The New Testament Library (London: SCM Press; Philadelphia: Westminster, 1966), pp. 112, 115 and 211; Jérôme Murphy-O'Connor, 'La genèse littéraire de la *Règle de la Communauté*', *RB*, 76 (1969), pp. 528-49 (p. 529); J. Pouilly, 'La Règle de la Communauté. Son evolution littéraire', *Cahiers de la Revue Biblique*, 17 (1976), p. 15; Christoph Dohmen, 'Zur Gründung der Gemeinde von Qumran (1QS VIII-IX)', *RevQ*, 11 (1982), 81-96; Knibb, *Qumran Community*, p. 129. For more recent discussion on the passage, see George J. Brooke, 'Isaiah 40:3 and the Wilderness Community', in *NQTS*, pp. 117-132; Uwe Glessmer, 'The Otot-texts and the Problem of Intercalations in the Context

of the 364-day Calendar', in *Qumranstudien: Vorträge und Beiträge der Teilnehmer des Qumranseminars auf dem internationalen Treffen der Society of Biblical Literature, Münster, 25.-26. Juli 1993*, ed. by Heinz-Josef Fabry, Armin Lange and Hermann Lichtenberger, Schriften des Institutum Judaicum Delitzschianum, 4 (Göttingen: Vandenhoeck & Ruprecht, 1996), pp. 125-164.

12 Hartmut Stegemann, *Die Essener, Qumran, Johannes der Täufer und Jesus: Ein Sachbuch* (Spektrum 4249; Freiburg, Basel, Wien: Herder, 1994), pp. 158-59.

13 J. T. Milik, in M. Baillet and others, 'Le Travail d'édition des fragments manuscrits de Qumrân' in *RB*, 63 (1956), 49-67 (pp. 60-62), dates the manuscript to the second half of the second century, but Cross, 'Paleographical Dates' says it was written about 50-25 BC.

14 See Sarianna Metso, 'The Primary Results of the Reconstruction of 4QS^e', *JJS*, 44 (1993), 303-308.

15 My analysis confirms the initial views expressed by J. T Milik and Geza Vermes, see Milik, 'Numérotation', p. 78, and Geza Vermes, 'Preliminary Remarks on Unpublished Fragments of the Community Rule from Qumran Cave 4, *JJS*, 42 (1991), 250-55 (p. 255). For a differing view, see Philip S. Alexander, 'The Redaction-History of Serekh ha-Yaḥad: a Proposal', *RevQ*, 17 (1996), 437-456.

16 This is clearly the case in 1QS V, 16b-19a, where the expository element 'For all those who are not counted in his covenant, they and everything that belongs to them are to be kept separate' has been brought into the text by the redactor. In 1QS VIII, 12b-16a the reminiscence of Isaiah 40:3 was obvious even before inserting the direct quotation, and the expository element 'This (way) is the study of the law w[hich] he commanded through Moses, that they should act in accordance with all that has been revealed from time to time and in accordance with what the prophets revealed by his holy spirit' was part of the original text already.

17 Murphy-O'Connor, 'La genèse littéraire', *RB*, 76 (1969), pp. 546-47; Knibb, *The Qumran Community*, p. 129.

18 DJD XV, pp. 150, 172 and 203.

19 Lawrence H. Schiffman, *The Halakhah at Qumran*, Studies in Judaism in Late Antiquity, 16 (Leiden: Brill, 1975), pp. 19-20.

20 Philip R. Davies, 'Halakhah at Qumran', in *A Tribute to Geza Vermes: Essays on Jewish and Christian Literature and History*, ed. by Philip R. Davies and Richard T. White, JSOTSup, 100 (Sheffield: JSOT Press, 1990), pp. 37-50 (pp. 43-49).

21 Moshe Weinfeld, *The Organizational Pattern and the Penal Code of the Qumran Sect: A Comparison with Guilds and Religious Associations of the Hellenistic-Roman Period*, Novum Testamentum et Orbis Antiquus, 2 (Fribourg Suisse: Universitätsverlag; Göttingen: Vandenhoeck & Ruprecht, 1986), pp. 71-76.

22 b. Ber, 35a; t. Ber. 4.1; see, for example Gordon D. Fee, *The First Epistle to the Corinthians*, The New International Commentary on the New Testament (Grand Rapids, MI: Eerdmans, 1987), p. 482; Hans Conzelmann: *1 Corinthians: A Commentary on the First Epistle to the Corinthians* (Philadelphia: Fortress Press, 1975), [trans. by James W. Leitch from *Der Erste Brief an die Korinther, Kritisch-Exegetischer Kommentar über das Neue Testament*, 5, 11th edn (Göttingen: Vandenhoeck & Ruprecht, 1969)], p. 242.

23 Conzelmann: *1 Corinthians*, p. 242, n. 17.

24 Ibid, p. 242.

THE CAVE 4 DAMASCUS DOCUMENT MANUSCRIPTS AND THE TEXT OF THE BIBLE

Eibert Tigchelaar

ONE YEAR after the Dead Sea Scrolls conference in Jerusalem which celebrated the fiftieth anniversary of the discovery of the first scrolls, a symposium marked the centenary of the discovery of the Damascus Document in the Cairo Genizah (CD) as well as the final publication of the Cave 4 Damascus Document manuscripts (4QD) in the series *Discoveries in the Judaean Desert*.[1]

The CD fragments were discovered by Solomon Schechter in 1897, and published in 1910,[2] while the 4QD fragments were found in 1952, and finally published in 1996.[3] As a result, for almost a century research of the Damascus Document has been based upon the medieval CD fragments, whereas now we can also take the fragments from Hellenistic and Roman times into account. Several scholars have dealt in detail with the relation of the Damascus Document to the Hebrew Bible, but on the whole their studies have not incorporated the Cave 4 materials, neither the 4QD manuscripts, nor the 4Q biblical fragments. Now that all of the Cave 4 texts are available, one may revisit the issue of the relation between the Damascus Document and the text of the Bible. This article will not attempt to consider the relation between the Bible and the Damascus Document in general, but will rather focus on the new evidence provided by the 4QD manuscripts.

THE DAMASCUS DOCUMENT AND THE BIBLE

In the introduction to his edition of CD, Schechter stated that

the quotations from the Scriptures are seldom correctly given, so that sometimes the source is hardly recognizable [...]. As a rule these deviations from the Massoretic text are mere textual corruptions of a careless scribe and not to be explained by the *variae lectiones* suggested by any known version, or quotation by any ancient authority.[4]

Subsequent scholarship disagreed with the view that most deviations are mere textual corruptions. It was recognized that there are more possibilities than scribal error and textual variant. Ottilie Schwarz recognizes two kinds of deviations: (1) unimportant and unintentional omissions or additions of single words, suffixes, prefixes or conjunctions, possibly because the author quoted from memory; and (2) intentional, exegetical, actualizing, adaptations of scripture.[5]

Schwarz's study focuses on the exegetical techniques of the Damascus Document, not its textual relation to the Hebrew Bible. Jan de Waard took a different approach.

Contrary to Schechter, who stated that deviations were not to be explained by variant readings suggested by any version, de Waard claims that some deviations are corruptions, but that thirty quotations in the Damascus Document 'show a reading deviating from the Masoretic Text (𝔐) which is supported by one or more of the old versions.'[6]

De Waard discusses only those quotations which are found both at Qumran and in the New Testament. In some cases he argues that deviations from the 𝔐 have a text-critical importance.

The past decades have seen many studies dealing with the use and quotation of the Hebrew Bible in the *Damascus Document* and in other Qumran literature. A few citations may serve to illustrate recent developments in the study of the use of Scripture in the *Damascus Document*. In a discussion of quotations in the 4QD manuscripts, Joseph Baumgarten states that

> ... the 'scriptural' citation under consideration appears to be, not a quotation in the literal sense, but the product of the interpretation applied by the Qumran exegetes to a combination of scriptural passages. A similar methodology may be illustrated elsewhere in the Damascus Document. [...] We may infer that the distinction between the biblical lemma and its interpretation was not as strictly drawn in the Damascus Document as it was, for example, in the *pesher* commentaries. [...] The foregoing examples of interpretations introduced as quotations are not, in my view, to be confused with cases where a citation formula is used to refer to the substance rather than the wording of a biblical passage.[7]

In short, Baumgarten identifies different kinds of quotations, namely exegetical combinations of scriptural passages, and references to the substance, rather than to the wording, of biblical texts.

On the whole, scholars nowadays tend to explain deviations from 𝔐 as exegetical. Yet recently John Elwolde indicated by means of a few examples 'how exegetical intention can be too hastily grasped at as a mean of explanation when more plausible motives are to be found in linguistic developments often beyond a writer's conscious control'.[8]

Jonathan Campbell, by contrast, argues that the text 'consistently draws upon a select body of scriptural contexts by way of citations and allusion.'[9] In a study of scriptural interpretation in the halakhic section of the *Damascus Document*, Aharon Shemesh recently argued that 'the Damascus Document contains textual units whose structure is based upon biblical verses, although the latter are not explicitly cited.'[10]

In short, a century of study of the *Damascus Document* has indicated that some of the differences between the Damascus Document and the Masoretic Text are scribal corruptions, some are supported by one or more of the ancient versions, some should be attributed to exegetical intention and techniques, whereas others need not be intentional. The techniques of quotation and of scriptural interpretation differ in the two main parts of the work, that is, the Admonition and the Laws. Also, one should not only examine *how* scripture is quoted, but also *which* particular units of scripture are cited or alluded to.[11]

BIBLICAL QUOTATIONS IN 4QD PARALLELED BY CD

By and large the 4QD fragments agree with the text of CD, and show that the majority of the manifold conjectures are not supported by any Qumran manuscripts.[12] At the same time, the 4QD manuscripts have established that the CD fragments preserve only part of the original composition. According to Hartmut Stegemann's preliminary reconstruction of the scroll, 4Q266 consisted of 31 columns, 17 of which corresponded to the sheets of CD.[13] In the cases where CD and 4QD overlap, there are relatively few important textual variants. Most of these variants have been recorded in Qimron's CD and Baumgarten's 4QD editions.[14] In the following cases 4QD and CD differ with regard to the text of biblical quotations or allusions (orthographical differences are disregarded).

1. CD I, 1 and Isaiah 51:7

CD I, 1 reads ועתה שמעו כל יודעי צדק, whereas 𝔐 has שמעו אלי ידעי צדק. 4Q266 2 i 6-7 agrees with CD I, 1, but 4Q268 1 9 has an additional לי, reading ועתה שמעו לי כול יודעי צדק. The latter clause, though belonging to a different section of the composition, is also found in 4Q270 2 ii 19. More שמעו admonitions are used in CD II, 2 ועתה שמעו אלי כל באי, and CD II, 14 ועתה בנים שמעו לי. The corresponding text of 4Q266 2 ii suggests that the 4QD manuscript reads here אלי instead of לי. These examples witness the interchange between לי and אלי, both within one manuscript and between manuscripts, so that the difference between שמעו לי in 4Q268 and 4Q270, and שמעו אלי in Isaiah 51:7 is therefore not unexpected.

2. CD I, 15, Psalm 107:40 and Job 12:24

CD I, 15 ויתעם בתוהו לא דרך corresponds exactly to the wording of the Masoretic Text's Psalms 107:40 and Job 12:24, but 4Q266 2 i 18-19 adds the conjunction: ויתעם בתהו ולא דרך. Also 4Q266 11 10-11, which refers to the same text, adds the conjunction: ותתעם בתהו ולו / ולו דרך (with dittography of ולו). It is unlikely that this is a textual or exegetical variant. Instead, the motive for the addition of the conjunction is probably to be found in the conscious or unconscious linguistic judgment of the scribe, who may have thought that the conjunction would make better Hebrew.

3. CD V, 16 and Isaiah 27:11

CD V, 16 כי לא עם בינות הוא corresponds exactly to 𝔐, whereas 4Q266 3 ii 4 [כי עם]בלא בינות הוא[suggests a different construction, presumably בלא בינות הוא[. How should one explain the difference? Constructions with בלוא and בלא are more common in the Dead Sea Scrolls than in Classical Hebrew, though preference for בלא/בלוא is found most in the Hodayot, Mysteries, and to a lesser extent in 4QInstruction. There are no other examples of בלוא in the Damascus Document.

Some phrases in the Hodayot are comparable to the word order in 4Q266: 1QH[a] IX, 24-25 (Sukenik I, 22-23); XII, 8 (Sukenik IV, 7) בלא בינה, and 1QH[a] X, 21 (Sukenik II, 19) לעם לא בינות.

4. CD VII, 11-12, CD XIV, 1, and Isaiah 7:17

CD VII, 11-12 provides a quotation of Isaiah 7:17. There are a few differences between the wording of CD and that of the Hebrew text of Isaiah.

CD VII, 11-12	יבוא עליך ועל עמך ועל בית אביך ימים
	אשר ‹לא› באו מיום סור אפרים מעל יהודה
𝔐 , 1QIsa[a]	יביא יהוה עליך ועל עמך ועל בית אביך ימים
	אשר לא באו למיום סור אפרים מעל יהודה

95

CD reads עליך יבוא whereas Isaiah 7:17 has יביא יהוה עליך. This difference is not surprising since, in all cases where the biblical text has the tetragrammaton, the Damascus Document changes the text in some way or another to avoid using the divine name.[15] However, as a result the text has a singular יבוא corresponding to a plural ימים, unless one assumes that יבוא is a scribal error for יביא.[16] The absence of לא in CD must be an error, whereas למיום of Isaiah has been changed to the easier form מיום.

No 4QD manuscript has preserved the text corresponding to CD VII, 11-12, but in CD XIV, 1 the same verse of Isaiah seems to be quoted, with the end of the quotation alone preserved, the bottom part of CD XIII having been lost:

CD XIV, 1   אשר לא באו מיום סור אפרים מעל יהודה

Again CD has מיום, but in other respects the text corresponds to the end of Isaiah 7:17. Elisha Qimron therefore supplies in his edition the text of Isaiah 7:17 at the end of CD XIII.

Parts of this text, corresponding to the lost end of CD XIII, and to CD XIV, 1 have been preserved in three 4QD manuscripts. 4Q266 9 iii, 4Q267 9 v and 4Q269 10 ii.[17] In view of the difficulties in reconstructing the texts, Baumgarten gives two different reconstructions in 4Q266 and 4Q267. It is clear, however, from the available space in the manuscripts, that the text is shorter than the text of Isaiah or of CD VII, and one should probably merely read יבואו על עמכה ימים, or in 4Q266 a singular יבו על עמכה יום, in contrast to the longer text עליך ועל עמך ועל בית אביך.

4Q266   [יבו עליך ועל עמך יום אשר] לו בא [מיום סור אפרים מעל יהודה]

4Q267   יבוא[ו על עמכה ימים אש]ר לוא באו [מ]יום סור או[פ]רים מעל [יהודה]

4Q269   [יבואו על עמכה ימים אשר לוא באו מיום] סור א[פר]ים מעל יהודה]

Contrary to the text of CD VII, 11, here the number of the verb יבואו has been adjusted to the plural ימים.

5. CD VIII, 3, CD XIX, 15 and Hosea 5:10

The text of CD XIX, 1-34 (CD-B) presents a different form of the text found in CD VII, 5—VIII, 21 (CD-A). In the case of the quotation of Hosea 5:10, the latter manuscript is close to the text of 𝔐, whereas the quotation in CD VIII, 3 seems to be 'defective and corrupt'.[18]

CD VIII   היו שרי יהודה אשר תשפוך עליהם העברה

CD XIX   היו שרי יהודה כמשיני גבול עליהם אשפך כמים עברה

𝔐   היו שרי יהודה כמסיני גבול עליהם אשפוך כמים עברתי

Sidnie White argues that CD-A contains an allusion to Hosea 5:10, and that a later scribe turned the allusion into a direct quotation. This scribe also added כאשר דבר to smooth the transition into the quotation.[19] This view should, however, be reconsidered on the basis of 4QD. 4Q266 3 iii-iv, though fragmentary, indicates a text that is different from both CD-A and CD-B. The text of 4Q266 is preserved on several fragments which are thought to belong to two subsequent columns. Thus, Baumgarten gives the following transcription of 4Q266 3 iii 25 and 3 iv 1:[20]

[ב]ליע[ל [הוא הי]ום אשר יפקדו [אל] כאשר [דבר] היו [שרי]

[יהודה ב]יום אשר [תשפוך עליהם העברה כי יחלו ללו ללו מרפא]

The translation in the DJD edition does not indicate that the text moves from one column to another column:

25. [B]elial. [That will be the da]y which [God] will appoint, as he [spoke: 'The princes] were

1. [... Judah on] the day that there [will be poured out the wrath upon them, for they shall be sick with no healing,][21]

Both the transcription and the translation are problematic. The lacuna between יפקדו (CD-A and CD-B have יפקד) and כאשר is much too large for אל, and it seems likely that היו, not שרי, was the last word of the line. Most important, however, the small fragments do not allow one to determine the amount of text missing in between 4Q266 3 iii 25 היו and 4Q266 3 iv 1] אשר יום[. It is quite possible to shift the fragments to the left in such a manner that one or more additional words could have fitted in. Moreover, the reading יום[in 4Q266 3 iv 1 is not at all certain. The first trace need not be a *yod*, and the letter read as *vav* could also be a *yod*. Thus one might also transcribe]ֹי, which could either belong to a plural noun or participle, or perhaps to אפֹ]רֹים. In the first case the letters would supply part of a predicate missing in CD-A.

On the whole, the 4QD fragments attest the text of CD-A (VII-VIII) as opposed to the text form of CD-B (XIX).[22] Here, however, we find that 4Q266 sides with CD-B in reading כאשר]דבר. On the other hand, the extant remains of 4Q266 3 iv 1 show that this text differs both from CD-A and CD-B.

6. CD XVI, 15 and Micah 7:2

The text of the quotation from Micah 7:2 is slightly damaged in CD XVI, 15, but Qimron's reading איש את רעיהו יצדו חרם is virtually certain. Micah 7:2 איש את אחיהו יצודו חרם reads אחיהו instead of רעיהו, but the text of CD is confirmed by 4Q271 4 ii 14 which reads רעהֹו (DJD XVIII), or רעה (see this idiosyncratic spelling in עם רעה 4Q266 8 ii 6) depending on whether the smudge on the border of the fragment is ink. This variant belongs to the category of 'synonymous readings' as defined and described by Shemaryahu Talmon.[23]

7. CD XI, 20-21 and Proverbs 15:8

The quotation of Proverbs 15:8 in CD XI, 20-21 differs in various respects from 𝔐. The change of 𝔐's תועבת יהוה to תועבה was due to the avoidance of the divine name. CD's ותפלת צדקם כמנחת רצון corresponds to the biblical ותפלת ישרים רצונו. The variant כמנחת רצון (see 1QS IX, 5) is an exegetical variant, but 4Q271 5 i 14 which has צדיקים confirms the judgment that CD צדקם is corrupt.

8. CD XIV, 2 and Proverbs 22:3; 27:12

It has long been recognized that CD XIV, 2 כי פתאום ונענשו is a corrupt allusion to Proverbs 22:3 פתאים עברו ונענשו or 27:12 פתאים עברו נענשו, and this is now supported by 4Q267 9 v 5-6 פֹֹֹתֹ]אֹים[עברון / ויענשו. Note not only the occurrence of עברו, but also the unattested reading ויענשו.

9. CD III, 7 and Deuteronomy 9:23

It is clear that the text of CD III, 7 עלו ורשו את רוחם, containing a reference to Deuteronomy 9:23 עלו ורשו את הארץ, is corrupt, and that some words have been lost between את and רוחם. Several reconstructions of the original text have been offered. The 4QD fragments do not supply parts of the missing text, but 4Q269 2 1-2 shows that some words may have dropped out from CD.

10. CD V, 17 and Deuteronomy 32:28

The text of CD V, 17 is not exactly identical to Deuteronomy 32:28. Space considerations suggest that 4Q266 3 ii 4 had a slightly different word order, perhaps reading]גוי אובַ[ד עצות והמה like 𝔐, as opposed to CD הם גוי אבד עצות.

11. CD IX, 1 and Leviticus 27:29

The wording of CD XI, 1 כל אדם אשר יחרים אדם מאדם, referring to Leviticus 27:29 (the introductory formula ואשר אמר is attested in 4Q266 8 ii) is suspect, and in DJD XVIII Baumgarten reconstructs כל חרם instead of כל אדם in 4Q266 8 ii 8 and 4Q270 6 iii 16.

In two cases the text of CD-A does not have an introductory formula, where the 4QD fragments provide such a formula. The first has been mentioned above: 4Q266 3 iii 25 reads]כאשרׄ דבר[, whereas the corresponding text of CD VIII, 3 has no such introduction. The other case is the quotation of Numbers 21:18 in CD VI, 3–4. The CD text has no introductory formula, but 4Q266 3 ii 10 has אשר אמר מושׄה, and 4Q267 2 9 אשר אמׄר מושה.

Summary

The number of differences between the fragments of 4QD and CD in the wording of biblical quotations, both attested and suggested by the available space, is considerable, including some minute differences. The differences do not belong to one single category, though on the whole the 4QD readings seem to be preferable to those of CD. One may note that there is not a consistent relation to 𝔐. In a few cases CD agrees with 𝔐, against 4QD, whereas some of the presumed corrupt variants in CD are not supported by the 4QD manuscripts.

EXPLICIT QUOTATIONS IN THE 4QD FRAGMENTS

The majority of the explicit quotations in CD are found in the part of the composition which is commonly called the Admonition, that is, CD I-VIII and XIX-XX. In the other part of CD, the so-called Laws, CD IX-XVI (or rather, XV-XVI and IX-XIV), few biblical quotations or allusions are introduced by a special formula. The 4QD texts which are not parallel with CD contain the following explicit quotations:

12. 4Q271 3 4-5 / Leviticus 25:14

In DJD XVIII, 4Q271 3 lines 4 and 5 are transcribed as follows:

4]גבר על איש ואשה[כׄאחת כי תועבה הׄיא *vac* ואשר אמר כי]תמכורׄ[

5]ממכר או קנה מיד[עֹמׄיתך לוא תונו איש את עמיתו *vac* וזהֹ פרוׄ]ש[

The clause between the two short *vacat*s, seems to be a quotation of Leviticus 25:14 introduced by ואשר אמר. The biblical text according to the Masoretic tradition runs as follows:

וכי תמכרו ממכר לעמיתך או קנה מיד עמיתך אל תונו איש את אחיו

There are several small differences between 4Q271 and 𝔐:

L. 4 וכי **]** כי 𝔐

L. 5 אל תונו **]** לוא תונו 𝔐

L. 5 אחיו **]** עמיתו 𝔐

In addition, DJD XVIII reconstructs a slightly different text from 𝔐:

L. 4 תכמרו **]** 𝔐 𝔊 𝖆𝖆𝖆 [ותמכור] 𝔐

L. 5 omitted in reconstruction **]** לעמיתך 𝔐

Baumgarten's omission of a word in line 5 seems plausible, but one cannot know *which* word has been left out. The text may alternatively have written ממכר, reading כי תמכור לעמיתך, or, alternatively, the scribe may have written an additional word at the end of line 4, in which case there is enough space in line 5 for the Masoretic wording.

The use of עמיתו instead of אחיו 𝔐 may be considered to be a synonymous reading, without real textual value. Thus, in a discussion of the variants אח and רע in 𝔐, CD and the Septuagint (LXX), de Waard claims that 'both words are constantly *confused*, in CD as well as in the LXX'.[24] I do not completely agree with him with regard to אח and רע, and certainly not with regard to עמית. Let us begin with the evidence of the Septuagint. The LXX reads here ἐὰν δὲ ἀποδῷ πρᾶσιν τῷ πλησίον σου ἐὰν καὶ κτήσῃ παρὰ τοῦ πλησίον σου, μὴ θλιβέτω ἄνθρωπος τὸν πλησίον, in which πλησίον occurs three times. In all instances where the Masoretic Text of Leviticus has עמית (11x), LXX renders with πλησίον, but πλησίον is first of all the rendering of רע (125x), and only very rarely (5x) 𝔐's אח (the figures are based on entries in the Hatch and Redpath Concordance to the Septuagint). In other words, it is more likely that LXX read a text, like the quotation in 4Q271, with three times עמית, than that the three times πλησίον is the rendering of עמית, עמית, and אח.

Coincidentally, one of the other four times where LXX has πλησίον and 𝔐 אח, is also found in a quotation in the Damascus Document. CD XVI, 15 and 4Q271 4 ii 14 quotes Micah 7:2 איש את אחיהו יצודו חרם,[25] 'they trap one another with a ban', where the Damascus Document reads רעהו instead of אחיהו. It is plausible that LXX read a text with רעהו, instead of אחיהו.

Here we may also discuss the other three occasions where, according to Hatch and Redpath, LXX uses πλησίον to render אח. In two of the remaining cases, the correspondence of Greek πλησίον to 𝔐's אח is found in the Alexandrinus, not in other major manuscripts, and the Göttingen edition reads there ἀδελφος.[26] The third case is Genesis 26:31 where 𝔐 has אחיו, but the Samaritan Pentateuch רעהו.[27] In other words, as far as I am concerned, the Damascus Document presents important evidence that the LXX does not render אח by πλησίον. In sum, both the Damascus Document and LXX are witnesses to the variants עמיתו and רעהו in Leviticus 25:14 and Micah 7:2.

13. 4Q271 3 8-9 / 4Q269 9 1 / 4Q270 5 15 / Deuteronomy 27:18

The composite text of the three fragments reads:

למה יביא עליו את משפט האררה אשר אמר משגה עור בדרך

lest he bring upon himself the judgment of the curse which is said (of the one) that 'makes the blind to wander out of the way'.[28]

The text quotes Deuteronomy 27:18a ארור משגה עור בדרך. The reading הארדה in 4QD is suggested by 4Q270 5 15, but not certain at all in 4Q269 9 1.

14. CD XVI, 1 / 4Q271 4 ii 3 / Exodus 34:27

The second part of the quotation is preserved in CD XVI, 1, while parts of the preceding text are found in 4Q271 4 ii 2-3. The word לאמור at the beginning of line 3 is presumably the end of an introductory formula, as in CD III, 20-21 and IV, 13-14. In the preceding lacuna Baumgarten reconstructs ועל הבר[י]ת ה[ז]את דבר ביד מושה.[29]

The quote corresponds to the text of Exodus 34:27 apart from the use of the preposition עם instead of את with כרת.[30] Exodus 34:27 reads ואת־ישראל, and CD XVI, 1 ועם כל ישראל. Baumgarten reconstructs in 4Q271 ועם[ישראל, but כול would still fit in the line.

15. 4Q272 1 i marginal / 4Q269 7 6 / 4Q273 4 ii / Leviticus 13:4-5

The section of the Damascus Document which deals with scale diseases has to be reconstructed on the basis of fragments of four manuscripts. In spite of the large number of fragments, the reconstruction of the first part of the section is not certain, although two manuscripts, 4Q269 7 6 and 4Q273 4 ii 2 both read the introductory אמר, probably to be expanded in both manuscripts to [כאשר] אמר. The remnants of 4Q272 1 i, 4Q269 7 and 4Q273 4 ii suggest that the quotation may have run as follows (the words in brackets are not preserved in any manuscript):

והסגירו [הכוהן שבעת ימים עד] אשר יצמח הבשר
וראה הכוהן ביום השביעי

[the priest] shall quarantine him [for seven days un]til the flesh grows. The priest shall examine (him) on the seventh day.[31]

The biblical text referred to is Leviticus 13:4b-5a (but see also the almost similar phrasing in Leviticus 13:31ff):

והסגיר הכהן את הנגע שבעת ימים:
וראהו הכהן ביום השביעי

The 4QD texts have replaced the explicit object את הנגע by the pronominal suffix, and have added the exegetical addition 'until the flesh grows'. The form וראה instead of וראהו 𝔐 corresponds to 𝔐 and 𝔊, but I am not convinced about the reading of 4Q269 7 7, which may perhaps read וראהו.

This quotation, if reconstructed properly, is a paraphrase which corresponds quite closely to the text of the Bible. Due to the poor condition of the preceding lines it is not completely clear why the biblical text is referred to. The verse may be quoted in view of the exegetical addition 'until the flesh grows', that is, the verse explains why the person stricken by the disease should be quarantined for seven days.

16. 4Q266 6 i 8-9 / 4Q272 1 i 17-18 / Leviticus 13:33, 54; 14:40

In the same section on skin disease the text refers to Leviticus 13:13, introduced by the formula כאשר אמר. The quotation differs in several respects from the Leviticus text, and has been adequately commented upon in DJD XVIII.

17. Explicit Quotations in the Final Section of the Damascus Document

At the bottom of CD XIV a new section begins, the remainder of which is preserved in the 4QD manuscripts, the Penal Code section which specifies the punishment for different kinds of unseemly behaviour.[32] This Penal Code continues with a so-called 'Expulsion Ceremony', after which the document ends with a few more lines.[33] This final part of the Damascus Document is preserved in two manuscripts, 4Q266 and 4Q270. The expulsion ceremony was first presented by J. T. Milik,[34] whereas the explicit citations in this passage have been discussed by Baumgarten.[35]

The Penal Code proper ends with a phrase which has been partially preserved, and can be reconstructed to read ואלה המ[שפטים א]שר ישפטו [בם כל המתיסרים, which Baumgarten renders 'And these are the laws by which all who are disciplined shall be ruled'. The reconstructed words are based on the heading of the Penal Code: וזה פרוש המשפטים אשר ישפטו בם, 'And this is the explication of the laws by which they shall be ruled'. Its conclusion adds the words כל המתיסרים to the words of the section heading. Baumgarten states that

Although התיסר denotes the general acceptance of sectarian laws in CD XX 31 and 1QS IX 10-11 [...], it is in our opinion evident that here, at the conclusion of the penal code, it refers to the punishment imposed on those guilty of infractions of discipline. The premise is that the sinners will voluntarily accept such punishment as an atonement.[36]

This comment seems to be based on Baumgarten's interpretation of the succeeding clauses, rather than on the meaning of the word itself. It is not clear to me why התיסר should refer here to punishment. The alternative meaning, namely 'those instructed', is imposed by the analysis of the following clauses, including the biblical quotation.

17a. 4Q266 11 1-3 / 4Q270 7 i (15-16)17-18 / Leviticus 4:2-4

A composite text from the DJD readings of 4Q270 7 i 15-17 and 4Q266 11 1-3 can be presented as follows:

כל אי[ש] אשר [יתיס]רֿ(?) יבוא וידיעהו לכוהן [המ]וֿפֿקֿד על הרבׄים
וקבל את משפטו מרצונו
כאשר אמר ביד מושה על הנפש אשר תחטֿא בשיגנה
אשר יביאו את חטאתו ואת אשמו

Any man who [is disciplined (?)] shall come and make it known to the priest appoin[ted over the Many and accept his judgement willingly, as He said through Moses concerning the soul that sins unwittingly, that they shall bring his sin-offering and his guilt-offering.[37]

Most of this section has been preserved in either one, or even in both manuscripts. I suggest reconstructing, at the beginning of the section in 4Q270 7 i 15, the conjunction *vav*, [ו]כל אי[ש], instead of [כל אי[ש; בשיגנה in 4Q266 should be read as a variant of בשגנה. However, the real problem is the five to six letter lacuna specifying what kind of man should come and make something known. Baumgarten tentatively reconstructs יתיס]רֿ, any man who 'is disciplined', but why should someone who has already been disciplined come to the priest and accept a judgment. In addition what then is the object expressed in וידיעהו, 'and he shall make it known'?

An alternative reconstruction may be based upon the following scriptural quotation, but what is the relation of this citation to the preceding statement? Baumgarten argues that accepting one's punishment willingly is like an atonement offering. If that is the case, why does the text refer to sins that are committed בשגגה, 'unwittingly', 'inadvertently'? The biblical quotation suggests that the text deals with a particular type of sinners, namely those who sin בשגגה, whereas a few lines later on, the text describes those who reject the regulations and despise instruction. These two categories of sinners seem to be distinct from each other. In that case, one need not interpret the preceding כל המתיסרים as 'those disciplined', but rather as 'those who are instructed', and instead of the reconstruction [ויתיס]ר, one may also restore [שנה ב]ם. Thus, one may present and translate the section as follows:

> [ואלה המ]שפטים א[שר ישפטו]בם כל המתיסרים[
> ו]כל אי[ש] אשר [שנה ב]ם יבוא וידיעהו לכוהן [המ]ו[פ]קד על הרב[ים
> וקבל את משפטו מרצונו
> כאשר אמר ביד מושה על הנפש אשר תחטא בשיגגה
> אשר יביאו את חטאתו ואת אשמו

And these are the laws by which all who are instructed shall be ruled. Any man who [sins unwittingly against] these, shall come and make it known to the priest appoin[ted over the Many and accept his judgement willingly, as He said through Moses concerning the soul that sins unwittingly, that they shall bring his sin-offering and his guilt-offering.[38]

The formulation of the scriptural reference is somewhat peculiar. It consists of a heading introduced by על, and the actual reference. However, the heading על הנפש אשר תחטא בשיגנה is almost a direct quotation of Leviticus 4:27 (or Numbers 15:27) ואם נפש אחת תחטא בשגגה, whereas the reference itself is quite imprecise. The texts in Leviticus 4 and 5 indeed use the verb הביא, often with the object קרבן, 'offering', and in Leviticus 5 we find the object אשמו. In Leviticus 4 the חטאת is mentioned as a sin-offering, but not as the object of הביא.

One might object that it would be strange for someone to have sinned unwittingly, to be aware of his sin and to tell it to the priest. Indeed, both in Leviticus, and in CD XV, 14, the sinner is told that he has sinned. Therefore, one may consider the possibility of an emendation to the text, namely וידיעהו הכוהן, instead of וידיעהו לכוהן.

17b. 4Q266 11 3-4 / 4Q270 7 i 18 / Leviticus 26:31

The reference to Leviticus 4:27 is followed by three other references to Scripture. Such an accumulation of four explicit scriptural references is unprecedented in the Damascus Document, or, for that matter, in the Dead Sea Scrolls. Charlotte Hempel claims that

only the first can [...] fruitfully be connected to what precedes, i.e., the admonition to accept one's punishment. The last three references seem to have been appended to the first citation with little regard for its overall context. [...] It seems likely that the last three references to scripture gradually came to be added to the first.[39]

She suggests that introductory formulae such as ובמקום אחר כתוב, 'and in another place it is written', are appropriate for a process of successive additions. Indeed, the formula ובמקום אחר כתוב is unique in the Damascus Document, but then this is the only section where we have such an accumulation of different quotations.

The first of these additional citations is introduced by ועל ישראל כתוב, 'and concerning Israel it is written'. The actual quotation runs in 4Q266 11 3-4 as follows:

> אלכה לי אל אל קצי [ה]שמים ולו אריח בריח ניחוחכם

I will get me to the ends of heaven and I will not smell the savour of your sweet odours.

4Q270 has the variant קצה השן‎מים. The second part of the quotation corresponds to Leviticus 26:31 ולא אריח בריח ניחחכם, but there is no biblical passage which matches the first part. Baumgarten argues that the 'ends of heaven' refers to Deuteronomy 30:4 אם יהיה נדחך בקצה השמים, 'if any of your outcasts are at the end of heaven', a section which like Leviticus 26 describes exile and chastisement. He argues:

It would appear that the Qumran exegetes saw the affinity between these two chapters of dire warnings and drew the inference that Israel's exile 'to the ends of heaven' in Deuteronomy can only be the result of God's self-concealment.

This seems a far-fetched explanation. A reference to the exile at the ends of heaven does not logically lead on to a statement about God's self-concealment at the ends of heaven. Yet, I must confess that I do not know *how* and *why* this first clause with a divine first person speech was presented as a scriptural quotation.

17c. 4Q266 11 5 supra / 4Q270 7 i 18-19 / Joel 2:13

Because of the lacunae in 4Q270 and the intralinear correction in 4Q266, it is not entirely clear how the quotations of Joel 2:13 and Joel 2:12 were introduced. In 4Q266 one should probably read first the intralinear addition וּבמקומׂ כתוב,[40] followed by the citation קרעו לבבכם ואל בגדיכם, and then the clause ובמקום אחר כתוב followed by לשוב אל אל בבכי ובצום. In 4Q270 7 i 18 there is enough space to reconstruct the first introduction as ובמקום אחר כתוב‎[, whereas the second quotation is simply introduced by וכתׂוב.

The quotation קרעו לבבכם ואל בגדיכם corresponds to the first words of Joel 2:13, apart from the omission of the conjunction of וקרעו.

17d. 4Q266 11 5 / 4Q270 7 i 19 / Joel 2:12+13

The next quotation, introduced by ובמקום אחר כתוב, or simply by וכתוב, seems to paraphrase Joel 2:12 and 2:13. The phrase לשוב אל אל corresponds to עדי שבו of Joel 2:12 or שבו אל-יהוה אלהיכם of Joel 2:13, whereas the words בבכי ובצום are taken from Joel 2:12 ובצום ובבכי ובמספד. The differences between the wording of the Damascus Document and the text of Joel are not really of a textual or exegetical nature, but rather due to paraphrasing the text.

18. 4Q270 3 iii 14

The letters שׁר הקן‎[in this tiny fragment can be restored to כא‎]שר הקים, as in CD III, 20-21 הקים אל ביד / כאשר‎, in which case it could be the introduction of a quotation, but the same words also occur in CD IV, 9 in a different context: כברית אשר הקים אל.

19. 4Q270 4 15

The word אמר‎[may be part of the introductory formula כאשר‎]אמר. In that case the following letters לא תׂ‎ן should be the beginning of a quotation.

20. 4Q266 1d 2

The reading אשר]צוׂה ביד מושׁה seems to introduce a quotation. Stegemann places fragments 1d and 1e in the lacuna in 4Q266 1a-b lines 9-13, but this does not help us to determine which passage is quoted.[41]

IMPLICIT QUOTATIONS OR ALLUSIONS
IN THE NEW 4QD MATERIALS

Since the 4QD materials are rather fragmentary one cannot always determine whether an introductory formula was present or not. Similarly, the fragmentary state of the materials makes it difficult to find all possible allusions. What follows below is therefore a selection.

21. 4Q270 2 ii 19 / 6Q15 5 5 and Isaiah 51:7

Isaiah 51:7 is alluded to in CD I, 1, but once again, and more completely, in 4Q270 2 ii 19, which DJD XVIII transcribes as follows:

ועתה שמעו לי כל יודׄעי צדק וׄ]שימו]תורׄת אל בלבכם

The reconstruction at the end is based on the parallel text of 6Q15 5,[42] albeit with the remarkable mistake of reading בלבכם instead of בלבבם.[43] In 6Q15 5 Baillet originally read ברׄיׄת, but the traces are better read as תורׄת. The reading [וׄ]שימו is consistent with the remaining trace and the available space, but is a mere guess. Note that the initial *vav* is not at all certain. Thus, one may compare the corrected composite text of 4QD/6QD with 𝔐 and 𝔊 of Isaiah 51:7:

4QD/6QD	ועתה שמעו לי כל יודׄעי צדק וׄן]תורׄת אל בלבבם
𝔐	שמעו אלי ידעי צדק עם תורתי בלבם

𝔊 ἀκούσατέ μου, οἱ εἰδότες κρίσιν, λαός μου, οὗ ὁ νόμος μου ἐν τῇ καρδίᾳ ὑμῶν

A reading וׄן עם]תורׄת אל בלבבם may be possible, but seems rather short for the lacuna. The substitution either of the divine name or of a divine first person suffix by אל is common in the Damascus Document.

22. 4Q266 5 i 10-12 / 4Q267 5 ii 3-5 and Jeremiah 11:9-10

The two relatively small overlapping fragments suggest that the text quoted Jeremiah 11:9-10. It is possible to reconstruct a composite text reading

יה כי נׄמׄ]צׄא[קשר לשוב]

This may be related to Jeremiah 11:9-10 which reads

נמצא קשר באיש יהודה ובישבי ירושלם: שבו על עונת אבותם

The remnants of 4Q266 5 i 10 יה·[may be read אשר אמר ירׄמׄיׄה, or ביד ירׄמׄיׄה. Baumgarten's reading of ובׄיושׄבׄיׄ / ירׄןׄשׄלׄיׄם in 4Q267 5 ii 4-5 is uncertain, especially since the letters שׄלׄיׄם seem to be the first letters of the line.

23. 4Q271 4 ii 2 and Jeremiah 31:30 (?)

In 4Q271 4 ii 2, DJD XVIII restores a lacuna on the basis of Jeremiah 31:30. Compare the following readings:

DJD 4Q271 4 ii 2	יכׄרׄוׄת]את בית ישראל ואת את בית יהודה] ברית
Jeremiah 31:30	וכרתי את בית ישראל ואת בית יהודה ברית חדשה

The reconstruction is impossible in view of the available space, but a shorter alternative restoration יכׄרׄוׄת]ואל עם בית ישראל]ברית fits.[44] Nonetheless, all that has been preserved are the words יכֹּרֹות and ברית, which is not enough to suggest an allusion to a specific scriptural passage.

24. 4Q266 6 ii 5-6 / Leviticus 12:2

In 4Q266 6 ii 5-6 the text deals with purification after childbirth, and paraphrases Leviticus 12:2 with small differences.

4Q266 6 ii 5-6	ואשה אשרֹן תזריֹןֹעֹ וילדה זכר
	[וטמאה אֹ[תֹ שבעת וֹהימים] / [כֹ]ן[מי נֹדֹתֹן]דאותה
ℳ Leviticus 12:2	אשה כי תזריע וילדה זכר
	וטמאה שבעת ימים כימי נדת דותה תטמא

The differences are linguistic, not exegetical.

25. 4Q266 11 10-11, CD I, 15, Psalm 107:40 and Job 12:24

4Q266 11 10-11 ולו דרך / ותתעם בתהו ולו (with dittography of ולו) alludes to Psalm 107:40 and Job 12:24. The same verses are referred to in CD I, 15 (see above no. 2). In CD I, 15 the subject of ויתעם is not God, as in Psalms and Job, but איש הלצון, 'the Man of Mockery'. Perhaps one may even see an analogy between שָׁפֵךְ in Psalm 107:40 and הטיף in CD I, 15. The combination of הטיף כזב, 'spreading of lies', and התעה, 'to make go astray'; is found in both CD I, 15 and 1QpHab X, 9. Yet in the prayer of the Expulsion Ceremony, the addressee is once again God, as in Scripture.

26. 4Q266 11 11-12 / Leviticus 18:5; Ezekiel 20:11, 13, 21

In the same section there is yet another scriptural reference, once more to a passage which was also referred to elsewhere in the composition. Hempel calls attention to the four words אשר יעשה האדם וחיה which occur both in 4Q266 11-12 and CD III, 15-16, and which are derived from Scripture, namely from Leviticus 18:5 and Ezekiel 20:11, 13, 21.

One should compare all these texts:

4Q266 11-12	ולזרעם נתתה חוקי אמתכה ומשפטי קודשכה
	אשר יעשה האדם וחיה
Ezekiel 20:11	ואתן להם את חקותי ואת משפטי הודעתי אותם
	אשר יעשה אותם האדם וחי בהם
Ezekiel 20:13	וימרו בי בית ישראל במדבר
	בחקותי לא הלכו ואת משפטי מאסו
	אשר יעשה אותם האדם וחי בהם
	ואת שבתתי חללו מאד
Ezekiel 20:21	וימרו בי הבנים
	בחקותי לא הלכו ואת משפטי לא שמרו לעשות אותם
	אשר יעשה אותם האדם וחי בהם
	את שבתותי חללו
Leviticus 18:5	ושמרתם את חקתי ואת משפטי
	אשר יעשה אתם האדם וחי (שׁ וְחיה) בהם
CD III, 14-16	שבתות קדשי ומועדי / כבודו עידות צדקו ודרכי אמתו וחפצי רצונו
	אשר יעשה / האדם וחיה בהם

Nehemiah 9:29 ולא שמעו למצותיך ובמשפטיך חטאו בם
אשר יעשה אדם וחיה בהם

In the four scriptural texts (Leviticus 18:5; Ezekiel 20:11, 13, 21) the things a man should do, אשר יעשה אתם האדם, are חוקתי, 'my statutes', and משפטי, 'my laws'. Here at the end of the Damascus Document the object is also חוקות and משפטים, but specified as חוקי אמתכה, 'your truthful statutes', and משפטי קודשכה, 'your holy laws'. The Leviticus and three Ezekiel passages are similar, but differ in minor respects. The allusion in the Damascus Document corresponds especially to Ezekiel 20:11 in that both mention that these statutes and laws are given by God (Ezekiel 20:11 ואתן, and here נתתה).

By contrast, the quotation אשר יעשה האדם וחיה בהם in CD III, 15-16 seems at first sight less connected to Leviticus and Ezekiel, as it only shares the phrase אשר יעשה האדם וחיה בם, and not the explicit mention of חוקתי, משפטי. More careful consideration, however, shows that in Ezekiel 20 three items are of importance, and are mentioned together all the time: חוקתי, 'my statutes', משפטי, 'my laws', and שבתותי, 'my Sabbaths'. The fact that the list of CD III, 14-16 of things a man should do to live begins with 'his holy sabbaths' strongly suggests that the author of this part of CD did not merely use a biblical phrase, but referred to Ezekiel 20. With regard to content, the two Damascus Document allusions are not related to Nehemiah 9:29. On the other hand, the CD and QD phrases are almost identical to the one in Nehemiah, omitting אותם and reading וחיה instead of וחי. One may surmise that וחיה is linguistically a younger form of the irregular וחי. See, however, 4Q504 6 17 which preserves ה]אדם וחי בם.

The change in the quotation in the Expulsion Ceremony from חוקתי to חוקי אמתכה, 'your truthful statutes', and משפטי to משפטי קודשכה, 'your holy laws', may be influenced by the other quotation in CD III, 15, which has a series of composite references: his *holy* Sabbaths, his *glorious* feasts, his *just* stipulations, and his *truthful* paths. Such genitival constructions with adjectivally used קודש and אמת are not unique, but rather rare in the Damascus Document. Such constructions are, however, found both in CD III, 14-16 and in the Expulsion Ceremony.

THE EXPULSION CEREMONY, THE RULE OF THE COMMUNITY, AND LEVITICUS 26

Milik and Hempel called attention to the correspondences between the Expulsion Ceremony proper (4Q266 11 5-14) and 1QS I, 16—III, 12.[45]

27. 4Q266 11 5-6 and 1QS II 25-26

| 4Q266 11 5-6 | וכול המואס במשפטים / האלה |
| 1QS II, 25-26 | וכול המואס לבוא / בברית א]ל |

Both clauses stand at the head of a subsection. One should also compare 4Q280 2 7 וכ]ול המואס לבוא [, which is a parallel to 1QS II, 25-26.[46] It is noteworthy that the combination of מאס with משפטי אל occurs in 1QS III, 5-6, since these are the only occurrences of מאס with משפטים in the Dead Sea Scrolls. In the Hebrew Bible the expression, always with משפטי, 'my regulations', is found in Leviticus 26:43 and Ezekiel 5:6; 20:13, 16, 24.

28. 4Q266 11 7 and 1QS II, 26—III, 1

The two clauses in 4Q266 11 7 כי געלה נפשו ביסורי הצדק and 1QS II, 26—III, 1 כיא געלה / נפשו ביסורי דעת are almost identical, and it is safe to assume some kind of relationship. One should also note though that the expression געלה נפש is not very common in the Hebrew Bible, and four out of five occurrences are found in Leviticus 26 (vv. 11, 15, 30, 43; with the fifth in Jeremiah 14:19). One should note that the combination of מאס במשפטים and געלה נפש is only found in 4Q266 11 15-17, 1QS II, 25—III, 1 and Leviticus 26:43, and that געל and מאס are used as synonyms in Leviticus 26:44.

29. 4Q266 11 6-7 and 1QS III, 1, 3-4

The formulation that the one who loathes disciplines 'shall not be reckoned among/with' is found in both sections. In 1QS III this is stated twice: in line 1 ועם ישרים לוא יתחשב, and in lines 3-4 לו יחשב / בכול בני אמתו / לוא יתחשב. 4Q266 11 6-7 reads בעין תמימים.

Other correspondences are found, for example the use of similar phrases such as חוקי אמת in 4Q266 11 11 and 1QS I, 15, an expression not used elsewhere in the Hebrew Bible or the Dead Sea Scrolls, except for 4Q215a 1 ii 6 חוקי האמת. Milik referred to the correspondence between הנוטה ימין / [ושמאול] in 4Q266 11 17-18 (which does not belong to the Expulsion Ceremony proper) and לסור ימין ושמאול in 1QS III, 10.[47] Compare also 1QS I, 15 ללכת ימין ושמאול. In addition, see the references to 'our fathers' (אבותינו) in both 1QS I, 26 and 4Q266 11 11, as well as the use of forms of the verb ארר in both sections. Hempel refers to the presence in our text of other 'expressions characteristic of the Community Rule — notably the use of the designation the many (הרבים)'[48] and concludes that it is likely that this section goes back to a late stage in the literary growth of the Damascus Document, although some of the incorporated traditions might be older.

I have referred above several times to Leviticus 26. Campbell indicated that this chapter was one of the sections of the Hebrew Bible used frequently by the text of the Admonition.[49] The influence of Leviticus 26 on the Damascus Document is apparent in quotations, allusions, and use of the same vocabulary, and thus one may draw the following list of correspondences:

a) CD I, 3 במועלם אשר עזבוהו (see also 4Q390 2 i 7-8) alludes to Leviticus 26:40 במעלם אשר מעלו בי (see also 4Q387 2 ii [*olim* frg. 3], 3 and *olim* 4Q387 5 1).

b) CD I, 4 and VI, 2 refer to Leviticus 26:45. Common to these phrases is זכר with ברית ראשנים.

c) Both CD I, 17-18 and CD XIX, 13 quote Leviticus 26:25 חרב נקמת נקם ברית.

d) 4Q266 11 3-4 quotes Leviticus 26:31 ולא אריח בריח ניחחכם.

e) The word קרי, 'contrary to', in CD XX, 29 בלכתנו קרי is only found in Leviticus 26 (vv. 21, 23, 24, 27, 28, 40, 41; in each case with הלך) and here.

f) The expression געלה נפש in 4Q266 11 7 is found five times in the Hebrew Bible, of which four times are in Leviticus 26 (vv. 11, 15, 30, 43).

g) The verb מאס has the object משפטים only in 4Q266 11 5, 1QS III, 5-6, Leviticus 26:43 and Ezekiel 5:6; 20:13, 16, 24. Note that in 4Q266 11, 1QS II-III, and Leviticus 26:15 and 43, the expressions געלה נפש and מאס are used as synonyms.

h) The expression הקים ברית in CD III, 13 is used several times in the Hebrew Bible instead of כרת ברית.[50] In Leviticus ברית is used hardly at all (2:13; 24:8; but seven

times in Leviticus 26), once with the expression הקים ברית (Leviticus 26:9
.(והקמתי את־בריתי אתכם).

i) The expression שמר מצות is used in, for example, CD II, 18, 21 and in Leviticus 26:3.

j) Like previous scholars, Campbell refers to CD III, 10 וארצם בו שממה as having the same language as Leviticus 26:33 והיתה ארצכם שממה, but he seems to favour an alternative possibility – that CD III, 10 is related to Ezekiel 33:28 ונתתי את הארץ שממה.[51]

It is not surprising that there are correspondences to Leviticus 26 in the Expulsion Ceremony. Leviticus 26 contains, after all, blessings and curses, and is also quoted in other Dead Sea Scrolls dealing with covenantal blessings or curses (see for example 4Q389 8 ii 4 quoting Leviticus 26:43, and 11Q14 1 ii 13-14 paraphrasing Leviticus 26:6). Yet it can hardly be a coincidence that allegedly late additions to the composition refer repeatedly to the same scriptural section as the so-called Admonition. This goes not only for the Expulsion Ceremony, but also for the quotation in 4Q266 11 3-4.

It is likely that the final sections of the Damascus Document are late additions. Apparently the editors who added these sections referred explicitly and implicitly to those parts of Scripture which were referred to in the composition, notably in the so-called Admonition.

CONCLUSIONS

On the whole, the results of this preliminary survey of the text of the Bible and of the 4Q manuscripts of the Damascus Document agree with scholarly opinions on the relation between the Bible and CD.[52]

This article has not listed the cases where the 4QD fragments confirm the text of CD. A comparison of the text of the biblical quotations in 4QD and CD shows that in items 1-8 there are differences between CD and one or more of the 4QD manuscripts, whereas considerations of space suggest some more variations (items 9-10). In a few cases the text of CD is clearly corrupted, and a 4QD manuscript provides a better reading (items 4, 7, 8; cf. also 9-10). Yet, differences between two or more 4QD manuscripts (items 1, 4, perhaps 13, 17b, 17c) indicate that one cannot prefer in all cases a 4QD reading against the CD one. This probably is the case in items 2, 3, and perhaps 5, where 4Q266 differs from both 𝔐 and CD. 4Q266 seems to have been somewhat carelessly written,[53] and an analysis of all the variants between 4Q266 and the other 4QD manuscripts is called for, in order to evaluate the textual character of 4Q266. In short, the 4QD manuscripts confirm that in some places biblical quotations in the text of CD have been corrupted. On the other hand, 4Q266 preserves some linguistic variants against 𝔐 and CD which should perhaps be attributed to the scribe of this manuscript, rather than to the authors of the document.

The second part of this survey listed biblical quotations found in 4QD but not in CD. In most cases the quotations and the contexts are fragmentary, but the final section of the document is well preserved and provides an interesting case. The accumulation of quotations (items 17a-d) indicates several stages of growth, and shows how Scripture was regarded as a treasury of authoritative texts on specific issues. The end product, with its string of quotations and the unprecedented reference to 'another place' (item 17d), betrays the hands of different authors.

Most interesting is the use of Scripture in the Expulsion Ceremony. This section refers to scriptural passages (items 25-26) which were already quoted earlier on in the document. Apparently, the editors consciously tried to relate this addition to the document. Most intriguing is the relation between the end of the *Damascus Document* and 1QS I, 16—III, 12. The fact that the *Damascus Document* repeatedly refers to Leviticus 26, and that this section of 1QS has similar references to Leviticus 26, suggests that 1QS I, 16—III, 12 is dependent on a source related to the *Damascus Document*.

NOTES

1   The proceedings of this symposium are published in Joseph M. Baumgarten, Esther G. Chazon, and Avital Pinnick (eds), *The Damascus Document: A Centennial of Discovery. Proceedings of the Third International Symposium of the Orion Center for the Study of the Dead Sea Scrolls and Associated Literature, 4-8 February 1998*, STDJ, 34 (Leiden: Brill, 2000).

2   Solomon Schechter, *Documents of Jewish Sectaries. 1. Fragments of a Zadokite Work: Edited from Hebrew Manuscripts in the Cairo Genizah Collection Now in the Possession of the University Library, Cambridge, and Printed with an English Translation, Introduction and Notes* (Cambridge: Cambridge University Press, 1910; repr. Ktav, 1970).

3   DJD XVIII. Preliminary publications of fragments or sections of the 4QD manuscripts were provided by Milik and Baumgarten in several articles, while Elisha Qimron's edition 'The Text of CDC', in *The Damascus Document Reconsidered*, ed. by Magen Broshi (Jerusalem: IES, 1992), presents in the critical apparatus most of the variant readings from the manuscripts found at Qumran, including those from Cave 4.

4   Schechter, *Documents*, pp. xi-xii.

5   Ottilie J. R. Schwarz, *Der erste Teil der Damaskusschrift und das Alte Testament* (Lichtland/Diest: Schwarz, 1965), pp. 97-98.

6   J. de Waard, *A Comparative Study of the Old Testament Text in the Dead Sea Scrolls and in the New Testament*, STDJ, 4 (Leiden: Brill, 1965), p. 30.

7   Joseph M. Baumgarten, 'A "Scriptural" Citation in 4Q Fragments of the Damascus Document' *JJS*, 43 (1992), 95-98 (p. 97).

8   John Elwolde, 'Distinguishing the Linguistic and the Exegetical: The Biblical Book of Numbers in the Damascus Document', *DSD*, 7 (2000), 1-25 (p. 25).

9   Jonathan G. Campbell, *The Use of Scripture in the Damascus Document 1-8, 19-20*, BZAW, 228 (Berlin: de Gruyter, 1995), p. ix.

10 Aharon Shemesh, 'Scriptural Interpretations in the Damascus Document and Their Parallels in Rabbinic Midrash', in *The Damascus Document: A Centennial of Discovery*, pp. 161-75 (p. 174).

11 See also Devorah Dimant, 'The Hebrew Bible in the Dead Sea Scrolls: Torah Quotations in the *Damascus Document*' (Hebrew with English Summary), in *"Sha'arei Talmon": Studies in the Bible, Qumran, and the Ancient Near East Presented to Shemaryahu Talmon*, ed. by Michael Fishbane and Emanuel Tov with the assistance of Weston W. Fields (Winona Lake, IN: Eisenbrauns, 1992), pp. 113*-122*.

12 The readings and emendations of the first decades of research are conveniently gathered in the first apparatus of Leonhard Rost, *Die Damaskusschrift neu bearbeitet*, Kleine Texte für Vorlesungen und Übungen, 167 (Berlin: de Gruyter, 1933).

13 Hartmut Stegemann, 'Towards Physical Reconstructions of the Qumran Damascus Document Scrolls', in *The Damascus Document: A Centennial of Discovery*, pp. 177-200.

14 Note that the lists of variants in the DJD edition are not exhaustive. Many variants are not noted.

15 See, for example, Donald W. Parry, 'Notes on Divine Name Avoidance in Scriptural Units of the Legal Texts of Qumran', in *Legal Texts and Legal Issues: Proceedings of the Second Meeting of the International Organization for Qumran Studies, Published in Honour of Joseph M. Baumgarten*, ed. by Moshe Bernstein, Florentino García Martínez and John Kampen, STDJ, 23 (Leiden: Brill, 1997), pp. 437-49.

16 As suggested by Schechter, *Documents*, p. xl. In that case the quotations would contain an ellipse of the Tetragrammaton (see Parry, 'Notes', p. 445).

17 The first two are published in DJD XVIII, whereas the latter is reconstructed in Hartmut Stegemann, 'More Identified Fragments of 4QD^d (4Q269)', *RevQ*, 18 (1998), 497-509, and in DJD XXXVI, p. 204.

18 Thus R. H. Charles in his notes to 'The Fragments of a Zadokite Work' in *The Apocrypha and Pseudepigrapha of the Old Testament in English with Introductions and Critical and Explanatory Notes to the Several Books. Vol. II Pseudepigrapha*, ed. by R. H. Charles (Oxford: Clarendon Press, 1913), pp. 785-834 (p. 817).

19 Sidnie Ann White, 'A Comparison of the "A" and "B" Manuscripts of the Damascus Document', *RevQ*, 12 (1987), 537-53 (p. 546).

20 DJD XVIII , pp. 44-45.

21 DJD XVIII, p. 45.

22 It seems to me that Géza Xeravits, 'Précisions sur le texte original et le concept messianique de *CD* 7:13-8:1 et 19:5-14', *RevQ*, 19 (1999), 47-59, plays down the evidence of the 4QD fragments which correspond by and large to the CD-A text, while quoting Milik who stated that a few fragments 'contain a text substantially the same as that in the B recension'. Examination of these fragments (4Q266 4 i; 4Q267 3; 4Q270 2 i 1-3) shows that these 'correspondences' are limited, not exact, and not pertinent to the issue of the relation between the A and B recension.

23 Shemaryahu Talmon, 'Synonymous Readings in the Textual Traditions of the Old Testament', in *Studies in the Bible*, ed. by Chaim Rabin, Scripta Hierosolymitana, 8 (Jerusalem: Magnes, 1961), pp. 335-83 (on רע – אח, cf. pp. 366-67).

24 de Waard, 'A Comparative Study', p. 35.

25 Unfortunately, 4QXII^g 96 only preserves here the suffix הו, not a preceding letter.

26 Deuteronomy 19:19 A and Jeremiah 38 (31):34 A.

27 Cf. also Talmon, 'Synonymous Reading', p. 366.

28 Baumgarten's translation.

29 It is not clear what Baumgarten wants to do with the small fragment within line 1 ויא[on the plate. The transcription and the placement on the plate do not correlate.

30 את is often replaced by other prepositions in the Dead Sea Scrolls. Only once do we find כרת ברית with את (4Q504 3 ii 13), whereas כרת ברית with עם or ל is more common (cf. 4Q372 3 9; 4Q434 7b 2; 4Q470 1 6; 11Q19 XXIX, 10).

31 Transcription and translation are more or less based upon the DJD edition.

32 Cf. Joseph M. Baumgarten, 'The Cave 4 Versions of the Qumran Penal Code', *JJS*, 43 (1992), 268-76; Charlotte Hempel, 'The Penal Code Reconsidered', in *Legal Texts and Legal Issues*, pp. 337-48.

33 Charlotte Hempel, *The Laws of the Damascus Document: Sources, Tradition and Redaction*, STDJ, 29 (Leiden: Brill, 1998), pp. 175-85 discusses the text under the heading 'Expulsion Ceremony and the End of the Document', but distinguishes five sections: a. Admonition to accept one's judgment willingly; b. Expulsion ceremony; c. Treatment of those who fail to ostracise the expelled member; d. The annual assembly of the members of the camps in the third month; e. The end of the document.

34 J. T. Milik, '*Milkî-ṣedeq et Milkî-rešaᶜ* dans les anciens écrits juifs et chrétiens', *JJS*, 23 (1972), 95–144 (pp. 135-36).

35 Baumgarten, 'A "Scriptural" Citation'. Cf. also the discussion in Hempel, *Laws*, pp. 175-85.

36 DJD XVIII, p. 166.

37 DJD XVIII, pp. 76 and 164, though these translations differ in some respects.

38 DJD XVIII, pp. 76 and 164, though these translations differ in some respects.

39 Hempel, *Laws*, p. 179.

40 Hempel, *Laws*, pp. 175 and 177, as well as *DSSSE*, I, p. 596, think that the text read ובמקום אחזר. However, more careful consideration shows that the supralinear text does read ובמקום, with a large space between the second *vav* and final *mem*, in order to avoid writing over the arm of *lamed* of line 5 לשוב. *DSSSE* also misleadingly suggests a different order of the two quotations.

41 Stegemann, 'Physical Reconstructions', pp. 193-97.

42 Presumably Baumgarten only observed the overlap in a late stage. In DJD XVIII the parallel is not mentioned in a heading parallels, and the text is not underlined. Baumgarten only refers to 6Q15 in the comments on lines 16-19.

43 In the comments 6Q15 5 5 is mistakenly quoted as reading בלבבכם instead of בלבבם.

44 Reading not only a shorter text, but also עם instead of עם (cf. the discussion of CD XVI, 1 / 4Q271 4 ii 3 / Exodus 34:27 above).

45 Milik, pp. 135-36; Hempel, *Laws*, pp. 180-82.

46 See Bilhah Nitzan's comments in DJD XXIX, p. 7.

47 Milik, p. 136.

48 Hempel, *Laws*, p. 185.

49 Campbell, pp. 58-59, 77, 173, 184, 201.

50 Genesis 6:18; 9:9, 11, 17; 17:7, 19, 21; Exodus 6:4; Leviticus 26:9; Deuteronomy 8:18; Ezekiel 16:60, 62. Cf. also Sirach 45:24; 50:24. In the Dead Sea Scrolls cf. 1QS 5:21-22 (4Q258 II, 1); 8:10 (4Q258 VI, 3); 1QSb 5:23; 4Q504 1-2 iv 6; 11Q13 ii 24

51 Campbell, pp. 77, 81.

52 For which cf. the section 'The Damascus Document and the Bible' above.

53 Cf. the discussion in DJD XVIII, p. 2.

BIBLICAL QUOTATIONS AND ALLUSIONS IN 4QAPOCRYPHAL LAMENTATIONS (4Q179)

Jesper Høgenhaven

4Q179 COMPRISES five fragments of a manuscript, originally published in 1968 by John Allegro, who entitled this text '4QLamentations'.[1] Allegro's title has been criticized for causing confusion by assigning to a non-biblical text the name of a canonical book, and has now given way in most scholarly literature to the more appropriate designation '4QApocryphal Lamentations A' or similar.

Fragment 1 is by far the largest surviving fragment of 4Q179, followed by fragment 2. Fragment 1 preserves the left part of one column with the remains of fifteen lines, and the right part of thirteen lines of the following column. Fragment 2 preserves the remains of ten lines of a third column, with three of these lines preserving both margins, thus indicating the column width of the manuscript. Fragments 3-5 are small with only a few words preserved on each.

The surviving text of fragments 1 and 2 may be presented as follows:

Column i (fragment 1)

TRANSCRIPTION[2]

[ ]·[	]	1
ל]·ר כל עוונותינו ואין לאל ידנו כי לוא שמענו[	]	2
]····דה לקרותנו כל אלה ברוע [	]	3
]· את בריתו vacat אוי לנ[ו	]	4
]היה לשרפת אש והפכה [	]	5
]·תפארתנו וניחוח אין בו במז[ו]בח[	]	6
]חצרות קודשנו היו	]	7
[ ]כ·[ ]··תים ירושלים עיר	]	8
מרב[ץ] לחיה ואין ע[ו]בר בה]ורחובותיה	]	9
א]ן הוי כל ארמונותיה שממו	]	10
]· ובאי מועד אין בם כל ערי	]	11
נ]חלתנו היתה כמדבר ארץ לוא	]	12
שמ[ח]ה לוא נשמעה בה ודורש	]	13
ל[ ]אנוש למכא[ו]בנו[ ]כול חובינו	]	14
פ]שעינו י·[ ]חטאותינו	]	15

bottom margin

113

Jesper Høgenhaven

NOTES ON READINGS

Line 2 ל־ר[. Traces of three letters are visible to the right of the *resh*. The first letter appears to be a *lamed*, which may suggest that the word is an infinitive.

Line 3 ה····[. Three or possibly four letter traces are visible to the right of the two legible letters. The first of these would seem to be either a *vav* or a *yod*.

Line 6 למזֿ[בח. Cf. the *zayin* in col. ii 4 (אכזרה). This reading is mentioned by Strugnell, p. 250, who, however, regards the *zayin* as impossible.

Line 10 ן[. The long stroke of a final *nun* is visible dropping below the line (as suggested by Strugnell, p. 250, who reads ן[ו), but there is no visible trace to the right of the *nun*.

Line 13 נשמשעה. The second (and superflous) *shin* was 'dotted', apparently marking a scribal error.

Line 14 ל[אנוש. As read by Strugnell, p. 251. Allegro, p. 75 reads ל[איש.

Line 14 למכֿאוֿבֿנֿו. The word with erasures and the supralinear addition of ת and י would seem to represent a correction of למכאובנו into למכתינו. Whether the *bet* was also erased is not clear.

Line 14 חובינו. As correctly read by Strugnell, p. 251.

TRANSLATION

2. [   ] ... all our sins. And it is not in the power of our hand, for we did not obe[y

3. [   ] ... so that all these things have happened to us because of the evil [

4. [   ] .. his covenant. *vacat* Woe to us [

5. [   ] has been burnt by fire, and an overthrow [

6. [   ] our beauty. And there is no pleasing odour in it on the al[tar

7. [   ] the courtyards of our sanctuary have become

8. [   ] ... Jerusalem, the city

9. [a lair] for wild beasts , and there is no one [passing by her,] and her streets

10. [   ] ... Alas! All her palaces are desolated

11. [   ] ... and those who come to the appointed feast are not among them. All the cities

12. [   ] our inheritance has become like a desert, a land not

13. [   ] j[o]y is not heard in her. And he who seeks

14. [   ] our wound is incurable [   ] all our guilt

15. [   ] our [tr]ansgressions [   ] our sins

Column ii (fragment 1)

TRANSCRIPTION

[	אוי לנוֿ כי אף אל על·ן	1
[	וננוללה עם המתים ·ן	2
[	כמשונאה יש·ן	3
[	לעוליהן ובת עמי אכזריהֿן	4
[	עלומיה שוממו בני פֿנֿמי	5
[	מלפני חורף בדל ידיהןֿ	6
[	אשפותות מדור בית·ן	7
[	שאלו מים ואיֿן מגירֿן	8
[	המסלאיֿםֿן בכתןֿסֿ נ·ן·ן	9
[	וחפץ אין בו יֿאמונים עלי תולֿןֿע	10
[	וכתם טוב עדים נושאים הלבוֿנֿשים	11
[	ומשי תכלת וריקמה מפֿנֿני	12
[	בנוֿיֿ ציון היקרים הרכות עֿמֿסֿן··	13

bottom margin

114

NOTES ON READINGS

Line 1 ל∙[. Allegro, p. 75 indicates a final *he* without any indication of uncertainty. The letter trace, however, is not identifiable (as noted by Strugnell, p. 251). Horgan, p. 232 reads יחר לנו.[3]

Line 5 שׁמֵי as suggested by Strugnell, p. 251.

Line 7 בית∙[. Strugnell, p. 251 reads ביתהן. Horgan, p. 233 reads ביתו (cf. Lamentations 4:5), but the angle of the letter trace preserved seems a little too sharp for a *vav*.

Line 12 ומשי. As read by Strugnell, p. 251 and Horgan, p. 234. Allegro, p. 76 reads ימשו.

Line 12 ורקמה. As read by Horgan, p. 234. Allegro, p. 76 reads ידי קמה, and Strugnell, p. 251 ורוקמה. Cf. Ezekiel 16:13; 27:24.

Line 13 בנ̇יֿ. The *tav* was added above the line to correct a scribal error. Emanuel Tov (private communication) has noted that the *vav* could equally be read as a *yod*. He then notes as a possibility that the scribe may originally have had masculine בני in mind (cf. היקרים), but when changing form, interpreted the third letter as a *vav*, added a *tav*, cancelled the masculine with dots, and added the feminine.

Line. 13 היקרים. The word was 'dotted', presumably to mark a scribal error.

Line. 13 שׁמֵם ∙∙[. Strugnell, p. 251 reads במעגל].

TRANSLATION

1. Woe to us, for the anger of God has gone up [
2. and we have polluted it with the dead ... [
3. like a hated woman ... [
4. their sucklings, but the daughter of my people is cruel [
5. her youth. The children of [my people] are desolate [
6. because of the winter. When their hands are weak [
7. ash heaps are the dwelling place where they spend the night [
8. they beg for water, but there is no one to pour out [
9. worth their weight [in gol]d... [
10. and there is no delight in it. Those who were brought up in purpl[e
11. and pure gold their ornament. Those who esteemed cloth[ing
12. and silk, purple, and embroidered cloth fro[m
13. the tender daughters of Zion with them...

Column iii (fragment 2)

TRANSCRIPTION

[∙ךֿ[ ]]			I
[∙נֿ∙∙[ ]∙[ ]]			2
[∙ע באהלך[ ]∙∙∙[ ]]			3
] איכה ישבה] בדר העיר] ∙ו∙[ ]לים ∙[ ]			4
]∙ים שרתי כל לאומים] שוממה כעזובה וכל]בנותיה עזובות [			5
כ]אשה עזו]בה כעצובה וכעזובת] כל ארמנותיה ורחו]מבותיה]			6
בעקרה וכמסככה כול אורחו]תי̇נֿה זֿה ⁷אשת מרורים			7
וכל בנותיה כאבלות על על בעוליהן כול שע̇ריה כמשכלות			8
ליחידיהן בכו תבכה ירו]שלים ז̇ו על לחיה על בניה			9
]ל ∙ והגנתה]∙[ ]∙[ ]			10

NOTES ON READINGS

Line 3 ∙[. The trace shows a long vertical stroke dropping beneath the line. Possibilities are final *kaf* or final *tsade*.

Line 4].·.[. Strugnell, p. 251 reads]שׁ לוֹ[.

Line 6 עזן]בה. The only identifiable letters are *ayin* and *he*. Before the *he*, the upper 'roof' of a letter is visible. Possibilities include *bet*, *kaf*, *mem*, or *resh*. Strugnell, pp. 251-52 reads ערוֹן]רֹיה. Horgan, p. 234 reads ערן]מה.

Line 6 [   ]. Allegro has [בע]לוֹה], but Strugnell, p. 252, correctly points out that there is no trace of a *lamed*.

Line 6 ורחון]בותיה, as correctly read by Strugnell, p. 252. Allegro reads וחן]מותיה, while Horgan, p. 234 suggests וחן]וצותיה.

Line 8 שע]ריה. The letter trace looks like either a *dalet* or *resh*.

TRANSLATION

3. [   ] ... in your tent [

4. [How] lonely [sits] the city [

5. [   ] ... a princess of all nation[s] is desolate like an abandoned woman, and all her [daug]hters are abandon[ed]

6. [like] a childless woman, like one abandoned and forsaken [   ] are all her palaces and her sq[uares]

7. like a barren woman and like a woman imprisoned are all [her] paths [   ] ... like a woman of grief.

8. And all her daughters are like women mourning for (for) [their] husb[ands   ] ... like those bereaved

9. of their only children. Jeru[salem] weeps bitterly [   ] upon her cheek because of her children

10. [   ] ... and she moans

The extant text may be characterized in general terms as a description of the desolate and miserable state of the city of Jerusalem, its sanctuary, and its inhabitants. In addition to this description, the text also contains a collective confession of guilt. The sins of the 'we' speaking in the text are presented as the cause of God's anger, which has led to the miserable situation described.

As noted in all scholarly treatments of 4Q179, the text is to a great extent inspired by and dependent upon biblical material. A number of scriptural quotations and allusions were pointed out by the first editor, Allegro, in DJD V. While Allegro's proposal to designate the text simply as '4QLamentations' has rightly been rejected, it remains true that there is a demonstrable and particularly strong link between 4Q179 and the biblical Book of Lamentations.

Maurya Horgan offered both a number of suggested readings and proposed restorations of lacunae, and also an attempt at interpreting the text, its genre and significance.[4] In reality, this attempt amounts to an identification of the numerous biblical background texts which are either quoted or alluded to and a discussion of the use made of this material in 4Q179.

Horgan's article leaves no doubt as to the importance of the biblical allusions for the composition and structure of 4Q179. In fact, 4Q179 may give the impression of being more or less a conglomerate or pastiche of biblical phrases. This latter expression is taken from a recent study by Adele Berlin.[5] Berlin's article constitutes an important step towards understanding the nature of the text's use of biblical material. Here, the use of Scripture is analyzed in the light of recent studies of exegesis and of interpretative strategies relating to ancient texts, since the use of biblical allusions is viewed as an important compositional and structuring device in 4Q179. Berlin also suggests interpreting the lament in 4Q179 in terms of 'Qumranic' polemics against the regime in Jerusalem, a suggestion which merits

Biblical Quotations and Allusions in 4QApocryphal Lamentations

further consideration. Our concern here, however, relates to the use of scriptural material in 4Q179, and an attempt will be made to offer some observations on the role of quotations and allusions in the compositional technique employed in the text.

First, some general remarks on compositional techniques in 4Q179 are in order. The fragmentary state of preservation of this text should caution us against drawing too swift or sweeping conclusions regarding its genre or literary structure. Neither the beginning nor the end of this literary work has survived, and we cannot even know whether the two columns of fragment 1 preceded or followed the column of fragment 2.

Nevertheless, certain observations on composition and structure can be made. The occurrence of a mid-line *vacat* in i 4 indicates a separation between sections of the text. Lines 1-4 preceding the *vacat* contain a collective confession of guilt, whereas, in the section following, the focus shifts to a description of the desolate state of Jerusalem and the temple.

That the extant text of 4Q179 is composed of several sections may be argued convincingly both from its form and its contents. As already mentioned, there are some demonstrable thematic shifts between sections. In i 1-4 a 'we' speaks of 'our sins' in the first person plural, and points – in the third person masculine singular – to God's punishing acts which have occurred as a consequence of the sins and transgressions committed by the 'we'-group. By contrast, in section i 4-14, the style is descriptive, depicting the desolate city which is spoken of in the third person feminine singular (i 8-10). Furthermore, reference is made to the sanctuary, its altar and courtyards, and to the population (i 11). The perspective is then widened to include the land, which has become like a desert with no joyful sound being heard (i 12-13).

The overall emphasis of the description is on the changes that the city, temple, land and people have suffered. This is brought out effectively by the contrast between past glory and present misery. The description moves from inside to outside, from centre to periphery, beginning with the temple and the altar, moving on to the city, its streets and palaces, then to the people, and finally to the land.[6] Interestingly, in i 14-15 the theme of 'confession of guilt' would seem to make its appearance again – at least, the two partly legible words of i 15 (חטאותינו and פ[ש]עינו) can plausibly be read as referring to 'our sins' and 'our transgressions'. Furthermore, at the end of i 14, one should probably read the word חוביֵנו, 'our guilt'.[7] This reference would thereby constitute a thematic bridge between the descriptive section and the preceding confession section. It might be argued that a sort of *inclusio* was intended, and, consequently, that this reference marks the end of the descriptive section. A further link between the confession and description sections is established by the employment of the first person plural at the beginning of the descriptive section (which is introduced by the words אוי לנו, i 4), and continuing throughout this section, relating the sanctuary and the land to 'us'.

The words אוי לנו occur again in column ii line 1, and it would seem natural to assume that here, too, they serve as an introduction to a new section. In fact, what we have in column ii may be understood as a second descriptive section, focusing on the image of the devastated city as a 'hated woman' (ii 3), then explaining and elucidating this image in terms of depicting the fate of her daughters and sons. Again, the first person plural occurs in the opening lines (ii 1-2), which point, first to the divine wrath that has hit 'us', and, secondly, echo the confession of guilt by stating that 'we' are defiling 'her/it', presumably the city. However, after these introductory lines, the 'we' does not reappear in this section. In fact, the first person plural gives way to a subtle interchange between the third person feminine singular (meaning both the personified city and the 'daughter of my people' (ii 4), i.e., the women of Jerusalem), the third person feminine plural, used of the 'daughters', and the third person masculine plural, used of the 'sons'.

The surviving part of a third column in fragment 2 would seem to exhibit a third descriptive section, again centred around the female metaphor used for the city. Here again in the preserved text, the third person feminine singular alternates with the third person feminine plural.

Despite the fragmentary state of 4Q179, all indications point to a carefully structured literary composition, the main focus of which is on describing the misery and desolation of Jerusalem within the framework of a theological perspective: it is God who has stricken the city in his anger because of the sins and failures of the 'we'-group who have broken his covenant and failed to listen to his commands. These literary and theological features connect 4Q179 with the genre that has been called 'penitential prayer', biblical examples of which are found in Daniel 9:4-19 and Nehemiah 1:5-11.[8] In terms of genre, however, 4Q179 is not, strictly speaking, a prayer text. God is never directly invoked or addressed in the second person, but consistently spoken of in the third person.[9] It is, of course, possible that this is simply due to the fragmentary state of the manuscript, but one may point to the canonical Book of Lamentations, where we have extensive descriptive sections, referring to God's punishing acts in the third person, and only at the end of these sections do the direct invocations occur. Something similar could have been the case in 4Q179. While such a possibility cannot be excluded, not a single example of direct invocation is found in the preserved text. The question of genre should be addressed in view of this fact, and the possibility that we are dealing with a text with affinities not only to 'penitential prayers' but also to documents of a more doctrinal or theological nature should be taken seriously.

At any rate, many questions concerning the literary character and structure of the original document represented by the manuscript 4Q179 must remain unanswered. What is preserved of the text, however, seems to reveal a carefully structured composition. We would therefore expect it to make a conscious and deliberate use of scriptural material. The examples below will demonstrate how biblical allusions and imagery have been employed in 4Q179 as a structuring principle, underlying and partly governing the shape of the text.

While biblical allusions in 4Q179 are numerous, regular verbatim quotations are relatively few, and those that can be identified tend to have a slightly different text when compared to the ancient biblical witnesses. One instance that would qualify as a regular quotation is found in ii 3-4:

[כמשונאה יש·]

[לעוליהן ובת עמי אכזריהן

Here the words ובת עמי אכזריה give the distinct impression of being a variant of Lamentations 4:3 בת עמי לאכזר. The impression that this is a quotation is corroborated by the preceding word לעוליהן. This would appear to be a variant of גוריהן, which in Lamentations 4:3 precedes the reference to the 'daughter of my people', forming the end of the phrase 'even the jackals give the breast and suckle their young', which expresses the contrast with the cruel, unnatural mothers of the hunger-smitten city. It seems, therefore, that this phrase from Lamentations 4:3 may be restored, with a high degree of certainty, at the end of ii 3. Whether or not the following words from Lamentations 4:3 'like ostriches of the desert' (כיענים במדבר) also followed in ii 4, we cannot know. The quotation has certainly broken off by the beginning of ii 5, although the text presumably continued to speak about 'her', i.e., the 'daughter of my people'. In other words, the quotation has become an integral part of the text's own literary structure.

Another example of biblical texts being directly quoted in 4Q179 is found in ii 9-11.

המסלאי֯ם֯ בכת֯ם֯ ֗נ֗[...]

וחפץ אין בו ֗האמונים עלי תול֗ע

וכתם טוב עדים נושאים הלב֗נ֯שים

This is an interesting case, illustrating how several quotations may be combined to create a new literary context. The clearly legible word המסלאים would seem to represent a quotation from Lamentations 4:2, which speaks of the 'precious sons of Zion' being 'weighed' or 'worth their weight' (המסלאים) in fine gold. Something similar in meaning to the biblical continuation בפז should probably be restored to follow המסלאים in ii 9. In the following line (ii 10), the phrase האמונים עלי תול֗ע ('those who were brought up in purple', the last word partly restored and the initial *he* added by the scribe supralinearly) is a direct quotation from Lamentations 4:5. This descriptive phrase was here combined or conflated with the description, similar in meaning, from Lamentations 4:2 to create a literary unit, an expanded description of those once used to luxury, in whom there is no delight any more. Column ii line 11 expands further on this description by means of a quotation from Ezekiel 16:13, which has been changed from second person to third person to fit its new context. Berlin remarks that this combination of biblical quotations may be more than merely a stylistic device. The context in Ezekiel, she observes, is a portrait of Jerusalem, who was dressed by God in finery, but then used her finery to attract her lovers. Accordingly, the employment of the Ezekiel quotation at this place may well have been intended to bring to mind the prophetic image of a sinful or guilty city that is being justly punished, thus adding a theological perspective to the mere contrast between past glory and present misery otherwise present in the text.

As we have seen identifying the specific biblical text or texts quoted or alluded to may be helpful in restoring lacunae and in elucidating the syntax and meaning of the preserved text of 4Q179. Another example of this may be found in i 9:

מרב֗ץ לחיה ואין ֗ע֯ובר בה]ורחובותיה

Here there seems to be an allusion to Zephaniah 2:15, from which verse we may restore the expression 'a lair for wild beasts' (מרב֯ץ לחיה), the second word being preserved in i 9. In the following lacuna, after the word ואין, Horgan suggests restoring the words ֗ע֯]ובר בה ('and there is no one passing through her'). This suggestion gains support from a similar phrase (עובר עלה) found in Zephaniah 2:15, although the context there is slightly different. In the Zephaniah text the reference is to everyone passing by the devastated city, who will hiss and shake their fists, whereas in 4Q179 the notion of anyone at all passing through the city is apparently denied, creating an image of complete emptiness and desolation. This change of perspective concurs with the use of biblical phrases as material for creating new contexts characteristic of 4Q179.

This use of scriptural references as a compositional technique or as a structuring principle may also be observed in the larger units of the text. In the text of the column preserved on fragment 2 (column iii) we have a direct quotation from the opening phrase of Lamentations 1:1. This quotation is then used as the starting-point for developing the metaphor of

Jerusalem as a mourning, abandoned woman, a metaphor which governs the entire following description. A biblical metaphor is thus made the structuring principle of the text, biblical allusions and materials being employed extensively to elaborate the metaphor, yet the context created is a new context in its own right. Something similar occurs in column ii. Here again we have a dominant metaphor (the 'hated woman' as an image of the city) governing the section. The metaphor is then elucidated, with various aspects of its meaning being brought out by means of a number of supplementary images: the cruel women denying food to their babies; the ash-heaps that have become their dwelling-places; the children begging for water without getting any; and finally, the elaborate image of the precious sons, who were once brought up in luxury, but who are no longer the delight of anybody. In this case the dominant metaphor, the 'hated woman', does of course echo the imagery of Lamentations as well as a number of biblical prophetic texts, but it is not drawn from one specific quotation or allusion. On the other hand, almost all the images employed to interpret the central metaphor represent biblical allusions, several of them being allusions to Lamentations 4, which forms the most important background text for this descriptive section of 4Q179. It would not be accurate, however, to characterize this section as a paraphrase of Lamentations 4, nor does the text constitute an interpretation, pesher, midrash, or the like, of the biblical text. Rather we are dealing with the deliberate employment of biblical images and phrases, drawn from a specific biblical context, and organized into a new literary unit, exhibiting a structure that is in some ways clearer or more easily perceived than that of the biblical text of Lamentations 4 itself.

It may be added that the general theme of 4Q179, the image of Jerusalem in ruins, is itself a strongly biblical theme, reflected as it is in Daniel, Psalms, and a great number of prophetic passages. The theme also occurs with theological significance in other writings from the Qumran library. In the light of this literary background there would seem little reason to look for any specific historical events as the background for 4Q179[10]. Such considerations, however, lie outside the scope of the present study.

NOTES

1 DJD V, p. 75-77, pl. XXVI. Cf. John Strugnell, 'Notes en marge du volume V des "Discoveries in the Judaean Desert of Jordan"', *RevQ*, 7 (1970), 163-276 (pp. 250-52).

2 All transcriptions have been made using the Brill microfiche photographs (PAM 41.320, 42.607, 43.425), and the fragments themselves have been examined at the Rockefeller Museum in Jerusalem.

3 Maurya P. Horgan, 'A Lament over Jerusalem ('4Q179')', *JSS*, 18 (1973), 222-34.

4 Horgan, 'Lament'.

5 Adele Berlin, 'Qumran Laments and the Study of Lament Literature', forthcoming and presently available as a paper at the Orion Center homepage, quoted with the permission of the author.

6 As pointed out by Berlin, 'Qumran Laments'.

7 This is a better reading than איבינו, 'our enemies', as read by J. M. Allegro in DJD V, p. 75.

8 Cf. Rodney Alan Werline, *Penitential Prayer in Second Temple Judaism: The Development of a Religious Institution*, SBL Early Judaism and Its Literature, 13 (Atlanta: Scholars Press, 1998). Reference to Werline's monograph and the genre of 'penitential prayer' is also made in Berlin, 'Qumran Laments'.

9 A possible exception is באהלך frg. 2 iii, 3. The second person suffix here could be understood as referring to God, but the reference is not clear since the context is missing.

10 The discussion concerning this point was opened by Strugnell with his remark: 'On se demandera à quelle destruction de Jérusalem l'auteur pensait' (Strugnell, p. 250). M. Horgan points to the account in 1 Maccabees 1:16-40 of an attack on Jerusalem by Antiochus IV Epiphanes, and suggests that the events mentioned there may underlie 4Q179 (Horgan, pp. 222-23).

4QTALES OF THE PERSIAN COURT (4Q550[A-E]) AND ITS RELATION TO BIBLICAL ROYAL COURTIER TALES, ESPECIALLY ESTHER, DANIEL AND JOSEPH

Sidnie White Crawford

THE PUBLICATION by J. T. Milik in 1992 of the Aramaic fragments 4Q550 stirred the community of Esther scholars, for Milik provocatively named the fragments 4QprotoEsther araméen.[1] Here at last was evidence that the Book of Esther was known at Qumran, at least in an Aramaic form. Or was it? In a 1996 article I endeavoured to demonstrate that, although several connections could be drawn between these fragments and the Hebrew and Greek Books of Esther, the fragments did not constitute a 'model, archetype or source'[2] for the Book of Esther.[3] This conclusion was also arrived at independently by Robert Eisenman and Michael Wise,[4] and followed by John Collins and Deborah Green, Edward Cook, and, most recently, Kristin de Troyer.[5] However, now that it has been sufficiently demonstrated that these fragments are not a prototype of the Book of Esther, it behoves us to ask what in fact they are. I began to answer this question by suggesting that these fragments were 'part of a cycle of tales about the Persian court', similar to the Daniel cycle, in general circulation in the middle to late Second Temple period.[6] That idea will be explored further in this paper. First, the transcriptions of the fragments, with translations and notes will be presented.[7]

4Q550[a][8]

1.	ומש]תמען לפטריזא אבוך[	
2.	בעבדי לבוש מלכותא בֿן]לן[	לֿ]מעבד
3.	עבידת מלכא כלֿוֿל דֿי קבל[	עין בה בשתא[
4.	ארכת רוחה די מלכא א.ן[	ספֿ]רֿי אבוהי התנקֿרֿיו קדמוהי ובין
5.	ספריא אשתכח מגלה חדה חתי]מה חתמֿ]ןֿ]שבעה בעזקתא די דריוש אבוהי עזינה	די כֿל אֿ]רֿעא
6.	דרֿ]וֿיש מלכא לעבדי שלֿטנא שלם פתיחת קרית השתכח כתיב בה די דריוש מלכא	
7.	]ולמלכין די ל]מלכון בתרי לעבדי שלֿטנא שלֿ]ום ידיע להוא לכן די כול אנוס ושקר	

NOTES

Line 1 ומש]תמען Milik, Collins-Green, *DSSSE*] Eisenman-Wise and Beyer read שמען]הון.

לפטריזא Collins-Green] Milik and Beyer read לפתריזא; *DSSSE* reads לפתרייזה; Eisenman-Wise reads לפתרונא.

Line 2 בעבדי Collins-Green] Milik reads ובעבדי; *DSSSE* reads ו]ןבעבדי; Eisenman-Wise reads לעבדי; Beyer reads ובון ען עבדי. I was unable to see traces of a letter before ב.

ל[בן Milik, Collins-Green, *DSSSE*] Eisenman-Wise and Beyer read בנכון‬ל.

Line 3 ככול Milik, Collins-Green, *DSSSE*, Beyer] Eisenman-Wise reads בכול.

קבול Collins-Green, Eisenman-Wise, Beyer] Milik reads קבולת; *DSSSE* reads קבנלון.

עין[Milik, Collins-Green, *DSSSE*] Eisenman-Wise reads ין·[; Beyer reads נין·[.

בשתא Collins-Green, *DSSSE*, Beyer] Milik correctly amends to בשעתא, which will be followed in the translation; Eisenman-Wise reads בשתה.

Line 4 א·[ ] Milik reads אעירדה; Collins-Green reads א[ן; *DSSSE* reads אען; Eisenman-Wise reads אל[ן; Beyer reads אדין.

ספ[ר]י Collins-Green, *DSSSE*, Beyer] Milik reads ס[פרי; Eisenman-Wise reads ·י[.

אבוהי Collins-Green] Milik, *DSSSE*, Eisenman-Wise and Beyer read אבנ[ו]הי.

התנקריו Collins-Green] Milik reads התקריו; *DSSSE* and Beyer read ו[א]תקריו; Eisenman-Wise reads ק·הי[ ]·.

קדמוהי Milik, Collins-Green, Eisenman-Wise, Beyer] *DSSSE* reads קדימוהי.

ובין Milik, Collins-Green, *DSSSE*, Beyer] Eisenman-Wise reads בין.

Line 5 אשתכח Milik, Collins-Green, Eisenman-Wise] *DSSSE* and Beyer suggest אשתכח(ת).

חנדה Collins-Green, *DSSSE*, Eisenman-Wise, Beyer] Milik reads חנתימה.

חתנ[ק]מה Collins-Green, *DSSSE*, Eisenman-Wise, Beyer] Milik reads פחנמה.

חתמין Collins-Green, Eisenman-Wise] Milik, *DSSSE* and Beyer read חתמין.

Line 6 At the beginning of the line, Milik indicates traces of two letters; Eisenman-Wise reads a ש; Beyer reads ו[ב]ה.

די כל א[ר]עא (supralinear) Milik, Collins-Green, *DSSSE*, Eisenman-Wise] Beyer reads די עול א[ר]עא.

פתיחת Milik, *DSSSE*, Eisenman-Wise, Beyer] Collins-Green reads ו[פ]תיחת.

Line 7 ולמלכין די ימלכון Milik] Collins-Green reads [מ]לכין; *DSSSE* reads ל· ... די ימלכון; Eisenman-Wise reads כתב לכול[ן] מלכין; Beyer reads ולבני די ימלכון.

ולעבדי Collins-Green, Eisenman-Wise] Milik, *DSSSE* and Beyer read ולעבדי.

שלום[ם] Milik, *DSSSE*, Eisenman-Wise, Beyer] שלם[ם] Collins-Green.

TRANSLATION

1. And] they [o]beyed Patireza your father...
2. among the servants of the royal wardrobe, in [...] to? [...] to perform...
3. the service of the king according to all that he received [...ob]eying(?) in that time...
4. the spirit of the king was long [...] the books of his father [...be] read before him and among
5. the books was found a scroll [... seal]ed with seven seal[s] with the signet ring of Darius his father. The subject:
6. ...Dar]ius the king, to the servants of the empire [of the w[hole e]arth], Peace! When it was opened and read, there was found written in it: Darius the king
7. to the kings who will] rule after me, to the servants of the realm, Pe[a]ce! Let it be known to you that any oppressor or liar...

NOTES ON THE TRANSLATION

Line 2 Cook translates 'among those who make the royal garments', which implies a lower level of servant than an official of the royal wardrobe.

Line 4 The first phrase is a literal translation of an enigmatic phrase. Other proposed translations include 'the king was unable to fall asleep' (Cook); 'the king's spirit was suffering' (*DSSSE*); 'the lengthening of the king's spirit' (García Martínez); 'the king was bored' (Collins-Green); and 'the king's patience' (Eisenman-Wise). Cook's translation is influenced by Esther 6:1; there is no mention of sleep in 4Q550[a].

4Q550^b

1. אנש להן ידזעַ] מלכא הֹן איתין
2. ולא יבד שמֹה טבא [וֹ]הימנותה
3. מלכא איתי לפתריזא בר יֹ]
4. נפלת עלוהי אימת בית ספרא
5. אושי מלכאֹ די תמֹֹר [וֹתתיהבן
6. ביתי [וֹנֹ]כֹסי לכול מֹה די יתנֹיהב
7. התכיל ותקבל עבידת אבוֹדן

NOTES

Line 1 ידזעַ] Milik, *DSSSE*, Eisenman-Wise, Beyer] Collins-Green reads ידע. I was unable to see traces of the ע.

Line 2 שמה Milik, Collins-Green, *DSSSE*, Beyer] Eisenman-Wise reads שהד.

[וֹ]הימנותה Milik, *DSSSE*, Beyer] Collins-Green reads [וֹ]הימנוֹ; Eisenman-Wise reads הימנו.

Line 3 לפתריזא Milik, *DSSSE*, Beyer] Collins-Green reads לפטריזא; Eisenman-Wise reads לפתרונא. The alternation between ט and ת in this name (assuming my readings are correct) is unexpected, since in Aramaic ט indicates either proto-Semitic ṭ or ṯ , while ת indicates proto-Semitic t.[9]

יֹ] *DSSSE*, Beyer] Milik reads יאיר and makes a connection with Yair the father of Mordecai in Esther 2:5; Collins-Green and Eisenman-Wise read יש. The letter traces could be a ש; א does not seem possible.

Line 4 אימת Milik, Collins-Green, Eisenman-Wise] *DSSSE* and Beyer read אומת.

ספרא Milik, *DSSSE*, Beyer] Collins-Green reads ספריא; Eisenman-Wise reads ספרא. The ר and א are clear on PAM 41.952.

Line 6 [וֹנֹ]כֹסי Eisenman-Wise] Milik, *DSSSE* and Beyer read ונכסי; Collins-Green reads [וֹנ]כֹסיֹ. The bottom stroke of the כ is visible on PAM 41.952, and possibly the bottom stroke of the נ.

יתנֹיהב Collins-Green] Milik reads יתנהב; *DSSSE* and Beyer read יתנ...; Eisenman-Wise reads [וֹיתנ.

Line 7 התכיל Milik, Collins-Green, *DSSSE*, Beyer] Eisenman-Wise reads התכול.

TRANSLATION

1. a man; but the king kno[ws] whether there is [
2. and his good name [and] his reputation are not ruined [...
3. O King, Patireza has a son, Y [...
4. the fear of the archives (literally: the house of the scribe) fell upon him [...
5. the herald of the king, that you shall spe[ak] and you shall be given [...
6. my house [and] my [pr]operty for everything that is [given...
7. it was measured and you will receive the position of your father [...

NOTES ON THE TRANSLATION

In the first three lines, a servant is apparently speaking to the king; in lines 5-7 the king is speaking (through the herald?) to Patireza's son.

Line 2 Another possible translation is: 'and his good name is not ruined, and they will do what is right [...' (see also Eisenman-Wise).

Line 3 It is also possible to translate the phrase איתי לפתריזא בר as 'Patireza son of ... has...' (see *DSSSE*, Eisenman-Wise). Cook construes the phrase as a question. Milik's reading of the final name as Yair (thus creating a parallel to Esther 2:5, where Mordecai is identified as the son of Yair) is without merit.[10]

Line 4 *DSSSE* and García Martínez take ספרא as a proper name, but it seems better to understand it as the definite form of the word 'book'; thus the king is worried about something related to what has just been read to him from the records (so also Collins-Green, Cook and Eisenman-Wise).

Line 5 The translation 'herald' is taken from the root אוש, 'to blow vehemently, make a noise, shout'.[11] *DSSSE* construes 'Ushay' as a proper name, while Cook and Eisenman-Wise derive their translation from אוש, 'foundation'.[12]

'you shall spe[ak]' understands תמ as the verb אמר (so also Collins-Green, García Martínez, Cook and Eisenman-Wise). *DSSSE* translates the word as a geographic name, 'Tamar'. However, the questions of what Tamar is or where it is located are unresolved.

Line 7 Both Cook and Eisenman-Wise construe this as a question.

4Q550ᶜ

]אׄושׄי מלכא די תמר לשרת·אן	]נה נדן	1.
]פתריזא אׄוׄבׄ]וׄךׄ] מן יומא די קם על עבידת]מלכאן קדם מלכא]		2.
]··עבד מן קׄוׄט ומׄן הׄיׄמׄני קׄ]דׄמׄוׄהי	]ה ען [	3.
]·א ואמר אושין		4.
]נה ארגׄ]ונא		5.
לן]לת שלן		6.

NOTES

Line 1 אושי *DSSSE*, Eisenman-Wise, Beyer] Milik reads אׄוׄ]שׄי; Collins-Green notes traces of letters.

מלכא Milik, Collins-Green, *DSSSE*, Beyer] Eisenman-Wise reads מלכה.

לשרת·אן] Milik reads לשרׄיׄתׄא אׄוׄנׄתׄהׄ; Collins-Green reads לשרתאן; *DSSSE* and Beyer read לשרתׄהׄא; Eisenman-Wise reads לשׄר·א. The mark I have transcribed as a circlet may be an erasure.

נה·]] Milik reads בנׄחׄתׄה; Collins-Green reads תׄה]; *DSSSE* reads נה]; Eisenman-Wise reads ·ה; Beyer reads נה] ·].

נדן] Collins-Green, *DSSSE*, Beyer] Milik reads נדיׄה].

Line 2 פתריזא Collins-Green, *DSSSE*, Milik, Beyer] Eisenman-Wise reads פתרונא.

אׄוׄבׄ]וׄךׄ] Milik, *DSSSE* and Beyer read אבנׄוׄךׄ]; Collins-Green and Eisenman-Wise read אׄוׄבׄוׄךׄ].

יומא Collins-Green, Eisenman-Wise, Beyer] Milik and *DSSSE* read חמא. A ח is a difficult reading; by way of comparison, the ח in רוחה, found in 4Q550ᵃ, line 4, does not have the pronounced triangle at the top of the left leg observable here.

עבידת Milik, Collins-Green, *DSSSE*, Beyer] Eisenman-Wise reads עבׄידׄתׄהן.

Line 3 ען Collins-Green] Milik reads עמׄהן; *DSSSE* and Beyer read ען·; Eisenman-Wise does not contain a reading.

··] Milik reads וׄהׄוׄהׄ]; Collins-Green does not contain a reading; *DSSSE* and Beyer read הׄוׄה]; Eisenman-Wise reads ·· לה]. Traces of two letters are visible, but I was unable to make a definitive reading.

ומן הׄיׄמׄני Collins-Green] Milik, *DSSSE* and Beyer read ומׄן הׄיׄמׄנו; Eisenman-Wise reads וׄפׄ·ה.

קׄ]דׄמׄוׄהי *DSSSE*, Eisenman-Wise, Beyer] Milik and Collins-Green read קׄ]דׄמׄיׄהה.

Line 4 א·] Milik, *DSSSE*, Beyer] Collins-Green reads א·].

Line 6 לׄת]לן Milik, Collins-Green] *DSSSE* and Beyer read לׄ]לׄתׄ]לׄת; Eisenman-Wise reads ·ל·ל.

שלן Collins-Green, Eisenman-Wise] Milik reads שׄ·ן; *DSSSE* and Beyer read שלׄ]טׄנא.

TRANSLATION

1.] herald(?) of the king, that you shall say to the princess [...

2.] Patireza [your] fa[the]r from the day he arose in the service of [the king?] before the king [...

3.] he served with uprightness and tr[uth b]efore him...

4QTales of the Persian Court (4Q550^{a-e})

4.] and the herald said [

5. ... purp[le...

NOTES ON THE TRANSLATION

Line 1 Translations vary depending on how אושי is understood. Along with Collins-Green, *DSSSE*, and García Martínez, I understand שרתא to be the definite form of שרה, 'princess'. Milik, followed by Cook, understands it as a proper name, while Eisenman-Wise translates the masculine form, 'prince (?)'.

Line 2 Those who read חמא translate it as a proper name, which Milik relates to Haman in the Book of Esther.[13] Cook translates 'Who has seen that he stood over the business of the [kingdom]...'

Line 3 García Martínez and Cook read the feminine 'before her', referring to the character in line 1.

Line 4 Translations vary depending on how אושי is understood.

4Q550^{d}, col. i

]ובחובי אבהתי	]לין	שפא לדן]]ונגדתן	ארו ידע אנתהן .1
]יך גבר	]ונגדתן	לה קאם לקבלה ובן]אן··	די חטו קדמיך ון .2
נב]רא טבוא	]לה קאם לקבלה ובן]אן··	יהודי מן רברבני מ]לכא	.3
די איתי]אפשר	מלכו]תא מה אעבד לכה ואנתה ידע [	גברא טבא עבד] .4
]ה אן	]ל·תך קאם באתר די אנתה קאם[	לנבר כותון להתבה] .5
	]א פקדני וכדי]תמז]ות אלקברנך בן	ב]נרם מה זד]י אנתה צנ[ב .6
כ]ול דין	עמר בכול אפשר די תעלית עבידתי קדם	.7

NOTES

Line 1 ארו Milik, Collins-Green, *DSSSE*, Beyer] Eisenman-Wise reads ארי.

Milik reads [·תן in the middle of the line, while *DSSSE* reads a תן]. I have been unable to verify this reading.

ובחובי] Collins-Green] Milik reads בחובתי ובחובי; *DSSSE* and Beyer read י] ובחובי; Eisenman-Wise reads בחובי.

Line 2 קדמיך Milik, *DSSSE*, Beyer] Collins-Green and Eisenman-Wise read קדמין. Only the tail of the final letter is visible. A material reading of ך or ן is possible, but the 2ms suffix agrees with the 2ms personal pronoun in line 1.

לדן] Milik reads לרחמנא]; Collins-Green reads לן]; *DSSSE*, Eisenman-Wise and Beyer read ל·[ן.

[·ונגדת] Milik reads [·ונגדת אן], in which the א belongs to the preceding word; Collins-Green reads ונגדתן]; *DSSSE* and Beyer read [·ונגדת]; Eisenman-Wise reads ונגדת·[ן.

]יך Collins-Green, Eisenman-Wise, Beyer] Milik and *DSSSE* read עבדו]יך.

Line 3 רברבני מ]לכא Collins-Green, *DSSSE*, Eisenman-Wise, Beyer] Milik reads דבר בנימן. The first letter is unlike other examples of ר on the fragments, but it is more likely than ד. In my previous article I followed Milik, but I have become convinced that his reading is materially impossible.

לה]·· Beyer] Milik and *DSSSE* read מנלה]; Collins-Green and Eisenman-Wise read לה].

ובן]א Collins-Green, Eisenman-Wise, Beyer] Milik and *DSSSE* read ובן]עא.

נב]רא Eisenman-Wise, Beyer] Milik reads פתוןרא; Collins-Green reads רא]; *DSSSE* reads פתן]רא. It may be that there was a dittography of the last two words of line 3 in the first two words of line 4.

Line 4 מלכו]תא Milik] Collins-Green and Eisenman-Wise read תא]; *DSSSE* and Beyer read מל]כא. The trace could be either a כ or a ת.

די איתי] My reconstruction is based on the amount of available space. Milik reconstructs

לא איתין]; Collins-Green reconstructs [די לא איתין; DSSSE and Beyer reconstruct [... איתין]; Eisenman-Wise reconstructs [די כול].

Line 5 כותני DSSSE, Beyer] Milik reads כותי; Collins-Green reads כותן; Eisenman-Wise reads כותונך].

כ·תך[ ] Milik and DSSSE read מל[כותך; Collins-Green reads תך[; Eisenman-Wise reads ביתך; Beyer reads כותך. The first visible letter has a bottom stroke; there is room for a short letter before the ת.

ה[Collins-Green] Milik reads אנה; DSSSE and Beyer read ה·[; Eisenman-Wise reads בה.

א[ן] Milik reads אסתתר; Collins-Green and Eisenman-Wise read אנן; DSSSE reads אן; Beyer reads אתן. Milik's reading of the name Esther would seem to clinch his argument regarding the relationship of these fragments to the Book of Esther; however, there is no evidence for a ס.

Line 6 בורם Milik, DSSSE, Beyer] Collins-Green reads ם[; Eisenman-Wise reads ק[או]ם.

די[ן Collins-Green, Eisenman-Wise] Milik, DSSSE and Beyer read די.

תמ[ות Milik, DSSSE, Beyer] Collins-Green does not transcribe any letters of [תמות]; Eisenman-Wise reads אמ[רת].

בן Milik, Eisenman-Wise] Collins-Green and Beyer do not have a reading at the end of line 6; DSSSE reads ·[. בקבר[ן, 'in a tomb', would be a possible restoration.

Line 7 תעלית Milik, DSSSE] Collins-Green and Beyer read תעל ית; Eisenman-Wise reads ויתעל ית (they do not read די). The question of whether or not a space exists can only be determined by a physical examination of the fragments, which I was unable to do.

עבידתי Collins-Green, Milik, Eisenman-Wise, Beyer] DSSSE reads עבדתי.

קודם Collins-Green, Eisenman-Wise, Beyer] Milik reads קו[ד]מיך.

כ[ול Milik, Collins-Green, DSSSE, Beyer] Eisenman-Wise reads וכ[ול.

TRANSLATION

1. Behold, you know [...] to me [...] and because of the sins of my fathers
2. which they sinned before you. And [...] ... [...] and I opposed [...] you. A man,
3. a Jew from the officers of the k[ing ...] ... arose before him/her and [ ] ... [ ] ... the go[od ma]n [...
4. the good man serves [...the kin]gdom. What can I do for you? But you know [that it is] possib[le
5. for a man like [me(?)] to respond [...li]ke (?) you, standing in the place that you stand [...
6. o[nl]y(?) what[ev]er you de[si]re command me; and when [you d]ie, I will bury you in [...
7. being master(?) in everything. It is possible that the rise of my service be[fore a]ll that [...

NOTES ON THE TRANSLATION

The first two lines contain a prayer; presumably the 'you' is God. Lines 4-7 contain the speech of a subordinate to a superior.

Line 2 Milik (followed by Cook) restores מתד[שפא לרח[מנ]א, 'praying to the merciful...' This is a plausible restoration. García Martínez suggests 'peaceful'.

'I opposed': 'she opposed' would be correct if the trace of the letter is restored as a י. Collins-Green, DSSSE, García Martínez and Eisenman-Wise translate 'followed after'; I have chosen 'oppose' because of the court conflict motif that I believe is present in the tale.

Line 3 Milik (followed by Cook and García Martínez), translates 'un des notables de la tribu de Benjam[in', based on his reading of line 3. This is one of his chief arguments for connecting 4QTales to the book of Esther, but his reading is unacceptable.

DSSSE and García Martínez transcribe מגלה and translate (dubiously) 'from the Diaspora'; Cook translates 'a scroll'.

Line 4 García Martínez suggests restoring 'attendant' instead of 'the king'.

4QTales of the Persian Court (4Q550[a-e])

Line 5 Milik, followed by *DSSSE* and García Martínez, translates 'qu'un homme Kûtéen', and uses that translation as one of his arguments for a date for the fragments.[14] In my 1996 article I followed his translation, but I have since been convinced by the arguments of Collins-Green that the translation 'like me' is the simpler and better reading.[15] Milik, *DSSSE* and García Martínez also restore 'your [kin]gdom' rather than 'li]ke you'.

Line 6 Eisenman-Wise restores 'you have [spo]ken' instead of 'you die', but given the following reference to burial, dying seems the proper antecedent.

Line 7 Collins-Green, Cook and Eisenman-Wise translate the first word as 'dwelling', taking the root from the Syriac.

DSSSE and García Martínez take the second phrase as a question.

4Q550[d], col. ii

‏שא גזרת מן‏ [‏·‏·‏·‏]‏א אזלן‏[	1.
‏ל‏[‏מכתב‏ ‏]‏לן‏ [‏·‏·‏א אזלו‏ ‏·‏ בלבושן‏[	2.
‏כ‏]‏ליל דהנבא על רי‏[‏שה וחמש ו‏]‏ש‏[‏נין אזלו‏[	3.
‏ב‏]‏להודוהי רן‏ ‏ש‏]‏תיתיא אזל ואמר‏	4.
‏כ‏]‏סף וד‏[‏ה‏]‏ב ונכסין די ו‏[‏אי‏]‏תי לבנושי בכפ‏[‏ל‏	‏למ‏]‏ן‏	5.
‏על בשלם בנסרו לדרת מלכא ו‏[	‏ושבניעיא אזלו‏	6.
‏ק‏]‏טיל אדין על ו‏[‏ב‏]‏נסרו לדנר‏[‏ת מלכא ש‏]‏ן‏	[‏·‏·‏·‏	‏]‏בה רן‏	‏בה ל‏[‏ן‏	‏בנושי‏ ‏]‏ב לן‏	7.
‏]‏ה ושקה ענה ואמר ב‏·‏רן בנסרו מן‏[	‏על רישה‏ ‏]	‏ואחדה ב‏[‏ו‏]‏נדה‏	8.

NOTES

Line 1 ‏מן‏ *DSSSE*, Eisenman-Wise, Beyer] Milik reads ‏ן‏·‏; Collins-Green does not have a reading.

‏[‏·‏·‏·‏]‏א‏ Milik, followed by *DSSSE* and Beyer, restores ‏ותנינ‏[‏א‏, based on the presence of 'third' in line 2. The remains of letters could be ‏ת‏ and ‏נ‏, but I was unable to verify the reading. Collins-Green reads ‏[   ]‏א‏; Eisenman-Wise reads ‏[‏א‏, with no letter traces.

Line 2 ‏ל‏[‏מכתב‏ Eisenman-Wise] Milik reads ‏מכתשיא‏; Collins-Green reads ‏מכתשיא‏; *DSSSE* reads ‏מבתן‏[; Beyer reads ‏למכתן‏[.

‏לן‏ [‏·‏·‏א‏] Milik, *DSSSE* and Beyer restore ‏ותל‏[‏י‏]‏תיא‏; Collins-Green reads ‏ל‏[ ]‏א‏; Eisenman-Wise reads ‏לן‏ [‏·‏א‏.

‏אזלן‏ Collins-Green, Eisenman-Wise] Milik, *DSSSE* and Beyer read ‏אזלו‏.

Line 3 ‏כ‏]‏ליל‏ Milik, *DSSSE*, Eisenman-Wise, Beyer] Collins-Green reads ‏כ‏]‏ליל‏.

‏דהנבא על רי‏[‏שה‏ Milik, Collins-Green] Eisenman-Wise reads ‏דהנב די מתקלה מא‏[‏ה‏; *DSSSE* and Beyer read ‏דנהב ברי\[‏שה‏.

‏וחמש ו‏]‏ש‏[‏נין‏] Milik reads ‏וחמש שנ‏[‏ין‏; Collins-Green reads ‏וחמש‏]‏שנין‏; *DSSSE* reads ‏וחמש‏[‏ש‏]‏ שנ‏[‏ין‏; Eisenman-Wise reads ‏וחמ‏[‏ן‏]‏שה‏; Beyer reads ‏וחמשיא‏.

‏אזלו‏ Beyer] Milik and *DSSSE* read ‏אזל‏[‏ה‏; Collins-Green and Eisenman-Wise read ‏אזל‏[‏ן‏.

Line 4 ‏ב‏]‏להודוהי‏ Collins-Green] Milik, *DSSSE*, Eisenman-Wise and Beyer see remnants of the ‏ב‏ at the beginning of the word.

‏ש‏]‏תיתיא‏ Collins-Green] Milik reads ‏וש‏]‏תיתיא‏; *DSSSE* and Beyer read ‏ו‏]‏שתיתיא‏; Eisenman-Wise read ‏תיתיא‏[.

‏אזל ואמר‏ Eisenman-Wise] Milik reads ‏אזלו אכ‏[‏ו‏]‏נמין‏; Collins-Green reads ‏אזל כן‏; *DSSSE* and Beyer read ‏א‏·‏אזלו ן‏.

In the photograph PAM 43.585, there is a small fragment that is placed so that its top line falls at the end of line 4. This top line contains an indiscernible letter; the second line contains ‏]‏לכה‏, and the third line contains ‏]‏ו‏·‏. Milik does not include this fragment in his publication, so its status as part of 4Q550 is unclear.[16]

Beginning with line 5 and continuing through line 8 Eisenman-Wise does not transcribe the first fragment of the column.

Line 5 למ] Milik, *DSSSE*, Beyer] Collins-Green reads למן.

תזדהב Collins-Green, Eisenman-Wise] Milik reads ודהב; *DSSSE* reads דהב; Beyer reads תכזל[. Milik and *DSSSE* (and evidently Beyer) transcribe supralinear writing on this line. There may be remnants of writing above line 5, but I was unable to make it out.

ונכסןין Milik, Collins-Green, *DSSSE*, Eisenman-Wise] Beyer reads ממזון].

בכפל Milik, Collins-Green, Eisenman-Wise] *DSSSE* and Beyer read בכפלין.

Line 6 על[Collins-Green, *DSSSE*, Eisenman-Wise, Beyer] Milik reads the remnant of ן before על.

בשלם] Milik, *DSSSE* and Beyer read בשולם[; Collins-Green reads בשלם[; Eisenman-Wise reads בשם.

בנסרו Milik, *DSSSE*, Beyer] Collins-Green and Eisenman-Wise read בנסרי. The last letter in this name is ו, since, according to Shaked, it should be connected to Iranian Baga-srū or Baga-srava.[17] Although I will no longer note it, I will follow this transcription throughout the fragments.

ו· Milik] Collins-Green, *DSSSE* and Beyer do not read the remnant of a letter; Eisenman-Wise reads ש.ו.

Line 7 בגושי]ב לן] Milik, *DSSSE* and Beyer read בנגושי תזב לן; Collins-Green reads בנוגשי]בן.

זבה רן[Collins-Green] Milik reads רזיבה רזיב; *DSSSE* reads רזבה רזב; Beyer does not transcribe.

ו··[*DSSSE*] Milik reads גזירו; Collins-Green and Beyer do not transcribe; Eisenman-Wise reads ו·[.

]ש *DSSSE*, Eisenman-Wise, Beyer] Milik reads שבויעיתא; Collins-Green reads ש.

Line 8 בידה Milik, Collins-Green, *DSSSE*, Eisenman-Wise] Beyer reads בזידרה[; he does not transcribe the intervening letters between the extant י and the extant ה.

ונשקה Milik, Collins-Green, *DSSSE*, Beyer] Eisenman-Wise read רבשקה.

ב·רן[ ] For the unidentified letter, Milik suggests a ס and/or a ת; the space seems too small to accommodate either or both. Collins-Green and *DSSSE* read זרן]ב; Eisenman-Wise reads בנסרי; Beyer reads בנסרו.

At the end of the line, Beyer reads אן].

TRANSLATION

1.]... decree from [...] ... they went[
2. to] writ[e...] ... he went [...] in the [royal] wardrobe [...
3.] a crown of go[ld upon] his h[ead.] And five years pass[ed...
4. by] himself [...] the [s]ixth passed, and he s[aid?
5. ... [... s]ilver and [g]old [and possess]ions which [belo]ng to Bagoshi in double amount.
6. and the se[venth passed?...] Bagasro entered the court of the king in peace ...
7. Bagosh[i ...] was [k]illed. Then [B]agasro entered the co[u]rt of the king...
8. And he seized him by the [hand...] upon [his] head [...] and he kissed him. He answered and said, "... Bagasro from..."

NOTES ON THE TRANSLATION

Line 1 Cook's 'I decreed' is also possible.

DSSSE, García Martínez and Cook, on the basis of the restoration, translate 'and the second ones went...'

Line 2 My restoration למכתנב, 'to write', agrees with Eisenman-Wise. I have chosen it rather than מכתנשיא ('plagues') of the other translations because of the presence of 'decree' in the line above.

DSSSE, García Martínez and Cook restore 'and the third ones went' instead of 'he went'.

4QTales of the Persian Court (4Q550^{a-e})

Line 3 Eisenman-Wise translates the last phrase as 'a gold crown weighing one hundred and fifty'. Collins-Green and Eisenman-Wise understand the final verb as a singular, 'and for five years he went...'

Line 4 Collins-Green translates 'the sixth, they went' (*DSSSE* also understands the verb as a plural); Eisenman-Wise does not translate תיתא[and understands the verb as a singular. García Martínez translates the final fragmentary word as 'bl[ack]'; he is following Milik, who understands the numbers in this column as referring to alternating periods of light and dark, as in 2 Baruch 53-74. There is no basis for this interpretation.[18]

Line 6 Eisenman-Wise: 'he entered the king's court in the name of Bagasri...'

Line 7 *DSSSE* and García Martínez restore 'Bagoshe returned to ... his judgment was judged ... and he was killed.' It is not entirely clear that the person who was killed was Bagoshi, but given the nature of a royal courtier tale (see below) in which a protagonist triumphs over an antagonist, it is the best understanding of the fragment.

Line 8 The subject in this line is presumably the king.

4Q550^d, col. iii

1. עליא די אנתון דחלין ו]פ[לחין הו שליט בכול ארן]עא כול די יצבא קריב בו] זד]ה ל·ן
2. כ]ול אנש די ימר מלהן באינ]שא על בנסרו בן   ית]קטל בדיל די לא איתין כ]ול
3. הט··ה לעו]למ]   ·] די ח]הן]   ]תרתין ואמר מלכא יכתוב
4.]·דן]   ]ל·ן]   ]אנון בדרת ב]ית מלכ]נא]·רבת]
5. יק]ומו]הן בתר בנסרו כרין בכתבא דנה
6. ב]אש]א באישתה תאבה עלן]·· כ]·ן
7.]ה   *vacat*

NOTES

Line 1 ו]פ[לחין Milik, Collins-Green, *DSSSE*, Beyer] Eisenman-Wise reads ופלחין.
בכול ארן]עא Collins-Green, *DSSSE*, Milik, Beyer] Eisenman-Wise reads בא]רן]עא.
בו]זד]ה Collins-Green] Milik reads בותה]; *DSSSE* reads בו·[ן; Eisenman-Wise reads בידה; Beyer reads בנ]סרון.
ל·ן] Milik reads ל]ן; Collins-Green, *DSSSE* and Beyer read ל]ן; Eisenman-Wise reads לו]מע]בוד.

Line 2 בנסרו בן *DSSSE*] Milik reads בנסרו נ]ביא; Collins-Green reads בנ]סרי נ; Eisenman-Wise reads בנסרי כן; Beyer reads בנסרו]·.
איתין כ]ול *DSSSE*, Beyer] Milik reads איתין כל]; Collins-Green reads איתין; Eisenman-Wise reads איתין]·.

Line 3 הט··ה] Milik and *DSSSE* read טה נפה]; Collins-Green and Eisenman-Wise read ה טובה; Beyer reads ל]ה טובה. I am not sure the letter remnants can support either reading.
·] די] *DSSSE*] Milik reads מ]א די; Collins-Green, Eisenman-Wise and Beyer read די]·.
ח]הן Collins-Green, *DSSSE*, Eisenman-Wise, Beyer] Milik reads ח]ה בן.

Line 4]·דן] Milik reads עז]ון; Collins-Green reads ז]ן; *DSSSE* indicates only letter traces; Eisenman-Wise reads חזה; Beyer does not transcribe.
]ל·ן] Collins-Green reads ל]ן; Milik and *DSSSE* read ש]לטון; Eisenman-Wise reads למלכא; Beyer does not transcribe.
אנון Collins-Green, *DSSSE*, Eisenman-Wise, Beyer] Milik reads ואנין.
מלכ]נא Milik, *DSSSE*] Collins-Green reads מלכ]ן; Eisenman-Wise and Beyer read מלכונת]א.
]·רבת] Milik and *DSSSE* read קרבתא; Collins-Green reads]רבת]·; Eisenman-Wise reads רבתא]א, where א is part of the preceding word מלכונת]א; Beyer, similarly, reads מלכונת]א רבתא.

Line 5 יק]ומו]הן *DSSSE*, Beyer] Milik reads יק]ומו]הן; Collins-Green reads קומ]ן; Eisenman-Wise reads ומן.

בנסרו] Milik, *DSSSE* and Beyer read בנסרו; Collins-Green reads בנסרי; Eisenman-Wise reads בנסרי.

Line 6 בןאישיא Milik, *DSSSE*, Eisenman-Wise, Beyer] Collins-Green reads אישן.

כ·· [ ] Milik reads רישןה כ; Collins-Green reads כן [; *DSSSE* reads ורישןה כן; Eisenman-Wise reads זה כזל; Beyer reads ונפשןה כזל.

Line 7 הן[Collins-Green, *DSSSE*] Milik and Beyer read זרןעה; Eisenman-Wise have only a *vacat* for this line.

On the photographic plate PAM 43.585 there is a small fragment placed before the beginning of lines 5-7. Milik transcribes this fragment under 'Fragments non placés'.[19] I essentially agree with Milik's readings; I have not transcribed the fragment here because I was not able to ascertain its place in the manuscript.

TRANSLATION
1. the Most High, whom you fear and [w]orship, rules over [all the ea]rth; everyone who wishes to bring an offering in his h[and...
2. Any man who says an [evi]l word against Bagasro [... will be put]to death, because there is noth[ing
3. ... for[e]ver. [...] ...that he saw [ ] the two. And the king said, Let him writ[e...
4. ...[...] them in the court of the kin[g's] house [...
5. ...they who] ari[s]e after Bagas[ro and] read in thi[s] book
6. ...e]vil, his own evil returns upon ...[

NOTES ON THE TRANSLATION
Line 1 Cook (following Milik) translates the last phrase as 'All who want to draw near to His Temple[...' Eisenman-Wise (closely approximated by Collins-Green) translates 'It is easy for him to [d]o anything that he desires...' Vermes translates 'Everyone whom he wishes (comes) near.' The proposed mention of the Temple would be anomalous in this group of fragments, which otherwise evinces no interest in Judaea or its institutions.
Vermes ends the line with 'Bagasro...'
Line 3 Collins-Green and Eisenman-Wise restore 'good' at the beginning of the line, while *DSSSE* and García Martínez (following Milik) restore 'barriers'.
Collins-Green (and Cook) uses 'that is customary' to translate חזה.
Line 4 There are a variety of translations for the first fragmentary words.
Cook has 'documents' rather than some form of the pronoun.

4Q550[e]

1. וֹ]קדם מלכא אֹ[
2. וֹ]הלך בקוריאֹ[ן
3. עֹזֹל אנפיכֹון
4. בֹ]נסרו כֹדֹב

Only Milik, *DSSSE* and Beyer transcribe this fragment. Because it mentions Bagasro, it certainly belongs to the story found in 4QTales. Since in line 4 Bagasro appears to be denying some charge, it is likely that this fragment should be placed somewhere before Bagasro's vindication in 4Q550[d], cols. ii and iii.

Line 1 אֹ[*DSSSE*] Milik reads אסןר; Beyer reads אסן.
Line 2 כדֹב Milik] *DSSSE* reads כן; Beyer reads כ·ן.

4QTales of the Persian Court (4Q550ᵃ⁻ᵉ)

TRANSLATION
1.] before the king ...[
2. he walks at the summons/in the villages [...(?)
3. up]on yo[ur] faces [
4. B]agasro den[ies

4QTALES OF THE PERSIAN COURT
AS A ROYAL COURTIER TALE

The fragments presented above can be understood as one or two stories concerning Jewish protagonists in the Persian court. The plot(s) can be summarized as follows: Patireza, probably a Jew (all the names in 4QTales are Persian)[20], was a servant of the Persian king, probably Darius I (although Darius II would also be possible). The story is addressed to Patireza's son (4Q550ᵃ, 1), and is set in the reign of Darius' successor, probably Xerxes (although again Artaxerxes II Memnon is also possible). Patireza evidently suffered some kind of injustice, uncovered in the archives of Darius, and the present king attempts to rectify this injustice by giving Patireza's son his father's office. A female character, a 'princess', is somehow involved. This may comprise one discrete story (4Q550ᵃ⁻ᶜ). If one accepts Wechsler's ordering of the fragments, this story would end with the proclamation of the king found in 4Q550ᵃ, after Patireza's son has been rewarded.[21] The second story, found in 4Q550ᵈ⁻ᵉ, concerns a Jew named Bagasro among the officers of the king. Although the plot is a little difficult to reconstruct, there appears to be some kind of conflict or intrigue between Bagasro and another courtier named Bagoshi, from which Bagasro emerges victorious. He is rewarded lavishly by the king, who also seems to praise Bagasro's God. It is also possible to take the two stories as separate episodes of one complete story. In that case, Bagasro would be the son of Patireza; following his elevation, he comes into conflict with Bagoshi, but ultimately triumphs. The king would be the same figure throughout.

This plot or plots appear(s) to fit the genre of the royal courtier tale, and specifically to take the form of a court conflict legend. A court conflict legend is defined as a narrative in which a protagonist begins within the court, is persecuted or conspired against by the other courtiers, but is finally vindicated before the king.[22] Other court conflict legends include Daniel 3 and 6, Bel and the Dragon 23-42, Hebrew and Greek Esther (although Esther is a longer and more complicated narrative) and Ahikar. The larger genre of royal courtier tales includes the other subgenre the royal contest legend, in which the protagonist, a member of the court, rises to prominence before the king by solving some problem or interpreting some sign that none of the other courtiers can interpret.[23] Examples of this type include Daniel 2, 4 and 5, Bel and the Dragon 1-22, the Prayer of Nabonidus (not certain), and 1 Esdras 3-4. The wider genre, that of the court tale, also includes Daniel 1 and Susanna (set in a judicial court), while the Joseph narrative, found in Genesis 37-50, contains both a conflict and a contest subplot. The book of Tobit, while not set in the court, is peripherally related to the genre. The book of Judith, although not part of the genre of royal courtier tale, does have some motival parallels with the genre and hence with these fragments. With the exception of Judith, all of these tales are set in the Diaspora, and, with the exception of Ahikar and Susanna, all of them include a conflict or contest in which a representative of a ruled ethnic group (the Jews) is pitted against a member of the ruling elite.[24] The majority of them are set in the Persian or neo-Babylonian courts. Although most of the examples of these royal courtier tales have come to us from the pens of Jewish scribes, we do have examples of non-Jewish royal courtier tales, such as Ahikar itself and the stories found in Herodotus concerning King Croesus of Lydia, appearing as a courtier in the palace of Cyrus of Persia.[25] These non-Jewish examples testify to the wide popularity of these tales in the Persian and early Hellenistic periods. In the Jewish world, they are 'diaspora tales', illustrating the lives of Jews under foreign domination and often providing role models for their Jewish diaspora audience.[26]

These diaspora tales have certain characteristics in common. The attitude toward the reigning monarch is often positive or at least neutral (some of the stories in Daniel 1-6 are exceptions). It is clearly acceptable for a courtier to be both Jewish and loyal to the foreign ruler.[27] The focus of the tales is on Jewish life in the Diaspora; a return to the land is not a priority. Rather, the goal is gaining status within the court hierarchy and achieving a peaceful co-existence with the Gentile 'other' (the exception to this is 1 Esdras 3-4, where the hero requests a return to the land).[28] Another characteristic is that God is not a prominent, active character in the story, but rather is part of the background, acknowledged but unseen. Instead, the human action is what drives the plot and gives it its dramatic interest. This is most obvious in Hebrew Esther, where God is not mentioned at all, and least true in Daniel, where God's miraculous intervention on behalf of Daniel and his companions is fundamental to the narrative. Finally, these narratives often feature important female characters, most notably Esther and Judith, but also Vashti and Zeresh, Susanna, Sarah and Anna, and Potiphar's wife.

The date of composition for these tales range from the early dates of the Joseph story and Ahikar, which may be originally pre-exilic, to Greek Esther, which is from the latter half of the second century BCE. Their original languages would appear to have been Hebrew or Aramaic, although parts of Greek Esther were actually composed in Greek.[29] Aramaic was the international language of the Persian court, and was adopted by the Jews as a literary language. Numerous new compositions in Aramaic have surfaced in the Qumran collection, including 4QTales of the Persian Court. The language of 4QTales is comparable to the Aramaic of Daniel 2-7 and the Aramaic portions of Ezra, with many overlaps in vocabulary. I do not see, however, any evidence for dependence in either direction. The provenance of the original forms of all of these court narratives, with the exception of the Joseph story, is probably the eastern diaspora; as Collins argues, 'the original composition of a group of tales which are set in a royal court can most plausibly be located in a milieu where such a court existed and was a focus of attention.'[30]

Our narrative fits the definition of court conflict legend in the following ways. There are at least two protagonists, Patireza and/or his son, and Bagasro (who, if all the fragments are understood to contain one story, may be Patireza's son). Patireza is a servant of the royal wardrobe; Bagasro is a courtier of some kind. The action takes place totally within the Persian court. The conflict may be reflected in the story concerning Patireza and his service, in which his son is eventually rewarded. There is certainly some kind of intrigue or plot in which Bagasro's reputation and loyalty are questioned, perhaps by Bagoshi (4Q550^d i 2-7; ii 5-7); Bagasro is eventually vindicated before the king. The attitude of the narrative toward the Persian king is neutral; he is not the antagonist of the conflict. The reward is higher office within the court hierarchy; no interest in Judah or a return is evinced. God is mentioned but not prominent (4Q550^d iii 1); it is the human characters that take centre stage. We may thus confidently locate 4QTales within the genre of royal courtier tale, and probably within the subgenre court conflict legend.

Specific elements of 4QTales will now be examined and compared to other examples from royal courtier tales. The purpose of this comparison is not to posit dependence of 4QTales on any other royal courtier tale, or vice versa, but to identify parallels on the generic level.[31]

4Q550^A

Milik has already noted that line 4 bears a close resemblance to Esther 6:1. In both instances the king commands the royal archives be read to him, in this case evidently to relieve tedium (not as a soporific as in Esther).[32] The motif of a king being read to in the night during a bout of insomnia also occurs in 1 Esdras 3. This motif is an important generic link among the royal courtier tales.

Lines 5-7 contain the actual text of the document discovered in the archive. As I have previously noted,[33] the closest parallel here is Ezra 6:1-5, where the edict of Cyrus concerning the restoration of the Temple in Jerusalem is read. We even find overlaps in vocabulary: דריוש מלכא (l. 6; Ezra 6:1); השתכח (l. 6; Ezra 6:2); מגלה חדה (l. 5; Ezra 6:2); כתיב (l. 6; Ezra 6:2). There are also reminiscences of Greek Esther Additions B and E, which contain the letters of the king to the empire. These letters are added to the text of Esther to give an air of historical verisimilitude; it is possible that this is one of the functions of Darius' decree in 4Q550^a.

4Q550^B

The plot appears to concern the reward of Patireza's son, who is given the position of his father. This calls to mind the plot of Ahikar, in which Nadin, Ahikar's adopted son, is given the position of his father (to no good results!).[34] If the translation 'herald' is correct, we find a motival overlap with Esther 6, in which Haman is commanded to proclaim Mordecai's honour in the manner of a herald, and the Joseph story, in which heralds cry out Joseph's honour (Genesis 41:43). In line 6, the king seems to be rewarding Patireza's son from his own property, which is in keeping with the expected largesse of the Persian kings.[35] This motif also appears in Esther 8 and 1 Esdras 4:42.

4Q550^C

The character of the 'princess' is introduced here. Although her function in the story is elusive, we have noted above that these tales often contain important female characters.

The mention of 'purple' in line 5 introduces an important motif in the royal courtier tales. Although the line is fragmentary, it is probable that the herald or the king is commanding that Patireza's son be clothed in purple, a royal colour. This motif of the courtier being dressed in special clothes (often purple) recurs throughout the tales. It is found in Genesis 41:42 (Joseph), Esther 6:8 (Mordecai), Esther 8:15, where a mantle of purple is specified (Mordecai), Daniel 5:29 (where Daniel is clothed in purple) and 1 Esdras 3:6 (the victorious courtier will be clothed in purple).

4Q550^D

Column I contains a prayer or a declaration of sin. The nature of the sin is unspecified; however, as Wills notes, general confessions of sin as a means of reinstituting or recalling the covenant between God and Israel became more common in this literature.[36] In the group of texts under consideration here, we find a confession of sin in Greek Esther Addition C and in Tobit 3, as well as more general prayers in Daniel 2, Judith 9 and Susanna.

The reference to burial in column i, line 6 is enigmatic. In biblical legends or stories, the reference is usually to sons burying parents, usually fathers (e.g. Genesis 25:9, 35:29, 49:29-32, 50:7, Tobit 14:11-12) or to husbands burying wives (e.g. Genesis 23:19, 35:19-20, 50:31); here, however, the dialogue is between a servant and master, with the servant speaking. Is the servant Bagasro?

The mention of a decree (נזרת) in column ii recalls the decree in Daniel 4:14 (verse 17 in the English versions), 21 (English: verse 24), where the same word is used, as well as more generally the decrees of the kings in Daniel 3 and 6 and Esther 3 and 8. The historical text of Ezra 1, 4 and 6 also contains decrees of the Persian kings. The mention of the 'royal wardrobe' (restored) in line 2 ties this fragment to 4Q550^a and may indicate that we are dealing with only one story.

The 'crown of gold' in line 3 has obvious connections with the royal courtier tale genre. Although the exact noun כליל does not appear in the other royal courtier tales, in Esther 1 the king orders Vashti to appear wearing the royal crown; the king crowns Esther in 2:17, and Mordecai appears in a crown in 8:15; in the Old Greek of Daniel 5:29 Belshazzar crowns Daniel. It is not clear who is being crowned in 4QTales; the possibilities include the king, Bagasro, Bagoshi or even the princess, if the suffix is read as a feminine. The five years that pass are identical to the amount of time that elapses between Esther's becoming queen and Haman's plot in the Book of Esther.[37] Evidently another two years pass in the narrative; seven years pass in 4QPrayer of Nabonidus. These parallels may be coincidental; however, the passage of time seems to be a common motif.

'Silver and gold' as indicative of wealth and reward are common in the royal courtier tales; the largesse and majesty of the king are symbolized by the amount of silver and gold he tosses about. This is especially apparent in Esther and Daniel 3 and 5 (recall also 1 Kings 10:14-25, concerning Solomon). In this case the silver and gold belong to Bagoshi.[38] Is Bagoshi forfeiting his possessions to Bagasro? Since in the next line Bagasro enters the king's court 'in peace', this scenario recommends itself. If it is Bagoshi who is killed in line 7, as seems most probable, then we have the denouement of the court conflict legend. Bagoshi and Bagasro have been in competition for the king's favour, and Bagasro has emerged victorious. The closest parallel to this is the Mordecai/Haman conflict in the Book of Esther, since Bagoshi has lost both his possessions and his life. Parallels also exist with Daniel 3 and 6 and Ahikar and Nadin. Bagasro's reception by the king in line 8 is similar to that of Esther by the king in Greek Esther Addition D.

Column iii begins with the divine title עליא, which, according to Bickerman, becomes popular in the third century BCE.[39] It occurs frequently in Daniel 3, 4 and 5. It would appear that the king is speaking, praising the god of Bagasro. This is a common motif in the royal courtier tales, occurring in Daniel 2, 3, 4 and 6, Bel and the Dragon, and the Prayer of Nabonidus.[40] It is interesting to note that in none of these examples, including 4QTales, does the monarch actually convert;[41] this is indicative of the international and tolerant flavour of these works. Only in Greek Esther 8:17 and Judith 14:10, narratives from a later and less tolerant time period, do we find the actual conversion of Gentiles to Judaism.[42] The king then interdicts any further intrigue against Bagasro, and evidently an edict is written (by Bagasro?) to this effect (cf. Esther 8).

4Q550^{E}

The phrase 'upon your faces' in line 3 recalls the practice of proskynesis, practiced in the Persian court. The practice is at the heart of the conflict in the book of Esther, since Mordecai refuses to genuflect to Haman (Esther 3:2). In positive examples of proskynesis, we find the king prostrating himself before Daniel in Daniel 2:46, Judith prostrating herself before Holofernes (Judith 10:23), and the Egyptians bowing to Joseph (Genesis 41:43), as well as Esther herself falling before Ahasuerus in Esther 8:3.

We have noted numerous parallels between 4QTales of the Persian Court with previously identified royal courtier tales from the Second Temple period, on the level of plot, characters and motifs. Thus we are justified in identifying 4QTales as yet another example of the royal courtier tale, probably belonging to the subgenre court conflict legend. The tale gives very little indication of date; if the Darius of 4Q550^{a} is Darius I, then the story is set in the reign of his son Xerxes (486-465 BCE) and must have been composed after that. The language is not a late Aramaic, and gives no evidence of Greek influence. That is a slender foundation on which to set a date; sometime in the Persian period, beginning in the late fifth century BCE, is perhaps the most that can be posited. As to provenance, the narrative evinces the flavour of other diaspora tales; it is set in the Persian court, displays no regard for or familiarity with Judah or its institutions, and is not interested in a return to the land. Therefore, like many of the other examples explored in this paper, 4QTales was most likely produced in the eastern diaspora, from where it circulated throughout the Jewish world.

What was the purpose of 4QTales? Like Ahiqar, Esther and the Daniel cycle, this work (or works) may have had the didactic purpose of illustrating the correct behaviour of a Jew in the court of a foreign king. While its purpose was didactic, its genre was meant to be entertaining; therefore it may well have been widely read and popular. This popularity may explain its presence in the Qumran caves, far from any foreign court.[43] While the generically similar stories of Esther and Daniel 1-6 eventually became part of the Jewish canon[44] and thus were preserved for later generations, 4QTales of the Persian Court did not and was eventually forgotten.[45] It is among the happy accidents of the Qumran discoveries that these fragments were preserved, and we thus have more evidence for the genre of the Royal Courtier Tale in the Second Temple period.

Sidnie White Crawford

NOTES

1   J. T. Milik, 'Les modèles araméens du livre d'Esther dans la Grotte 4 de Qumrân', *RevQ*, 15 (1992), 321-99 (hereinafter cited as 'Milik'). J. Strugnell informs me that J. Starcky, the original editor, informally named the fragments 'A Jew in the Persian Court'. I would like to thank Professor Strugnell for his close reading of and helpful comments on this article. Beyer publishes the work under the title of 'Die Urkunde des Dareios' [Klaus Beyer, *Die aramäischen Texte vom Toten Meer*, Supplementary Edition (Göttingen: Vandenhoeck & Ruprecht, 1994), pp. 113-17 (hereinafter Beyer)].

2   Milik, p. 321.

3   Sidnie White Crawford, 'Has *Esther* been found at Qumran? 4QProto-Esther and the *Esther* Corpus', *RevQ*, 17 (1996), 307-25.

4   Robert H. Eisenman and Michael Wise, *The Dead Sea Scrolls Uncovered* (New York: Penguin Books, 1992), pp. 99-103, who titled the work 'Stories from the Persian Court'.

5   John J. Collins and Deborah A. Green, 'The Tales from the Persian Court (4Q550[a-e])', in *Antikes Judentum und Frühes Christentum*, ed. by Bernard Kollman, Wolfgang Reinbold and Annette Steudel, Festschrift für Hartmut Stegemann zum 65. Geburtstag, BZNW, 97 (Berlin: de Gruyter, 1999), pp. 39-50; Edward Cook, 'The Tale of Bagasraw', in *The Dead Sea Scrolls: A New Translation*, ed. by Michael Wise, Martin Abegg, Jr. and Edward Cook (San Francisco: HarperCollins, 1996), pp. 437-39; Kristin de Troyer, 'Once more, the so-called Esther fragments of Cave 4', W. H. Brownlee Lecture, Claremont, CA, 1999 (unpublished). I would like to thank Professor de Troyer for supplying me with a copy of her paper prior to its publication.

6   Crawford, '4Qproto-Esther', p. 324.

7   In my 1996 article, I almost always accepted Milik's readings. However, after further examination of the fragments, I found myself in disagreement with Milik at several points. Therefore the transcription and translation found here is my own, although I have consulted the following transcriptions: Milik, Collins and Green (cited as Collins-Green), Eisenman and Wise (cited as Eisenman-Wise), Beyer (it should be noted that Beyer does not indicate supralinear letters), and *DSSSE*, II, pp. 1096-1103. I have also compared the following English translations: Collins-Green, Cook, Florentino García Martínez, *The Dead Sea Scrolls Translated*, trans. by W. G. E. Watson (Leiden: Brill, 1994), pp. 291-92 (cited as García Martínez), *DSSSE*, Eisenman-Wise, and Geza Vermes, *The Complete Dead Sea Scrolls in English,* 5th edn (New York: Penguin Books, 1998), pp. 578-79. I have not included 4Q550[f] in this discussion, since it is unlikely that this fragment is part of the cycle 4QTales of the Persian Court (Crawford, '4Qproto-Esther', p. 323; Collins-Green, p. 40, n.6). Michael G. Wechsler's article 'Two Para-Biblical Novellae from Qumran Cave 4: A Reevaluation of 4Q550', *DSD*, 7 (2000), 130-72) came to my attention too late to thoroughly incorporate his conclusions into this article. I will briefly summarize his main contribution: Wechsler argues that 4Q550[a-f] represent three independent, non-successive works, the first of which (4Q550[d-e]) he entitles '4QAramaic Ezra-Nehemiah Sequel' and the second (4Q550[b-c,a]) which he names '4QAramaic Esther Prequel'. 4Q550[f] he separates from the other fragments and considers an unrelated composition. Wechsler connects the characters in 4Q550[d-e] with actual historical characters in the Persian period, while he agrees with Milik that Patireza in 4Q550[b-c,a] should be identified with Mordecai's father Yair; thus the addressee of the fragments is Mordecai (p. 163). His separation of the fragments into two distinct stories is helpful; his subsequent conclusions are less convincing.

8   The final PAM photographs for 4Q550 are 43.584 and 43.585. Other photographs are 40.585, 40.619, 41.444, 41.512, 41.952, 41.956, 42.081, 42.439, and 43.443.

9   Franz Rosenthal, *A Grammar of Biblical Aramaic*, 6th edn, Porta Linguarum Orientalium, Neue Serie, 5 (Wiesbaden: Harrassowitz, 1995), p. 18.

10   Milik, p. 332; cf. Collins and Green, p. 41.

11   So also Milik, pp. 370-71; Collins-Green, p. 42.

12   Shaked suggests that אוש could be a borrowing from the Old Iranian word for 'ear, intelligence, understanding', and as such refers to a highly placed official of the king. Shaul Shaked, 'Qumran: Some Iranian Connections', in *Solving Riddles and Untying Knots: Biblical, Epigraphic and Semitic Studies in Honor of Jonas C. Greenfield*, ed. by Ziony Zevit, Seymour Gitin and Michael Sokoloff (Winona Lake, IN: Eisenbrauns, 1995), pp. 277-81 (pp. 278-79).

13   Milik, p. 335.

14 Milik, p. 344.

15 Collins-Green, p. 44.

16 See also Collins-Green, p. 45.

17 Shaked, p. 278.

18 Collins-Green, p. 45.

19 Milik, p. 358.

20 Shaked, p. 278.

21 Wechsler, pp. 170-71.

22 Lawrence M. Wills, *The Jewish Novel in the Ancient World* (Ithaca: Cornell University Press, 1995), pp. 41-42.

23 Wills, *Novel*, p. 41.

24 Lawrence M. Wills, *The Jew in the Court of the Foreign King: Ancient Jewish Court Legends* (Minneapolis, MN: Fortress Press, 1990), pp. 60-68.

25 Wills, *Jew in the Court*, p. 55.

26 W. Lee Humphreys, 'A Life-Style for Diaspora: A Study of the Tales of Esther and Daniel', *JBL*, 92 (1973), 211-23; Sidnie Ann White, 'Esther: A Feminine Model for Jewish Diaspora', in *Gender and Difference in Ancient Israel*, ed. by Peggy L. Day (Minneapolis, MN: Fortress Press, 1989), pp. 161-77.

27 The historical figure of Nehemiah presented a real-life example of this notion.

28 Susan Niditch and Robert Doran, 'The Success Story of the Wise Courtier: A Formal Approach', *JBL*, 96 (1977), 179-93 (p. 184); Wills, *Novel*, p. 239.

29 Sidnie White Crawford, 'The Additions to Esther', in *The New Interpreter's Bible*, (Nashville, TN: Abingdon Press, 1999), III, pp. 943-72 (pp. 953, 966).

30 John J. Collins, 'The Court-Tales in Daniel and the Development of Apocalyptic', *JBL*, 94 (1975), 218-34 (p. 220).

31 For a closer comparison of these fragments with the books of Esther, see Crawford, '4QProto-Esther'. However, since I no longer accept some of Milik's readings (e.g. חמא אנ in 4Q550^c, 2 or 'Cuthite' in 4Q550^d i, 5), some of the linkages that I proposed in that article I no longer find tenable.

32 Milik, p. 328; Crawford, '4QProto-Esther', p. 311.

33 Crawford, '4QProto-Esther', p. 311.

34 For the Aramaic text of Ahikar, see A. Cowley, *Aramaic Papyri of the Fifth Century B.C.* (Oxford: Clarendon Press, 1923). Ahikar is identified as a scribe, ספרא, but that vocabulary overlap is coincidental.

35 Sidnie White Crawford, 'The Book of Esther', in *The New Interpreter's Bible*, (Nashville, TN: Abingdon Press, 1999), III, pp. 853-941 (p. 892).

36 Wills, *Novel*, p. 53.

37 Crawford, '4QProto-Esther', p. 319.

38 For comment on Bagoshi's identity, see Crawford, '4QProto-Esther', p. 319. De Troyer disputes any connection with 'Bougaion' in Greek Esther.

39 Elias J. Bickerman, *The Jews in the Greek Age* (Cambridge, MA: Harvard University Press, 1988), p. 60.

40 Collins-Green, p. 49.

41 Wills, *Novel*, p. 199.

42 Hebrew Esther 8:17 contains the verb מתיהדים, but it is not clear if this verb indicates actual conversion or the mere identification with the Jews. For further discussion see Jon D. Levenson, *Esther* (Louisville, KY: John Knox/Westminster, 1997), p. 117.

43 Milik notes in this connection the very small size of the (reconstructed) scroll (pp. 363-64). Perhaps 4QTales was one of the 'paperbacks' of the Second Temple period!

44 Susanna, Tobit and Judith became part of the Septuagint canon, but not part of the Hebrew canon.

45 It is perhaps less surprising that 4QTales did not become part of the canon than that the book of Esther did. Esther's entry into the canon was facilitated by its relationship to the popular festival of Purim.

THE BIBLICAL TEXTS FROM THE JUDAEAN DESERT – AN OVERVIEW AND ANALYSIS OF THE PUBLISHED TEXTS[1]

Emanuel Tov

I. INTRODUCTION AND STATISTICS

IN MANY WAYS the newly discovered texts have revolutionized the study of the text of the Hebrew Bible, as well as that of the Greek Bible. Many aspects of the transmission of the biblical text can now be illustrated by the texts from the Judaean Desert, and occasionally this applies also to the last stages of the literary growth of the biblical books. In the scholarly writing it may sound a little bombastic to speak of 'revolutionizing' the field, but this term probably describes the finds from the Judaean Desert correctly, especially the ones from Qumran. Some may claim that the texts found outside Qumran in Wadi Murabbaʿat, Wadi Sdeir (= Naḥal David), Naḥal Ḥever, Naḥal Ṣeʾelim, and Masada are uninteresting, as they 'merely' confirm the medieval Masoretic Text (MT), but these texts, too, are in many ways remarkable.[2] The novel aspects relating to all these texts from the Judaean Desert pertain not only to the new data, but also to a better understanding of the sources known prior to the Qumran finds.[3]

The analysis of these texts would have been different had the texts from cave 4 been published prior to or simultaneously with those from cave 1. As it happened, the texts that have been most researched are the ones that became known first, that is, 1QIsaᵃ (1951) and subsequently the texts published by E. L. Sukenik (Jerusalem 1954, 1955) and the ones published in DJD I. The only texts from cave 4 that were known in the early 1950s were two columns of 4QSamᵃ (1953), one column of 4QSamᵇ (1955), and 4QQoh (1954). It is therefore not surprising that in the minds of many scholars, consciously or not, the special characteristics of the large Isaiah scroll were considered to be the norm for the textual nature and scribal features of all the Qumran texts. The impressive length of 1QIsaᵃ, which is unequalled among the other biblical texts, and is second in length only to 11QTᵃ, also gave much weight to that scroll. With the publication of the other texts, however, it has now become clear that this scroll is not typical of the Qumran finds. If anything, 1QIsaᵃ may be considered typical of the texts written by the Qumran scribal school, but even such a characterization would be imprecise, since within that group 1QIsaᵃ is idiosyncratic because of its many Aramaizing readings, internal inconsistencies in orthography, and its manifold corrections.

The present survey of the biblical texts is the first to cover all the sites in the Judaean Desert, including beyond Qumran also Wadi Murabbaʿat, Wadi Sdeir (= Naḥal David),

Naḥal Ḥever, Naḥal Ṣeʾelim, and Masada, and it is the first to include indirect evidence embedded in non-biblical Qumran texts.

Now that all the known Hebrew/Aramaic biblical texts from the Judaean Desert have been published in a final form, with the exception of the three Samuel scrolls from cave 4, we can assess their evidence well. The biblical texts have been published in the following volumes: DJD I (Qumran cave 1), II (Murabbaʿat), III (minor caves of Qumran), IV (11QPs[a]), IX, XII, XIV–XVI (all: Qumran cave 4), XXIII (Qumran cave 11), XXXVIII (sites other than Qumran), *Masada VI* (all the Masada biblical texts).[4] These volumes are joined by the editions of 1QIsa[b] by Sukenik,[5] of 1QIsa[a] by Qimron-Parry,[6] and of 11QLev[a] by Freedman-Mathews.[7] The DJD edition of the Isaiah scrolls from cave 1 will follow suit (vol. XXXII). The *tefillin* and *mezuzot* were published in various additional editions.[8]

The final count of the biblical scrolls amounts to around 200 fragmentary scrolls (five of which span more than one biblical book) from Qumran, of the Hebrew/Aramaic Bible and twenty-three fragmentary scrolls from other sites in the Judaean Desert. The slight fluctuation for Qumran pertains to 4QGen[h1] and 4QGen[h2] which may or may not reflect one scroll according to its editor, James Davila. But also beyond this item many doubts remain in matters of detail. Do the various fragments of Mur 1 (Genesis, Exodus, Numbers) reflect one, two, or three manuscripts? Further, it is often unclear whether the separation of several groups of fragments into different manuscripts or their combination into one manuscript is correct. Are 4QJer[b,d,e] indeed three manuscripts as was claimed in DJD XV, and are the Deuteronomy and Exodus segments of 4QDeut[j] indeed part of the same manuscript as was claimed by Julie Duncan in DJD XIV? As a result of these and similar problems, the totals for the manuscripts of the biblical books are approximate only.

In the analysis of the biblical texts from the Judaean Desert, the definition of the scope of the biblical corpus is unclear as we are uncertain regarding the canonical conceptions of the persons who left these texts behind. Our analysis, however, takes no stand on these issues, and refers only to the books contained in the traditional canon of the Hebrew/Aramaic Bible.

Furthermore, although the notion of what exactly constitutes a fragment of a biblical text as opposed to a parabiblical text or pesher is sometimes unclear, our figures are based on the views of the scholars who have published these texts. We regard as biblical texts items which have been given names of the biblical books, such as 1QIsa[a]. Phylacteries and *mezuzot*, although containing segments of Hebrew Scripture are excluded from the statistics, since they are not biblical texts in the usual sense of the word. By the same token one could exclude other texts which may have served liturgical purposes, such as scrolls containing both biblical Psalms and other Hymnic material (e.g., 4QPs[f], 11QPs[a], and 11QPs[b]), but as these scrolls have been given biblical names, they are included in our statistics. Other Qumran compositions, which contain anthologies of biblical texts (especially 4QTest [4Q175]) are also excluded from the list as they too do not represent biblical scrolls in the regular sense of the word.

Because of this procedure, the overall number of the biblical scrolls includes different types of biblical texts. Most texts represent regular biblical scrolls, but some biblical texts may represent abbreviated or excerpted compositions[9] (e.g., 4QExod[d], 4QCant[a], and 4QCant[b]).[10]

The Biblical Texts from the Judaean Desert

Within the Qumran corpus of some 900 texts, the 200 biblical texts constitute 22% (not counting the *tefillin* and *mezuzot*), while in the Masada corpus the biblical texts constitute a larger percentage, 47% or 44% depending on whether fifteen or sixteen literary texts are counted at Masada. *Within* the biblical corpus, a special interest in the Torah is visible in all the sites in the Judaean Desert: eighty-seven texts or 44% of the Qumran biblical corpus represent the books of the Torah. In the sites beyond Qumran this percentage is even greater: fifteen of the twenty-five texts or 62.5%.

The number of the copies for the individual books shows the different measure of interest in the books. The exceptionally large number of copies of Deuteronomy (30), Isaiah (21), and Psalms (36) probably reflects the interest of the Qumran Covenanters in these books.

Occasionally one of the extremities of a biblical scroll has been preserved, and rarely both (1QIsa[a], 4QIsa[b]). The beginnings of fifteen (8%) of the 200 biblical texts from Qumran and two from other sites have been found.[11] Likewise, the ends of seven biblical Qumran scrolls (3.5% of all the biblical scrolls) and two from Masada have been preserved. The extremities of these scrolls are recognizable because of conventions practised by scribes and scroll manufacturers (uninscribed areas, handle sheets), while often segments of the first or last columns have been preserved. In any event, no differences are recognizable between the biblical and non-biblical scrolls with regard to the practices used in the beginnings and ends of scrolls. Some have large uninscribed areas in the beginning or end, while others have handle sheets at one of the extremities, while rarely these two conventions were used at the same time.

II. EXTERNAL DATA ON THE BIBLICAL SCROLLS

1QIsa[a] is the only scroll which has been preserved in its entirety, fifty-four columns in seventeen sheets. Substantial though fragmentary remains have been preserved of 1QIsa[b], 4QpaleoExod[m], 4QNum[b], 4QSam[a], 4QIsa[c], 4QJer[a], 11QpaleoLev[a], 11QPs[a], MurXII, and 11QtgJob, while the preserved remains of all other scrolls are even more fragmentary. Sometimes a tiny inscribed piece is the only evidence for a biblical scroll identified by its content and/or script (e.g. 4QIsa[h—r]).

If two or more biblical books were contained in a single scroll, these books must have constituted a larger unit, namely the Torah, Minor Prophets, or Five Scrolls. Evidence for scrolls containing such large units, however, is scanty, and there is also reverse evidence for single books which were demonstrably *not* part of such large units. Of course, scrolls starting with Genesis (4QGen[b,g,k]), Joshua (XJosh), Kings (5QKgs), Isaiah (1QIsa[a] and MurIsa), or the Minor Prophets (4QXII[d]), preceded by a handle sheet or a large uninscribed area, should cause no surprise. Nor should it cause surprise that MasDeut, MasPs[b], and 11QPs[a] ended with a final handle sheet or an uninscribed surface. At the same time, there is some evidence for larger units.

Thus the inclusion in one scroll of more than one biblical book is evidenced for four, five, or six Torah scrolls: 4QGen-Exod[a] (36 lines [evidence unclear]), 4QpaleoGen-Exod[l] (55–60 lines), 4QExod[b] (c. 50 lines), and possibly also 4QExod-Lev[f] (c. 60 lines), 4QLev-Num[a] (43 lines), and Mur 1 (c. 60 lines), the latter possibly containing Genesis, Exodus, and Numbers (see DJD III, pp. 75–78 and plates XIX–XXI). In all these cases the spaces between the two books have been preserved together with some letters or words of the adjacent book, but in no instance has the full evidence been preserved. The large column size of several of these scrolls confirms the assumption that they indeed contained two or more books, since a large number of lines per column usually implies that the scroll was long. On the basis of their large parameters, it may be presumed that other Torah scrolls likewise contained two or more books, such as 4QGen[e] (c. 50 lines), 4QExod[e] (c. 43), MasDeut (42), SdeirGen (c. 40), and 4QGen[b] (40).

It is thus likely that several of the scrolls found at Qumran contained more than one book of the Torah, and possibly all of the Torah, in which case they would have measured 25–30 metres. According to *Sof.* 3.4, two of the books of the Torah should not be combined if there was no intention to add the other three books to them. If this rule was followed in the case of the scrolls found at Qumran, all the mentioned instances of two attached books of the Torah would have contained the other three Torah books as well. It is unknown, however, whether this rule was followed in the case of the Qumran scrolls.

The books of the Minor Prophets were included in one scroll in MurXII, 4QXII[b] and 4QXII[g]: a space of three lines was left between various books in MurXII, as evidenced by the transition between Jonah and Micah, Micah and Nahum, and Zephaniah and Haggai (see DJD III, pp. 182, 192, 197, 200, 202, 205 and pls LXI, LXVI, LXIX, LXXI, LXXII). This practice follows the instruction in *b. B. Bat.* 13b for combining these books in one unit, while in 4QXII[b] fragment 3, line 5 only one line is left between Zephaniah and Haggai and in 4QXII[g] fragments 70–75 one-and-a-half lines were left between Amos and Obadiah.

While most of the extant Qumran copies of the Five Scrolls were probably contained in separate scrolls (note their small dimensions), there may be indirect evidence for one scroll (4QLam) containing all five *Megillot* or at least one additional book beyond Lamentations. The first preserved column of 4QLam starts at the top with Lamentations 1:1b והיתה כא[ולמנה רבתי בנוים שרׄתי במדינות היתה למס], and since the column length of the scroll is known (ten or eleven lines), the preceding column would have contained at least the first line of the book, a few empty lines between Lamentations and the preceding book, and the end of the preceding book.

At the same time, there is also evidence for several scrolls which contain a single biblical book and are not part of a larger unit such as described above: 11QpaleoLev[a], ending with a ruled uninscribed area of 15.6 cm, covering a complete column, as well as with a separate handle sheet, was not followed by Numbers. 4QLev[c] and 4QDeut[h], both starting at the top of a column, probably started a new scroll, although they could also have been preceded by the previous biblical books ending somewhere on the previous column. 6QDeut? (6Q20), starting with an initial margin of 5.0+ cm was not part of a larger scroll of the Torah. 1QIsa[a], which was not followed by an additional book (no sheet was stitched unto it), formed a single scroll, probably preceded by an uninscribed handle page.

Some general conclusions on the scope of the biblical scrolls written on leather can be formulated, although many details remain nebulous, for example concerning scrolls that probably contained only parts of biblical books.

Torah: Probably the average scroll of a single book of the Torah contained 20–30 lines. Scrolls of a smaller size would not have contained the complete books, and the longer ones (40–50, even 55 and 60 lines) would have contained two or more books. Thus in Genesis five longer copies (4QGen[b,e], SdeirGen, MurGen-Num, 4Q[Gen-]Exod[b]) contain 40–50 lines, while intermediate copies contain 24 and 25 lines. The smaller ones, 4QGen[d,g,f], contain 11, 14, and 17 lines respectively. It would be hard to imagine that 4QGen[d] with a mere 11 lines per column would have contained all of Genesis with an assumed length of 14 metres. This pertains also to 4QExod[e] with 8 lines. In the case of Deuteronomy, 4QDeut[j,n,q] probably contained liturgical excerpts.

Greater Prophets: Average copies of a single scroll contained 30–40 lines in the case of Isaiah and Ezekiel and 20–30 lines in the case of Jeremiah. 4QEzek[b] with 11 lines is an exception and according to Judith Sanderson,[12] it is highly unlikely that this scroll would have contained the entire text of Ezekiel, which would have been 32 metres long with 280 columns.

Psalms: The smaller scrolls were of a limited scope, containing only Psalm 119 (such as 1QPs[a], 4QPs[g], 4QPs[h], 5QPs; for the latter two and 1QPs[a] no measurements can be made), Psalm 104 (4QPs[l]), or a small anthology (such as 4QPs[f], 11QPs[a], or 11QPs[b]), while the longer ones contained all or most of the biblical psalms. At the same time, we lack specific data on the contents of the Psalms scrolls which are known in a variety of sizes, from 8 to 60+ lines.

Five Scrolls: All known copies of the Five Scrolls (with the exception of 4QQoh[a] (Qumran practice) with 20 lines of 37 letter-spaces) are small: 2QRuth[a] (8 lines), 4QRuth[b] (11 lines), 4QLam (10, 11 lines), 5QLam[a] (7 lines), 4QCant[a] (14 lines), 4QCant[b] (14, 15 lines), 6QCant (7 lines). With the exception of 4QLam, which probably was preceded by another book (see above), possibly all preserved specimens of the Five Scrolls contained merely a single book.

Daniel: 4QDan[a,b,c,e] contained 16–22 lines while 4QDan[e] was smaller (9 lines).

III. BIBLICAL AND NON-BIBLICAL SCROLLS

The texts from the Judaean Desert show that very little distinction, if any, was made between the writing of biblical and non-biblical texts and more generally, of sacred and non-sacred texts. It may very well be that in some circles a limited or even rigid distinction was made between the two types of texts (see, for example, the regulations in the rabbinic literature for the writing of sacred texts), but such a distinction is not documented in the Qumran texts.

The two types of texts share all scribal features relating to writing, ruling, stitching of sheets, size and shape of the columns, correction systems, scribal signs, etc. Sacred texts display no idiosyncrasies in any of these features, nor in the matter of the length of scrolls, number of columns per sheet, height of columns, margins, paragraphing, repair-stitching, patching, initial and final handle sheets, use of guide dots, spelling, careful writing, nor even in the employment of the paleo-Hebrew tetragrammaton, found in some biblical manuscripts as well as in non-biblical texts (more in the latter). The leather used for sacred texts was not finer, since *tefillin* and *mezuzot* were written on leather of inferior quality.

Like the non-biblical scrolls, the biblical Qumran scrolls show no evidence for verse division. The only evidence of this kind which was spotted in 4QDan[a] actually is not relevant, as it pertains to small section divisions.[13] While early written evidence for verse division in Hebrew sources is very scarce, if present at all, it does exist for ancient witnesses of the Aramaic and Greek translations, the earliest of which are contemporary with the witnesses of the Hebrew Bible from Qumran. Thus one of the earliest copies of the Targum, 4QtgLev, evidences the use of spacing with dicola (:) in accord with the tradition of writing in that language and script, while the earliest Greek evidence for verse division pertains to spacing between small sense units, verses (Qumran, Naḥal Ḥever, Egyptian papyri). Only later were these spaces filled in with graphic indicators in accord with the tradition of Greek writing, namely the dicolon and dot, usually the high dot.

All the sub-systems used for paragraphing are shared by biblical and non-biblical manuscripts, relating to small and large spaces, spaces in the line and at the end of the line, completely empty lines, and indentations. At the same time, the *paragraphos* signs are used more frequently in non-biblical texts.

Poor tanning, scar tissue,[14] and stitching[15] forced scribes to leave uninscribed certain areas in both biblical and non-biblical scrolls. Papyrus strips, which may be either inscribed or uninscribed (4QpapUnclassified Fragments [4Q51a]), were sometimes attached in antiquity to the back of the leather (e.g. 4QSam[a]) for support. It is unclear how many words in the texts from the Judaean Desert were re-inked in antiquity when the ink had become faint.[16] The final column of 1QIsa[a] was probably damaged in antiquity, possibly since it did not have a handle sheet or an uninscribed section for handling; as a result, the ends of lines 1–4, 6, 7, 9, 10 were re-inked.

Use of scribal signs in biblical scrolls was more limited than in non-biblical scrolls. Cancellation dots and strokes (above and below single letters, and in the case of 1QIsa[a] also for complete words) were found in several scrolls written in the Qumran system (4QDeut[j], 4QSam[c], 4QXII[e], 1QIsa[a]), as well as in other texts: 4QExod[c], 4QDeut[c], 4QJer[a], 4QIsa[d], 4QIsa[h]. Some letters were crossed out with a line in 4QDeut[c], 1QIsa[a], 4QQoh[a], and 4QDan[a], all written in the Qumran system, as well as in 4QJer[c]. Parentheses were used in 4QJer[a], 4QQoh[a], and 4QCant[b], and single paleo-Hebrew letters were written in the margin of 1QIsa[a], 4QCant[b], 4QPs[b], 5QLam[a] and MasDeut. A sign of undetermined nature is found in the top right corner of 4QExod[k], and *tetrapuncta* for the divine name are found in 1QIsa[a] and 4QSam[c].

Since it is rare that we can see the recurrence of a scribal hand in two different Qumran documents, little is known about scribes who wrote both sacred and non-sacred documents. An exception is the scribe who wrote 1QS, 1QSa, and 1QSb as well as the biblical 4QSam[c] and some of the corrections in 1QIsa[a]. This scribe employed the same system and notations throughout all five texts (including the *tetrapuncta*). In addition, 1QS and 1QIsa[a] also share three unusual marginal signs, which were probably inserted by this scribe.

Thus the Qumran texts display a distinction in very few details between biblical and non-biblical texts, although this was not necessarily characteristic of all of ancient Israel, since in rabbinic circles different approaches for the writing of sacred and non-sacred documents may have been developed. In the following areas differences are recognizable:

(a) Biblical texts were inscribed on only one side of the parchment unlike some non-biblical opisthographs.

(b) Biblical texts found in the Judaean Desert were almost exclusively written on parchment (thus also *m. Meg.* 2:2; *y. Meg.* 1.71d). The relatively small number of biblical papyrus fragments (4-6 copies out of a total of 200 manuscripts) possibly served as personal copies. On the other hand, papyrus was frequently used for documentary texts and some literary works.

(c) A single *vav* in the palaeo-Hebrew or square script serving as a paragraphing device is found only in three biblical scrolls in the middle of closed sections: 4QpaleoExod^m, 11QpaleoLev^a, 4QNum^b. This type of *vav* is generally placed in an open or closed section when the first word of the new section would have started with a (usually conversive) *vav* which is now omitted.

(d) A special arrangement for the writing of several poetical sections was devised for many biblical scrolls (including Ben Sira [2QSir and MasSir]), but not for any of the non-biblical compositions. An exception is the non-biblical 4QMessianic Apocalypse (4Q521) fragment 2 ii which is written in a simple stichographic arrangement. Within the Bible, this stichographic arrangement is evidenced for two poems in the Torah (Exodus 15; Deuteronomy 32), and for the books of Psalms (especially Psalms 119 and 104), Proverbs, Lamentations, and Job in 30 biblical scrolls, but not in the other 27 biblical scrolls which span poetic passages (four scrolls have a mixture of both systems: 1QPs^a, 4QPs^d, 11QPs^{a,b}). It is hard to determine the background of the use of the stichographic arrangements, but it may have been determined by liturgical needs, though not in all instances.

This summary shows that the rules for the writing of sacred texts recorded in *Massekhet Soferim* and in earlier sources in the Talmud are somewhat misleading, since most details recorded there pertain to aspects of the writing which were practised also for non-sacred texts written in the Second Temple period. For example, *Sof.* 1:15 states that texts which deviate from the norm regarding the indication of open and closed sections cannot be used as sacred writings. But this practice, which is basically a paragraphing system, was also followed in most other compositions written in the Qumran period, biblical and nonbiblical. Thus, it is not the practice that was sacred, but the tradition to use an open section rather than a closed one in a specific verse. Likewise, larger bottom margins than top margins were the norm in all texts, and not only in Torah scrolls. In other cases, new restrictions were imposed on the writing of sacred scrolls: a scroll in which a complete line was erased (*Sof.* 3:9), scrolls containing more than a certain number of mistakes (3:10), scrolls mixing medial and final letters (2:20), or scrolls which had letters written beyond the vertical left-hand margin (2:3) could not be used.

(e) Large de luxe editions, especially of MT, and especially in scrolls from 50 BCE onwards, seem to be specific to biblical scrolls. This category, not recognized previously, possibly coincides with the 'exact copies' (ἠκριβωμένα) which were fostered by the temple circles in Saul Lieberman's description.[17] The assumption of such de luxe scrolls is based on the data included in the Appendix to this paper.

IV. TEXTUAL CHARACTER

A. SITES OTHER THAN QUMRAN

All the twenty-three texts found outside Qumran are almost identical to the medieval consonantal text of MT, even more so than the proto-Masoretic Qumran texts. This grouping comprises the following sites and texts: Masada (Genesis, Leviticus [2], Deuteronomy, Ezekiel, and Psalms [2]),[18] Wadi Sdeir (Genesis), Naḥal Ṣeʾelim (Numbers), Naḥal Ḥever (Numbers [2], Deuteronomy, Psalms) and Murabbaʿat (Genesis, Exodus, Numbers, Deuteronomy, Isaiah, Minor Prophets), as well as three scrolls of unknown origin.[19] The only differences with the medieval text pertain to orthography, a few minute details, paragraphing, and the layout of individual Psalms, and these variations resemble the internal differences between the medieval manuscripts of MT themselves.[20]

B. QUMRAN

As in the past, the main sources for our knowledge of the biblical text in Qumran remain those containing a running biblical text, but our information about these manuscripts can now be supplemented by other sources which have not been used much in the past. The information from these sources is significant, although the amount of information embedded in them is limited. We refer to biblical quotations in the non-biblical compositions as well as to excerpted and abbreviated biblical manuscripts. At the same time, the biblical manuscripts remain the most obvious source. The differences between the various Qumran documents are taken as reflecting variant readings or exegesis by the scribes or authors of the non-biblical compositions; E. L. Greenstein, on the other hand, has suggested that when encountering variations in the biblical and non-biblical texts, one's first inclination should be to assume the scribe's faulty memory.[21] In our view, this approach would be valid in only a few instances.

1. THE BIBLICAL TEXT REFLECTED IN THE NON-BIBLICAL COMPOSITIONS

A full analysis of the biblical text in Qumran ought to include the quotations from the Bible in the non-biblical documents which add to our knowledge of the variety of biblical texts in the period under investigation. In the past, these non-biblical texts have not been used much in text-critical analyses, with some justification, since it is often difficult to extract from them reliable information about the biblical text quoted. These difficulties are caused by the fact that biblical quotations and stretches of biblical text are found in a variety of compositions, each of which requires a different type of analysis. Thus the evaluation of the textual deviations reflected in the biblical quotations in these compositions differs not only from one category of compositions to the other, but also from one composition to the next. The following three categories of compositions are distinguished.[22]

A. FREE QUOTATIONS AND ALLUSIONS

Several non-biblical compositions, both sectarian and non-sectarian, freely quote from and allude to passages in the Bible. In the case of the sectarian writings this is understandable, since the Bible held a very central position in the life of the Qumranites, so that the *Hodayot*, the *Rules*, 4QShirShabb, and the various sapiential compositions abound with biblical quotations. This also pertains to non-Qumranic compositions such as 4QNon-Canonical Psalms A–B (4Q380-81). Most of these quotations are free, involving changes in the biblical text and combinations of different biblical texts, which accordingly cannot be utilized easily within the context of a text-critical discussion. The textual background of some compositions has been studied, but few solid conclusions have been reached.[23]

B. PESHARIM

Pesharim are composed of quotations from the biblical text (lemmas) and their exposition (pesher). These lemmas in the eighteen running pesharim on biblical books or parts of them from caves 1 and 4 contain long stretches of biblical text, which, when combined, would amount to running biblical manuscripts, were it not for the fact that they often have been preserved only fragmentarily. However, in 1QpHab, 4QpNah, 4QpPs, and some sections of the pesharim on Isaiah, such running texts may be reconstructed. In addition, the exposition in the pesher itself sometimes also reflects a few additional readings differing from the biblical text on which the pesher comments.[24]

Different views have been voiced regarding the text-critical value of the biblical text contained in and reflected by these pesharim. A positive position was taken by the editors of textual editions who incorporated readings from these pesharim in their textual apparatuses (*BHS* and *BHQ*[25] for 1QpHab, and *HUBP*[26] for the pesharim on Isaiah). A negative position was taken by other scholars, who ascribed most non-Masoretic readings in the pesharim to their contextual exegesis.[27] Although the biblical text of the pesharim reflects contextual exegesis by the authors of the pesharim, including a few cases of sectarian exegesis,[28] the positive approach is generally more realistic. However, it remains difficult to determine the amount of manuscript variation. A maximalistic approach regarding the number of variants from MT underlies the lists of presumed variant readings for 1QpHab by William Brownlee (see n. 28) and for all the pesharim by Timothy Lim.[29] Thus, according to Lim (p. 90), seventeen percent of all the words of the MT of Nahum differ from the corresponding preserved segments of 4QpNah. The number of readings of 4QpNah which, according to Lim, differ from MT is substantial, but they include morphological variations and a large number of contextual changes, both of which are problematic. If, according to the minimalist approach, these elements were inserted by the authors of the pesharim, the underlying biblical text was probably not very different from MT. Unfortunately, however, there are hardly any criteria for deciding between the two options, although the mentioned sectarian changes (see n. 26) make us believe that the authors of the pesharim themselves were very free in their approach to the biblical text. But it is also possible that this *Vorlage* already included the morphological variations and contextual changes, so that those manuscripts resembled 1QIsa[a] and similar texts. Believing that this was the case, several scholars[30] indeed characterized the underlying text of the pesharim as 'vulgar' texts.[31]

The pesharim from caves 1 and 4 in Qumran often differ from the Masoretic tradition regarding the division of the units in the biblical text quoted in the lemmas. Thus, while the lemmas quoting the biblical text in 1QpHab sometimes conform to what is now a verse in the Masoretic tradition of Habakkuk (1:5, 11, 12, 17; 2:14, 15, 16), more frequently they comprise half-verses or even smaller segments (1:3a, 3b, 4bα, 1:4bβ, 6a, 6b, 10a, 10b, 1:13aα, 13b; 2:3a, 3b, 4a, 4b, 8b, 17a, 17b), or one-and-a-half verses (1:1–2a; 1:6bβ–7; 1:12b–13a; 2:7–8a), or stretches of two (2:1–2, 5–6, 12–13, 19–20), or three (1:14–16; 2:9–11) verses. Similar deviations from the verse division of MT are reflected in the lemmas of 1QpMic, 4QpIsa^d (4Q164), 4QNah (4Q169), and to a lesser degree 4Qpap pIsa^c (4Q163), 4QpHos^a (4Q166), and 4QpPs^a (4Q171). At the same time, 4QpIsa^{a,b,e} present the text mainly in clusters of two or more verses. These different types of quotation characterize the systems of quoting in the pesharim and the Talmud in which the subject matter sometimes requires the mentioning of a larger or smaller unit than a verse in MT. This deviating evidence therefore is not indicative of the oral tradition concerning the extent of early verses.

C. REWRITTEN BIBLICAL COMPOSITIONS

The group of rewritten biblical compositions provides substantial information relevant to our knowledge of the biblical text. These rewritten biblical compositions reformulate the content of the Bible, especially of the Torah, adding and omitting minor and major details, as well as changing many a word. Each composition was a unicum, inserting a different amount of changes into the biblical text. Some compositions were very close to the biblical text, such as 4QRP (4QReworked Pentateuch)[32] and the Temple Scroll (especially as contained in 11QT^a), both of which contain very long stretches which run parallel to the biblical text. In fact, 4QRP^{a-e}, which has been preserved well in its five different manuscripts (including 4QRP^a = 4Q158), is almost in the nature of a regular biblical manuscript to which a thin layer of exegetical changes was added. It is often very hard to recognize these exegetical changes in the above compositions. This applies to compositions whose names contain the elements 'ps(eudo)' and 'apocr', such as 2QapocrMoses? (2Q21), 4QapocrMos$^{a-b,c?}$ (4Q375, 4Q376, 4Q408), 4QapocrJosh$^{a-b,c?}$ (4Q378, 4Q379, 4Q522), 4QpsEzek^{a-e} (4Q385, 4Q385c, 4Q386, 4Q388, 4Q391), and 4QapocrJer A-C (4Q383, 4Q384, 4Q385a, 4Q385b, 4Q387, 4Q387a, 4Q388a, 4Q389, 4Q390), 4QapocrLam A, B (4Q179, 4Q501), 4QapocrElisha (4Q481a), 4QapocrDan ar (4Q246), 4QapocrPent. A, B (4Q368, 4Q377), 4QapocrLevi^{a-b} ar (4Q540, 4Q541), as well as to 4QExposition on the Patriarchs (4Q464) and 4QparaGen-Exod (4Q422). Because of the difficult distinction in these compositions between the biblical text and the more substantial added layer of exegesis and rewriting, it is hard to incorporate the underlying biblical text in text-critical analyses. In the case of the first mentioned compositions, however, the underlying biblical text is often recognizable. For example, there is strong evidence that three of the manuscripts of 4QRP (4Q158, 364 and 365 = 4QRP^{a,b,c}) are close to the Samaritan Pentateuch and hence to the so-called pre-Samaritan manuscripts.[33] A similar text is reflected in the biblical quotations in the book of Jubilees, although there is more evidence available pertaining to the Ethiopic 'grand-daughter' translation of that book than to the fragmentary Qumran texts.[34] Also for 11QT^a much textual evidence is available, especially for columns LI–LXVI. That composition does not show a close textual relation to any of the known textual witnesses of the Bible, and its text should probably be characterized as reflecting an independent textual tradition.[35]

The Biblical Texts from the Judaean Desert

Although the amount of information on the biblical text reflected in the non-biblical compositions from Qumran is limited, these sources need to be further explored for text-critical purposes. Among other things, an attempt should be made to examine possible links between the biblical quotations in the non-biblical Qumran texts, especially the sectarian ones, and the biblical texts found in Qumran. This is a difficult assignment, since it is not easy to determine on which specific biblical manuscript a quotation in a non-biblical composition is based. Characteristic readings of the biblical texts need to be isolated in the quotations, and this is possible only when the differences between the manuscripts themselves are sufficiently distinctive. For example, in Isaiah the differences between 1QIsa[a] (sometimes agreeing with 4QIsa[c]) on the one hand and on the other hand the proto-Masoretic 1QIsa[b] and most of the Isaiah manuscripts from cave 4 are quite distinct, as are the differences in Jeremiah between (1) 4QJer[b,d] and the Septuagint (LXX), (2) the Masoretic 4QJer[a,c], and (3) the idiosyncratic 2QJer. At the same time, it remains difficult to determine close affinities between brief quotations from these two books in non-biblical compositions and specific Qumran biblical manuscripts. A few special links between such quotations and Qumran manuscripts have been noticed, but research of this type is still in its infancy.[36]

2. BIBLICAL MANUSCRIPTS

A. EXCERPTED AND ABBREVIATED TEXTS

The existence of excerpted biblical texts among the Qumran manuscripts has been recognized for some time.[37] With the publication of additional texts, especially from the Torah, this category has been extensively analyzed by the present author.[38] Due to the fragmentary nature of these excerpted texts, their essence is not always clear, nor is the background of the excerpting. Most excerpted texts were probably made for liturgical purposes:[39] all the *tefillin*, several manuscripts of Exodus and Deuteronomy,[40] and a long list of Psalm texts from caves 4 and 11 containing major transpositions of Psalms and segments of Psalms (e.g., 4QPs[n] in which Psalm 135:12 is followed by 136:22 ff.)[41] as well as omissions and additions of Psalms. Other manuscripts contain an abbreviated text as well. Thus 4QExod[d] (Exodus 13:15-16; 15:1 ff) omits 13:17 ff and all of chapter 14; 4QCant[a] omits 4:7-6:11, and 4QCant[b] omits Cant 3:6-8 and 4:4-7.[42] Again other texts are suspected as abbreviated texts because of their small size, such as 4QGen[d], 4QDeut[h,n,q], 4QEzek[b], 4QPs[g], and 4QDan[e]. If the characterization of these scrolls as excerpted and abbreviated texts is correct, their major omissions and transpositions should be disregarded in the text-critical analysis, but other details in the texts should be taken into consideration. Likewise, the *tefillin* containing combinations of four different biblical texts, often agree with one of the other textual witnesses, and their readings should thus be included in the text-critical analysis of Exodus and Deuteronomy. Some of these readings agree with the Masoretic family, and others with LXX or SP, in the latter case, especially in harmonizing readings.[43] Again, other readings agree with certain Qumran scrolls.

The textual character of some excerpted texts is significant. Thus the first biblical quotation in 4QTest which combines Deuteronomy 5:28-29 and 18:18-19 is close to SP and 4QRP[a] (4Q158, of a pre-Samaritan character). At the same time, the third quotation in 4QTest, from Deuteronomy 33:8-11, is very close to 4QDeut[h], and may have been based on that scroll or a similar one.[44] These two quotations thus show that the author of 4QTest used at least two biblical scrolls of a different character, that is a pre-Samaritan text and 4QDeut[h], a textually independent text. This unintentional mixture must have resulted from the author's use of these particular scrolls, and probably neither he nor the other authors took notice of the different textual character of the scrolls consulted.

Another feature of the excerpted and abbreviated texts is that none of these texts, with the exception of some *tefillin* and *mezuzot*, is close to MT.[45] This feature indicates a certain milieu for these anthologies, whose purpose differed from that of the writing of regular Scripture texts.

B. BEGULAR BIBLICAL TEXTS

(1). BACKGROUND

The great majority of the 200 Hebrew biblical texts come from cave 4, while smaller quantities were found in caves 1, 2, 3, 5, 6, 8, and 11.[46] How uncertain we are regarding the number of texts originally deposited in the caves is shown by the sixty-eight reinforcing leather tabs found in cave 8. Each reinforcing tab was probably attached to a single scroll, and although this cave probably contained a leather workshop or depository, it is not impossible that many scrolls decayed in this cave and that the reinforcing tabs are the evidence of the existence at one time of many scrolls, much more than the remains of four manuscripts would indicate.[47]

Preferably the Qumran biblical texts should be classified according to objective criteria, but there hardly is such a criterion. For one thing, the contents of each of the caves are not homogeneous, with the sole exception of cave 7 which contained only Greek papyri, probably all biblical, and of cave 11 containing mainly texts written in the Qumran scribal practice (biblical and non-biblical). The main depository of texts was cave 4, which contained copies of all the books of the Hebrew Bible, with the exception of Esther.[48] It is significant that virtually all the so-called canonical books were represented in this cave, which probably implies that an effort was made to store in that cave among other things all the books which were considered authoritative at that stage, at least in certain Jewish circles, and which became authoritative at a later stage for all of Judaism. On the other hand, only a few books of the Apocrypha, and the so-called Pseudepigrapha, were represented in cave 4 (*Tobit, Jubilees, Levi ar, TJud ar, TNaph*). Cave 4 thus may have served as a central depository for the written material owned by the Qumran community, including some Greek texts, *tefillin*, and *mezuzot*. It is probably not coincidental that most Qumran copies of the biblical books which are considered to be significant for the textual analysis of the Hebrew Bible were found in cave 4. While a text like 1QIsa[a] may be important to our understanding of the textual transmission of the Bible, it contains so many secondary features that its importance for the reconstruction of the original text of the Bible is limited. Cave 4 does contain texts of the type of 1QIsa[a], but on the other hand, the caves other than cave 4 hardly contain any texts which are of major significance for text-critical analysis.

The Biblical Texts from the Judaean Desert

(2). TEXTS IN THE PALAEO-HEBREW SCRIPT

The great majority of the texts from Qumran and the other sites in the Judaean Desert are written in the square script, and they reflect a textual variety. A similar variety, though on a smaller scale, is reflected in the texts written in the palaeo-Hebrew script, so that the textual character of these texts cannot serve as a key for unscrambling the riddle of the writing in this script. The twelve biblical texts written in the palaeo-Hebrew script differ from the texts written in the square script with regard to the scribal characteristics inherent in writing in that script, with regard to the almost complete lack of scribal intervention in them, and in additional scribal features.[49]

At Qumran, fragments of twelve biblical texts written in the palaeo-Hebrew script have been found as well as a few palaeo-Hebrew texts of uncertain nature:[50] 1QpaleoLev, 1QpaleoNum (same scroll as 1QpaleoLev?), 2QpaleoLev, 4QpaleoGen-Exod[l], 4QpaleoGen[m], 4QpaleoExod[m], 4QpaleoDeut[r,s], 4QpaleoJob[c], 6QpaleoGen, 6QpaleoLev, and 11QpaleoLev[a]. Three texts (4Q124–125 and 11Q22) are unidentified. 4QpaleoParaJosh, probably not a biblical text, contains parts of Joshua 21.

Beyond Qumran two non-biblical texts, Mas 1o (Mas pap paleoText of Sam. Origin [recto] and Mas pap paleoUnidentified Text [verso]) are also written in palaeo-Hebrew characters.[51]

The fragments of the Bible texts written in the palaeo-Hebrew script contain only texts of the Torah and Job – note that the latter is traditionally ascribed to Moses (cf. *b. B. Bat.* 14b-15a; cf. also manuscripts and editions of the Peshitta in which Job follows the Torah). Note also that only one of the books of the Torah (Leviticus) and Job Targumim were found in Qumran written in the palaeo-Hebrew script. The longest preserved texts written in the palaeo-Hebrew script are 4QpaleoExod[m] and 11QpaleoLev[a].

These texts, rather than pre-dating writing in the square script, were actually written at a relatively late period, probably as a natural continuation of the tradition of writing in the 'early' Hebrew script, and were concurrent with the use of the square script. This can be demonstrated by an examination of the palaeography of the palaeo-Hebrew script,[52] and of their orthography which is *no more* archaic than that of the texts written in the square script. While it is tacitly assumed by most scholars that, with the revival of the palaeo-Hebrew script in the Hasmonean period, texts were transformed from the square to the palaeo-Hebrew script,[53] it would be more natural to assume that the habit of writing in the palaeo-Hebrew script had never ceased through the centuries. Possibly the palaeo-Hebrew texts from Qumran derived from the circles of the Sadducees, the major argument for this assumption being the fact that most palaeo-Hebrew texts reflect MT,[54] while writing in this script was forbidden by the Pharisees.[55] One of the special characteristics of the palaeo-Hebrew texts is that they display virtually no scribal intervention. It is further possible that the Qumran scribes were influenced by this Sadducean tradition when writing the tetragrammaton and other divine names in palaeo-Hebrew characters in biblical and non-biblical texts, in order that these words, whose sanctity was determined by the writing in this script, would not be erased.

(3). TEXTUAL VARIETY

The textual variety of the Qumran biblical texts is now accepted by scholars as established.[56] It is probably equally accepted by many scholars that these texts derived from different places in ancient Israel, not only from Qumran. Presently scholars are not as naive as the first generation of Qumran scholars who ascribed all the texts found in Qumran to the Qumran community, while some of them even tried to locate in them the characteristic ideas of that community.[57] On the other hand, we do not have to go as far as Norman Golb, who denied any connection between the scrolls found in the caves and the Qumran community living in Khirbet Qumran very close to cave 4.[58] We prefer a middle course, according to which some of the Qumran texts (probably not more than twenty percent) were copied by the scribes of the Qumran community, while the remainder were brought to Qumran from outside. We believe that there are criteria in the realm of orthography, morphology, and scribal practices for distinguishing between the two groups (see below, 4a). As a result, if this opinion is correct, in our view it is justifiable to look for sectarian readings in 1QIsa[a] (although I have not been able to locate them), but it is not justifiable to look for them in any text whose connection with the Qumranites has not been established, such as 4QSam[a], for example.

3. CLASSIFICATION OF THE TEXTS ACCORDING TO TEXTUAL CHARACTER

The classification of the Qumran texts remains a difficult assignment. The texts should not be grouped by cave, since the contents of each individual cave were not homogeneous. Nor should they be classified by origin (copied by the Qumranites/brought from outside), since this distinction is neither firmly secured nor sufficient. Nor should the texts be classified by date, by palaeographical or codicological criteria, since none of these criteria are firm. Probably the best criterion for classification is according to textual character, even though this criterion is also problematic. However, since one of our main interests is gaining insights into the textual nature of the individual texts and of the collection as a whole, we nevertheless have to attempt to classify the texts according to this criterion. The first step in this classification is an attempt to determine the principles for describing five textual groups, and to fill in the details for each group. The second step is to see how these groups are distributed in the individual books of the Bible even though we should not forget that the preservation of the Qumran fragments depends to a large degree on coincidence. Yet even with these limitations, it is relevant to examine, for example, how many texts belonging to the Masoretic family have been preserved in each of the books of the Bible, and whether the various biblical books present a different textual picture from each other.[59]

The principle behind this classification is the recognition that all texts can be grouped according to the degree of closeness to MT, LXX, or SP without accepting the claim that these three texts are the central pillars (recensions, texts, text types, etc.) of the biblical text. One of the groups in this corpus comprises texts which are not close to any of these three entities (group *e* below). It may be rather unusual to classify ancient texts according to the degree of their closeness to later textual witnesses, certainly if these are medieval (MT and SP), but this comparison is necessary, since these texts already existed in the last centuries before the turn of the Era.

This classification can only be approximate, not only because the texts are fragmentary (texts which are too fragmentary are not included in the analysis), but also because, in the stretches covered by several fragmentary texts, there is insufficient opposition between MT and SP in the Torah and MT and LXX in Isaiah and Ruth. The recognition of this aspect as well as the coverage of all the texts from the Judaean Desert allows us to correct our statistics published earlier. In the calculation of the percentages for the various groups of texts, the numbers are based on a list of 128 biblical texts (the remaining 72 texts are too fragmentary for textual analysis). In this calculation, the following principles are employed: (1) Questionable attributions to textual groups are counted as regular ones. (2) In accord with statistical probability, texts which are equally close to MT and SP in the Torah and to MT and the LXX in other books are counted as MT. (3) Texts written according to the Qumran practice (group a) are not included separately in the statistics, since these texts are already counted in other groups in accord with their textual affiliation. (4) Texts which are characterized as both 'independent' and close to the LXX or the SP are counted as 'independent'. (5) Since the texts like the SP are not evidenced for books other than the Torah, statistics for the Torah are separated from those of the other books, but they are rather similar.

In the forty-six Torah texts that are sufficiently extensive for analysis (out of a total of fifty-two such texts included in the calculation), twenty-four texts (fifty-two percent) reflect MT (or are equally close to the MT and SP), seventeen are non-aligned (thirty-seven percent), three reflect the SP (6.5 percent), and two the LXX (4.5 percent). In the remainder of the Bible, in the seventy-five texts included in the calculation that are sufficiently extensive for analysis (out of a total of seventy-six such texts), thirty-three texts (forty-four percent) reflect MT (or are equally close to MT and LXX), forty are non-aligned (fifty-three percent), two reflect the LXX (three percent). The overall preponderance of the Masoretic and non-aligned texts in the Qumran corpus is thus evident, in the Torah more the MT and in the other books more the non-aligned texts.

a) Texts Written in the Qumran Practice

It has been suggested, especially by the present author, that a large group of Qumran texts stand apart from the others because of their common use of a distinctive orthography, morphology,[60] and set of scribal practices.[61] It was thus recognized that a series of scribal features occurs almost exclusively in texts which display a certain system of orthography and morphology. The fact that virtually all the sectarian texts from Qumran reflect this combined set of features has led to the suggestion that these texts had been copied by the group of people who left the texts behind in the Qumran caves, possibly written in Qumran itself, although this is not a necessary part of the hypothesis. It is not suggested that these mentioned features are characteristic of the Qumran scribal school only. It is only claimed that, within the corpus of the texts found at Qumran, these features display a peculiar distribution.[62] Likewise, *tefillin* that were written by the Qumran scribal school do not reflect the rabbinic prescriptions for the contents of the *tefillin*, while the *tefillin* not written in the Qumran scribal practice, do so.[63] On the basis of these criteria, it is now possible to identify a group of biblical texts reflecting the Qumran scribal practice.[64] The great majority of these texts reflect a free approach to the biblical text which manifests itself in adaptations of unusual forms to the context,[65] in frequent errors, in numerous corrections, and sometimes, also, in careless handwriting. This approach seemingly contradicts the strict approach of the Qumran Covenanters to their Bible interpretation, but this contradiction is only apparent, as different aspects of life are involved.

An examination of the textual affinities of all the biblical texts represents a novel element in this analysis. Some of the texts written by the Qumran scribal school must have been copied from proto-Masoretic texts, but they can no longer be identified, since the scribes made too many changes in the course of copying. Thus, for instance, 1QIsa[a] could have been copied from 1QIsa[b] or a similar text, but because of the free approach of 1QIsa[a], this assumption cannot be verified. In other cases, the textual background of the texts can be identified more readily, as in the case of texts copied by a Qumran scribe from a text close to SP (e.g., 4QNum[b]; see further group c below). The sectarian scribe of 4QSam[c] probably copied from a text which was both close to MT and to the Lucianic text of 2 Samuel 14–15, which in that section probably reflects the Old Greek translation, and should therefore be deemed independent. The majority of the texts written in the Qumran practice (twenty-one texts) are characterized as textually independent (group e below), since their many contextual changes made the text into independent entities: 2QExod[a[?]], 2QExod[b[?]], 4QExod[b], 11QLev[b], 4QDeut[j], 4QDeut[k1], 4QDeut[k2], 4QDeut[m], 4QSam[c], 1QIsa[a], 4QIsa[c], 2QJer, 4QXII[c], 4QXII[e], 4QXII[g], 11QPs[a], 11QPs[b], 11QPs[c], 11QPs[d[?]], 4QQoh[a], 4QLam. For other texts in this group the textual affinity cannot be determined: 2QExod[b[?]], 4QExod[j[?]], 4QLev[g?], 2QNum[b], 1QDeut[a], 2QDeut[c], 4QPs[o].

The twenty-seven documents written in the Qumran practice, often described as typical Qumran texts, comprise a sizable group among the Qumran biblical texts. Probably the base text of most pesharim, reflecting all the elements of the Qumran practice, belonged to this group as well. The percentage of this group within the corpus of Qumran biblical texts is not expressed in statistical terms in the overall statistical analysis, since the great majority of the texts are included in the statistics of the other four categories, which together add up to 100 percent. At the same time, it is noteworthy that twenty-one percent of the Qumran biblical scrolls were copied by the Qumran community, a far cry from the percentage which was assumed during the first two generations of Qumran research, namely 100 percent

b) Proto-Masoretic (or Proto-Rabbinic) Texts

Proto-Masoretic (or Proto-Rabbinic) texts contain the consonantal framework of MT, one thousand years or more before the time of the Masorah codices, and they do not seem to reflect any special textual characteristics beyond their basic agreement with MT. These texts are usually named proto-Masoretic, but the term 'proto-rabbinic,' used by Frank Cross,[66] probably better describes their nature.

The exclusive closeness of some twenty-four Qumran texts to the medieval texts is remarkable, while textual identity is spotted only for the texts from the other sites in the Judaean Desert (see n. 20). 4QGen-Exod[a], 4QpaleoGen-Exod[l], 4QGen[b], 4QExod[c], 4QJosh[b], 1QSam, 4QSam[b], 4QKgs, 1QIsa[b], 4QJer[a], 4QJer[c], 4QEzek[b[?]], 11QEzek, 4QXII[b[?]], 4QXII[f[?]], 4QPs[c], 4QPs[g], 4QPs[m[?]], 4QJob[a[?]], 4QpaleoJob[c[?]], 4QProv[a], 4QProv[b], 1QDan, 4QEzra.[67] In other cases in which no opposition between MT and SP can be discerned in passages covered by the Qumran texts, twenty Qumran texts are equally close to the medieval texts of MT and to SP in the Torah, while nine Isaiah texts and four texts of Ruth are equally close to MT and LXX: 4QGen^c, 4QGen^d, 4QGen^e, 4QGen^f, 4QGen^g, 4QGen^j, 1QExod, 1QpaleoLev, 4QLev^b, 4QLev^c, 4QLev^e, 4QLev-Num^a, 1QDeut^b, 4QDeut^d, 4QDeut^e, 4QDeut^f, 4QDeut^g, 4QDeut^i, 4QDeut^o, 4QpaleoDeut^r, 4QIsa^a, 4QIsa^b 4QIsa^d, 4QIsa^e, 4QIsa^f, 4QIsa^g, 4QIsa^h, 4QIsa^m, 4QIsa^o, 2QRuth^a, 2QRuth^b, 4QRuth^a, 4QRuth^b.

These fifty-seven texts comprise some fifty-two percent of the Qumran biblical texts in the Torah (24 texts) and forty-four percent in the other books (33 texts).[68]

c) Pre-Samaritan (or: Harmonistic) Texts

The pre-Samaritan Qumran texts (4QpaleoExod^m, 4QExod-Lev^f, and 4QNum^b, and secondarily also 4QDeut^n and possibly 4QLev^d) reflect the characteristic features of SP with the exception of the latter's ideological readings, but they occasionally deviate from it. It appears that one of the texts of this group formed the basis of SP, and that the Samaritan ideological changes and phonological features were subsequently inserted into that text. A characteristic feature of these texts is the preponderance of harmonistic readings, and as a result the group as a whole was termed harmonistic by Eshel.[69] F. M. Cross prefers to name this group 'Palestinian',[70] and there is much justification for this characterization, since these texts are not evidenced outside Palestine. The use of this term is, however, problematic, since it may imply that no other texts or groups of texts were extant in Palestine. Of the rewritten Pentateuch compositions, the following reflect a pre-Samaritan biblical text: 4Q158, 4Q364, and 4Q365 (all three containing 4QRP). 4QTest also reflects a similar text.

The three pre-Samaritan texts together comprise no more than 6.5 percent of the Qumran biblical texts of the Torah. Although this is a small group it is very significant for our understanding of the transmission of the Hebrew Bible.[71]

d) Texts Close to the Presumed Hebrew Source of LXX

Although no text was found in Qumran that is identical or almost identical to the presumed Hebrew source of LXX, a few texts are very close to that translation: 4QJer^{b,d} bear a strong resemblance to LXX in characteristic details, with regard both to the arrangement of the verses and to their shorter text.[72] Similarly close to LXX, though not to the same extent, are 4QLev^d (also close to the SP), 4QDeut^q, and secondarily also 4QSam^a (close to the main tradition and the Lucianic manuscripts of LXX; see further below, group *e*),[73] 4QNum^b, and according to Cross (DJD XII, p. 84) also 4QExod^b. Individual agreements with LXX are also found in additional texts, in a somewhat large proportion in 4QDeut^{c,h,j}, but these texts actually belong to group *e*.

There is insufficient evidence for speculating on the internal relation between the texts which are close to LXX. In any event, they should not be considered a textual group. They do not form a closely-knit textual family like the Masoretic family or the pre-Samaritan group, nor have these texts been produced by a scribal school, like the texts written in the Qumran practice (group *a*). They represent individual copies that in the putative stemma of the biblical texts happened to be close to the Hebrew text from which LXX was translated. Since the *Vorlage* of LXX was a single biblical text, and not a family, recension, or revision, the recognition of Hebrew scrolls that were close to the *Vorlage* of LXX is thus of limited importance to our understanding of the relation between these texts, but it does have bearing on our understanding of the nature of LXX and its *Vorlage*. The four texts which are close to LXX comprise 4.5 percent of the Qumran biblical texts in the Torah (two texts) and three percent in the other books (two texts).[75]

e) Non-Aligned Texts

Many Qumran texts are not exclusively close to either MT, LXX, or SP and are therefore considered non-aligned, that is, they agree, sometimes with MT against the other texts and sometimes with the SP and/or LXX against the other texts. They furthermore contain readings not known from other texts, so that they are not exclusively close to one of the other texts or groups. Usually the employment of the term *non-aligned* merely implies that the texts under consideration follow an inconsistent pattern of agreements and disagreements with MT, LXX and SP, e.g., 4QGen[k], 2QExod[a], 4QExod[b], 4QExod[e?], 4QExod-Lev[f], 11QpaleoLev[a], 4QDeut[b,c,h,k1,k2,m], 5QDeut, 4QSam[c], 6QpapKings, 1QIsa[a], 4QIsa[c], 4QIsa[k?], 2QJer, 4QEzek[a], 4QXII[a,c,d?,e,g], 4QPs[l?], 4QQoh[a], 4QDan[a,b[?],c[?],d[?]], 6QCant, 4QLam, 6QpapDan and 4QChron[?]. But the texts which are most manifestly non-aligned, and actually independent, are texts which contain (groups of) readings that diverge significantly from the other texts, such as 4QJosh[a] and 4QJudg[a]. 4QSam[a] holds a special position in this regard, since it is closely related to the *Vorlage* of LXX, while reflecting independent features as well. A special sub-group of non-aligned texts are scrolls written for a specific purpose, especially 'liturgical' or 'excerpted' texts, such as 4QExod[d], 4QDeut[j,n], most Psalm texts from caves 4 and 11 (4QPs[a,b,d,e,f,,k,n,q,x], 11QPs[a,b,c,d]), and 4QCant[a,b]. These fifty-seven texts comprise thirty-seven percent of the Qumran biblical texts in the Torah (seventeen texts) and fifty-three percent in the other books (forty texts). However, if the Qumran Psalters, which are not regular biblical texts, are excluded from the statistics, the number of independent texts would be smaller.

Whether we assume that all the aforementioned texts were written at Qumran or that only some were written there, while others were brought from elsewhere, the coexistence of the different categories of texts in the Qumran caves is noteworthy. The fact that all these different texts were found in the same caves probably reflects textual plurality for the period between the third century BCE and the first century CE. Within that textual plurality the large number of proto-Masoretic texts probably indicates their importance, while the large number of independent texts underline the special condition of the transmission of the biblical text. Since there is no evidence concerning the circumstances of the depositing of the scrolls in the caves or concerning their possibly different status within the Qumran sect, no solid conclusions can be drawn about the approach of the Qumranites towards the biblical text, but it is safe to say that they paid no special attention to textual differences such as those described here.

That all these different groups of texts coexisted in Qumran, and in Palestine as a whole, shows that no fixed text or textual family had been accepted as the central text for the country as a whole. That conclusion may, however, be misleading, since in certain milieus in Palestine one of the texts or textual families could still have been the only accepted text. This, we believe, was the case for the Masoretic family which probably was the only acceptable text in Temple circles and therefore very influential elsewhere.[76] In a way this text should be considered a preferred text, and this assumption would explain the large number of copies of this text found at Qumran and its exclusive presence in Masada, as well in the later finds from Wadi Sdeir (= Naḥal David), Naḥal Ḥever, Wadi Murabbaʿat, Naḥal Ṣeʾelim. The sociological data known about Masada fits into this picture since the community which lived there would have adhered to the rabbinic text. This assumption also applies to the other sites, reflecting a reality from the time of the Second Jewish Revolt (135 CE).

If the recognition of the aforementioned five groups of texts is correct, by definition some of the textual theories which have been suggested in the last century cannot be maintained, especially because of our fifth group, which is composed of texts not connected with MT, LXX, or SP. The existence of this group allows for an endless number of individual texts, thus eliminating the possibility that all the Qumran texts, and in fact all ancient Hebrew texts, ultimately derived from a tripartite division of the textual sources. Elsewhere we have tried to refute that view,[77] claiming that the textual sources of the Bible cannot be reduced to three traditions and that these textual traditions are no recensions or text types, but that they are simply 'texts'. It should however be conceded that my own view, like all other views, is based on certain suppositions; it is equally subjective, and like other views, cannot be proven. The texts themselves should remain our point of departure, but a study by Davila on Genesis and Exodus shows how difficult it is to find mutually acceptable criteria.[78] In the wake of others before him, Davila takes as his point of departure that within these books, the MT and SP traditions represent different text types, rather than texts, and he suggests that they, together with the Qumran texts, belong to the same text type, and that LXX reflects a different text type.[79] Most of the Qumran texts of Genesis and Exodus examined by Davila are indeed close to MT, but the material is simply too fragmentary to prove that the Qumran texts together with MT and SP comprise one textual entity and that this entity is a text type. Had the fragments been more extensive, we would probably have been able to recognize the proximity between some Qumran fragments and SP. For example, one of the rewritten Bible texts, 4QRP[b] (4Q364), reflects significant harmonizing additions in Genesis and Exodus, and if the biblical text upon which this text is based had been found, the statistical picture for these two books would have been different.

The status of the Greek manuscripts from the Judaean Desert runs parallel to that of the Hebrew manuscripts. The Hebrew manuscripts from Qumran reflect a variety of textual forms, among them proto-Masoretic texts, while those of the later sites of Naḥal Ḥever, Wadi Sdeir, Murabbaʿat, and Naḥal Ṣeʾelim (as well as the earlier site of Masada) exclusively reflect the proto-Masoretic texts (also named proto-rabbinic texts) later to be contained in MT (to be precise, the texts from the sites other than Qumran are closer to the medieval text than the Qumran proto-Masoretic texts). Similarly, at least some of the Greek Torah texts from Qumran probably reflect an earlier form of Greek Scripture, while 8ḤevXII gr reflects a later Jewish revision toward MT deriving from proto-rabbinic Jewish circles. Both the Hebrew and Greek texts from Qumran thus reflect a community which practised openness at the textual level, without being tied down to MT, while the other sites represent Jewish nationalistic circles which adhered only to the proto-rabbinic (proto-Masoretic) text in Hebrew and the Jewish revisions of the Septuagint towards that Hebrew text. As a result, the differences between the texts and sites is probably due primarily to their different socio-religious background, while their different chronological background (late date of some texts found in sites other than Qumran) is also partly responsible for this situation.

APPENDIX

The theory of de luxe scrolls above is based on the data included in this Appendix.

1. A large de luxe editions format was used especially for biblical scrolls (see list below), though also for some non-biblical texts. Some manuscripts are of better quality than others with regard to their contents (precision in copying) and external shape (regularity of the ruling, quality of the leather, aesthetics of the layout, and adherence to a neat column structure), e.g. 1QM, 1QIsa[b], 11QPs[a], 11QT[a] (11Q19), 11QT[b] (11Q20), MasEzek, MasPs[a]. It seems, however, that the use of large top and bottom margins is a major criterion for establishing that a manuscript was meant as a de luxe edition, together with fine writing, the proto-rabbinic text form, and the paucity of scribal intervention. MasPs[a] probably serves as the best sample of such a choice text.

The following table presents *all* the texts from the Judaean Desert with large-size top and bottom margins (beyond 3.0 cm). The purpose of the table is to establish that these parameters were used especially for de luxe editions of biblical texts. For these texts other data is recorded as well (number of lines, height, date, and textual character for the biblical texts). In this table 'r' signifies 'reconstructed'. In other cases ('—') the relevant evidence is lacking. Since top and bottom margins usually measure 1-2 cm in the Qumran texts, margins such as MurNum (7.5 cm), 2QNum[a] (5.7+ cm), 4QDeut[g] (5.7+ cm), and XHev/SeNum[b] (7.2-7.5 cm) are quite unusual.

Biblical texts

Name	Top margin	Bottom margin	Number of lines	Height in cm	Date of MS	Textual character	Number of lines b/n corrections
2QNum[a]	—	5.7+	—	—	c.30 –1 BCE	MT	17+
4QGen[b]	3.2	—	40 r	35 r	c.50 – 68 CE	MT	62
4QExod[c]	4.0-4.4	3.1	c.43r	c.38 r	33–1 BCE	MT	17
4QpaleoGen-Exod[l]	—	4.0	55–60 r	38 r	100–50 BCE	MT +/-	105
4QpaleoExod[m]	3.0-3.5	4.3-4.5	32-33	35+	c.100–25 BCE	pre-Samarit.	197
4QDeut[g]	—	5.7+	—	—	c.1–25 CE	MT	43
4QDeut[k1]	—	3.2+			c.30–1BCE	Q-ortho; independ	12
4QJudg[b]	—	5.3	—	—	c.30–1BCE	MT	8
4QSam[a]	2.2-2.6	2.9-3.1	42-44	30.1 r	c.50–25 BCE	independ	110
4QJer[c]	—	2.5-4.5	18	25.3-26.3	30–1 BCE	MT +/-	25
4QEzek[a]	3.0	—	42 r	29 r	c.50 BCE	MT	50
4QPs[c]	1.5+	3.2+	33	c.26	c.50 –68 CE	MT	52
MurGen[(a)]	5.2	—	46.5 r	c.50 r	c.100–125 CE	MT	23+
MurNum	—	7.5	46.5 r	c.50 r	c.100–125 CE	MT	—
MurXII	2.6-4.0	4.5-5.0	39	35.5		MT	75
XHev/SeNum[b]	—	7.2-7.5	—	44 r	c.50–68 CE	MT	28+
34ṢeNum (34Ṣe 2)	5.0	—	—	—	—	—	—
MasDeut	3.4	—	42	33	50–1BCE	MT	17
MasPs[a]	2.4	3.0	29	25.5	25–1 BCE	MT	74+
XJosh	—	4.0	27	c.24	40 BCE–68 CE	MT	—

Non-biblical texts

Name	Top margin	Bottom margin	Number of lines	Height in cm	Date of MS	Textual character	Number of lines b/n corrections
1QM	2.7-3.5	—	20 or 23–25 r	—	*c.* 25 BCE–25 CE	—	12
1QapGen	2.2-3.1	2.6-3.0	34	30.5	*c.* 25 BCE–50 CE	—	17
4QCommGen C (4Q254)	3.8	—	—	—	25–1 BCE	—	40
4Qcrypt A Lunisolar Cal. (4Q317)	2.9-3.1	22				—	
4QpapHist. Text C (4Q331)	3.0	—	—	—	*c.* 50 BCE	—	—
4QpapRitPur B (4Q512)	3.0	—	—	—	*c.* 100–75 BCE	—	32
4QapocrLevi^b? ar (4Q541)	1.1+	3.0	—	—	*c.* 100 BCE	—	35

The number of biblical texts among the manuscripts with large top and bottom margins is very high. Among this group of twenty-seven texts, twenty (or 71%) are biblical, which implies that the writing in a large format was used especially for the books of the Hebrew Bible.

One might claim that large margins were connected with any large scroll, not necessarily biblical scrolls, as large margins would be aesthetically appropriate for any large writing surface. However, among the Qumran scrolls there are more non-biblical long scrolls than the seven scrolls in the table. In fact, half of the large scrolls are non-biblical. It therefore remains correct to say that the large format of the margins was used especially for the biblical scrolls, and that this format was used to create a de luxe edition as would be fitting for the biblical scrolls.

In most cases, the combined size of the top and bottom margins equals some 20% of the total height of the leather, while in the case of MurXII these margins amount to 25%. These proportions conform with the Herculaneum Greek papyri as described by G. Cavallo.[80]

Greek de luxe editions of literary papyri often have large margins as well, such as the Thucydides papyri P.Oxy. 4103–4112 with margins of 4-8 cm (four texts dating to the second century CE) and various Herculaneum papyri with 5-6 cm (see Cavallo, quoted in n. 17). See further the observations on Greek de luxe papyrus rolls by Turner.[81]

2. In the above examples of de luxe editions, large margins usually go together with a large format of the text. On the other hand, in other large scrolls of 30–50 lines (even 60 lines), no such large margins are found.

3. The great majority of the biblical scrolls written in de luxe format reflect the medieval text of MT, in an exact form in the texts from sites other than Qumran (7), and slightly less so in the texts from Qumran (6), with two scrolls deviating a little more from MT. On the other hand, 4QpaleoExod^m resembles SP, 4QDeut^k1 was written in the Qumran practice, and 4QSam^a was independent. Since the de luxe format was used

Emanuel Tov

mainly for the scrolls of the Masoretic family, we assume that many of them were produced in the spiritual centre of Judaism, the same centre which subsequently was to formulate the rules for writing which have been transmitted in the Talmud and *Massekhet Soferim*.

It is not impossible that these scrolls are the corrected copies mentioned in *b. Pes.* 112a: 'when you teach your son, teach him from a corrected copy (ספר מוגה)'. As this teaching was performed anywhere in ancient Israel, it stands to reason that these precise scrolls had been corrected according to a central document and were then used anywhere, so that the scrolls found in the Judaean Desert could have been of that type.

4. As a rule, de luxe format scrolls are characterized by a limited amount of scribal intervention, expressed in the last column in the table as the number of lines between each instance of scribal intervention (supralinear corrections, deletions, erasures, and reshaping of letters). Much scribal intervention is evidenced, for example, in a scroll like 1QIsa[a] which is far from being a de luxe scroll (one correction in every four lines). One correction per twenty lines or more should probably be considered a low amount of scribal correction, but most scrolls in the table have much fewer corrections: 4QGen[b], 4QpaleoExod[m], 4QDeut[g], 4QJer[c], 4QEzek[a], MurXII (for details see the table). More scribal intervention is evidenced in 4QExod[c] and 4QDeut[kɪ]. Other scrolls of the MT family from Qumran which were not written as de luxe scrolls sometimes have little scribal intervention as well, while scrolls beyond the Masoretic family display more such activity.

The impression created by this data is that we should posit a group of de luxe Bible scrolls, especially among the later scrolls, as indicated by large top and bottom margins, a large number of lines, a proximity to MT, and a low incidence of scribal intervention. In fact, almost all the leather texts from Naḥal Ḥever, Murabbaʿat, and Masada are of this type. At the same time, some de luxe texts are of a different nature, as is shown by 4QpaleoExod[m] and 4QSam[a].

NOTES

1 The present article rewrites my 1995 study published in 1998: Emanuel Tov, 'The Significance of the Texts from the Judaean Desert for the History of the Text of the Hebrew Bible: A New Synthesis', in *QONT*, pp. 277-309. For bibliographical references relating to the published and unpublished documents the reader is referred to Emanuel Tov, 'Texts from the Judean Desert for the History of the Text of the Hebrew Bible', in *The SBL Handbook of Style: For Ancient Near Eastern, Biblical, and Early Christian Studies*, ed. by Patrick H. Alexander and others (Peabody, MA: Hendrickson, 1999), pp. 176-233. I would like to express my thanks to my fellow editor, Edward D. Herbert, for his much appreciated remarks on my paper, and to Steve Delamarter for sharing with me his thoughts on the classification of the Qumran texts.

2 The provenance of the biblical texts is usually rather stable. At the same time, 4QPs[q] may derive from Naḥal Ḥever (see Patrick W. Skehan, Eugene Ulrich and Peter W. Flint, DJD XVI, p. 145). The provenance of XJosh is equally unclear.

3 For earlier summaries of my own, see Emanuel Tov, 'A Modern Textual Outlook Based on the Qumran Scrolls', *HUCA*, 53 (1982), 11-27; Emanuel Tov, 'Hebrew Biblical Manuscripts from the Judaean Desert: Their Contribution to Textual Criticism', *JJS* 39 (1988), 5-37; *TCHB*. For additional summaries, in chronological order, see: Patrick W. Skehan, 'Littérature de Qumran. - A. Textes bibliques' in L. Pirot and A. Robert (eds), *Dictionnaire de la Bible: Supplément,* vol. IX (Paris: Letouzey & Ané, 1979), pp. 805-822; Florentino García Martínez, 'Lista de MSS procedentes de Qumrán', *Henoch*, 11 (1989), 149-232; Eugene Ulrich, 'The Biblical Scrolls from Qumran Cave 4: An Overview and a Progress Report on Their Publication', *RevQ*, 14 (1989), 207-28; Adam S. van der

Woude, 'Fünfzehn Jahre Qumranforschung (1974-1988)', *Theologische Rundschau*, 55 (1990), 245-307 (274-307); 57 (1992), 1-57; George J. Brooke, 'Torah in the Qumran Scrolls', in *Bibel in jüdischer und christlicher Tradition. Festschrift für Johann Maier zum 60. Geburtstag*, ed. by Helmut Merklein and others, Athanäuns Monografien Theologie, 88 (Frankfurt am Main: Hain, 1993), pp. 97-120; Eugene Ulrich, 'The Dead Sea Scrolls and the Biblical Text', in *DSSAFY*, I, pp. 79-100; Eugene Ulrich, 'The Qumran Biblical Scrolls–The Scriptures of Late Second Temple Judaism', in *DSSTHC*, pp. 67-87; Eugene Ulrich, 'The Qumran Scrolls and the Biblical Text', in *The Dead Sea Scrolls: Fifty Years After Their Discovery: Proceedings of the Jerusalem Congress, July 20-25, 1997*, ed. by Lawrence H. Schiffman and others (Jerusalem: IES, 2000), pp. 51-59.

4   Shemaryahu Talmon, 'Hebrew Fragments from Masada', in Shemaryahu Talmon and Yigael Yadin, *Masada VI, The Yigael Yadin Excavations 1963-1965, Final Reports, Hebrew Fragments from Masada* (Jerusalem: IES, 1999), pp. 1-149.

5   E. L. Sukenik (ed.), *The Dead Sea Scrolls of the Hebrew University* (Jerusalem: Magnes Press, 1955).

6   Donald W. Parry and Elisha Qimron, *The Great Isaiah Scroll (1QIsaᵃ): A New Edition*, STDJ, 32 (Leiden: Brill, 1999).

7   D. N. Freedman and K. A. Mathews, with a contribution by Hanson Richards, *The Paleo-Hebrew Leviticus Scroll (11QpaleoLev)* (Winona Lake, IN: ASOR, 1985). Three texts were published elsewhere: 4QGenⁿ (DJD XXV); 4Qpap cryptA Levʰ? (DJD XXXVI); Mur? (Émile Puech, 'Fragment d'un Rouleau de la Genèse provenant du Désert de Juda (Gen 33, 18-34, 3)', *RevQ*, 10 (1980), 163-66).

8   DJD I, II, III, VI, XXXVIII; Yigael Yadin, *Tefillin from Qumran* (Jerusalem: IES and The Shrine of the Book, 1969). Since the same sections are contained in both *tefillin* and *mezuzot*, it is hard to distinguish between the two in fragmentary texts (note especially 4QPhyl S and U and 4QMez G)., the main criterion for the distinction being their physical features (see J. T. Milik, DJD VI, pp. 35-37).

9   See Emanuel Tov, 'Excerpted and Abbreviated Biblical Texts from Qumran', *RevQ*, 16 (1995), 581-600.

10   Two aspects remain problematical:

    a)   Some of the very fragmentary texts which have been named biblical may actually have been part of compositions which included among other things long stretches of Bible texts, such as pesharim and other commentaries, or paraphrases such as 4QReworked Pentateuch (4QRPᵃ⁻ᵉ). For example, the text which has been published as 4QpapIsaᵖ (4Q69) contains only a few words, and could therefore also have represented a pesher like 4Qpap pIsaᶜ. By the same token, the list includes a minute fragment inscribed in the cryptic A script, described by Stephen J. Pfann (DJD XXXVI) as a fragment of the book of Leviticus: (pap cryptA Levʰ?), but more likely it reflects only a quotation from that book. Likewise, the 'biblical' 2QExodᵇ may actually contain a rewritten Bible text.

    b)   The manuscripts entitled 4QReworked Pentateuchᵃ⁻ᵉ (4QRPᵃ⁻ᵉ [4Q158, 4Q364-367]) are not included in the list of biblical texts because they were not published as such. However, according to two scholars these compositions represent an aberrant biblical text which may be named 4QPentateuch, in which case it ought to be included in the list of biblical manuscripts. See Michael Segal, 'Biblical Exegesis in 4Q158: Techniques and Genre', *Textus*, 19 (1998), 45-62; Eugene Ulrich, 'The Qumran Biblical Scrolls', esp. p. 76.

11   1QIsaᵃ, 4QGenᵇ, 4QGenᵍ, 4QGenᵏ, 4QLevᶜ, 4QDeutʰ, 4QIsaᵃ, 4QIsaᵇ, 4QIsaʲ, 4QXIIᵈ, 4QRuthᵃ, 4QRuthᵇ, 5QKgs, 6QDeut? (6Q20), 6QCant, MurIsa, XJosh.

12   DJD XV, p. 216.

13   It was suggested by Stephen Pfann and Eugene Ulrich that small spaces in 4QDanᵃ,ᵈ represent such a verse division: see Stephen Pfann, 'The Aramaic Text and Language of Daniel and Ezra in the Light of Some Manuscripts from Qumran', *Textus*, 16 (1991), 127-37 (136); Stephen J. Pfann, '4QDanielᵈ (4Q115): a Preliminary Edition with Critical Notes', *RevQ*, 17 (1996), 37-71 (pp. 49-52); E. Ulrich, DJD XVI, p. 225. However, the evidence for 4QDanᵈ (after Daniel 3:25; 4:6, 13; 7:19) is insufficient and may well refer to section indications. 4QDanᵃ has spaces after some verses (2:20, 25, 27, 29, 30, 32 [?], 34, 49; 5:17), but these spaces could also indicate small section divisions, like in 4QEnᵃ ar (4Q201) and 1QIsaᵇ where the different size of the spaces probably indicates different degrees of subdivision. Besides, such spaces are not indicated after other verses in 4QDanᵃ (2:35, 43; 8:3, 5, 27; 10:19, 20).

14   The scribe of 4QGenᵍ left an interval of eight letter-spaces between the first and the second word of Genesis 1:5 because of an uneven surface. The scribe of 4QDeutⁿ avoided writing on many lines (col.

III, line 9 and col. IV, lines 1-4, 7-8; the empty line 5 in col. I was probably uninscribed for the same reason). The intervals in col. IV, lines 1, 7-8 could have been intentional, but those in III, line 9 and IV, 2-4 are not. Besides, the leather shows bad surface in all these lines. The scribe of 11QpaleoLevᵃ avoided writing in frg. H, 6 and col. 3, line 6.

15 4QGenᵍ was stitched in the middle of the text before Genesis 1:20 prior to the writing. Several tears in 1QIsaᵃ were stitched before the writing (for example, col. XVII, line 4 from bottom) or after the parchment was inscribed (for example, cols XVI and XII, in the latter case with stitches in the full height of the column). Tears in 4QJerᶜ were stitched both before the writing (cols. IV, XXI and XXIII) and afterwards (for example, col. XXIII). It is hard to know when the stitches in col. XVI were inserted. Note also stitches in the bottom margins of 4QCantᵇ frg. 1 and of 4QLevᶜ frg. 5 (with the preservation of parts of the threads). The two fragments of 4QPsᵏ were stitched together in antiquity by way of repair.

16 Some examples are listed by Malachi Martin, *The Scribal Character of the Dead Sea Scrolls*, 2 vols, Bibliothèque du Muséon, 44 and 45 (Louvain: Publications Universitaires, 1958), II, p. 424, but it is difficult to evaluate their validity.

17 Saul Lieberman, *Hellenism in Jewish Palestine*, 2nd edn, Texts and Studies of the Jewish Theological Seminary of America, 18 (New York: Jewish Theological Seminary of America, 1962), pp. 20-27.

18 For the publication and an analysis, see Talmon, *Masada VI*. For my own analysis, see Emanuel Tov, 'A Qumran Origin for the Masada Non-biblical Texts?', *DSD*, 7 (2000), 57-73.

19 For the first three sites, see the texts published by Peter W. Flint, Matthew Morgenstern, and Catherine Murphy in DJD XXXVIII. For the last site, see the texts published by J. T. Milik in DJD II.

20 As a result, Barthélemy considers MurXII a characteristic sample of the textual standardization which took place between the two revolts and which is therefore more properly proto-Masoretic, so to speak, than the earlier Qumran texts of the Minor Prophets and of other books: Dominique Barthélemy, *Critique textuelle de l'Ancien Testament*, OBO, 50, 3 vols (Fribourg: Universitaires; Göttingen: Vandenhoeck & Ruprecht, 1992), III, p. cxiii.

21 E. L. Greenstein, 'Misquotation of Scripture in the Dead Sea Scrolls', in *The Frank Talmage Memorial Volume*, ed. by Barry Walfish (Haifa: Haifa University Press, 1993), pp. 71-83. A similar theory had been advanced previously for 1QIsaᵃ by Harry M. Orlinsky, 'Studies in the St. Mark's Isaiah Scroll', *JBL*, 69 (1950), 149-66 (p. 165).

22 Excerpted and abbreviated biblical manuscripts, analyzed below as a subgroup of biblical manuscripts, are not included in this group.

23 M. H. Gottstein, 'Bible Quotations in the Sectarian Dead Sea Scrolls', *VT*, 3 (1953), 79-82; Jean Carmignac, 'Les citations de l'Ancien Testament dans "La Guerre des Fils de Lumière contre les Fils de Ténèbres"', *RB*, 63 (1956), 234-60, 375-90; Menahem Mansoor, 'The Thanksgiving Hymns and the Massoretic Text (Part II)', *RevQ*, 3 (1961), 387-94; J. de Waard, *A Comparative Study of the Old Testament in the Dead Sea Scrolls and in the New Testament*, STDJ, 4 (Leiden: Brill, 1965); Geza Vermes, 'Biblical Proof Texts in Qumran Literature', *JSS*, 34 (1989), 493-508; Jonathan G. Campbell, *The Use of Scripture in the Damascus Document 1-8, 19-20*, BZAW, 228 (Berlin: de Gruyter, 1995); John Elwolde, 'Distinguishing the Linguistic and the Exegetical: The Biblical Book of Numbers in the Damascus Document', *DSD*, 7 (2000), 1-25.

24 The relevant instances have been discussed in scattered analyses, and also in a monograph by Ilana Goldberg, 'Variant Readings in Pesher Habakkuk', *Textus*, 17 (1994), ‏ס-כד‎ (Heb.).

25 *Biblia Hebraica Quinta*, in preparation.

26 See Moshe H. Goshen-Gottstein (ed.), *The Hebrew University Bible: The Book of Isaiah* (Jerusalem: Magnes Press, 1995).

27 E.g., Georg Molin, 'Der Habakukkommentar von 'En Fešḥa in der alttestamentlichen Wissenschaft', *Theologische Zeitschrift*, 8 (1952), 340-57; George J. Brooke, 'The Biblical Texts in the Qumran Commentaries: Scribal Errors or Exegetical Variants?' in *Early Jewish and Christian Exegesis: Studies in Memory of William Hugh Brownlee*, ed. by Craig A. Evans and William F. Stinespring (Atlanta, 1987), pp. 85-100 with references to earlier studies. Brooke argues, p. 87: '... in more cases than are usually recognized the variants in the biblical texts in the Qumran commentaries have been deliberately caused by the desire of the Qumran commentator to make this text conform with his exegetical understanding.'

28 The most clear-cut examples are 1QpHab VIII 3 (Habakkuk 2:5) הון (MT: הוין); 1QpHab XI 3
(Habakkuk 2:15) מועדיהם (MT: מעוריהם). For an analysis of these readings, see William H. Brownlee,
The Text of Habakkuk in the Ancient Commentary from Qumran, JBL Monograph Series, 11
(Philadelphia: Society of Biblical Literature and Exegesis, 1959), pp. 113-18.

29 Timothy H. Lim, *Holy Scripture in the Qumran Commentaries and Pauline Letters* (Oxford:
Clarendon Press, 1997), chapter IV.

30 J. van der Ploeg, 'Le Rouleau d'Habacuc de la grotte de 'Ain Feshḫa', *BO,* 8 (1951), 2-11 (p. 4) Karl
Elliger, *Studien zum Habakuk-Kommentar vom Toten Meer*, Beiträge zur historischen Theologie, 15
(Tübingen: Mohr-Siebeck, 1953), p. 48; P. Kahle in a review of Elliger in *TLZ,* 79 (1954), 478-79
(p. 479); S. Segert, 'Zur Habakuk-Rolle aus dem Funde vom Toten Meer VI', *Archiv Orientální,* 23
(1955), 575-619 (p. 608). These scholars probably go too far when describing the biblical quotations
in the pesharim as reflecting a distinct textual recension deviating from the other textual sources. A
similar conclusion was reached by M. Collin, mainly on the basis of an analysis of 1QpMic, which
was characterized by him as reflecting a third recension of the biblical book, alongside MT and LXX:
Matthieu Collin, 'Recherches sur l'histoire textuelle du prophète Michée', *VT,* 21 (1971), 281-97.
This characterization was rejected by Lawrence A. Sinclair, 'Hebrew Text of the Qumran Micah
Pesher and Textual Traditions of the Minor Prophets', *RevQ,* 11 (1983), 253-63.

31 For a discussion of why many scholars name 'vulgar texts', see *TCHB,* pp. 193-97.

32 See Emanuel Tov and Sidnie White: '4QReworked Pentateuch[b-e]', in DJD XIII, pp. 187-352.

33 See Emanuel Tov, 'The Textual Status of 4Q364-367 (4QPP)', in *MQC,* pp. 43-82. On the other
hand, if these manuscripts are considered an aberrant biblical manuscript (see above n. 2), they need
not be analyzed in the present context.

34 For an analysis see James C. VanderKam, *Textual and Historical Studies in the Book of Jubilees,*
HSM, 14 (Missoula, MT: Scholars Press, 1977).

35 See Emanuel Tov, 'The "Temple Scroll" and Old Testament Textual Criticism', Hebrew with English
summary, *ErIsr,* 16 (Archaeological, Historical and Geographical Studies [Harry M. Orlinsky
Volume]), 100-111.

36 See the discussion of the quotation from Deuteronomy 33:8-11 in 4QTest below. See further the
examples listed by Tov, 'Hebrew Biblical Manuscripts', p. 34. G. Vermes, 'Biblical Proof Texts'
mentions a few cases of difference between MT and the text quoted in Qumran compositions, e.g. cf.
1QS V, line 17 לכם agreeing with MT Isaiah 2:22 differing from לכמה in 1QIsa[a]; cf. also הואה with הוא
in 1QIsa[a].

37 See especially Hartmut Stegemann, 'Weitere Stücke von 4 Q p Psalm 37, von 4 Q Patriarchal Blessings
und Hinweis auf eine unedierte Handschrift aus Höhle 4 Q mit Exzerpten aus dem Deuteronomium',
RevQ, 6 (1967), 193-227 (217-27); Brooke, 'Torah in the Qumran Scrolls'.

38 Tov, 'Excerpted and Abbreviated Biblical Texts'.

39 The background of the scrolls containing merely Deuteronomy 32 (4QDeut[q]) and Psalm 119 (4QPs[g,h]
and 5QPs) is unclear.

40 4QExod[e] (Exodus 13:3-5); 4QDeut[j] (Exodus 12:43ff.; 13:1-5 and fragments of Deuteronomy 5, 6, 8,
11, 30 [?], 32); 4QDeut[k] (Deuteronomy 5, 11, and 32); 4QDeut[n] (Deut 8:5-10; 5:1-6:1).

41 For details, see Peter W. Flint, 'The Psalms Scrolls from the Judaean Desert: Relationships and Textual
Affiliations', in *NQTS,* pp. 31-52.

42 For both texts, see Tov, 'Excerpted and Abbreviated Biblical Texts', and Emanuel Tov, 'Three
Manuscripts (Abbreviated Texts?) of Canticles from Qumran Cave 4', *JJS,* 46 (1995), 88-111. The
texts have been published in DJD XVI.

43 See Esther Eshel, '4QDeut[n]—A Text That Has Undergone Harmonistic Editing', *HUCA,* 62 (1991),
117-54.

44 See Emanuel Tov, 'The Contribution of the Qumran Scrolls to the Understanding of the LXX', in
SSCW, pp. 11-47 (pp. 31-35); Julie A. Duncan, 'New Readings for the "Blessing of Moses" from
Qumran', *JBL,* 114 (1995), 273-90.

45 For an analysis, see Tov, 'Excerpted and Abbreviated Biblical Texts'.

46 In the past the number of the biblical texts has changed with new insights into the nature of the
fragments, in particular due to the separation of groups of fragments. Thus, Patrick W. Skehan listed
172 different scrolls in 1965: 'The Biblical Scrolls from Qumran and the Text of the Old Testament',

BA, 28 (1965), 87-100. Subsequently, the first edition of the *Companion Volume* (1993) to the Microfiche edition (see n. 1) listed 189 biblical texts, slightly more than a decade ago. The list in Emanuel Tov and Stephen J. Pfann (eds), *The Dead Sea Scrolls on Microfiche: A Comprehensive Facsimile Edition of the Texts from the Judean Desert* (Leiden: Brill and IDC, 1993) includes the following figures for biblical Hebrew/Aramaic texts: Cave 1: 15; Cave 2: 17; Cave 3: 3; Cave 4: 129; Cave 5: 7; Cave 6: 7; Cave 8: 2; Cave 11: 9. In the second edition of this *Companion Volume to the Dead Sea Scrolls Microfiche Edition* (Leiden: Brill and IDC, 1995) four items were added. The contents of the different fragments of biblical texts have been listed by several scholars: Uwe Glessmer, 'Liste der biblischen Texte aus Qumran', *RevQ*, 16 (1993), 153-92; Harold Scanlin, *The Dead Sea Scrolls and Modern Translations of the Old Testament* (Wheaton, IL: Tyndale House, 1993); Eugene Ulrich, 'An Index of the Passages in the Biblical Manuscripts from the Judaean Desert (Genesis–Kings)', *DSD*, 1 (1994), 113-29; Eugene Ulrich, 'An Index of the Passages in the Biblical Manuscripts From the Judean Desert (Part 2: Isaiah–Chronicles)', *DSD*, 2 (1995), 86-107.

47   See J. Carswell, 'Fastenings on the Qumran Manuscripts', in DJD VI, pp. 23-28 (p. 24).

48   The absence of this book should probably be ascribed to coincidence (decaying of the material) rather than to any other factor.

49   See Emanuel Tov, 'Scribal Practices Reflected in the Paleo-Hebrew Texts from the Judaean Desert', *Scripta Classica Israelica*, 15 (Studies in Memory of Abraham Wasserstein, vol. I, 1996), 268-73; Emanuel Tov, 'The Socio-Religious Background of the Paleo-Hebrew Biblical Texts Found at Qumran', in *Geschichte – Tradition – Reflexion, Festschrift für Martin Hengel zum 70. Geburtstag*, ed. by Hubert Cancik, Hermann Lichtenberger and Peter Schäfer, 2 vols (Tübingen: Mohr-Siebeck, 1996), I, 353-74.

50   See Mark D. McLean, *The Use and Development of Paleo-Hebrew in the Hellenistic and Roman Periods* (unpublished doctoral thesis, Harvard University, 1982), pp. 41-47; DJD IX.

51   Talmon, *Masada VI*, pp. 138-47.

52   See Richard S. Hanson, 'Paleo-Hebrew Scripts in the Hasmonean Age', *BASOR*, 175 (1964), 26-42.

53   Thus K. A. Mathews: 'The Background of the Paleo-Hebrew Texts at Qumran', in *The Word of the Lord Shall Go Forth: Essays in Honor of David Noel Freedman in Celebration of His Sixtieth Birthday*, ed. by Carol L. Meyers and M. O'Connor, ASOR Special Volume Series, 1 (Winona Lake, IN: Eisenbrauns, 1983), pp. 549-68.

54   Thus Ulrich, 'The Palaeo-Hebrew Biblical Manuscripts', p. 128.

55   See *m. Yad.* 4.5; *b. Sanh.* 21b; and cf. *b. Meg.* 9a; *t. Sanh.* 5.7; *y. Meg.* 1.71b-c. For details, see Tov, 'Socio-Religious Background'.

56   For recent discussions, see Eugene Ulrich, 'Pluriformity in the Biblical Text, Text Groups, and Questions of Canon', *MQC*, I, p. 23-41; Ulrich, 'Dead Sea Scrolls and the Biblical Text'.

57   The only clearly recognizable sectarian readings in biblical manuscripts which exclusively reflect the views of one of the religious groups in ancient Israel are of Samaritan background. On the other hand, although many of the Qumran biblical manuscripts were presumably copied by the Qumran scribes (see below), they do not contain readings which reflect the views of the Qumran Covenanters (such readings are, however, included in the biblical text quoted and expounded in 1QpHab and possibly in other pesharim as well). According to I. L. Seeligmann, a further exception should be made for Isaiah 53:11 in 1QIsa[a] and LXX, see 'Δεῖξαι αὐτῷ φῶς', *Tarbiz*, 27 (1958), 127-41 (Heb. with Eng. summ.).

58   Norman Golb, 'The Problem of Origin and Identification of the Dead Sea Scrolls', *Proc. Am. Phil. Soc.*, 124 (1980), 1-24; Norman Golb, 'Who Hid the Dead Sea Scrolls?' *BA*, 48 (1985), 68-82; idem, 'Khirbet Qumran and the Manuscripts of the Judaean Wilderness: Observations on the Logic of Their Investigation', *JNES*, 49 (1990), 103-114; Norman Golb, *Who Wrote the Dead Sea Scrolls: The Search for the Secret of Qumran* (New York: Scribner, 1995).

59   For earlier analyses, see Tov, *TCHB*, pp. 114-117; Emanuel Tov, 'Groups of Biblical Texts Found at Qumran', in *A Time to Prepare the Way in the Wilderness. Papers on the Qumran Scrolls by Fellows of the Institute for Advanced Studies of the Hebrew University, Jerusalem, 1989-1990*, ed. by Devorah Dimant and Lawrence H. Schiffman, STDJ, 16 (Leiden: Brill, 1995), pp. 85-102.

60   Emanuel Tov, 'The Orthography and Language of the Hebrew Scrolls Found at Qumran and the Origin of These Scrolls', *Textus*, 13 (1986), 31-57; idem, 'Hebrew Biblical Manuscripts' (see n. 2);

TCHB, pp. 108-110; idem, 'Further Evidence for the Existence of a Qumran Scribal School', in *Dead Sea Scrolls: Fifty Years After Their Discovery*, ed. by Schiffman and others, pp. 199-216. See also John Lübbe, 'Certain Implications of the Scribal Process of 4QSam^c', *RevQ*, 14 (1989), 255-65. Cross describes the orthography of these texts as a 'baroque style' and he includes the morphological features under the heading of orthography: Frank Moore Cross, 'Some Notes on a Generation of Qumran Studies', in *MQC*, I, pp. 1-14. See also my reply, Emanuel Tov, 'Some Notes on a Generation of Qumran Studies (by Frank M. Cross): Reply by Emanuel Tov', in *MQC*, I, pp. 15-21.

61 Emanuel Tov, 'Scribal Markings in the Texts from the Judaean Desert', in *Current Research and Technological Developments on the Dead Sea Scrolls: Conference on the Texts from the Judean Desert, Jerusalem, 30 April 1995*, ed. by Donald W. Parry and Stephen D. Ricks, STDJ, 20 (Leiden: 1996), pp. 41-77; Tov, 'Further Evidence'.

62 See my article, Emanuel Tov, 'Scribal Practices Reflected in the Documents from the Judaean Desert and in the Rabbinic Literature: A Comparative Study', in *Texts, Temples, and Traditions: A Tribute to Menaham Haran*, ed. by Michael V. Fox and others (Winona Lake, IN: Eisenbraun, 1996), pp. 383-403.

63 Emanuel Tov, '*Tefillin* of Different Origin from Qumran?' in *A Light for Jacob, Studies in the Bible and the Dead Sea Scrolls in Memory of Jacob Shalom Licht*, ed. by Yair Hoffman and Frank H. Polak, (Jerusalem: University of Tel Aviv, Bialik Institute, 1997), pp. 44*-54*.

64 Sound evidence for the Qumran practice exists with regard to the following texts: 1QDeut^a, 1QIsa^a, 2QExod$^{a,b[?]}$, 2QNum^b[?], 2QDeut^c, 2QJer, 3QLam, 4QNum^b, 4QExod^b, 4QDeut^{h,j,k1,k2,m}, 4QSam^c, 4QIsa^c, 4QXII^{c,e,g}, 4QPs^f, 4QLam, 4QQoh^a, 11QLev^b (?), 4QPhyl A,B,G-I,J-K,L-N,O,P,Q. To this group also belong *all* the sectarian compositions written by the Qumran Covenanters (such as 1QH^{a,b}, 1QM, 1QS, and the pesharim) and the following biblical paraphrases and collections of Psalms: 4Q158, 4Q364, 4Q365 (all three containing 4QRP), 4QPs^o, 11QPs$^{a,b,c,d(?)}$. Although there is no characteristic representative of this group, 1QIsa^a, which contains the longest Qumran text of a biblical book, is often referred to (incorrectly) as if it were the main text written in the Qumran practice.

65 This feature is illustrated in *TCHB*, pp. 110-11. See further two brief studies by Arie Rubinstein illustrating the same point: 'Notes on the Use of the Tenses in the Variant Readings of the Isaiah Scroll', *VT*, 3 (1953), 92-95; 'Formal Agreement of parallel Clauses in the Isaiah Scroll', *VT*, 4 (1954), 316-21. In his 1953 article, Rubenstein exemplifies the simplification of the tense system and, in his 1954 article, the adaptation of small grammatical elements in 1QIsa^a to the parallel stich.

66 For the use of the term and the conception behind it, see Cross, 'Some Notes'.

67 The Qumran proto-Masoretic group ought to be investigated also with regard to possible clusters within this group regarding spelling and content, but because of the paucity of overlapping Qumran texts, this investigation has to be very limited. A possible clustering of 1QIsa^{a,b} and 4QIsa^{c,d} (of which 1QIsa^a and 4QIsa^c reflect the Qumran orthography), against the medieval text, is visible. Such clusters, if detected, could show how MT has developed since the Qumran period. It should thus be possible to pinpoint readings in which the medieval text reflects a later development.

68 This calculation is based on the statistical probability that most of the texts which are equally close to MT and SP and equally close to MT and LXX should be counted as MT texts.

69 Eshel, '4QDeut^n'.

70 Oral communication.

71 The statistics include only the pre-Samaritan texts which are exclusively close to the SP. Qumran texts which are equally close to both SP and MT are counted with MT (group *b*).

72 See the discussion in *TCHB*, pp. 319-27.

73 For an analysis, see Tov, 'The Contribution of the Qumran Scrolls'.

74 For an analysis, see Tov, 'The Contribution of the Qumran Scrolls'.

75 In Isaiah MT and LXX are fairly close to each other, so that most of the extant Qumran Isaiah texts from cave 4 are equally close to MT and LXX. These numbers (6) are not included in the statistics for LXX.

76 For details, see *TCHB*, pp. 32-33.

77 *TCHB*, pp. 155-60.

78 James R. Davila, 'Text-Type and Terminology: Genesis and Exodus as Test Cases', *RevQ*, 16 (1993), 3-37.

79 In our view, however, the MT and SP of Genesis and Exodus differ sufficiently in order to be considered different texts, often recensionally different. LXX reflects yet a third text, again often recensionally different, especially in the genealogies and in Genesis 31. But this evidence does not suffice to prove either our theory nor the views of Davila (reiterating those of others before him).

80 Guglielmo Cavallo, *Libri scritture scribi a Ercolano: Introduzione allo studio dei materiali greci*, Cronache Ercolanesi Supplemento, 1 ([Naples]: Macchiaroli, 1983), pp. 18, 48.

81 E. G. Turner, *Greek Manuscripts of the Ancient World*, 2nd edn, revised and enlarged by P. J. Parsons; Institute of Classical Studies, Bulletin Supplement, 46 (London: University of London, Institute of Classical Studies, 1987), p. 7.

1. Large Isaiah Scroll (1QIsaᵃ), col XLIII (Isa 51:13–52:12). Qumran, *c.* 125–100 BCE. Israel Museum, Jerusalem

2. Manual of Discipline (1QS), cols IV–V. Qumran, 1st century CE (IM photo 7105). Israel Museum, Jerusalem

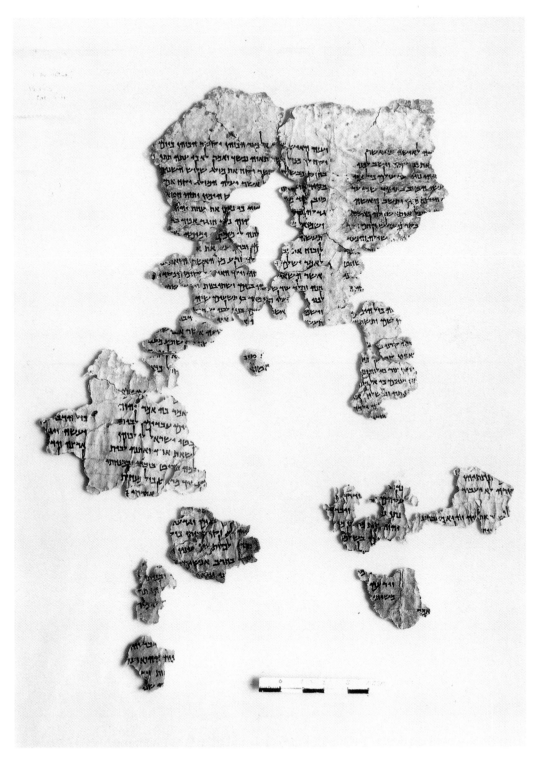

3. 4QSamuelᵃ, cols II–III. Qumran, *c.* 25–50 BCE (PAM photograph 43.122).
Israel Antiquities Authority

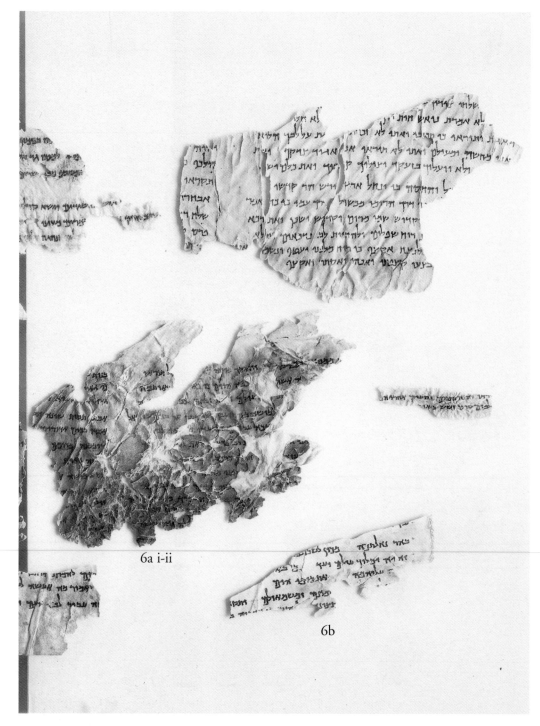

6a i–ii

6b

4. 4QReworked Pentateuch^c (4Q365), frgs 6a i–ii and 6b (PAM photograph 43.373). Israel
Antiquities Authority

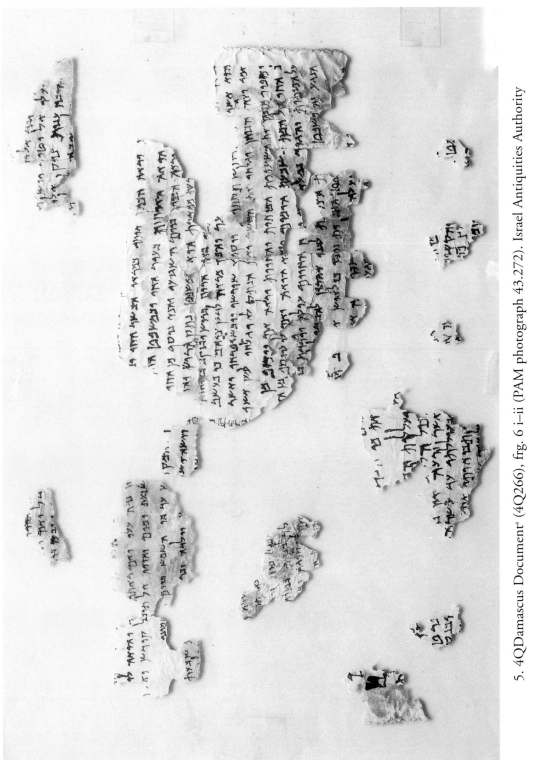

5. 4QDamascus Document[a] (4Q266), frg. 6 i–ii (PAM photograph 43.272). Israel Antiquities Authority

Column II, lines 24–29

Column III, lines 1–8

6. 4QEnoch[b] ar (4Q202, PAM photograph 43.203), col II, lines 24–29 and col III, lines 1–8.
Israel Antiquities Authority

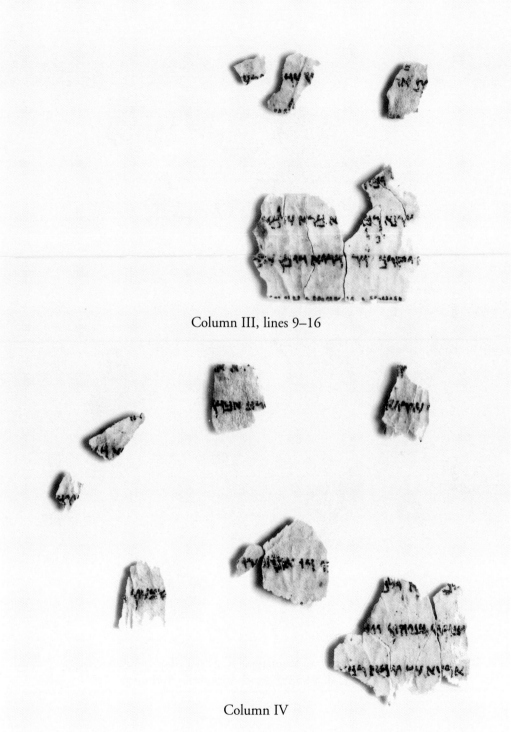

Column III, lines 9–16

Column IV

7. 4QEnochᵇ ar (4Q202, PAM photograph 43.203), col III, lines 9–16 and col IV.
Israel Antiquities Authority

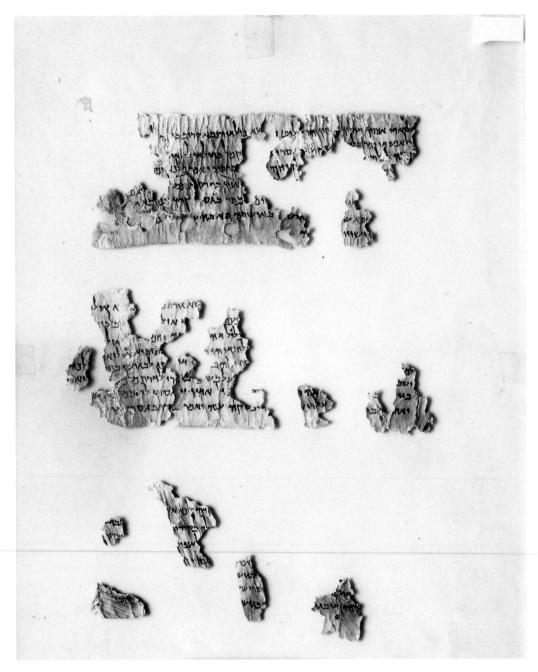

8. 4QTales of the Persian Court[a-e] ar *also* named 4QprotoEsther[a-e] (4Q550, 4Q550[a-e]; PAM photograph 43.585). Israel Antiquities Authority

THE TEXTUAL CRITICISM
OF THE HEBREW BIBLE
BEFORE AND AFTER
THE QUMRAN DISCOVERIES

Arie van der Kooij

1. INTRODUCTION

THIS PAPER EXPLORES the textual criticism of the Hebrew Bible, the Old Testament, before and after the Qumran discoveries.[1] Since it is not possible in the brief confines of this paper to give a detailed picture of the way textual criticism has been practiced before and after Qumran, I will only highlight key issues which characterize these periods.

2. BEFORE QUMRAN

In the course of the sixteenth and seventeenth centuries, scholars realized that the Hebrew text, such as it was attested in the editions of the time (*Biblia Rabbinica*), was not the only text of the Hebrew Bible.[2] Study of the Samaritan Pentateuch and of the Septuagint (LXX) led to a great deal of textual comparison. From this it became clear that there are variant readings which required evaluation. The same realization prompted B. Kennicott and G. B. de Rossi in the eighteenth century to publish the many variant readings extant in a range of medieval manuscripts. The reliability of the Masoretic Hebrew text (MT) could not longer be taken for granted.

2.1. LECTIO FACILIOR OR DIFFICILIOR

The first issue I would like to mention concerns the evaluation of the textual evidence. Opinions have differed from the outset. Scholars like L. Cappellus were of the opinion that, as a rule, the *lectio facilior* was to be regarded as superior (*potior*); whilst others, including his colleague J. Buxtorf, Jr., opposed this view.[3] Similarly in the eighteenth century, C. F. Houbigant, who was rather critical of the Hebrew text, shared the view of Cappellus,[4] and he was criticized by Semitist scholars such as E. F. C. Rosenmüller.[5]

In the nineteenth century, O. Thenius argued that the rule of *lectio difficilior potior* should be limited to the poetical parts of the Bible. For the prose sections, however, such as the historical books like Samuel, one should prefer the other rule, *lectio facilior potior*, because, as he argued, 'die hebr. Erzählungsweise eine durchaus *schlichte* und völlig *natürliche* ist'.[6]

The critical view concerning MT Samuel was shared by J. Wellhausen. To explain why the text contains so many errors and omissions, he argued that there must have been a period in the early days 'wo man von streng philologischer Treue und gar von mechanischer Pedanterie gar keinen Begriff hatte, vielmehr gar oft in ungenierter Naivetät den Buchstaben dem Sinne opferte'.[7] In his view, one should not explain all incorrect readings as mechanical errors, since some of them had resulted from the attempt by ancient readers and writers to produce a text which would make sense: 'Von jeher hat sich [...] bei den die israel. Profangeschichte behandelden Büchern die Auslegung des Textes in die Überlieferung desselben gemischt und der letzteren einen schwankenden fliessenden Character gegeben'.[8]

Generally speaking, one may say that, particularly since the second half of the nineteenth century, a rather critical attitude had arisen towards the quality of the MT. The MT was considered to represent a text that has been transmitted rather carelessly at several places, with many readings viewed as having arisen from mechanical errors.[9]

In the first half of the twentieth century, this view of the MT was criticized by scholars such as H. S. Nyberg and P. A. H. de Boer.[10] As in the debates of the previous centuries, the issue at stake was basically the evaluation of the MT from a philological point of view. It was argued that one should not emend the MT too easily, because the fact that we as modern scholars consider readings (words, expressions, syntactical constructions, or stylistic elements) to be incorrect or examples of bad Hebrew might be due, among other things, to an insufficient knowledge of Classical Hebrew. Thus, for the books of Samuel, de Boer did not argue on the basis of the rule *lectio facilior potior*, which was adhered to by Thenius. A 'smooth' and 'harmonized' text was considered by him to be secondary; instead, he preferred the alternative rule, *lectio difficilior potior*.

2.2. SCOPE OF TEXTUAL CRITICISM

Textual criticism started with textual comparison based on the available evidence, but later on, particularly since the nineteenth century, it was extended to cases where the text was considered to be difficult and where no variants were attested. The picture that emerges from commentaries and from the editions of *Biblia Hebraica* (edited by R. Kittel *BHK*1 [1905-1906], 2 [1912], 3 [1937]), is that of numerous 'problems' in the MT, including morphological, syntactical, matters of style (e.g., *metri causa*), and literary critical issues (e.g., glosses). In a large number of instances, these difficulties in the MT were viewed as being due to scribal errors. Of course, the proposals made and the text critical decisions taken often differed from scholar to scholar. It is interesting to note that, generally speaking, grammarians of the time, like W. Gesenius, F. Böttcher, and E. König, were less inclined to state that something was 'incorrect' Hebrew.

2.3. ATTENTION TO CONTEXT

For the most part, in the period under review there was a strong tendency, especially by exegetes, to do textual criticism on an *ad hoc* basis as far as the ancient versions were concerned; most cases are dealt with on a word level, with no attention given to the immediate context in those ancient witnesses involved. Although there were exceptions to this (e.g., W. Gesenius (Isaiah), S. R. Driver (Samuel),[11] and volumes in the International Critical Commentary series), the study of the ancient versions was not yet well advanced, and the main interest was with the Hebrew text; that is to say, readings in the ancient witnesses were only used for the purpose of establishing a better Hebrew text.

2.4. AIM OF TEXTUAL CRITICISM

Finally, the issue of the aim of textual criticism needs to be mentioned; namely, the question of the original text of a particular biblical book. From the beginning, the aim was to establish the original wording of the biblical text, later on designated as the 'archetype' or 'Urtext'. Gradually, however, the question was raised whether this goal was achievable. In a lecture delivered at Leipzig in 1901 entitled: *Über die Notwendigkeit und Möglichkeit einer neuen Ausgabe der Hebräischen Bibel*,[12] Rudolf Kittel stated that the aim should be the reconstruction of the 'Urschrift' of the biblical writers. What he meant by this term, however, points to some ambivalence: the text of the 'autographon' of the biblical authors, on the one hand, but the *ipsissima verba* of a prophet like Isaiah, on the other. This, of course, reflected modern (nineteenth century) theories about the literary history of biblical books. However, according to Kittel, since this aim is a matter of much uncertainty, it is more realistic to define the goal as 'die Rückbildung des massoretischen Textes in der Richtung auf die Urschrift bis zu einem bestimmten, zwischen der Urschrift und der Masora liegenden, Punkte'.[13] He has in mind here the text of biblical books as read by the Jewish communities circa 300 BCE. This idea was similar to that expressed by other scholars later in the twentieth century; namely, that the purpose of textual criticism should be the text of a book in its earliest attainable form, or the text of a book at the time of its 'final redaction'.[14]

As is clear from commentaries, however, this theory did not work in practice. As a rule, the critical evaluation of a text was made from the perspective of the pericope or chapter concerned, rather than from that of the final redaction of the book. This means that, in the case of books that were considered to contain earlier sources and traditions, the evaluation was made on the basis of these assumptions. Thus, in practice, the aim was to reconstruct each part of a composite book, even to the point of what might have been the *ipsissima verba* (albeit in written form) of a prophet like Isaiah. This explains the ambivalence of the meaning of 'Urschrift' noted above. As the editions of Kittel and commentaries of the time show, this approach led to text-critical proposals in the form of the deletion of all kinds of glosses. In a sense, the underlying aim was, to quote Kittel again, to establish 'eine kritisch gereinigte Ausgabe des hebräischen Bibeltextes'.[15]

3. AFTER QUMRAN

The major contribution of the discoveries in the Dead Sea region, in the years 1947-1956, is, of course, the fact that a great number of biblical texts were found at Qumran, Masada, Naḥal Ḥever, and Wadi Murabbaʿat. Most of these texts are written in the language of the Hebrew Bible, i.e., Hebrew or Aramaic, thus representing a 'direct' witness, in contrast to 'indirect' witnesses such as the ancient versions (translations). The biblical texts of Qumran are most significant because they date from the earliest period in which the biblical text is attested, viz. the third century BCE up to the first century CE.

In comparison to the other witnesses of this period (LXX and Samaritan Pentateuch (SP)), the Qumran texts have an additional value in that they constitute manuscript evidence that goes back directly to this period, and not indirectly (i.e., via a reconstruction of the text on the basis of manuscripts of a later date). On the other hand, it is frustating that the Qumran evidence is so fragmentary (except in the case of the 'great' scroll of Isaiah (1QIsaᵃ)).

Basically, the Qumran biblical texts are significant for text-critical studies in three primary ways:

(a) They provide clear evidence that the MT represents a very old textual tradition;
(b) They offer a large amount of variant readings (variants, pluses and minuses);
(c) They contain cases of remarkable differences compared with the MT tradition: differences that pertain to clauses, sentences, pericopes, and even the structure of a book;
(d) They attest to a variety of textual traditions, especially those which seem to be related to the LXX and the Samaritan Pentateuch.

As far as main issues that have been placed on the agenda of the textual critic since the discoveries of Qumran are concerned, I would like to mention the following seven:

3.1. PLURIFORMITY AND UNIFORMITY

One issue concerns the fascinating matter of the diversity or variety of biblical texts in the earliest period of textual attestation. The discussion of how to evaluate and explain this diversity is ongoing. A well-known theory, advanced by Frank Cross in the late sixties, was based on the idea that the diversity could be explained on the basis of 'local text types' (Palestinian, Egyptian, Babylonian),[16] but since the different texts have all been found in one region (Palestine), this theory has turned out to be unsatisfactory.[17]

A crucial matter is the question of pluriformity vis-à-vis uniformity in the period of the third century BCE to the first century CE. Some scholars regard the textual variety as evidence of a 'fluidity' of the biblical text in the sense of a continuing process of textual change and reworking, a process which is seen as the continuation of the literary history of a given book; textual uniformity comes only after the previously mentioned period.[18] This may be true to some extent, but this theory also raises several crucial questions, particularly whether the development of a book during its literary history is similar to changes attested in the period under discussion. To give an example, the early history of a book like Isaiah is characterized by a literary development in the sense of the insertion or addition of large sections (pericopes, chapters), but the evidence from Qumran (21 manuscripts) does not testify to an ongoing 'growth' in the sense of adding new sections to the book as was the case in the early history of the book.

Other scholars do not share the view that uniformity followed only after a period of pluriformity. They are of the opinion, rightly so in my view, that the available evidence strongly suggests that an essentially uniform textual tradition existed *alongside* a pluriform tradition in Palestinian Judaism.[19] These scholars base their argument upon the fact that the later MT is attested by a large number of biblical texts dating to the period before 70 CE which have been found in the Dead Sea region (biblical texts found at Qumran and at Masada, some phylacteries, and the so-called kaige-recension/Theodotion are of great interest in this regard).[20]

Some scholars have suggested that this situation might be accounted for by the assumption that, at least since the late first century BCE, a particular group within Judaism, probably that of the Pharisees, adhered to, or even preferred, this proto-MT textual tradition.[21]

Be this as it may, the fact that this textual tradition is attested – in a few cases, it is attested as early as the late third century BCE (e.g., 4QJer[a]) – indicates that there must have been a scribal milieu in which texts were copied in an accurate and conservative manner. It may well be that the milieu responsible for a conservative transmission was to be found in Temple circles, since the Temple was the primary place where ancient books were kept.[22] This is not to say that this type of text was considered to be a standard text, or a fixed text, because the emphasis on an accurate transmission in these circles does not need to be seen as part of a religious ideology (such as the idea of canonicity); rather, the accurate transmission may be due to the fact that the work was done by 'official', in the sense of highly trained, copyists.

3.2. THE SEPTUAGINT IN THE LIGHT OF QUMRAN

I would like to touch upon the fact that the LXX, which was the only witness dating to the earliest period of attestation apart from the SP until 1950, has gained textual company. It has become obvious that the Qumran evidence is very important for the study of (the *Vorlage* of) the LXX. Remarkable agreements between Qumran and the LXX have come to light, with telling examples such as the text of Samuel. These agreements have suggested the notion to some scholars that the books of the LXX should be viewed as fairly literal translations.[23] However, this view might be challenged on the following grounds:

(a) The available evidence supports this view only to some extent. Even in the case of Samuel, there are not only agreements but also differences between the Old Greek and Qumran (4QSam[a]);

(b) The situation differs from book to book (as far as the available evidence goes). In the case of Isaiah, for instance, the agreements between 1QIsa[a] and the LXX are very small in number;

(c) The LXX is characterized by a great diversity as far as the style of translation is concerned; that is to say, diversity is not only the hallmark of the Qumran texts, but also of the biblical books in Greek which together make up the LXX. Some books are the result of a rather literal type of translation, while others are the product of more creative authors, just as is the case with the later versions/translations; see below (6)(c);[24]

(d) Agreements between some Qumran texts and the LXX does not necessarily mean that the parent text of the LXX contained the same reading. It has been argued in recent times that the books of the LXX were not produced by translators who did their work on an *ad hoc* basis (like a dragoman), or intuitively (cf. the Helsinki school),[25] but by scholars who belonged to the milieu of learned scribes.[26] If this is correct, then one has to consider the possibility that agreements between biblical texts from Qumran and the LXX could have arisen from a common or similar interpretation of a given passage.[27]

3.3. TEXTUAL CRITICISM AND LITERARY CRITICISM

I would like to comment briefly on the relationship between textual criticism and literary/redaction criticism.[28] An important issue at stake is whether biblical texts, attested by versions either in Hebrew (Qumran) or in Greek (LXX), which differ strongly from the MT in a quantitative manner, represent an earlier stage than the (proto-)MT. It is true, in principle, that textual criticism has to do with the transmission history and that redaction criticism has to do with the literary history of a book, but the real question concerns which text might be seen as the end product of the literary history of a book: the proto-MT, or an earlier version, the pre-MT. If the proto-MT is considered to be the end product, then the earlier (pre-MT) version should be regarded as a (late) stage in the redaction history of a book.[29] However, if one asserts that a pre-MT version marks the end product of the literary development of a book, then the conclusions are very different. In this case, the proto-MT may represent the result of a reworking of the first (pre-MT) edition. Thus, it would be comparable to 'reworked' texts such as 4QRP, which presuppose, in their turn, the proto-MT textual tradition as the prior edition. It is a matter of definition.

Related to this is the question of how to determine whether a divergent text or edition is prior or subsequent to (proto-)MT. One could argue that the shorter text is prior to the longer version for the simple reason that a shorter version normally comes first. This is not a bad argument, but nor is it a strong one, since there are also examples of the other way around: a longer text which was shortened later on (LXX Job; Tobit).[30] Of course, additional arguments are necessary. Divergent text forms, due to literary creativity, require an evaluation which is not only based on text-critical arguments, but which also takes literary critical observations and considerations into account.

Due to the ongoing specialization within the field of Old Testament studies, text-critical research and literary critical research is currently being carried out in separate scholarly circles. Dialogue, or co-operation between these two areas of research is only in its infancy.[31] (An intriguing issue in this regard, which asks for more study, concerns the question whether the type of redactional growth of biblical books in the sense of literary strata is similar to the type of reworking in the so-called 'reworked' texts). One might object to the idea of co-operation on the grounds that, methodologically speaking, textual criticism should come first, and literary criticism next. In theory this makes good sense, but in practice it does not work. Considering the complexities involved in both types of research, it is better in my view to apply both approaches simultaneously and in interaction with each other.

3.4. QUMRAN HEBREW

The Dead Sea scrolls add much to our knowledge of a particular phase in the history of the Hebrew language.[32] This can be helpful for the evaluation of variant readings. The linguistic analysis of the great Isaiah scroll by E. Y. Kutscher is, of course, a good illustration of this aspect.[33] It also demonstrates clearly that the date of a text (manuscript) is not very important. Even though it is the oldest scroll of the book, linguistically speaking 1QIsa[a] is secondary in comparison to the MT, whose manuscripts are of a much later date.

In addition, as far as lexicography is concerned, the study of Qumran Hebrew will also contribute to a more adequate evaluation of equivalents in the LXX; equivalents which may seem unusual from the perspective of Classical Hebrew.

3.5. QUMRAN AND BIBLE INTERPRETATION

The Dead Sea scrolls testify, at least from the second century BCE onwards, to a strong interest in the study and interpretation of biblical texts which, as such, presuppose an authoritative status for these texts. For one reason or another, the period of writing of the scrolls was a time of intensive study of the ancient, or ancestral,[34] books. As a collection, these books were referred to from around the middle of second century BCE as 'the Law, the Prophets and those of David' (4QMMT). This study was limited, of course, to scholarly circles such as those of priests and scribes.

An analysis of the pesharim and other exegetical writings will help us to understand the way the biblical text in Hebrew was 'read' (in the sense of vocalization and syntactical understanding) and interpreted at that time. It may shed light on variant readings ('reading' in the triple sense of the word: _ketib_, _qere_, syntax) in the Qumran-texts as well as in the LXX. It was typical of the pre-Qumran textual criticism to regard the readings in the LXX that differ from MT – as far as morphology, vocalization, or syntax of the Hebrew are concerned – as arising from an 'incorrect' understanding of the MT. However, such an evaluation of ancient versions like the LXX does not do them justice from the point of view of reception history. Exegesis in Qumran and in the books of the LXX actually represent a stage in the reception history (or history of interpretation) of a given biblical text. Instead of labelling a specific reading as incorrect, it would be more appropriate to regard divergent readings in the LXX, such as those reflecting a different vocalization, as attesting a particular interpretation of a particular period.[35] This understanding is the more plausible if, as was stated above, the authors who were responsible for parts of the LXX were members of the just mentioned intellectual elite (scholar-scribes) of that time.[36]

3.6. SCOPE OF TEXTUAL CRITICISM

The Dead Sea discoveries have strengthened the well-founded idea that the earliest period of textual attestation is the most important one for textual criticism. But, although it is true that the later versions (Aquila, Symmachus, Targum, Peshitta, Vulgate) are not that significant for the reconstruction of the earliest text of the Hebrew Bible, they are nevertheless of great value in other respects, for they widen the text historical horizon in the following ways:

(a) The later versions show a variety of styles of translation, which is very helpful for the study of the LXX;

(b) They are most important from the perspective of the history of the 'reading' and interpretation of the Hebrew text. In this respect, too, the later versions can shed light, at least by analogy, on variant readings in the early witnesses (Qumran; LXX);

(c) The later versions, specifically the targumim, may be very useful in clarifying the phenomenon of literary creativity in the early texts. It would be interesting to study the cases of reworking and expanded versions in Qumran and in the LXX in the light of similar cases in the targumim. The latter provide several types of exegetical reworking, both in the sense of addition and rephrasing. This process can even go so far as to result in a completely new literary composition (e.g., Targum Canticles), which may be comparable to the type of rewritten Bible.

3.7. AIM OF TEXTUAL CRITICISM

Finally, a few words on the purpose of textual criticism are in order. Generally speaking, textual criticism aims at the reconstruction of the original form of a literary work. In principle, textual criticism of the Old Testament does not form an exception to this rule, but a disputed question is, what do we mean by the 'original text'? One may doubt the idea of an original text, but, as have been argued by scholars, it is likely that there has been an original text of a biblical book in the sense of the first (complete) edition.[37]

A related question is whether one should define the goal of textual criticism as the establishment of the proto-MT or of an earlier, pre-MT, version. This, of course, depends on the available textual data and their evaluation. In my view, one should aim at the 'original' (complete) text in the sense of the text/edition, whether it is proto-MT or pre-MT, that underlies available copies and/or editions. That is to say, one should go as far back as the textual evidence allows and requires.[38]

Of course, it is a completely different question whether, or to what extent, this goal can be achieved. It is interesting to note that there is a tendency in the field of Old Testament studies to date the redactional completion of biblical books later than was done by scholars in the past. The distance between these datings and the first period of textual attestation is becoming smaller. To give an example, if scholars are correct in dating the first (complete) edition of the book of Isaiah about 300 BCE,[39] one may assume that this 'original' text was still available in the temple of Jerusalem in the second and first centuries BCE[40] because, in line with the practice of the ancient (Semitic) world, literary works were deposited in an archive or library of a temple, or palace, if the literary work was considered to be significant (see also above).

4. FINAL REMARKS

It may be clear that due to the Qumran discoveries the agenda of the textual critic has become fuller and more demanding than ever before. The life of the textual critic in the post-Qumran era is more complicated, but also more exciting. His or her menu is sometimes a bit heavier but also richer and more varied than before. As an all-round textual critic, one is supposed to be familiar with many areas of research: Hebrew grammar, both biblical and post-biblical (especially Qumran Hebrew); biblical exegesis; literary and redactional criticism as well as literary analysis of the Hebrew text; study of the Qumran biblical texts and of the ancient versions, each in its own right; and the history of interpretation.[41]

Of course, the basic work that still needs to be done is the evaluation of the individual cases. The discussion about the *lectio facilior* and *difficilior* will still be part of the game, but the scenery has changed. The context of text-critical work has become very different as is evident from the seven issues mentioned above. For example, one not only needs to consider the question of *lectio facilior* or *difficilior*, but also the issue of *textus facilior* or *difficilior*.

Furthermore, as a result of the Qumran discoveries another shift is to be mentioned. In contrast to pre-Qumran textual criticism, the emphasis now is focused more on *all* the available evidence. The great number of variant readings and variant texts demands our attention. This shift becomes fully clear when one compares the *Hebrew University Bible* edition[42] with the editions of Kittel and the *Biblia Hebraica Stuttgartensia*. This applies also to the forthcoming edition of the *Biblia Hebraica Quinta*, although this one will allow reconstructed readings to be noted in the apparatus even where no variants exist.

In earlier days textual criticism was considered to be 'lower criticism'. In the light of the developments which have been outlined in this paper, there is good reason to assert that textual criticism in the post-Qumran era can be regarded as a part of 'higher criticism'. We may congratulate ourselves on this promotion.

NOTES

1　The expression 'Qumran discoveries' will be taken here to include the discoveries elsewhere in the Dead Sea region (Naḥal Ḥever, Masada, and Murabbaʿat).

2　For the early history of textual criticism, see Dominique Barthélemy, *Critique textuelle de l'Ancient Testament*, 3 vols, OBO 50 (Fribourg: Éditions Universitaires; Göttingen: Vandenhoeck & Ruprecht, 1982), I, pp. 1*-63*; M. H. Goshen-Gottstein, 'The Textual Criticism of the Old Testament: Rise, Decline, Rebirth', *JBL*, 102 (1983), 365-99 (pp. 365-86).

3　L. Cappellus, *Critica sacra* (Paris: Cramoisy, 1650); J. Buxtorf, Jr., *Anticritica* (Basel: Ludovici Regis, 1653).

4　C. F. Houbigant, *Biblia Hebraica cum notis criticis et versione latina ad notas criticas facta,* 4 vols (Paris: Lutetiae-Parisiorum, 1753).

5　E. F. C. Rosenmüller, *Handbuch für die Literatur der Biblischen Kritik und Exegese*, 4 vols (Göttingen: Vandenhoeck & Ruprecht, 1797-1800).

6　O. Thenius, *Die Bücher Samuels* (Leipzig: Hirzel, 1842), p. ix.

7　Julius Wellhausen, *Der Text der Bücher Samuelis* (Göttingen: Vandenhoeck & Ruprecht, 1871), p. 16.

8　Wellhausen, p. 22.

9　See, e.g., Felix Perles, *Analekten zur Textkritik des Alten Testaments* (München: Ackermann, 1895); Friedrich Delitzsch, *Die Lese- und Schreibfehler im Alten Testament* (Berlin: de Gruyter, 1920).

10　H. S. Nyberg, 'Das textkritische Problem des Alten Testaments am Hoseabuche demonstriert', *ZAW*, 52 (1934), 241-54; Pieter Arie Hendrik de Boer, *Research into the Text of 1 Samuel I-XVI: A Contribution to the Study of the Books of Samuel* (Amsterdam: Paris, 1938).

11　Wilhelm Gesenius, *Der Prophet Jesaia*, 3 vols (Leipzig: Vogel, 1820-1821); S. R. Driver, *Notes on the Hebrew Text and the Topography of Samuel; with an Introduction on Hebrew Palaeography and the Ancient Versions*, 2nd edn (Oxford: Clarendon Press, 1913).

12　Rudolf Kittel, *Über die Notwendigkeit und Möglichkeit einer neuen Ausgabe der Hebräischen Bibel* (Leipzig: Edelman, 1901).

13　Kittel, p. 36.

14　See, e.g., Ernst Würthwein, *Der Text des Alten Testaments*, 4th edn (Stuttgart: Württembergische Bibelanstalt, 1973), p. 102.

15　Kittel, p. 3.

16　See the contributions of Frank Moore Cross in *QHBT*: 'The History of the Biblical Text in the Light of Discoveries in the Judaean Desert', pp. 177-95; 'The Contribution of the Qumrân Discoveries to the Study of the Biblical Text', pp. 278-92; 'The Evolution of a Theory of Local Texts', pp. 306-20.

17　For the question of how to describe the plurality of texts, see *TCHB*, p. 191; Émile Puech, 'Qumrân et le texte de l'Ancien Testament', in *Congress Volume Oslo 1998*, ed. by A. Lemaire and M. Saebø, SVT, 80 (Leiden: Brill, 2000), pp. 437-64 (pp. 458-60); and Eugene Ulrich, 'The Dead Sea Scrolls and the Biblical Text', *DSSAFY*, I, pp. 79-100 (pp. 83-86).

18　See Eugene Ulrich, *The Dead Sea Scrolls and the Origins of the Bible* (Grand Rapids: Eerdmans; Leiden: Brill, 1999), pp. 24-25, 76-78.

19　See Adam S. van der Woude, 'Pluriformity and Uniformity: Reflections on the Transmission of the Text of the Old Testament', in *Sacred History and Sacred Texts in Early Judaism: A Symposium in Honour of A.S. van der Woude,* ed. by J. N. Bremmer and F. García Martínez, Contributions to Biblical Exegesis and Theology, 5 (Kampen: Kok Pharos, 1992), pp. 151-69; *TCHB*, pp. 189-92; and Adam S. van der Woude, 'Fifty years of Qumran Research', in *DSSAFY* (Leiden: Brill, 1998), I, pp. 1-45 (p. 42).

20 As for Masada, see now S. Talmon and Y. Yadin, *Masada VI: The Yigael Yadin Excavations 1963-1965, Final Reports, Hebrew Fragments from Masada* (Jerusalem: IES, 1999), pp. 1-149. For the phylacteries of the 'Pharisaic' type which attest the proto-MT tradition, see DJD VI, 39.

21 See, e.g., Dominique Barthélemy, *Études d'histoire du texte de l'Ancien Testament*, OBO, 21 (Fribourg: Éditions Universitaires; Göttingen: Vandenhoeck & Ruprecht, 1978), p. 303. Here we touch upon the question of the relationship between textual pluriformity and pluriformity within Judaism of the time.

22 See *TCHB*, p. 191, and Van der Woude, 'Pluriformity', p. 163. Concerning the Temple as the place where the ancient books were kept, see A. van der Kooij, 'The Canonization of Ancient Books Kept in the Temple of Jerusalem', in *Canonization and Decanonization: Papers presented to the International Conference of the Leiden Institute for the Study of Religions (LISOR) held at Leiden 9-10 January 1997*, ed. by A. van der Kooij and K. van der Toorn (Leiden: Brill, 1998), pp. 17-40. For a different view, namely that the pluriformity of Qumran points to a pluriformity in the temple of Jerusalem, see Puech, p. 463.

23 See, e.g., Ulrich, pp. 42-44; Ronald S. Hendel, *The Text of Genesis 1-11: Textual Studies and Critical Edition* (New York/Oxford: Oxford University Press, 1998), pp. 16-39.

24 For the latter type, see, e.g., LXX Proverbs. Cf. Johann Cook, *The Septuagint of Proverbs: Jewish and/or Hellenistic Proverbs? Concerning the Hellenistic Colouring of LXX Proverbs*, VTSup, 69 (Leiden: Brill, 1997).

25 See Ilmari Soisalon-Soininen, 'Zurück zur Hebraismenfrage', in *Studien zur Septuaginta - Robert Hanhart zu Ehren Aus Anlaß seiner 65. Geburtstages*, ed. by Detlef Fraenkel, Udo Quast and John William Wevers, Abhandlungen der Akademie der Wissenschraften in Göttingen, Philologisch-Historische Klasse, Folge 3, Mitteilungen des Septuaginta–Unternehmens, 20, 190 (Göttingen: Vandenhoeck & Ruprecht, 1990), pp. 35-51 (p. 36).

26 See Martin Rösel, *Übersetzung als Vollendung der Auslegung. Studien zur Genesis-Septuaginta*, BZAW, 223 (Berlin: de Gruyter, 1994), p. 158; Arie van der Kooij, 'Perspectives on the Study of the Septuagint: Who are the Translators?' in *Perspectives on the Study of the Old Testament and Early Judaism: A Symposium in Honour of Adam S. van der Woude on the Occasion of his 70th Birthday*, ed. by Florentino García Martínez and Ed Noort, VTSup, 73 (Leiden: Brill, 1998), pp. 214-29.

27 This is a well-known phenomenon as far as specific agreements between Targum and Peshitta are concerned. See Yeshayahu Maori, *The Peshitta Version of the Pentateuch and Early Jewish Exegesis* (Jerusalem: Magnes Press, 1995), pp. 285-318; M. P. Weitzman, *The Syriac Version of the Old Testament: An Introduction*, University of Cambridge Oriental Publications, 56 (Cambridge: Cambridge University Press, 1999), pp. 86-129.

28 See, e.g., *TCHB*, pp. 313-49, and Arie van der Kooij, 'Zum Verhältnis von Textkritik und Literarkritik: Überlegungen anhand einiger Beispiele', in *Congress Volume Cambridge 1995*, ed. by J. A. Emerton, VTSup, 66 (Leiden: Brill, 1997), pp. 185-202.

29 See *TCHB*, p. 317.

30 See H. Jürgen Tertel, *Text and Transmission: An Empirical Model for Literary Development of Old Testament Narratives*, BZAW, 221 (Berlin: de Gruyter, 1994).

31 For an interesting example, see Klaus Bieberstein, *Josua - Jordan – Jericho: Archäologie, Geschichte und Theologie der Landnahmeerzählungen Josua 1-6*, OBO, 143 (Freiburg, Schweiz: Universitätsverlag; Göttingen: Vandenhoeck & Ruprecht, 1995).

32 On Qumran Hebrew, see Takamitsu Muraoka, 'Hebrew', in *EDSS*, I, pp. 340-45 and the literature cited there.

33 E. Y. Kutscher, *The Language and the Linguistic Background of the Isaiah Scroll (1 Q Isa^a)*, STDJ, 6 (Leiden: Brill, 1974). See also Elisha Qimron, *The Hebrew of the Dead Sea Scrolls*, HSS, 29 (Atlanta: Scholars Press, 1986).

34 Cf. Prologue to Wisdom of Ben Sira, l. 10.

35 See Arie van der Kooij, 'Textual Witnesses to the Hebrew Bible and the History of Reception: The Case of Habakkuk 1:11-12', in *Die Textfunde vom Toten Meer und der Text der Hebräischen Bibel*, ed. by Ulrich Dahmen, Armin Lange, Hermann Lichtenberger (Neukirchen-Vluyn: Neukirchener Verlag, 2000), pp. 91-108.

36 See van der Kooij, 'Perspectives', p. 227.

37 See *TCHB*, pp. 164-180, and Hendel, p. 11 ('the literary and editorial completion of the original text' of a given biblical book).

38 For a similar view, see Hermann-Josef Stipp, 'Das Verhältnis von Textkritik und Literarkritik in neueren alttestamentlichen Veröffentlichungen', *BZ* Neue Folge, 34 (1990), 16-37 (p. 33).

39 See Odil Hannes Steck, *Studien zu Tritojesaja*, BZAW, 203 (Berlin: de Gruyter, 1991), p. 159.

40 Compare 1QIsa[a] which was available from the middle of the second century BCE to about 65 CE.

41 It should be noted that the last fifty years have been marked not only by the Qumran discoveries but also by a great progress in the study of the ancient versions, notably that of the LXX, kaige recension/Theodotion, Targumim, and Peshitta.

42 Up to the present, the following books have been published: *The Hebrew University Bible: the Book of Isaiah*, ed. by Moshe H. Goshen-Gottstein (Jerusalem: Magnes Press, 1995); *The Hebrew University Bible: The Book of Jeremiah*, ed. by C. Rabin, S. Talmon, and E. Tov (Jerusalem: Magnes, 1997).

THE ABSENCE OF 'SECTARIAN VARIANTS' IN THE JEWISH SCRIPTURAL SCROLLS FOUND AT QUMRAN

Eugene Ulrich

WHEN I WAS ORIGINALLY asked to address the topic of 'sectarian elements' in the biblical scrolls from Qumran, I replied somewhat ungraciously that my article would require only about one page in the volume. That is because in all my years working on the biblical scrolls, I do not remember having seen one sectarian variant. I did suggest — especially since titles can be instructive — that I could offer a paper on the *absence* of sectarian variants in the scrolls, since that absence teaches us a quite valuable lesson.

The article will discuss: (1) some issues and problems involved with the idea of 'sectarian' variants; (2) some examples of sectarian variants in order to clarify what the object of the search would look like; (3) a search through the biblical manuscripts in quest of such variants; and (4) some specific probes of selected other manuscripts for clues.

The scope of the paper must be confined to the *c.* 230 biblical scrolls, in order to ensure clarity of focus and usefulness of results. A similar, broader study of the quotations and use of scriptural texts (both for books that eventually became canonical and for other authoritative books that did not) in biblical commentaries as well as other nonbiblical, parabiblical, and 'rewritten' biblical scrolls, would be highly desirable.[1] The present analysis of the strictly biblical manuscripts should form a more solid basis for that broader study.

The focus here will be on individual textual variants in the attempt to discover variants that were sectarian in origin or motivation. For this purpose, other levels will not be treated: orthographic differences, variant literary editions, or disputed books. The level of orthographic differences will be ignored insofar as those are almost by definition meaningless. Also ignored will be routine minor variants, such as initial *vav*, the definite article, את, כל, etc. Should orthographic differences or minor variants appear to point to significant variant readings or interpretations, they will of course be examined. On the other hand and perhaps more importantly, the scope of this paper does not permit discussion either of variant literary editions of books as possibly sectarian in origin or motivation, or of possible variation between Jewish parties with regard to whether disputed books did or did not have authoritative status. Those questions, however, are ripe for detailed investigation.

Eugene Ulrich

I. ISSUES AND PROBLEMS

I see two main issues raised by the question of 'sectarian variants'. The first centres around the value we should assign to the biblical scrolls found at Qumran. Are they aberrant or 'vulgar'[2] texts and thus of relatively small value for our knowledge of the history of the biblical text, or are they 'the oldest, the best, the most authentic'[3] manuscripts of the Bible and thus of highest importance for the history of the biblical text?

The second issue centres around increased knowledge of Judaism in the late Second Temple period. If the variants highlighted by the scrolls are 'sectarian' — whether the secondary variants are in the scrolls, in the Masoretic Text (MT), in the Septuagint (LXX), or in other witnesses — what can this teach us about Judaism in the late Second Temple period and about the history of the biblical text?

There are also two points that cry out for immediate discussion, since many biblical scholars and students will probably begin with predictable assumptions. The first involves texts, the second sects: first, clarification concerning the proper stance for assessing the MT vs. the Qumran manuscripts; and second, clarification concerning the proper stance for assessing the Pharisees or rabbis vs. the Qumranites or Covenanters or Essenes.

In the period with which we are dealing, the MT and the Pharisaic party are simply not the principal points for reference or comparison. With regard to texts, the MT was not the 'standard text' of 'the Bible', nor was it even an identifiable text (in the collective singular) or even an identifiable collection of disparate texts. The text of the various books of Scripture was pluriform, and there is abundant evidence that this pluriformity was widely accepted. The text form for each book that was later incorporated into the MT collection was simply one of several forms of the text as they circulated in Judaism during the Second Temple period. There was no 'proto-MT' of the Tanak — or at least it still remains to be demonstrated that there was a 'proto-MT' — in the late Second Temple period in the sense of a unified, identifiable collection of texts that together (in contrast to other texts) would move ahead through history and become the Masoretic collection of texts that emerged in the sixth to ninth centuries. There was no standard text.[4] Thus, those texts which differ from the MT are not aberrant; it is only the presuppositions of those who would so claim that are aberrant.

Similarly, with regard to sects or parties within Judaism, the Pharisees did not constitute mainstream 'normative Judaism'. That is an outdated reconstruction prevalent in the first half of last century, to be sure, but it has been corrected in many revised descriptions.[5] It is not the case that orthodox belief and practice were represented by the Pharisees, while those who diverged or disagreed with them were unorthodox sects in the modern Western sense of that term. 'The Pharisees were one group among many, vying for power against others.'[6] If the term 'sect' is used for the Essenes, it is similarly to be used for the Pharisees, Sadducees, and other late Second Temple groups.[7]

So it is a misconception that the Pharisees represented 'normative' Judaism, and thus even if there were an identifiable textual collection that could be labelled the 'proto-MT', and even if it could in the second or first century BCE be linked to the Pharisees, there is no evidence to substantiate the claim that the proto-MT was to be considered the dominant or standard text.[8]

The Absence of 'Sectarian Variants'

With those points made, the focus can return to the main question: whether there are sectarian variants in the MT, the LXX, or the scrolls. The logic itself stumbles. If one group tampered with the text of Scripture in order to promote its views, it would be open to immediate demonstrable refutation. The analogous problem was beginning only a short time later regarding the problem of the differing Hebrew vs. Greek texts. In both rabbinic and early Christian circles, the discrepancies between texts eventually became glaringly clear in religious debates, and so began the Greek recension process of 'correcting' Greek texts 'back' toward the 'original' Hebrew text (which was soon assumed to be exclusively the rabbinic text-traditions that developed into the Masoretic).[9] All the actors had limited viewpoints, but all apparently agreed that the text of the 'original' Scriptures should not be altered, and if there were problems, the texts should be corrected toward the 'original'. Here, it pays to recall the words of Chaim Rabin:

> The conviction of the [Qumran] sect that they were actors in a drama described in the O.T. in all details naturally led them to apply to their own situation those Scripture verses which in their view predicted it. The very fact that there were such verses at hand was a guarantee that their analysis of the situation was right. The place of an event in the divine plan was, so to say, adequately plotted if the verse for it could be found. For this reason, the extensive use of quotation and allusion in the argumentation [. . . is] an intrinsic part of the argument. [. . .] These allusions were meant to be taken by the reader or listener as proof of the identity of the 'prophecy' and the situation to which it was applied.

> Now it appears an inescapable conclusion that if one quotes scripture for such purposes, one does — in intent at least — quote it literally. Failure to do so will mean that the reader either misses the point or will be able to raise objections from the correct text.[10]

This does not mean, of course, that no ancient scribe ever made a sectarian variant; but it does mean that intentional sectarian-motivated alteration of Scripture would not be a problem-free action and therefore that a scholar making such a claim would need clear and thorough-going proof.

II. EXAMPLES OF SECTARIAN VARIANTS

A. *Sectarian Variants.* If the search is for sectarian variants, it is important to know what a sectarian variant looks like. What qualifies, and what does not? The Samaritan Pentateuch (SP) offers a few clear examples of sectarian variants.

1. In Deuteronomy, where the MT and LXX have the frequent Deuteronomistic formula about 'the place where the Lord will choose' to have his name dwell (Deuteronomy 12:5; 14:23; 16:2; 17:8; 18:6; 26:2; etc.), the SP routinely has 'the place where the Lord has chosen'. The polemic here, of course, is that, in the minds of the Samaritans, the Lord had at the time of Moses and Joshua chosen Mount Gerizim as true Israel's central shrine, and that should not change; indeed in the Hebrew Bible Shechem retained its status as a revered central shrine during the period of Joshua. For the Judaeans, however, Jerusalem would become the central shrine established by David and Solomon, and from that temporal point of reference, the Lord's choice of Jerusalem still lay in the future.

2. Similarly, after Exodus 20:17[14] in the SP a long commandment is added, stipulating that an altar be built on Mount Gerizim after the Lord has led the people into the land. The commandment is repeated in the SP after the second

recitation of the commandments in Deuteronomy 5:21[18] as well. This commandment, though clearly added by the Samaritans, is not a specifically Samaritan creation; it consists mostly of the stipulations given to Moses in Deuteronomy 27:2-7 in both the MT and the SP. The glaring difference is the localization of the altar 'on Mount Gerizim' in the SP vs. 'on Mount Ebal' in the MT at Deuteronomy 27:4. The SP reading is clearly a variant inspired by Samaritan (or at least northern, Samarian) concerns.

3. But is 'Mount Ebal' at Deuteronomy 27:4 in the MT the original reading? 4QJosh[a] strongly suggests that it is not. That oldest extant manuscript of Joshua apparently assumes Gilgal as the location of the first altar after Israel had crossed into the land. There are persuasive reasons to indicate that 4QJosh[a] offers the earliest preserved narrative (indeed followed by Josephus), placing the altar naturally at the point of entry immediately after the crossing of the Jordan. This would assume a text in Deuteronomy 27:4 which, like Deuteronomy 27:2-3, had no place name but assumed that the altar would be built at the point of entry. At a second level 'Mount Gerizim' was inserted due to northern concerns, and at a third level that insertion was not deleted but was countered by Judaeans with the anomalous substitution of 'Mount Ebal'.[11] Insofar as this interpretation be correct, it should be noted that this variant is not a sectarian variant made at Qumran but a double sectarian variant made first by the Samarians and subsequently by the Judaeans.

Finally, it is to be noted that (1) each of these examples is clearly a *secondary* reading; (2) each was clearly *intentional* and (3) was *particular* to the Samaritans (or at least to northern worshippers), except for the 'Mount Ebal' reading, which was specifically and jarringly anti-Samaritan; and (4) that the specifically Samaritan theme in the variants is found *repeated*.

B. Non-Sectarian Variants. In contrast, it is probably helpful to note that there are numerous variants which are intentionally made in texts transmitted in the MT, the LXX, and the scrolls, but that they should not be considered sectarian. That is, they are characteristic of Jewish authors or scribes in general. They are not peculiar to any particular group.

1. For example, 4QJudg[a] highlights a theological insertion into the MT of Judges (Judges 6:7-10), but the MT should not be accused of a sectarian variant.[12] The text of 4QJudg[a] retains the old, uninterrupted folk narrative on a single fragment, continuing from Judges 6:2-6 directly on to 6:11-13. The narrative is about Gideon during the Midianite raids and tells how each time the Israelites would plant their crops, the Midianites would come and destroy the land. Becoming impoverished, the Israelites cried out to the Lord; then the messenger of the Lord came (Judges 6:12). Just before this last element a short paragraph with the cyclical pattern reminiscent of Deuteronomistic theology is inserted in the MT:

When the Israelites cried to the Lord on account of the Midianites, the Lord sent a prophet to the Israelites; and he said to them, 'Thus says the Lord, the God of Israel: I led you up from Egypt, and brought you out of the house of slavery; and I delivered you from the hand of the Egyptians, and from the hand of all who oppressed you, and drove them out before you, and gave you their land; and I said to you, "I am the Lord your God; you shall not pay reverence to the gods of the Amorites, in whose land you live." But you have not given heed to my voice' (Judges 6:7-10 NRSV).

This must be considered a general Jewish insertion, based on ancient Deuteronomistic theology, not a sectarian variant.

2. Similarly, in 1 Samuel 1:23, after Hannah's vow about her new-born Samuel, Elkanah replies:

4QSam[a] LXX OL [אך יקם יהו]ה היוצא מפיך
only let the Lord confirm what has come from your mouth.

MT אך יקם יהוה את דברו
only let the Lord confirm his word.

It is probable that 4QSam[a] preserves the earlier reading and that the tradition in the MT has been influenced by the Deuteronomistic concern for linking isolated prophetic words with subsequent events and connecting these originally free-standing elements into a prophecy-fulfilment motif.[13] Again, this would be a theologically motivated intentional variant, but it is a general Jewish variant, based on traditional theology, and not a sectarian variant.

III. THE MANUSCRIPTS OF THE JEWISH SCRIPTURES FOUND AT QUMRAN

For this section there is, ironically, both too much to discuss and nothing to report. Since the books of Deuteronomy, Isaiah, Psalms, and (relative to its size) Daniel were the most widely attested biblical books at Qumran, and since the prophetic books appear the most fertile sources for possible sectarian variants, the discussion will focus on Isaiah, Psalms, and Daniel, but the negative conclusions hold for the other biblical books as well.

A. Isaiah. In 1QIsa[a] there are roughly a thousand variants from the other Qumran manuscripts and the MT, depending upon one's definition of and criteria for variants. In 1QIsa[b], though that manuscript is usually described as virtually identical with the MT, there are more than a hundred textual variants, in addition to the hundred-plus orthographic differences. In the Cave 4 Isaiah manuscripts there are over 460 variants.[14]

The most dramatic variants in the book of Isaiah highlighted by the scrolls are the ten large additions of about one to five verses.[15] Some of these appear in 1QIsa[a], some appear in the LXX; interestingly, all these secondary additions are incorporated into the MT, making the received text the latest of our witnesses, at least from this perspective. But none of these dramatic long insertions should be labelled sectarian in nature.

Moreover, of all the thousand-plus Isaiah variants, in my view none should be classified as sectarian. Two suspicious possibilities may be adduced as examples, plus one which has in fact been suggested as a sectarian variant:

1. Isaiah 44:25: יסכל ('to render their knowledge *foolish*' 1QIsa[a], 1QIsa[b], 4QIsa[b], LXX) vs. ישכל ('to render their knowledge *wise*'[?] MT). In light of James Harding's recent article,[16] one is tempted to examine whether the Isaiah variant is possibly sectarian. But first, the most plausible explanation is not that the MT has substituted 'wise' for 'foolish', but that a scribe in the MT tradition simply confused sibilants; confusion of ס/שׂ is not infrequent, and the context and parallelism do not permit 'wise'. Thus, there is no true variant, only a minor lapse. Much less can it support the claim

of a sectarian variant, as is confirmed by the wider support of the third- or early-second-century BCE Greek translation. Secondly, it should be stated explicitly that Harding does not claim that there are sectarian variants in the biblical texts. He correctly finds that

> wordplay [. . .] is a crucial literary device within the 'sectarian' scrolls. The wordplay studied here derives from texts within the [Hebrew Bible], and so this study also has implications for the way in which we perceive the nature of the 'Qumranian' appropriation of 'scriptural' texts. [. . .] The 'sectarian' scrolls therefore draw on ideas present in the wider context of Second Temple Judaism and develop them in a way which would define their position against other groups (p. 80).

Harding makes the important distinction that significant words in scriptural texts are taken and used to develop particular positions by different Second Temple groups within Judaism; but the arguments are developed in the secondary 'sectarian' works, while the texts of the Scriptures are left unchanged.

2. Isaiah 53:11: יראה ('he will see' MT) vs. יראה אור ('he will see light' 1QIsa^a, 1QIsa^b, 4QIsa^d, LXX). In the light of the sharp contrast drawn in the Rule of the Community between בני אור and בני חושך, one might be tempted to see this addition of אור as sectarian, but again, careful analysis leaves no substance to such a claim. First, the verb is probably from the root רוה ('be filled, saturated; drink one's fill'), not ראה ('see'), as the parallelism with the following שבע ('be sated, satisfied') suggests.[17] Thus, none of our witnesses contains the 'original' text. The MT transmits an erroneous consonantal text, losing the *lectio difficilior*; once it had been understood as 'see', a natural complement was added as the direct object, and most of the textual tradition, including even 1QIsa^b (which often displays close similarities to the MT) transmits the tertiary reading. The broader attestation by 1QIsa^b and LXX deflates claims of sectarian motivation, whereas all Jews would immediately resonate with the confession יהוה אורי (as in Psalm 27:1).

3. Isaiah 41:22: או אחרונות או הבאות ('or the last things or the things to come' 1QIsa^a) vs. אחריתן או הבאות ('their end or the things to come' MT). Arie van der Kooij sees the author of 1QIsa^a as relating the prophecies of Isaiah to his own time, 'actualizing' the prophecies in the same way as the author(s) of the pesharim; the suggestion is even made that the 'author' of 1QIsa^a might be the Teacher of Righteousness.[18] The reading of Isaiah 41:22, however, and the others adduced to exemplify the actualizing interpretation are not in my view sufficient to support his claim. His book is carefully worked and his claim, if valid, would be important, so it deserves more space than is available here. But I do not agree with it and can offer here only a few points:

(a) The assumption that אחריתן in the MT is the earlier, neutral reading and אחרונות in 1QIsa^a the altered, 'actualizing' interpretation is questionable. In the previous colon הראשנות is parallel, and when used in pairs in Isaiah, אחרון usually follows ראשון (8:23; 41:4; 44:6; 48:12) and אחרית follows ראשית (46:10). Regarding the 'actualization', if such were operative, אחרית (הימים) could be claimed as potentially as eschatological as אחרונות.

(b) Even if the 1QIsa^a reading were the secondary one, how can we know that it was the specific scribe of that manuscript — as opposed to a previous scribe of one of its *Vorlagen* — who introduced the change?

(c) In Isaiah 47:7 the same pair of variants occurs (אחרונה in 1QIsa^a, אחריתה in the MT) with clearly no significance; this 'end' is clearly something in the past or the extended present. In the oracle on the fall of Babylon the text in both 1QIsa^a and the MT reads:

The Absence of 'Sectarian Variants'

[5]Sit in silence, [. . .] daughter Chaldea! [. . .]
[7]You said: 'I will be mistress forever',
But you did not take these things to heart,
nor were you mindful of their end.

(d) Moreover, אחרון is used for both the simple future (8:29[9:1]; 30:8) and the cosmic or eschatological future (41:4; 44:6; 48:12) with both 1QIsa[a] and the MT in agreement.

(e) The claim that a scribe intentionally changed the meaning of the Isaianic prophecies is a serious one, requiring clear and sustained proof. For van der Kooij, part of the broader proof lies in his conviction that the roughly contemporaneous translator of the LXX of Isaiah engaged in the same type of actualizing exegesis.[19] But neither do I think that the claim for the LXX translator can be sustained.[20] It is helpful to recall the lifelong experience of the former director of the Septuaginta-Unternehmen in Göttingen, Robert Hanhart:

With regard to the original form of the Greek translation, [. . .] deviations from the MT must be noticed but should only in the rarest cases be taken as the peculiar expression of the translator by means of which he wants to interpret — let alone reinterpret — his *Vorlage*. The LXX — and this is true for all the books translated — is *interpretation* only insofar as a decision is made between various possibilities of understanding which are already inherent in the formulation of the Hebrew *Vorlage* and thus given to the translator. Furthermore, the LXX is the *actualization* of the contemporary history of the translator only when the choice of the Greek equivalent is capable of doing justice both to the factuality and history of the original Hebrew witness and also to the contemporary history of the translator. The LXX is essentially *conservation*.[21]

In sum, the first two Isaiah readings that looked suspiciously as though they could have been sectarian turn out not to be so. For the third reading, methodology argues against it. The 1QIsa[a] reading may well have been the original, not the changed reading, and even if it were the secondary reading, it is not clear that it was intentional — it recurs later in the text with no significance attached; it was not specific to the Qumran Covenanters; and it was not consistently applied or repeated when the scribe had the opportunity to do so. Thus I conclude that for the book of Isaiah no variants adduced to date indicate intentional sectarian change.

B. Psalms. The Psalms scrolls highlight over five hundred variants in comparison with the MT and the LXX.[22] By far the most instructive variants are at the level of literary editions: Psalters showing the inclusion of additional Psalms beyond the familiar 151 and variations in the order in which the Psalms occur. With respect to individual textual variants among the witnesses, however, remarkably few increase our knowledge beyond what intelligent conjectures could have produced. That is, for each Psalm line-by-line, in general only a single text tradition seems to have been transmitted. Thus there emerges a long series of minor isolated individual textual variants or errors, often frustratingly small and meaningless, despite their high number. None of these appears to be sectarian in origin, whether in the MT, in the LXX, or in the scrolls.

There is a notable set of variants in Psalm 145 attested by 11QPs[a]. This manuscript copies the Psalm together with a repeated refrain drawn from the wording of 145:1-2, just as Psalm 136 is copied in the MT and LXX with a recurring refrain from 136:1. Other Psalms also were probably sung antiphonally (cf. ויענו בהלל Ezra 3:11, and especially the NRSV and *Good News Bible* translations), whether the antiphon was copied out or not. Moreover, 11QPs[a] preserves, as does one Masoretic manuscript, the LXX, and the Peshitta, the *nun* verse at 145:13 which had been lost from most of the MT tradition.[23] Though otherwise instructive, these variants show no sectarian influence.

The most dramatic group of variants in all the Psalms, of course, is the variant edition of the entire (last third of the) Psalter exhibited by 11QPs[a]. This edition, as such, is not sectarian and probably originated prior to the origins of the Qumran community, but it does contain a significant variant that can be seen as sectarian. In the section entitled 'David's Compositions', a number of claims are made: Davidic authorship of the Psalter, divine inspiration, and prophetic origin of the Psalms (col. XXVII, 2-11). None of those is sectarian; all Jews would agree with them, but yet another claim is made: that the year has 364 days (col. XXVII, 6-7). The date of origin of that claim remains to be determined, and so it is uncertain whether the claim was, when composed, already polemical or whether it became so only later. But the claim for the solar calendar vs. the lunar calendar, which eventually emerged as successful in Judaism, was undoubtedly clear when this particular manuscript was copied 'in the first half of the first century' CE (DJD V, 9).[24]

It is important to analyse the separate aspects of this reading. The place where this scroll was *copied* is unknown, whether in Jerusalem, in broader Palestine, or at Qumran; a claim for the latter would certainly have to be proved and may not be assumed. The place where this edition was first *composed* is even more difficult to determine. There is good reason to think that it was composed well before the specific manuscript 11QPs[a] was copied. The composition may well have predated the Qumran period, just as the book of *Jubilees*, also advocating the 364-day year, was composed prior to the Qumran period but was brought to Qumran and was read and popular there. Thus, though the group at Qumran apparently agreed with the 364-day year, there are no grounds for claiming that a specifically Qumran scribe was responsible for composing 'David's Compositions'.

Moreover, the person responsible for first adding 'David's Compositions' onto the earlier Psalter of which 11QPs[a] is a late copy probably thought he was writing, not Scripture, but a colophon or appendix to a scriptural manuscript. It is arguable that an earlier edition of this work ended with Psalm 149, 150, and the 'Hymn to the Creator' (cf. col. XXVI). After that conclusion two appendices were added: 'David's Last Words' (2 Samuel 23:1-7) and 'David's Compositions', providing credentials and praise of the author.[25] At a later stage several other Psalms were added, as frequently happens at the end of hymnbooks: Psalms 140, 134, and finally 151 (with which the LXX also concludes).

Though originally 'David's Compositions' was probably not considered Scripture but an appendix to Scripture, now it should be considered part of a 'scriptural' scroll, just as the similar passage praising Solomon and enumerating his proverbs and songs in 1 Kings 4:29-32, though probably not originally considered Scripture, has now been incorporated into a book that became Scripture. It would still remain a valid principle unviolated by the original author of 'David's Compositions' that no change in the text of *Scripture* was made for sectarian motives. The variant ends up as a sectarian variant in a scriptural manuscript, but it did not originate as a sectarian variant in Scripture. It would not be in the same category with the 'Mount Ebal' reading in the MT at Deuteronomy 27:4.

C. Daniel. There are close to seventy variants between the scrolls and the MT in Daniel, but none of them is such that it should be considered partisan to any group in Judaism. [26] In fact, there is not a single variant that is even worth mentioning or considering for our present task. That is highly significant for a book whose composition (at least for the twelve-chapter edition) was roughly contemporary with the origins of the Qumran Covenanters, shared the Covenanters' intense interest in apocalypticism, and indeed served as a source for some of their concepts (e.g., 'Time of the End') and religious vocabulary (e.g., משכיל, הרבים). If there is not a single variant worth considering as a possible sectarian variant in the Book of Daniel, it would seem all the more dubious that such would be found in other books.

D. Other Books. Both in my working through all the Cave 4 biblical manuscripts for publication in DJD and in a recent review of their variants, I found nothing that I would categorize as a sectarian variant, except for the variant in 4QJosh[a] about Gilgal as the location of the first altar after Israel had crossed into the land. That variant was not a Qumranic sectarian variant but a double Samarian-then-Judaean variant in the SP-[Old Greek?]-Old Latin, and in the MT-LXX, respectively.

IV. OTHER MANUSCRIPTS AND PERSPECTIVES

Thus far, the focus has been on books whose content the Covenanters might have found especially fertile for sectarian variants, but since direct evidence that a specific manuscript was copied at Qumran itself is rare, focus on manuscripts that most likely *were* copied at Qumran could prove illuminating.

A. 4QSam[c]. This manuscript in particular should be examined closely for Qumranic sectarian variants since it has perhaps the strongest claim to being a biblical text that was copied at Qumran. It is clearly a biblical manuscript, and it is highly probable that it was copied at Qumran because the same scribe copied the main manuscript of the Rule of the Community from Cave 1 (1QS). Its script is markedly idiosyncratic and is detectable in several other manuscripts, including the Testimonia (4Q175) and a correction in the Great Isaiah Scroll (1QIsa[a]) at Isaiah 40:7-8. Moreover, the point could be argued that this copyist may have been a high-ranking leader in the community: his skill as a scribe or copyist is remarkably low, and thus he may have had some other basis for his role, such as his leadership position; his selection of the Rule of the Community and the Testimonia (a meditation on leadership, good and bad) may be indications of his role as a leader; and he had the authority to correct the scroll of Isaiah.

A review of the variants in 4QSam[c] produces interesting results. The extant remains preserve one small scrap from 1 Samuel 25:30-31 and multiple fragments from three contiguous columns with text from 2 Samuel 14:7–15:15. In the sixty-seven partially surviving lines, the scribe stumbled twenty-one times (almost one out of every three lines!). Despite his high rate of errors, corrections, and insertions, the text he produced is still superior to the Masoretic *textus receptus*. 4QSam[c] has nineteen extant readings superior to those in the MT (and twelve more that can be reconstructed), whereas the MT has thirteen readings superior to those extant in 4QSam[c] (with four more that can be reconstructed). Five of the superior readings in 4QSam^c are unique, while a number are also attested in the Greek.[27]

When the focus sharpens to specifically sectarian variants, again the indicator falls to zero. All of the variants in the scroll, the MT, the Old Greek, the later Greek manuscripts, and the Old Latin are virtually meaningless. They consist of minor, routine intentional variants, such as the explicit adding of implicit elements (subject, direct or indirect object, or particles), or minor, routine unintentional variants, such as spelling mistakes, parablepsis, or substitution of more familiar forms or expressions. Not a single variant in the scroll, the MT, or the LXX will sustain the claim that it could be an intentional variant by any of the Jewish parties.

B. *4QTestimonia (4Q175)*. This manuscript, copied by the same scribe as for 4QSam^c, consists of four quotations selected for the theme of leadership: three positive quotations from Scripture focusing on prophet (Exodus 20:18^b in the SP, Deuteronomy 5:28-29 and 18:18-19 in the MT), king (Numbers 24:15-17), and priest (Deuteronomy 33:8-11), and a negative quotation from the *Apocryphon of Joshua* focusing on an accursed man who rebuilds Jericho (4Q389; cf. Joshua 6:26).

If the text of the four quotations is compared with the MT, numerous variants emerge.

1. For the first, the MT of Exodus does not have the passage at all, whereas the MT of Deuteronomy has variants:

4QTest	וידבר •••• אל מושה לאמור שמעת
MT SP (Deuteronomy)	ויאמר יהוה אלי שמעתי

If, however, one avoids the presupposition that the MT is the point of comparison and turns to other available witnesses to the Hebrew Bible, here the SP, 4QTest is seen to quote the SP of Exodus almost verbatim:

4QTest	וידבר •••• אל מושה לאמור שמעת
SP (Exodus)	וידבר יהוה אל משה לאמר שמעתי

Instead of having to claim that 4QTest adapts the wording and excerpts from two different passages in Deuteronomy, it can be seen that the full quotation derives from Exodus 20:18^b in a Jewish variant literary edition of Exodus in circulation at the time.[28] The quotations also naturally unfold in the established chronological order of the books: Exodus, Numbers, Deuteronomy, Joshua.

Specifically with regard to Exodus, in the early first century BCE when 4QTest was copied, there were at least three forms of Exodus in use in Jewish circles. The earliest form attested in our manuscripts is preserved in the LXX; it is close to the edition attested in the MT, except that it exhibits an earlier literary edition of the section comprising chapters 35-40.[29] The second variant literary edition is that presented in the MT. The third is that illustrated by 4QpaleoExod^m, the edition that was used as a basis by the Samaritans.

The Christians eventually inherited the early edition, the rabbis the medial edition, and the Samaritans the late edition; there appears to be no evidence suggesting that any of those parties consciously chose their specific text on either ideological or textual grounds. Indeed, it can be argued that the same general principle was at work in the MT edition's development beyond the LXX edition of Exodus 35–40 that was at work in the 4QpaleoExod^m-SP edition's development beyond the MT edition of the full book. The 4QpaleoExod^m-SP edition routinely expanded the text to note that Moses did in fact perform the tasks commanded by God.[30] Similarly in the Tabernacle Account, 'the MT [of Exodus 35–40] repeats most of the details of the first section [Exodus 25–31]..., and its development was motivated by the idea that the realization of the tabernacle in all its detail should correspond to the instructions.'[31]

2. In the second quotation from Numbers 24:15-17, the text of 4Q175 is for all practical purposes the same as that in the SP, the MT, and the LXX. Unfortunately, none of the Judaean Desert scrolls of Numbers preserves this passage.

3. In the third quotation from Deuteronomy 33:8-11, 4QTest contains a reading 'Give to Levi' which is lacking in the MT and SP, but 4QDeut^h and the LXX also attest this reading, again making it virtually certain that the clause was in the text being faithfully quoted by the Qumran scribe. Moreover, the clause was either original and lost in the MT-SP tradition or a clarifying explication of what was implicit; at any rate there is no change of meaning, and the fact that the third-century BCE LXX had the reading clearly removes it from consideration as an intentional sectarian variant.

4. The fourth quotation in 4Q175 appears to be a quotation of Joshua 6:26 plus a typical Qumran pesher, but it turns out that the entire passage is a quotation of a text also preserved in 4QApocryphon of Joshua^b (4Q389 22 ii 7-15).[32] Not only did this Qumran scribe not alter his source text, in this case it should be noted that the MT exhibits a secondary form of Joshua 6:26 with three additions (ויקום, לפני יהוה, and את יריחו).

Thus, 4QTestimonia is a composition consisting of three biblical passages plus a fourth biblical passage already amplified in another Qumran text. The four passages were selected and juxtaposed as a quasi-meditation on the theme of leadership, positive and negative. It is not a biblical manuscript, but a free selection of scriptural passages, and thus it might be understandable if the author altered the text of the quotations to suit the community's views. But even here the author or scribe did not. Although 4QTestimonia was possibly composed by, or at least almost certainly copied by an inhabitant of Qumran, there is no reason to suspect that any textual variants were introduced into the scriptural text in order to shape the original text toward the beliefs or views of the Qumran community.

C. A Correction in 1QIsa^a. Finally, this same scribe made a correction inserted into the Great Isaiah Scroll at Isaiah 40:6-8. For that well-known passage the base text of 1QIsa^a reads:

> All flesh is grass,
> and all its beauty like the flowers of the field.
> The grass withers, the flowers fade,
> but the word of our God stands forever.

Subsequently, the scribe of 4QSam^c-1QS-4QTest added, to be inserted after the word 'fade', the text in italics:[33]

> All flesh is grass,
> and all its beauty like the flowers of the field.
> The grass withers, the flowers fade,
> *when the breath of •••• blows upon it.*
> *(Surely the people is the grass.)*
> *The grass withers, the flowers fade*
> but the word of our God stands forever.

There are two possible explanations for this scribal phenomenon. First, note that the text copied by the scribe of 1QIsa[a] may have been original, with the later insertion by the scribe of 4QSam[c]-1QS-4QTest seen as a secondary amplification; clearly the parenthetical identification of the 'grass' is a secondary amplification. The alternate possibility is that the fuller text was original and the 1QIsa[a] scribe simply committed parablepsis, skipping from the first occurrence of 'the flowers fade' to the second, and thus lost a line. In favour of the first alternative, however, is the fact that the OG also has the same short text, which makes sense as it is, in exact agreement with the text copied by the original scribe. At any rate, one Hebrew tradition contained the longer text, and the scribe of 4QSam[c] knew that tradition and revised 1QIsa[a] on the basis of it. The main point to be made in the present context is that the Qumran scribe, who also copied 4QSam[c], 1QS, and 4QTest without 'sectarian' variants, inserted text into this scriptural manuscript but penned the insertion faithfully, in basic accordance with the text tradition mirrored by the MT and the Hexapla, and without sectarian variants.

Thus, one of the scribes with the strongest claim to being a specifically Qumran scribe copied biblical and nonbiblical and excerpted biblical texts without any sign of introducing changes motivated by sectarian concerns.

Before concluding, it can be noted that none of the main proposals concerning the history of the biblical text in the light of the scrolls appeals to sectarian variants. Frank Moore Cross argued for a local-text theory, that different text types had developed in different localities — Palestine, Egypt, and (probably) Babylon.[34] Though it is quite probably true that there were different examples of textual growth that took place in different localities, to my knowledge there is no specific evidence that causally links any particular form of growth with any particular locality. There are no sectarian variants known to be due to the different localities.

Shemaryahu Talmon, in contrast to Cross's local-text theory which attempted to explain how a single text developed into three, proposed a theory of many text forms being reduced to only three. His socio-religious idea of *Gruppentexte* explained why, out of the plethora of text forms of the books of Scriptures that were generally circulating in the first century CE, only three text forms emerged — those saved by the Jews, the Samaritans, and the Christians.[35] It did not, however, explain why each particular community chose its particular text. Why specifically did the rabbis end up with the collection found in the MT, the Samaritans with the expanded form of the text, and the Christians with the collection found in the LXX? Are there any features that are *group-specific* in any of those texts (other than the three SP features described above)? And if the Qumran community had eventually chosen its own single text form for each book, is there any way to know which of the several available texts for a given book it would have chosen? The challenge for this theory is to discover any evidence that a group changed its form of the text in a manner attributable to the ideology of that group.

The Absence of 'Sectarian Variants'

Neither Emanuel Tov's reconstruction of the history of the biblical text in *TCHB*,[36] nor my idea of variant literary editions appeal to variants due to sectarian motivation.

V. CONCLUSION

This article, in the attempt to discover textual variants that were 'sectarian' in origin or motivation, has focused on individual textual variants highlighted by the Qumran biblical scrolls in contrast with each other and with the Masoretic Text, the Samaritan Pentateuch, and the Septuagint. Its limited scope could not include either variant literary editions as possibly sectarian in origin or the authoritative status of disputed books as possibly promoted or discounted by vying Jewish parties.

Despite the fact that the question regarding sectarian basis seems so obvious, so instinctual, so needing to be asked, both the resulting evidence and the logic of the question point toward a negative answer.

With regard to the textual evidence: no variants emerged to indicate that any group — whether Pharisaic, Sadducean, Samaritan, Essene, Christian, or other — had tampered with Scripture in order to bolster their particular beliefs, except for the two Samaritan beliefs that God 'had chosen' Mount Gerizim and had commanded the central altar there, and possibly except for the Mount Gerizim/Mount Ebal variant.

With regard to the logic: if one group tampered with the text of Scripture in order to promote its views, it would have been open to immediate demonstrable refutation. All the groups had limited viewpoints, but all apparently agreed that the text of the 'original' Scriptures should not be altered, and if there were problems, the texts should be corrected toward the 'original', not reshaped according to secterian ideology.

The following is what the ancient scribes seem to have done. Almost always, the scribes tried simply to copy faithfully the text that lay before them, or at least the text their eye or mind perceived. Occasionally, they introduced changes into the text, either making inadvertent mistakes (some of which were corrected, while some remained) or attempting to make the text clearer or smoother; these were intended not as changes in content but as minor improvements to bring out the inherent sense more clearly or to make the grammar flow more smoothly.

Rarely, probably less than once per century for any given book, a creative religious leader or theologian produced a new edition of a work — analogous to the revised edition of the Gospel According to Mark produced by the redactor of Matthew or Luke — that transmitted the traditional content faithfully but creatively reshaped it in light of the contemporary historical, theological, or cultural situation. In form, such could be termed a new literary edition of the work; in content and motive, it was a new theological edition. None of the new literary editions show indications of sectarian motivation, with the single exception of the Samaritan focus on Gerizim.

Very rarely, indeed virtually never, did a scribe introduce a theological change, and when this happened, it was not sectarian but in line with general Jewish views or impulses.

Now it is fully possible, of course, that there are some sectarian variants that I have not noticed or have not correctly understood. It is also true that the biblical variants illuminated by the manuscripts of the Scriptures found at Qumran form a tantalizing collection of data. And we all know that, if there is an attractive mistake waiting to be made, there is probably an eager scholar itching to make that mistake.

So I offer a few criteria that may help scholars either discover true sectarian variants, if there are such, or not make the mistake of hastily claiming that a variant is a 'sectarian' variant if it is not.

1. A sectarian variant must be clearly *secondary* (or later). It cannot be either an original (or earlier) reading or what Shemaryahu Talmon has helpfully categorized as a synonymous variant. It should perhaps be jarring or arresting in the context (as, e.g., כדויד in Amos 6:5).

2. The variant must be *intentional*. It must be clear that an author or scribe was concerned to change one natural, sound reading into a reading important to his particular group.

3. The variant must be *specific* to one group or sect vs. another, or supporting a major theme or word peculiar to a specific group as opposed to Jews in general. It is unlikely, for example, that the presence of אור in Isaiah 53:11 constitutes a sectarian variant inspired by the motif of בני אור vs. בני חושך when all Jews could immediately identify with יהוה אורי in Psalm 27:1.

4. The variant ought to be *repeated* or consistently made or accompanied by other similarly sectarian variants in the same manuscript, not a single, isolated variant. It should not be easily explainable by simpler, more frequent classes of variants, such as metathesis, confusion of laryngeals or sibilants, confusion of palaeographic forms ד / ר / ו / י, or similar phenomena; these happen so frequently where no meaning is involved that such a variant would be highly implausible without other solid corroboration.

In the light of the thousands of biblical variants which involve neither significant meaning nor sectarian influence, but which are readily assignable to the normal, dull categories of textual variants, there is a Herculean burden of proof on the person who wishes to claim that a particular variant — especially an isolated variant — is sectarian in nature. In most instances where theological *Tendenz* is seen in readings in the Septuagint, or where sectarian variants will surely be claimed in the scrolls, the basis disappears upon analysis. First, sectarian manipulation or theological *Tendenz* is usually only one of several possible explanations of the variant, and usually a maximalist interpretation. Second, the phenomenon is not sustained in other possible occurrences where it would have been expected to be repeated. Third, additional examples of the alternate and usually less exciting explanation often occur, counter-indicating the sectarian or tendentious claim. In short, one should rarely be convinced of sectarian motivation or theological *Tendenz* in textual variants.[37]

NOTES

1   See George Brooke's insightful paper in this volume.

2   Paul Kahle, *Die hebräischen Handschriften aus der Höhle* (Stuttgart: Kohlhammer, 1951), pp. 183–84. See also the discussions in E. Y. Kutscher, *The Language and Linguistic Background of the Isaiah Scroll (1 Q Isaᵃ)*, STDJ, 6 (Leiden: Brill, 1974), pp. 77–89; and TCHB, pp. 193–95.

3   Eugene Ulrich, 'The Dead Sea Scrolls and the Hebrew Scriptural Texts', in *The Bible and the Dead Sea Scrolls: Proceedings of the Jubilee Celebration at Princeton Theological Seminary*, vol. 1: *The Hebrew Bible and Qumran*; ed. by James H. Charlesworth (North Richland, TX: Bibal Press, 2000), pp. 105–133 (p. 133).

4   For a discussion of the issues involved, see Eugene Ulrich, 'The Qumran Biblical Scrolls — The

Scriptures of Late Second Temple Judaism', in *DSSTHC*, pp. 67–87.

5   See, e.g., E. P. Sanders, *Judaism: Practice and Belief 63 BCE–66 CE* (London: SCM Press; Philadelphia: Trinity Press International, 1992); Lawrence H. Schiffman, *From Text to Tradition: A History of Second Temple and Rabbinic Judaism* (Hoboken, NJ: Ktav, 1991); Albert I. Baumgarten, 'Pharisees' in *EDSS*, II, pp. 657–63 (p. 661); and Ulrich, 'Scriptures of Judaism', pp. 81–87.

6   Baumgarten, p. 661.

7   For a judicious analysis see Anthony J. Saldarini, 'Sectarianism', in *EDSS*, II, pp. 853–57 (p. 854). See also Schiffman, *From Text to Tradition*, p. 98: 'The designation of these groups as "sects" and of this phenomenon as "sectarianism" is admittedly problematic, since these two terms usually assume a dominant or normative stream from which others have diverged. Rabbinic tradition claimed such a status for Pharisaic Judaism but it is difficult to consider a minority, no matter how influential, to be a mainstream'.

8   See Ulrich, 'The Scriptures of Judaism', pp. 81–87.

9   It is interesting to note that those ancient textual scholars, including Origen, made an error analogous to that of modern scholars who presume that the MT was the standard text in that period. A valuable witness to the ancient Hebrew text was destroyed when the Old Greek (OG) translation was 'revised' toward the rabbinic text. The OG was generally a faithful translation of one form of the Hebrew text. Such alternate Hebrew texts were eventually lost after the Jewish revolts, and often their witnesses in Greek were also lost through the 'revisions' toward the lone rabbinic form of the texts, in the mistaken notion that the latter were the 'original'.

10 Chaim Rabin, 'The Dead Sea Scrolls and the History of the O.T. Text', *JTS*, New Series, 6 (1955), 174–82 (pp. 174–75).

11 For the critical edition of the text plus details of the argument see Eugene Ulrich, '47. 4QJosh[a]', in DJD XIV, pp. 143–52; and Eugene Ulrich, '4QJoshua[a] and Joshua's First Altar in the Promised Land', in *NQTS*, pp. 89–104. 'Mount Gerizim' is also attested by the Old Latin (OL) at Deuteronomy 27:4, suggesting that the OG or an early form of the LXX also had that reading.

12 For the critical edition and a discussion see Julio Trebolle Barrera, '49. 4QJudg[a]', in DJD XIV, pp. 161–64; and Julio Trebolle Barrera, 'Textual Variants in 4QJudg[a] and the Textual and Editorial History of the Book of Judges', in *The Texts of Qumran and the History of the Community: Proceedings of the Groningen Congress on the Dead Sea Scrolls (20–23 August 1989)*, I: *Biblical Texts*, ed. by Florentino García Martínez (Paris: Gabalda (= *RevQ*, 14, no. 54) 1989), pp. 229–45.

13 I first heard this point argued by Robert Kugler in 'The Deuteronomist's Text of 1 Samuel 1', presented in the Textual Criticism of the Hebrew Bible Section at the annual meeting of the Society of Biblical Literature, San Francisco, November 1992. It is persuasively in line with Gerhard von Rad, 'The Deuteronomic Theology of History in I and II Kings', in *The Problem of the Hexateuch and Other Essays*, trans. by E. W. Trueman Dicken (London: SCM Press, 1966), pp. 205–21.

14 See *DSSB*, pp. 267–381.

15 These occur in the MT and either 1QIsa[a] or the LXX at Isaiah 2:9b-10, 22; 34:17[fin]–35:2; 36:7; 37:4-7; 38:20; 40:7, 14b-16; 51:6; and 63:3[fin]. For brief commentary see *DSSB*, pp. 274–75, 322–24, 326, 331–33, 355, and 375. For more detailed discussion see Eugene Ulrich, The Developmental Composition of the Book of Isaiah: Light from 1QIsa[a] on Additions in the MT', *DSD*, 8 (2001), 288–305.

16 James E. Harding, 'The Wordplay between the Roots כשל and שכל in the Literature of the *Yaḥad*', *RevQ*, 19 (1999), pp. 69–82.

17 This is also suggested by D. Winton Thomas in *BHS* note 53:11[a].

18 Arie van der Kooij, *Die alten Textzeugen des Jesajabuches: Ein Beitrag zur Textgeschichte des Alten Testaments*, OBO, 35 (Freiburg, Schweiz: Universitätsverlag; Göttingen: Vandenhoeck & Ruprecht, 1981), pp. 95–96: 'Der Verfasser von Q[a] Prophezeiungen des Jesajabuches auf seine eigene Zeit bezog. Das bedeutet, dass er die überlieferten Prophezeiungen auf genau die Weise aktualisierte, wie es auch in den Pescharim geschah. Er und mit ihm andere Mitglieder der Qumrangemeinde waren davon überzeugt, dass die prophetischen Worte von "den kommenden Ereignissen" auch "die letzten Ereignisse" darstellten. [. . .] der Verfasser-Schriftgelehrter von Q[a] ist mit dem (ersten) Lehrer der Gerechtigkeit gleichzusetzen.'

19 Arie van der Kooij, *The Oracle of Tyre: The Septuagint of Isaiah XXIII as Version and Vision*,

VTSup, 71 (Leiden: Brill, 1998), p. 186: 'In contrast to MT which is about a destruction of Tyre, LXX refers to a destruction of Carthage with its serious consequences for Tyre'.

20 Briefly: (a) In several readings the Qumran Isaiah MSS show that the LXX was not translating from a *Vorlage* like the MT but faithfully attempting to translate a text which was simply a different Hebrew text.

(b) Peter W. Flint ('The Septuagint Version of Isaiah 23:1-14 and the Massoretic Text', *BIOSCS*, 21 (1988), 35–54) has written countering the actualizing interpretation of Isaiah 23, and Ronald L. Troxel ('Ἔσχατος and Eschatology in LXX-Isaiah', *BIOSCS*, 25 (1992), 18–27), countering the eschatological use of ἔσχατος by the LXX translator.

(c) Van der Kooij's view is partly influenced by Seeligmann who had earlier proposed this Carthage hypothesis. But Seeligmann's work, published in 1948, was written prior to the new knowledge provided by the scrolls and needs a methodological revision. Moreover, van der Kooij objects both to Seeligmann's isolated approach to individual readings rather than the full context, and to his specific understanding of πλοῖα in 23:1 as the subject of ἀπώλετο.

(d) The title of the oracle in 23:1 is משא צר, translated faithfully as τὸ ὅραμα Τύρου; and thus the oracle as presented by the Greek translator is against Tyre, not Carthage.

(e) In 23:5 the Greek 'sorrow about Tyre' is a free but faithful translation of the Hebrew 'report about Tyre', faithfully but more pointedly and less ambiguously making explicit that the translator understands that it is Tyre, not Carthage, which has suffered.

(f) The immediately following words (23:6) are 'Depart to Carthage!' suggesting that Tyre is destroyed and thus they should depart to Carthage which is safe.

(g) Both the Hebrew and the Greek of 23:8 say: 'Who has counselled this against Tyre [. . .] whose merchants were princes, rulers of the world?' Thus, presumably it is the formerly mighty Tyre which has fallen, not Carthage.

In short, several places are indeed ambiguous, capable of being interpreted either way. But the Cave 1 and Cave 4 Isaiah MSS offer examples of the Hebrew forms seen and faithfully translated by the Greek translator, and other parts of the Greek passage demonstrate that it is Tyre, not Carthage, that has fallen and is to be lamented.

21 Robert Hanhart, 'The Translation of the Septuagint in Light of Earlier Tradition and Subsequent Influences', in *SSCW*, pp. 339–79 (pp. 342–43). See also now the responses by Ronald S. Hendel, 'On the Text-Critical Value of Septuagint Genesis: A Reply to Rösel', *BIOSCS*, 32 (1999), 31–34, and William P. Brown, 'Reassessing the Text-Critical Value of Septuagint-Genesis 1: A Response to Martin Rösel', *BIOSCS*, 32 (1999), 35–39 to Martin Rösel's excessive claims in 'The Text-Critical Value of Septuagint-Genesis', *BIOSCS*, 31 (1998), 62–70 for 'theological intention' (p. 63) by the LXX translator.

22 See *DSSB*, pp. 505–89.

23 See *DSSB*, pp. 570–72.

24 For a recent, solid, and clear analysis of calendrical issues, see James C. VanderKam, *Calendars in the Dead Sea Scrolls: Measuring Time* (London: Routledge, 1998).

25 Appendices occur at or near the end of several books or major sections thereof, e.g., Judges, Samuel, Isaiah, and perhaps Leviticus and Deuteronomy.

26 See *DSSB*, pp. 482–501.

27 For the edition and text-critical analysis of 4QSam^c, see Eugene Charles Ulrich, '4QSam^c: A Fragmentary Manuscript of 2 Samuel 14–15 from the Scribe of the *Serek Hay-yaḥad*' (1QS)', *BASOR*, 235 (1979), 1–25.

28 4Q158 frg. 6 also quotes this form of the Exodus text, as Brant James Pitre pointed out in 1999 in an unpublished paper on 4Q175.

29 The LXX edition of Exodus 35–40, however, is not the earliest form of this section but already shows signs of editorial development; see Anneli Aejmelaeus, 'Septuagintal Translation Techniques — A Solution to the Problem of the Tabernacle Account', in *On the Trail of Septuagint Translators* (Kampen: Kok Pharos, 1993), pp. 116–30.

30 See DJD IX, pp. 53–130; and Judith E. Sanderson, *An Exodus Scroll from Qumran: 4QpaleoExod^m and the Samaritan Tradition*, Harvard Semitic Studies, 30 (Atlanta: Scholars Press, 1986).

31 Aejmelaeus, 'Septuagintal Translation Techniques', p. 127.

32 See Carol Newsom, in DJD XXII, pp. 278–81.

33 It need not be mentioned that the scribe made several errors in his insertion, misspelling two words and continuing the insertion one or two words beyond where he should have stopped.

34 Frank Moore Cross, 'The Evolution of a Theory of Local Texts', in *QHBT*, pp. 306–20.

35 Shemaryahu Talmon, 'The Old Testament Text', in *The Cambridge History of the Bible. I: From the Beginnings to Jerome*, ed. by P. R. Ackroyd and C. F. Evans (Cambridge: Cambridge University Press, 1970), pp. 159–99 (pp. 197–99) (repr. in *QHBT*, pp. 1–41 (pp. 40–41)); Shemaryahu Talmon, 'Aspects of the Textual Transmission of the Bible in the Light of Qumran Manuscripts', *Textus*, 4 (1964), 95–132 (pp. 125–32) (repr. in *QHBT*, pp. 226–63 (pp. 256–63)); Shemaryahu Talmon, 'The Textual Study of the Bible—A New Outlook', *QHBT*, pp. 321–400.

36 See *TCHB*, p. 266, n. 37.

37 See the quotation from Professor Hanhart in III. A. 3. (e) above.

THE KAIGE RECENSION OF SAMUEL: LIGHT FROM 4QSAM^A

Edward D. Herbert

THE EXTANT REMAINS of 4QSam[a], a fragmentary manuscript of the books of Samuel, preserve about eight per cent of the original scroll, spread across their chapters, containing elements (at least one letter) of one third of the verses. The value of the scroll arises particularly from three observations. Firstly, it 'stands in the same general tradition as the Hebrew text upon which the Septuagint was based';[1] secondly, it shares readings with Chronicles against the Masoretic Text of Samuel (MT)[2] and finally, according to some,[3] it supplies new potentially primitive readings that have been hitherto lost in a book where the MT is generally recognised as less well preserved than in other books of the Hebrew Bible. The scroll therefore is valuable not only in clarifying the text critical value of the witnesses to Samuel and in contributing readings which may resolve certain text critical conundra, but also in providing an important window on the history of the biblical text around the turn of the era.

H. St J. Thackeray's 1907 article laid the foundation for later work on the Septuagint of Samuel-Kings.[4] He distinguished five divisions of the Greek text of Reigns: α (1 Samuel); ββ (2 Samuel 1:1 - 11:1); βγ (2 Samuel 11:2 – 1 Kings 2:11); γγ (1 Kings 2:12 - 21:43) and γδ (1 Kings 22 – 2 Kings 25). He believed that these represented four different translators, sections βγ and γδ being the work of a single (later) translator, which he labelled βδ. Thackeray identified a markedly different translation technique in βδ, and listed a range of distinctive translation characteristics that were apparent in βδ, but not in α, ββ or γγ.

Dominique Barthélemy in his programmatic work *Les devanciers d'Aquila* demonstrated that Thackeray's βδ was not an independent translation, but rather a recension, in the sense of an attempt to conform the existing Old Greek text towards the Hebrew.[5] This recension was labelled the 'kaige recension' (KR) on the basis of one of the more striking characteristics of βδ, namely the translation of גם or וגם by και γε. The clearest evidence that this was a recension rather than a translation was that the 'Lucianic' manuscripts boc₂e₂ (hereafter, L) deviated much more sharply from the LXX (in this article LXX represents the Septuagint excluding L) in βδ than in α, ββ or γγ, whilst retaining the translational characteristics present in α, ββ and γγ throughout Samuel-Kings. He also identified βδ as one of a number of witnesses apparent at different points within the Old Testament Greek witnesses in which the same 'kaige recension' has been preserved. He furthermore sought to identify KR as from Theodotion, hence the name 'kaige-Theodotion' sometimes used for this recension.

An attempt will be made below to reconsider KR in Samuel in the light of an analysis of 4QSam[a] (hereafter, 4Q) to test and develop some aspects of the work of Thackeray,

Barthélemy and later scholars. This will be achieved by constructing statistics concerning the pattern of agreements between the key textual witnesses (MT, 4Q, LXX and L) and considering how these relate to the theories regarding the KR in Samuel. The analysis will build on the relationships which have already been established between the key textual witnesses.[6]

The wisdom of seeking to categorize textual witnesses according to their relationships has been questioned, especially by Emanuel Tov, who has categorized thirty-seven percent of Torah scrolls and fifty-three percent of other biblical scrolls as 'non-aligned' rather than linked with key textual tradition groupings.[7] This view has been particularly argued on the grounds that such scrolls contain a significant number of unique readings. However, manuscripts have been copied from manuscripts which have been copied from others in turn, and so on. It is therefore possible, at least in principle, to link manuscripts by constructing a stemma. Unique readings are merely the inevitable fruit of corruption and adaptation in the process of copying. The presence of unique readings, therefore, does not affect its relationships as such, but merely the transmission history of the witnesses *after* the separation of their underlying traditions. In other words, supposedly 'non-aligned' manuscripts still have ancestor manuscripts and are thus related in some way to the wider manuscript tradition.[8]

The fact that all manuscripts have an ancestry does not imply that they were not subject to contamination from readings from another tradition. Indeed it is clear that such contamination is a reality in many instances, as is apparent, for instance, in LXX recensional activity towards proto-MT, the employment of Hexaplaric readings widely among LXX manuscripts, and the presence of doublets in most extant traditions. In the light of this, any method for constructing and utilizing stemmas must take full account of the all too real possibility of contamination of one tradition by readings from another. Such a method for constructing stemmas and applying insights from them to text critical problems, that is fully cognizant of the reality of contamination between traditions, has already been developed, and the stemma relating to Samuel which has been derived in that process is shown below.[9] Since the primary points of contamination between traditions which have been identified in the above article are not material to the discussion below, these have been excluded from the stemma.

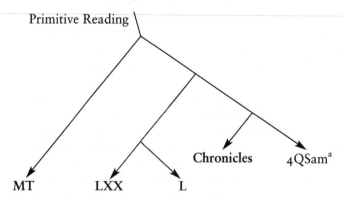

Fig. 1 Stemma of key textual relationships in Samuel
(black represents Hebrew transmission; grey represents Greek transmission)

The Kaige Recension of Samuel

1. TESTING BARTHÉLEMY'S THEORY OF A KAIGE RECENSION IN SAMUEL

Barthélemy postulates that L is the only part of the Septuagint tradition unaffected by the recension, whereas LXX was subject to it in sections βγ and γδ but not in α, ββ or γγ. This would mean that LXX, but not L, has been 'drawn towards' MT in the kaige sections and thus away from Old Greek (OG) out of which L (and LXX) arose. The revised stemma below reflects Barthélemy's theory of movement of KR towards LXX in the kaige sections of Samuel.

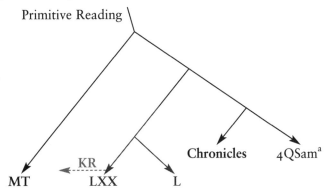

Fig. 2 Stemma of key textual relationships in Samuel (sections βγ and γδ) (including impact of kaige recension on LXX)

If Barthélemy is correct, we would expect to see:

1. a greater deviation between LXX and L in the kaige sections than in the non-kaige sections, since LXX in the kaige sections has been corrected away from both Old Greek and L towards MT;

2. LXX agreeing significantly more with MT against 4Q in the kaige sections compared to the non-kaige sections, since LXX has been corrected towards MT in the kaige sections;

3. L displaying approximately the same pattern of agreements with MT and 4Q in the kaige and non-kaige sections, since L, according to Barthélemy, was unaffected by the KR.

There are 351 variation units[10] in 1-2 Samuel where the readings of MT and 4Q differ from each other and where it is possible with reasonable confidence to determine which of the two is followed by LXX and which is followed by L.[11] Two thirds are in the non-kaige section and one third in the kaige section. Analysis of these variation units results in the statistics tabulated at the top of the next page concerning relationships between traditions. The final two columns express these statistics in percentages for ease of comparison.

In the non-kaige section, which acts as a 'control' for the analysis of the impact of KR on the textual relationships, LXX agrees with 4Q (with or without the support of L) on 58% (i.e. 53%+5%) of occasions and with MT on 42% of occasions. On the other hand, L agrees with 4Q against MT on 56% (i.e. 53%+3%) of occasions and with MT in the remaining 44% of occasions. It, is thus apparent that, where KR is not present, L and LXX each agree with 4Q in approximately the same proportion of occasions as each other.

	Non-kaige (frequency)	kaige (frequency)	Non-kaige (%)	kaige (%)
MT=LXX/L ≠ 4Q	92^{12}	59^{13}	39	51
MT=L ≠ 4Q=LXX	12^{14}	2^{15}	5	2
MT ≠ 4Q=LXX/L	125^{16}	20^{17}	53	17
MT=LXX ≠ 4Q=L	6^{18}	35^{19}	3	30
TOTAL	235	116	100	100

Table 1: Pattern of agreements between key witnesses in Samuel
where MT and 4Q readings differ

In the kaige section, LXX agrees with 4Q in only 19% of variation units (i.e. 17%+2%), only one third of the level of agreements (58%) of LXX with 4Q in the non-kaige sections. The recensional impact of KR is thus seen to be significant indeed. Interestingly, however, L agrees with 4Q on 47% of occasions in the kaige section, i.e., significantly below that of the 56% L=4Q agreement in the non-kaige section. The drop of 9% between non-kaige and kaige sections for L=4Q agreements is statistically significant, but is only around one quarter of the drop for LXX=4Q between these sections.

The substantial differential between the impact of KR on LXX=4Q and that on L=4Q supports Barthélemy's theory.[20] The significant reduction in the proportion of L=4Q agreements in the kaige section relative to the non-kaige section, however, also warrants an explanation, since random statistical variation alone is inadequate to explain this reduction. An explanation is required of how the KR has impacted L, albeit to a much lesser degree than KR's impact on LXX.

Again we find that Barthélemy's work provides the raw materials for an explanation. He argues that the fifth column of Origen's *Hexapla* actually contained the KR in βδ, and it is already known that L contains many Hexaplaric readings.[21] Consequently, in the kaige sections, a higher proportion of the readings picked up from the fifth column of the Hexapla would be proto-MT-related. This being the case, we would expect L to have a slightly higher proportion of agreements with MT in the kaige section than in the non-kaige section, although L itself was never subject to the KR.

The above analysis suggests that Barthélemy's theory of a recension in the latter part of Samuel towards MT is well founded, even though the impact on L might not have been anticipated on the basis of his basic theory.

2. THE NATURE OF THE KAIGE RECENSION

Now that the general nature of KR has been established, it would be useful to consider whether there are particular *types* of agreements with 4Q, such as pluses or minuses, that are more likely to be transformed into agreements with MT by KR. To achieve this, all the 351 variation units have been categorised as to whether the text of 4Q is longer, shorter or of similar size to that of MT.[22] The results are displayed below in terms of the percentage of the particular type of variant (e.g. 4Q longer than MT) in the non-kaige section and then in the kaige section that displays a certain pattern of textual agreements. The figures in brackets are the actual number of variation units represented.

		4Q longer than MT % [frequency]	4Q similar to MT % [frequency]	4Q shorter than MT % [frequency]	TOTAL % [frequency]
Non-kaige	All variations	100 [92]	100 [92]	100 [51]	100 [235]
kaige	All variations	100 [39]	100 [48]	100 [29]	100 [116]
Non-kaige	4Q = LXX	50 [46]	71 [65]	51 [26]	58 [137]
kaige	4Q = LXX	23 [9]	21 [10]	10 [3]	19 [22]
Non-kaige	4Q = L	51 [47]	70 [64]	39 [20]	56 [131]
kaige	4Q = L	41 [16]	60 [29]	34 [10]	47 [55]

Table 2: Analysis by type of variation: percentage of variation units reflecting specified pattern of textual agreements [frequency in brackets]

For all types of variant, LXX is considerably further from 4Q (and correspondingly closer to MT) in the kaige section. Particularly striking, though, is that, whilst almost 50% of the 4Q=LXX agreements in the non-kaige sections have been retained in the variation units where 4Q is longer than MT (23% as against 50%), only 30% have been retained, where 4Q is the same length as MT (21% as against 71%), and just over 20% where 4Q is shorter than MT (10% as against 51%). In other words, the recensionist appears to have been much happier to add text on the basis of proto-MT (pMT) than to remove Septuagint text on the basis of its absence from pMT. Perhaps there was a wariness at excising potentially valuable elements from Scripture. By contrast, the statistics suggest that the impact on L was independent of whether the variation unit was longer in MT or 4Q.

Whilst the number of variation units relating to the pattern of LXX agreements in the non-kaige section is adequate for statistical analysis, the number of variation units for the kaige section is less than one would desire. It is, nevertheless, appropriate to seek to explore further the impact of the relative length of the MT or 4Q readings on the pattern of agreements of LXX in the kaige section.

We have noted that the likelihood of the recensionist conforming his text to that of MT was partly dependent upon whether the reading of MT represented a plus or a minus relative to LXX. If, as appears to be the case, the recensionist tended to prefer to add material rather than remove material from his Septuagint archetype, it becomes appropriate to examine the few (three)[23] instances where the recensionist apparently failed to embrace longer MT readings. Interestingly, all three of these exist where MT's reading appears to be secondary. Since, of course, the recensionist would not actually have had access to MT in its current form, but rather proto-MT (pMT), there is a real possibility that these corruptions occurred in the MT tradition *after* KR had taken place. They may therefore not be examples of the recensionist failing to take into his Greek text pluses that were available from 'his MT'.

Half of the ten 4Q=LXX variation units in the kaige section where 4Q's reading is of similar length to MT[24] and one third of the nine variation units where 4Q's reading is longer than MT[25] are examples where MT appears to be secondary. This means that there are still at least five variation units where 4Q and MT readings are of similar length and at least six variation units where MT's reading is shorter than that of 4Q where the recensionist failed to conform his Greek text to 'his MT'. This suggests that the recensionist may have been keen to take in pluses from pMT and make changes to his text on the basis of pMT, but was willing to leave some minor differences, and was reluctant to excise sections of LXX on the basis of their absence from pMT.

Of particular interest are the six readings (up to nine if some of the readings where MT is secondary arose earlier than KR) where the recensionist chose not to correct to pMT. Two of these are major pluses (2 Samuel 13:21 and 13:37a) with the other four comprising only single words. These can be compared to the seven readings in the kaige section where 4Q is longer than MT and where MT=LXX but where L still agrees with 4Q,[26] as these appear to be the variation units where the recensionist decided to remove text from his Greek source to conform it to pMT. One of these is a major plus (2 Samuel 18:3) and one other may be significant (2 Samuel 22:37), but the other five are minor additions of only one or two words. Despite the strong recension towards MT represented by KR, the recensionist therefore appears to have been reluctant to remove elements from his source text. Indeed only in around half of the variation units where MT was shorter than 4Q did the recensionist actually appear to have been willing to cut text. The desire to conform the Greek text to the Hebrew appears to be tempered by a wariness to risk potentially losing a piece of valuable Scripture which might have been occasioned by the removal of an element of the Septuagint that was not represented in the Hebrew.

This has implications when considering the impact of other recensions or of contamination between textual traditions. The above suggests that caution should be exercised before assuming that Greek pluses would have been removed when contact with a Hebrew text without the plus in question occurs. If even the recensionist responsible for KR was less than keen to cut text, then less thorough recensions can be expected to have reflected even less enthusiasm. The implications of this observation for text criticism have been introduced in my 1997 article.[27]

Ulrich noted 'Thus, none of the 20 agreements of 4Q G [i.e. 4Q=LXX in our notation] in section βγ appear to be part of the kaige recensional stratum of the KR text but rather part of the OG substratum of the text',[28] a conclusion which appears to be supported by Tov.[29] In other words, KR was not consistent in conforming all readings to MT. The above analysis confirms this, but has sought to contribute to the question by indicating the *types* of readings where the recensionist is most likely to have allowed the OG substratum to remain unchanged – those where the Hebrew text is shorter than the Greek text which is being subject to recension.

3. TWO KEY SEPTUAGINT MANUSCRIPT GROUPS

There is an interesting distinction between manuscript B(h/y)a$_2$Acx and the rest of the LXX tradition, which warrants further consideration. B(h/y)a$_2$, in the kaige sections where 4Q deviates from MT, deviates from the majority LXX (hereafter LXXmaj) a total of eight times.[30] In all of these cases, B(h/y)a$_2$ follows MT, and in seven of these cases, B(h/y)a$_2$ is followed by A and usually also by cx.[31]

Bya$_2$, often supported by Acx, also remains a significant grouping within the non-kaige sections, with six independent instances where Bya$_2$ reflects a different loyalty to LXXmaj,[32] supported by Acx in three of these occasions.[33] In contrast to the uniformity of textual affinities noted in the kaige section, there is no consistent pattern. Out of these six instances, Bya$_2$ agrees four times with 4Q, once with MT (2 Samuel 5:8) and once with neither MT nor 4Q (2 Samuel 5:1). Thus in the non-kaige section, Bya$_2$ deviates from the remainder of LXX in a markedly different way to that in the kaige sections. In the non-kaige section, Bya$_2$ has a tendency to move away from MT (towards 4Q), sometimes independently of Acx, whilst in the kaige section, B(h/y)a$_2$ deviates consistently towards MT in tandem with Acx.

An explanation should be sought that will explain the different movements experienced by B(h/y)a$_2$ (and Acx) in the kaige and non-kaige sections. The first question is whether B(h/y)a$_2$Acx was subjected to the above distinctive changes before or after certain sections of Samuel-Kings Septuagint were subject to KR. If these changes had occurred before Samuel-Kings had become part kaige and part non-kaige, then we would need to presume that KR had *independently* had an impact on the different manuscript groupings (B(h/y)a$_2$Acx and LXXmaj) *and* that these two groupings were independently combined with non-kaige material *with exactly the same* points of transition between kaige and non-kaige. Since this combination of circumstances is implausible, it is clear that the movement within B(h/y)a$_2$Acx must have occurred *after* LXX had been subjected to KR.

It is hard to conceive a single set of changes which would have moved B(h/y)a$_2$Acx towards MT in kaige sections *and* generally towards 4Q in non-kaige sections. This is particularly the case since LXX has already been drawn towards MT in the kaige sections relative to the non-kaige sections through the impact of KR. Barthélemy claims that the group Acx has issued from the fifth column of the Hexapla, while Ba$_2$ is the only direct witness to the basic text used by Origen to construct this fifth column.[34] This again suggests that the explanation does not reside with B(h/y)a$_2$ and Acx moving relative to LXXmaj (i.e. LXX, excluding B(h/y)a$_2$ and Acx), but rather with LXXmaj moving relative to B(h/y)a$_2$ and Acx.

For LXXmaj to have moved, this would require an archetype of LXXmaj to have been subjected to influences after the divergence of the traditions behind B(h/y)a$_2$Acx from the LXXmaj tradition. This being the case, an influence should be sought which can explain LXXmaj's movement towards 4Q in the kaige sections and towards MT, though with less consistency, in the non-kaige sections. The Hexapla is unlikely to be the cause, since this would fail to explain the movements away from MT in the kaige sections. The Lucianic tradition is unlikely, since, although L often agrees with B(h/y)a$_2$ and Acx, it rarely agrees with them against 4Q. The most likely explanation is that the archetype of LXXmaj has been influenced by the Old Greek or at least by a pre-kaige manuscript related to the Old Greek. This would explain why the impact on the kaige section is both more marked and more consistent, than in the non-kaige section, since LXX has already moved away from the Old Greek in the kaige sections due to KR. LXX in the non-kaige sections still approximates to the Old Greek so that the impact of the acceptance of a few readings from the Old Greek should be both less marked and less consistent in direction.

4. THE BOUNDARIES OF THE KAIGE RECENSION

James Shenkel argued that the KR began at the start of 2 Samuel 10, rather than at 2 Samuel 11:2 as had been argued by Barthélemy on the basis of Thackeray's original work.[35] Shenkel rightly pointed out that Thackeray had put forward no textual evidence for this point of division, but had rather depended upon theological grounds, namely that 11:2 represented a cut-off point for which he could suggest an explanation as to why the original translator might have chosen to omit the chapters that followed.[36] He was also correct that Barthélemy had accepted Thackeray's divisions without further investigation. Shenkel argued that KR began with chapter 10 of 2 Samuel rather than chapter 11. The most telling evidence was the presence of historic presents in L in chapter 10, which were replaced by aorists in the majority LXX – exactly as in the kaige sections.

The primary problem with Shenkel's analysis, however, is that none of the characteristics that distinguish kaige from non-kaige that were identified by Thackeray (pp. 267-76) or Shenkel (pp. 113-16) are apparent between 2 Samuel 9:6 and 10:6. Thus, on the basis of the evidence provided, it is not possible to identify the starting point of KR any more specifically than it is somewhere between 2 Samuel 9:6 and 10:6.

This raises the question as to whether 4QSam^a can provide any leads in this respect. Since KR represents a thorough-going attempt to revise the Greek text towards MT, the structure of agreements between the witnesses in the kaige sections is markedly different to those elsewhere. Arising from this, it has been observed above that the proportion of variation units where 4Q=LXX is much lower in the kaige than the non-kaige sections, with a consequently higher incidence of 4Q=L alone (with LXX=MT).

An examination of the agreements with 4Q in 2 Samuel 10 yield no examples of L agreeing with 4Q alone, despite the existence of eleven variation units. However, the fact that there are only two variation units where LXX and L do not follow MT means that there were only two variation units where the interrelationships of the witnesses could be expected to have changed as a result of a recension of LXX towards MT.

These two units occur in 10:5 and 10:6. In 10:6, MT has the clearly corrupt reading איש טוב ('a good man') in place of the place name, אישטוב, which is reflected in 4Q, LXX and L. If this corruption occurred at a later stage in the transmission history of MT than the point at which the recension towards MT occurred, then this example is perfectly compatible with Shenkel's suggestion that this is within a section of Samuel for which LXX had undergone KR. In 10:4, 4Q, Chronicles, LXX and L all reflect the addition of על אנשים into the verse for the purposes of clarification. It is reasonably clear that MT's omission of this gloss represents the superior reading, but the fact that it has already been noted that Theodotion appeared to retain some Greek pluses which were not present in his Hebrew text suggests that 10:4 is equally compatible with its presence within kaige as within non-kaige. Consequently 4Q is unable to help to locate the start of KR, which, on the basis of KR characteristics identified by scholars, cannot be specified more closely than somewhere between 2 Samuel 9:6 and 10:6.

Eugene Ulrich, on the basis of his study of 4Q, MT, Chronicles and LXX in 2 Samuel 6, concludes

> Thackeray and Barthélemy separate 2 S 1-11:1 sharply from the second half of 2 S, assigning 2 S 6 to the "older translator" or the "Old Greek". While their division retains much of its justification, there is, nonetheless, evidence in this chapter of revision, at least some of which is by the hand of the "later translator" or the "*kaige* recension."[37]

Whilst Ulrich highlights good evidence of hebraising revision (doublets reflecting the readings of 4Q and MT), it is not so clear that this arises from the kaige recension, since the nature of this recension appears to be to pull LXX readings towards MT leaving L alone supporting 4Q. However, within 2 Samuel 6, in which there are twenty-four variation units where 4Q deviates from MT, only one case exists (6:9) where L alone follows 4Q, which is of the approximate proportion which we might expect in the non-kaige sections of Samuel. Thus it is seen to be unlikely that KR applied to any substantial degree within 2 Samuel 6. Not only are his two arguments weak for KR, but this should not be seen as the source of the doublets which he highlights, since these are present in L as well as LXX.

Richard Nysse suggests from his study of the Lament of David (2 Samuel 1:19-27) that LXX has been subject to KR in this section too, and seems to imply that this may point to a general extension of KR back to this point, where he states that the aim of his study 'involves a search for the best witness to the Old Greek (OG) in 2 Samuel 1-9'.[38] Unfortunately, 4Q is not extant in 2 Samuel 1:19-27, so that 4Q cannot test the possibility that there might be an isolated section of KR at this point. However, the idea of such a section seems unlikely, for there is no evidence of any such sections of KR within 1 Samuel 1 - 2 Samuel 10. It is most unlikely that such an oasis of KR activity, if it existed, could extend much beyond the end of chapter 1, since eleven variation units exist in 2 Samuel 2:5-16, with five agreements of LXX/L with 4Q, with no cases of L alone following 4Q. A similar picture is apparent in the nineteent variation units within 2 Samuel 2:29-31.

CONCLUSIONS

It can be confidently affirmed that Barthélemy's theory of a thorough-going kaige recension in much of 2 Samuel is well founded, as is the (lesser) impact of KR on L in these sections (probably via the Hexapla). Analysis of the LXX manuscript tradition has also revealed that the majority LXX tradition (excluding B(h/y)a$_2$, Acx and L) has together been subject to further changes after those inserted by KR. These would also have occurred after the (post-KR) divergence of the tradition behind the majority LXX from the traditions behind B(h/y)a$_2$ and Acx. The source of these post-KR changes was a non-Hexaplaric tradition related to the Old Greek.

It is desirable that further consideration of the nature of recensional activity, both in Samuel-Kings and elsewhere, be undertaken to confirm whether the reluctance of the recensionist in 2 Samuel to remove elements from the Septuagint text on the basis of a shorter proto-MT is a characteristic of recensions in general rather than just of the kaige recensionist.

The point at which KR begins in 2 Samuel is *somewhere* between 2 Samuel 9:6 and 10:6. The more precise claims of Thackeray, Barthélemy and Shenkel are unfounded. The point at which the transition to KR takes place, however, could be identified more closely by comparing LXX and L in these chapters to see where the 'textual distance' between them markedly increases from the level present in the non-kaige section to that present in the kaige section of Samuel. This is an appropriate test because L is a reasonable witness, both in the kaige and the non-kaige sections, to the Old Greek,[39] since KR was applied to LXX rather than L in the kaige section.

NOTES

1   Frank M. Cross, Jr., 'A New Qumran Biblical Fragment Related to the Original Hebrew Underlying the Septuagint', *BASOR*, 132 (1953), 15-26 (p. 23).

2   Frank M. Cross, Jr., *Ancient Library of Qumran and Modern Biblical Studies*, Haskell Lectures 1956-57 (London: Duckworth, 1958), pp. 140-42. See also Werner E. Lemke, 'The Synoptic Problem in the Chronicler's History', *HTR*, 58 (1965), 349-63 (pp. 353, 356-57).

3   Frank Moore Cross, 'The Ammonite Oppression of the Tribes of Gad and Reuben: Missing Verses from 1 Samuel 11 Found in 4QSamuel[a]', in *The Hebrew and Greek Texts of Samuel: 1980 Proceedings IOSCS – Vienna*, ed. by Emanuel Tov (Jerusalem: Academon, 1980), pp. 105-119, for instance, argued that the extra material in 4QSam[a] which explains why Nahash the Ammonite was determined to gouge out every right eye of the inhabitants of Jabesh Gilead should be viewed as original (1983). In this, he is followed by Eugene Charles Ulrich, Jr., *The Qumran Text of Samuel and Josephus*, HSM, 19 (Missoula, MT: Scholars Press: 1978), pp. 166-70 and Eugene C. Ulrich, 'The Qumran Biblical Scrolls – The Scriptures of Late Second Temple Judaism', in *DSSTHC*, pp. 67-87 (p. 77), and P. Kyle McCarter, Jr., *I Samuel: A New Translation with Introduction, Notes & Commentary*, Anchor Bible, 8 (Garden City, NY: Doubleday, 1980), pp. 199-200. This conclusion is disputed by Rofé and myself on different grounds: Alexander Rofé, 'The Acts of Nahash according to 4QSam[a]', *IEJ*, 32 (1982), 129-33. Edward D. Herbert, '4QSam[a] and its Relationship to the LXX: an Exploration in Stemmatological Analysis', in *IX Congress of the International Organization for Septuagint and Cognate Studies: Cambridge, 1995*, ed. by Bernard A. Taylor, SBL Septuagint and Cognate Studies Series, 45 (Atlanta, GA: Scholars Press, 1997), pp. 37-55.

4   H. St J. Thackeray, 'The Greek Translators of the Four Books of Kings', *JTS*, 8 (1907), 262-78.

5   Dominique Barthélemy, *Les devanciers d'Aquila*, VTSup, 10 (Leiden: Brill, 1963), pp. 92-102.

6   See especially Ulrich, *Qumran Text of Samuel*, and Herbert, '4QSam[a] and its Relationship'.

7   See his paper in this volume, and his earlier comments in *TCHB*, pp. 114-17, where the non-aligned category was seen as 10% of the biblical scrolls at Qumran).

8   Cf. Frank Moore Cross, 'Some Notes on a Generation of Qumran Studies', in *MQC*, pp. 1-14 (pp. 6-9), where he argues for the appropriateness of analyzing manuscripts into families which represent filial relationships, and for the identification of shared secondary readings as the basis for distinguishing these relationships. See also Tov's response in Emanuel Tov, 'Some Notes on a Generation of Qumran Studies (by Frank M. Cross): Reply by Emanuel Tov' in *MQC*, pp. 15-21 (pp. 18-21).

9   Herbert, '4QSam[a] and its Relationship'.

10 A variation unit is a section of text which features alternative readings among key witnesses. It may be shorter or longer, but if different parts of a section of text have diverged in different ways in different witnesses, then more than one variation unit is assigned to the section. It is therefore possible to have several variation units in one verse or to have a variation unit which spans more than one verse.

11 4Q readings include those which have been derived by reconstruction on the basis of space considerations where there is 'reasonable certainty' of that deviation existing. This corresponds to deviations designated by '?' or '??' in Appendix D of Edward D. Herbert, *Reconstructing Biblical Dead Sea Scrolls: A New Method Applied to the Reconstruction of 4QSam[a]*, STDJ, 22 (Leiden: Brill, 1997), pp. 221-46 as described on p. 221 of that volume. Details of the deviations in 2 Samuel are

provided in that Appendix. Those for 1 Samuel remain unpublished. Variation units where LXX or L appear not to agree with either MT or 4Q have been excluded from the data.

12   1 Sam 1:11 (x2), 22 (x2), 23, 24, 28; 2:16 (x4), 19, 21, 22 (x2), 25, 26, 27/8, 29, 35; 4:10-12; 5:8 (x2); 6:2, 5, 18; 8:9/10, 11, 18/19; 19:6/7, 7; 10:5, 8, 17/18, 18, 26, 27-11:1; 11:9 (x2), 9/10; 14:24, 31/2, 33, 49; 15:30; 17:5/6; 24:4, 9, 14, 15, 21; 25:4 ,9/10, 20/21; 26:11, 12, 21/2; 27:10; 28:1, 2; 30:27; 2 Sam 2:9/10; 3:7/8, 10, 25 (x2), 28, 29, 34 (x2), 35 (x3), 39; 4:4, 11, 12; 5:4/5, 6, 8, 14-16; 6:2 (x2), 3, 5, 13, 16, 18; 7:25/6, 28; 8:1, 6.

13   2 Sam 10:6 (x3); 11:2, 3, 4, 5, 6, 8, 11, 16; 12:14 (x2), 15 (x2), 16 (x2), 17, 31; 13:3 (x2), 5, 6, 16, 17/18, 19/20, 25, 26, 32; 14:2, 2/3; 15:2 (x2), 4, 6, 28; 16:1 (x2); 18:3 (x2), 4, 5, 9 (x2), 10; 19:6/7, 8, 14/15, 25; 21:1, 6; 22:31/2, 36, 37, 48; 24:16, 20 (x3).

14   1 Sam 1:25; 2:21, 24, 27, 28, 31/2; 11:7; 14:50; 27:10/11; 2 Sam 3:7; 8:3, 4.

15   2 Sam 11:5; 13:31.

16   1 Sam 1:11, 13, 23, 24 (x5), 26; 2:2 , 9, 10 (x2), 16 (x2), 17, 20 (x4), 21 (x3), 22 (x2), 23/4, 25 (x2), 27, 29 (x4), 30, 33, 34, 36; 5:8 (x2), 10, 11; 6:2, 3 (x3), 4, 20; 8:17, 18; 9:11, 18, 19, 21; 10:25, 26 (x2), 27; 11:1, 8; 12:8; 14:30 (x3), 47, 48, 49; 15:27, 28/9, 29; 17:4; 24:15 (x2), 20; 25:3, 11, 22; 27:10 (x2); 30:29; 2 Sam 1:12; 2:5, 7, 13, 15 (x2), 31 (x2); 3:3 (x2), 4, 7, 8 (x2), 10/11, 23, 29, 33, 34 (x2), 36; 4:1, 2, 3, 11, 12 (x2); 5:6, 8, 9, 10, 13; 6:2, 3/4, 5 (x2), 6, 9, 13, 16; 7:23 (x3); 8:4, 7; 10:5.

17   2 Sam 10:6; 11:6; 13:21, 25, 27, 37 (x2); 14:19; 15:2; 18:7, 9; 19:8, 10; 20:11; 22:39, 43, 44; 23:3; 24:16, 17.

18   1 Sam 5:9, 10; 6:2; 9:11; 2 Sam 3:28; 6:9.

19   2 Sam 12:1, 15, 16, 17; 13:3, 24, 25, 28, 29, 32; 15:2 (x2), 29/30; 18:3, 9, 11; 19:7, 20:10 (x2), 13 (x2); 21:6; 22:24, 37, 39, 40, 41, 43, 46 (x2), 49, 51; 23:4; 24:16, 18.

20   Cf. conclusions reached by Frank Moore Cross, 'The Evolution of a Theory of Local Texts', in *QHBT*, pp. 306-20 (p. 313), and Emanuel Tov, 'The Textual Affiliations of 4QSam[a]', *JSOT*, 14 (1979), 37-53 (p. 43), both of whom tend to consider only the impact of KR on LXX.

21   Barthélemy, *Devanciers*, pp. 135-36; Sebastian P. Brock, *The Recensions of the Septuagint Version of 1 Samuel* (Oxford D.Phil. dissertation), pp. 174-75; now published as *The Recensions of the Septuagint Version of 1 Samuel*, Quaderni di Henoch, 9 (Turin: Zamorani, 1996); and Herbert, '4QSam[a] and its Relationship', pp. 46-48.

22   For this purpose, if the variant reading of 4Q takes up not more than 5mm more or less space (approximately 2 characters) in the scroll of 4Q than would the reading of MT, then it is treated as being of similar size. If the variation is more than 5mm, then it is designated a plus or minus relative to the text of MT as appropriate. 'Variant reading' is intended here to be a neutral term, indicating nothing concerning the superiority or otherwise of one reading over another.

23   2 Sam 20:11; 22:39, 43.

24   2 Sam 10:6; 11:5; 13:25; 13:31; 14:19; 15:2; 18:9; 22:44; 23:3 and 24:16 contain 4Q=LXX readings in the kaige section. In 10:6; 13:25; 13:31 and 18:9, MT's reading appears secondary, and in 13:31, 4Q's reading appears to be secondary.

25   2 Sam 11:6; 13:21, 27, 37 (two variation units); 18:7; 19:8, 10 and 24:17 contain 4Q=LXX readings in the kaige section. In 13:27; 19:8 and 24:17, MT's reading appears secondary.

26   2 Sam 12:1, 16; 18:3; 20:13; 22:37, 43 and 46.

27   Herbert, '4QSam[a] and its Relationship', pp. 51-52.

28   Ulrich, *Qumran Text of Samuel*, p. 93.

29   Emanuel Tov, 'Textual Affiliations', p. 44.

30   2 Sam 12:16; 13:39; 16:1; 18:11; 20:13; 21:6; 22:45/6; 24:16. 2 Samuel 13:39 and 22:45/6 have not been included in the preceding lists of variation units as L appears to deviate from both MT and 4Q.

31   In the one case (2 Sam 21:6) where A does not follow B(h/y)a[2]'s distinctive reading, a Ketib/Qere alternative for MT makes the textual affinities less clear cut.

32   1 Sam 5:11; 6:20; 17:4; 2 Sam 5:1, 8; with both 2 Sam 3:8 and 4:12 relating to the name of Ishbosheth/ Mephibosheth.

33   2 Sam 5:1, 8 and 4:12, with 3:8 supported by cx.

34   Barthélemy, *Devanciers*, pp. 138-39;

35   James Donald Shenkel, *Chronology and Recensional Development in the Greek Text of Kings*, HSM, 1, (Cambridge, MA: Harvard University Press, 1968), pp. 117-20.

36 The same could be said for Barthélemy, see Barthélemy, *Devanciers*, pp. 140-41.
37 Ulrich, *Qumran Text of Samuel*, p. 197.
38 Richard W. Nysse, 'An Analysis of the Greek Witnesses to the Text of the Lament of David', in Tov, *1980 Proceedings IOSCS*, pp. 69-104 (p. 69).
39 This is not to say that L preserves the Old Greek more or less intact (as Barthélemy, *Devanciers*, p. 140 proposes), since comparison of L and LXX in the non-kaige sections of Samuel – Kings indicates recensional activity, or at least significant textual developments and corruptions, within L (see Brock, *Recensions of the Septuagint*).

UNIQUE READINGS IN 4QSAM^A

Donald W. Parry

INTRODUCTION AND BACKGROUND

4QSAM^A IS ONE of three manuscripts of Samuel unearthed in Qumran Cave 4 by Roland de Vaux and Lankester Harding in September 1952. The material, at that time consisting of approximately twenty-seven fragments, was buried under more than three feet of deposit. The Samuel manuscript is the best preserved of the biblical manuscripts from Cave 4, in part because the leather was reinforced with a glued papyrus backing, an indication that the scroll was well worn before it was placed in Cave 4.

Subsequent to its discovery, scholars have valued 4QSam^a for its multiple, variant readings which offer new understanding to the text of Samuel. In 1953, Frank Cross published a study which set forth textual affinities between 4QSam^a and the Septuagint.[1] Others, too, have provided examples of individual variant readings of 4QSam^a that establish that the Septuagint is based on a *Vorlage* that is more similar to this Qumran scroll than the Masoretic text (𝔐).[2]

Subsequently, other studies, most notably by Eugene Ulrich, have indicated agreements in readings between 4QSam^a and Josephus.[3] In approximately half a dozen occasions, Josephus presents readings of Samuel in his *Antiquities* that correspond with 4QSam^a, but are not extant in either the Masoretic text or LXX. In addition, Josephus, 4QSam^a, and LXX share almost three dozen readings against those in the Masoretic text.[4]

Moreover, where the book of Chronicles parallels 1 and 2 Samuel, the readings of Chronicles clearly belong to the 4QSam^a rather than the Masoretic textual tradition.[5] Ulrich concludes that 'Chronicles never agrees with M against 4QSam^a, except for [a single reading]. On the other hand, Chronicles agrees with 4QSam^a against 𝔐 in 42 readings, some of which are quite striking.'[6]

While textual affinities between 4QSam^a and the Septuagint, Josephus, and parallel passages in Chronicles have been established, the Qumran witness is less known for its unique readings, that is, variant readings that are not attested in other ancient textual witnesses.[7]

PRELIMINARY NOTES

1. The 81 unique readings of 4QSam^a, from 1 Samuel 1:22 to 2 Samuel 22:37, are presented without detailed comment.[8]

Donald W. Parry

2. The list does not present orthographic variants between the Samuel texts of 4QSam[a] and the Masoretic Text, nor does it list the parallel passages in Chronicles or Psalm 18. Neither does the list include unique readings which are based entirely on reconstruction on the basis of space considerations, e.g.:

1 Samuel 8:11   𝔐 מרכבתו] [ברכב]ו

1 Samuel 9:6   𝔐𝔊𝕮𝕾𝖁 > [ ] [האיש אלוהים]

1 Samuel 12:31   הברזל 1 Chr 20:3; 𝔐𝕮 ובמגרות; ובמגזרת הברזל [[ובמגזרה] 𝔊ᴸ: > 𝔊ᴮ ובמגזרת

2 Samuel 2:5   𝔊ᴬ החסד האלהים 𝔊ᴸ; החסד 𝔐𝕾𝕮𝖁 החסד הזה [[החסד האלהים הז]ה

3. There are several readings where 4QSam[a] differs from 𝔐, but where it is hard or impossible to tell which reading is being followed by the ancient versions. These have not been included in the above list of variant readings. Some examples of such instances are noted below:

1 Samuel 2:16   𝔐 בחזקה] בחזק

1 Samuel 6:2   𝔐 למקומו] אל מקומו

1 Samuel 14:32   𝔐 אל] על

1 Samuel 28:23   𝔐 מהארץ] מן [הא]רץ

2 Samuel 2:6   𝔐 עמכם] אתכם

2 Samuel 2:27   𝔐 מהבקר] מן [הבקר

2 Samuel 3:24   𝔐 הנה] הן

2 Samuel 3:29   𝔐 ואל] ו[לו]א

2 Samuel 3:32   𝔐 את קולו] קולו

2 Samuel 6:2   𝔐 את [> 1 Chr 13:6

2 Samuel 11:6   𝔐 שלח] שלחה

2 Samuel 11:8   𝔐 לאוריה] אל אוריה

2 Samuel 12:18   𝔐 ואיך] ואינ[כ]ה

2 Samuel 13:15   𝔐 מאהבה] מן האהב[ה

UNIQUE READINGS IN 4QSAM^A

I SAMUEL

1) 1:11   יעבור [יעלה 𝔐𝔊𝔖𝔙

2) 1:22   עד אשר [עד 𝔐

3) 1:22   [יהוה] וישב לפני [וישב 𝔐𝔊𝔗𝔖𝔙

4) 1:22+   [חייו] כול ימי [< 𝔐𝔊𝔗𝔖𝔙

5) 1:24   ותעל אותו שילה] και ανεβη μετ αυτου εις Σηλωμ 𝔊; ותעלהו עמה 𝔐𝔗𝔖𝔙

6) 1:24   [בקר משלש [בפר בן] εν μοσχω τριετιζοντι 𝔊; בתורא תולתא 𝔖; בפרים שלשה 𝔐𝔗

7) 1:28   [ליהוה] וישתחוו שם [ותעזב]הו שם ותשתחון ליהוה] > 𝔊^B; וישתחו שם ליהוה 𝔐𝔗; וישתחוו שם ליהוה 𝔖𝔙; וישתחוו ליהוה 𝔊^L

8) 2:4   חתה [חתים 𝔐

9) 2:9   [חס]ידיו ודרך [רגלי חסידו 𝔐; cf. 𝔐^q𝔖𝔙; > 𝔊

10) 2:10+   [יהוה] מי ק[דוש כ] Κυριος αγιος 𝔊; > 𝔐𝔖𝔙

11) 2:10+   [ ] ת[ם בשלמ·] > 𝔐𝔊𝔖𝔙

12) 2:10+   [ ] מל[ן] > 𝔐𝔊𝔖𝔙

13) 2:16   ויאמר האיש הזבח 𝔊 [ועה האיש ו[אומ]ר אל נער הכוהן] ויאמר אליו האיש 𝔐𝔗𝔖; cf. 𝔙

14) 2:16   הכוהן כיום] כיום 𝔐𝔊𝔖𝔙

15) 2:16   ול[ק]חתי [ואם לא לקחתי 𝔐 cf. 𝔊𝔖𝔙

16) 2:16+   long plus] > 𝔐𝔊𝔗𝔖𝔙

17) 2:18   חונר [חגור 𝔐

18) 2:21   [שמואל] ויג[ד]ל שם [ויגדל הנער שמואל 𝔐𝔊𝔗𝔖𝔙

19) 2:22   בן תשעים שנה [> 𝔐𝔊𝔗𝔖𝔙

20) 2:22   [עו]שים בניו 𝔗𝔖] יעשון בניו 𝔐

21) 2:23   𝔐 אנכי שמע] אני [שר]מ[ע]

22) 2:25   𝔐𝔊𝔗𝔖 לקול אביהם כי] ל[]קול כיא

23) 5:8   𝔐𝔊^BO𝔗𝔖𝔙; cf. 𝔊^L   יסב ארון] ו[י]סבו א[ו]ת ארון

24) 5:11   𝔊^B (συγχυσις); מהומת מות] מ[ה]המת יהוֹה 𝔐𝔊^LO𝔗𝔖𝔙

25) 5:11   𝔐; > 𝔊^L𝔙   שם] ש[מ]ה

26) 6:2   > 𝔐𝔊𝔗𝔖𝔙   ולמעל[ני]ם

27) 6:5   עפליכם] העפ[לי]ם 𝔐𝔊^O𝔗𝔖; > 𝔊^BL

28) 6:5   𝔐𝔊𝔗𝔖𝔙 אולי] ו[אנ]לי

29) 10:8   𝔐 להעלות =] לע[לו]ת

30) 10:14   𝔐 דוד שאול; 𝔊 דודו] דוד

31) 10:18   > 𝔐𝔊𝔗𝔖𝔙   כול

32) 11:9   תהיה לכם תשועה 𝔐𝔊𝔗𝔖^O; cf. 𝔊^L לכם תשועה 𝔊^B] [לכם]מיהוה התשו[עה]

33) 11:9+   > 𝔐𝔊𝔗𝔖   [לכם פתחו השׁ]ער

34) 14:34   𝔐𝔊 פצו] נפצו

35) 14:49   𝔐𝔊𝔖𝔙 וישוי] וא[נ]ש בעל

36) 24:19   𝔐𝔗 את אשר] א[שׁ]ר

37) 25:10   𝔐 המתפרצים] [המתפר]שׂים

38) 27:10   𝔐 ועל נגב הירחמאלי ואל נגב] ואל נגב ירח[מ]אל ו[על נגב

39) 28:1   [למ]לחמה יזרעא[לה]; cf. Jos, Ant. 6.325 [εις τον πολεμον εις ρεγ(γ)αν] 𝔊𝔖 למלחמה אתה ואנשיך; 𝔐𝔗𝔙 אתה ואנשיך במחנה

2 SAMUEL

40) 3:10   𝔐𝔊 ועל יהודה] [ו]יהודה

41) 3:25   𝔐 לפתתך] הלפתותך

42) 3:29   𝔐𝔊𝔗𝔖𝔙 אביו] יואב

43) 3:30   [ונג]נ̇ו] הרגו 𝔐𝔖; 𝔊 διεπαρετηρουντο

44) 3:34   בזקים] או [ידיך לא אסרות 𝔐𝔊𝔗𝔖𝔙

45) 3:34   הגש] הגשו 𝔐

46) 3:34   כל [+ העם 𝔐𝔊^{BAL}𝔗𝔖

47) 3:35   לפי] לפני 𝔐𝔊𝔗𝔖

48) 3:35   אוכל] או כל 𝔐𝔊𝔗

49) 4:3   נת[ני]ם] נתימה 𝔐

50) 4:4   ויהי] היה 𝔐; 𝔊 והוא και ουτος)

51) 4:10   לאמ[ור] הנה לאמר] 𝔐𝔗𝔖; cf. 𝔊^L (οτι)

52) 5:6   הסית[?]] הסירך 𝔐; cf. 𝔖; αντεστησαν 𝔊 ante te steterunt 𝔏

53) 6:6   נודן] נכון 𝔐; Νωδαβ 𝔊; כיד 1 Chr 13:9 cf. Jos., *Ant.* VII.81 (Χειδωνος)

54) 7:25   [יהוה] ועתה הדבר] ועתה יהוה הדבר 1 Chr 17:23 cf. הדב 𝔊; ועתה ואדני הדב ועתה יהוה אלהים הדבר 𝔐𝔖

55) 7:28   ודבריך] ודבריך 𝔐𝔊𝔖; > 1 Chr 17:26

56) 11:4   מתקדשת [+ מטמאתה 𝔐𝔊𝔗𝔖

57) 11:10   [ו]יגד] ויגדו 𝔐𝔊𝔗𝔖

58) 12:14   את דבר Co] את איבי 𝔐𝔊^{B(O)}𝔗𝔏𝔖; cf. 𝔊^L; את יהוה 𝔊^C

59) 12:17   ברה] ברא 𝔐

60) 12:17   אותם] אתם 𝔐𝔊𝔗𝔖

61) 12:31   [ובמ]חרצי] ובחריצי 𝔐𝔊𝔗; cf. 𝔖; 1 Chr 20:3

62) 13:3   שמעיה] שמעה 𝔐𝔊 Σαμαα; cf. 1 Chr 20:7 שמעא

63) 13:6   [אחותי] תמר] תמר אחתי 𝔐𝔗𝔖𝔙

64) 13:25   נכביד] נכבד 𝔐𝔊

65) 13:28   והמתם] ומתתם 𝔐

66) 13:31   בנדיו [בנדים 𝔐; cf. 𝔊ᴸ; בנדיהם 𝔊ᴮᴼℭℨℭ𝔖

67) 13:32   את כל הנערים 𝔐𝔊ℨ; cf. 𝔖 [הנערים כול

68) 15:28   דבר מעמכם 𝔐𝔊 (הדבר) 𝔊ᴸ ℭ𝔳; cf. 𝔖 [מן עמכם דבר]

69) 15:29   ירושלם 𝔐 [ירו]שלי מה]

70) 18:3   ישימו 𝔐𝔊ᴮᴬᴸℭ [יו]שי[ם

71) 18:3   אלינו 𝔐𝔊ᴮᴬᴸ [לנו

72) 18:5   שמעו 𝔐ℭ; cf. 𝔖 [שמעים

73) 20:11   ומי אשר לדוד 𝔐ℭ [ומי לד]ויד]

74) 21:16   > 𝔐𝔊 [ומב]חורה

75) 22:36   וענותך 𝔐; וענתך 𝔐ᵠ𝔊𝔖𝔳ℭ [ועזרתך

76) 22:37   תרחיב צעדי תחתי 𝔐; cf. 𝔊𝔊ᵠ𝔖 תרחיב צעדי תחתני [תר]חי[ב צעדי 𝔐ᵠ

77) 22:40   תכריע 𝔐𝔐ᵠ [ותכרע

78) 22:43   אדקם ארקעם 𝔐ℭ; cf 𝔳; אדקם 𝔊ᴮᴼ; cf 𝔊ᴸ; אריקם 𝔐ᵠ [ארקעם

79) 22:46   בני נכר יבלו 𝔐𝔐ᵠ; cf. 𝔖 [לא

80) 22:48   הנתן 𝔐𝔐ᵠ𝔊ᴸ𝔖; cf. 𝔊ᴮᴼ [נתן

81) 22:48   וידבר 𝔐𝔖; ומוריד 𝔐ᵠ [ומרדד

ANALYSIS

1. The unique readings are scattered throughout 1 and 2 Samuel, located in twenty-six chapters of the forty-six chapters for which 4QSamᵃ is extant. The readings belong to various prose and poetic-type literary genres such as historical narrative (e.g., 1 Samuel 5:8, 11; 6:2, 5; 10:8, 14; 11:9), song (e.g., Royal Song of Thanksgiving, 2 Samuel 22:37, 40, 43, 46, 48), lament (e.g., 2 Samuel 3:34), prayer (Prayer of Hannah, see 1 Samuel 2:9-10; Prayer of David; 2 Samuel 7:25, 28), prophecy (e.g., prophecy against Eli's House; 2 Samuel 12:14), genealogical list (1 Samuel 14:49), dialogue (1 Samuel 24:19), oath formula (2 Samuel 4:10), and curse (2 Samuel 3:29-30).

While the readings are scattered throughout Samuel, there exist several clusters of unique readings. For example, a large cluster – six in number – is located in David's lament of Abner (2 Samuel 3:30-38).[10] The majority of these unique readings are relatively insignificant, producing minor variant readings. Two readings, however, have consequence to the understanding of David's lament of Abner. These two readings are

בזקים] או and הגיש, both from 2 Samuel 3:34.[11] All other ancient witnesses unanimously reflect ידיך לא אסרות for the first expression and הגשו for the second.

Other clustered unique readings are located in the following pericopes: six in the section detailing the birth and consecration of Samuel (1 Samuel 1:22-23, 28; three in verse 22, two in verse 24, and one in verse 28), two in the latter part of the Song of Hannah (1 Samuel 2:9, 10), eight in the section describing the sins of the sons of Eli (four in 1 Samuel 2:16, two in verse 22, and once each in verses 23 and 25 of the same chapter), eight in the Murder of Abner pericope (2 Samuel 3:22-39; one each in verses 25, 29, 30, and two in verse 35 and three in verse 34), two within seven verses describing the Second Ammonite Campaign (2 Samuel 11:1-27, one each in verses 4 and 10), two in the section on the death of Bathsheba's child (two in 2 Samuel 12:17), and seven in the Royal Song of Thanksgiving (2 Samuel 22; one each in verses 36, 37, 40, 43, 46 and two in verse 48).

The statistics listed above do not present an accurate overall picture of the unique readings in 4QSam^a, because the scroll is so fragmentary – only eight per cent of the text is extant.[12] Moreover, the eight per cent that is extant requires much reconstruction, thus creating an incomplete and oft-times distorted picture.

2. The socio-religious background of the versions was not immediately apparent in my own analysis; nor was there unmistakable evidence of scribal reworking for theological purposes, except for the euphemistic gloss in 2 Samuel 12:14.[13] This euphemism is especially peculiar because both of the Hebrew witnesses provide different euphemistic expressions in verse 14. 4QSam^a stands unique while the Masoretic Text is followed by the other versions. The 4QSam^a text has Nathan telling David, 'you have utterly spurned the word of the Lord', whereas the Masoretic Text reads, 'you have utterly spurned the enemies of the Lord.' 4QSam^a likely was influenced by 12:9, which reads 'why have you shown contempt for the word of the Lord [...] ?', the term דבר preceding the Divine name here and again in verse 14. The original text likely read 'you have utterly scorned the Lord.'[14]

3. Many unique readings are the result of activity on the part of the copyists, whether from the scribe of 4QSam^a, or one of its antecedents, or from a scribe from the proto-Masoretic or Masoretic tradition, since the uniqueness of 4QSam^a may as easily have arisen from scribal activity within the Masoretic tradition as from that of 4QSam^a.

Scribal activity has resulted in mechanical changes of many types and forms in numerous readings in the traditions of the Masoretic text, 4QSam^a, or both. There are examples of pluses, minuses, graphic confusion, transposition of texts, metathesis, misdivision of words, secondary expansion, synonymous readings, and others. A single type of reading does not dominate the deviations between 4QSam^a and other witnesses, where 4QSam^a is unique. The following examples serve to illustrate the variety of variant readings listed above:

A) GRAPHIC SIMILARITY

2 Samuel 22:43 ארקעם] ארקעם אדקם 𝔐ℭ; cf 𝔙; אדקם 𝔊^{BO}; cf 𝔊^L; אריקם 𝔐^Ψ

The three Hebrew variants have comparable appearances – each has an *alef*, *resh* or *dalet*, *qof*, and final *mem*. The 4QSam^a and Psalms texts each have an additional letter –

ayin or *yod*. These graphically similar words may have originated from a single word, and were eventually recorded and understood as three different roots: אריקם from ריק/רוק,[15] ארקעם from רקע,[16] and ארדקם from דקק.[17] The Greek renderings are difficult to equate to the Hebrew and can only be approximated.[18]

It appears that 𝔐's two words for the single word in 4QSam[a] and Psalms arose from dittography with subsequent graphic confusion, writing *resh* for *dalet*. Hence, ארדקם is probably secondary, and, of the two words that remain (אריקם and ארקעם), the latter would serve best as the parallel for ואשחקם that appears in the first half of this couplet.

2 Samuel 3:35   לפי] לפני 𝔐𝔊𝔗𝔖

The 4QSam[a] reading qualifies as the *lectio difficilior*. In any case, the graphic similarity is responsible for the variant readings.

B) MISDIVISION OF WORDS

2 Samuel 3:35   או כל] אוכל 𝔐𝔊𝔗

The reading of 4QSam[a] arose from a scribe failing to divide the words properly. The Greek texts reflect 𝔐.

C) INTERCHANGE OF LETTERS

2 Samuel 3:29   אביו] יואב 𝔐𝔊𝔗𝔖𝔙

Did the scribe of 4QSam[a] anticipate בית יואב located in the latter part of the verse? אביו sufficiently resembles יואב that the scribe's confusion is not surprising.

D) TRANSPOSITION OF WORDS

2 Samuel 13:6   תמר אחתי] [אחותי] תמר 𝔐𝔊𝔖𝔙

Perhaps 4QSam[a] transposes אחותי before תמר.

E) VARIATION OF VERBS

2 Samuel 4:4   היה 𝔐; 𝔊 והוא και ουτος] ויהי

2 Samuel 6:13   וה̇ל̇דת̇ן] ויהי 𝔐

F) PROPER NAMES

1 Samuel 14:49   וישוי] וא̇נ̇ש בעל 𝔐𝔊𝔖

A calculation of the letters reveals that there is enough space to read ואיש בעל or ואשבעל versus the shorter name attested in 𝔐.

2 Samuel 13:3   שמעה] שמעיה 𝔐𝔊 Σαμαα; cf. 1 Chronicles 20:7 שמעא

The name is probably to be read *šmʿ* hypocoristic for *šmʿyhw*. Cf. 1 Samuel 16:9 (שמה); 17:13 (שמה); 2 Samuel 21:21 (שמעי *ketib*; שמעה *qere*).

G) PLUSES AND MINUSES

1 Samuel 1:22   וישב] וישב לפני [יהוה] 𝔐𝔊𝔖𝔙

Unique Readings in 4QSam^a

The expression לפני יהוה echoes 1 Samuel 1:11 לפניך (4QSam^a), ליהוה (𝔐), and is probably a secondary expansion.

1 Samuel 1:22+ כול ימי [חיין]] > 𝔐𝔊𝕮𝕾𝓥

This phrase echoes 1:11 𝔐. It is interesting, however, that 1:11 𝔊 (εως ημερας θανατου) echoes Judges 13:7 (cf. 16:17). This is probably an expansion in view of the character of haplography and the unanimity of the other witnesses in omitting it.

2 Samuel 3:34 כל¹⁹] + העם 𝔐𝔊^{BAL}𝕮𝕾

The phrase כל העם occurs six times in this section regarding Abner's funeral (verses 31-38). In 34b 4QSam^a omits העם although it appears after כל just six words later in 35b.

2 Samuel 22:37 תרחיב צעדי תחתי] תרן־חיןב צעדי 𝔐^ψ תרחיב צעדי תחתני 𝔐; cf. 𝔊𝔊^ψ𝕾

Both 𝔐 and Psalms, with the inclusion of תחתי, have a 3+3 metrical arrangement, a common pattern in Hebrew poetry.[20] 4QSam^a's omission of the preposition and suffix presents a 3+2 pattern, also attested in Hebrew poetry. Of all the witnesses, 4QSam^a alone lacks תחתי, perhaps as a result of a scribal error, for the same expression is found on the fragment directly two lines below. תחתני appears three times in the Hebrew Bible, only in this Royal Psalm (here and in verses 40 and 48). The form תחת is well attested in the Bible.

Donald W. Parry

NOTES

1   Frank M. Cross, Jr. was the first to note the Septuagint's affinity to this Qumran scroll. See especially his article, 'A New Qumrân Biblical Fragment Related to the Original Hebrew Underlying the Septuagint', *IEJ*, 16 (1966), 81-95.

2   See, for example, Eugene Charles Ulrich, Jr., *The Qumran Text of Samuel and Josephus*, HSM, 19 (Missoula, MT: Scholars Press, 1978), pp. 39-117; Donald W. Parry, '4QSamᵃ (4Q51): A Preliminary Edition of 1 Samuel 25:3-31:4', in *The Provo International Conference on the Dead Sea Scrolls: Technological Innovations, New Texts and Reformulated Issues*, ed. by Donald W. Parry and Eugene Ulrich, STDJ, 30 (Leiden: Brill, 1999), pp. 58-71; Emanuel Tov, 'The Contribution of the Qumran Scrolls to the Understanding of the LXX', in SSCW, pp. 11-47.

3   Ulrich, *Qumran Text*, see especially pp. 165-91.

4   Ibid.

5   Frank Moore Cross, Jr., 'The History of the Biblical Text in the Light of Discoveries in the Judaean Desert', *HTR*, 57 (1964), 281-99 (p. 293); F. M. Cross, Jr., 'The Contribution of the Qumrân Discoveries to the Study of the Biblical Text', *IEJ*, 16 (1966), 81-95 (p. 88); and Werner E. Lemke, 'The Synoptic Problem in the Chronicler's History', *HTR*, 58 (1965), 349-63.

6   Ulrich, *Qumran Text*, p. 163. For a discussion of parallel passages in Chronicles, see Cross, 'History of the Biblical Text', 293; Cross, 'Contribution of Qumran Discoveries', 88; and Lemke, 'Synoptic Problem', 349-363; Steven L. McKenzie, *The Chronicler's Use of the Deuteronomistic History*, HSM, 33 (Atlanta, GA: Scholars Press, 1985), presents the most complete treatment on textual affinities between Chronicles and 4QSamᵃ.

7   A unique reading is defined as one that is exclusive to a single witness, a sole reading among witnesses. The formulas 4QSamᵃ≠MT=LXX and 4QSamᵃ≠ MT ≠LXX (and so on) serve to describe the unique readings of 4QSamᵃ.

8   Both the count of unique readings and their presentation is preliminary and will be fine-tuned in DJD XVII. The key to the lists is as follows: Septuagint (𝕲), Syriac (𝕾), Targum (𝕿), Vulgate (V), Coptic (𝕮), Josephus (Jos), Old Latin (𝕷), Masoretic Text of Psalms (𝔐ᵂ), Septuagint Psalms (𝕲ᵂ).

9   The apparatus of BHS errs with its reading of the Qumran text (לו]בר).

10   For a discussion of these readings, see my article, Donald W. Parry, 'The Aftermath of Abner's Murder', *Textus*, 20 (2000): 83-96.

11   For discussion of this unique reading, see Parry, 'Aftermath of Abner's Murder'. This article discusses various approaches to the reconstruction of this phrase in 4QSamᵃ, concluding, with Herbert (Edward D. Herbert, *Reconstructing Biblical Dead Sea Scrolls: A New Method Applied to the Reconstruction of 4QSamᵃ*, STDJ, 22 (Leiden: Brill, 1997), p. 113), that the previously published reconstruction אוסרות ידיך לאן בזקים does not fit the space requirements of the line.

12   Edward D. Herbert, '4QSamᵃ and its Relationship to the LXX: an Exploration in Stemmatological Analysis', in *IX Congress of the International Organization for Septuagint and Cognate Studies, Cambridge 1995*, ed. by Bernard A. Taylor, SBL Septuagint and Cognate Studies Series, 45 (Atlanta, GA: Scholars Press, 1997), pp. 37-55 (p. 38).

13   There exist many euphemisms in the books of Samuel, e.g., 1 Sam 5:6, 9, 12; 6:4, 5; 20:15-16; 24:3; 25:22; 29:4. A classic example of euphemism is located in 1 Sam 3:13, where in the text describes the Lord's curse upon the house of Eli because of Eli's failure to correct his sons for their sins. The Masoretic Text reads: 'I am judging his house forever because he has known that his sons have been cursing themselves.' The reading avoids a direct offence against the Deity by omitting the *alef* of אלהים, thus reading להם, 'to them' or 'themselves.' See Marvin H. Pope, 'Bible, Euphemism and Dysphemism in the', in *ABD*, I, pp. 720-25 (p. 724).

14   S. R. Driver, *Notes on the Hebrew Text and the Topography of the Books of Samuel*, 2nd edn (Oxford: Clarendon, 1913), p. 292. The observation of Herbert, *Reconstructing Biblical Dead Sea Scrolls*, p. 147 that 'את דבר יהוה is supported only by the Coptic' is significant and deserves further attention.

15   See Ludwig Koehler and Walter Baumgartner, *The Hebrew and Aramaic Lexicon of the Old*

Testament, 4 vols (Leiden: Brill, 1994-99, subsequently revised by Walter Baumgartner and Johann Jacob Stamm; translated and edited under the supervision of M. E. J. Richardson), III, p. 1228.

16   Ibid., III, p. 1292.

17   Ibid., I, p. 229.

18   See Ulrich, *Qumran Text*, 104. Although the Greek renderings are difficult to equate to the Hebrew, Herbert correctly notes, 'While the *Vorlagen* of PLXX [𝕲Ψ] and SL [𝕲^L] are therefore, uncertain, it is clear that SB/SL/*AE*/PMT/PLXX [𝕲^{B+} 𝕲^L *Armenian Ethiopic* 𝔐Ψ 𝕲Ψ] agree with 4QSam^a in attesting only one word here', Herbert, *Reconstructing Biblical Dead Sea Scrolls*, p. 189.

19   BHS in the apparatus incorrectly registers that 4QSam^a lacks כל.

20   Wilfred G. E. Watson, *Classical Hebrew Poetry: A Guide to its Techniques* (Sheffield: JSOT, 1984), p. 98.

1QISA^A AND 1QISA^B: A REMATCH

Martin G. Abegg, Jr.

THIS STUDY REPRESENTS a preliminary examination of the character of the two Isaiah scrolls found in Cave 1 (1QIsa^a and 1QIsa^b), focusing on the character of the smaller 1QIsa^b. This scroll has been somewhat neglected, in part because of the consensus assessment that it is very close to the Masoretic Text and in part because of the attention garnered by its much more dramatic cousin, the Great Isaiah Scroll (1QIsa^a).

1QIsa^b was published by E. L. Sukenik in 1954-55 with the War Scroll and the Hodayot,[1] supplemented by the publication of seven additional fragments from the beginning of the scroll in DJD I.[2] These combined publications present a manuscript with extant fragments ranging from Isaiah 7:22 to 66:24, totalling about twenty per cent of the overall text. The style of the scribal hand dates the scroll to the Herodian period.

In the nearly fifty years since the first biblical manuscripts became available, there has been a notable evolution among scholars concerning the character of the biblical text in the Second Temple period. The first attempt by Frank Cross, who theorized the existence of three local texts – Babylonian, Palestinian, and Egyptian – has been nuanced by Emanuel Tov to include texts written in Qumran practice and those which show no alignment.[3] Tov's initial figures as to the distribution are as follows:

Qumran Practice	20%
Proto-Masoretic	60%
Pre-Samaritan	5%
Pre-Septuagint	5%
Non-Aligned	10%

In the nearly ten years since these figures were published, Tov has modified the Proto-Masoretic category downward to fifty-two (Torah) or forty-four per cent (other biblical) with a concurrent expansion taking place in the Non-Aligned group.[4] In a forthcoming article, Tov writes: '... the more I consult the Qumran biblical manuscripts and the evidence of the Greek LXX in my work, the less I feel drawn to consider MT the central text'.[5] In this he echoes the earlier sentiments of S. Talmon who wrote in 1971,

[I]n the Qumran material coalesce the phase of creative authoring of biblical literature with the ancillary phase of text transmission ... in ancient Hebrew literature no hard and fast lines can be drawn between authors' conventions of style and tradents' and copyists' rules of reproduction and transmission.[6]

Our attachment to MT both as to text and to the more conservative scribal school which produced and maintained it appears now to be anachronistic when projected onto the Second Temple period.

In a similar vein Eugene Ulrich has developed a theory of variant literary editions. To discern these he has proposed:

(1) the removal of any purely orthographic differences, on the conviction that the specific orthographic profile of a manuscript is seldom related to any particular edition of that work;

(2) the temporary removal of individual textual variants that do not seem related to the pattern of variants by which an author or tradent or scribe systematically reworked an existing edition of a work into a revised edition.[7]

Elsewhere he writes:

> The fundamental principle guiding this proposal is that the Scriptures, from shadowy beginnings until the final, perhaps abrupt, freezing point of the Masoretic tradition, arose and evolved through a process of organic development. The major lines of that development are characterized by the intentional, creative work of authors or tradents who produced new, revised editions of the traditional form of a book or passage.[8]

Ulrich subsequently demonstrated the development of successive literary editions using the evidence from Exodus, Numbers, and Joshua. The twenty-one manuscripts of Isaiah[9] seem to present a different picture, as suggested by Peter Flint and Eugene Ulrich: 'Though large-scale variant editions are preserved for some other books, for Isaiah the scrolls and the other ancient witnesses preserve apparently only one edition of this book, with no consistent patterns of variants or rearrangements'.[10] While this description is generally correct, a closer look at the evidence suggests that the Qumran Isaiah scrolls do have their own contribution to make to our evolving understanding of the history of the biblical text.

1. DATA

The following chart contains preliminary data that despite their partial nature will allow a more quantitative description of the character of Isaiah in the Dead Sea Scrolls. In the chart, the second column refers to inflected 'word units' ignoring morphological boundaries between inseparable morphemes. For example, ולמספרו, is considered as one word, not four units. This procedure produces an increase in the percentages (about thirty per cent) in both the variant and orthography columns, but it does not affect the relationship between the results recorded in the rows of the chart which would change little if at all. Further, the figures in columns III and V are given in comparison to the Masoretic Text. 1QIsa[a] could have been used, as it is also nearly everywhere extant, but the special nature of this text as compared to the rest of the corpus ruled against this decision for present purposes. Finally, the columns chosen for 1QIsa[a] were made more or less at random aside from two factors: 1) at least one column after column XXVIII was chosen in order to test the early suspicion that a shift in scribal character had occurred at this point in the manuscript,[11] and 2) the variant catalogue for DJD XXXII is currently complete only to Isaiah 44.

Manuscript	Words	Variants to MT[12]	%	Orthography	%
1QIsa[a]	17212[13]				
X	383	38	9.9%	33	8.6%
XX	289	36	12.5%	33	11.4%
XXXV	276	51	18.5%	52	18.8%
1QIsa[b]	3317	142	4.3%	122	3.7%
4QIsa[a] (4Q55)	410	21	5.1%	16	3.9%
4QIsa[b] (4Q56)	1019	49	4.8%	37	3.6%

1QIsa^a and 1QIsa^b: A Rematch

Manuscript	Words	Variants to MT[12]	%	Orthography	%
4QIsa^c (4Q57)	862	71	8.2%	81	9.4%
4QIsa^d (4Q58)	470	28	6.0%	32	6.8%
4QIsa^e (4Q59)	327	23	7.0%	16	4.9%
4QIsa^f (4Q60)	331	19	5.7%	15	4.5%
4QIsa^g (4Q61)	84	3	3.6%	4	4.8%
4QIsa^h (4Q62)	45	3	6.7%	1	2.2%
4QIsa^i (4Q62a)	24	0	0	0	0
4QIsa^j (4Q63)	20	1	5.0%	1	5.0%
4QIsa^k (4Q64)	42	6	14.3%	5	11.9%
4QIsa^l (4Q65)	14	0	0	2	14.3%
4QIsa^m (4Q66)	37	0	0	2	5.4%
4QIsa^n (4Q67)	21	7	33.3%	2	9.5%
4QIsa^o (4Q68)	39	2	5.1%	0	0
4QIsa^p (4Q69)	11	1	9.1%	0	0
4QIsa^q (4Q69a)	5	0	0	0	0
4QIsa^r (4Q69b)	3	0	0	0	0
5QIsa (5Q3)	7	0	0	0	0
MurIsa (Mur 3)	34	0	0	0	0
MurXII (Mur 88)	3822	33	0.9%	20	0.5%

The following observations can be made:

1) The unique nature of 1QIsa^a can easily be seen by figures. The number of actual variants (orthographic and morphological differences separated out) stands at 9.9%, 12.5% and 18.5% for columns X, XX and XXXV respectively. This sets it apart from all of the Cave 4 and 5 scrolls except the rather scanty remains of 4QIsa^k and 4QIsa^n and to a lesser degree 4QIsa^c.

2) The notable increase in both real and orthographic variants after column XXXV of 1QIsa^a as compared to columns X and XX is also important to note. It has been suggested from the very early days of research on the Great Isaiah Scroll that the change of scribal style from column XXVIII-LIV is evidence of the beginning of a second hand. This decision has been based in large part on the noted change in favour of the 'heavy' pronominal suffixes at this point: hemah, henah, kemah, kenah. E. Y. Kutscher's examination of the manuscript determined that the scribe of 1QIsa^a did not change, but it remains a distinct possibility that this substitution might have occurred in one of the scroll's ancestors.[14] Otherwise we must conclude, with Kutscher, that for some unknown reason the scribe notably modified his style at this point. A full examination of the latter half of the manuscript may help clarify this issue.

3) Although Ulrich has suggested the removal of orthographic variants in the determination of literary editions,[15] columns IV and VI suggest a relationship between real and orthographic variants. In scrolls with twenty or more words, a high percentage of orthographic variants is echoed by a high percentage of real variants. This indicates that scribes who exercised greater freedom in their approach to spelling conventions

were also apt to exhibit 'creative authoring' in other areas as well. Similar studies of the biblical scrolls corpus will be needed to determine whether there is a comparable relationship between orthographic and real variants elsewhere.

4) Tov and others have grouped 4QIsa[c] with 1QIsa[a] in discussions concerning categorization; this decision is born out by the higher percentage of orthographic variants for 4QIsa[c], a key characteristic of Qumran Practice.

5) Although in text critical analyses 1QIsa[b] has been ignored to a large degree because of the assumption that it is nearly the equal of the Masoretic Text, when it is compared to the Minor Prophets scroll from Murabbaʿat (MurXII found at the bottom of the chart), it looks much more like the majority of the somewhat mixed scrolls from Cave 4. This also raises the question of just how many orthographic (and morphological) variants are allowable in Tov's schema before a scroll no longer warrants the classification Proto-Masoretic and is termed Qumran (or some other qualifier) Practice. There is a perhaps more important converse question: if orthographic or morphological variants of the Qumran Practice are excluded from the discussion, and the majority of real variants can be shown to be secondary, is not the overall position of the Proto-Masoretic text type subsequently strengthened? In other words, is not the category Qumran Practice simply a sub-category of Proto-Masoretic?

2. ORTHOGRAPHY

In regards to orthography, 1QIsa[b] is demonstrably more conservative (i.e., more like the Masoretic Text) than 1QIsa[a] (3.7% compared with 13.2%) and does not regularly reflect what Tov has called Qumran practice.[16] Nonetheless, it does exhibit a certain regular approach to spelling. The following patterns set it apart from being categorized as strictly Masoretic.

1. *Qal* participles regularly appear with fully written 'o' vowel (25x): e.g. Isaiah 26:5, יושבי (MT: יֹשְׁבֵי)

2. Demonstrating a norm in the reverse of the first pattern, there are no fully written 'o' or 'u' theme vowels in the large majority of noun formations (21x): Isaiah 47:11, שאה (MT: שֹׁאָה). To this number could be added a substantial number of similar occurrences among adjectives and verbs (apart from *Qal* active participles).

3. Also seeming to work contrary to the first pattern is the fact that most feminine plural forms are without a fully written 'o' vowel (12x): Isaiah 44:26, וחרבתיה (MT: וְחׇרְבוֹתֶיהָ).

3. MORPHOLOGY

There are a small number of morphological variants which perhaps reflect some familiarity with Qumran practice. Otherwise, 1QIsa[b] exhibits a similar morphology to MT-Isaiah. As such, there are no lengthened pronominal suffixes (second and third plural), no pausal inflections used as free forms, no verbal forms with pronominal suffixes which are inflected as *y^{e}quṭlenu*, no lengthened second person plural (*q^{e}ṭaltemah*), no מואדה, מאודה, or מודה with the adverbial ending-*ah*, and no long forms of the second masculine singular perfect ending in -*ah*.[17]

1QIsa^a and 1QIsa^b: A Rematch

1. Lengthened Independent Pronouns

Isaiah 65:24	1QIsa^b	ואני אענה עוד המה מדברים
	MT	וַאֲנִי אֶעֱנֶה עוֹד הֵם מְדַבְּרִים

Note, however, 1QIsa^b at Isaiah 56:11 and 65:23 where the reverse occurs. Twelve of the twenty-one occurrences of הם in Isaiah are long in MT compared to three of six in 1QIsa^b.

2. Lengthened Future Forms

Isaiah 43:4	1QIsa^b	ואתנה אדם תחתיך
	MT	וְאֶתֵּן אָדָם תַּחְתֶּיךָ

See also 1QIsa^b at 57:18; 63:5 (2x), and 6 (2x), but note 1QIsa^b at Isaiah 56:12 where the reverse occurs.

3. Other Qumran/Second Temple Hebrew Spellings

a) Isaiah 52:9	1QIsa^b	פצחו רננו יחדיו
	MT	פִּצְחוּ רַנְּנוּ יַחְדָּו

This spelling also occurs in 1QIsa^b at Isaiah 60:13 whereas all instances of יחד are written defectively in MT. Among the six extant occurrences of the word in Qumran sectarian literature only 4Q374 2 ii, 1 is spelled defectively, with 4Q163 4-7 21; 4Q271 3 10; 11QT^a LII, 11, 13; and 11QT^{a}LIII, 4 all spelled *plene*.

b) Isaiah 55:3	1QIsa^b	חסדי דויד הנאןמנ֯ים
	MT	חַסְדֵי דָוִד הַנֶּאֱמָנִים

Of the twenty-nine cases of the name David in Qumran literature only three (all in the medieval manuscript A of CD) are spelled defectively (דוד). In MT, seventy-three per cent are defective (including all ten instances in Isaiah). Almost all of the longer forms are found in the books of Ezra, Nehemiah and 1-2 Chronicles.

4. TEXT CRITICISM AND 1QISA^B

Now we must look at a few text critical examples; not only because we are drawn here eventually, even if our assigned task is linguistics and scribal practice, but because in several instances the examinations of orthography and morphology allow for more nuanced text-critical decisions. In other words we have satisfied a main tenet of text-critical discussion: we have got to know the scribe or scribal school of the text reflected in 1QIsa^b.

The only reading from 1QIsa^b which has been accepted by modern English translations (NIV, NRSV) is the addition of the word אור (light) to Isaiah 53:11.

Isaiah 53:11	1QIsa^a	מעמל נפשוה יראה אור וישבע
	1QIsa^b	מעמל נפשו יראה אור וישׄ֯ן֯בע
	MT	מֵעֲמַל נַפְשׁוֹ יִרְאֶה יִשְׂבָּע
	LXX	ἀπὸ τοῦ πόνου τῆς ψυχῆς αὐτοῦ δεῖξαι αὐτῷ φῶς
	NRSV	Out of his anguish he shall see light;
		he shall find satisfaction (through his knowledge)

The coincidence of 4QIsa[a-b], 4QIsa[d] and the LXX is striking and provides the necessary object of the seeing that is evidently lacking in MT. However, the fact that a scribe is more apt to add what seems to be lacking than omit both object and the following conjunction makes this reading suspect.[18] Perhaps a better solution, although not reflected in any of the witnesses, is an ancient confusion of ראה, 'to see', with the less common רוה, 'to be saturated, satiated'.[19] This proposal provides an appealing parallel with ישבע as well as a logical source of the misread יראה without the expected object.

The evidence of 1QIsa[b] has been denied in favour of 1QIsa[a] in three further instances by the NRSV.

1.	Isaiah 45:2	1QIsa[a]	אני לפניכה אלך והררים יאושר
		1QIsa[b]	אנין לפניך אלך והדורים אושׁנר
		MT	אֲנִי לְפָנֶיךָ אֵלֵךְ וַהֲדוּרִים אוֹשֵׁר
		LXX	ἐγὼ ἔμπροσθέν σου πορεύσομαι καὶ ὄρη ὁμαλιῶ
		NRSV	I will go before you and level the mountains

In this instance it is noteworthy that the scribe of 1QIsa[b] has abandoned his usual pattern of representing nouns and verbs without theme vowels. The more difficult reading, which gains some degree of support by the uncharacteristic spelling of 1QIsa[b], is certainly וַהֲדוּרִים, which might refer to swellings – a rough road – that were levelled to allow an army to approach with ease. Although the graphically similar *resh* and *dalet* with the later addition of a *vav* for sense might have produced this difficult reading, 'mountains' with 1QIsa[a] and the Septuagint is more logically secondary.[20]

2.	Isaiah 56:12	1QIsa[a]	אתיו ונקח יין
		1QIsa[b]	אתיו אקח יין
		MT	אֵתָיוּ אֶקְחָה יַּיִן
		LXX	–
		NRSV	'Come', they say, 'let us get wine'

1QIsa[a] and MT probably reflect two early exegetical solutions to the harder text of 1QIsa[b]. The fact that the scribe of 1QIsa[b] normally lengthened first person imperfects argues for the originality of its reading. It is also more difficult to imagine how the first plural would have developed from a first singular in this context.

3.	Isaiah 60:19	1QIsa[a]	השמש לאור יומם ולנ׳גה הירח בלילה
		1QIsa[b]	השמש לאור יומם ולנגה הירח
		MT	הַשֶּׁמֶשׁ לְאוֹר יוֹמָם וּלְנֹגַהּ הַיָּרֵחַ
		LXX	ὁ ἥλιος εἰς φῶς ἡμέρας οὐδὲ ἀνατολὴ σελήνης φωτιεῖ σοι τὴν νύκτα
		NRSV	The sun shall no longer be your light by day, nor for brightness shall the moon give light to you by night

The reading of 1QIsa[a] and the LXX fills in the expectant gap left open in MT and 1QIsa[b]. It is too obviously secondary to be considered as the 'better' text.

One additional reading is worth further consideration:

Isaiah 28:16	1QIsa^a^	הנני מיסד בציון אבן
	1QIsa^b^	הנני יוסד [בציון אבן
	MT	הִנְנִי יִסַּד בְּצִיּוֹן אָבֶן
	LXX	ἰδοὺ ἐγὼ ἐμβαλῶ εἰς τὰ θεμέλια Σιων λίθον
	NRSV	See, I am laying in Zion a foundation stone

In Isaiah 28:16 none of the modern translations examined note the LXX or Qumran readings, although they translate the difficult Hebrew as if they had. Here, given our scribe's propensity to write *Qal* active participle forms fully, it is difficult to know what his exemplar read, but a participle following הנני would certainly be expected. Although an asyndetic relative clause ('It is I who laid...') is theoretically possible, it is striking that this is the only instance in the Hebrew Bible where הנה with pronominal suffix is followed by a perfect form of the verb without agreement in person. There are, by contrast, 144 examples of a participle following. Despite the normally helpful guide of *lectio difficilior*, MT as pointed is probably contextually unacceptable, so that 1QIsa^b^ preserves the best reading.

5. CONCLUSIONS

1) Although clearly close to MT and most of its Cave 4 Isaiah contemporaries, 1QIsa^b^ evidences some clear decisions that its scribe (or scribal school) had made concerning a particular course through the possible orthographic and morphological permutations. These decisions were more conservative than 1QIsa^a^, but they form a fingerprint by which the scribe or scribal school might be recognized should other biblical scrolls be examined in this way, as in this study.

2) On the basis of the orthographic practice used, it is not likely that 1QIsa^b^ is a direct descendant or ancestor of the scroll whose offspring survives in MT. It is possible to imagine a more primitive scroll – with defective spellings – that had two offspring, one which fully spelled participles and one which fully spelled nouns and feminine plural endings. 1QIsa^a^, on the other hand, might have descended directly from either the family of MT or of 1QIsa^b^.

3) Following the preceding point, a study still in progress using 1QIsa^a^ as a base text has produced data which emphasizes the similarity of MT to 1QIsa^b^ as well as to most of the Cave 4 scrolls. Looked at from this perspective, MT is simply another representative of the main stream for the book of Isaiah at Qumran: MT-like texts, siblings and cousins of the manuscript which survived in the collection known as the Masoretic Text.

4) It does not appear that the selection of the manuscripts which eventually led to the individual books of MT was random. The evidence suggests that there was an effort to dodge the more radical of the available manuscripts. In the case of Isaiah, this meant the exclusion of those manuscripts exhibiting Qumran scribal practice; for the Pentateuch, the same decision would have also required a setting aside of the pre-Samaritan group.

The conclusions reached in this preliminary study will probably gain a degree of clarity upon a full review of all of the data evidenced by the twenty-two Isaiah manuscripts from the Judaean desert. As witnessed by the unique characteristic of 1QIsa[b], it is likely that other scribal patterns will surface that will allow the identification of additional scribal 'schools' alongside that which is labelled 'Qumran Practice' by Tov. Looking forward from the time of the Qumran sectarians, some further focus is likely to be gained concerning the family history of that manuscript which eventually survived in the Masoretic collection. Moving into the past, perhaps some lost details of the previous generations of Isaiah scribal activity will become evident as well.

NOTES

1   E. L. Sukenik, *The Dead Sea Scrolls of the Hebrew University* (Jerusalem: Magnes, 1955).

2   DJD I, p. 66-69.

3   Frank Moore Cross, 'The Evolution of a Theory of Local Texts', in *QHBT*, pp. 306-20; *TCHB*, pp. 114-17.

4   See Tov's study in the present volume.

5   Emanuel Tov, 'The Place of the Masoretic Text in Modern Text Editions of the Hebrew Bible: The Relevance of Canon', as yet unpublished study, 2000.

6   Shemaryahu Talmon, 'The Textual Study of the Bible — A New Outlook', in *QHBT*, pp. 380-81.

7   Eugene Ulrich, 'The Dead Sea Scrolls and the Biblical Text', in *DSSAFY*, I, pp. 79-100 (p. 83).

8   Eugene Ulrich, 'Multiple Literary Editions: Reflections toward a Theory of the History of the Biblical Text', in *Current Research and Technological Developments on the Dead Sea Scrolls: Conference on the Texts from the Judean Desert, Jerusalem, 30 April 1995*, STDJ, 20, ed. by Donald W. Parry and Stephen D. Ricks (Leiden: Brill, 1996), pp. 78-105 (p. 89).

9   Isaiah is the third most prevalent biblical book in the Qumran corpus, following Psalms and Deuteronomy.

10   *DSSB*, p. 267.

11   E. Y. Kutscher, *The Language and Linguistic Background of the Isaiah Scroll (1 Q Isa^a)*, STDJ, 6 (Leiden: Brill, 1974), pp. 564-66.

12   These variants are called 'real' variants in the following discussion, that is, variants which cannot be explained by orthographic or morphological changes.

13   Based on a word count of the Masoretic Text.

14   Kutscher, pp. 564-66.

15   Ulrich, 'The Dead Sea Scrolls', p. 83.

16   *TCHB*, p. 114.

17   For a complete list see *TCHB*, p. 110.

18   I. L. Seeligmann, 'Δεῖξαι αὐτῷ φῶς', *Tarbiz*, 27 (1958), pp. 127-41, has suggested this may be the rare instance of Qumran ideology reflected in a biblical manuscript.

19   This suggestion has been made by both Shemaryahu Talmon and Eugene Ulrich in private conversation.

20   See *TCHB*, p. 254 for the opposite conclusion. Charles H. Southwood, 'The problematic h^a durîm of Isaiah XLV 2', *VT*, 25 (1975) pp. 801-802.

THE BOOK OF ISAIAH
IN THE DEAD SEA SCROLLS

Peter W. Flint

1. INTRODUCTION

OF THE ISAIAH SCROLLS discovered near the Dead Sea, some are more familiar to scholars – notably the 'Great' and 'Small' Isaiah Scrolls from Cave 1 (1QIsa[a], 1QIsa[b]) – while others are less known since they were only recently published. The present article introduces the Isaiah scrolls from Qumran and other sites, comments on the editions of the Isaiah Scrolls in the DJD series ('Discoveries in the Judaean Desert'), and then offers several observations on these ancient manuscripts, and discusses the interpetation of Isaiah at Qumran. Two appendices follow: a table with data on the Isaiah Scrolls from the Judaean Desert and an index of the contents of the Isaiah Scrolls by chapter and verse.

2. THE ISAIAH SCROLLS FROM QUMRAN AND OTHER SITES[1]

To the best of our present knowledge (see section 3.1 below), a total of twenty-two copies of Isaiah have been identified at Qumran and other sites. Two scrolls were discovered in Cave 1, eighteen in Cave 4, one in Cave 5, and one more at Murabba'at further down the western coast of the Dead Sea. The first two Isaiah scrolls to be discovered were 1QIsa[a] and 1QIsa[b] in 1947. Because of its importance and size, the Great Isaiah Scroll has been published in several preliminary editions, the first (ed. Burrows *et al.*) appearing as early as 1950.[2] The single Isaiah manuscript from Cave 5 was found in 1952 by archaeologists while they were excavating Cave 4 nearby, the Murabba'at Isaiah scroll was discovered by the Bedouin in October of the previous year, and the Cave 4 scrolls were found in 1952.

All the Isaiah scrolls from Caves 4 and 5 as well Murabba'at had been published in the official DJD series.[3] Although the two manuscripts from Cave 1 have appeared in valuable preliminary editions,[4] and a portion of 1QIsa[b] in DJD I, comprehensive critical editions of 1QIsa[a] and 1QIsa[b] are currently being prepared by Peter W. Flint and Eugene Ulrich for publication in DJD XXXII.

2.1 THE ISAIAH SCROLLS FROM CAVE 1 AND CAVE 5

(a) 1QIsa[a] (The 'Great Isaiah Scroll' or the 'Isaiah Scroll of St. Mark's Monastery') [See Burrows, Trever and Brownlee, *Scrolls of St. Mark's Monastery I*; Cross and others, *Scrolls from Qumrân Cave I*, pp. 13–123; Francis James Morrow, *The Text of Isaiah at Qumran* (doctoral diss., Washington, DC: Catholic University of America, 1973); E. Y. Kutscher, *The Language and Linguistic Background of the Isaiah Scroll (I Q Isa[a])*,

STDJ, 6 (Leiden: Brill, 1974); E. Qimron, *E. Y. Kutscher, The Language and Linguistic Background of the Isaiah Scroll (1QIsaᵃ): Indices and Corrections*, STDJ, 6A (Leiden: Brill, 1979); Parry and Qimron, *The Great Isaiah Scroll (1QIsaᵃ): A New Edition*, STDJ, 30 (Leiden: Brill, 1999); Flint and Ulrich, DJD XXXII (in preparation)].

The Great Isaiah scroll was discovered among the first group of manuscripts by the Bedouin in 1947, preserved virtually intact since it was well stored in its jar. 1QIsaᵃ is the longest of all the preserved biblical scrolls at 7.34 m; among the non-biblical scrolls, only one (11QTᵃ, at 8.148 m) is longer. This manuscript preserves all sixty-six chapters of Isaiah in its fifty-four columns, except for small lacunae (notably in cols I–IX), resulting from leather damage. Since it is one of the few complete manuscripts to emerge virtually intact from the caves and became the focus of early scholarly attention, the Great Isaiah Scroll has been published in several preliminary editions and has dominated research of the text of Isaiah at Qumran. This is the earliest of all twenty-two Isaiah scrolls. Palaeographic analysis shows that the manuscript was copied in about 150-125 BCE,[5] while more recent radiocarbon tests yield a possibly earlier date of 335-122 BCE.[6] The orthography is full with a liberal use of *matres lectionis*. While the text of this document is usually in agreement with the received Masoretic Text (𝔐), it also contains many variant readings that are of great interest to scholars, as well as many errors and corrections.

It is not surprising that 1QIsaᵃ has been the subject of numerous monographs and articles (see section 3.4 below). Several characteristic features have been identified, such as the presence of many errors and corrections;[7] unusual scribal markings at several points of the scroll, only some of which are readily understood;[8] the presence of more Aramaisms than in most other Qumran scrolls; and the neat division of the manuscript into two parts (chapters 1–33 and 34–66), each written by a different scribe.[9]

(b)   1QIsaᵇ (1Q8) (The 'Small Isaiah scroll' from Cave 1 or the 'Hebrew University Isaiah Scroll') [DJD I, pp. 66–68 + pl. xii; Sukenik, *Scrolls of the Hebrew University*; DJD XXXII (in preparation)]. Although not as well-known to scholars as 1QIsaᵃ, this manuscript is significant in that it preserves a large amount of the text of Isaiah. The late script dates the scroll to the Herodian period. The orthography is rather sparing and close to 𝔐, and less full than that of 1QIsaᵃ. 1QIsaᵇ preserves text ranging from Isaiah 7:22 to 66:24; material from every chapter of Isaiah is included (often very fragmentarily), except for chapters 1–6, 9, 11, 14, 17–18, 21, 27, 31–34, 36, and 42.[10]

(c)   5QIsa (5Q3) [DJD III, p. 173 + pl. xxxvi]. Judging from the very small amount of extant text, J. T. Milik dated this manuscript to the Herodian period ('Écriture tardive', p. 173; cf. p. 167). 5QIsa features but one orthographic difference from 1QIsaᵃ (מי at 40:18; cf. מיא 1QIsaᵃ) and none from 𝔐; however, too little text remains for a proper orthographic assessment to be made. The scroll preserves just a few words from Isaiah 40:16, 18-19 plus one more unplaced word.

2.2 THE ISAIAH SCROLLS FROM CAVE 4

This cave contained a total of eighteen Isaiah manuscripts, of which two are substantial (4QIsaᵇ, 4QIsaᶜ) but most are very fragmentary. The critical edition was published in the DJD series by Eugene Ulrich, who used and thoroughly expanded the unpublished edition prepared by Patrick Skehan before his death on 9 September, 1980 (cf. Skehan and Ulrich, 'Isaiah' in DJD XV, pp. 7–143 + pls. i–xxiii).

(a)   4QIsa^a (4Q55) [DJD XV, pp. 7–18 + pls. i–ii; Muilenburg, 'Fragments of Another Qumran Isaiah Scroll', pp. 28–32]. This scroll is written in a late Hasmonaean formal hand that dates from approximately the third quarter of the first century BCE. The orthography is 'somewhat more full' than that of 𝔐 but 'less so than that of 1QIsa^a. The manuscript preserves portions of the following chapters from the book of Isaiah: 1–2, 4–6, 11–13, 17, 19–23, 33.

(b)   4QIsa^b (4Q56) [DJD XV, pp. 19–43 + pls. iii–vi]. This manuscript has features characteristic of both the late Hasmonaean and the Herodian scripts, and is dated to approximately the third quarter of the first century BCE. The orthography may be described as 'mixed', since it is often less full, but sometimes fuller, than that of 𝔐, whereas fuller spellings in 1QIsa^a are far more regular. Parts of the following chapters are preserved: 1–3, 5, 9, 11–13, 17–22, 24, 26, 35–37, 39–46, 48–49, 51–53, 61, 64–66.

(c)   4QIsa^c (4Q57) [DJD XV, pp. 45–74 + pls. vii–xii]. Inscribed in a formal, developed Herodian hand and a few Palaeo-Hebrew words, 4QIsa^c dates from about the middle third of the first century CE. The orthography is 'quite full' in comparison with that of 𝔐, 1QIsa^a and 1QIsa^b. An interesting feature is the scribe's regular use of Palaeo-Hebrew letters for the divine name יהוה. Other words associated with God are usually written in Palaeo-Hebrew: e.g. אלוהים (Isaiah 44:6), צבאות (Isaiah 44:6, following יהוה), and אדוני (22:1 and 30:15). However, these words also occur in Aramaic script (אלוהיכה 55:5; צבאות 54:5; (apparently) צ[ב]אות 51:15; אדני 24:1; and כאדוניו 24:2 (referring to a human)). The fragments preserve portions of the following chapters: 9–12, 14, 22–26, 28, 30, 33, 44–46, 48–49, 51–55, 66.

(d)   4QIsa^d (4Q58) [DJD XV, pp. 75–88 + pls. xiii–xv]. This scribe wrote in a late Herodian formal hand which dates the manuscript to approximately the middle of the first century BCE. The orthography is sparing, being less full than that of 1QIsa^a, 1QIsa^b and 𝔐. Parts of the following chapters are preserved: 45–49, 52–54, 57–58.

(e)   4QIsa^e (4Q59) [DJD XV, pp. 89–97 + pls. xvi–xvii; Ulrich and Skehan, 'Edition of 4QIsa^e', 3–16; Morrow, *Isaiah at Qumran*, pp. 29–32, 38]. This scroll is written in an early Herodian hand and is dated to the late first century BCE. The orthography is somewhat fuller than that of 𝔐, and portions of the following chapters are preserved: 2, 7–14, 59.

(f)   4QIsa^f (4Q60) [DJD XV, pp. 99–111 + pls. xviii–xx]. Inscribed in a typical Hasmonaean hand, this manuscript dates from approximately the first half of the first century BCE. The orthography appears to be sparing, although 4QIsa^f has *vav* once, *yod* once and *he* once where these letters are not found in 1QIsa^a or in 𝔐. The scroll preserves parts of the following chapters: 1–2, 5–8, 20, 22, 24, 27–29(?).

(g)   4QIsa^g (4Q61) [DJD XV, pp. 113–15 + pl. xxi]. This manuscript is written in a formal hand of the early Herodian – or perhaps late Hasmonaean – period, and is dated to approximately the latter half of the first century BCE. The orthographic character, which is not altogether clear owing to the small amount of preserved text, appears to be mixed (with 𝔐 adding *vav* twice and 4QIsa^g adding *vav* twice), but is less full than that of 1QIsa^a (which adds *vav* three times). Only the following verses are still preserved: Isaiah 42:14-25; 43:1-4, 16-24.

(h)   4QIsa^h (4Q62) [DJD XV, pp. 117–19 + pl. xxi; Morrow, *Isaiah at Qumran*, 29–32, 38]. The manuscript dates to approximately the first half of the first century

BCE, and is written in a careful, distinctive Hasmonaean hand. Despite the small amount of remaining text, the orthography seems to be sparing since it is noticeably less full than that of 1QIsa^a and rather less full than that of 𝔐. Only Isaiah 42:4-11 has been preserved.

(i) 4QIsa^i (4Q62a) [DJD XV, pp. 121–22 + pl. xxi]. The scribe wrote in a 'bold, decisive Hasmonaean script' which dates from approximately the first half of the first century BCE. To judge from the small amount of text that remains, the scroll's orthography is similar to that of both 𝔐 (except for a single *vav* reconstructed on the basis of spacing) and 1QIsa^a (except for a single verbal suffix: שמת at 57:8; cf. שמתה 1QIsa^a). The surviving portions are from Isaiah 56:7-8 and 57:5-8.

(j) 4QIsa^j (4Q63) [DJD XV, p. 123 + pl. xxii]. This manuscript is written in a late Hasmonaean hand that dates from approximately the third quarter of the first century BCE. To judge from the few words that are preserved, the orthography agrees with that of 𝔐, although Isaiah 1:2 indicates the quiescence of the radical *alef* (וֹהזֹנֹי; cf. והאזיני 1QIsa^a 𝔐) and the longer pronominal form והמה (thus also 1QIsa^a; cf. והם 𝔐). The single fragment preserves only seven complete and ten partial words from Isaiah 1:1-6, including the opening word of the book.

(k) 4QIsa^k (4Q64) [DJD XV, pp. 125–27 + pl. xxii]. This scribe wrote in a late Hasmonaean hand that dates from approximately the middle of the first century BCE. Despite the small amount of surviving text, the orthography may be described as fuller than that of 𝔐 and possibly even that of 1QIsa^a. The five surviving fragments preserve text from Isaiah 28:26–29:9.

(l) 4QIsa^l (4Q65) [DJD XV, pp. 129–30 + pl. xxii; Ulrich and Skehan, 'Edition of 4QIsa^e', 3–16]. The scroll is written in a late Hasmonaean hand that dates from approximately the middle of the first century BCE. To judge from the small amount of surviving text, the orthography seems to be fuller than that of 𝔐 but more sparing than that of 1QIsa^a. The text that survives is from Isaiah 7:14-15 and 8:11-14.

(m) 4QIsa^m (4Q66) [DJD XV, pp. 131–32 + pl. xxii]. This manuscript is inscribed in a Hasmonaean hand dated to about the first half of the first century BCE. The expanded orthography appears to be similar to that of 1QIsa^a and fuller than that of 𝔐 (cf. 61:1, where 4QIsa^m reads לקרוא with 1QIsa^a, whereas 𝔐 has לקרא). The surviving fragments preserve text from Isaiah 60:20–61:1, 3-6.

(n) 4QIsa^n (4Q67) [DJD XV, pp. 133–34 + pl. xxiii; Morrow, *Isaiah at Qumran*, pp. 155–56]. The scribe wrote in a 'bold and inconsistent Hasmonaean hand' using thick, large letters with semicursive tendencies, and dating from approximately the first half century BCE. With respect to orthography, the small amount of surviving text displays quiescence of *alef* (וקרת; cf. וקראתה 1QIsa^a, וקראת 𝔐) and assimilation of *dalet* (וכבתה; cf. וכבדתו 1QIsa^a 𝔐) at 58:13. The single fragment that survives preserves portions of Isaiah 58:13-14.

(o) 4QIsa^o (4Q68) [DJD XV, pp. 135–37 + pl. xxiii]. This scroll is written in a thick, bold Hasmonaean script that displays semicursive tendencies and similarities to the scripts of the earlier 4QDan^c (4Q114) and the later 4QMMT^e (4Q398). It was copied in approximately the first half of the first century BCE. The text preserved in frg. 1 is from Isaiah 14:28–15:2; a second fragment may contain 16:7-8, but this seems to be unlikely.

(p) 4QpapIsa^p (4Q69) [DJD XV, p. 139 + pl. xxiii]. The few letters that remain suggest that the scribe wrote in a Hasmonaean hand that has semicursive tendencies, and which dates to approximately the first half of the first century BCE. Any accurate assessment of the orthographic character is compromised by the small amount of remaining text, which is from Isaiah 5:28-30. It is also by no means certain that this was a manuscript of the complete Book of Isaiah.

(q) 4QIsa^q (4Q69a) [DJD XV, p. 141 + pl. xxiii]. To judge from the few preserved letters, this scroll is written in an early Herodian script. No orthographic differences against 1QIsa^a or 𝔐 are evident; however, there appears to be one morphological variant against 1QIsa^a (מרחמן֜ 4QIsa^q 𝔐; cf. מרחמכי 1QIsa^a). The small amount of extant text is from Isaiah 54:10-13.

(r) 4QIsa^r (4Q69b) [DJD XV, p. 143 + pl. xxiii]. One small fragment remains for this manuscript, which is written in a Hasmonaean hand. Too little text remains for an assessment of the orthographic character to be reached, but the scribe appears to have employed the medial form of *mem* also in final position. Only two lines remain, with most of three words from Isaiah 30:23 in the first line and traces of another word in the second.

2.3 ISAIAH SCROLLS FROM OTHER JUDAEAN SITES

It is perhaps surprising that no copies of Isaiah have been found at sites other than Qumran, except for the lone copy among the fragments discovered at Wadi Murabbaʿat.

(a) MurIsa (Mur 3) [DJD II, pp. 79–80 + pl. xxii]. The scribe wrote in a late hand that dates from about the time of the First Jewish Revolt (66–73/74 CE). The preserved text and orthography are identical to that preserved in 𝔐. MurIsa is a very fragmentary manuscript, preserving only portions of Isaiah 1:4-14.

3. OBSERVATIONS ON THE ISAIAH SCROLLS

3.1 THE PRECISE NUMBER OF MANUSCRIPTS

It is very likely that the exact number of Isaiah scrolls will never be known. One reason is because further Isaiah material may yet be recognized among the unidentified fragments in the Rockefeller Museum. Furthermore, the small size and incompleteness of most of the Isaiah fragments makes it difficult to reach a precise figure. As Emanuel Tov stated in 1997:

> The number of the copies of the biblical books found at Qumran should always be considered conjectural. Most of the fragments are small, containing no more than one-tenth of a biblical book. The script of the texts serves as the main criterion for distinguishing between the supposedly different copies even when only tiny fragments have been preserved. Therefore, one has to be cautious when making an estimate of the number of the scrolls on the basis of small fragments. For example, if a scroll of Isaiah was written by more than one scribe, any two fragments of that book written in different scripts could have belonged to that scroll [....] a group of fragments which previously had been ascribed to a single scroll, is sometimes ascribed to two different ones.[11]

Two earlier calculations of the total of Isaiah scrolls at Qumran and other sites were offered by Patrick Skehan in 1956 and 1979, at sixteen[12] and eighteen,[13] respectively. However, to the best of our present knowledge, a total of twenty-two copies of Isaiah have now been identified at Qumran and one other site (see Appendix 1: 'Isaiah Scrolls from the Judaean Desert').

3.2 CONTENTS OF THE ISAIAH SCROLLS

For a full listing of the contents of the Isaiah scrolls by chapter and verse, see Appendix 2. Strictly speaking, none of the Isaiah scrolls preserves every word of this prophetic book; however, 1QIsa^a preserves all sixty-six chapters, with the exception of a few small lacunae. Other scrolls that are relatively well preserved are – in descending order of contents – 1QIsa^b, 4QIsa^b, 4QIsa^c, 4QIsa^a, and 4QIsa^f. Conversely, manuscripts preserving just a few words or verses are 4QIsa^i, 4QIsa^j, 4QIsa^l, 4QIsa^p, 4QIsa^q, and 4QIsa^r. While there is no evidence to indicate that all twenty-two Isaiah scrolls originally contained less than the book in its entirety (chapters 1 to 66), it is possible that some very fragmentary scrolls may have contained only part of the book or may even have been part of a pesher.[14]

Both the beginning of the book (1:1) and its end (66:24) are preserved in three scrolls: 1QIsa^a, 1QIsa^b, and 4QIsa^b. The beginning of Isaiah is also preserved in 4QIsa^a and 4QIsa^j, and the end is extant in 4QIsa^c. As can be expected, the vast majority of Isaiah's sixty-six chapters are represented in more than one of the twenty-two Isaiah scrolls. However, chapters 31, 32, and 34 are preserved in only one manuscript: the Great Isaiah Scroll.

Finally, while there is no evidence to suggest that First and Second Isaiah were written on different manuscripts, it may be noted that material from chapters 1–39 alone is found in nine scrolls: 4QIsa^a, 4QIsa^f, 4QIsa^j, 4QIsa^k, 4QIsa^l, 4QIsa^o, pap4QIsa^p, 4QIsa^r, and MurIsa. Text from chapters 40–66 alone is preserved in eight scrolls: 4QIsa^d, 4QIsa^g, 4QIsa^h, 4QIsa^i, 4QIsa^m, 4QIsa^n, 4QIsa^q, and 5QIsa. Only five scrolls preserve material from both chapters 1–39 and 40–66: 1QIsa^a, 1QIsa^b, 4QIsa^b, 4QIsa^c, 4QIsa^e. Also to be noted is the division of 1QIsa^a into two parts (chapters 1–33 in cols i–xxvii and chapters 34–66 in cols xxviii–liv); see section 4.1 below.

3.3 COMPARATIVE DATINGS

On the basis of palaeographic analysis (see Appendix 1),[15] at least eighteen Isaiah scrolls were copied before the Common Era.[16] The oldest of these are 1QIsa^a (100 CE) and seven Cave 4 manuscripts that date to the first half of the first century BCE.[17] Two of the Qumran scrolls are generally classified as 'Herodian' (30 BCE to 70 CE),[18] one is placed in the middle third of the first century CE,[19] and the sole manuscript from Murabbaʿat was copied at the very end of the Herodian period.[20]

3.4 THE SPECIAL POSITION OF 1QISA^A AND 1QISA^B

Research on Isaiah in the Scrolls has been dominated by the two Cave 1 manuscripts: very obviously by 1QIsa^a, and to a lesser extent by 1QIsa^b.

More aspects have been studied of the Great Isaiah Scroll than any other Dead Sea manuscript, which makes it the best known of all Qumran texts, both biblical and non-biblical. Around one hundred scholarly articles or monographs have been written on various aspects of this scroll.[21] Although 1QIsa^a has been published in two facsimile editions and one transliteration (see section 2.1 above), the lack of a critical edition is to be noted. On the other hand, this manuscript has been the subject of several noted and ground-breaking studies, including Malachi Martin's early monograph on the scribal character of the Dead Sea Scrolls,[22] Joseph Rosenbloom's literary analysis (1970),[23] and E. Y. Kutscher's investigation of the language and linguistic background of 1QIsa[a] (1974).[24] Numerous other aspects of 1QIsa[a] have been treated, including its marginal notations;[25] its orthographic and morphological features;[26] its relationship to ancient versions such as the Septuagint,[27] the Peshitta and Targums,[28] and the Vulgate;[29] and the possible presence of exegetical elements in the scroll (see section 3.5 below).

The influence of 1QIsa[b] on research on Isaiah at Qumran has not been as dramatic as that of 1QIsa[a], yet remains significant. Both 1QIsa[a] and 1QIsa[b] were published relatively very early, and at a time when the contents of very few other biblical texts were known, and so came to represent for many scholars the character of the biblical scrolls. Since 1QIsa[b] is considered to be very close textually to the received Masoretic Text, while 1QIsa[a] is more divergent, several scholars came to regard the Qumran biblical scrolls as generally identical with the Masoretic Text (allowing for differences in small details),[30] with some scrolls (notably 1QIsa[a]) containing secondary or corrupted readings. It thus comes as no surprise that, for Isaiah, variant readings from these two scrolls feature in the Apparatus of the seventh edition of *Biblica Hebraica*,[31] of *Biblia Hebraica Stuttgartensia*,[32] and of the *Hebrew University Bible*.[33]

With respect to the Cave 1 Isaiah scrolls in general, and 1QIsa[a] in particular, Emanuel Tov concludes:

The study of the biblical (and nonbiblical) texts from Qumran would have been different had the texts from cave 4 been published first or simultaneously with the texts from cave 1. As it happened, in the minds of the scholars the special characteristics of 1QIsa[a] were often considered to be the norm for the Qumran texts, with regard to all aspects of these texts. True, other, nonbiblical, Qumran texts were known in the early days of the research of the scrolls, especially from cave 1, but it so happened that many of their scribal features ran parallel to those of 1QIsa[a]. As a result, the description of the other biblical texts, more than that of the nonbiblical texts, depended much on 1QIsa[a].[34]

3.5 THE DIVERGENT CHARACTER OF 1QISA[A]

It is clear that the Great Isaiah Scroll contains hundreds of variant readings in comparison with the Masoretic Text, the Septuagint, and other Qumran manuscripts. Many of these variants should not be attributed to a different textual base or *Vorlage*, but are simply errors on the part of the scribe or corrections made by himself, by another hand, or by a scribe of an archetype of the scroll. For example, the shorter form of Isaiah 4:5-6 in 1QIsa[a] is not evidence of a shorter text, but came about when the scribe or the scribe of an archetype of the scroll skipped from יומם, 'by day', in verse 5 to יומם in verse 6:

1QIsa[a]	Masoretic Text
⁵ויברא יהוה על כול מכון הר ציון ועל מקראה ענן יוממ	⁵ובּרא יהוה על כל⁻מכון הר ציון ועל מקראה ענן יומם ועשן ונגה אש להבה לילה כי על כל כבוד חפה ⁶וסכה תהיה לצל יומם
⁶מחרב ולמחסה ולמסתור מזרם וממטר	מחרב ולמחסה ולמסתור מזרם וממטר פ

Many other variants, however, were most likely present in the scribe's *Vorlage*, since they are also attested by additional Isaiah scrolls or by the Septuagint (for several examples, see sections 4.2 and 4.3 below).

The fact that many variant readings in 1QIsa[a] are attested elsewhere shows such divergences from the Masoretic Text or from other Isaiah scrolls cannot automatically be ascribed to carelessness or error on the part of the scribe of the scroll or of an immediate archetype. Moreover, if it can be shown that such readings make good sense by themselves (see section 4.2 below), the likelihood increases that they are viable alternative forms of ancient origin.

4. SOME OBSERVATIONS ON THE ISAIAH SCROLLS

Study of the Isaiah scrolls raises a number of issues which have been investigated to a larger or lesser extent by scholars. Some of the proposals and conclusions put forward may be viewed as provisional since they were arrived at without recourse to the Cave 4 material, which was only published in 1997.[35] Here I draw attention to three issues which have been treated by others but which merit further discussion. It is my intention to revisit these topics more thoroughly at a later date.

4.1 THE 'BISECTION' OF THE GREAT ISAIAH SCROLL

An interesting feature of 1QIsa[a] is its 'bisection' or division into two parts (chapters 1–33 and 34–66), each written by a different scribe. Many scholars agreed early on that a second scribe commenced writing at the beginning of a new sheet with chapter 34:1 (col. XXVIII) of 1QIsa[a],[36] but others maintain that both segments were written by the same scribe.[37] Although two or more hands are visible also in other Qumran scrolls (e.g. 1QH[a], 1QpHab, and 11QT[a]), according to Tov ('Text of Isaiah', p. 501), 'in no source is the text so neatly divided as in the Isaiah scroll'. Further evidence for the bipartition of the scroll has been presented, e.g. with recourse to palaeography, and also the second scribe's use of fuller orthography, a larger amount of gutturals and specific scribal marks.[38]

Is there any significance to this bisection? The Great Isaiah Scroll offers no textual evidence for any division between the major blocks that have been identified by scholars: First Isaiah (chapters 1–39) and Second Isaiah (40–66) or, for that matter, between Isaiah 1–35, 36–39, 40–55 and 56–66. However, the division at chapters 33/34 is at least interesting, and possibly complex if we accept that a second scribe commenced writing at this point. Since 1QIsa[a] has fifty-four columns, the beginning of a second half of the scroll would be appropriate at col. XXVIII; perhaps a new scribe simply took over here the task of copying this very large manuscript. On the other hand, could those who copied this scroll have seen some significance in the more universal emphasis on the nations found in Isaiah 34, and thus viewed chapters 1–33 and 34–66 as two parts of the book on the basis of content?

4.2 THE TEXT OF ISAIAH IN THE SCROLLS

Several studies on the text of Isaiah in the Dead Sea Scrolls have appeared, including overview essays,[39] complete monographs,[40] and studies of specific chapters or passages.[41] Three more recent discussions on the text of Isaiah in Qumran, which do take into account the Cave 4 texts, have been offered by Paulson Pulikottil, Emanuel Tov and Eugene Ulrich.[42]

There is general agreement among scholars that the textual evidence from the Isaiah scrolls, as well as from the Masoretic Text and the Septuagint, 'all points to a single main edition of [Isaiah] circulating in Judaism in the late Second Temple period.'[43] A (literary) 'edition' in this context is understood as:

a literary unit [...] appearing in two or more parallel forms [...] which one author, major redactor, or major editor completed and which a subsequent redactor or editor subsequently changed to a sufficient extent that the resultant form should be called a revised edition of that text.[44]

It has also been stated that the textual data for Isaiah indicates 'a picture of textual unity, [...] Isaiah presents a much more closely-knit textual tradition than the books of the Pentateuch, or [...] Jeremiah and Ezekiel.'[45] For Tov, this textual unity is so evident that he regards the main textual feature for the Isaiah texts not on the level of variant editions or readings, but in 'the existence of two different scribal traditions, recognizable in differences in the area of orthography, morphology, and scribal habits.'[46]

However, the many variant readings in the Great Isaiah Scroll – some of them major – indicate that, in at least this manuscript, the textual tradition may not be as closely-knit as many scholars suppose. While granting that a large number of these variants are simply errors or corrections, many others were most likely present in the scribe's *Vorlage* (see section 3.5). It is also clear that such readings often make good sense by themselves. For example, in the call-narrative of Isaiah 40:6-8, the original scribe of 1QIsa[a], supported by the Septuagint, had a shorter text. A later scribe, however, has inserted supralinearly an addition that is also found in the Masoretic Text. Verse 7 now has three cola (versus one in the original hand of 1QIsa[a]) and verse 8 has two (versus one by the original scribe):

1QIsa[a]	Masoretic Text
⁶קול אומר קרא ואומרה מה אקרא	⁶קול אמר קרא ואמר מה אקרא
כול הבשר חציר	כל הבשר חציר
וכול חסדיו כציץ השדה	וכל חסדו כציץ השדה
⁷יבש חציר נבל ציץ	⁷יבש חציר נבל ציץ
	כי רוח יהוה נשבה בו
	אכן חציר העם
	⁸יבש חציר נבל ציץ
⁸ודבר אלוהינו יקום לעולם	ודבר אלהינו יקום לעולם

In the above example, it may be argued that the scribe's eye skipped from יבש חציר נבל ציץ, 'The grass withers, the flowers fade' in verse 7 to the same colon in verse 8, resulting in the loss of the intervening text. However, it is far more likely that 1QIsa[a] copied a text with the earlier, shorter form since it makes better sense than the longer (expansionistic?) form found in the Masoretic Text, towards which the later scribe of

1QIsa[a] corrected the manuscript.[47] This likelihood is enhanced by the fact that the Septuagint has the identical short form, which indicates that for verses 7-8 the Greek translator had before him a Hebrew text like 1QIsa[a] and not one like the Masoretic Text.

A second, more complex example is found in col. XXXII of 1QIsa[a], which ends Hezekiah's hymn with the first two words of Isaiah 38:20, while the Masoretic Text (and the Septuagint) contains a longer text:[48]

1QIsa[a]	Masoretic Text
[19]חי חי הוא יודכה כמוני היום	[19]חי חי הוא יודך כמוני היום
אב לבנים יודיע אל אמתכה	אב לבנים יודיע אל אמתך
[20]יהוה להושיעני	[20]יהוה להושיעני
חי חי יודך כמוני היום	
אב לבנים והודיע אלוה אמתך	
יהוה להושיעֵנ	
ונגנותי נגנן כול ימי חיינו על בית יהוה	ונגנותי נגנן כל־ימי חיינו על בית יהוה
[21]ויאומר ישעיהו דבלת תאנים וימרחו	[21]ויאמר ישעיהו ישאו דבלת תאנים וימרחו
על השחין ויחי [22]ויאמר חזקיה מה	על השחין ויחי [22]ויאמר חזקיהו מה
אות כי אעלה בית יהוה	אות כי אעלה בית יהוה ס

In this example, the original scribe of 1QIsa[a] left two and one-half lines blank after להושיעני, presumably for text to be supplied at a later time. Apparently a second scribe then filled in the wrong text, reduplicating all of verses 19-20. Yet a third scribe added vv. 21-22 (which occur earlier in the parallel passage in 2 Kings 20, at verses 7-8) in the remaining space on the column (line 14), and vertically down the left margin since he had run out of space. With respect to our understanding of Isaiah 38, this complex passage in 1QIsa[a] suggests that (a) the original form of Isaiah 38 or an early form of it lacked verses 21-22; (b) at some point a form of the two verses found at 2 Kings 20:21-22 were inserted into Isaiah 38 as verses 21-22 (as in '𝔐' used to represent 'Masoretic Text'), although they are out of place here; (c) the earlier form of this passage (lacking verses 21-22) was copied by the original scribe of 1QIsa[a]; (d) the two verses were inserted by a later scribe, apparently for the purpose of conforming to a proto-Masoretic textual form, at least at this point in the scroll; (e) the intervention by the later scribe effectively results in an inferior reading.

Examples such as these suggest that, even if the original scribe of 1QIsa[a] was careless and the text in its present form contains corrections, this scroll contains readings that are significant for textual criticism of Isaiah. While a different literary edition cannot be identified in 1QIsa[a] or any of the other Isaiah scrolls, scholars should carefully consider whether some of the preserved variants constitute evidence for alternative earlier or preferred readings in the book itself. It is my intention to explore this question systematically in the near future.

4.3 SPECIFIC VARIANT READINGS

A significant contribution of the Isaiah scrolls to biblical scholarship in general, and to textual studies in particular, is on the level of individual variants. Many useful articles have been written on specific variant readings in the Isaiah scrolls, especially 1QIsa[a].[49] Depending on their approaches to the Hebrew text, individual scholars would accept a greater or lesser number of these readings as earlier or superior textual forms in Isaiah.

One example is found at Isaiah 1:15, which describes the Lord's revulsion at those who stretch out their hands to worship when they have committed murder and violent oppression. In 4QIsa[f] and the Masoretic Text the verse concludes with 'your hands are filled with blood', but 1QIsa[a] adds 'your fingers with iniquity' (אצבעותיכם בעאון). Another example occurs at Isaiah 2:20, where the Masoretic Text describes the idols of silver and of gold as those 'which they have made for themselves to worship' (אשר עשו לו להשתחות), while 1QIsa[a] reads 'which their fingers have made to worship' (אשר [עשו אצ]בעותיו להשתחות). Of these two examples, the first variant appears to be a preferred reading since it completes the parallelism in Isaiah 1:15. The second variant, however, is a viable alternative reading, but not necessarily a better one, to the form found in the Masoretic Text of Isaiah 2:20.

A most interesting reading occurs at Isaiah 53:11, where the presence of a single word ('light') in 1QIsa[a] renders the meaning of the verse very different to that in 𝔐 which lacks the word:

1QIsa[a]	Masoretic Text
מעמל נפשוה יראה אור וישבע ובדעתו יצדיק צדיק עבדו לרבים ועוונותם הואה יסבול	מעמל נפשו יראה ישבע בדעתו יצדיק צדיק עבדי לרבים ועונתם הוא יסבל

It has been suggested[50] that here the Masoretic reading יראה ('he will see'), which is also found in the Syriac and the Vulgate but is awkward in this context, is another form of ירוה ('he will be satisfied'), which makes better sense. In that case, אור could be viewed as an addition on the part of 1QIsa[a] or of the text he was copying. On the other hand, the reading 'light' is attested in all three Qumran witnesses that preserve the relevant text (1QIsa[a], 1QIsa[b], 4QIsa[d]) and by the Septuagint (δεῖξαι αὐτῷ φῶς). It is interesting to note that the longer text is now translated by most modern English Bibles, including the *NRSV, NIV, NEB, REB, JB* and *NAB*.

5. THE INTERPRETATION OF ISAIAH AT QUMRAN

Isaiah is fairly prominent in several writings that are distinctive to the Qumran community, including the six pesharim on this book (3Q4, 4Q161, 4Q162, 4Q163, 4Q164, 4Q165), but just how do these pesharim interpret Isaiah, and in what context are Isaianic passages cited in other writings from Qumran? Eugene Ulrich points out:

'Unlike such figures as Enoch, Moses, and Daniel, the person of Isaiah does not emerge as a clear actor in the writings found at Qumran.'[51] Instead of dwelling on the person of the prophet himself, the Qumran commentators and other authors focused on God's message as revealed in his book – a message vitally applicable to their own situation, and in their eyes often referring to the Yaḥad in specific terms. While a great deal may be written on this community's use and interpretation of Isaiah, the present essay focuses on four aspects – in many cases not mutually exclusive – that are evident in the writings from Qumran.

5.1 AUTHORITATIVE STATUS AND LEGITIMATION

On occasion Isaiah is specifically termed a נביא, for instance in col. 7:10 of the Damascus Document (CD): עליהם בבוא הדבר אשר כתוב בדברי ישעיה בן אמוץ הנביא ('to them that is when the oracle that is written in the words of the prophet Isaiah son of Amoz came true'); see also CD IV, 13-14 ('as God spoke by the prophet Isaiah son of Amoz'), quoting Isaiah 24:17.

The authoritative standing of the book of Isaiah is clearly underscored by the CD passage when it introduces Isaiah 7:17 with a quotation formula (הדבר אשר כתוב, 'the oracle that is written'), followed by the citation in lines 11-12. The same quotation formula is found in the Community Rule (1QS), one of the Qumran community's central texts, which introduces (כאשר כתוב) and quotes Isaiah 2:22 in V, 17. Other examples of passages introduced by this formula are found in: 4QFlorilegium (4Q174), quoting Isaiah 8:11 in frgs. 1-2 i 15-16; in 4QMiscellaneous Rules (4Q265), quoting Isaiah 54:1-2 in frg. 2, lines 3-5; and in 11QMelchizedek (11Q13), quoting Isa 52:7 in II, 23. Two other relevant texts, which use somewhat different quotation formulas, are CD's introduction of Isaiah 24:17 with 'as God spoke' in IV, 13-14; and 1QM's statement that in times past 'you' (i.e., God himself) foretold the appointed time (XI, 11-12), quoting Isaiah 31:8.

The high regard which the Qumran community had for Isaiah is further evidenced by it being one of relatively few biblical books on which pesharim (commentaries) were written (the others being Hosea, Micah, Nahum, Habakkuk, Zephaniah, Malachi, and the Psalms). It is generally agreed among scholars that biblical books on which pesharim were written were viewed by the commentators as authoritative prophetic literature.[52]

Another work that makes extensive use of Isaiah is 4QTanḥumim (4Q176), which resembles the pesharim in some respects.[53] Near the beginning of this fascinating document (frgs. 1–2 i 4), there is specific reference to the book of Isaiah as containing the very words of God himself: 'And from the book of Isaiah, words of comfort: [... 'Comfort, comfort my people], says your God,"' followed by the full quotation of Isaiah 40:1-5 (lines 5-9). 4Q176 as a whole is a compilation of consoling words from prophetic literature; quoted most prominently is the book of Isaiah (eleven quotations), but there are also citations from Zechariah and Psalms (one each).[54]

The community's use of, and appeal to, Isaiah as an authoritative prophet served to legitimate the admonitions made or interpretations offered in the text that preceded or followed the various quotations.

5.2 FAITHFULNESS TO THE COVENANT

Not surprisingly, many quotations of Isaiah in writings that were specific to Qumran underscore the fulfilment of prophecy. One example is the quotation of Isaiah 7:17 (in a somewhat adapted form) in CD VII, 11-12, which was introduced in the preceding line 10:

[11]which says: "Days are coming upon you and upon your people and upon your father's house that [12]have never come before, since the departure of Ephraim from Judah."[55]

When this and several other passages are considered, one strong theme that emerges is the need of the Yaḥad or Qumran community to remain faithful to the Covenant by keeping the commandments of God. Line 9 of the column reads 'But those who reject the commandments and the rules <shall perish>,'[56] which hints at the purpose of the quotation of Isaiah 7:17 in CD: that the fulfilment of prophecy confirms the inevitability of God's judgement on those who reject his laws. The lesson to be learnt: '[1]... And such is the verdict on all members of the covenant who [2]do not hold firm to these laws: they are condemned to destruction by Belial' (CD VIII, 1-2).[57]

An allied interpretation of Isaiah is found in column V of the Community Rule (1QS), which outlines general rules and foundational precepts with respect to entry into the Qumran community's New Covenant, and provides stipulations for the examination of initiates. After the quotation of Isaiah 2:22 in line 17, the column focuses on what is expected of those who belong to the Yaḥad and to the Covenant:

[13] ... None of the perverse men is to enter purifying waters used by the Men of Holiness and so contact their purity.... [15] None belonging to the Yaḥad is to discuss [16]with such men matters of Law or legal judgment, nor to eat or drink what is theirs, nor yet to take anything from them [17]unless purchased, as it is written "Turn away from mere mortals, in whose nostrils is only breath; for of what account are they?" (Isaiah 2:22). Accordingly, [18]all who are not reckoned as belonging to His covenant must be separated out, along with everything they possess ... (1QS V, 13-18).[58]

5.3 A SEPARATE AND RIGHTEOUS PEOPLE

The admonitions to righteous living and keeping the commandments are reinforced by the harsh reality of an evil age as described by the use of Isaiah 24:17 in CD IV, 12-14 of the Damascus Document:

[12] ... But in the present age [13]Belial is unrestrained in Israel, just as God said by Isaiah the prophet, the son of Amoz, [14]saying, "Fear and pit and snare are upon thee, dweller in the land" (Isaiah 24:17). The true meaning of this verse [15]concerns the three traps of Belial about which Levi son of Jacob said [16]that Belial would catch Israel in, so he directed them towards three kinds of [17]righteousness.[59]

The passage continues by explaining this base text in terms of the three traps of Belial, and in so doing discloses several ethical principles that differentiated the Qumran group from others. The implication is clear: the Qumran Covenanters were to avoid the traps of Belial by living as a separate people with strict and distinctive ethical norms.

The interpretation of Isaiah 2:22 in 1QS V was discussed above (in relation to the Covenant). Following the quotation of Isaiah 2:22, the text emphasizes the need for those belonging to the belonging to the Yaḥad to live separately from outsiders:[60]

Accordingly, [18]all who are not reckoned as belonging to His covenant must be separated out, along with everything they possess; the Man of Holiness must not rely upon futile [19]actions, whereas all who do not know His covenant are futility itself. All those who despise His word, He shall destroy from upon the face of the earth. Their every deed is an abomination [20]before Him, all that is theirs being infested with impurity (1QS V, 17-20).[61]

While the admonition to separate from the ungodly is not prominent in the Isaiah pesharim, the notion of the wicked in contrast to those who follow righteousness is sometimes evident. For example, 4QpIsa[b] (4Q162) interprets Isaiah 5:11-14 as referring to the 'men of mockery who are in Jerusalem,' and proceeds to define them in terms of Isaiah 5:24-25 ('the ones who have rejected the Law of the Lord, ...'). The ungodly also seem to be denoted in the fragmentary 4Qpap pIsa[c] (4Q163), which quoted Isaiah 30:15-18 and apparently refers to the Pharisees who have rejected the Law: [10]'This passage is for the last days and refers to the company of Flattery-Seekers [11]who are in Jerusalem [...] [12]in the Law and not [...] [13]heart, for to trample [...].'[62]

Another frequently cited passage is in 1QS VIII, which quotes Isaiah 40:3 in affirming the community's self-identity. This text clearly illustrates their self-understanding as a holy people who were set apart from the 'session of perverse men' and proceeding to the wilderness:

When these men have been grounded in the instruction of the Yaḥad for two years – provided they be blameless in their conduct – [11]they shall be set apart as holy in the midst of the men of the Yaḥad. No biblical doctrine concealed from Israel but discovered by the [12]Interpreter is to be hidden from these men out of fear that they might backslide. When such men as these come to be in Israel, [13]conforming to these doctrines, they shall separate from the session of perverse men to go to the wilderness, there to prepare the way of truth, [14]as it is written, "In the wilderness prepare the way of the Lord, make straight in the desert a highway for our God" (Isaiah 40:3).[63] (1QS VIII, 10-14)

5.4 AN ESCHATOLOGICAL EMPHASIS

The passage just quoted also reveals the eschatological aspect of the community's self-identity: they went 'to the wilderness, there to prepare the way of truth, as it is written, "In the wilderness prepare the way of the Lord, ..."' (1QS VIII, 13-14). The similar use of Isaiah 40:3 by all four Gospel writers[64] as pointing to John the Baptist's ministry in the wilderness for the purpose of ushering in the eschaton has often been noted.

Another text that makes use of Isaiah in reference to the end times is 4QFlorilegium (4Q174), which one translator has termed 'The Last Days: A Commentary on Selected Verses.'[65] Quoting Isaiah 8:11, the author makes it clear that those who have turned aside from the path of the wicked are fulfilling Isaiah's prophecy with respect to the End Times:

[14]The interpretation of "Happy are those who do not follow the advice of the wicked" (Ps 1:1a). The meaning is, [th]ey are those who turn aside from the path of [the wicked], [15]as it is written in the book of Isaiah the prophet in reference to the Last Days, "And it came to pass, while His hand was strong upon me, [that He warned me not to walk in the way of] [16]this people" (Isa 8:11). These are they about whom it is written in the book of Ezekiel the prophet, namely, "They shall ne[ver again defile themselves with] [17]their idols" (Ezek 37:23). They are the Sons of Zadok, and the m[e]n of the[i]r council who pu[rsue righ]teousness and follow them to join the Yaḥad (4Q146 1-2 i 14-17).[66]

Isaiah is also quoted in 11QMelchizedek (11Q13) with reference to the End Times and the coming Messiah. Weaving together passages from Isaiah, the Psalms and the Torah, 11Q13 includes commentary for the purpose of explaining the eschatological fulfilment of these texts. With the most prominent citation from Isaiah (in column II), the figure of the messenger – an Anointed one who comes with a message from God — is described, but then he shall be 'cut off.'

> This vi[sitation] [15]is the Day of [Salvation] that He has decreed [through Isai]ah the prophet [concerning all the captives], inasmuch as scripture sa[ys, "How] beautiful [16]upon the mountains are the fee[t of] the messeng[er] who [an]nounces peace, who brings [good] news, [who announces salvat]ion, who [sa]ys to Zion, 'Your [di]vine being [reigns]'" (Isaiah 52:7). [17]This scripture's interpretation: "the mounta[ins" are the] prophet[s], they w[ho were sent to proclaim God's truth and to] proph[esy] to all I[srael]. [18]"The messenger" is the [An]ointed of the spir[it,] of whom Dan[iel] spoke, "[After the sixty-two weeks, an Anointed one shall be cut off" (Daniel 9:26). The "messenger who brings] [19]good news, who announ[ces salvation]" is the one of whom it is wri[tt]en, "[to proclaim the year of the LORD's favor, the day of vengeance of our God]; [20][to comfo[rt all who mourn" (Isaiah 61:2).[67] (11Q13 II, 14-20)

Eschatological and messianic themes are also evident in some of the pesharim's interpretation of Isaianic passages. For example, 4QpIsa[a] (4Q161) understands Isaiah 10:24-27 as referring to the 'Ruler of the Nation' or Davidic Messiah:

> [13][This refers to ...] [14][...] when they return from the "wilderness of the Gentiles" (cf. Ezek. 20:35) ... [15][... the Staff is the] Ruler of the Congregation, and afterward he will remove [the yoke] from them.[68] (4Q161 ii 13-15)

There follows a quotation of 10:28-32, a passage that originally referred to the advance of the Assyrians on Jerusalem; but now the pesher interprets this as prophesying the Messiah's progress to the holy city:

> [26]This saying [refers to] the latter days still to come [...] [27][the Ruler of the Na]tion, when he marches inland from the Plain of Akko to fight against [... the Ruler of [28]the Na]tion, for there is none like him in all the cities of [....] [29]up to the border of Jerusalem [...].[69] (4Q161 ii 22-24)

Specific reference to the Messiah as the 'Branch of David' is later provided in the document's interpretation of Isaiah 11:1-5:

> [22][This saying refers to the Branch of] David, who will appear in the lat[ter days, ...] [23][...] his enemies; and God will support him with [a spirit of] strength [...] [24][... and God will give him] a glorious throne, [a sacred] crown, and elegant garments. [25][... He will put a] scepter in his hand, and he will rule over all the G[enti]les, even Magog [26][and his army ... all] the peoples his sword will control. As for the verse that says, "He will not [27][judge only by what his eyes see], he will not decide only by what his ears hear," this means that [28][he will be advised by the Zadokite priests], and as they instruct him, so shall he rule, and at their command [29][he shall render decisions; and always] one of the prominent priests shall go out with him, in whose hand shall be the garments of [...].[70] (4Q161 iii 18-25)

Other Isaiah pesharim also interpret the biblical text with reference to the End Times or the Messiah. See, for example, 4QpIsa[b] (1Q162), which understands Isaiah 5:10 as referring 'to the last days, when the land itself is condemned by sword and famine; so it shall be [2]at the time when the land is punished' (column ii 1-2).[71] Another example is in 4Qpap pIsa[c] (4Q163), where the citation of Isaiah 10:20-22 is followed by the comment 'This passage is for the last [days ...]' (frgs. 4–6 ii 12).[72]

6. SUMMARY AND CONCLUSION

The twenty-two Isaiah scrolls provide a rich resource for studying Judaean biblical manuscripts, and the book of Isaiah itself. They include the best preserved and most complete of all the Dead Sea Scrolls (1QIsa[a], the 'Great Isaiah Scroll'), as well as several others that are relatively well preserved (1QIsa[b], 4QIsa[b], 4QIsa[c], 4QIsa[a], and 4QIsa[f]). A special position continues to be held by 1QIsa[a] because of the circumstances surrounding its discovery, its virtually complete state, and the fact that it diverges qualitatively from the Masoretic Text more than any other Isaiah scroll.

While all the Isaiah scrolls point to a single main edition of Isaiah, they contain many variant readings that are of text-critical value. Some of these variants are substantial – involving several cola – while others involve only a word or two. Many variant readings, at times supported by the Septuagint, attest to textual forms that are earlier or preferred than those found in the Masoretic Text. Other variant readings, however, must be attributed to carelessness or error by the scribe of 1QIsaᵃ in particular. Since the Cave 4 Isaiah scrolls were published relatively recently (1997), a detailed assessment of their value in relation to each other and to 1QIsaᵃ, 1QIsaᵇ, the Masoretic Text and the Septuagint has yet to be made.

Isaiah was used extensively in several writings that are distinctive to the Qumran community and is the subject of six pesharim. Unlike figures such as Enoch, Moses, and Daniel, Isaiah himself is not prominent in the writings found at Qumran, but the larger book attributed to him is extensively quoted and interpreted in a variety of ways. While the Qumran community's interpretation of Isaiah may be treated in several ways, this essay has focused on four ways in which they made use of this book in relation to their own time: to underscore authoritative status and legitimation; to demonstrate their faithfulness to the Covenant; to declare themselves as a separate and righteous people; and to add weight to the eschatological emphasis of their faith.

NOTES

1   For an earlier description of the Isaiah scrolls, see Peter W. Flint, 'The Isaiah Scrolls from the Judean Desert', in *Writing and Reading the Scroll of Isaiah. Studies of an Interpretative Tradition*, ed. by Craig C. Broyles and Craig A. Evans, 2 vols, FIOTL, I, 1 and 2; VTSup, 70, 1 and 2 (Leiden: Brill, 1997), II, pp. 481-89.

2   See section 2.1 (a) below.

3   DJD III, p. 173 and pl. xxxvi; DJD II, pp. 79-80 and pl. xxii; and P. W. Skehan and E. Ulrich, 'Isaiah' in DJD XV, pp. 7-143 + pls i-xxiii; see also James Muilenburg, 'Fragments of Another Qumran Isaiah Scroll', *BASOR*, 135 (1954), 28-32; Eugene Ulrich and Patrick W. Skehan, 'An Edition of 4QIsaᵉ, Including the Former 4QIsaᵇ', *RevQ*, 17 (Milik Festschrift, 1996), 23-36.

4   DJD I, pp. 66-68 and pl. xii; Millar Burrows with John C. Trever and William H. Brownlee (eds.), *The Dead Sea Scrolls of St. Mark's Monastery. Volume I: The Isaiah Manuscript and the Habakkuk Commentary* (New Haven, CT: ASOR, 1950); Frank Moore Cross, David Noel Freedman and James A. Sanders (eds). *Scrolls from Qumrân Cave I: The Great Isaiah Scroll, the Order of the Community, the Pesher to Habakkuk* (Jerusalem: The Albright Institute of Archaeological Research and The Shrine of the Book, 1972), pp. 13-123; Donald W. Parry and Elisha Qimron (eds), *The Great Isaiah Scroll (1QIsaᵃ): A New Edition*, STDJ, 32 (Leiden: Brill, 1999); E. L. Sukenik (ed.), *The Dead Sea Scrolls of the Hebrew University* (Jerusalem: Magnes, 1955).

5   See Frank Moore Cross, *The Ancient Library of Qumran*, 3rd edn. (Sheffield: Sheffield Academic Press, 1995), p. 176.

6   See A. J. Timothy Jull and others, 'Radiocarbon Dating of Scrolls and Linen Fragments from the Judaean Desert', *Radiocarbon*, 37 (1995), 11-19. An earlier radiocarbon examination performed in Switzerland suggested 199-120 BCE; see G. Bonani and others, 'Radiocarbon Dating of the Dead Sea Scrolls', *'Atiqot*, 20 (1991), 27-32.

7   The corrections to 1QIsaᵃ were made both by the original scribe and by a later hand. According to Emanuel Tov, 'The Text of Isaiah at Qumran', in Broyles and Evans, *Writing and Reading the Scroll of Isaiah*, II, pp. 491-511 (p. 502): 'of all the Qumran texts, this text contains the relatively largest amount of corrections, viz. an average of one scribal intervention in every four lines of text', cf.

Emanuel Tov, 'The Textual Base of the Corrections in the Biblical Texts Found at Qumran', in *The Dead Sea Scrolls – Forty Years of Research*, ed. by D. Dimant and U. Rappaport, STDJ, 10 (Jerusalem: Magnes; Leiden: Brill, 1992), pp. 299-314.

8   In three cases these signs are virtually identical with those in 1QS, and were most likely produced by the scribe who wrote the text of 1QS, 1QSa, 1QSb, and 4QSam[c]; see Eugene Charles Ulrich, '4QSam[c]: A Fragmentary Manuscript of 2 Samuel 14-15 from the Scribe of the *Serek Hay-yaḥad* (1QS)', *BASOR*, 235 (1979), 1-25; cf. Tov, 'Text of Isaiah', p. 501. Some scribal markings are written in the palaeo-Hebrew script, and others are similar to the Cryptic A script. Since it is now clear that the Cryptic A script was used for sectarian texts, it appears that Qumran texts such as 1QIsa[a] 'were either used by the Qumran community or copied by its scribes' (Tov, 'Text of Isaiah', p. 501).

9   See section 4.1 below.

10 For a precise list of contents, see Appendix 2: 'Contents of the Isaiah Scrolls by Chapter and Verse'.

11 Tov, 'Text of Isaiah', p. 491, n. 1.

12 P. W. Skehan, 'The Qumran Manuscripts and Textual Criticism', in *Volume du Congrès: Strasbourg 1956*, VTSup, 4 (Leiden: Brill, 1957), pp. 148-58 (p. 150).

13 P. W. Skehan, 'Qumran, Littérature de Qumran – A. Textes bibliques', *DBSup*, 9 (1979), cols 805-22 (col. 810).

14 For example, 4QpapIsa[p] (see DJD XV, p. 139), the only Isaiah fragment that was written on papyrus. For the proposal that some copies of biblical books written on papyrus – which is a rare phenomenon among the biblical scrolls – were personal rather than official copies, see Michael Owen Wise, *Thunder in Gemini: And Other Essays on the History, Language and Literature of Second Temple Palestine*, JSPSup, 15 (Sheffield: JSOT Press, 1994), pp. 103-57 (pp. 130-32); and Tov, 'Text of Isaiah', p. 493, n. 10.

15 For a grouping of the eighteen Cave 4 Isaiah scrolls in four categories (Hasmonaean, late Hasmonaean/early Herodian, early Herodian, late Herodian), see Eugene Ulrich, 'Isaiah, Book of', in *EDSS*, I, pp. 384-88, (p. 385).

16 1QIsa[a], 4QIsa[a], 4QIsa[b], 4QIsa[d], 4QIsa[e], 4QIsa[f], 4QIsa[g], 4QIsa[h], 4QIsa[i], 4QIsa[j], 4QIsa[k], 4QIsa[l], 4QIsa[m], 4QIsa[n], 4QIsa[o], 4QIsa[p], 4QIsa[q], 4QIsa[r].

17 4QIsa[f], 4QIsa[h], 4QIsa[i], 4QIsa[m], 4QIsa[n], 4QIsa[o], 4QpapIsa[p].

18 1QIsa[b] and 5QIsa.

19 4QIsa[c].

20 MurIsa, *c*. 70 CE.

21 This number is obviously an approximation. In 1997 Tov stated that 'more than 75 scholarly articles' had been written on various aspects of 1QIsa[a] ('Text of Isaiah', p. 496).

22 Malachi Martin, *The Scribal Character of the Dead Sea Scrolls*, 2 vols. Bibliothèque du Muséon, 44 and 45 (Louvain: Publications Universitaires, 1958).

23 Joseph R. Rosenbloom, *The Dead Sea Isaiah Scroll – A Literary Analysis. A Comparison with the Masoretic Text and the Biblia Hebraica* (Eerdmans: Grand Rapids, 1970). See also William Hugh Brownlee, *The Meaning of the Qumrân Scrolls for the Bible: with Special Attention to the Book of Isaiah* (New York: Oxford University Press, 1964).

24 Kutscher, *Language and Linguistic Background*.

25 See most recently Emanuel Tov, 'Scribal Markings in the Texts from the Judean Desert', in *Current Research and Technological Developments on the Dead Sea Scrolls: Conference on the Texts from the Judean Desert, Jerusalem, 30 April 1995*, ed. by Donald W. Parry and Stephen D. Ricks, STDJ, 20 (Leiden: Brill, 1996), pp. 41-77. Earlier studies include J. L. Teicher, 'The Christian Interpretation of the Sign x in the Isaiah Scroll', *VT*, 5 (1955), 189-98; and Martin, *Scribal Character*, passim.

26 In addition to the monographs by Martin, *Scribal Character* and Kutscher, *Language and Linguistic Background*, see the following more recent studies: Jean Koenig, 'Réouverture du débat sur la Première Main rédactionnelle du rouleau ancien d'Isaïe de Qumrân (1 Q Is[a]) en 40, 7-8', *RevQ*, 11 (1983), 219-37; Emanuel Tov, 'The Orthography and Language of the Hebrew Scrolls Found at Qumran and the Origin of These Scrolls', *Textus*, 13 (1986), 31-57; and F. M. Cross, Jr., 'Some Notes on a Generation of Qumran Studies', in *MQC*, pp. 1-14.

27 For example, Joseph Ziegler, 'Die Vorlage der Isaias-Septuaginta (LXX) und die Erste Isaias-Rolle von Qumran (1QIs[a])', *JBL*, 78 (1959), 34-59.

28 For example, M. H. Gottstein, 'Die Jesaia-Rolle im Lichte von Peschitta und Targum', *Biblica*, 35 (1954), 51-71.

29 For example, Angelo Penna, 'La Volgata e il manoscritto 1QIsᵃ', *Biblica*, 38 (1957), 381-95.

30 This view was developed early on by Harry M. Orlinsky, 'Studies in the St. Mark's Isaiah Scroll', *JBL*, 69 (1950), 149-66; *JNES*, 11 (1952), 153-56; *JJS*, 2 (1950-51), 151-54; *JQR*, 43 (1952-53), 329-40; *IEJ*, 4 (1954), 5-8; and *HUCA*, 25 (1954), 85-92.

31 Kittel, Rudolph (ed.), *Biblia Hebraica*, 3rd edn (Stuttgart: Württembergische Bibelanstalt Stuttgart, 1937-1962), with readings from the Dead Sea Scrolls listed in a third, separate apparatus.

32 D. Winton Thomas, 'Librum Jesaiae' (1968), in *Biblia Hebraica Stuttgartensia* ed. by K. Elliger and W. Rudolph (Stuttgart: Deutsche Bibelgesellschaft, 1967-77).

33 *The Hebrew University Bible: The Book of Isaiah,* ed. Moshe H. Goshen-Gottstein (Jerusalem: Magnes, 1995).

34 Tov, 'Text of Isaiah', p. 495.

35 See Patrick W. Skahan and Eugene Ulrich, 'Isaiah', in DJD XV, pp. 7-143 + pls. i-xxiii.

36 For example, M. Noth, 'Eine Bemerkung zur Jesajarolle vom Toten Meer', *VT*, 1 (1951), 224-26; and Curt Kuhl, 'Schreibereigentümlichkeiten: Bemerkungen zur Jesajarolle (DSIa)', *VT*, 2 (1952), 307-33, (pp. 332-33).

37 For example, Martin, *Scribal Character*, pp. 65-73; Kutscher, *Language and Linguistic Background*, pp. 564-66; and Johann Cook, 'Orthographical Peculiarities in the Dead Sea Biblical Scrolls', *RevQ*, 14 (1989; The Texts of Qumran and the History of the Community: Proceedings of the Groningen Congress on the Dead Sea Scrolls (20-23 August 1989), vol. I: Biblical Texts), 293-305, (pp. 303-304).

38 See especially William H. Brownlee, 'The Literary Significance of the Bisection of Isaiah in the Ancient Scroll of Isaiah from Qumran', in *Proceedings of the 25th Congress of Orientalists*, 2 vols (Moscow: Izdatel'stvo Vostochnoi Literatury, 1962-63), I, pp. 431-37; Kent H. Richards, 'A Note on the Bisection of Isaiah', *RevQ*, 5 (1965), 257-58; Johann Cook, 'The Dichotomy of 1QIsaᵃ', in *Intertestamental Essays in Honour of Józef Tadeusz Milik*, ed. by Zdzislaw J. Kapera, Qumranica Mogilanensia, 6, Studies Offered to Józef Tadeusz Milik, Part I (Kraków: Enigma, 1992), pp. 7-24; and Tov, 'Text of Isaiah', pp. 498-99, esp. n. 37.

39 For example, Patrick W. Skehan, 'The Text of Isaias at Qumrân', *CBQ*, 17 (1955), 158-63 (pp. 162-63); Florentino García Martínez, 'Le livre d'Isaïe à Qumran', *Le monde de la Bible*, 49 (1987), 43-45.

40 For example, Kutscher, *Language and Linguistic Background*; F. D. James, *A Critical Examination of the Text of Isaiah, Based on the Dead Sea Scroll of Isaiah (DSIa), the Masoretic Text, the Septuagint* (doctoral diss., Boston: Boston University, 1959); Morrow, *Isaiah at Qumran*; Jean Koenig, *L'Herméneutique analogique du Judaïsme antique d'après les témoins textuels d'Isaïe*, VTSup, 33 (Leiden: Brill, 1982); and Dominique Barthélemy, *Critique textuelle de l'Ancien Testament*, 3 vols, OBO, 50 (Fribourg: Universitaires; Göttingen: Vandenhoeck & Ruprecht, 1992), III: Ézéchiel, Daniel et les 12 Prophètes.

41 For example, Wᴍ H. Brownlee, 'The Text of Isaiah vi 13 in the Light of DSIa', *VT*, 1 (1951), 296-98; J. Carmignac, 'Six Passages d'Isaïe éclairés par Qumran', in *Bibel und Qumran: H. Bardtke Festschrift*, ed. by S. Wagner (Berlin: Evangelische Haupt-Bibelgesellschaft, 1968), pp. 37-46; Jesper Hoegenhaven, 'The First Isaiah Scroll from Qumran (1QIsᵃ) and the Massoretic Text: Some Reflections with Special Regard to Isaiah 1-12', *JSOT*, 28 (1984), 17-35.

42 Paulson U. Pulikottil, *Transmission of Biblical Texts in Qumran: The Case of the Large Isaiah Scroll 1QIsaᵃ* JSPSup, 34 (Sheffield: Sheffield Academic Press, 2001); Tov, 'Text of Isaiah', pp. 491-511; Ulrich, 'Isaiah, Book of', pp. 384-88.

43 Ulrich, 'Isaiah, Book of', p. 386.

44 See Eugene Ulrich, 'Multiple Literary Editions: Reflections Toward a Theory of the History of the Biblical Text', in Eugene Ulrich, *The Dead Sea Scrolls and the Origins of the Bible* (Grand Rapids: Eerdmans; Leiden: Brill, 1999), pp. 99-120, (p. 107).

45 Tov, 'Text of Isaiah', p. 505.

46 *Ibid.*

47 Cf. Ulrich, 'Isaiah, Book of', p. 386.

48 In the left column, the italicized words were copied by a second scribe and the words in bold by a third scribe.

49 Early articles (in the 1940s and 1950s) include: Millar Burrows, 'Variant Readings in the Isaiah Manuscript', *BASOR*, 111 (1948), 16-24 and 113 (1949) 24-32; J. M. P. Bauchet, 'Note sur les variantes de sens d'Isaïe 42 et 43 dans le manuscrit du désert du Juda', *La nouvelle revue théologique*, 71 (1949), 304-305; Otto Eissfeldt, 'Varianten der Jesaia-Rolle', *Theologische Literaturzeitung*, 74 (1949), cols 221-26; Brownlee, 'Text of Isaiah VI 13'; Samuel Loewinger, 'New Corrections to the Variae Lectiones of O. Eissfeldt', *VT*, 4 (1954), 80-87; Samuel Loewinger, 'The Variants of DSI II', *VT*, 4 (1954), 155-63; Arie Rubinstein, 'Isaiah LII 14 – משחת – and the DSIa Variant', *Bib*, 35 (1954), 475-79; Arie Rubinstein, 'Isaiah lvii 17 וַאֶקְצֹף הַסְתֵּר and the DSIa Variant', *VT*, 4 (1954) 200-201; Arie Rubinstein, 'The Theological Aspect of Some Variant Readings in the Isaiah Scroll', *JJS*, 6 (1955), 187-200; Samuel Iwry, 'Maṣṣēbāh and Bāmāh in 1Q Isaiah[A] 6 13', *JBL*, 76 (1957), 225-32. Articles after the 1950s include the following: John Sawyer, 'The Qumran Reading of Isaiah 6 13', *Annual of the Swedish Theological Institute*, 3 (1964), 111-13; Samuel Iwry, 'והנמצא – A Striking Variant Reading in 1QIs[a]', *Textus*, 5 (1966), 34-43; Mitchell Dahood, 'Isaiah 19,11 ḥkmy and 1QIsa[a] ḥkmyh' *Biblica*, 56 (1975), 420; Craig A. Evans, 'The Text of Isaiah 6 9-10', *ZAW*, 94 (1982), 415-18; Koenig, 'Réouverture du débat'; Arie van der Kooij, '1QIsa[a] Col. VIII, 4-11 (Isa 8, 11-18): A Contextual Approach of Its Variants', *RevQ*, 13 (Mémorial Jean Carmignac, 1988), 569-81; Shemaryahu Talmon, 'Observations on Variant Readings in the Isaiah Scroll (1QIsa[a])', in Shemaryahu Talmon, *The World of Qumran from Within: Collected Studies* (Jerusalem: Magnes; Leiden: Brill, 1989), pp. 117-30; David S. New, 'The Confusion of taw with waw-nun in Reading 1QIsa[a] 29:13', *RevQ*, 15 (1992), 609-10; J. Gerald Janzen, 'Isaiah 41:27: Reading הנה הנומא in 1QIsa[a] and הנה הנם in the Masoretic Text', *JBL*, 113 (1994), 597-607.

50 I. L. Seeligmann, 'Δεῖξαι αὐτῷ φῶς', *Tarbiz*, 27 (1958), 127-41. See also note 11[a] in *BHS*.

51 Eugene Ulrich, 'Isaiah, Book of,' in *EDSS*, I, 384-88 (387).

52 For the large Psalms scroll from Cave 11 (11QPs[a]) as compiled by the Prophet David, see col. XXVII, 11, which states that David authored a large number of psalms "through the spirit of prophecy which had been given him from the Most High." David is also described as a prophet in the New Testament (Acts 2:25-31) and by Josephus (*Ant.* 8 §§109-10).

53 Edward Cook terms this work 'A Commentary on Consoling Passages in Scripture' in *DSSNT*, p. 239.

54 See James E. Bowley, 'Prophets and Prophecy at Qumran,' in *DSSAFY*, II, pp. 354-78 (p. 355).

55 *DSSNT*, p. 57.

56 *DSSNT*, p. 57.

57 *DSSNT*, p. 58.

58 *DSSNT*, pp. 132-33.

59 *DSSNT*, p. 55

60 The implication is that 'involvement with such people was a dangerous attraction for some members of the community' (*DSSNT*, p. 132).

61 *DSSNT*, pp. 132-33.

62 *DSSNT*, p. 213. See also Moshe J. Bernstein, 'Pesher Isaiah', in *EDSS*, II, pp. 651-53 (652).

63 *DSSNT*, p. 138.

64 See Matt 3:3; Mark 1:2-3 (conflating material from Isa 40:3 with Exod 23:20 and Mal 3:1); Luke 3:4-6 (quoting Isa 4:3-5); and John 1:23.

65 *DSSNT*, p. 225.

Peter W. Flint

APPENDIX 1

ISAIAH SCROLLS FROM THE JUDAEAN DESERT

Details of the twenty-two Isaiah scrolls are summarized in the Table below. Column III ("Range of Contents") lists a manuscript's earliest and latest verses in terms of their Masoretic order. But here it must be emphasized that many scrolls are very fragmentary, and thus contain only part of the specified content. Column V ("Date or Period when Copied") indicates the approximate date of each manuscript on the basis of palaeographic analysis. Column VI ("Publication") details publication in the DJD series, unless otherwise indicated.

ISAIAH SCROLLS FROM THE JUDAEAN DESERT

I. By Siglum	II. By Number	III. Range of Contents	IV. Orthography	V. Date or Period when Copied	VI. Publication
1QIsa^a	—	1:1 to 66:24	full	150–125 BCE	1. Burrows, Trever & Brownlee (1950) 2. Cross, Freedman & Sanders (1972) 3. Qimron and Parry (1999)
1QIsa^b	1Q8	7:22 to 66:24	sparing	Herodian	1. DJD 1.66–68 + pl. xii 2. Sukenik (1955)
4QIsa^a	4Q55	1:1 to 33:17(?)	fuller than 𝔐	3rd quarter of 1st c. BCE	DJD 15.7–18 + pls. i–ii
4QIsa^b	2Q56	1:1 to 66:24	mixed	3rd quarter of 1st c. BCE	DJD 15.19–43 + pls. iii–vi
4QIsa^c	3Q57	9:3 to 66:24	fuller than 𝔐	middle 3rd of 1st c. CE	DJD 15.45–74 + pls. vii–xii
4QIsa^d	4Q58	45:20 to 58:7	sparing	mid-1st c. BCE	DJD 15.75–88 + pls. xii–xv
4QIsa^e	4Q59	2:1 to 59:16	fuller than 𝔐	late 1st c. BCE	DJD 15.89–97 + pls. xvi–xvii
4QIsa^f	4Q60	1:1 to 29:8?	sparing/mixed	1st half of 1st c. BCE	DJD 15.99–111 + pls. xviii–xx
4QIsa^g	4Q61	42:14 to 43:24	mixed?	2nd half of 1st c. BCE	DJD 15.113–15 + pl. xxi
4QIsa^h	4Q62	42:4–11	sparing	1st half of 1st c. BCE	DJD 15.117–19 + pl. xxi
4QIsa^i	4Q62a	56:7 to 57:8	mixed?	1st half of 1st c. BCE	DJD 15.121–22 + pl. xxi
4QIsa^j	4Q63	1:1–6	mixed/like 𝔐	3rd quarter of 1st c. BCE	DJD 15.123 + pl. xxii
4QIsa^k	4Q64	28:26 to 29:9	full	mid-1st c. BCE	DJD 15.125–27 + pl. xxii
4QIsa^l	4Q65	7:14 to 8:14	fairly full	mid-1st c. BCE	DJD 15.129–30 + pl. xxii
4QIsa^m	4Q66	60:20- to 61:6	full	1st half of 1st c. BCE	DJD 15.131–32 + pl. xxii
4QIsa^n	4Q67	58:13–14	sparing?	1st half of 1st c. BCE	DJD 15.133–34 + pl. xxiii
4QIsa^o	4Q68	14:28 to 16:8?	?	1st half of 1st c. BCE	DJD 15.135–37 + pl. xxiii
4QpapIsa^p	4Q69	5:28–30	?	early Herodian	DJD 15.139 + pl. xxiii
4QIsa^q	4Q69a	54:10–13	?	Hasmonaean	DJD 15.141 + pl. xxiii
4QIsa^r	4Q69b	30:23	?	Herodian	DJD 15.143 + pl. xxxvi
5QIsa	5Q3	39:3? to 40:19	?	Herodian	DJD 3.173 + pl. xxxvi
MurIsa	Mur 3	1:4–14	mixed/like 𝔐	ca. 70 CE	DJD 2.79–80 + pl. xxii

The Book of Isaiah in the Dead Sea Scrolls

APPENDIX 2

CONTENTS OF THE ISAIAH SCROLLS BY CHAPTER AND VERSE

For earlier listings of contents by chapter and verse, see Eugene Ulrich, 'An Index of the Passages in the Biblical Manuscripts From the Judean Desert (Part 2: Isaiah-Chronicles)', *DSD*, 2 (1995) 86-107 (pp. 88-92); Eugene Ulrich, 'Appendix I: Index of Passages in the Biblical Scrolls', in *The Dead Sea Scrolls After Fifty Years: A Comprehensive Assessment*, ed. by Peter W. Flint and James C. VanderKam, 2 vols (Leiden: Brill, 1998-99), II, 649-65, (pp. 656-58); and Peter W. Flint, 'Appendix: Index of Passages in the Biblical, Apocryphal, and "Pseudepigraphal" Scrolls', in *Judaism in Late Antiquity, Part Five: The Judaism of Qumran: A Systematic Reading of the Dead Sea Scrolls. Volume One: Way of Life*, ed. by Alan J. Avery-Peck, Jacob Neusner and Bruce D. Chilton, Handbuch der Orientalistik Judastik (Leiden: Brill, 2000), pp. 87-103 (pp. 93-95).

1:1 to 66:24	1QIsa^a	8:2-14	4QIsa^e
1:1-31	1QIsa^a	8:11-14	4QIsa^l
1:1-6	4QIsa^b	9:1-20	1QIsa^a
1:1-6	4QIsa^j	9:3-12	4QIsa^c
1:1-3	4QIsa^a	9:10-11	4QIsa^b
1:4-8, 11-14	MurIsa	9:17-20	4QIsa^e
1:10-16, 18-31	4QIsa^f	10:1-34	1QIsa^a
2:1-22	1QIsa^a	10:1-10	4QIsa^e
2:1-4	4QIsa^e	10:16-19	1QIsa^b
2:1-3	4QIsa^f	10:23-33	4QIsa^c
2:3-16	4QIsa^b	11:1-16	1QIsa^a
2:7-10	4QIsa^a	11:4-11, 14-16	4QIsa^c
3:1-26	1QIsa^a	11:7-9	4QIsa^b
3:14-22	4QIsa^b	11:11-15	4QIsa^a
4:1-6	1QIsa^a	11:14-15	4QIsa^e
4:5-6	4QIsa^a	12:1-6	1QIsa^a
5:1-30	1QIsa^a	12:1-6	4QIsa^e
5:1	4QIsa^a	12:1	4QIsa^c
5:13-14, 25	4QIsa^f	12:2	4QIsa^b
5:15-28	4QIsa^b	12:3-6	1QIsa^b
5:28-30	4QpapIsa^p	12:4-6	4QIsa^a
6:1-13	1QIsa^a	13:1-22	1QIsa^a
6:3-8, 10-13	4QIsa^f	13:1-16	4QIsa^a
6:4-8	4QIsa^a	13:1-8, 16-19	1QIsa^b
7:1-25	1QIsa^a	13:1-4	4QIsa^e
7:14-15	4QIsa^l	13:3-18	4QIsa^b
7:16-18, 23-25	4QIsa^f	14:1-32	1QIsa^a
7:17-20	4QIsa^e	14:1-13, 20-24	4QIsa^e
7:22-25	1QIsa^b	14:1-5, 13(?)	4QIsa^c
8:1-23	1QIsa^a	14:28-32	4QIsa^o
8:1, 4-11	4QIsa^f	15:1-9	1QIsa^a
8:1	1QIsa^b	15:1-2	4QIsa^o

Reference	Siglum	Reference	Siglum
15:3-9	1QIsa^b	28:6-14	4QIsa^c
16:1-14	1QIsa^a	28:6-9, 16-18(?), 22, 24(?)	4QIsa^f
16:1-2, 7-12	1QIsa^b	28:15-20	1QIsa^b
17:1-14	1QIsa^a	28:26-29	4QIsa^k
17:8-14	4QIsa^b	29:1-24	1QIsa^a
17:9-14	4QIsa^a	29:1-9	4QIsa^k
18:1-7	1QIsa^a	29:1-8	1QIsa^b
18:1, 5-7	4QIsa^b	29:8?	4QIsa^f
19:1-25	1QIsa^a	30:1-33	1QIsa^a
19:1-25	4QIsa^b	30:8-17	4QIsa^c
19:7-17, 20-25	1QIsa^b	30:10-14, 21-26	1QIsa^b
19:24-25	4QIsa^a	30:23	4QIsa^r
20:1-6	1QIsa^a	31:1-9	1QIsa^a
20:1-6	4QIsa^a	32:1-20	1QIsa^a
20:1-4	4QIsa^b	33:1-24	1QIsa^a
20:1	1QIsa^b	33:2-8, 16-23	4QIsa^c
20:4-6	4QIsa^f	33:16-17(?)	4QIsa^a
21:1-17	1QIsa^a	34:1-17	1QIsa^a
21:1-16	4QIsa^a	35:1-10	1QIsa^a
21:11-14	4QIsa^b	35:4-6	1QIsa^b
22:1-25	1QIsa^a	35:9-10	4QIsa^b
22:10-14, 23	4QIsa^c	36:1-22	1QIsa^a
22:11-18, 24-25	1QIsa^b	36:1-2	4QIsa^b
22:13-25	4QIsa^a	37:1-38	1QIsa^a
22:14-22, 25	4QIsa^f	37:8-12	1QIsa^b
22:24-25	4QIsa^b	37:29-32	4QIsa^b
23:1-18	1QIsa^a	38:1-22	1QIsa^a
23:1-12	4QIsa^a	38:12-22	1QIsa^b
23:1-4	1QIsa^b	39:1-8	1QIsa^a
23:8-18	4QIsa^c	39:1-8	1QIsa^b
24:1-23	1QIsa^a	39:1-8	4QIsa^b
24:1-15, 19-23	4QIsa^c	39:3? (or 41:25?)	5QIsa
24:1-3	4QIsa^f	40:1-31	1QIsa^a
24:2, 4	4QIsa^b	40:1-4, 22-26	4QIsa^b
24:18-23	1QIsa^b	40:2-3	1QIsa^b
25:1-12	1QIsa^a	40:16, 18-19	5QIsa
25:1-8	1QIsa^b	41:1-29	1QIsa^a
25:1-2, 8-12	4QIsa^c	41:3-23	1QIsa^b
26:1-21	1QIsa^a	41:8-11	4QIsa^b
26:1-9	4QIsa^c	41:25? (or 39:3?)	5QIsa
26:1-5, 7-19	4QIsa^b	42:1-25	1QIsa^a
26:1-5	1QIsa^b	42:2-7, 9-12	4QIsa^b
27:1-13	1QIsa^a	42:4-11	4QIsa^h
27:1, 5-6, 8-12	4QIsa^f	42:14-25	4QIsa^g
28:1-29	1QIsa^a	43:1-28	1QIsa^a

43:1-13, 23-27	1QIsa^b	53:11-12	4QIsa^b
43:1-4, 16-24	4QIsa^g	54:1-17	1QIsa^a
43:12-15	4QIsa^b	54:1-11	4QIsa^d
44:3-7, 23	4QIsa^c	54:1-6	1QIsa^b
44:1-28	1QIsa^a	54:3-5, 7-17	4QIsa^c
44:19-28	4QIsa^b	54:10-13	4QIsa^q
44:21-28	1QIsa^b	55:1-13	1QIsa^a
45:1-25	1QIsa^a	55:1-7	4QIsa^c
45:1-13	1QIsa^b	55:2-13	1QIsa^b
45:1-4, 6-8	4QIsa^c	56:1-12	1QIsa^a
45:20-25	4QIsa^b	56:1-12	1QIsa^b
45:20	4QIsa^d	56:7-8	4QIsa^i
46:1-13	1QIsa^a	57:1-21	1QIsa^a
46:1-3	4QIsa^b	57:1-4, 17-21	1QIsa^b
46:3-13	1QIsa^b	57:5-8	4QIsa^i
46:8-13	4QIsa^c	57:9-21	4QIsa^d
46:10-13	4QIsa^d	58:1-14	1QIsa^a
47:1-15	1QIsa^a	58:1-14	1QIsa^b
47:1-14	1QIsa^b	58:1-3, 5-7	4QIsa^d
47:1-6, 8-9	4QIsa^d	58:13-14	4QIsa^n
48:1-22	1QIsa^a	59:1-21	1QIsa^a
48:6-8	4QIsa^b	59:1-8, 20-21	1QIsa^b
48:8-22	4QIsa^d	59:15-16	4QIsa^e
48:10-15, 17-19	4QIsa^c	60:1-22	1QIsa^a
48:17-22	1QIsa^b	60:1-22	1QIsa^b
49:1-26	1QIsa^a	60:20-22	4QIsa^m
49:1-15	1QIsa^b	61:1-11	1QIsa^a
49:1-15	4QIsa^d	61:1-3	4QIsa^b
49:21-23	4QIsa^b	61:1-2	1QIsa^b
49:22	4QIsa^c	61:1, 3-6	4QIsa^m
50:1-11	1QIsa^a	62:1-12	1QIsa^a
50:7-11	1QIsa^b	62:2-12	1QIsa^b
51:1-23	1QIsa^a	63:1-19	1QIsa^a
51:1-10	1QIsa^b	63:1-19	1QIsa^b
51:1-2, 14-16	4QIsa^b	64:1-11	1QIsa^a
51:8-16	4QIsa^c	64:1, 6-8	1QIsa^b
52:1-15	1QIsa^a	64:5-11	4QIsa^b
52:2, 7	4QIsa^b	65:1-25	1QIsa^a
52:4-7	4QIsa^d	65:1	4QIsa^b
52:7-15	1QIsa^b	65:17-25	1QIsa^b
52:10-15	4QIsa^c	66:1-24	1QIsa^a
53:1-12	1QIsa^a	66:1-24	1QIsa^b
53:1-12	1QIsa^b	66:20-24	4QIsa^c
53:1-3, 6-8	4QIsa^c	66:24	4QIsa^b
53:8-12	4QIsa^d		

TEXTUAL INFLUENCE
OF THE QUMRAN SCROLLS
ON ENGLISH BIBLE VERSIONS[1]

Stephen C. Daley

I. INTRODUCTION

A. THE MOTIVATING QUESTION

SHORTLY AFTER 1948, when the discovery of biblical scrolls at Qumran quickly became global news, scholars began the slower and usually less sensational process of studying the scrolls in detail. Gradually, the text-critical implications of the scrolls, with their numerous small or large differences (variants) from the traditional Hebrew text, began to be appreciated. The process of examining the scrolls and evaluating the variants found in them has continued to the present and is not yet complete. From our vantage point at the turn of the millennium, we look back across five decades of scholarship on the scrolls, and, more pertinent to the present study, five decades of English Bible translations produced by translators with access to at least some data from the scrolls. Has the availability of numerous ancient Hebrew variants from the scrolls influenced the wording of the English Bible?

Stating the question in this manner involves a figure of speech, for ancient texts do not influence modern translations directly. Between the ancient texts and the modern translations stand the translators themselves. Instead of inquiring into the influence of the scrolls on the translations, we might turn the question and focus on the human agent. We may inquire as to how often a given translator or translation committee has decided to follow a variant reading from the scrolls. Where possible, the human perspective should be maintained, since it is less abstract and more realistic than its figurative counterpart, and in this study specific information on the textual views of the translators is incorporated where it is available.

In general, however, the proceedings of translation committees are not published, and individual translators do not always provide complete notes of the kind that would be of most help to the textual critic. The ancient texts may be examined freely by the researcher, and the modern translations are readily available, but it is often difficult to locate precise information about the discussions of committees or the thinking of specific translators. For this practical reason, we cast the question that motivates the present study in the abstract: How much textual influence have the Qumran scrolls exerted on the modern English versions of the Bible?[2]

B. THE SCOPE OF THE STUDY

1. THE SCROLLS

The study is limited to the systematic examination of the influence of sample portions of two scrolls. The first is the Great Isaiah Scroll, 1QIsaᵃ, and the portions examined, XI, 30 – XIII, 5 and XL, 28 – XLI, 28, correspond to Isaiah 14 and 49. The Isaiah scroll was chosen because it was among the first scrolls discovered, the first published, and the first to have an influence on an English translation.[3] Also, because of its excellent state of preservation, the Great Isaiah Scroll has maintained pride of place among the Qumran scrolls, perhaps typifying the scrolls in the thinking of the general public.[4]

Chapters 14 and 49 of Isaiah were selected after a preliminary survey of the 1QIsaᵃ readings adopted by the RSV, NAB, and NEB. In chapters 14 and 49, these versions display a pattern of significant scroll use combined with significant disagreement as to which scroll variants are to be preferred. In chapter 14 there are six scroll readings that are preferred by at least one of the versions surveyed but only one scroll reading that is adopted by all three. In chapter 49 there are five scroll readings that are preferred by at least one of the three versions but, again, only one that is adopted unanimously. Because of this pattern of significant use with significant disagreement, these chapters provide zones of turbulence where the text-critical praxis of all the English versions might be meaningfully sampled.

The second scroll to be examined is 4QSamᵃ, and the portion included in this study, columns I-IV, preserves parts of 1 Samuel 1-3.[5] These columns were chosen because of the relatively early publication of parts of them by Frank M. Cross and because of the textual difficulties present in the corresponding chapters of the Masoretic Text (𝔐).[6] Difficulties in 𝔐 provide translators with a motive for text-critical intervention, and 4QSamᵃ provides a number of readings that could be regarded as preferable. As with the sections of 1QIsaᵃ chosen for study, it was estimated that an analysis of the initial columns of 4QSamᵃ would yield results indicative of the text-critical position of the each of the English versions vis-à-vis the scroll.

2. THE ENGLISH VERSIONS

The English versions (EVs) examined are represented by their abbreviations in Figure 1, below, which provides a chronological overview and displays approximate lines of revision.[7]

The Revised Standard Version (RSV) was completed in 1952, just late enough to reflect some readings from 1QIsaᵃ but too early to reflect any from 4QSamᵃ. It therefore belongs partially to the pre-Qumran (pre-𝔔) era and partially to the post-Qumran (post-𝔔) era. To the left of the RSV are other pre-𝔔 translations. Beginning with the KJV, these versions form a control group that provides a basis for comparing text-critical praxis before and after the availability of the scrolls and allows the influence of the scrolls to be seen in greater relief.

To the right of the RSV in Figure 1 are the post-𝔔 translations which are the focus of this study. Among these, the translation that accompanies the scholarly commentary of Kyle McCarter on 1 Samuel is listed as [McC], the brackets serving as a reminder that it pertains to 1 Samuel but not Isaiah.[8] Because McC is based on a careful analysis of 4QSam[a], as well as other textual data, it supplies an additional point of comparison. As the pre-Ⓠ EVs exemplify the absence of scroll influence, so McC approximates maximum scroll influence.

Figure 1. The Chronology and Revision Lines of the English Versions

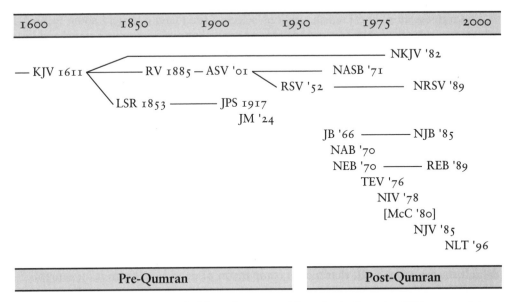

Translations that are preceded by a horizontal line, including the KJV, are revisions of earlier work, while all others are largely independent. Three post-Ⓠ translations, the RSV (in Isaiah), JB, and NEB, have themselves undergone revision in the NRSV, NJB, and REB, respectively.[9] In sections III.A.4, III.B.4, and IV.E the possibility that these revisions of post-Ⓠ translations may reflect a different assessment of the scroll data than do their predecessors is examined in detail.

C. THE TRANSLATOR'S PERSPECTIVE

The relationship between Bible translation and textual criticism may be typified as uneasy. Primarily, translators produce Bible versions that are intended for use in a community of faith, whose members regard the biblical text as ancient, unchanging, and inspired. What then is the place of text-critical scholarship in the task of the translator? Ellingworth has written of the attitudes that the Christian Church at large might hold toward textual scholarship. After describing hypothetical extremes consisting of a dogmatically negative attitude as opposed to a dogmatically positive one, he cautiously suggests some principles that would bolster a middle way.[10] More recently, Tov has argued that the tentative views of textual scholarship ought not be incorporated into biblical translations intended for the general public, in particular, he opposes the textual eclecticism of the great majority of the recent translations.[11]

As debate over the basic issues continues, the area of textual criticism is generally viewed as daunting and overly complex. Field translators, who often invest several years in formal theological and linguistic training before beginning translation projects, are rarely afforded the opportunity of developing expertise in textual criticism. Furthermore, the aids available to them, such as model translations, commentaries, the BHS textual apparatus, and the Hebrew Old Testament Text Project,[12] may express conflicting viewpoints, leaving the translator to decide the most technical of issues somewhat independently.

The translators of the English versions selected for this study held some technical advantages over the typical field translator portrayed above. First, most translated into their mother tongue and so did not need to concern themselves with the mastery of a new language and culture. Second, most were biblical scholars by profession and some were well known textual scholars. For example, Burrows worked on the *Revised Standard Version*, Barthélemy on the *Jerusalem Bible*, Driver on the *New English Bible*, Cross on the *New American Bible*, and Orlinsky on the *New Jewish Publication Society Version*.[13] For such reasons, several of the translations included here are considered model translations and are recommended as the basis for translations being produced in many parts of the world. In recommending model English translations to follow in issues of text, Barclay Newman[14] listed the RSV, JB, NEB, NAB, NIV, and GNB,[15] all of which, and several more, are included in this study.

Finally, all of the translators whose work is examined here began with 𝔐 and departed from it only when they judged that there was due cause.[16] The fact that the definition of due cause differs from one translator or committee to another does not prevent their translations from sharing a default source in common. It is the shared default source, namely 𝔐, that makes comparison of departures from it meaningful.

D. THE CHALLENGE

The general complexity of determining the *Vorlagen* of the English versions has at times been underestimated. For example, in the introduction to his translation of the Bible, James Moffatt wrote the following with regard to his work on the Old Testament:[17]

> Since nearly every page [of the translation] contains some emendation of the traditional text in the interest of accuracy and point, it has been impossible to annotate them. Scholars and students will recognize them readily, and I must ask the general reader to believe that none has been admitted except upon what the translator regards as sufficient evidence [...]. It would have swollen the book inordinately to have justified either the readings or, for the matter of that, the renderings one after another (xviii-xix).

Though the difficulty of including full, technical notes is appreciated, Moffatt's expectation that scholars and students would *readily* recognize his emendations is too optimistic.[18] The difficulty lies in the possible confusion of the effects of what Moffatt terms 'readings' and 'renderings'. There are cases in which a rendering, particularly a non-literal or dynamic one, may hide the association lines that would lead the analyst back to its reading, i.e., its textual base or *Vorlage*. It is at such points that notes from the translator are needed.[19] Without such notes, some level of uncertainty may accompany the analysis; what the translator held clearly in mind at the moment when a text-critical or translational decision was made may not be recoverable by the later analyst who has only the final rendering by which to judge.

The difficulties involved in determining the *Vorlagen* of the EVs must not be overstated. Some of these translations do include textual notes and some committees have published textual information about their work in separate volumes.[20] Even without notes, many, though not all, departures from 𝔐 can be identified with some degree of certainty, so that available data may lead to meaningful conclusions.[21] In this study, conclusions regarding the textual influence of the Qumran scrolls on the English versions are approached by means of a three-stage procedure, which is presented in the next section.

II. PROCEDURE

A. THEORETICAL FRAMEWORK

The most fully developed theoretical framework for studying a translation and its *Vorlage* is set forth by Emanuel Tov.[22] Since many of the issues that arise in determining the *Vorlage* of the Septuagint also arise in work on the *Vorlage* of an English version, the theoretical approach presented in Tov's work may provide the groundwork for the present study. In particular, the three stages of analysis that are defined as such and utilized in our treatment of the English versions are already implied in Tov's treatment of Septuagint data. Yet, because the goals of the present study differ from the goals of Septuagint scholarship and because a different set of textual relations must continually be described, different terminology is needed. Before proceeding with an overview of the three-stage procedure employed, a limited set of terms must be defined.

VARIANT (v). A (textual) variant or variant reading is any textual difference that exists between the text discussed and 𝔐. The term is used in a broad sense and covers differences of orthography and linguistic differences, as well as differences that alter meaning.

TRANSLATABLE VARIANT (tbv). A reading characterized by a variation that is distinguishable in translation is called a translatable variant. Normally, orthographic variation is not translatable, while pluses, minuses, substitutions, and some transpositions are translatable. Variants that are indistinguishable in translation are referred to as non-translatable variants (ntbv).

CORRESPONDENCE (c). A correspondence is a reading in an EV that is formally similar to a parallel reading in the source under consideration. For clarity, 'formal correspondence' is used in some contexts and with the same meaning. To say that an EV (formally) corresponds to 𝔔 in a specific reading means that it is similar to 𝔔 at that point. When an EV reading does not resemble the alternate source, it may be labeled as a non-correspondence (nc).

TEXTUAL CORRESPONDENCE (tc). When the translator of an EV decides to adopt a variant in 𝔔 as *Vorlage*, the rendering that results, directly reflecting the scroll, is referred to as a textual correspondence; it textually corresponds to the scroll. Only some (formal) correspondences qualify as textual correspondences, and any correspondence arising for reasons other than direct textual influence is marked as a non-textual correspondence (ntc).

Non-textual correspondence may be best clarified with the help of an example. In variant 1a of Isaiah 49 (see Table 6) 𝔔 שמעו [...] הקשיבו 'Hear [...]. Pay attention [...]' differs from 𝔐 שִׁמְעוּ [...] וְהַקְשִׁיבוּ 'Hear [...] and pay attention [...]' in lacking the conjunction –ı 'and'. Seven post-Ⓠ EVs also lack 'and' and so formally correspond to the scroll (JB, NAB, NEB, NIV, NJB, NRSV, and REB). Does this correspondence indicate direct influence from the scroll and, thus, textual correspondence? That the NEB committee, for example, omitted this conjunction in English on stylistic grounds is confirmed by archived notes,[23] and it is likely that the other EVs listed, none of which is particularly literal, reflect stylistic adjustments rather than text-critical decisions to follow Ⓠ. The renderings of all seven of these EVs are marked as non-textual correspondences.

B. OVERVIEW OF THE PROCEDURE

As preparation for the three stages of analysis employed in this study, a selected scroll portion is collated with 𝔐 and all its variants are identified.[24] In Figure 2 below, the abbreviation 'v' represents this preliminary list of variants. At stage one of the analysis, each Qumran variant (v) is evaluated and classified as either translatable (tbv) or non-translatable (ntbv), according to the nature of the variation involved. At stage two, the translatable variants identified at stage one are collated with the appropriate renderings in the EVs, and each of these renderings is classified as either corresponding (c) or not corresponding (ntc) to the scroll variant. The focus at this stage is on formal resemblance rather than textual affiliation. At stage three of the analysis the correspondences identified in stage two are evaluated and classified as either textual correspondences (tc) or non-textual correspondences (ntc).

Figure 2. *Overview of Three-Stage Procedure*

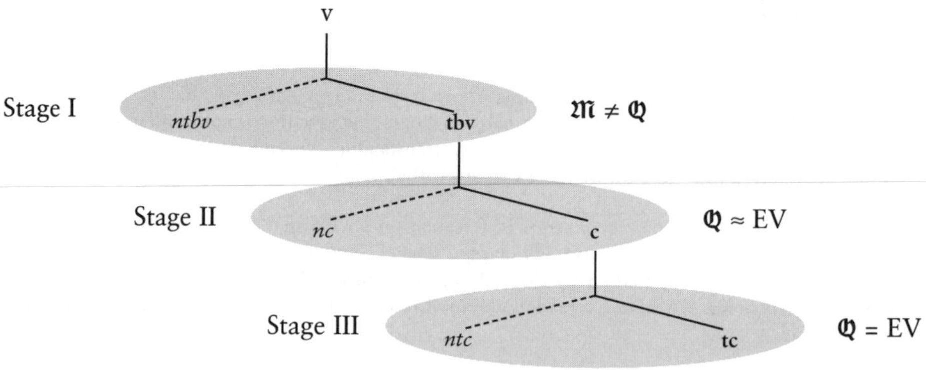

The equations on the right side of Figure 2 indicate the relationship that is defined at each stage. The study as a whole is mainly concerned with locating readings in which a scroll variant is adopted by one or more English versions, readings for which the description 𝔐 ≠ Ⓠ = EV is valid. As a means of illustrating the operation of this three-stage procedure, it will now be applied to data from Isaiah 14:2.

C. THE THREE STAGES OF ANALYSIS

When 1QIsaᵃ is compared with 𝔐, a relatively large number of variants is observed. Taking Isaiah 14:2 as a short sample, the following table presents the 1QIsaᵃ variants, and a note describes the nature of each.

Table 1

Complete List of Textual Variants for a Sample of 1QIsaᵃ (Isaiah 14:2)

Variant		𝔐	1QIsaᵃ	Nature
2	i	עַמִּים	עמים רבים	plus
	ii	אֶל־מְקוֹמָם	אל אדמתם ואל מקוממ	plus
	iii	עַל אַדְמַת יְהוָה	אל אדמת יהוה	preposition א/ע
	iv	שָׁבִים	שובן׳[ם ׳	orthography
	v	לְשִׁבְיֵהֶם	לשוביהם	orthography
	vi	וְרָדוּ	ורדים	tense/aspect
	vii	בְּנֹגְשֵׂיהֶם	בנוגשיהם	orthography

Three of the variants of Table 1 differ from 𝔐 in orthography alone, and in each of these *vav* is added word-medially as a *mater lectionis* representing *holem* (2 iv, v, vii). Such variants are expressions of the *scriptio plena* that is typical of 1QIsaᵃ and that contrasts with the largely *defectiva* spelling of 𝔐.[25] Variants that are not strictly orthographic in nature are also found in significant number, however, and in Table 1 there are two textual pluses (2 i, ii), a replacement of the preposition על with אל (2 iii),[26] and a change of verb tense/aspect (2 vi). As a prerequisite to stage one of the analysis, all variants are listed in this manner and briefly described.

1. STAGE ONE: TRANSLATABLE AND NON-TRANSLATABLE VARIANTS

The task of stage one is to determine which of all the variants present in the scroll are translatable and which are non-translatable. Augmenting the definition of 'translatable variant' given above in section II.A, a translatable variant is a textual variant that when rendered literally into English[27] has a different form and meaning than a similarly literal rendering of the parallel portion of 𝔐. By this criterion, only four of the variants listed in Table 1 qualify as translatable (2 i, ii, iii, and vi), and all others (2 iv, v, and vii) are non-translatable.[28] While non-translatable variants are set aside, translatable variants must be considered further; they may exert a textual influence on an EV.

As indicated by Table 2, variant 2a involves the addition of רבים 'many', while variant 2b involves the addition of ו- אל אדמתם 'to their land'. Regarding variant 2c, it is conceivable that a literal translation would have different equivalents for על 'on, over' and אל 'to, toward'. Similarly, the features by which 𝕼 differs from 𝔐 in variant 2d, (i.e., verb tense and/or aspect), may be readily indicated in English. All of these variants are clearly translatable.[29]

Table 2

Translatable Variants of 1QIsaᵃ (Isaiah 14:2)

	Variant	𝔐	1QIsaᵃ	Nature
2	a	עַמִּים	עמים רבים	plus
	b	אֶל־מְקוֹמָם	אל אדמתם ואל מקומם	plus
	c	עַל אַדְמַת יְהוָה	אל אדמת יהוה	preposition א/ע
	d	וְרָדוּ	ורדים	tense/aspect

2. STAGE TWO: CORRESPONDENCE AND NON-CORRESPONDENCE

The task of the second stage of analysis is to compare the translatable variants of the scroll with the appropriate rendering in each of the EVs. English renderings that resemble a scroll variant in specific details are termed correspondences while those that do not resemble the variant in those details are called non-correspondences.

When the rendering of an EV is examined, the question that is asked is whether or not it shares with the scroll the features of divergence associated with the variant under consideration. For example, when testing the EVs for correspondence to 1QIsaᵃ in variant 2a, the presence or absence of an adjective similar to 'many' is decisive. If an EV has 'many peoples', or similar wording, it is marked as a correspondence, if it has only 'peoples' it is marked as a non-correspondence. An EV rendering corresponding to variant 2b would include a phrase resembling 'to their land and (to their place)', and a correspondence to variant 2c would have 'to' or 'toward' rather than 'on' or 'upon'. Variant 2d differs from 𝔐 with regard to tense/aspect, and each EV would be examined for these features. Evaluating the EVs in this way yields the distribution of the correspondence (c) and non-correspondence (nc) indicated in Table 3:

Table 3

Correspondence and Non-correspondence of EVs to 1QIsaᵃ (Isaiah 14:2)

Variant	𝔐	1QIsaᵃ	R	J	N	N	N	T	N	N	N	N	R	N	N
			S	B	A	E	A	I	J	J	R	E	K	L
			V		B	B	S	V	V	B	V	S	B	J	T
						B						V	V		
2 a	עַמִּים	עמים רבים	nc	nc	nc	c	nc	c	nc	nc	nc	nc	nc	nc	nc
b	אֶל־מְקוֹמָם	אל אדמתם ואל מקומם	nc	nc	nc	nc	nc	nc	nc	nc	nc	nc	nc	nc	nc
c	עַל	אל	nc	nc	nc	nc	nc	nc	nc	nc	nc	nc	nc	nc	nc
d	וְרָדוּ	ורדים	nc	nc	c	nc	nc	nc	nc	nc	c	nc	nc	nc	nc

It may be observed that only two ℚ variants have correspondences among the EVs, 2a and 2d. In variant 2a, only the NEB and TEV correspond to 1QIsaᵃ in the addition of 'many'. The NEB reads, 'Many nations (shall escort Israel [...])', and the TEV reads, 'Many nations (will help the people of Israel [...])'. Others follow 𝔐 with 'people/s'

(RSV, NASB, NJV, NJB, and NKJV) or 'nations' (NIV, NRSV, REB, and NLT). The NAB rendering does not correspond to the scroll variant, nor does it resemble 𝔐. It involves an emendation[30] in which the translator read עִמָּם 'with them' in place of עַמִּים 'peoples'.[31]

Among the EVs that correspond to variant 2d, the NAB has the rendering '(making captives of its captors) and ruling over (its rulers)', which corresponds to 1QIsaᵃ by having a participle 'and ruling' where the scroll has ורדים. With the nominal rendering 'and masters', the NJV also corresponds to 1QIsaᵃ. The other EVs resemble 𝔐, though they tend to tighten its loose parallelism.

3. STAGE THREE: TEXTUAL AND NON-TEXTUAL CORRESPONDENCE

The essential task of stage three is the text-critical evaluation of the correspondences registered at stage two. Important sources of information for this stage are the textual notes that accompany some EVs and the front matter of several translations. While notes may offer specific information about particular readings, the text-critical and translational policies are often briefly discussed in a preface. Whatever the source of information, the more one understands about the usage, tendencies, and overall approach of a particular EV, the less one is likely to mistake translation adjustments for textual correspondence to a scroll variant.[32] Table 4 displays the textual correspondences (tcs) and non-textual correspondences (ntcs) of the sample under consideration.[33]

Table 4

Textual and Non-textual Correspondences of the EVs to 1QIsaᵃ (Isaiah 14:2)

Variant	𝔐	1QIsaᵃ	RSV	JB	NAB	NEB	NASB	TEV	NIV	NJB	NJV	NRSV	REB	NKJV	NLT
2 a	עַמִּים	עמים רבים				tcⁿ		tc							
b	אֶל־מְקוֹמָם	אל אדמתם ואל מקוממ													
c	עַל	אל													
d	וְרָדוּ	ורדים			ntc						ntc				

There are only four correspondences to be evaluated in v. 2. Regarding variant 2a, 𝔐 עַמִּים is translated literally as 'peoples' (RSV and NASB) or 'nations' (NRSV). It is also rendered fairly literally by the collective singular 'people' (NKJV). There is a tendency to qualify 'peoples' or 'nations' with the definite article (RSV, NASB, and NRSV), and the NLT adds qualification in its rendering 'the nations of the world'.[34] Unqualified, the renderings 'peoples' and 'nations' leave the reader to ask, 'How many?' or even 'Which ones?' Because it answers the first question, the Q reading עמים רבים is contextually smoother than 𝔐.[35] That the NEB has been directly influenced by Q in variant 2a is indicated by a footnote in the translation itself[36] and by Brockington, p. 180. The TEV, however, includes no note. It is estimated that a contextual adjustment on the part of the TEV translators would have added less information, and may have consisted of the inclusion of the definite article. Apart from the influence of the Qumran variant at this point, the presence of the word 'many' in the TEV rendering is difficult to explain. In variant 2d, a preference for parallelism is enough to explain the (formal) correspondence of the NJV and the NAB with the scroll, and for this reason both are marked as non-textual correspondences (ntc).

III. THE TEXTUAL INFLUENCE OF 1QISA^A

A. ISAIAH 14

1. OVERVIEW

The results of applying of the three-stage procedure described above to all of Isaiah 14 are indicated statistically in the following chart:

Figure 3. *Overview of Results for Isaiah 14*

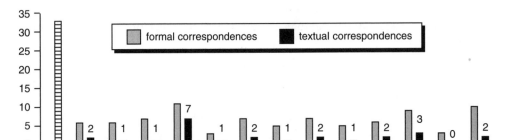

As Figure 3 indicates, the scroll contains thirty-three translatable variants ($\mathfrak{Q}$ tbvs) for this chapter of Isaiah. This number expresses the outcome of stage one of the analysis. As for the results of stage two, the unlabeled, left-hand bar of each pair represents the number of correspondences found in each EV. The exact values range from two (NKJV) to twelve (NEB). The results of stage three are indicated by the numbered, right-hand bars of each pair. The numbers show that the NEB, with seven, has the most textual correspondences to the scroll. The NKJV has none. The JB, NAB, NASB, NIV, and NJV have one textual correspondence each, while the RSV, TEV, NJB, NRSV, and NLT have two each. The REB has three textual correspondences to the scroll.

In terms of relative certainty, textual correspondences may be separated into three groups: (1) those that are confirmed by a note (labeled 'tc^n' in full data tables) and practically certain, (2) those that are estimated in the absence of notes as possible and likely (labeled 'tc'), and (3) those that are estimated in the absence of notes as possible but unlikely, or for which available the data is suggestive but inconclusive (˜tc). In the totals of Figure 3, textual correspondences that are certain (tc^n) or likely (tc) are included. Textual correspondences regarded as possible but unlikely (˘tc) are excluded from the counts.[37]

2. THE DATA

In Table 5 below, the results of each of the three analytical stages may be examined in detail. The translatable variants (tbvs) of stage one are listed in the third column alongside 𝔐 (BHS) in the second column. Where possible, the features of divergence, or points of variation, that define each translatable variant are indicated by shading.[38] The results of stage two may be inferred from notations appearing in the fourth through sixteenth columns. Empty cells indicate non-correspondence at stage two while non-empty cells represent stage-two correspondence. The results of stage three are indicated explicitly using the notations introduced above, i.e., tc (textual correspondence), ntc (non-textual correspondence) and the indicators for the three levels of certainty.

3. TEXTUAL CORRESPONDENCES

The textual correspondences (tcs) displayed in Table 5 bear the following brief comments.[39] Regarding variant 4a, factors such as the difficulty posed by 𝔐 מַרְהֵבָה (derived from דהב 'gold'?), the contextual appropriateness of 𝕼 מרהבה (from רהב 'assail'), and the slight graphic difference between the two (ר/ד) allow several EVs to adopt the scroll reading. All the pre-𝕼 EVs, except JM, follow 𝔐; all the post-𝕼 EVs, except NKJV, reflect 𝕼. While NKJV maintains the KJV rendering, JM anticipates the scroll reading by following the versions. With twelve textual correspondences among the EVs, 𝕼 appears as highly influential in this reading.

By way of contrast, there are several variants from the scroll that are adopted by only one EV. The REB alone renders 1QIsaᵃ in variant 11a, where 𝔐 has הֲמַת נְבָלֶיךָ 'the music of your harps' (JB and most EVs) but 𝕼 has המות נבלתך, 'the throng of your victims' (according to the REB). In this instance the REB translators revise the NEB in the direction of the scroll. In turn, the NEB is alone in following 1QIsaᵃ in four variants, 24a, 25a, 25b, and 31a, the last of which involves a difference of *mem* and *bet*, letters that are similar in the script of 1QIsaᵃ and in the Hasmonean script in general. Without directly mentioning graphic similarities, Kutscher suggested that an original בודד may have become מודד under the influence of the *mem* of the following word, בְּמוֹעֲדָיו.[40] In any case, both readings are contextually difficult and, using various interpretive strategies, the EVs generally follow 𝔐. With regard to the TEV and NLT, formal alignment is difficult at stage two, but given their dynamic translation technique, both may be regarded as reflecting 𝔐. The alignment of the NEB with 𝕼 would itself be uncertain if it were not confirmed by Brockington, who notes that the NEB translators did read 𝕼 אין מודד, pointing the verb to reflect the *Pual* conjugation.[41] A case involving even more uncertainty presents itself in variant 32a, where it appears possible but unlikely that the NKJV reflects the scroll.[42]

The only other variant of 1QIsaᵃ to be reflected in the EVs is 30a, where the scroll reads אהרוג 'I will slay' and 𝔐 has יַהֲרֹג 'he/it will slay'. Because both 𝕼 and 𝔐 have the first person form והמתי 'and I have killed' in the previous clause, the third person form יַהֲרֹג may be viewed as contextually dissonant. The scroll itself reads smoothly since both clauses have first person subjects. Among the pre-𝕼 EVs, JM anticipates the reading of

Table 5

Isaiah 14: Textual and Non-textual Correspondences of the EVs to 1QIsaᵃ

Variant	𝔐	1QIsaᵃ	RSV	JB	NAB	NEB	NASB	TEV	NIV	NJB	NJV	NRSV	REB	NKJV	NLT
2 a	עַמִּים	עמים רבים				tc[n]		tc							
2 b	אֶל־מְקוֹמָם	אל אדמתם / ואל מקוממם													
2 c	עַל	אל													
2 d	וְרָדוּ	ורדים			ntc						ntc				
3 a	עֻבַּד	עבדו													
4 a	מַדְהֵבָה	מרהבה	tc[n]	tc[n]	tc[n]	tc[n]	tc	tc	tc[n]	tc[n]	tc[n]	tc[n]	tc[n]		tc
8 a	לְבָנוֹן	הלבנון													
8 b	לֹא־יַעֲלֶה	ולוא יעלה													
9 a	עוֹרֵר	עור[ר]ה				ntc		ntc							
9 b	הֵקִים	הקימה				ntc						ntc			
11 a	הֱמַת נְבָלֶיךָ	המות נבלתך											tc[n]		
12 a	מִשָּׁמַיִם	מהשמים		ntc	ntc					ntc					
12 b	גּוֹיִם	גוי													
16 a	מַרְגִּיז הָאָרֶץ	המרניז הארץ													ntc
16 b	מַרְעִישׁ מַמְלָכוֹת	המרעיש ממלכות מרעיש ממלכות													ntc
17 a	וַעֲרָיו הָרָס	עריו הר[ס]			ntc			ntc					ntc		ntc
18 a	כֻּלָּם שָׁכְבוּ בְכָבוֹד	שכבו בכבוד	~ntc	~ntc	ntc[n]		~ntc	ntc	ntc			~ntc			ntc
19 a	יוֹרְדֵי	יורדו				ntc		ntc					ntc		ntc
20 a	לֹא־תֵחַד אִתָּם	לוא תחת אותם													
20 b	לֹא־יִקָּרֵא	[ל]וא יקראו	ntc								ntc				
22 a	וּשְׁאָר וָנִין	ושארית נין	ntc	ntc	ntc	ntc	ntc	ntc	ntc	ntc	ntc	ntc	ntc		
23 a	וְשִׂמְתִּיהָ	ושמתי											ntc		ntc
23 b	וְאַגְמֵי־מָיִם	אגמי מים		ntc		ntc			ntc	ntc			ntc		ntc
23 c	וְטֵאטֵאתִיהָ	וטאטאתי								ntc					
24 a	כֵּן הָיָתָה	כן תהיה	ntc	ntc	ntc	tc[n]		ntc	ntc	ntc	ntc	ntc	ntc	ntc	ntc
25 a	וְסָר מֵעֲלֵיהֶם	וסר מעליכמה				tc[n]									
25 b	שִׁכְמוֹ	שכמכה				tc[n]									
27 a	וְיָדוֹ	וידיו													
30 a	יָהֲרֹג	אהרוג	tc[n]			tc[n]				tc[n]		tc[n]	tc[n]		tc
31 a	בּוֹדֵד	מודד				tc[n]									
31 b	בְּמוֹעָדָיו	במודעיו													
32 a	יַעֲנֶה	יענו												~tc	
32 b	מַלְאֲכֵי־גוֹי	מלכי גוי													

Stage I	Translatable Variants	Total = 33													
Stage II	Formal Correspondences	Totals =	6	6	7	12	3	7	5	7	5	6	9	2	10
Stage III	Textual Correspondences	Totals =	2	1	1	7	1	2	1	2	1	2	3	1	2

the scroll, either by following the Latin Vulgate ($\mathcal{V}$) or by contextual adjustment in keeping with the idea that if the Lord should send a famine, and people die as a direct result, then the Lord (speaking in the first person) is the controlling agent. The divine passives that appear in the ASV and RV may be explained as euphemisms. Regarding the EVs marked in Table 5 as having adopted the scroll reading, five of the six include textual notes indicating that 1QIsa^a has indeed been followed. The NLT has no note, but it is possible and seems likely that its formal correspondence to the scroll is also the result of direct textual influence.

4. REVISIONS OF POST-QUMRAN TRANSLATIONS

A diachronic perspective of the influence of the 1QIsa^a on chapter 14 of the EVs is gained through a comparison of EVs completed early in the post-$\mathcal{Q}$ period with revisions of the same EVs that date from later in the post-$\mathcal{Q}$ period. Available for such a comparison are three pairs of translations, RSV/NRSV, JB/NJB, and NEB/REB, in which the second member of each pair is a revision of the first.

Regarding the use of 1QIsa^a in chapter 14, the RSV and NRSV are identical. Both adopt scroll readings in variant 4a and 30a and both include textual notes at those points. Both have non-textual correspondences to the scroll with regard to variants 18a, 20b, 22a, and 24a. In short, both have six (formal) correspondences and two textual correspondences to the scroll.

When the JB and its revision the NJB are compared, the only reading in which they are found to agree in accepting a scroll reading is variant 4a, where both have textual notes. The only other textual correspondence is that of the NJB to variant 30a. The JB does not follow the scroll in this variant, so in this detail the NJB moves closer to the scroll. While the JB has six (formal) correspondences and only one textual correspondence, the NJB has seven correspondences and two textual correspondences.

The NEB is revised in the REB. The NEB contains seven textual correspondences to 1QIsa^a in chapter 14, but the REB reduces this number to three textual correspondences, reversing decisions by the NEB committee and no longer following the scroll in variants 2a, 24a, 25a, 25b, and 31a. In the opposite direction, the REB committee accepted variant 11a into the text (cf. section III.A.3) though the NEB had it only in a footnote. The three textual correspondences of the REB to the scroll in this chapter thus involve variants 4a, 11a, and 30a.

While the REB committee was more conservative than that of the NEB with regard to the acceptance of readings from 1QIsa^a, the NJB committee adopted one more reading from the scroll than the JB, and the NRSV reflects the same evaluation of 1QIsa^a as the RSV. Based on this data, no general trend either toward or away from an acceptance of readings from the Isaiah scroll may be observed.

B. ISAIAH 49

1. OVERVIEW

Figure 4 offers a statistical overview of the results obtained when the three stages of analysis are applied to 1QIsa^a and the EVs in Isaiah 49.

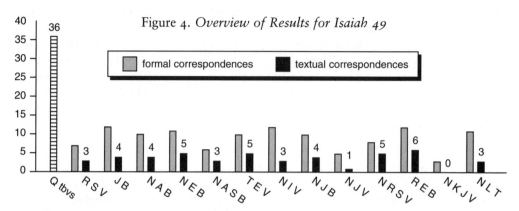

Figure 4. *Overview of Results for Isaiah 49*

Stage one of the analysis reveals thirty-six translatable variants in the scroll (𝕼 tbvs) for this chapter, three more than for chapter 14. The unlabeled, left-hand bar of each pair represents the number of correspondences found in each EV, ranging from four (NKJV) to fifteen (JB, NIV, and REB), and represents the results of stage two. The results of stage three are indicated by the numbered, right-hand bars of each pair. These numbers show that the REB, with six, has the most textual correspondences to the scroll, while the NKJV, as in chapter 14, has none. Other EVs have five (NEB, TEV, and NRSV), four (JB, NAB, and NJB), or three (RSV, NASB, NIV, and NLT). The NJV has only one textual correspondence to the scroll.

2. THE DATA

In Table 6 the stage-three correspondences of the EVs to the scroll, textual and otherwise, are indicated. As in Table 5, all stages of the analysis may be deduced from what appears. The translatable variants (tbvs) of stage one are listed in column three, the features of divergence being marked by shading, and the correspondences (cs) of stage two appear as non-blank cells in columns four through sixteen, where blank cells are vestiges of non-correspondence (nc). Finally, the outcome of stage-three analysis is explicitly indicated as textual correspondence (tc) or non-textual correspondence (ntc), with relative certainty also shown.

3. TEXTUAL CORRESPONDENCES

There are nine variants in 1QIsa[a] that have textual correspondences among the EVs in Isaiah 49. Variant 5b involves 𝔐 *ketib* לא / *qere* לו and a 1QIsa[a] reading identical to the *qere*. With the exception of the KJV, all of the pre- and post-𝕼 EVs prefer לו 'to him'. Since the form לו is shared by the scroll and the 𝔐 *qere*, a situation emerges in which nearly all of the EVs correspond to 𝕼 against the 𝔐 *ketib*. Since the outcome of following the 𝔐 *qere* or 𝕼 would be the same, the isolation of scroll influence is something of a methodological fine point. By means of a textual note, the NJB indicates its reliance on the scroll and is the only EV for which influence from 𝕼 can be confirmed. With nothing to indicate the contrary, the remaining formal correspondences are regarded as reflecting the 𝔐 *qere* and on that basis marked as non-textual correspondences (ntcs) vis-à-vis 𝕼. Other variants having but a single textual

Table 6

Isaiah 49: Textual and Non-textual Correspondences of the EVs to 1QIsaᵃ

Version header (letters read top-to-bottom per column):

```
        R  J  N  N  T  N  N  N  N  R  N  N
        S  B  A  E  A  E  I  J  J  R  E  L
        V  B  B  S  V  V  B  V  S  B  J  T
              B     B              V     V
```

Variant		𝔐	1QIsaᵃ	RSV	JBB	NABB	NESB	TAVB	NEVB	NIB	NJV	NJSV	RRB	NEJV	NLT
1	a	שִׁמְעוּ [...] הַקְשִׁיבוּ שִׁמְעוּ וְהַקְשִׁיבוּ	שמעו [...] הקשיבו שמעו והקשיבו	ntc	ntc	ntc			ntc	ntc		ntc	ntc		
4	a	וַאֲנִי	אני					ntc			ntc				ntc
	b	וְהֶבֶל	ולהבל			ntc			ntc	ntc		ntc	ntc	ntc	
5	a	יֹצְרִי	יוצרך												
	b	לוֹ ק / לֹא	לו	ntc	ntc	ntc	ntc	ntc	ntc	tc[n]	ntc	ntc	ntc	ntc	
	c	עֻזִּי	עזרי												
6	a	יִשְׂרָאֵל [...] יַעֲקֹב יִשְׂרָאֵל	יעקב [...] ישראל												
	b	קְצֵה	קצוי	ntc	ntc	ntc			ntc	ntc		ntc	ntc		
7	a	∅	אדוני												
	b	גֹּאֵל	גואלכה												
	c	לִבְזֹה	לבזוי	ntc	tc[n]	tc[n]		tc	tc	tc	tc[n]	tc	tc	tc	tc
	d	יִרְאוּ	ראו												
	e	שָׂרִים	ושרים	ntc	ntc			ntc							
	f	וְיִשְׁתַּחֲוּוּ	יהשתחוו												
	g	וַיִּבְחָרֶךָ	יבחרכה												
8	a	עֲנִיתִיךָ	אענכה		ntc			ntc	ntc						ntc
	b	עֲזַרְתִּיךָ	אעזרכה		ntc			ntc	ntc						ntc
9	a	לַאֲשֶׁר	ולאשר			ntc		ntc	ntc			ntc			
	b	עַל־דְּרָכִים	על כול הרים		tc								tc		
	c	עַל־דְּרָכִים	על כול הרים					tc							
12	a	סִינִים	סונים	ntc	tc[n]	tc[n]		tc[n]	tc[n]		tc[n]		tc[n]		tc[n]
13	a	וּפִצְחוּ ק / ופצחו	פצחו	ntc	ntc	ntc	ntc		ntc	ntc	ntc	ntc	ntc		ntc
	b	נִחַם	מנחם	ntc	ntc			ntc							
14	a	וַאדֹנָי	ואלהי ואדוני				tc[n]								
17	a	בָּנָיִךְ	בוניך	tc	tc[n]	tc[n]	tc		tc		tc[n]		tc	tc	
	b	מְהָרְסַיִךְ	מהורסיך	tc			tc						tc	tc	
21	a	גֹּלָה	וגולה												
	b	וְאֵלֶּה	אלה	ntc	ntc	ntc			ntc	ntc			ntc		ntc
22	a	∅	כיא												
	b	אֲדֹנָי יְהוִה	יהוה												
	c	עַמִּים	העמים	ntc	ntc	ntc	ntc	ntc	ntc	ntc		ntc	ntc	ntc	ntc
24	a	הֲיֻקַּח	היקחו												
	b	וְאִם	אם								ntc				ntc
	c	צַדִּיק	עריץ	tc[n]	tc[n]	tc[n]	tc[n]	tc	tc	tc[n]	tc		tc[n]	tc[n]	tc[n]
25	a	שְׁבִי [...] מַלְקוֹחַ וּמַלְקוֹחַ	שבי [...] ומלקוח												
	b	יְרִיבֵךְ	ריבך	ntc	ntc	ntc	ntc		ntc	ntc	ntc	ntc	ntc		ntc

Stage I	Translatable Variants	Total = 36													
Stage II	Formal Correspondences	Totals =	9	15	13	14	7	13	15	12	6	10	15	4	14
Stage III	Textual Correspondences	Totals =	4	4	4	5	3	5	3	4	1	5	6	0	3

correspondence among the EVs are variant 9c, where it is theoretically possible that the TEV follows 𝕼, and 14a, where textual correspondence to 𝕼 is supported by a note in the NEB.

In variant 7c 𝕼 נפש לבזוי 'to one despised of soul' differs from 𝔐 נפש לבזה 'to him whom man despiseth' (KJV) and is adopted by up to ten post-𝕼 EVs. Before the discovery of the scrolls, there was certainly a recognition of the difficulty of 𝔐 נפש לבזה, as well as a tendency to correct in the direction of נפש לבזוי. The latter was the emendation recommended by BH in its note 'l לִבְזוּי' (p. 616, note 7a) and previously by Duhm.[43] The RSV seems to reflect this emendation rather than the scroll itself and, with some reservation, is marked as a non-textual correspondence (~ntc).[44] Influence from 𝕼 is confirmed by notes in three EVs (JB, NAB, and NJB) and estimated for seven more (NASB, TEV, NIV, NJV, NRSV, REB, and NLT). Besides 7c, other variants with fairly broad acceptance among the EVs are variants 12a, 17a, and 24c. Variant 17b (where 𝔐 is pointed as a *Piel* participle 'your destroyers' while 𝕼 has comparative *mem* 'than your destroyers') is best considered along with variant 17a, though it is not adopted as often.[45]

The two EVs that formally correspond to 𝕼 in variant 9b are JB 'on every roadway' and REB 'along every path', and in both of these EVs 'every' provides a formal equivalent to the textual plus כול 'every' of the scroll. The text of the Septuagint (𝕲) ἐν πάσαις ταῖς ὁδοῖς 'in all the ways' also includes a formal equivalent to the plus of the scroll (כול // πάσαις). There is no note in either the JB or REB to indicate that a non-𝔐 *Vorlage* has, in fact, been adopted, and the addition of 'every' to the first member of the bicolon may be seen as stylistically attractive, since כ(ו)ל is supported by the parallel member וּבְכָל־שְׁפָיִם מַרְעִיתָם 'and their pastures [shall be] in all high places' (KJV). On balance, however, it must be noted that the addition of 'every' is not common among the EVs, nor does its inclusion serve English style. It seems preferable, therefore, to posit textual influence, so that both the JB and the REB reflect textual correspondences (tcs) to the scroll at this point.

4. REVISIONS OF POST-QUMRAN TRANSLATIONS

With regard to revisions of EVs that were completed early in the post-𝕼 period, the same translation / revision pairs are examined here as were examined above: RSV/NRSV, JB/NJB, NEB/REB (cf. section III.A.4).

Regarding the first of these pairs, the NRSV maintains the three scroll readings found in the RSV (17a, 17b, and 24c) but accepts two more (7c and 12a). Of interest here is that the renderings of the NRSV are the same as those of the RSV in both 7c and 12a. What has changed, however, is the textual base that supports these renderings. The RSV has no textual note accompanying variant 7c whereas the NRSV is clearly based on the scroll. Similarly, variant 12a was apparently not recognized by the RSV translators, for they gave its English equivalent on the basis of an emendation. Again, the NRSV maintains the same rendering, but bases it on the scroll.

Though both JB and NJB have four textual correspondences each in this chapter, there are some differences to be noted. As discussed previously, variant 5b involves a *ketib-qere* pair in 𝔐 and a scroll reading that agrees with the *qere*. The change introduced by the NJB is that, according to the accompanying note, the scroll is explicitly followed. There is no actual change of reading, only an apparent change of textual perspective and citation. With regard to variant 9b, however, a change of reading is clear, for where JB has 'on every roadway' ('every' = כול) NJB reads 'along the roadway' and no longer aligns with the scroll.

The third post-𝔔 translation/revision pair is NEB/REB. Relative to the NEB, the REB aligns with the scroll in two additional readings while removing an alignment in another location. It has additional textual correspondences at variants 7c and 9b, and returns to 𝔐 at variant 14a, where the NEB, alone among the EVs, reads 'my God' instead of 'my Lord' on the basis of a scribal correction in the scroll.

By comparing earlier post-𝔔 EVs with their later revisions, we gain a diachronic perspective that allows us to observe that textual data from 1QIsaᵃ was re-evaluated, at least in some details, by each of the committees responsible for the RSV, NJB, and REB. Most striking is that this re-evaluation may lead to further acknowledgment of scroll influence in cases where no change of rendering takes place, as in the NRSV at 7c and 12a and in the NJB at 5b. Other differences in scroll use suggest only minor adjustments and imply no general trend in the evaluation of variants from 1QIsaᵃ (cf. III.A.4 where a similar conclusion was reached regarding data from Isaiah 14).

C. ISAIAH 14 AND 49 RESULTS COMBINED

When the results of the analysis of chapters 14 and 49 are combined, we find that the NEB, with a total of twelve tcs, registers the highest number of textual correspondences to 1QIsaᵃ. Its revision, the REB, has three fewer. At the opposite extreme are the NKJV, which in chapters 14 and 49 of Isaiah has no textual correspondences to the scroll, and the NJV which has only two.[46] Indicated by the numbered, right-hand columns of Figure 5 are the total number of textual correspondences located in Isaiah 14 and 49 of the EVs (arranged by decreasing number of total tcs).

Figure 5. *Isaiah 14 and 49: Textual Correspondences of the EVs to 1QIsaᵃ*

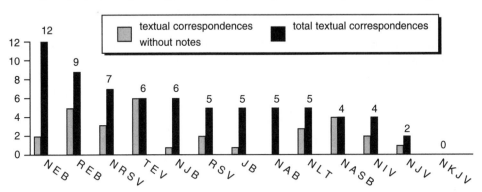

The left-hand columns of each pair give the number of textual correspondences that, in the absence of textual notes, have been estimated for each EV by means of the three-stage procedure for internal analysis. By means of the same procedure, the scroll readings that are indicated in notes have been confirmed.

The number of tcs estimated in the absence of notes is significant for several reasons. First, it provides an indication of the margin of error in the overall counts. The fewer the estimated readings, the more certain the overall count. For example, the NEB has twelve tcs overall and only two of the twelve are estimated. All others are confirmed externally by notes. By contrast, the TEV has six tcs overall and all six of these have been estimated in the absence of notes. The margin of possible error in the TEV data is larger than in the NEB data.

The number of estimated readings is also an indicator of the amount of difference that exists between the results of internal analysis and the results of a strict count of textual notes that acknowledge Qumran influence. If both the internal analysis and the notes are precise, they should both indicate the same textual correspondences. This is indeed the case for the NAB, whose five tcs are all indicated by notes and these five and no others are identified by the procedure of internal analysis. With regard to the NKJV, neither external evidence (notes) nor internal analysis identifies any viable tcs, so that the two agree at zero. With regard to the other EVs, some questions remain. From a certain perspective, the tcs that are identified by internal analysis but not confirmed by a note constitute an unresolved tension, an experimental residue requiring further study.

IV. THE TEXTUAL INFLUENCE OF 4QSAM[A]

A. BACKGROUND

The difference of physical appearance between 1QIsa[a] and 4QSam[a], appreciated at a glance, is analogous to the difference of textual nature between them. In working with the *complete* Isaiah Scroll there is seldom a material gap in the text, and very often its variants are letter-sized, involving a *vav*, a *yod*, an article, a pronoun, sometimes a word or two. By contrast, the Samuel scroll is preserved as an association of fragments, whether large or small. In a relatively well preserved section, half of the text, or more, is likely to be physically absent; at the same time, many of its variants are textually significant.

A ratio that answers the question 'How many translatable variants per verse?' can be used to emphasize the contrasting natures of the two scrolls. In the sections of 1QIsa[a] that were examined, Isaiah 14 and 49, there are 69 translatable variants in 55 verses, according to 𝔐, for a ratio of 1.25 translatable variants per verse. By contrast, in the first four columns of the Samuel scroll there are 63 translatable variants and about 44 verses, or 1.4 translatable variants per verse. This figure, however, is very conservative since it counts all but five poorly attested verses as if fully preserved but only counts extant variants.[47] A more accurate representation can be drawn from a well preserved partial column, the top of column III.[48] This section represents parts of 10 verses and contains 25 translatable variants, or 2.5 translatable variants per verse, a ratio twice as high as for the Isaiah data. These statistics help to illustrate the contrast between the two scrolls by indicating that one meets a translatable variant around twice as often in the Samuel scroll as in the Isaiah scroll.

While applying the basic procedure to 1 Samuel 1:11–3:4 (4QSam[a] cols I–IV),[49] one is confronted with the challenge of differentiating influence from the scroll from influence from the versions. Before the discovery of 4QSam[a], the English versions adopted a significant number of readings from the ancient versions, the Syriac Peshitta (𝔖), the Aramaic Targums (𝔗), 𝔙 and, in particular, 𝔊. This use of the ancient versions has continued into the post-𝔔 period. In some of the post-𝔔 EVs there is already a layer of non-𝔐 readings from the ancient versions, and the influence of the scroll is introduced as an additional layer. These two layers are not always easily distinguishable. The fact that the text of 4QSam[a] often resembles that of 𝔊, for example, blurs the distinctions considerably, and sometimes scroll influence and versional influence coalesce.

In order to differentiate, as far as possible, a committee's use of the scroll from its reliance on the ancient versions, greater attention to the latter is necessary when treating the 4QSam[a] data than it was when treating 1QIsa[a]. Thus, to illustrate the formal and textual relationships that exist between the EVs, the ancient versions, and the scroll, a kind of charting that was not necessary in the discussion of the 1QIsa[a] data is employed. Examples of the charting are given below in section D.

B. OVERVIEW

The figure below gives the results of the three-stage analysis of the 4QSam[a] fragments and the EVs in 1 Samuel 1:11-3:4. The EVs are presented in chronological order.[50]

Figure 6. *Overview of Results for 1 Samuel 1:11-3:4*

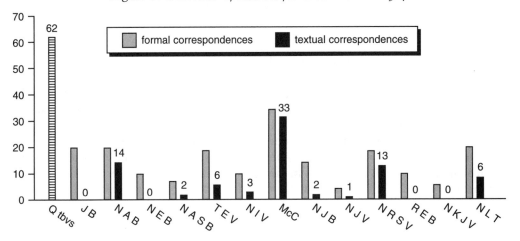

The sixty-two translatable variants (ℚ tbvs) identified in the scroll represent the outcome of stage one of the analysis. An impression of the number of correspondences identified at stage two is given in the left-hand column for each EV, while the number of textual correspondences, determined at stage three, is given in the right-hand columns. Of the sixty-two readings (tbvs) that might be adopted from the scroll, McC, the translation prepared for McCarter's critical commentary, renders just over half (thirty-three tcs). McC is included in the comparison as an indicator of maximum scroll influence. The NAB accepts just under a quarter (fourteen tcs). The NRSV, with thirteen, has only one less textual correspondence than the NAB. Other EVs have nine (NLT), six (TEV), three (NIV), two (NASB and NJB), one (NJV) or zero (JB, NEB, REB, and NKJV).

Included in the counts of Figure 6 are a number of textual correspondences that must be qualified as uncertain.[51] These are readings that correspond to the scroll formally, but for any of a number of reasons cannot be convincingly identified as either textual correspondences or non-textual correspondences. With additional information, these may prove to be places where the committees actually were influenced by scroll variants. While such difficult or doubtful textual correspondences were few in the Isaiah data, they are significantly numerous in the Samuel data and should not be ignored. Figure 7 shows which translations contain uncertain readings (˜tcs).

Figure 7. *Uncertain Textual Correspondences in 1 Samuel 1-3*

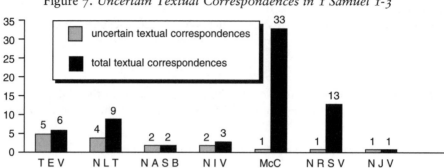

The presence of a single uncertain reading in McC and NRSV is not very significant, since the overall number of scroll readings in these EVs is high. The presence of an uncertain textual correspondence in the NJV, however, is more important. Did the NJV allow a Qumran reading into the text? Similarly, the NASB may have adopted a scroll variant in two readings, but both of these are questionable. Did the NASB translators consider 4QSam[a] at all? Significant questions remain regarding the TEV, NLT, and even the NIV in this regard, and while these questions stand, the higher numbers, shown in Figure 6, will be included in the general statistics and will serve as a reminder of the need for further investigation.

C. THE DATA

Represented in Table 7 below are the textual and non-textual correspondences of the English versions to the translatable variants extant in 4QSam[a] columns I-IV. Though the results that are most clearly displayed in Table 7 are those of stage three of the analysis, other stages may be deduced from what appears (see section III.A.2 and the explanation of Table 5). With regard to notation, the abbreviation 'tc$_{-\mathfrak{Q}}$' marks a post-$\mathfrak{Q}$ rendering that essentially agrees with the scroll against $\mathfrak{M}$ but actually has $\mathfrak{G}$ or one of the other ancient versions as *Vorlage*. The absence of scroll influence in such a reading is sometimes indicated by textual notes that list sources other than the scroll but at times must be deduced by means of circumstantial evidence. Readings with 'tc$_{-\mathfrak{Q}}$' are found only in the JB, NJB, NEB, REB, and TEV. Empty parentheses '( )' indicate that the $\mathfrak{Q}$ reading is given in margin but not in the text. Such an indication may co-occur with other notations, for example, the NAB is marked 'ntc ( )', meaning that a non-textual correspondence occurs in the text, while the $\mathfrak{Q}$ reading is given in a footnote.

Table 7

1 Samuel 1:11-3:4: Textual and Non-textual Correspondences of the EVs to 4QSam[a]

Table 7, continued...

Variant	𝔐	4QSamᵃ
[2:14a]		
2:16 a		
b		
c		
d		
e		
f		
2:17 a		
2:18 a		
2:20 a		
b		
c		
d		
e		
2:21 a		
b		
c		
d		
e		
2:22 a		
b		
c		
d		

Table 7, continued...

Variant	𝔐	4QSam^a	JB	NAB	NEB	NASB	TEV	NIV	NJB	NRSV	REB	NKJV	...	...	...
Stage I Translatable Variants Total = 62															
Stage II Formal Correspondences Totals =			21	21	11	7	19	10	35	15	4	19	10	6	21
Stage III Textual Correspondences Totals =			0	14	0	2	6	3	33	2	1	13	0	0	9

(Variants listed: 2:24 a; 2:25 a, b; 2:27 a; 2:28 a; 2:29 a, b, c; 2:30 a; 2:31 a; 2:32 a, b, c; 2:33 a, b; 2:36 a; 3:4 a)

D. SELECTED READINGS

While a general discussion of all variants with textual correspondences was presented for Isaiah 14 and 49, a more detailed discussion of only two variant readings from 4QSam^a is presented below. Variants 1:24c and 1:28b were chosen to help illustrate the interplay of different textual influences on the EVs and the method by which these influences may be at least partially isolated.

1. VARIANT 1:24C

Where 𝔐 has בְּפָרִים שְׁלֹשָׁה 'with three bulls' the scroll reads [בפר בן] בקר משלש '[with a bull ca]lf three years old'. The textual plus בקר [בן] '[ca]lf' is unique to the scroll, and none of the EVs reflect this longer reading, which McCarter refers to as expansive (pp. 56-7). Several EVs do, however, reflect the text of the scroll in משלש [בפר] '[with a] three-year-old [bull],' a reading that is reflected by 𝔊 and 𝔖.

From the KJV (1611) to JPS (1917), all the pre-Ⴕ EVs read 'three bulls', though the RV (1885) includes a note that mentions the variant. JM was the first of the EVs to include the reading of 𝔊 and 𝔖 in the text, while the RSV did the same later.

Among the post-Ⴕ EVs, all reflect the reading 'three-year-old bull' except two, NJV and NKJV. Both of these render 𝔐 in nearly all cases and do so here. The NJV acknowledges 𝔊 and Ⴕ in a note but follows 𝔐 in the text. The stage-two alignments are thus as follows:

Stage-two Detail: Variant 1:24c

		EVs	Ancient Versions	Hebrew Sources
1.	three bulls	KJV LSR RV ASV JPS NJV NKJV	𝕮𝖁	𝔐
2.	a three-year-old bull	JM RSV JB NAB NEB NASB TEV NIV McC NJB NRSV REB NLT	𝔊𝔖	4QSam^a (also adds 'calf')

A number of EVs adopt the reading transmitted by the scroll, but not on the basis of the scroll itself. In this reading, the JB, NEB, TEV, NJB, and REB all accept the variant on the authority of the versions, and though each of these EVs includes a note regarding this reading, none of them mentions the 4QSam^a. The EVs that do accept the variant and cite the scroll among the evidence are the NAB, NIV, McC, NRSV, and NLT.

With regard to the NASB, where no note appears with the reading 'a three-year-old bull', there is some uncertainty as to whether or not 4QSam^a was involved in this textual choice. Almost certainly, 𝔊 and perhaps 𝔖, were involved in the decision, and the scroll may have been considered, as well. In any case, there is no uncertainty regarding the fact that a non-𝔐 variant has been followed.

A significant facet of this and a number of other scroll readings is that where there are agreements between the scroll and the Septuagint, the reading may have, in essence, been available to scholars before the Qumran texts were discovered. By retroverting 𝔊, for example, the BHK editors were already able to recommend the reading בפר משלש 'with a three-year-old bull'.[52]

Stage-three Detail: Variant 1:24c

Pre-𝕼 EVs							Post-𝕼 EVs											
K	L	R	A	J	J	R	J	N	N	N	T	N	M	N	N	N	R	N	N
J	S	V	S	P	M	S	B	A	E	A	E	I	c	J	J	R	E	K	L
V	R		V	S		V	B	B	S	V	V	C	B	V	S	B	J	T
							B									V	V

𝔐𝕮𝓥 · · · · ·   𝔐𝕮𝓥   ·   ·

𝕲𝕾   n   · ·ⁿ   4QSamᵃ𝕲𝕾   xⁿ ·ⁿ xⁿ ~ xⁿ ·ⁿ ·ⁿ xⁿ ⁿ ·ⁿ xⁿ   ·ⁿ

2. VARIANT 1:28B

𝕼 has ותשת[ח]ו[ן] 'and she worshiped', making Hannah the subject, while 𝔐 has וַיִּשְׁתַּחוּ 'and he worshiped', with Elkanah as subject. In this variant the EVs are divided in following one of four readings from the ancient sources, while in variant 1:28a (see Table 7) the scroll aligns with 𝕲 and the other ancient versions align with 𝔐, leaving two attested options. For this reason variant 1:28a and 1:28b must be treated separately.

𝔐 and 𝕮 have the masculine singular form of the verb וַיִּשְׁתַּחוּ 'and he worshiped'. This form is reflected by the earliest of the EVs, and is found in all the pre-𝕼 translations up until James Moffatt's translation (JM), which here, as in variant 1:28a, follows the text of 𝕲. Among the post-𝕼 EVs, the JB and NRSV also reflect 𝕲, and thus, like JM, lack an equivalent to וַיִּשְׁתַּחוּ. The earliest EV in which appears the masculine plural form וַיִּשְׁתַּחֲווּ 'and they worshiped' is the RSV, the last EV of the pre-𝕼 period,[53] though several of the post-𝕼 EVs, specifically NEB, TEV, NJB, NJV, REB, NKJV, and NLT, also read the plural. The two EVs that employ the feminine singular 'and she worshiped' align with 4QSamᵃ in this detail, as well as with 𝕲 at 2:11a. The formal relationships between the witnesses and the EVs may be displayed as follows:

Stage-two Detail: Variant 1:28b

	EVs	Ancient Versions	Hebrew Sources
1. and he worshiped the LORD there	KJV LSR RV ASV JPS NASB NIV	𝕮	𝔐
2. (and she left him there) Ø	JM JB NRSV	𝕲	
3. and they worshiped the LORD there	RSV NEB TEV NJB NJV REB NKJV NLT	LXXᴸ 𝕾𝓥	
4. (and she left him there) and she worshiped the LORD	NAB McC	𝕲 2:11	4QSamᵃ

Regarding the EVs associated with (1), only the NASB and NIV follow 𝔐 literally in the post-𝕼 era. That more EVs do not follow 𝔐 is testimony, perhaps, to the contextual difficulty of the masculine singular of וַיִּשְׁתַּחוּ 'and he worshiped'. Conspicuous by its absence is the NKJV, which in this reading revises the KJV away from 𝔐, a rare occurrence that again confirms the perceived difficulty of 𝔐. With respect to (2), a textual note in JB offers a cross reference to 2:11a, where the JB itself has 'she left' against 'Elkanah went' of 𝔐. Though 𝔊 is not specifically mentioned it is followed at both places. The note in the NRSV is more complete, citing both 𝔊 and 𝔔. Again, it is 𝔊 that is specifically followed in variant 1:28b.

There are instructive notes in several of the EVs listed in (3). The notes of the NEB and REB, for example, cite 𝔖 in support of the plural, while the NJV gives a cross reference to (NJV) 2:11 where the name (Hannah) has been added. The note goes on to cite the Talmudic tractate *b.* Ber. 61a in support of the fact that Elkanah was present as well as Hannah, thus making the plural verb appropriate at this point in the text and leading to the addition of Hannah's name, in parentheses, at 2:11. These are contextual adjustments, rather than text-critical decisions, and the result is a rendering like the ones that are based on LXX[L] 𝔖 and/or 𝔳, though a direct line of textual influence cannot be drawn to any of these sources on the evidence of the NJV footnote. Finally, in (4), come the two EVs that follow the scroll specifically. Both have notes. That of the NAB is succinct and reads, 'cf. 4QSam[a], LXX 2:11'. The comments of McCarter are more detailed but likewise confirm that the reading of the scroll has been preferred. The textual associations determined at stage three are illustrated below.

Stage-three Detail: Variant 1:28b

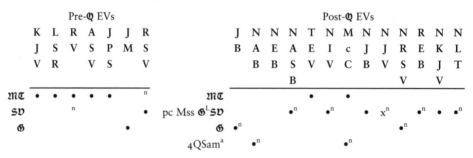

This variant is of particular interest with respect to the topic of revisions, which is covered more thoroughly below. It is important to note here, however, that NJV and NKJV, two EVs that normally follow 𝔐 quite closely, both have the plural, the latter in contrast to the KJV, itself. Also, the NJB revises JB, bringing the latter somewhat closer to 𝔐, though NJB, too, prefers the plural.

E. REVISIONS OF POST-QUMRAN TRANSLATIONS

Theoretically, an increase or decrease in the influence of 4QSam[a] on the EVs would be indicated in a comparison of translations completed early in the post-𝔔 period and revisions of the same translations carried out later in the post-𝔔 period. When a similar comparison was carried out on data from Isaiah 14 and 49 (cf. sections III.A.4 and B.4) three translation/revision pairs were available, RSV/NRSV, JB/NJB, and NEB/REB. However, there are only two such pairs available with regard to the data from 1 Samuel 1–3: JB/NJB and NEB/REB;[54] in order to gain a meaningful diachronic perspective on the influence of 4QSam[a] the comparison must be broadened to include the NRSV and the NAB, on one hand, and McC and the NAB, on the other.

Textual Influence of the Qumran Scrolls

Any account of the influence of 4QSam[a] on the English versions must begin with Frank M. Cross and his 1953 publication of the two partial columns of the scroll. By 1970, though, when Cross's translation of the books of Samuel was published as part of the NAB, more fragments had been identified and the reconstruction had progressed. In fact, the textual notes to the NAB show that scroll readings were adopted throughout the books of 1 Samuel and 2 Samuel and in significant number. In 1 Samuel 1:11-3:4, there are fourteen readings in which scroll variants have been adopted.

Though showing some affinity to the translation by Cross, McCarter's translation differs in kind from all the other translations treated here. Intended to accompany a critical commentary, it reflects McCarter's estimation of the original shape of the biblical text. He is free, for example, to leave a large gap of several lines in the rendering of 1 Samuel 2:10, where these lines in the scroll are unintelligible but indicate a lengthy plus. The Septuagint also has a long plus, and McCarter himself believes that the original text included a plus that is not reconstructable from available evidence. In McC, this ellipsis is marked with three points. While some EVs do use points to indicate an apparent ellipsis in the text, none meant for public use has gone so far as McCarter in this regard.[55] Thus, while the translations of both McCarter and Cross reflect a critical analysis of the scroll data, McCarter adopts thirty-three scroll variants in 1 Samuel 1:11-3:4, more than twice the number reflected in the NAB.

2. JB AND NJB

The 1966 publication of the Jerusalem Bible (JB) preceded that of the NAB by only a few years. It is conceivable, therefore, that the translation of the book of 1 Samuel might have adopted textual variants from the scroll, at least with regard to the fragments published by Cross in 1953. Available evidence seems to indicate the opposite, however, and points to the conclusion that no 4QSam[a] readings are adopted, as such, by the JB translator. Rather, the correspondences to 4QSam[a] in JB can be attributed to the influence of the versions, particularly the Septuagint. The fact that there is no mention of the scroll even in the most complete edition of the JB notes also supports this conclusion. As a direct revision of JB, the NJB is textually more conservative than its predecessor. In at least five readings, for example, it reverses an earlier decision to follow a non-𝕸 *Vorlage*.

That the scroll was consulted by the NJB revisers is evident from the fact that it is mentioned in a footnote to 2:20. Neither here nor elsewhere, however, does awareness of the scroll lead to any new readings being adopted from the scroll. In fact, all the non-𝕸 readings of the NJB[56] were already present in the JB and are simply maintained in the revision. In this sample, then, the NJB represents a moderate revision toward 𝕸.

3. NEB AND REB

Like the New American Bible (NAB), the New English Bible (NEB) was published in 1970. Its revision, the Revised English Bible (REB) was published in 1989. It will be recalled that the NEB adopted more 1QIsa[a] variants into its translation of chapters 14 and 49 of Isaiah than any of the other EVs. The REB ranked a close second. Because of this marked preference for scroll readings in Isaiah, one might expect readings from

4QSam^a to have made there way from Cross's preliminary publication into the text of the new translation. The evidence does not confirm any such expectation, however, and it appears that in no reading does the NEB reflect direct influence from 4QSam^a. Those renderings in which the NEB formally corresponds to the scroll may all be viewed as the result of influence from the versions. The textual notes to the NEB prepared by Brockington confirm this explanation, as Brockington mentions 1QIsa^a over seventy times in his notes on that book, while 4QSam^a is nowhere cited by him. Furthermore, the REB does not make any textual changes either toward or away from 4QSam^a and in the readings examined for this study is identical to its predecessor with regard to *Vorlage*.

4. NRSV COMPARED TO NAB

With regard to 4QSam^a, the RSV belongs to the pre-𝒬 era, while the 1989 NRSV is among the most important examples of EVs that make use of the scroll. The NRSV adopts at least twelve and perhaps thirteen readings from the scroll in 1 Samuel 1:11-3:4. Thus the NRSV very nearly equals the NAB in the number of readings adopted from the scroll. In fact, the two adopt the same scroll variant against 𝔐 in nine places, making their agreements, so defined, more numerous than their disagreements. A further two scroll variants adopted into the NAB are relegated to the notes of the NRSV.

V. CONCLUSIONS

By means of a three-stage procedure, the textual influence of the Qumran scrolls on the English versions may be analysed. Stage one of the procedure locates all translatable variants in the scroll, stage two identifies formal correspondences to these variants in the English versions, and stage three eliminates the correspondences that occur for reasons other than textual influence. The outcome of the analysis is an identification of textual correspondences, which are those readings in each EV that are likely to have arisen from the influence of the scroll.

Following this procedure in an examination of portions of 4QSam^a (1 Samuel 1:11-3:4) and 1QIsa^a (Isaiah 14 and 49) yielded a multifaceted view of the influence of selected portions of the Qumran scrolls on the English versions. At the same time, aspects of the text-critical praxis reflected in the EVs were illustrated. In Figure 8 the results from all scroll portions discussed are combined.[57]

In Figure 8, data relating to the EVs are ordered along a continuum so as to illustrate overall scroll usage.[58] At the extreme left of the continuum is McCarter's translation. While aiming at a reconstructed *Urtext*, McCarter has included over twice as many readings from 4QSam^a as any other EV and stands alone in this regard. At the opposite extreme is the NKJV, which accepts no 4QSam^a variants and only one variant from 1QIsa^a. Translations close to the NKJV's end of the continuum follow 𝔐 closely. Again, the discussions of specific non-𝔐 readings may be located via the data charts which are keyed to the sample readings. Between these extremes are positioned all the other post-𝒬 EVs.[59]

Of note is the erratic pattern of usage apparent for 4QSam^a as compared to the somewhat more consistent usage of 1QIsa^a. In this regard, the low values associated with 4QSam[a] are lower (NEB, REB, JB, and NKJV all have zero), while its high values are higher than those of 1QIsa[a]. Even if McC is not considered, both the NAB and NRSV adopt more readings from 4QSam[a] than the NEB adopts from 1QIsa[a], and the NEB adopts more 1QIsa[a] readings than any other EV.

Figure 8. *Scroll Use in 1 Sam 1:11-3:4 and Isaiah 14 & 49*

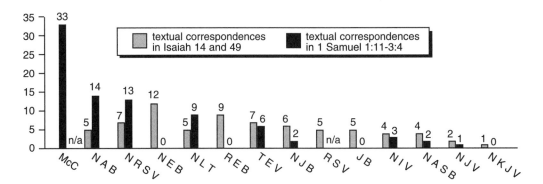

The non-use of 4QSam[a] that is indicated for several EVs runs contrary to expectation, particularly with respect to the NEB, REB, and JB. The NKJV, which renders 𝔐 wherever possible, has found no reason to adopt scroll readings into 1 Samuel 1:11-3:4. It may rely instead on contextual exegesis, which sometimes allows an English translation to read more smoothly than its base text. The topic of contextual exegesis as an alternative to the adoption of non-𝔐 readings in textually conservative EVs should be studied further. In contrast to the NKJV, the NEB, REB, and JB do adopt non-𝔐 readings fairly readily, and a reader who is familiar with the variants of 4QSam[a] may gain the impression that the scroll has in fact been followed at certain points in these EVs. This impression, however, is due to the textual affiliation of 4QSam[a] and 𝔊 and the fact that readings from 𝔊 have been adopted by these three translations. Only when the details of each variant are examined does it become clear that 4QSam[a] leaves no mark on these versions.

The primary motive for adoption of non-𝔐 readings by the EVs is difficulty in 𝔐 itself. If one were to characterize the environment in which non-𝔐 readings are favoured, the contextual difficulty of 𝔐 would feature prominently. Some of the readings where the influence of a scroll variant is seen in greatest relief involve elements of 𝔐 that were long recognized as contextually difficult. Variant 4a of Isaiah 14, for example, involves a nearly unintelligible word in 𝔐, with regard to which an interpretive tradition had developed. Though an alternative was available in the ancient versions, it was not followed until the Hebrew reading from the scroll emerged. Subsequently, nearly all the EVs adopted the reading of the scroll. Most examples are not as clear cut, but many have some contextual difficulty in 𝔐 as a starting point. This aspect of the text-critical praxis reflected by the EVs would indicate that a textually plausible and contextually appropriate reading is often preferred over the most difficult one, contrary to what some have regarded as among fundamentals of textual studies, namely, *lectio difficilior praeferenda*, 'the more difficult reading is to be preferred'. In practice, translators must translate meaning and must locate the same in their *Vorlage.*[60]

An additional aspect of the EVs and the text-critical praxis they reflect is portrayed in Figure 5 for Isaiah 14 and 49 and Figure 7 for 1 Samuel 1:11-3:4. The latter indicates that the place of 4QSam[a] in the TEV, NLT, NASB, and NIV must be clarified, since the analysis of the influence of the scroll on these translations remains uncertain in a significant number of readings. Featured in both of these figures is an indication of how many readings are estimated to reflect actual influence from the scrolls in the absence of explicit textual notes. Given the present situation in which there is no general agreement as to precisely which readings are preferable, text-critical decisions should be systematically documented by translators as the translation is produced. It cannot be claimed that those who need to know about them will readily recognize departures from 𝔐,[61] and the textual information provided in the preface of several translations is usually too general actually to guide the reader to details of the base text.

A final aspect of the text-critical praxis of the EVs emerges from the consideration of EVs completed early in the post-𝔔 era that have undergone revision in more recent years. Three such translation/revision pairs were considered with regard to 1QIsa[a], while the comparison was broadened with regard to 4QSam[a] (cf. sections III.A.4 and B.4 and IV.D). The outcome of this aspect of the study is negative, since no clear trend either toward or away from the scrolls is indicated by the data, though there are some significant changes of perspective in certain translations with regard to specific variants. The one general observation that does emerge is that the NEB is revised toward 𝔐 by the REB in Isaiah 14 and 49.

ABBREVIATIONS

ASV   *The American Standard Version* (Nashville: Nelson, 1901)

JB   *The Jerusalem Bible* (London: Darton, Longman & Todd, Ltd., 1966)

JM   *A New Translation of the Bible Containing the Old and New Testaments,* trans. by James Moffatt (London: Hodder and Stoughton Ltd., 1924)

JPS   *The Jewish Publication Society Version* (Philadelphia: The Jewish Publication Society of America, 1917)

KJV   *The King James Version* (Nashville: Nelson, 1982)

LSR   *The Twenty-Four Books of the Holy Scripture,* trans. by Isaac Leeser (New York: Hebrew Publishing Company, 1853)

McC   The English translation in P. Kyle McCarter, Jr., *1 Samuel: A New Translation with Introduction, Notes & Commentary,* The Anchor Bible, 8 (Garden City, NY: Doubleday, 1980).

NAB   *The New American Bible* (New York: Nelson, 1970)

NASB *The New American Standard Bible* (Nashville: Holman, 1971)

NEB   *The New English Bible* (Cambridge: Cambridge University Press, 1970)

NIV   *The New International Version* (Grand Rapids: Zondervan, 1978)

NJB   *The New Jerusalem Bible* (London: Darton, Longman & Todd, 1985)

NJV   *The New Jewish Publication Society Version* (Philadelphia: The Jewish

Publication Society of America, 1985)

NKJV *The New King James Version* (Nashville: Nelson, 1982)

NLT *The New Living Translation* (Wheaton: Tyndale, 1996)

NRSV *The New Revised Standard Version* (Grand Rapids: Zondervan)

REB *The Revised English Bible* (Cambridge: Cambridge University Press, 1989)

RSV *The Revised Standard Version* (London: World, 1952)

RV *The Revised Version* (Cambridge: Cambridge University Press, 1885)

TEV The Good News Bible or Today's English Version (New York: American Bible Society, 1976)

NOTES

1 I would like to thank my doctoral supervisor, Prof. Emanuel Tov, for his even-handed guidance in my research and comments on the present study. I am also grateful to Harold P. Scanlin for stimulating interaction on a number of key points.

2 The question of the influence of the scrolls on the modern translations is only one part of the larger issue of the textual basis or *Vorlage* of the translations overall. From the time of Tyndale to the present, the English translations have adopted readings, whether few or many, from various sources other than the Masoretic Text (𝔐), so that a full treatment of the *Vorlagen* of the English versions would have to take into consideration the textual influence of the Syriac Peshitta (𝔖), the Aramaic Targums (𝔗), the Latin Vulgate (𝔙), the Old Latin (𝔏), and, most importantly, the Septuagint (𝔊).

3 1QIsa^a was among the original seven scrolls taken from Cave 1, probably in 1947. For comments on discovery date, see James C. VanderKam, *The Dead Sea Scrolls Today* (Grand Rapids, MI: Eerdmans, 1994), p. 3. Early photographs by John C. Trevor and a transcription appeared in *The Isaiah Manuscript and the Habakkuk Commentary*, the first volume of *The Dead Sea Scrolls of St. Mark's Monastery*, ed. by Millar Burrows, 2 vols (New Haven, CT: ASOR, 1950). A group of readings from 1QIsa^a were adopted into the text of the RSV, which was published in 1952.

4 In large measure, this seems still to be the case today, though, from a critical standpoint, it is generally acknowledged that 1QIsa^a represents a popular or 'vulgar' edition of the biblical book and most of its numerous small variations from 𝔐 do not represent preferable readings.

5 For the precise limits of the material included from 4QSam^a, see Plate 121 in the first volume of Robert H. Eisenman and James M. Robinson, *A Facsimile Edition of the Dead Sea Scrolls*, 2 vols (Washington, D.C.: Biblical Archaeology Society, 1991), where PAM 40.971 is reproduced. For further details regarding the content of the fragments, see Edward D. Herbert, *Reconstructing Biblical Dead Sea Scrolls: A New Method Applied to the Reconstruction of 4QSam^a*, STDJ, 22 (Leiden: Brill, 1997), where Appendix B (pp. 205-213) lists the range of verses covered by each fragment and takes account of recent identifications.

6 Frank M. Cross, Jr., 'A New Qumran Biblical Fragment Related to the Original Hebrew Underlying the Septuagint', *BASOR*, 132 (1953), 15-26.

7 These revision lines will not be rigorously proved or systematically demonstrated here. In most cases, however, they represent the acknowledgments of the translators or committees themselves and are not controversial.

8 P. Kyle McCarter, Jr., *1 Samuel: A New Translation with Introduction, Notes & Commentary*, The Anchor Bible, 8 (Garden City, NY: Doubleday, 1980).

9 While three translation/revision pairs (RSV/NRSV, JB/NJB, and NEB/REB) are examined with respect to Isaiah 14 and 49, only two pairs (JB/NJB and NEB/REB) may be examined from this perspective in 1 Samuel 1-3, since the RSV is among the pre-𝔔 translations. In the 1 Samuel data, it is expedient to broaden the comparison so as to include the NAB as it relates to McC and the NRSV (cf. IV.E).

10 Paul Ellingworth, 'Theological Reflections on the Textual Criticism of the Bible', *The Bible Translator*, 46 (1995) 119-25 (pp. 121-23).

11 Emanuel Tov, 'The Textual Basis of Modern Translations of the Hebrew Bible: The Argument against Eclecticism', *Textus*, 20 (2000), 193-211

12 Dominique Barthélemy and others, *Preliminary and Interim Report on the Hebrew Old Testament*

Text Project, 5 vols (New York: United Bible Societies, 1979-80).

13   The New Jewish Publication Society Version is abbreviated as NJV throughout this paper so as to avoid the five letter acronym NJPSV which is sometimes difficult to fit into compact data charts.

14   Barclay M. Newman, Jr., 'Some Hints on Solving Textual Problems', *The Bible Translator*, 33 (1982) 430-35 (p. 434).

15   The Good News Bible (GNB) is also known as Today's English Version and is referred to as the TEV throughout the present work.

16   Excluded from the study, therefore, are English translations based on texts other than 𝔐, such as: *The Holy Bible from Ancient Eastern Manuscripts*, trans. by George M. Lamsa (Philadelphia: Holman, 1957), which is a rendering of the Syriac Peshitta; *The Old Testament: Newly Translated from the Latin Vulgate*, trans. by Ronald A. Knox (London: Burns, Oats, and Washbourne, 1949); and *The Septuagint Version of the Old Testament with an English Translation*, trans. by Lancelot C. L. Brenton (London: Bagster, 1879).

17   Moffatt's translation (JM) is the only pre-𝔔 translation included in this study that is not a revision in the KJV line. Because it reflects a significant number of readings from the ancient versions, particularly 𝔊, it serves as evidence for one translator's appraisal of 𝔊 in the pre-𝔔 period.

18   In Moffatt's usage, the term 'emendation' refers to any attempt to 'patch up' the traditional text, whether on the basis of the versions or otherwise. Moffatt also speaks of 'conjectures' (Introduction, xviii). In the present article, the term 'emendation' is a technical term for what others may refer to as 'conjectural emendation' while an extant reading adopted from any ancient source is simply a 'preferred reading' as defined in *TCHB*, pp. 351-6. See also note 30 below.

19   That is, they are needed from the perspective of the present study. Whether the intended audience of the translation would have been helped by such textual notes is a different matter.

20   The best examples are the textual notes published separately for the NAB in *Textual Notes on the New American Bible*, ed. by Louis F. Hartman (Paterson, NJ: St. Anthony's Guild, 1970) and for the NEB in L. H. Brockington, *The Hebrew Text of the Old Testament* (Oxford: Oxford University Press, 1973). In addition, some information regarding the text of the RSV is provided in Millar Burrows, *Diligently Compared: The Revised Standard Version and the King James Version of the Old Testament* (London: Nelson, 1964), pp. 210-23.

21   The precise reasoning that leads the translator or committee to prefer one reading over another is often irrecoverable, even when the *Vorlage* is determined with some degree of certainty, and, ideally, notes would include this more illusive information as well.

22   Emanuel Tov, *The Text-Critical Use of the Septuagint in Biblical Research*, 2nd edn, Jerusalem Biblical Studies, 8 (Jerusalem: Simor, 1997).

23   Box four of the papers of J. A. Emerton at the Bible Society Archives at the Cambridge University Library contains a booklet, dated July 1962, that was sent to the Old Testament panel of the NEB from the literary panel. At Isaiah 49:1 there is a note indicating that 'and' should be omitted. Because the omission originates from the literary panel, there is little question of textual influence from 1QIsaᵃ. The author wishes to thank Ingrid Roderick of the British and Foreign Bible Society for granting him access to the archive and the librarians, particularly Kathleen Caan, for their gracious assistance.

24   𝔐 is used as the basis for comparison and terms such as textual 'plus', 'minus', and 'replacement' are intended in a strictly formal sense. These terms do not pertain to the textual value of a given variant. The term 'variant' itself is to be similarly regarded, since it marks a formal difference from 𝔐 without commenting on whether or not the variant is preferable to 𝔐.

25   Drawing on E. Y. Kutscher, *The Language and Linguistic Background of the Isaiah Scroll (1 Q Isaᵃ)*, STDJ, 6 (Leiden: Brill, 1974), pp. 5-8, and Elisha Qimron, *The Hebrew of the Dead Sea Scrolls*, HSS, 29 (Atlanta, GA: Scholars Press, 1986), §100, Schniedewind summarizes the situation well. He writes, 'The most characteristic feature of Qumran orthography is the use of *scriptio plena*, or "full writing". This is particularly true of the use of *waw*, which comes to represent long and short *ḥōlem*, *šûreq*, *qibbûṣ*, *qāmeṣ ḥaṭup*, *ḥaṭep qāmeṣ*, and even sometimes *vocal shewa*'. See, William M. Schniedewind, 'Qumran Hebrew as an Antilanguage', *JBL*, 118 (1999) 235-52 (p. 247).

26   This variant may have developed as an accidental interchange of weakened guttural letters (cf. Kutscher, pp. 505-511).

27   To some extent, differentiating translatable and non-translatable variants is a language-specific

operation that depends in part on the alignment of the source language and the receptor language in specific linguistic details.

28 While in this one-verse sample it may appear that there is a simple division between orthographic variants (as non-translatable) and other variants (as translatable), there are instances in which this division does not hold. For example, in Isaiah 14:4 there is a variant that involves the addition of the direct object marker אֵת. In that instance, a literal English translation would be the same with or without this function word, since there is no direct equivalent for אֵת in English and since the function it signals, marked via different linguistic mechanisms in English, is already indicated by context in Hebrew.

29 Deciding that a variant is translatable reflects a linguistic rather than text-critical judgment and does not relate to the issue of whether or not the variants are preferable to 𝔐. No text-critical evaluation is performed at this point.

30 When, in the view of one or more scholars, the original reading is not directly reflected by any of the extant sources, a new reading, extrapolated from extant ones, is sometimes suggested as preferable to all others and closer to the original. In this work, the term 'emendation' applies only to such readings (see note 18).

31 Many details concerning the *Vorlage* of the NAB are given in Hartman, *Textual Notes*.

32 Emanuel Tov emphasizes this principle where he writes, 'the more one knows about the nature of the translation, and the more thoroughly inner-translational deviations are analysed, the less one is inclined to ascribe translational deviations to Hebrew variants' (*Text-Critical Use of the Septuagint*, p. 44).

33 A superscript 'n' (e.g., tc[n]) is added where an evaluation is based on a textual note.

34 As already mentioned, the NAB follows neither 𝔐 nor the 𝔔 variant but the conjectural emendation עִמָּם 'with them'.

35 Tov regards this Qumran variant as a contextual change, which, in this instance, amounts to a scribal addition most likely motivated by the scribe's wish to improve the literary style of the text (*TCHB*, p. 263).

36 The note 'So Scroll; Heb. om'. is found only in the Old Testament volume of the three volume Library Edition of the NEB. The one volume Standard Edition does not have a note at this point.

37 Only one textual correspondence, located in the NKJV, has been omitted from the counts of Figure 3 as possible but unlikely. Even this tc is counted, however, in Table 5, where the tcs of stage three are totaled. Regarding textual correspondences identified as possible and likely, five have been identified. They occur in the following EVs (quantity in parenthesis): NASB (1), TEV (2), and NLT (2). All the other textual correspondences included Figure 3 are supported by notes.

38 For example, in variant 2a, רבים 'many' is shaded since the EVs were examined for correspondence to this textual plus. When shading appears in both the BHS and 1QIsa[a] columns, it highlights the contrasting element that defines the variant. Normally, only one segment is shaded from each text (e.g. variant 2c); however, more than one segment may be shaded when multiple contrasting features characterize a single variant (e.g. variant 11a).

39 The discussion of variant 2a may be found in section II.C.3 above.

40 Kutscher, p. 253.

41 Brockington, p. 180.

42 At variant 32a, the pre-𝔔 JM has, 'What answer shall my people give [...]?' and anticipates the reading of the scroll to the extent that 'people' is more easily regarded as denoting a many-membered entity (i.e., a plurality). To the same extent, the presence of this reading in a pre-𝔔 EV may be taken as further indication that that the plural 'they' of the NKJV need not correspond textually to the scroll.

43 Bernhard Duhm, *Das Buch Jesaia, Handkommentar zum Alten Testament* (Göttingen: Vandenhoeck & Ruprecht, 1902), p. 334.

44 This reading is not included by Burrows in his list of readings adopted into the RSV from 1QIsa[a]. Another place where the RSV is based on an emendation is in variant 12a of Isaiah 49.

45 The nature and value of variants 17a and b are discussed in some detail in David Flusser, 'The Text of Isa. xlix, 17 in the DSS', *Textus*, 2 (1962), 140-42.

46 The NKJV does contain one rendering that has been evaluated as a possible but unlikely textual

correspondence (˜tc). The scroll variant involved is found in v. 32 of chapter 14 and is 32a, 𝔐 יְעֲנֶה // יענו 𝔔. Like the scroll reading, the NKJV rendering is plural but may reflect a contextual adjustment. As mentioned above, textual correspondences considered unlikely are not included in the tc totals.

47 Column I is represented in two fragments preserving small parts of 1 Samuel 1:11-13 and 17-18 (?). Column II preserves parts of 1:22-2:6 and 2:8-10. Column III preserves parts of 2:16-36. A fragment that probably fit near the top of column IV (or bottom of III?) preserves words from 3:1-4. A cluster of words forming the beginning of at least three lines (the top of a *lamed* in a fourth) are preserved in column IV and fit into 3:18-20. Counting all but 1:17-18 and 3:18-20 yields a total of forty-four verses.

48 Portions of Columns II and III were referred to as column I and II in the initial publication by Cross, and his transcription of these portions (p. 26) is followed with minor alterations. For the portions of columns I-IV not covered by Cross, PAM 40.971, reproduced as Plate 121 in Eisenman, *A Facsimile Edition*, was consulted (cf. note 5 above).

49 The extant material from columns I-IV of 4QSam[a] makes up the sample that is examined in this study. Because no part of 1 Samuel 1:1-10 has been identified, 1 Samuel 1:11 is set as the *terminus ad quo*. The last fragment of col. IV preserves a small part of 3:18-20 but contains no translatable variants. Thus the *terminus ad quem* is set at 1 Samuel 3:4, where a significant variant does occur. Though this section may be described as 1 Samuel 1:11-3:4, it is to be understood that significant gaps exist in the scroll, even between these limits, and that the sample is at all points determined by what is extant in the scroll.

50 As mentioned above (see Figure 1), the RSV was completed in 1952, just late enough to allow the incorporation of readings from 1QIsa[a] but too early to include any from 4QSam[a]. The RSV is therefore absent from Figure 6, for it is among the pre-𝔔 EVs with regard to 4QSam[a], though it was counted among the post-𝔔 EVs in discussions of 1QIsa[a].

51 For the Isaiah data, the abbreviation ˜tc marked readings that were considered possible but unlikely. Such readings were not included in the statistics. Different dynamics are at work in the 4QSam[a] data, however, and the abbreviation ˜tc marks readings that are regarded as simply uncertain.

52 The exact note that appears in *BHK* is ' *l* c בְּפַר מְשֻׁלָּשׁ ' (p. 406, n. 24a).

53 It is important to recall that the RSV is among the post-𝔔 EVs with regard to 1QIsa[a] but among the pre-𝔔 EVs with regard to 4QSam[a], cf. Figure 1 and the comments that elucidate it.

54 As a translation / revision pair, the RSV/NRSV cannot be included here because the RSV is pre-𝔔 in 1 Samuel. See Figure 1 and the comments associated with it.

55 The NJV, for example, uses points to indicate an apparent ellipsis in Genesis 4:8, where it translates, 'Cain said to his brother Abel … and when they were in the field, Cain set upon his brother and killed him'.

56 Note that this pertains to the readings examined, which are determined by the location of translatable variants in the scroll.

57 This juxtaposition also allows a comparison of the use of the selected portions of 1QIsa[a] and 4QSam[a] within each of the EVs. The values shown in Figure 9 may be read as the actual number adopted out of the total number possible. The fact that the total possible (= number of translatable variants) in the Isaiah data (sixty-nine) is similar to the number found in the I Samuel data (sixty-two) ensures that the comparison is germane.

58 In ordering the EVs, the highest of the two values shown for each EV was considered first. When two such highs were identical, the lows for each EV were compared. In this way, for example, the NLT (5, 9) is ranked higher than the REB (9, 0). Where lows are also identical, the EVs are presented in chronological order. Thus, RSV (5, n/a =0) appears before JB (5, 0).

59 Throughout the discussion, the RSV has been treated as post-𝔔 with respect to 1QIsa[a] but pre-𝔔 with respect to 4QSam[a].

60 How to treat difficult readings in 𝔐 is perhaps the chief textual challenge for translators and may provide the best criterion by which to group the EVs vis-à-vis text-critical praxis. Translations might be broadly categorized into (1) those that accept the text of 𝔐 even when it is difficult or practically unintelligible and render it into smooth English on the basis of contextual exegesis or an interpretive tradition, and (2) translations that recognize some of the difficulties of 𝔐 as points of textual

corruption that must be restored. Translations of the latter kind follow their *Vorlage* more closely, while translations of the former kind may require a looser semantic connection between *Vorlage* (i.e. 𝔪) and rendering.

61 See the quotation of Moffatt's preface and the associated comments in section I.D.

TEXT, TRUTH AND TRADITION: THE PUBLIC'S VIEW OF THE BIBLE IN THE LIGHT OF THE DEAD SEA SCROLLS

Harold P. Scanlin

WHAT THE PUBLIC DOES AND DOES NOT KNOW ABOUT THE DEAD SEA SCROLLS

THE COVER STORY of the US tabloid, *Sun* (18 April 2000) declared, 'FOUND! Dead Sea Scroll written by Jesus reveals . . . EXACT DATE OF MY RETURN!' Although this type of journalism does not really need any facts on which to base its stories, in this case the writers may have picked up on accounts in the general press about the recently 'discovered' Angel Scroll, purported to be from Qumran.[1] While it may be difficult to gauge to what degree the public accept the veracity of such stories, it does reflect the public interest in the Dead Sea Scrolls and their inclination to suspect the sensational against the sober judgments of the academic world.[2] Apparently, the public's appetite for sensationalism is matched by naïve assumptions regarding the nature and transmission of ancient religious texts.

POPULAR NOTIONS OF BIBLE AS TEXTUAL ACCURACY OR ICONIC VALUE

There is a phenomenal interest in religious, biblically based themes among the American public. In June 2000, the number one fiction bestseller on the *New York Times* bestseller list, starting at number 2 and rising to number 1 in only its second week on the list, was *The Indwelling* by Tim LaHaye and Jerry B. Jenkins,[3] 'the seventh in a series of novels about true believers who confront the Antichrist after the rapture of the saved'.[4]

Despite such popular interest in such biblical themes, surveys consistently demonstrate that the American public holds the Bible in high regard while also demonstrating their serious lack of knowledge about its contents. In a poll conducted by *US News* and published in its 4 April 1994 issue, 34% of respondents said that the Bible is 'the actual word of God to be taken literally word for word'; 46% said it is 'the inspired word of God, but not everything can be taken literally'; and only 16% said that it is 'an ancient book of legends, history and moral precepts, recorded by man'. Yet the actual knowledge of basic facts about the Bible was far below what one would expect of a society that, by a large percentage, claims they accept the Bible as the actual, inspired word of God. For example, a Barna Report poll conducted in the year 2000 confirms the earlier statistics regarding the authority of Scripture, but offers some interesting contrasts. Only 49% of those polled said that the book of Jonah is in the Old Testament; one would expect 50% by sheer guesswork. Furthermore, nearly every household has a Bible – 92% have at least one Bible, and households on average own three.[5] So, while people claim to accept the authority of Scripture and have their own copy, they seem to have an inadequate knowledge of its contents.

A 1980 Gallup Poll, conducted on behalf of *Christianity Today* also found the same dichotomy between popular reverence for the Bible but a lack of readership and a limited knowledge of its contents.[6] Gallup's more recent surveys confirm these earlier results.[7]

How should one explain this discrepancy? Paul Gutjahr demonstrates that when Protestants developed a wide variety of Bible-related publications the notion of *Sola Scriptura*[8] was lost: 'God's word never reaches readers in pure, unmediated form'.[9] The nineteenth-century publishing practices that made the Bible the most widely available book of all time may in reality have contributed to its downfall as the preeminent text of the American print culture.[10] If Gutjahr is right, the risk at the turn of the millennium may be even greater, with the appearance of many new translations and all kinds of repackaged study Bibles. Add to this the proliferation of new media presentations of the Bible, the tension between fixed text and pluriform presentations will only increase.

A major controversy arose in mid-nineteenth century when the American Bible Society decided to publish a slightly edited King James Version with modernised spelling, some readers' aids such as headings and paragraph divisions, and a few minor textual changes. Edward Robinson and other prominent American biblical scholars of the day headed the committee. Objections were raised by mainline denominations on the grounds that these changes were unwarranted tampering with the Word of God. The critics of this King James edition, which by today's standards was a very modest revision, ultimately pressured the American Bible Society into withdrawing the edition. In protest, the revision committee resigned. This episode suggests that the public resists tampering by biblical scholars of its sacred book, but it seems that they do not bother to appropriate its content.

Into this milieu enters information on the Dead Sea Scrolls. How does the public gain access to this information? By what criteria do they judge the validity of popular reports in the press and on television? It may be safe to say that the public does not necessarily take at face value what it reads in the United States tabloid, *Sun* and other tabloids. However, the popularity of general books on the Dead Sea Scrolls seems to be in direct proportion to the controversy level promoted by the author(s). How can the sober judgments of conferences such as this one counteract misinformation so widely disseminated in the popular press? Up to this point, the sensationalism and mystique of the 'hidden scrolls' seems to have made little impact on peoples' attitude towards and knowledge of the Bible. Scholars work away at the tedium of textual research and believe that great strides are being made in advancing our knowledge of the text of Scripture in its pluriform witnesses during the centuries at the turn of the era, but only infrequently do they have the opportunity to mediate this knowledge to the general reading public. One of the few opportunities – with potentially the greatest impact – is in Bible translation, but here, too, the impact at the moment is minimal. The cynic might say that this does not matter, since the Bible is a book mostly owned, not read.

TEXT, TRUTH AND TRADITION – A THESIS

The linkage of text, truth, and tradition in popular views of the authority of Scripture is a phenomenon that has developed in a context which overlooks the diversity of textual witnesses and shifts the locus of scriptural authority to that which stresses iconic value rather than Scripture's truth claims. The Dead Sea Scrolls as a corrective to this notion may, in the final analysis, be the most significant influence on Bible translation.

THE DEAD SEA SCROLLS BIBLE

The general public now has access to an excellent translation of virtually all biblical texts found at Qumran.[11] The translators capably place the nature of the evidence in its historical, text-critical context. Unfortunately, the public's introduction to the topic as presented on the dust jacket of the book misrepresents the nature of the case in almost every line. The title and sub-title, *The Dead Sea Scrolls Bible: The Oldest Known Bible: Translated for the First Time into English*, is likely to leave general readers with the impression that there was a 'Bible', a fixed collection of canonical books bound in black leather and so designated, at least *de facto*, by the Covenanters at Qumran. It is a 'book' that is older and perhaps radically different from the Bible of pre-Qumran discovery days.[12] The additional jacket blurb, 'Over 1000 years older than any previously discovered manuscripts' is plainly wrong.

More subtle is the potentially misleading phrase, 'the oldest known Bible'. Does this set up a false dichotomy in the mind of the general reader – our present Bibles versus an older Bible found at Qumran? The CenturyOne Foundation polls its visitors to its Internet bookstore on various topics of current interest. When they first offered *The Dead Sea Scrolls Bible*, they posed the following question: 'When the Dead Sea Scrolls Bible differs from our standard traditional Hebrew text, which should we give weight to? The older or the traditional?' Results as of 21 May 2000 were: Older [Dead Sea Scrolls] 66%; Traditional [Hebrew Text] 25%; Don't Know 9%. The results of the poll, which CenturyOne clearly labels as unscientific, are, nevertheless quite revealing. Assuming most of the respondents were not textual scholars, it is remarkable that people were willing to express an opinion. The clear preference for 'older' is likely to be based on the presupposition that in such matters 'older is better'. The textual critic, however, realises that the situation is more complex than that. While age of a reading is a significant factor, the decidedly mixed witnesses of the Qumran biblical manuscripts, including witnesses that lend support to the traditional text, demonstrate the complexity of the Qumran evidence and caution against simplistic conclusions. The ultimate problem seems to be that pluriformity of texts contradicts an iconic view of the Bible.

QUMRAN – ON THE WAY TO CANON

During the first centuries BCE and CE evidence is lacking for a developed notion of 'canon', or even that it occurred to religious leaders to ask about the notion of canonicity, at least as a global concept.[13] On the other hand, there are sufficient contemporary references to authoritative (or at least highly regarded) texts that were distinguished from other writings in the way they were copied[14] and used. This was a dynamic period of theological dialogue in an environment that tolerated, or even welcomed, pluriform texts. For example, contemporaneous different text editions open up the possibility of adaptability to the exegetical concerns of the community. The tension between stable text form and dynamic interpretation would continue to exist until the dawn of a different century with different socio-political realities.

What can be said about the existence and nature of authoritative texts among the Covenanters at Qumran? Some texts are consulted with greater frequency – especially in contexts where authoritative texts are called for – but how can one know if and when these criteria are met? If there is no exact description of such functionality by the Covenanters themselves, it may nevertheless be possible to make reasonable assumptions based on the evidence, or, at the very least, make some educated guesses. The following indicators are relevant:

- The number of copies of certain texts, e.g. Deuteronomy, Isaiah, Psalms, the pesharim (grouped as a genre), and multiple copies of books other than the twenty-four of the Hebrew canon of later formulation.
- The use made of these texts. It is (only) an authoritative text that forms the basis of a theological explanation of the contemporary situation. Typical examples are the exegetical method found in the pesharim and the function of authoritative liturgical texts in worship.
- Formulaic introductions – similar in function, if not in exegetical principle to pesher.
- Quotation and allusion in sectarian writings. The New Testament, a first century CE document which can be described as a collection of Jewish sectarian writings that clearly regarded the Hebrew Bible as authoritative, uses a variety of formulae to introduce quotations which establish a continuity they see between the Hebrew Bible and their messianic beliefs.
- Intertextuality. In one New Testament book, Revelation, there are no direct quotes, but John of Patmos clearly regarded the Old Testament as scripture and makes extensive intertextual use of it.

These criteria are not sufficient to establish a fixed list, but they do indicate that some texts were more highly regarded for their authority than others.[15]

Although it is rightly argued that there is no evidence for comprehensive discussions of canonicity during the period (the purported evidence for Jamnia hardly qualifies as a systematic discussion of canonical issues), there are some contemporary analogous statements made about Greek and Roman literature. For example, for Dio Cassius (164-229 CE) Thucydides was 'the canon'.[16] Actual lists of authoritative works began to show up as early as the third to second century BCE. In Alexandria the term οι ενκριθεντης, 'the select authors' was being used to categorise certain works as enjoying a special status. Thus, the concept of authoritative text was current during the Qumran era, even if there is no direct evidence of the existence of such lists in the community's literature. The question still remains regarding the degree of textual stability of authoritative texts.

Text, Truth and Tradition

FIXED OR FLUID AUTHORITATIVE TEXT?

Canon(ization) and fixity of texts may have more to do with sociology than textual criticism. On this side of Shemaryahu Talmon's great divide dating from about the end of the first century CE, the highly stable Masoretic Text, earlier forms of which may be seen for example in Murabba'at and Masada, nevertheless allowed for a certain degree of 'wiggle room'. Once socio-religious factors and historical circumstances led to a very stable edition of the Hebrew Bible which came to be called the proto-Masoretic Text, there remained variants, albeit minor, within the tradition. In Harry Orlinsky's words, there is no such thing as *'the* [emphasis mine] Masoretic text'.[17] Tolerance for minor variations was established precisely because, rather than in spite of the fact that, there was a theological need to have a fixed text. Once fixity became the essential virtue the religious community had to deal with the, admittedly small, residue of textual variants that remain in the process of fixing the text. This phenomenon can be seen in the way Western Christian communities deal with textual criticism in their Bible translations.

Another issue that factors into the public's attitude toward the tolerance of textual uncertainty is the matter of authorial intent and canonical form. To give a modest example, Christian worshippers sing Charles Wesley's famous Christmas hymn, 'Hark the Herald Angels Sing'. Yet this is not the original form of the hymn, which actually begins, 'Hark how all the welken rings, Glory to the King of Kings'. Wesley's authorial intent is not the canonical form of the hymn. In this case Charles's brother John disliked the hymn. Another famous religious leader of the day, George Whitfield, recommended the change in lyrics that finally persuaded John to allow the hymn in the Methodist hymnal and established its canonical form as one of the most familiar Christmas hymns sung today. This example illustrates the fact that a degree of 'wiggle room' is tolerated in religious texts. Tension arises when we desire to have a fixed text, presumably with the best chance of encapsulating the words of the divine revelation in the language(s) that God chose to use, but are faced with pluriform texts which arose not only through the accidents of scribal transmission but through a willingness to re-formulate sacred text for evolving situations.

Christianity has always lived with the tension between the emotional security of having the *ipsissima verba* of the divine revelation and the translatability of that divine message, so necessary to a religion that claims a universal mission and a zeal to win converts. This is not to say that other religions are not confronted with similar concerns, but of the three 'religions of the Book',[18] Christianity has actively pursued a translation enterprise that has resulted in Scriptures in over two thousand languages, with at least eight hundred translation projects under way today.

THE IMPACT, PRACTICAL AND THEOLOGICAL, ON BIBLE TRANSLATIONS[19]

The Bible translator is constantly aware of the potential anxiety over textual criticism in a target audience that believes the original text is the fixed Word of God and may not want to be told that even minor variants exist in the base text, let alone more major differences both in length and editorial perspective. The Qumran discoveries have heightened the focus of modern translators on the issue, but the principle is far from new.

Harold P. Scanlin

THE KING JAMES VERSION AND MARGINAL NOTES

After a process which took nearly fifty years, the KJV supplanted its greatest rival, the Geneva version (first edition, 1560). Its durability influenced the popular perception in the English-speaking world of what a sacred text should be like. Its archaic language has become in the popular mind the canonical form of sacred language, even though the language of the KJV was not archaic in the early seventeenth century. Over the years, popular editions of the KJV dropped all marginal notes, notes that could have led the reader to recognise the existence of textual variants and the honest admission of the translators that there are some difficulties in understanding some Hebrew words and phrases.

To understand how the form of the original KJV, with its textual notes and its presentation of alternate renderings, was superceded by contemporary presentations of the text, we should look at the reasons why James I came to authorise this translation project. James, the Scottish monarch who was called to succeed Elizabeth I on the English throne in 1603, had to deal with a simmering conflict between Anglican regulars and the Puritans. The Anglican Church had an official Bishops Bible, but the Puritans were fond of their favourite Bible translation, the Geneva Bible, with its numerous anti-monarchical marginal notes. James convened a conference at Hampton Court in the hope of resolving a number of conflicts between the religious parties. Apparently, a Bible revision was not on the agenda, but a brilliant compromise was offered by John Rainolds who 'moved his majesty that there be a new translation of the Bible because those which were allowed in the reign of Henry the eighth and Edward the sixth were corrupt and not answerable to the truth of the original'[20]. This appealed to James I, because he was a bookman and had even dabbled in Bible translation. The compromise translation project would please the Puritans, with their cadre of biblical scholars, and give the Crown the opportunity to do away with the despised anti-monarchical notes of the Geneva Bible. To ensure the removal of the offensive notes, the King himself promoted the idea first put forward by John Bancroft, Bishop of London, that there be no marginal notes in his new translation. The notes of the Geneva Bible were the target of this declaration, but Bancroft's 'Rules to Be Observed in the Translation of the Bible' did allow for the affixing of marginal notes 'for the Explanation of the *Hebrew* or *Greek* Words which cannot without some circumlocution, so briefly and fitly be expressed in the Text' (Rule 6).[21] In practice, the use of such marginal notes offered both alternate textual readings and explanations of difficult renderings. The KJV preface, 'The Translators to the Reader', unfortunately omitted from almost all current editions, goes on to explain that, in a modern rendering,

Some persons perhaps would want to have no alternative readings or renderings placed in the margin, for fear that any appearance of uncertainty might undermine the authority of Scripture as definitive. But we do not consider their judgment to be prudent on this point.[22]

Over the years, most editions of the KJV gradually dropped the marginal notes. The trend was made nearly universal by the policy of the British and Foreign Bible Society, followed by other Bible societies including the American Bible Society, that Bibles be published 'without note or comment'.[23] The motivation was similar to the desire expressed at the Hampton Court conference to avoid doctrinal controversy promoted by biased notes, but the net result served to camouflage issues of textual and exegetical difficulties and lent tacit support to notions of textual fixity.

Text, Truth and Tradition

TEXTUAL CRITICISM
AND THE RELIABILITY OF SCRIPTURE

Despite popular notions of textual fixity in the Bible, the overwhelming majority of biblical scholars, including those of Protestant evangelical persuasion, recognise the reality of textual variants, both unintentional and intentional. Yet some have specifically emphasised the essential reliability of the biblical texts we now possess. For example, F. F. Bruce said, 'If the variant readings are so numerous, it is because the witnesses are so numerous. But all the witnesses and all the types that they represent, agree on every article of Christian belief and practice'.[24]

More recently, however, some textual scholars have chosen to emphasise intentional differences. Bart Ehrman claims that theologically-motivated textual changes were introduced during the period in early Church history when Christian orthodoxy was defining itself against heterodox and heretical thought.[25] He cites as one example the addition of 'Son of God' in Mark 1:1 as an effort to reinforce the orthodox view of the divinity of Jesus Christ. More cautiously, and with a less provocative title, David Parker points out that in some of the most doctrinally crucial texts there are significant textual variants.[26] This is true, for example, of the Lord's Prayer and Jesus' teaching on divorce.

The same phenomenon occurs in the Hebrew Bible, as well. For example, the Ten Commandments not only appear in two different recensions in Exodus and Deuteronomy, but the form of the text in the Nash papyrus, probably the oldest extant manuscript of the Hebrew Bible before the discovery of the Dead Sea Scrolls, also contains textual variants. Two silver amulets, dating from the early sixth century BCE and containing the so-called Aaronic benediction were recently discovered near Jerusalem. The two amulets show textual differences between themselves as well as against the Masoretic Text of Numbers 6:24-26.[27]

MODERN VIEWS OF THE TEXTUAL BASE

Based on their presuppositions regarding biblical inerrancy and verbal inspiration, often embracing a form of 'dictation theory', Protestant Fundamentalists strongly favour the Masoretic Text (MT). Curiously, there is currently a lively debate in fundamentalist circles regarding the Greek textual base of the New Testament, some arguing for the *textus receptus*, the Greek text used by the KJV translators, while others are prepared to accept, at least on a limited basis, contemporary approaches to textual criticism resulting in an eclectic text.

In a recent volume of essays by Fundamentalists defending the eclectic text view against 'KJV-Only' views, they nevertheless seem to be less open to a similar approach to the textual criticism of the Hebrew Bible. They describe the value of the Dead Sea Scrolls for the study of the Hebrew Bible as 'the most significant impact on their discovery has been their confirmation of the accuracy of the Hebrew text of the Old Testament in use today'.[28]

Other similar claims by Fundamentalists, both in writing and in verbal defenses, often pick up on half of the story of the biblical text at Qumran – that there are witnesses to a proto-MT text – while neglecting to consider witnesses that do not support, wholly or in part, the MT tradition. In 1993 I discussed the impact of Qumran discoveries on Bible translation and concluded, '(1) the scrolls confirm the reliability of the Masoretic Text, thereby adding almost a thousand years to the antiquity of the Hebrew text. (2) They reestablish the Septuagint as a textual authority. (3) The scrolls are a source of reliable variant readings'.[29] Some readers have cited only point (1), but the complete picture requires a recognition of all three aspects of the textual history of Qumran witnesses.

The extremely popular New International Version (NIV), still holding its ranking as the best selling version in the United States, strikes a more conciliatory note, and, in fact, does not rely entirely on MT as the base text, describing itself as 'balanced'[30] in its approach to textual criticism as well as translation theory and practice. The NIV Preface says, 'The Dead Sea Scrolls contain material bearing on an earlier stage of the Hebrew text'. Kenneth Barker concludes, after citing a number of cases of MT departures, that these 'are the exceptions that prove the general rule that the NIV adhered rather rigidly to the MT'[31]. One notable exception, not, however cited by Barker, is Isaiah 53:11 NIV, which, along with most other modern versions, accepts the 1QIsa^a and 1QIsa^b reading אור 'the light [of life]' which also tends to support an individual suffering servant interpretation. Contrast this with the New Jewish Publication Society (NJPS) translation. It is by its own claim a translation of the traditional Hebrew text which not only rejects the Qumran reading, but adds a footnote referring to the text 'he shall see it', explaining that 'it' refers to the arm of the Lord, i.e. his vindication.[32]

The New Living Translation (NLT), a thorough revision of the Living Bible and now translated directly from the original texts, also generally takes a conservative approach to textual matters, generally preferring the Masoretic Text. There are only thirteen places in the entire Hebrew Bible where the text follows a Qumran reading, and almost always with additional support of the ancient versions. In an additional four passages, a Qumran reading is given in a textual note. In a revision of NLT currently under way, greater use will be made of the Qumran evidence. I have had the opportunity to check the drafts of Isaiah, and the number of Qumran readings has more than doubled from six to thirteen. While hardly a major shift in text base, it does suggest a trend towards greater valuation of the Qumran evidence. It was reported to me that in the revision of Samuel there will be a significantly greater use made of the Qumran material, but specific details are not yet available. While it may be risky to offer generalizations based on the limited evidence of one book and a relatively low number of adoptions of Qumran readings, I think it is fair to say that the trend in this and other new translations and revisions will be toward an increased use of the textual evidence from Qumran.

Qumran influence in Bible translation has reached as far as Nigeria, where a new Old Testament translation into Berom has accepted one Qumran reading, the large plus at 1 Samuel 10:27.[33] Curiously, this is the only Qumran reading that the translators have followed. They may have been influenced by the NRSV in adopting this reading, a practice which is frequently followed by translation teams that may be competent in Hebrew but may lack expertise in textual criticism and are inclined to follow textual decisions made by other translations.

Most major Bible translations of the second half of the twentieth century use footnotes to explain their text-critical decisions. While intellectually honest, this approach may create a tension between reader expectations for an authoritative text, especially for the 'religious' reader, and the historical reality of textual transmission. Edouardo Crisafulli discusses reader expectation and a translator's attitude toward text-critical issues in the case of a well-known nineteenth century English translation of Dante's *Comedy* by H. F. Cary.

Cary complies with the expectation of the reading public that he will recover the original meaning; on the other hand, he takes great pains to flout such expectation in the footnotes by suggesting that the task of "faithfully" representing the source text is a chimera, given its fragmented state.[34]

There seems to be a developing trend in some recent Bible translations to provide a very minimum of textual notes but also to provide, in supplementary publications, the full documentation regarding textual (and exegetical) decisions for readers interested in the translators' presuppositions on textual criticism and the practical results of such decisions. The 1992 Danish Bible (published in 1995 by the Danish Bible Society and intended to be the standard translation for the Danish Churches) does not offer textual notes. The translation team, however, including Bertil Albrektson and other highly competent Danish Old Testament scholars, departed from MT over 1,500 times. Svend Holm-Nielsen examines all the cases where the translators have abandoned MT[35] either because 'other textual witnesses are more trustworthy' or because the Hebrew text is incomprehensible.[36] Despite the many departures from the Masoretic Text there is a remarkable paucity of use of the Qumran evidence, especially significant since the translators clearly established an eclectic text as their base text. In 1 Samuel, there is only one case where Qumran evidence is cited (2:20). There are more Qumran citations in 2 Samuel, usually lending its support to an Old Greek reading that the translators chose to follow. The way Qumran evidence is cited in this and many other translations can be misleading. By citing any Qumran evidence with just one siglum such as 'Q' the general reader is left with the false impression that there is a degree of uniformity in the Qumran textual witnesses. While this *may* be true for some books, for example Isaiah, the evidence is frequently just the opposite: the biblical texts at Qumran offer a surprising diversity of text editions (text types) which amply testify to an attitude to 'authoritative text' that would not move towards fixity until later centuries.

WHAT TO TRANSLATE?

It must be recognised that by some standards, the Qumran evidence has been greatly under-utilised, with few exceptions, in modern translations. Should greater use be made of the evidence? An answer to this question depends on recognising the base text philosophy of the translation. In the case of translations for religious Jewish audiences (such as NJPS and the Stone edition of the Tanak) the obvious choice is still 'the traditional text'. So, too, for many theologically conservative Christians. In both cases, the assumption is that MT most accurately preserves the canonical form of the sacred text, whether or not the scholars, or at least the religious community, are aware of the diversity of textual witnesses at the turn of the era.

Others will utilise Qumran evidence primarily as a tool for recovering the 'best' text. This is a textual procedure on the way to an eclectic text, which, nevertheless, is a difficult enterprise in light of the limited evidence. Still others with a theological preference for the Septuagint (especially in the case of the Eastern Orthodox Churches) might be expected to welcome the Qumran evidence. Yet even here there is an underutilisation of the Qumran evidence.

The statement of the KJV translators made nearly 400 years ago is equally appropriate today as a guideline for the use of Qumran evidence in modern Bible translations:

Some persons perhaps would want to have no alternative readings or renderings placed in the margin, for fear that any appearance of uncertainty might undermine the authority of Scripture as definitive. But we do not consider their judgment to be prudent on this point.[37]

NOTES

1   *The Jerusalem Report* announced the purported discovery in September 1999 and featured it as its cover story in the 11 October 1999 issue, 'the Mystery of the Angel Scroll: Elaborate Hoax or Find of the Century?' For an academic analysis of the topic, see Stephen J. Pfann's discussion at www.csec.ac.uk/benpadia.htm (22 October 1999).

2   Fiona C. Black takes a whimsical look at the phenomenon of sensationalist reporting of purported Bible related discoveries in 'Lost Prophecies! Scholars amazed! *Weekly World News* and the Bible', *Sem*, 82 (1998), 127-49.

3   Tim LaHaye and Jerry B. Jenkins, *The Indwelling* (Wheaton: Tyndale, 2000).

4   *The Indwelling*, quote taken from dustjacket.

5   Barna Research Online: the Bible, www.barna.org.cgi-bin/PageCategory.asp, (25 April 2000).

6   See Walter Elwell, 'Belief and the Bible: A Crisis of Authority? The Christianity Today – Gallup Poll shows the Bible is highly revered but seldom used', *Christianity Today,* 21 March 1980, pp. 18-21.

7   See The Gallup Organization. Gallup Poll Topics: Religion, at www.gallup.com/poll/indicators/indreligion.asp.

8   *Sola Scriptura*, a crucial distinction in Protestant theology, especially in its Reformation dispute with the Roman Catholic Church, stressed the role of Scripture as the only source of authority in matters of faith and doctrine. This was not intended, however, to do away with the function either of the Church or of reason.

9   Paul Gutjahr, *An American Bible: A History of the Good Book in the United States, 1777-1880* (Stanford, CA: Stanford University Press, 1999).

10   Peter Thuesen makes a similar point in his review of Gutjahr, entitled 'The Leather-Bound Shrine in Every Home', in *Books and Culture*, (March/April 2000, 20-22). In the same issue, Gutjahr reviews Thuesen's new book, *In Discordance with the Scriptures: American Protestant Battles over Translating the Bible* (New York: Oxford University Press, 1999).

11   Martin Abegg, Jr., Peter Flint and Eugene Ulrich, *The Dead Sea Scrolls Bible: The Oldest Known Bible Translated for the First Time into English* (San Francisco: HarperCollins, 1999).

12   The British publisher, T&T Clark, advertises the book as 'The Dead Sea Scrolls Bible – the most ancient versions of the books of the Bible', a more accurate and less sensational description (Edinburgh: T&T Clark, 1999).

13   See the article by Shemaryahu Talmon in this volume.

14   We think here of both qualitative and quantitative issues. In assessing this type of evidence, it must be kept clearly in mind that we are dealing with criteria of relative, not absolute, weight.

15   When discussing 'canon' it is important to distinguish between the formal historical process that led to official statements regarding the precise limits of authoritative texts for a particular religious community and a more general notion of canon. Robert Alter, *Canon and Creativity* (New Haven: Yale University Press, 2000) defines canon in the latter sense, 'as a designation for the corpus of secular literary works implicitly or explicitly endorsed by established cultural authority as worthy of preservation through reading and study' (p. 1). This is a helpful definition even for religious literary works.

16   John F. A. Sawyer, *Sacred Languages and Sacred Texts* (London and New York: Routledge, 1999).

17   Harry Orlinsky, 'The New Jewish Version of the Torah', *JBL*, 82 (1963), 260.

18   Judaism, Christianity and Islam are often so described because of the fundamental role of their written scriptures.

19 Elsewhere in this volume, Stephen Daley has detailed the use of Qumran textual evidence in a number of major Bible translations that have appeared since the 1950s.

20 Olga S. Opfell, *The King James Bible Translators* (Jefferson, NC and London: McFarland, 1982), pp. 6-7.

21 Olga S. Opfell, *The King James Bible Translators* cites the full list of fifteen rules on pp. 139-40.

22 Erroll F. Rhodes and Liana Lupas, eds, *The Translators to the Readers* (New York: American Bible Society, 1997), p. 82.

23 William Canton, *A History of the British and Foreign Bible Societies* (London: John Murray, 1904), vol. I, p. 17.

24 F. F. Bruce, *The Books and the Parchments* (London: Pickering and Inglis, 1971), p. 189. Compare his full treatment in F. F. Bruce, *The New Testament Documents: Are they Reliable?*, 5th edn (London: Inter-Varsity, 1960).

25 Bart D. Ehrman, *The Orthodox Corruption of Scripture: The Effect of Early Christological Controversies on the Text of the New Testament* (New York: Oxford University Press, 1993).

26 D. C. Parker, *The Living Text of the Gospels* (Cambridge: Cambridge University Press, 1997).

27 Gabriel Barkay, 'The Priestly Benediction on Silver Plaques: the Significance of the Discovery at Ketef Hinnom' [in Hebrew], *Cathedra*, 52 (1989), 37-76.

28 James B. Williams, ed., *From the Mind of God to the Mind of Man* (Greenville, NC and Belfast: Ambassador-Emerald International, 1999), p. 222.

29 Harold P. Scanlin, *The Dead Sea Scrolls and Modern Translations of the Old Testament* (Wheaton, IL: Tyndale House, 1993), p. 139.

30 Kenneth Barker, *The Balance of the NIV: What Makes a Good Translation* (Grand Rapids: Baker, 1999), especially Chapter 3, 'A Balanced Textual Basis', pp. 23-40.

31 Barker, *The Balance of the NIV*, p. 31.

32 For a fuller treatment of the adherence of NJPS to the Masoretic Text, see my article, ' "...According to the Traditional Hebrew Text" as a Translation Principle in *Tanakh*', in *I Must Speak to You Plainly*, ed. by Roger L. Omanson (Carlisle: Paternoster, 2000), pp. 23-37.

33 Reported in personal correspondence with the primary translator, Hanni Kuhn of the Summer Institute of Linguistics, the sponsor of the translation. As of 2000, the translation has not been published, so it is not certain if this decision will remain unchanged.

34 Edouardo Crisafulli, 'The Translator as Textual Critic and the Potential of Transparent Discourse', *The Translator*, 5 (1999), 83-107.

35 Surprisingly, not in Genesis 4:8.

36 Svend Holm-Nielsen, *Noter til bibeloversaettelsen af 1992: Rettelser I den hebraiske tekst* (Danish Bible Society, 1997).

37 Rhodes and Lupas, *Translators to the Readers*, p. 82.

ABBREVIATIONS

JOURNALS

BA	*Biblical Archaeologist*
BASOR	*Bulletin of the American Schools of Oriental Research*
BHS	*Biblia Hebraica Stuttgartensia*
Bib	*Biblica*
BHQ	*Biblia Hebraica Quinta*
BO	*Bibliotheca Orientalis*
BIOSCS	*Bulletin of the International Organization for Septuagint and Cognate Studies*
CBQ	*Catholic Biblical Quarterly*
DJD	*Discoveries in the Judaean Desert*
DSD	*Dead Sea Discoveries*
ErIsr	*Eretz-Israel*
HTR	*Harvard Theological Review*
HUCA	*Hebrew Union College Annual*
IEJ	*Israel Exploration Journal*
JBL	*Journal of Biblical Literature*
JJS	*Journal of Jewish Studies*
JSOT	*Journal for the Study of the Old Testament*
JSS	*Journal of Semitic Studies*
JTS	*Journal of Theological Studies*
NTS	*New Testament Studies*
RB	*Revue Biblique*
RevQ	*Revue de Qumrân*
Sem	*Semitica*
VT	*Vetus Testamentum*
ZAW	*Zeitschrift für die alttestamentliche Wissenschaft*

BOOKS

ABD	David Noel Freedman and others (eds), *Anchor Bible Dictionary*, 6 vols (New York: Doubleday, 1992)
CRC	Eugene Ulrich and James VanderKam (eds), *The Community of the Renewed Covenant: The Notre Dame Symposium on the Dead Sea Scrolls*, Christianity and Judaism in Antiquity Series, 10 (Notre Dame, IN: University of Notre Dame Press, 1994)
DSSAFY	Peter W. Flint and James C. VanderKam (eds), *The Dead Sea Scrolls after Fifty Years: A Comprehensive Assessment*, 2 vols (Leiden: Brill, 1998-99)
DSSB	Martin Abegg, Jr., Peter Flint, and Eugene Ulrich (eds), *The Dead Sea Scrolls Bible: The Oldest Known Bible Translated for the First Time into English* (San Francisco: HarperSanFrancisco, 1999)
DSSSE	Florentino García Martínez & Eibert J.C. Tigchelaar (eds), *The Dead Sea Scrolls Study Edition*, 2 vols (Leiden: Brill; Grand Rapids, MI: Eerdmans, 1997-1998)
DSSTHC	Timothy H. Lim and others (eds), *The Dead Sea Scrolls in Their Historical Context* (Edinburgh: T&T Clark, 2000)

Abbreviations

EDSS   Lawrence H. Schiffman and James C. VanderKam (eds), *Encyclopedia of the Dead Sea Scrolls*, 2 vols (Oxford: Oxford University Press, 2000)

MQC   Julio C. Trebolle Barrera and Luis Vegas Montaner (eds), *The Madrid Qumran Congress—Proceedings of the International Congress on the Dead Sea Scrolls—Madrid, 18–21 March, 1991*, STDJ, 11, 2 vols (Leiden: Brill, 1992)

NQTS   George J. Brooke and Florentino García Martínez (eds), *New Qumran Texts and Studies: Proceedings of the First Meeting of the International Organization for Qumran Studies, Paris 1992*, STDJ, 15 (Leiden: Brill, 1994)

QHBT   Frank Moore Cross and Shemaryahu Talmon (eds), *Qumran and the History of the Biblical Text* (Cambridge, MA: Harvard University Press, 1975)

QONT   Frederick H. Cryer and Thomas L. Thompson (eds), *Qumran between the Old and New Testaments*, Journal for the Study of the Old Testament Supplement Series, 290, Copenhagen International Seminar, 6 (Sheffield: Sheffield Academic Press, 1998)

SSCW   George J. Brooke and Barnabas Lindars (eds), *Septuagint, Scrolls, and Cognate Writings: Papers Presented to the International Symposium on the Septuagint and Its Relations to the Dead Sea Scrolls and Other Writings (Manchester, 1990)*, SBL Septuagint and Cognate Studies Series, 33 (Atlanta, GA: Scholars Press, 1992)

TCHB   Emanuel Tov, *Textual Criticism of the Hebrew Bible* (Minneapolis: Fortress; Assen: Van Gorcum, 1992); 2nd edn (Minneapolis: Augsburg Fortress, 2001)

SERIES

ASOR   American Schools of Oriental Research
BZAW   Beihefte zur Zeitschrift für die alttestamentliche Wissenschaft
BZNW   Beihefte zur Zeitschrift für die neutestamentliche Wissenschaft
HSM   Harvard Semitic Monographs
HSS   Harvard Semitic Studies
IES   Israel Exploration Society
IOSCS   International Organization for Septuagint and Cognate Studies
JPS   Jewish Publication Society
JSNTSup   Journal for the Study of the New Testament: Supplement Series
JSOTSup   Journal for the Study of the Old Testament: Supplement Series
JSPSup   Journal for the Study of the Pseudepigrapha: Supplement Series
OBO   Orbis biblicus et orientalis
SBL   Society of Biblical Literature
STDJ   Studies on the Texts of the Desert of Judah
VTSup   Supplements to Vetus Testamentum

MISCELLANEOUS

CD   Damascus Document
𝕲/LXX   Septuagint
𝕲^A LXX: Codex Alexandrinus
𝕲^B LXX: Codex Vaticanus
𝕲^L LXX: Lucianic manuscripts
𝕲^O LXX: Hexapla (Origen)
HUBP   Hebrew University Bible Project
JB   Journal for the Pseudapigrapha: Supplement Series

Abbreviations

JSPSup	Jerusalem Bible
KJB	King James Version
£/OL	Old Latin
𝔪/MT	Masoretic Text
NAB	New American Bible
NEB	New English Bible
NIV	New International Version
NJPS	New Jewish Publication Society
NRSV	New Revised Standard Version
OG	Old Greek
Ψ	Psalms
REB	Revised English Bible
RSV	Revised Standard Version
𝔪/SP	Samaritan Pentateuch
𝔖	Syriac Peshitta
𝔗	Targums
𝔳	Vulgate

DISCOVERIES IN THE JUDAEAN DESERT

DJD I	D. Barthélemy, O.P. and J. T. Milik, *Qumran Cave 1* (Oxford: Clarendon Press, 1955)
DJD II, IIa	P. Benoit, O.P., J. T. Milik, and R. de Vaux, *Les grottes de Murabbaᶜat* (Oxford: Clarendon Press, 1961)
DJD III, IIIa	M. Baillet, J. T. Milik, and R. de Vaux, *Les 'petites grottes' de Qumrân* (Oxford: Clarendon Press, 1962)
DJD IV	J. A. Sanders, *The Psalms Scroll of Qumrân Cave 11 (11QPsᵃ)* (Oxford: Clarendon Press, 1965)
DJD V	J. M. Allegro with A. A. Anderson, *Qumrân Cave 4.I* (Oxford: Clarendon Press, 1968)
DJD VI	R. de Vaux and J. T. Milik, *Qumrân grotte 4.II: I. Archéologie; II: Tefillin, Mezuzot et Targums (4Q128–4Q157)* (Oxford: Clarendon Press, 1977)
DJD VII	M. Baillet, *Qumrân grotte 4.III (4Q482–4Q520)* (Oxford: Clarendon Press, 1982)
DJD VIII	E. Tov with the collaboration of R. A. Kraft, *The Greek Minor Prophets Scroll from Naḥal Ḥever (8ḤevXIIgr) (The Seiyâl Collection I)* (Oxford: Clarendon Press, 1990; repr. with corrections, 1995)
DJD IX	P. W. Skehan, E. Ulrich, and J. E. Sanderson, *Qumran Cave 4.IV: Palaeo-Hebrew and Greek Biblical Manuscripts* (Oxford: Clarendon Press, 1992)
DJD X	E. Qimron and J. Strugnell, *Qumran Cave 4.V: Miqṣat Maᶜaśe ha-Torah* (Oxford: Clarendon Press, 1994)
DJD XI	E. Eshel et al., in consultation with J. VanderKam and M. Brady, *Qumran Cave 4.VI: Poetical and Liturgical Texts, Part 1* (Oxford: Clarendon Press, 1998)
DJD XII	E. Ulrich, F. M. Cross, et al., *Qumran Cave 4.VII: Genesis to Numbers* (Oxford: Clarendon Press, 1994 [repr. 1999])
DJD XIII	H. Attridge et al., in consultation with J. VanderKam, *Qumran Cave 4.VIII: Parabiblical Texts, Part 1* (Oxford: Clarendon Press, 1994)
DJD XIV	E. Ulrich, F. M. Cross, et al., *Qumran Cave 4.IX: Deuteronomy, Joshua, Judges, Kings* (Oxford: Clarendon Press, 1995 [repr. 1999])
DJD XV	E. Ulrich et al., *Qumran Cave 4.X: The Prophets* (Oxford: Clarendon Press, 1997)

Abbreviations

DJD XVI   E. Ulrich et al., *Qumran Cave 4.XI: Psalms to Chronicles* (Oxford: Clarendon Press, 2000)

DJD XVII F. M. Cross, D. W. Parry, and E. Ulrich, *Qumran Cave 4.XII: 1–2 Samuel* (Oxford: Clarendon Press, forthcoming)

DJD XVIII J. M. Baumgarten, *Qumran Cave 4.XIII: The Damascus Document (4Q266–273)* (Oxford: Clarendon Press, 1996)

DJD XIX   M. Broshi et al., in consultation with J. VanderKam, *Qumran Cave 4.XIV: Parabiblical Texts, Part 2* (Oxford: Clarendon Press, 1995)

DJD XX   T. Elgvin et al., in consultation with J. A. Fitzmyer, S.J., *Qumran Cave 4.XV: Sapiential Texts, Part 1* (Oxford: Clarendon Press, 1997)

DJD XXI   S. Talmon, J. Ben-Dov, U. Glessmer, *Qumran Cave 4.XVI: Calendrical Texts* (Oxford: Clarendon Press, 2001)

DJD XXII G. Brooke et al., in consultation with J. VanderKam, *Qumran Cave 4.XVII: Parabiblical Texts, Part 3* (Oxford: Clarendon Press, 1996)

DJD XXIII F. García Martínez, E. J. C. Tigchelaar, and A. S. van der Woude, *Qumran Cave 11.II: 11Q2–18, 11Q20–30* (Oxford: Clarendon Press, 1998)

DJD XXIV M. J. W. Leith, *Wadi Daliyeh I: The Wadi Daliyeh Seal Impressions* (Oxford: Clarendon Press, 1997)

DJD XXV   É. Puech, *Qumran Cave 4.XVIII: Textes hébreux (4Q521–4Q528, 4Q576–4Q579)* (Oxford: Clarendon Press, 1998)

DJD XXVI P. Alexander and G. Vermes, *Qumran Cave 4.XIX: 4QSerekh Ha-Yaḥad and Two Related Texts* (Oxford: Clarendon Press, 1998)

DJD XXVII H. M. Cotton and A. Yardeni, *Aramaic, Hebrew, and Greek Documentary Texts from Naḥal Ḥever and Other Sites, with an Appendix Containing Alleged Qumran Texts (The Seiyâl Collection II)* (Oxford: Clarendon Press, 1997)

DJD XXVIII D. M. Gropp, *Wadi Daliyeh II: The Samaria Papyri from Wadi Daliyeh*; E. Schuller et al., in consultation with J. VanderKam and M. Brady, *Qumran Cave 4.XXVIII: Miscellanea, Part 2* (Oxford: Clarendon Press, 2001)

DJD XXIX E. Chazon et al., in consultation with J. VanderKam and M. Brady, *Qumran Cave 4.XX: Poetical and Liturgical Texts, Part 2* (Oxford: Clarendon Press, 1999)

DJD XXX   D. Dimant, *Qumran Cave 4.XXI: Parabiblical Texts, Part 4: Pseudo-Prophetic Texts* (Oxford: Clarendon Press, 2001)

DJD XXXI É. Puech, *Qumran Cave 4.XXII: Textes araméens, première partie: 4Q529–549* (Oxford: Clarendon Press, 2001)

DJD XXXII P. W. Flint and E. Ulrich, *Qumran Cave 1.II: The Isaiah Scrolls* (Oxford: Clarendon)

DJD XXXIII D. Pike, A. Skinner, in consultation with J. VanderKam and M. Brady, *Qumran Cave 4.XXIII: Unidentified Fragments* (Oxford: Clarendon Press, 2001)

DJD XXXIV J. Strugnell, D. J. Harrington, S.J., and T. Elgvin, in consultation with J. A. Fitzmyer, S.J., *Qumran Cave 4.XXIV: 4QInstruction (Mûsār lᵉMēvîn): 4Q415 ff.* (Oxford: Clarendon Press, 1999)

DJD XXXV J. Baumgarten et al., *Qumran Cave 4.XXV: Halakhic Texts* (Oxford: Clarendon Press, 1999)

DJD XXXVI S. J. Pfann, *Cryptic Texts*; P. Alexander et al., in consultation with J. VanderKam and M. Brady, *Miscellanea, Part 1: Qumran Cave 4.XXVI* (Oxford: Clarendon Press, 2000)

DJD XXXVII É. Puech, in consultation with J. VanderKam and M. Brady, *Qumran Cave 4.XXVII: Textes araméens, deuxième partie: 4Q550–575, 580–582* (Oxford: Clarendon Press, forthcoming)

DJD XXXVIII J. Charlesworth et al., in consultation with J. VanderKam and M. Brady, *Miscellaneous Texts from the Judaean Desert* (Oxford: Clarendon Press, 2000)

DJD XXXIX E. Tov (ed.), *The Texts from the Judaean Desert: Indices and an Introduction to the Discoveries in the Judaean Desert Series* (Oxford: Clarendon Press, 2002)

BIBLIOGRAPHY

Abegg, Martin G., Jr., Peter W. Flint, and Eugene Charles Ulrich (eds), *The Dead Sea Scrolls Bible: The Oldest Known Bible Translated for the First Time into English* (San Francisco: HarperSanFrancisco, 1999) [= *DSSB*]

Aejmelaeus, Anneli, *On the Trail of Septuagint Translators* (Kampen: Kok Pharos, 1993)

Alexander, Philip S., 'From Son of Adam to Second God: Transformations of the Biblical Enoch', in Michael E. Stone and Theodore A. Bergren (eds), *Biblical Figures outside the Bible* (Harrisburg, PA: Trinity Press International, 1998), pp. 87-122

– 'Retelling the Old Testament', in D. A. Carson and H. G. M. Williamson (eds), *It is Written: Scripture Citing Scripture: Essays in Honour of Barnabas Lindars, SSF* (Cambridge: Cambridge University Press, 1988), pp. 99-121

– 'The Redaction-History of Serekh ha-Yaḥad: a Proposal', *RevQ*, 17 (1996), 437-56

Alter, Robert, *Canon and Creativity* (New Haven: Yale University Press, 2000)

Anderson, G. W., 'Canonical and Non-Canonical', in P. R. Ackroyd and C. F. Evans (eds), *The Cambridge History of the Bible. I: From the Beginnings to Jerome* (Cambridge: Cambridge University Press, 1970), pp. 113-59

Aune, D. E., 'On the Origins of the "Council of Javneh" Myth', *JBL*, 110 (1991), 491-93

Avigad, N., 'The Palaeography of the Dead Sea Scrolls and Related Documents', in Chaim Rabin and Yigael Yadin (eds), *Aspects of the Dead Sea Scrolls*, Scripta Hierosolymitana, 4 (Jerusalem: Magnes, 1958), pp. 56-87

Baillet, M., and others, 'Le Travail d'édition des fragments manuscrits de Qumrân', *RB*, 63 (1956), 49-67

Barkay, Gabriel, 'The Priestly Benediction on Silver Plaques: the Significance of the Discovery at Ketef Hinnom' [in Hebrew], *Cathedra*, 52 (1989), 37-76

Barker, Kenneth, *The Balance of the NIV: What Makes a Good Translation* (Grand Rapids: Baker, 1999)

Barthélemy, Dominique, *Critique textuelle de l'Ancien Testament*, 3 vols, OBO 50 (Fribourg: Éditions Universitaires; Göttingen: Vandenhoeck & Ruprecht, 1982)

– *Études d'histoire du texte de l'Ancien Testament*, OBO, 21 (Fribourg: Éditions Universitaires; Göttingen: Vandenhoeck & Ruprecht, 1978)

– *Les Devanciers d'Aquila*, VTSup, 10 (Leiden: Brill, 1963)

– , and others, *Preliminary and Interim Report on the Hebrew Old Testament Text Project*, 5 vols (New York: United Bible Societies, 1973-80)

Barton, John, 'The Significance of a Fixed Canon of the Hebrew Bible', in Magne Sæbø (ed.), *Hebrew Bible/Old Testament: The History of Its Interpretation*, vol. 1, part 1 (Göttingen: Vandenhoeck & Ruprecht, 1996), pp. 67-83

Bauchet, J. M. P., 'Note sur les variantes de sens d'Isaïe 42 et 43 dans le manuscrit du Désert du Juda', *La nouvelle revue théologique*, 71 (1949), 304-5

Baumgarten, Albert I., 'Pharisees', in *EDSS*, II, pp. 657-63

Baumgarten, Joseph M., 'The Cave 4 Versions of the Qumran Penal Code', *JJS*, 43 (1992), 268-76

– 'A "Scriptural" Citation in 4Q Fragments of the Damascus Document', *JJS*, 43 (1992), 95-98

Bibliography

Beckwith, Roger, *The Old Testament Canon of the New Testament Church and its Background in Early Judaism* (Grand Rapids, MI: Eerdmans, 1985)

Ben-Dov, Jonathan, 'A Presumed Citation of Esther 3:7 in 4QD^b', *DSD*, 6 (1999), 282-84

Bernstein, Moshe J., '4Q252 i 2 לעולם באדם רוחי ידור לא: Biblical Text or Biblical Interpretation', *RevQ*, 16 (1994), 421-27

– 'Introductory Formulas for Citation and Re-citation of Biblical Verses in the Qumran Pesharim', *DSD*, 1 (1994), 30-70

– 'Pentateuchal Interpretation at Qumran', in *DSSAFY*, I, pp. 128-59

– 'Scriptures: Quotation and Use', in *EDSS*, II, pp. 839-42

– , with Florentino García Martínez and John Kampen (eds), *Legal Texts and Legal Issues: Proceedings of the Second Meeting of the International Organization for Qumran Studies, Cambridge 1995, Published in Honour of Joseph M. Baumgarten*, STDJ, 23 (Leiden: Brill, 1997)

Beyer, Klaus, *Die aramäischen Texte vom Toten Meer*, Ergänzungsband (Göttingen: Vandenhoeck & Ruprecht, 1994)

Bickerman, Elias J., *The Jews in the Greek Age* (Cambridge, MA: Harvard University Press, 1988)

Bieberstein, Klaus, *Josua–Jordan–Jericho: Archäologie, Geschichte und Theologie der Landnahmeerzählungen Josua 1-6*, OBO, 143 (Freiburg: Universitätsverlag; Göttingen: Vandenhoeck & Ruprecht, 1995)

Black, Fiona C., 'Lost Prophecies! Scholars Amazed! *Weekly World News* and the Bible', *Sem*, 82 (1998), 127-49

Black, Matthew, *Apocalypsis Henochi Graece*, Pseudepigrapha Veteris Testamenti Graece, 3 (Leiden: Brill, 1970)

– *The Book of Enoch or I Enoch*, Studia in Veteris Testamenti Pseudepigrapha, 7 (Leiden: Brill, 1985)

Bloch, J. S., *Studien zur Geschichte der althebräischen Literatur* (Leipzig: Leiner, 1875)

Boer, Pieter Arie Hendrik de, *Research into the Text of 1 Samuel I-XVI: A Contribution to the Study of the Books of Samuel* (Amsterdam: Paris, 1938)

Bonani, G., and others, 'Radiocarbon Dating of the Dead Sea Scrolls', *'Atiqot*, 20 (1991), 27-32

Brenton, Lancelot C. L., *The Septuagint Version of the Old Testament with an English Translation* (London: Samuel Bagster, 1879)

Brock, Sebastian P., *The Recensions of the Septuagint Version of 1 Samuel* (Oxford D.Phil. dissertation); now published as Sebastian P. Brock, *The Recensions of the Septuagint Version of 1 Samuel*, Quaderni di Henoch, 9 (Turino: Zamorani, 1996)

Brockington, L. H., *The Hebrew Text of the Old Testament* (Oxford: Oxford University Press, 1973)

Brooke, George J., '*E Pluribus Unum*: Textual Variety and Definitive Interpretation in the Qumran Scrolls', in *DSSTHC*, pp. 107-19

– 'Isaiah 40:3 and the Wilderness Community', in *NQTS*, pp. 117-32

– 'Psalms 105 and 106 at Qumran', *RevQ*, 14 (1989), 267-92

– 'Rewritten Bible', in *EDSS*, II, pp. 777-81

– 'The Biblical Texts in the Qumran Commentaries: Scribal Errors or Exegetical Variants?', in Craig A. Evans and William F. Stinespring (eds), *Early Jewish and Christian Exegesis: Studies in Memory of William Hugh Brownlee*, Homage Series, 10 (Atlanta, GA: Scholars Press, 1987), pp. 85-100

– 'The Temple Scroll and LXX Exodus 35-40', in *SSCW*, pp. 81-106

– 'The Textual Tradition of the *Temple Scroll* and Recently Published Manuscripts of the Pentateuch', in Devorah Dimant and Uriel Rappaport (eds), *The Dead Sea Scrolls: Forty Years of Research*, STDJ, 10 (Leiden: Brill; Jerusalem: Magnes, 1992), pp. 261-82

Bibliography

- 'Torah in the Qumran Scrolls', in Helmut Merklein and others (eds), *Bibel in jüdischer und christlicher Tradition: Festschrift für Johann Maier zum 60. Geburtstag*, Athanäums Monografien Theologie, 88 (Frankfurt am Main: Hain, 1993), pp. 97-120

- , and Barnabas Lindars (eds), *Septuagint, Scrolls, and Cognate Writings: Papers Presented to the International Symposium on the Septuagint and Its Relations to the Dead Sea Scrolls and Other Writings (Manchester, 1990)*, SBL Septuagint and Cognate Studies Series, 33 (Atlanta, GA: Scholars Press, 1992) [=SSCW]

- , and Florentino García Martínez (eds), *New Qumran Texts and Studies: Proceedings of the First Meeting of the International Organization for Qumran Studies, Paris 1992*, STDJ, 15 (Leiden: Brill, 1994) [=NQTS]

Brown, William P., 'Reassessing the Text-Critical Value of Septuagint-Genesis 1: A Response to Martin Rösel', *BIOSCS*, 32 (1999), 35-39

Brownlee, William H., 'The Habakkuk Midrash and the Targum of Jonathan', *JJS*, 7 (1956), 169-86

- 'The Jerusalem Habakkuk Scroll', *BASOR*, 112 (1948), 8-18

- 'Biblical Interpretation Among the Sectaries of the Dead Sea Scrolls', *BA*, 14 (1951), 54-76

- 'The Literary Significance of the Bisection of Isaiah in the Ancient Scroll of Isaiah from Qumran', in *Proceedings of the 25th Congress of Orientalists*, 2 vols (Moscow: Izdatel'stvo Vostochnoi Literatury, 1962-63), I, pp. 431-37

- *The Text of Habakkuk in the Ancient Commentary from Qumran*, JBL Monograph Series, 11 (Philadelphia: Society of Biblical Literature and Exegesis, 1959)

- *The Meaning of the Qumrân Scrolls for the Bible with Special Attention to the Book of Isaiah* (New York: Oxford University Press, 1964)

- 'The Text of Isaiah vi 13 in the Light of DSIa', *VT*, 1 (1951), 296-98

Bruce, F. F., *The Books and the Parchments* (London: Pickering and Inglis, 1971)

- *The New Testament Documents: Are They Reliable?*, 5th edn (London: Inter-Varsity Fellowship, 1960)

Budde, Karl, *Der Kanon des Alten Testaments* (Giessen: Ricker, 1900)

Buhl, Frants, *Canon and Text of the Old Testament*, trans. by John Macpherson (Edinburgh: T&T Clark, 1892)

Burkert, Walter, *The Orientalizing Revolution: Near Eastern Influence on Greek Culture in the Early Archaic Age*, Revealing Antiquity, 5 (Cambridge, MA: Harvard University Press, 1992)

Burrows, Millar, 'Variant Readings in the Isaiah Manuscript', *BASOR*, 111 (1948), 16-24 and 113 (1949), 24-32

- *Diligently Compared: The Revised Standard Version and the King James Version of the Old Testament* (London: Nelson, 1964)

- , with John C. Trever and William H. Brownlee (eds), *The Dead Sea Scrolls of St. Mark's Monastery, vol 1: The Isaiah Manuscript and the Habakkuk Commentary* (New Haven, CT: ASOR, 1950)

Buxtorf, J., Jr., *Anticritica* (Basel: Ludovici Regis, 1653)

Campbell, Jonathan G., *The Use of Scripture in the Damascus Document 1-8, 19-20*, BZAW, 228 (Berlin: de Gruyter, 1995)

Cappellus, L., *Critica sacra* (Paris: Cramoisy, 1650)

Carmignac, Jean, 'Six Passages d'Isaïe éclairés par Qumran', in S. Wagner (ed.), *Bibel und Qumran: H. Bardtke Festschrift* (Berlin: Evangelische Haupt-Bibelgesellschaft, 1968), pp. 37-46

- 'Les citations de l'Ancien Testament dans "La Guerre des Fils de Lumière contre les Fils de Ténèbres"', *RB*, 63 (1956), 234-60, 375-90

Cassuto, U., *A Commentary on the Book of Genesis, vol. 1: From Adam to Noah (Genesis I-VI 8)*, trans. by Israel Abrahams (Jerusalem: Magnes, 1961)

Bibliography

Catastini, Alessandro, *Isaia ed Ezechia: Studio di storia della tradizione di II Re 18-20 // Is. 36-39*, Studi Semitici Nuova serie, 6 (Rome: Università degli Studi "La Sapienza", 1989)

Cavallo, Guglielmo, *Libri scritture scribi a Ercolano: Introductione allo studio dei materiale greci*, Cronache Ercolanesi Supplemento, 1 ([Naples]: Macchiaroli, 1983)

Charles, R. H., *The Book of Enoch or 1 Enoch*, 2nd edn (Oxford: Clarendon Press, 1912)

– , (ed.), *The Apocrypha and Pseudepigrapha of the Old Testament in English With Introductions and Critical and Explanatory Notes to the Several Books. vol. II Pseudepigrapha* (Oxford: Clarendon Press, 1913)

– *The Book of Jubilees or The Little Genesis* (London: Black, 1902; reprinted Jerusalem: Maqor, 1972)

Childs, Brevard S., *Introduction to the Old Testament as Scripture* (Philadelphia: Fortress Press, 1979)

Collin, Matthieu, 'Recherches sur l'histoire textuelle du prophète Michée', *VT*, 21 (1971), 281-97

Collins, John J., 'The Court-Tales in Daniel and the Development of Apocalyptic', *JBL*, 94 (1975), 218-34

– , and Deborah A. Green, 'The Tales from the Persian Court (4Q550^{a-e})', in Bernd Kollmann, Wolfgang Reinbold and Annette Steudel (eds), *Antikes Judentum und Frühes Christentum: Festschrift für Hartmut Stegemann zum 65. Geburtstag*, Beihefte zur Zeitschrift für die neutestamentliche Wissenschaft, 97 (Berlin: de Gruyter, 1999), pp. 39-50

Conzelmann, Hans, *1 Corinthians: A Commentary on the First Epistle to the Corinthians*, trans. by James W. Leitch (Philadelphia: Fortress Press, 1975); translated from *Der erste Brief an die Korinther*, Kritisch-Exegetischer Kommentar über das Neue Testament, 5, 11th edn (Göttingen: Vandenhoeck & Ruprecht, 1969)

Cook, Edward, 'The Tale of Bagasraw', in *DSSB*, pp. 437-39

Cook, Johann, 'Orthographical Peculiarities in the Dead Sea Biblical Scrolls', *RevQ*, 14 (1989; The Texts of Qumran and the History of the Community: Proceedings of the Groningen Congress on the Dead Sea Scrolls (20-23 August 1989), vol. 1: Biblical Texts), 293-305

– 'The Dichotomy of 1QIsa^a', in Zdzislaw J. Kapera, *Intertestamental Essays in Honour of Józef Tadeusz Milik*, Studies Offered to Jósef Tadeusz Milik, Qumranica Mogilanensia, 6, Part I (Kraków: Enigma, 1992), pp. 7-24

– *The Septuagint of Proverbs: Jewish and/or Hellenistic Proverbs? Concerning the Hellenistic Colouring of LXX Proverbs*, VTSup, 69 (Leiden: Brill, 1997)

Cowley, A., *Aramaic Papyri of the Fifth Century B.C.* (Oxford: Clarendon Press, 1923)

Crawford, Sidnie White, 'Has *Esther* been found at Qumran? *4QProto-Esther* and the *Esther* Corpus', *RevQ*, 17 (1996), 307-25

– 'Reworked Pentateuch', in *EDSS*, II, pp. 775-77

– 'The "Rewritten Bible" at Qumran: A Look at Three Texts', *ErIsr*, 26 (Archaeological, Historical and Geographical Studies (Frank Moore Cross Volume, 1999)), 1*-8*

– 'The Book of Esther', in *The New Interpreter's Bible* (Nashville, TN: Abingdon Press, 1999), III, pp. 853-941

– 'The Additions to Esther', in *The New Interpreter's Bible* (Nashville, TN: Abingdon Press, 1999), III, pp. 943-72

Crisafulli, Edouardo, 'The Translator as Textual Critic and the Potential of Transparent Discourse', *The Translator*, 5 (1999), 83-107

Cross, Frank M., Jr., 'The Contribution of the Qumrân Discoveries to the Study of the Biblical Text', *IEJ*, 16 (1966), 81-95

– 'A New Qumran Biblical Fragment Related to the Original Hebrew Underlying the Septuagint', *BASOR*, 132 (1953), 15-26

Bibliography

– , and Shemaryahu Talmon (eds), *Qumran and the History of the Biblical Text* (Cambridge, MA: Harvard University Press, 1975) [=*QHBT*]

– 'Paleographical Dates of the Manuscripts', in James H. Charlesworth, and others (eds), *The Dead Sea Scrolls: Hebrew, Aramaic, and Greek Texts With English Translations*, I: *Rule of the Community and Related Documents* (Tübingen: Mohr-Siebeck; Louisville: Westminster John Knox, 1994), p. 57

– 'Some Notes on a Generation of Qumran Studies', in *MQC*, I, pp. 1-14

– 'The Ammonite Oppression of the Tribes of Gad and Reuben: Missing Verses from 1 Samuel 11 Found in 4QSamuel^a', in Emanuel Tov (ed.), *The Hebrew and Greek Texts of Samuel: 1980 Proceedings IOSCS – Vienna* (Jerusalem: Academon, 1980), pp. 105-19

– 'The Evolution of a Theory of Local Texts', in *QHBT*, pp. 306-20

– , David Noel Freedman and James A. Sanders (eds), *Scrolls from Qumrân Cave I: The Great Isaiah Scroll, the Order of the Community, the* Pesher *to Habakkuk* (Jerusalem: The Albright Institute of Archaeological Research and The Shrine of the Book, 1972)

– *From Epic to Canon: History and Literature in Ancient Israel* (Baltimore: Johns Hopkins University Press, 1998)

– 'The History of the Biblical Text in the Light of Discoveries in the Judaean Desert', *HTR*, 57 (1964), 281-99

– 'The History of the Biblical Text in the Light of Discoveries in the Judaean Desert, in *QHBT*, pp. 177-95

– *The Ancient Library of Qumrân and Modern Biblical Studies: The Haskell Lectures 1956-1957* (London: Duckworth, 1958); *The Ancient Library of Qumran* (3rd edn, Sheffield: Sheffield Academic Press, 1995)

Cryer, Frederick H., and Thomas L. Thompson (eds), *Qumran between the Old and New Testaments*, JSOTSup, 290, Copenhagen International Seminar, 6 (Sheffield: Sheffield Academic Press, 1998) [= *QONT*]

Dahood, Mitchell, 'Isaiah 19,11 ḥkmy and 1QIsa^a ḥkmyh', *Bib*, 56 (1975), 420

Davies, Philip R., 'Halakhah at Qumran', in Philip R. Davies and Richard T. White (eds), *A Tribute to Geza Vermes: Essays on Jewish and Christian Literature and History*, JSOTSup 100 (Sheffield: JSOT Press, 1990), pp. 37-50

Davila, James R., 'Text-Type and Terminology: Genesis and Exodus as Test Cases', *RevQ*, 16 (1993), 3-37

Delitzsch, Friedrich, *Die Lese- und Schreibfehler im Alten Testament* (Berlin: de Gruyter, 1920)

Dillmann, A., 'Beiträge aus dem Buch der Jubiläen zur Kritik des Pentateuch-Textes', in *Sitzungsberichte der königlichen preussischen Akademie der Wissenschaften zu Berlin*, 1 (Berlin: Verlag der königlichen Akademie der Wissenschaften, 1883), pp. 323-40

– 'Das Buch der Jubiläen oder die kleine Genesis: aus dem Äthiopischen übersetzt', *Jahrbücher der Biblischen Wissenschaft*, 3 (1851), 1-96

– *Genesis: Critically and Exegetically Expounded*, trans. by Wm B. Stevenson, 2 vols (Edinburgh: T&T Clark, 1897)

Dimant, Devorah, 'The Hebrew Bible in the Dead Sea Scrolls: Torah Quotations in the *Damascus Document*' [Hebrew with English summary], in Michael Fishbane and Emanuel Tov with the assistance of Weston W. Fields (eds), *"Sha'arei Talmon": Studies in the Bible, Qumran, and the Ancient Near East Presented to Shemaryahu Talmon* (Winona Lake, IN: Eisenbrauns, 1992), pp. 113*-22*

– 'The Qumran Manuscripts: Contents and Significance', in Devorah Dimant and Lawrence H. Schiffman (eds), *A Time to Prepare the Way in the Wilderness: Papers on the Qumran Scrolls by Fellows of the Institute for Advanced Studies of the Hebrew University, Jerusalem, 1989–1990*, STDJ, 16 (Leiden: Brill, 1995), pp. 23-58

Bibliography

– 'Use and Interpretation of Mikra in the Apocrypha and Pseudepigrapha', in Martin Jan Mulder and Harry Sysling (eds), *Mikra: Text, Translation, Reading and Interpretation of the Hebrew Bible in Ancient Judaism and Early Christianity*, Compendia Rerum Iudaicarum ad Novum Testamentum, II, 1 (Assen: Van Gorcum; Philadelphia: Fortress Press, 1988), pp. 379-419

Dohmen, Christoph, 'Zur Gründung der Gemeinde von Qumran (1QS VIII-IX)', *RevQ*, 11 (1982), 81-96

Driver, S. R., *Notes on the Hebrew Text and the Topography of the Books of Samuel*, 2nd edn (Oxford: Clarendon Press, 1913)

Duhm, Bernhard, *Das Buch Jesaia, Handkommentar zum Alten Testament* (Göttingen: Vandenhoeck & Ruprecht, 1902)

Duncan, Julie A., 'New Readings for the "Blessing of Moses" from Qumran', *JBL*, 114 (1995), 273-90

Ehrman, Bart D., *The Orthodox Corruption of Scripture: The Effect of Early Christological Controversies on the Text of the New Testament* (New York: Oxford University Press, 1993)

Eisenman, Robert H., and James M. Robinson, *A Facsimile Edition of the Dead Sea Scrolls*, 2 vols (Washington, D.C.: Biblical Archaeology Society, 1991)

– , and Michael Wise, *The Dead Sea Scrolls Uncovered: The First Complete Translation and Interpretation of 50 Key Documents Withheld for Over 35 Years* (New York: Penguin, 1992)

Eissfeldt, Otto, 'Varianten der Jesaja-Rolle', *Theologische Literaturzeitung*, 74 (1949), cols 221–26

– *Einleitung in das Alte Testament*, 3rd edn (Tübingen: Mohr-Siebeck, 1964); = *The Old Testament: An Introduction*, trans. by Peter R. Ackroyd (Oxford: Blackwell, 1965; repr. 1974)

Elliger, Karl, *Studien zum Habakuk-Kommentar vom Toten Meer*, Beiträge zur historischen Theologie, 15 (Tübingen: Mohr-Siebeck, 1953)

– , and W. Rudolph, *Biblia Hebraica Stuttgartensia*, (Stuttgart: Deutsche Bibelgesellschaft, 1967/77)

Ellingworth, Paul, 'Theological Reflections on the Textual Criticism of the Bible', *The Bible Translator*, 46 (1995), 119-25

Elwolde, John, 'Distinguishing the Linguistic and the Exegetical: The Biblical Book of Numbers in the Damascus Document', *DSD*, 7 (2000), 1-25

Eshel, Esther, '4QDeut[n]—A Text That Has Undergone Harmonistic Editing', *HUCA*, 62 (1991), 117-54

Eshel, H., 'The Historical Background of the Pesher Interpreting Joshua's Curse on the Rebuilder of Jericho', *RevQ*, 15 (1992), 409-20

Evans, Craig A., 'The Text of Isaiah 6: 9-10', *ZAW*, 94 (1982), 415-18

Eybers, I. H., 'Some Light on the Canon of the Qumran Sect', in Sid Z. Leiman (ed.), *Papers Read at 5th Meeting of Die OT Werkgemeenskap in Suid-Afrika* (1961), pp. 1-9; republished in Sid Z. Leiman (ed.), *The Canon and Masorah of the Hebrew Bible* (New York: Ktav, 1974), pp. 23-36

Fabry, Heinz-Josef, 'Der Umgang mit der kanonisierten Tora in Qumran', in Erich Zenger (ed.), *Die Tora als Kanon für Juden und Christen*, Herders Biblische Studien, 10 (Freiburg: Herder, 1996), pp. 293-327

– 'Die Qumrantexte und das biblische Kanonproblem', in Beyerle, Stefan, Günter Mayer, and Hans Strauß (eds), *Recht und Ethos im Alten Testament – Gestalt und Wirkung, Festschrift for H. Seebass* (Neukirchen-Vluyn: Neukirchner Verlag, 1999), pp. 251-71

Fee, Gordon D., *The First Epistle to the Corinthians*, The New International Commentary on the New Testament (Grand Rapids, MI: Eerdmans, 1987)

Fitzmyer, Joseph A., 'The Use of Explicit Old Testament Quotations in Qumran Literature and in the New Testament', *NTS*, 7 (1960-61), 297-333

Flint, Peter W., 'Appendix: Index of Passages in the Biblical, Apocryphal, and "Pseudepigraphal" Scrolls', in Alan J. Avery-Peck, Jacob Neusner, and Bruce D. Chilton (eds), *Judaism in Late Antiquity, Part Five: The Judaism of Qumran: A Systematic Reading of the Dead Sea Scrolls. Volume One: Way of Life*, Handbuch

Bibliography

der Orientalistik. Judaistik. (Leiden: Brill, 2000), pp. 87-103

– 'The Isaiah Scrolls from the Judean Desert', in Craig C. Broyles and Craig A. Evans (eds), *Writing and Reading the Scroll of Isaiah: Studies of an Interpretative Tradition*, 2 vols, FIOTL, I, 1 and 2; VTSup, 70, 1 and 2 (Leiden: Brill, 1997), II, pp. 491-511

– 'The Psalms Scrolls from the Judaean Desert: Relationships and Textual Affiliations', in *NQTS*, pp. 31-52

– 'The Septuagint Version of Isaiah 23:1-14 and the Massoretic Text', *BIOSCS*, 21 (1988), 35-54

– , and James C. VanderKam (eds), *The Dead Sea Scrolls after Fifty Years: A Comprehensive Assessment*, 2 vols (Leiden: Brill, 1998-99) [=DSSAFY]

– *The Dead Sea Psalms Scrolls and the Book of Psalms*, STDJ, 17 (Leiden: Brill, 1997)

Flusser, David, 'The Text of Isa. xlix, 17 in the DSS', *Textus*, 2 (1962), 140-42

Freedman, D. N., and K. A. Mathews (with contributions by R. S. Hanson), *The Paleo-Hebrew Leviticus Scroll (11QpaleoLev)* (Winona Lake, IN: American Schools of Oriental Research, 1985)

Freedman, David Noel, and others (eds), *The Anchor Bible Dictionary*, 6 vols (New York: Doubleday, 1992) [=ABD]

Friedman, Meir, (ed.), *Mekhilta Beshallaḥ* (repr. New York: OM, 1948)

Fürst, J., *Der Kanon des Alten Testaments nach den Überlieferungen in Talmud und Midrasch* (Leipzig: Dörffling & Franke, 1868)

García Martínez, Florentino, 'Le livre d'Isaïe à Qumran', *Le Monde de la Bible*, 49 (1987), 43-45

– 'Lista de MSS procedentes de Qumran', *Henoch*, 11 (1989), 149-232

– , and Eibert J.C. Tigchelaar (eds), *The Dead Sea Scrolls Study Edition*, 2 vols (Leiden: Brill; Grand Rapids, MI: Eerdmans, 1997-1998) [=DSSSE]

– *The Dead Sea Scrolls Translated: The Qumran Texts in English*, trans. by Wilfred G. E. Watson (Leiden: Brill, 1994)

Gebhard, C., (ed.), *Spinozae Opera: Im Auftrag der Heidelberger Akademie der Wissenschaften* (Heidelberg: Carl Winters Universitätsbuchhandlung, 1925)

Geller, M. J., 'The Survival of Babylonian Wissenschaft in Later Tradition', in Sanna Aro and R. M. Whiting (eds), *The Heirs of Assyria: Proceedings of the Opening Symposium of the Assyrian and Babylonian Intellectual Heritage Project Held in Tvärminne, Finland, October 8-11, 1998: Melammu Symposia*, vol. 1 (Helsinki, 2000), pp. 1-6

Gerhardsson, Birger, *Memory and Manuscript: Oral Tradition and Written Transmission in Rabbinic Judaism and Early Christianity*, Acta Seminarii Neotestamentici Upsaliensis, 22, trans. by Eric J. Sharp (Lund: Gleerup; Copenhagen: Munksgaard, 1961); republished in *Tradition and Transmission in Early Christianity*, Coniectanea Neotestamentica, 20, trans. by Eric J. Sharp (Grand Rapids, MI: Eerdmans; Livonia: Dove, 1998)

Gese, Hartmut, 'Die dreifache Gestaltwerdung des Alten Testaments', in Martin Klopfenstein and others (eds), *Mitte der Schrift? Ein jüdisch-christliches Gespräch: Texte des Berner Symposions vom 6.-12. Januar 1985*, Judaica et Christiana, 11 (Bern: Peter Lang, 1987), pp. 299-328

Gesenius, Wilhelm, *Der Prophet Jesaia*, 3 vols (Leipzig: Vogel, 1820-1821)

Glessmer, Uwe, 'Liste der biblischen Texte aus Qumran', *RevQ*, 16 (1993), 153-92

– 'The Otot-texts and the Problem of Intercalations in the Context of the 364-day Calendar', in Heinz-Josef Fabry, Armin Lange and Hermann Lichtenberger (eds), *Qumranstudien: Vorträge und Beiträge der Teilnehmer des Qumranseminars auf dem internationalen Treffen der Society of Biblical Literature, Münster, 25.-26. Juli 1993*, Schriften des Institutum Judaicum Delitzschianum, 4 (Göttingen: Vandenhoeck & Ruprecht, 1996), pp. 125-64

Golb, Norman, 'Khirbet Qumran and the Manuscripts of the Judaean Wilderness: Observations on the Logic of Their Investigation', *Journal of Near Eastern Studies*, 49 (1990), 103-14

– 'The Problem of Origin and Identification of the Dead Sea Scrolls', *Proceedings of the American Philosophical Society*, 124 (1980), 1-24

– 'Who Hid the Dead Sea Scrolls?, *BA*, 48 (1985), 68-82

– *Who Wrote the Dead Sea Scrolls: The Search for the Secret of Qumran* (New York: Scribner, 1995)

Goldberg, Ilana, 'Variant Readings in Pesher Habakkuk' [Hebrew], *Textus*, 17 (1994), כ-כד

Goshen-Gottstein, M. H., 'The Psalms Scroll (11QPsª): A Problem of Canon and Text', *Textus*, 5 (1966), 22-33

– 'The Textual Criticism of the Old Testament: Rise, Decline, Rebirth', *JBL*, 102 (1983), 365-99

– (ed.), *The Hebrew University Bible: The Book of Isaiah* (Jerusalem: Magnes, 1995)

Gottstein, M. H., 'Bible Quotations in the Sectarian Dead Sea Scrolls', *VT*, 3 (1953), 79-82

– 'Die Jesaia-Rolle im Lichte von Peschitta und Targum', *Bib*, 35 (1954), 51-71

Grabbe, Lester L., *Judaism from Cyrus to Hadrian*, 2 vols (London: SCM Press, 1992)

Graetz, H., 'Der Abschluss des Kanons des Alten Testaments und die Differenz von kanonischen und extrakanonischen Büchern nach Josephus und Talmud', *Monatschrift für Geschichte und Wissenschaft des Judentums*, 35 (1886), 281-98

Greenfield, Jonas C., 'The Words of Levi son of Jacob in Damascus Document IV, 15-19', *RevQ*, 13 (1988), 319-22

Greenspahn, Frederick E., 'Why Prophecy Ceased', *JBL*, 108 (1989), 37-49

Greenstein, E. L., 'Misquotation of Scripture in the Dead Sea Scrolls', in Barry Walfish (ed.), *The Frank Talmage Memorial Volume* (Haifa: Haifa University Press, 1993), pp. 71-83

Gutjahr, Paul, *An American Bible: A History of the Good Book in the United States, 1777-1880* (Stanford, CA: Stanford University Press, 1999)

– *In Discordance with Scriptures: American Protestant Battles over Translating the Bible* (New York: Oxford University Press, 1999)

Hallo, William W., 'The Concept of Canonicity in Cuneiform and Biblical Literature: A Comparative Appraisal', in K. Lawson Younger, Jr., William W. Hallo, and Bernard Frank Batto (eds), *The Biblical Canon in Comparative Perspective: Scripture in Context 4*, Ancient Near Eastern Texts and Studies, 11 (Lewiston, NY: Mellen Press, 1991), pp. 1-19

Hanhart, Robert, 'The Translation of the Septuagint in Light of Earlier Tradition and Subsequent Influences', in *SSCW*, pp. 339-79

Hanson, Richard S., 'Paleo-Hebrew Scripts in the Hasmonean Age', *BASOR*, 175 (1964), 26-42

Harding, James E., 'The Wordplay between the Roots כשל and שכל in the Literature of the *Yaḥad*', *RevQ*, 19 (1999), 69-82

Harrington, Daniel J., 'Palestinian Adaptations of Biblical Narratives and Prophecies I: The Bible Rewritten (Narratives)', in Robert A. Kraft and George W. E. Nickelsburg (eds), *Early Judaism and Its Modern Interpreters*, The Bible and Its Modern Interpreters, 2 (Philadelphia: Fortress Press; Atlanta, GA: Scholars Press, 1986), pp. 239-47

– 'The Biblical Text of Pseudo-Philo's *Liber Antiquitatum Biblicarum*', *CBQ*, 33 (1971), 1-17

Hartman, Louis F., (ed.), *Textual Notes on the New American Bible* (Paterson, NJ: St. Anthony's Guild, 1970)

Hartmut Stegemann, 'The Qumran Essenes – Local Members of the Main Jewish Union in Late Second Temple Times', in *MQC*, I, pp. 83-166

Hempel, Charlotte, 'Methodologische Beobachtungen zur Frage der Kriterien zur Bestimmung "essenischer Verfasserschaft" von Qumrantexten', in Jörg Frey and Hartmut Stegemann (eds), *Brennpunkte gegenwärtiger Qumranforschung* (Paderborn: Bonifazius, forthcoming)

Bibliography

- 'The Penal Code Reconsidered', in Moshe Bernstein, Florentino García Martínez and John Kampen (eds), *Legal Texts and Legal Issues: Proceedings of the Second Meeting of the International Organization for Qumran Studies, Cambridge 1995, Published in Honour of Joseph M. Baumgarten*, STDJ, 23 (Leiden: Brill, 1997), pp. 337-48

- *The Laws of the Damascus Document: Sources, Tradition and Redaction*, STDJ, 29 (Leiden: Brill, 1998)

Hendel, Ronald S., 'On the Text-Critical Value of Septuagint Genesis: A Reply to Rösel', *BIOSCS*, 32 (1999), 31-34

- 'Scriptures: Translations', in *EDSS*, II, pp. 836-39

- *The Text of Genesis 1-11: Textual Studies and Critical Edition* (New York: Oxford University Press, 1998)

Herbert, Edward D., '4QSam^a and its Relationship to the LXX: an Exploration in Stemmatological Analysis', in Bernard A. Taylor (ed.), *IX Congress of the International Organization for Septuagint and Cognate Studies, Cambridge 1995*, Society of Biblical Literature Septuagint and Cognate Studies Series, 45 (Atlanta, GA: Scholars Press, 1997), pp. 37-55

- *Reconstructing Biblical Dead Sea Scrolls: A New Method Applied to the Reconstruction of 4QSam^a*, STDJ, 22 (Leiden: Brill, 1997)

Hoegenhaven, Jesper, 'The First Isaiah Scroll from Qumran (1QIs^a) and the Massoretic Text: Some Reflections with Special Regard to Isaiah 1-12', *JSOT*, 28 (1984), 17-35

Holm-Nielsen, Svend, *Noter til bibeloversaettelsen af 1992: Rettelser I den hebraiske tekst* (København: Danish Bible Society, 1997)

Horgan, Maurya P., 'A Lament over Jerusalem ('4Q179')', *JSS*, 18 (1973), 222-34

- 'Palestinian Adaptations of Biblical Narratives and Prophecies, II: The Bible Explained (Prophecies)', in Robert A. Kraft and George W. E. Nickelsburg (eds), *Early Judaism and Its Modern Interpreters*, The Bible and Its Modern Interpreters, 2 (Philadelphia: Fortress Press; Atlanta, GA: Scholars Press, 1986), pp. 247-53

- *Pesharim: Qumran Interpretations of Biblical Books*, CBQ Monograph Series, 8 (Washington, DC: Catholic Biblical Association of America, 1979)

Horowitz, Haim S., and Israel A. Rabin, *Mechilta d'Rabbi Ismael cum Variis Lectionibus et Adnotationibus* (Jerusalem: Bamberger & Wahrman, 1960)

Houbigant, C. F., *Biblia Hebraica cum notis criticis et versione latina ad notas criticas facta* (Paris: Lutetiae-Parisiorum, 1753)

Housman, A. E., 'The Application of Thought to Textual Criticism', *Proceedings of the Classical Association*, 18 (1922), 67-84

Humphreys, W. Lee, 'A Life-Style for Diaspora: A Study of the Tales of Esther and Daniel', *JBL*, 92 (1973), 211-23

Hunzinger, Claus-Hunno, 'Fragmente einer älteren Fassung des Buches Milḥamā aus Höhle 4 von Qumrān', *ZAW*, 69 (1957), 131-51

Iwry, Samuel, 'והנמצא—A Striking Variant Reading in 1QIs^a', *Textus*, 5 (1966), 34-43

- '*Maṣṣēbāh* and *Bāmāh* in 1Q Isaiah^a 6 13', *JBL*, 76 (1957), 225-32

Jacobson, Howard, *A Commentary on Pseudo-Philo's* Liber Antiquitatum Biblicarum *with Latin Text and English Translation*, Arbeiten zur Geschichte des antiken Judentums und des Urchristentums, 31, 2 vols (Leiden: Brill, 1996)

James, F. D., *A Critical Examination of the Text of Isaiah, Based on the Dead Sea Scroll of Isaiah (DSIa), the Masoretic Text, the Septuagint* (doctoral diss., Boston: Boston University, 1959)

Janzen, J. Gerald, 'Isaiah 41:27: Reading הנה הנומא in 1QIsa^a and הנה הנם in the Masoretic Text', *JBL*, 113 (1994), 597-607

Bibliography

Jarick, John, 'The Bible's "Festival Scrolls" among the Dead Sea Scrolls', in Stanley E. Porter and Craig A. Evans (eds), *The Scrolls and the Scriptures: Qumran Fifty Years After*, JSPSup, 26, Roehampton Institute London Papers, 3 (Sheffield: Sheffield Academic Press, 1997), pp. 170-82

Jellicoe, Sidney, *The Septuagint and Modern Study* (Oxford: Clarendon Press, 1968)

Jellinek, Adolph, *Bet ha-Midrasch*, 6 vols, 2nd edn (Jerusalem: Bamberger & Wahrmann, 1938)

Jepsen A., 'Zur Kanongeschichte des Alten Testaments', *ZAW*, 71 (1959), 114-36

Jull, A. J. Timothy, and others, 'Radiocarbon Dating of Scrolls and Linen Fragments from the Judaean Desert', *Radiocarbon*, 37 (1995), 11-19

Kahle, P., review of Elliger, Karl, *Studien zum Habakuk-Kommentar vom Toten Meer*, Beiträge zur historischen Theologie, 15 (Tübingen: Mohr, 1953), *Theologische Literaturzeitung*, 79 (1954), 478-79

– *Die hebräischen Handschriften aus der Höhle* (Stuttgart: Kohlhammer, 1951)

Kittel, Rudolf, *Über die Notwendigkeit und Möglichkeit einer neuen Ausgabe der Hebräischen Bibel* (Leipzig: Edelman, 1901)

– , (ed.), *Biblia Hebraica*, 3rd edn (Stuttgart: Württembergische Bibelanstalt Stuttgart, 1937-1962)

Knibb, Michael A., *The Ethiopic Book of Enoch*, 2 vols (Oxford: Clarendon Press, 1978)

– *The Qumran Community*, Cambridge Commentaries on Writings of the Jewish and Christian World 200 BC to AD 200, 2 (Cambridge: Cambridge University Press, 1987)

Knox, Ronald A., *The Old Testament: Newly Translated from the Latin Vulgate* (London: Burns, Oats, and Washbourne, 1949)

Koehler, Ludwig, and Walter Baumgartner, *The Hebrew and Aramaic Lexicon of the Old Testament*, 4 vols (Leiden: Brill, 1994-99)

Koenig, Jean, 'Réouverture du débat sur la première main rédactionnelle du rouleau ancien d'Isaïe de Qumrân (1QIs^a) en 40, 7-8', *RevQ*, 11 (1983), 219-37

– *L'Herméneutique analogique du Judaïsme antique d'après les témoins textuels d'Isaïe*, VTSup, 33 (Leiden: Brill, 1982)

Kraemer, David, 'The Formation of Rabbinic Canon: Authority and Boundaries', *JBL*, 110 (1991), 613-30

Kuhl, Curt, 'Schreibereigentümlichkeiten: Bemerkungen zur Jesajarolle (DSIa)', *VT*, 2 (1952), 307-33

Kutscher, E. Y., *The Language and Linguistic Background of the Isaiah Scroll (1 Q Isa^a)*, STDJ, 6 (Leiden: Brill, 1974)

LaHaye, Tim, and Jerry B. Jenkins, *The Indwelling* (Wheaton: Tyndale, 2000)

Lamsa, George M., *The Holy Bible from Ancient Eastern Manuscripts* (Philadelphia: Holman, 1957)

Lane, William R., 'Pešer style as a reconstruction tool in 4Q Pešer Isaiah b', *RevQ*, 2 (1959-60), 281-83

Lange, Armin, 'Kriterien essenischer Texte', in Jörg Frey and Hartmut Stegemann (eds), *Brennpunkte gegenwärtiger Qumranforschung* (Paderborn: Bonifazius, forthcoming)

– 'The Essene Position on Magic and Divination', in Moshe Bernstein, Florentino García Martínez and John Kampen (eds), *Legal Texts and Legal Issues: Proceedings of the Second Meeting of the International Organization for Qumran Studies, Cambridge 1995, Published in Honour of Joseph M. Baumgarten*, STDJ, 23 (Leiden: Brill, 1997), pp. 377-435

– *Weisheit und Prädestination: Weisheitliche Urordnung und Prädestination in den Textfunden von Qumran*, STDJ, 18 (Leiden: Brill, 1995)

Leaney, A. R. C., *The Rule of Qumran and Its Meaning*, The New Testament Library (London: SCM Press; Philadelphia: Westminster, 1966)

Leiman, Sid Z., *The Canonization of Hebrew Scripture: The Talmudic and Midrashic Evidence*, Transactions of the Connecticut Academy of Arts and Sciences, 47 (Hamden, CT: Archon Books, 1976)

Lemke, Werner E., 'The Synoptic Problem in the Chronicler's History', *HTR*, 58 (1965), 349-63

Bibliography

Levenson, Jon D., *Esther* (Louisville, KY: Westminster/John Knox Press, 1997)

– *The Hebrew Bible, the Old Testament, and Historical Criticism* (Louisville, KY: Westminster/John Knox Press, 1993)

Lewis, Jack P., 'What Do We Mean By Jabneh?', *Journal of Bible and Religion*, 32 (1964), 125-32

Lichtenberger, Hermann, *Studien zum Menschenbild in Texten der Qumrangemeinde*, Studien zur Umwelt des Neuen Testaments, 15 (Göttingen: Vandenhoeck & Ruprecht, 1980)

Lieberman, Saul, *Hellenism in Jewish Palestine*, Texts and Studies of the Jewish Theological Seminary of America, 18, 2nd edn (New York: Jewish Theological Seminary of America, 1962)

Lim, Timothy H., 'The Chronology of the Flood Story in a Qumran Text (4Q252)', *JJS*, 43 (1992), 288-98

– 'The Qumran Scrolls, Multilingualism and Biblical Interpretation', in John J. Collins, and Robert Kugler (eds), *Aspects of the Religion of the Dead Sea Scrolls* (Grand Rapids, MI: Eerdmans, 2000), pp. 57-73

– , and others (eds), *The Dead Sea Scrolls in Their Historical Context* (Edinburgh: T&T Clark, 2000) [=*DSSTHC*]

– *Holy Scripture in the Qumran Commentaries and Pauline Letters* (Oxford: Clarendon Press, 1997)

Loewinger, Samuel, 'New Corrections to the Variae Lectiones of O. Eissfeldt', *VT*, 4 (1954), 80-87

– 'The Variants of DSI II', *VT*, 4 (1954), 155-63

Lübbe, John, 'Certain Implications of the Scribal Process of 4QSam^c', *RevQ*, 14 (1989), 255-65

Maier, Johann, *Die Qumran-Essener: Die Texte vom Toten Meer*, vol. 2: *Die Texte der Höhle 4*, Uni-Taschenbücher, 1863 (München and Basel: Ernst Reinhardt, 1995)

– *Die Qumran-Essener: Die Texte vom Toten Meer*, vol. 1: *Einführung, Zeitrechnung, Register und Bibliographie*, Uni-Taschenbücher, 1916 (München and Basel: Ernst Reinhardt, 1996)

Mansoor, Menahem, 'The Thanksgiving Hymns and the Massoretic Text (Part II)', *RevQ*, 3 (1961), 387-94

Maori, Yeshayahu, *The Peshitta Version of the Pentateuch and Early Jewish Exegesis* (Jerusalem: Magnes, 1995)

Margolis, M. L., 'How the Song of Songs Entered the Canon', in W. H. Schoff (ed.), *The Song of Songs: A Symposium* (Philadelphia: JPS, 1924), pp. 9-17

– *The Hebrew Scriptures in the Making* (Philadelphia: Jewish Publication Society, 1922)

Martin, Malachi, *The Scribal Character of the Dead Sea Scrolls*, 2 vols, Bibliotèque du Muséon, 44 and 45 (Louvain: Publications Universitaires, 1958)

Martone, Corrado, *La 'Regola della Comunité': Edizione critica*, Quaderni di Henoch, 8 (Torino: Zamorani, 1995)

Mathews, K. A., 'The Background of the Paleo-Hebrew Texts at Qumran', in Carol L. Meyers and M. O'Connor (eds), *The Word of the Lord Shall Go Forth: Essays in Honor of David Noel Freedman in Celebration of His Sixtieth Birthday*, ASOR Special Volume Series, 1 (Winona Lake, IN: Eisenbrauns, 1983), pp. 549-68

McCarter, P. Kyle, Jr., *1 Samuel: A New Translation with Introduction, Notes & Commentary*, Anchor Bible, 8 (New York: Doubleday, 1980)

McKenzie, Steven L., *The Chronicler's Use of the Deuteronomistic History*, HSM, 33 (Atlanta, GA: Scholars Press, 1985)

McLean, Mark D., *The Use and Development of Paleo-Hebrew in the Hellenistic and Roman Periods* (doctoral diss., Harvard University, 1982)

Metso, Sarianna, 'The Primary Results of the Reconstruction of 4QS^e', *JJS*, 44 (1993), 303-8

– 'The Use of Old Testament Quotations in the Qumran Community Rule', in *QONT*, pp. 217-31

– *The Textual Development of the Qumran Community Rule*, STDJ, 21 (Leiden: Brill, 1997)

Milik, J. T., 'Les modèles araméens du livre d'Esther dans la Grotte 4 de Qumrân', *RevQ*, 15 (1992), 321-99

Bibliography

- 'Milkî-ṣedeq et Milkî-reša' dans les anciens écrits juifs et chrétiens', *JJS*, 23 (1972), 95-144
- 'Numérotation des feuilles des rouleaux dans le scriptorium de Qumrân', *Sem*, 27 (1977), 75-81
- with the Collaboration of Matthew Black, *The Books of Enoch: Aramaic Fragments of Qumrân Cave 4* (Oxford: Clarendon Press, 1976)

Molin, Georg, 'Der Habakukkommentar von 'En Fešḫa in der alttestamentlichen Wissenschaft', *Theologische Zeitschrift*, 8 (1952), 340-57

Morrow, Francis James, *The Text of Isaiah at Qumran* (doctoral diss., Washington, DC: Catholic University of America, 1973)

Muilenburg, James, 'Fragments of Another Qumran Isaiah Scroll', *BASOR*, 135 (1954), 28-32

Muraoka, Takamitsu, 'Hebrew', in *EDSS*, I, pp. 340-45

Murphy-O'Connor, Jérôme, 'La genèse littéraire de la *Règle de la Communauté*', *RB*, 76 (1969), 528-49

Neusner, Jacob, 'Accommodating Mishnah to Scripture in Judaism: The Uneasy Union and its Offspring', *Michigan Quarterly Review*, 22 (1983), 465-79
- 'Mishnah and Messiah', in Jacob Neusner, William Scott Green and Ernest S. Frerichs (eds), *Judaisms and Their Messiahs at the Turn of the Christian Era* (Cambridge: Cambridge University Press, 1987), pp. 265-82
- *Early Rabbinic Judaism: Historical Studies in Religion, Literature and Art*, Studies in Judaism in Late Antiquity, 13 (Leiden: Brill, 1975)
- *Oral Tradition in Judaism: The Case of the Mishnah*, The Albert Bates Lord Studies in Oral Tradition, 1, Garland Reference Library of the Humanities, 764 (New York: Garland, 1987)

New, David S., 'The Confusion of *taw* with *waw-nun* in Reading 1QIsaᵃ 29:13', *RevQ*, 15 (1992), 609-10

Newman, Barclay M., Jr., 'Some Hints on Solving Textual Problems', *The Bible Translator*, 33 (1982), 430-35

Newsom, Carol A., '"Sectually Explicit" Literature from Qumran', in William Henry Propp, Baruch Halpern and David Noel Freedman (eds), *The Hebrew Bible and its Interpreters*, Biblical and Judaic Studies from The University of California, San Diego, 1 (Winona Lake, IN: Eisenbrauns, 1990), pp. 167-87
- '4Q378 and 4Q379: An Apocryphon of Joshua', in Heinz-Josef Fabry, Armin Lange and Hermann Lichtenberger (eds), *Qumranstudien: Vorträge und Beiträge der Teilnehmer des Qumranseminars auf dem internationalen Treffen der Society of Biblical Literature, Münster, 25.-26. Juli 1993*, Schriften des Institutum Judaicum Delitzschianum, 4 (Göttingen: Vandenhoeck & Ruprecht, 1996), pp. 35-85
- 'The "Psalms of Joshua" from Qumran Cave 4', *JJS*, 39 (1988), 56-73

Nickelsburg, George W. E., 'The Bible Rewritten and Expanded', in Michael E. Stone (ed.), *Jewish Writings of the Second Temple Period: Apocrypha, Pseudepigrapha, Qumran Sectarian Writings, Philo, Josephus*, Compendia Rerum Iudaicarum ad Novum Testamentum, II/2 (Assen: Van Gorcum; Philadelphia: Fortress Press, 1984), pp. 89-156

Niditch, Susan, and Robert Doran, 'The Success Story of the Wise Courtier: A Formal Approach', *JBL*, 96 (1977), 179-93

Noth, M., 'Eine Bemerkung zur Jesajarolle vom Toten Meer', *VT*, 1 (1951), 224-26

Nyberg, H. S., 'Das textkritische Problem des Alten Testaments am Hoseabuche demonstriert', *ZAW*, 52 (1934), 241-54

Nysse, Richard W., 'An Analysis of the Greek Witnesses to the Text of the Lament of David', in Emanuel Tov (ed.), *The Hebrew and Greek Texts of Samuel: 1980 Proceedings IOSCS – Vienna* (Jerusalem: Academon, 1980), pp. 69-104

Ohler, Annemarie, *Studying the Old Testament from Tradition to Canon*, trans. by David Cairns (Edinburgh: T&T Clark, 1985)

Opfell, Olga S., *The King James Bible Translators* (Jefferson, NC and London: McFarland, 1982)

Oppenheim, A. Leo, *Ancient Mesopotamia: Portrait of a Dead Civilization*, 2ⁿᵈ edn (Chicago: University of

Bibliography

Chicago Press, 1977)

Orlinsky, Harry M., 'Studies in the St. Mark's Isaiah Scroll', *JNES*, 11 (1952), 153-56; *JJS*, 2 (1950-51), 151-54; *JQR*, 43 (1952-53), 329-40; *IEJ*, 4 (1954), 5-8; and *HUCA*, 25 (1954), 85-92; *JBL*, 69 (1950), 149-66

– *Essays in Biblical Culture and Translation* (New York: Ktav, 1974)

– 'The New Jewish Version of the Torah', *JBL*, 82 (1963), 249-64

Parker, D. C., *The Living Text of the Gospels* (Cambridge: Cambridge University Press, 1997)

Parry, Donald W., '4QSam^a (4Q51): A Preliminary Edition of 1 Samuel 25:3-31:4', in Donald W. Parry, and Eugene Ulrich, *The Provo International Conference on the Dead Sea Scrolls: Technological Innovations, New Texts and Reformulated Issues*, STDJ, 30 (Leiden: Brill, 1999), pp. 58-71

– 'Notes on Divine Name Avoidance in Scriptural Units of the Legal Texts of Qumran', in Moshe Bernstein, Florentino García Martínez and John Kampen (eds), *Legal Texts and Legal Issues: Proceedings of the Second Meeting of the International Organization for Qumran Studies, Cambridge 1995, Published in Honour of Joseph M. Baumgarten*, STDJ, 23 (Leiden: Brill, 1997), pp. 437-49

– 'The Aftermath of Abner's Murder', *Textus*, 20 (2000), 83-96

– , and Elisha Qimron (eds), *The Great Isaiah Scroll (1QIsa^a): A New Edition*, STDJ, 32 (Leiden: Brill, 1999)

Penna, Angelo, 'La Volgata e il manoscritto 1QIs^a', *Bib*, 38 (1957), 381-95

Perles, Felix, *Analekten zur Textkritik des Alten Testaments* (München: Ackermann, 1895)

Pfann, Stephen J., '4QDaniel^d (4Q115): a Preliminary Edition with Critical Notes', *RevQ*, 17 (1996), 37-71

– 'The Aramaic Text and Language of Daniel and Ezra in the Light of Some Manuscripts from Qumran', *Textus*, 16 (1991), 127-37

Pietersma, Albert, *The Apocryphon of Jannes and Jambres the Magicians*, Religions in the Graeco-Roman World, 119 (Leiden: Brill, 1994)

Pope, Marvin H., 'Bible, Euphemism and Dysphemism in the', in *ABD*, I, pp. 720-25

Pouilly, J., *La Règle de la Communauté de Qumrân: Son evolution littéraire*, Cahiers de la Revue Biblique, 17 (Paris: Gabalda, 1976)

Puech, Émile, 'Fragment d'un Rouleau de la Genèse provenant du Désert de Juda (Gen. 33, 18-34, 3)', *RevQ*, 10 (1980), 163-66

– 'Qumrân et le texte de l'Ancien Testament', in A. Lemaire and M. Saebø (eds), *Congress Volume Oslo 1998*, VTSup, 80 (Leiden: Brill, 2000), pp. 437-64

Pulikottil, Paulson U., *Transmission of Biblical Texts in Qumran: The Case of the Large Isaiah Scroll 1QIsa^a*, JSPSup, 34 (Sheffield: Sheffield Academic Press, 2001)

Qimron, E., E. Y. Kutscher, *The Language and Linguistic Background of the Isaiah Scroll (1QIsa^a): Indices and Corrections*, STDJ, 6A (Leiden: Brill, 1979)

– 'The Text of CDC', in Magen Broshi (ed.), *The Damascus Document Reconsidered* (Jerusalem: The Israel Exploration Society, The Shrine of the Book, Israel Museum, 1992), pp. 9-49

– , and James H. Charlesworth (with an Appendix by F. M. Cross), 'Cave IV Fragments Related to the Rule of the Community (4Q255-264 = 4QS MSS A-J)', in James H. Charlesworth, and others (eds), *The Dead Sea Scrolls: Hebrew, Aramaic, and Greek Texts With English Translations*, I: *Rule of the Community and Related Documents* (Tübingen: Mohr-Siebeck; Louisville: Westminster John Knox, 1994), pp. 53-103

– *The Hebrew of the Dead Sea Scrolls*, HSS, 29 (Atlanta, GA: Scholars Press, 1986)

Rabin, C., 'The Dead Sea Scrolls and the History of the O.T. Text', *JTS*, new series, 6 (1955), 174-82

– , S. Talmon, and E. Tov, (eds) *The Hebrew University Bible: The Book of Jeremiah* (Jerusalem: Magnes, 1997)

Rad, Gerhard von, *The Problem of the Hexateuch and Other Essays*, trans. by E. W. Trueman Dicken (London: SCM Press, 1966)

Bibliography

Reeves, John C., *Jewish Lore in Manichaean Cosmogony: Studies in the* Book of Giants *Traditions*, Monographs of the Hebrew Union College, 14 (Cincinnati: Hebrew Union College Press, 1992)

Rhodes, Erroll F., and Liana Lupas (eds), *The Translators to the Readers* (New York: American Bible Society, 1997)

Richards, Kent H., 'A Note on the Bisection of Isaiah', *RevQ*, 5 (1965), 257-58

Rodrigue-Shwartzwald, Ora and Michael Sokoloff, *A Hebrew Dictionary of Linguistics and Philology* (Even-Yehuda: Reches, 1992)

Rofé, Alexander, 'The Acts of Nahash according to 4QSamᵃ', *IEJ*, 32 (1982), 129-33

– 'The Editing of the Book of Joshua in the Light of 4QJoshᵃ', in *NQTS*, pp. 73-80

– 'The End of the Book of Joshua According to the Septuagint', *Henoch*, 4 (1982), 17-36

Rösel, Martin, 'The Text-Critical Value of Septuagint-Genesis', *BIOSCS*, 31 (1998), 62-70

– *Übersetzung als Vollendung der Auslegung. Studien zur Genesis-Septuaginta*, BZAW, 223 (Berlin: de Gruyter, 1994)

Rosenbloom, Joseph R., *The Dead Sea Isaiah Scroll—A Literary Analysis: A Comparison with the Masoretic Text and the Biblia Hebraica* (Eerdmans: Grand Rapids, 1970)

Rosenmüller, E. F. C., *Handbuch für die Literatur der Biblischen Kritik und Exegese*, 4 vols (Göttingen: Vandenhoeck & Ruprecht, 1797-1800)

Rosenthal, Franz, *A Grammar of Biblical Aramaic*, Porta Linguarum Orientalium, Neue Serie, 5, 6ᵗʰ edn (Wiesbaden: Harrassowitz, 1995)

Rosenzweig, Franz, *Kleinere Schriften* (Berlin: Schocken, 1937)

Rost, Leonhard, *Die Damaskusschrift neu bearbeitet*, Kleine Texte für Vorlesungen und Übungen, 167 (Berlin: de Gruyter, 1933)

Rubinstein, Arie, 'Formal Agreement of parallel Clauses in the Isaiah Scroll', *VT*, 4 (1954), 316-21

– 'Isaiah LII 14 – מִשְׁחַת – and the DSIa Variant', *Bib*, 35 (1954), 475-79

– 'Isaiah lvii 17 – וָאֶקְצֹף הַסְתֵּר and the DSIa Variant', *VT*, 4 (1954), 200-201

– 'Notes on the Use of the Tenses in the Variant Readings of the Isaiah Scroll', *VT*, 3 (1953), 92-95

– 'The Theological Aspect of Some Variant Readings in the Isaiah Scroll', *JJS*, 6 (1955), 187-200

Ryle, Herbert Edward, *The Canon of the Old Testament* (London: Macmillan, 1892)

Saldarini, Anthony J., 'Sectarianism', in *EDSS*, II, pp. 853-57

Sanders, E. P., *Judaism: Practice and Belief 63 BCE–66 CE* (London: SCM Press; Philadelphia: Trinity Press International, 1992)

Sanders, James A., 'Adaptable for Life: The Nature and Function of Canon', in Frank Moore Cross, Werner E. Lemke and Patrick D. Miller, Jr., (eds), *Magnalia Dei: The Mighty Acts of God: Essays on the Bible and Archaeology in Memory of G. Ernest Wright* (New York: Doubleday, 1976), pp. 531-60

– '"Spinning" the Bible', *BR*, 14/3 (1998), pp. 22-29, 44-45

– 'Canon', in *ABD*, I, pp. 837-52

– 'Text and Canon: Concepts and Method', *JBL*, 98 (1979), 5-29

– 'The Scrolls and the Canonical Process', in *DSSAFY*, II, pp. 1-23

– *Canon and Community* (Philadelphia: Fortress Press, 1984)

– *From Sacred Story to Sacred Text* (Philadelphia: Fortress Press, 1987)

Sanderson, Judith E., *An Exodus Scroll from Qumran: 4QpaleoExodᵐ and the Samaritan Tradition*, HSS, 30 (Atlanta: Scholars Press, 1986)

Sandmel, Samuel, 'On Canon', *CBQ*, 28 (1966), 203-7

Sawyer, John F. A., *Sacred Languages and Sacred Texts* (London and New York: Routledge, 1999)

– 'The Qumran Reading of Isaiah 6. 13', *Annual of the Swedish Theological Institute*, 3 (1964), 111-13

Bibliography

Scanlin, Harold P., ' "...According to the Traditional Hebrew Text" as a Translation Principle in *Tanakh*', in Roger L. Omanson (ed.), *I Must Speak to You Plainly* (Carlisle: Paternoster, 2000), pp. 23-37

– *The Dead Sea Scrolls and Modern Translations of the Old Testament* (Wheaton, IL: Tyndale House, 1993)

Schäfer, Peter, 'Die sogenannte Synode von Jabne. Zur Trennung von Juden und Christen im ersten/zweiten Jh. n. Chr. II. Der Abschluss des Kanons', *Judaica*, 31 (1975), 116-24

Schechter, S., 'The Quotations from Ecclesiasticus in Rabbinic Literature', *Jewish Quarterly Review*, old series, 3 (1891), 682-706

– *Documents of Jewish Sectaries. 1. Fragments of a Zadokite Work: Edited from Hebrew Manuscripts in the Cairo Genizah Collection Now in the Possession of the University Library, Cambridge, and Provided with an English Translation, Introduction and Notes* (Cambridge: Cambridge University Press, 1910; repr. New York: Ktav, 1970)

Schiffman, Lawrence H., 'The Septuagint and the Temple Scroll: Shared "Halakhic" Variants', in *SSCW*, pp. 277-97

– , and James C. VanderKam (eds), *Encyclopedia of the Dead Sea Scrolls*, 2 vols (Oxford: Oxford University Press, 2000) [=*EDSS*]

– , and others (eds), *The Dead Sea Scrolls: Fifty Years After Their Discovery: Proceedings of the Jerusalem Congress, July 20-25, 1997* (Jerusalem: IES, 2000)

– *From Text to Tradition: A History of Second Temple and Rabbinic Judaism* (Hoboken, NJ: Ktav, 1991)

– *The Halakhah at Qumran*, Studies in Judaism in Late Antiquity, 16 (Leiden: Brill, 1975)

Schniedewind, William M., 'Qumran Hebrew as an Antilanguage', *JBL*, 118 (1999), 235-52

Schuller, Eileen M., 'The Psalm of 4Q372 1 Within the Context of Second Temple Prayer', *CBQ*, 54 (1992), 67-79

– *Non-Canonical Psalms from Qumran: A Pseudepigraphic Collection*, HSS, 28 (Atlanta, GA: Scholars Press, 1986)

Schürer, Emil, *The History of the Jewish People in the Age of Jesus Christ (175 B.C.-A.D. 135)*: A new English version revised and edited by Geza Vermes, Fergus Millar and Martin Goodman (Edinburgh: T&T Clark, 1986)

Schwarz, Ottilie J. R., *Der erste Teil der Damaskusschrift und das Alte Testament* (Lichtland/Diest, 1965)

Seeligmann, I. L., 'Δεῖξαι αὐτῷ φῶς', (Heb. with Eng. summ.), *Tarbiz*, 27 (1958), 127-41

Segal, M., '4Qreworked Pentateuch or 4QPentateuch?', in Lawrence H. Schiffman, and others (eds), *The Dead Sea Scrolls: Fifty Years After Their Discovery: Proceedings of the Jerusalem Congress, July 20-25, 1997* (Jerusalem: IES, 2000), pp. 391-99

– 'Biblical Exegesis in 4Q158: Techniques and Genre', *Textus*, 19 (1998), 45-62

Segert, Stanislav, 'Zur Habakuk-Rolle aus dem Funde vom Toten Meer I-IV', *Archiv Orientální*, 21 (1953), 218-39; 22 (1954), 99-113, 444-59; 23 (1955), 178-83, 364-73 and 575-619

Shaked, Shaul, 'Qumran, Some Iranian Connections', in Ziony Zevit, Seymour Gitin and Michael Sokoloff (eds), *Solving Riddles and Untying Knots: Biblical, Epigraphic, and Semitic Studies in Honor of Jonas C. Greenfield* (Winona Lake, IN: Eisenbrauns, 1995), pp. 277-81

Shemesh, Aharon, 'Scriptural Interpretations in the Damascus Document and Their Parallels in Rabbinic Midrash', in Joseph M. Baumgarten, Esther G. Chazon, and Avital Pinnick (eds), *The Damascus Document: A Centennial of Discovery. Proceedings of the Third International Symposium of the Orion Center for the Study of the Dead Sea Scrolls and Associated Literature, 4-8 February 1998*, STDJ, 34 (Leiden: Brill, 2000), pp. 161-75

Shenkel, James Donald, *Chronology and Recensional Development in the Greek Text of Kings*, HSM, 1 (Cambridge, MA: Harvard University Press, 1968)

Bibliography

Sinclair, Lawrence A., 'Hebrew Text of the Qumran Micah Pesher and Textual Traditions of the Minor Prophets', *RevQ*, 11 (1983), 253-63

Skehan, P. W., 'Qumran, IV Littérature de Qumran: – A. Textes bibliques', in L. Pirot and others (eds), *Dictionnaire de la Bible: Supplément,* vol. IX (Paris: Letouzey & Ané, 1979), pp. 805-22

– 'The Qumran Manuscripts and Textual Criticism', in P. A. H. de Boer (ed.), *Volume du Congrès: Strasbourg 1956*, VTSup, 4 (Leiden: Brill, 1957), pp. 148-58

– 'The Biblical Scrolls from Qumran and the Text of the Old Testament', *BA*, 28 (1965), 87-100

– 'The Period of the Biblical Texts from Khirbet Qumrân', *CBQ,* 19 (1957), 435-40

– 'The Text of Isaias at Qumrân', *CBQ,* 17 (1955), 158-63

Soisalon-Soininen, Ilmari, 'Zurück zur Hebraismenfrage', in Detlef Fraenkel, Udo Quast and John Wm Wevers (eds), *Studien zur Septuaginta – Robert Hanhart zu Ehren. Aus Anlaß seiner 65. Geburtstages,* Mitteilungen des Septuaginta-Unternehmens, 20, Abhandlungen der Akademie der Wissenschaften in Göttingen, Philologisch-Historische Klasse, Folge 3, 190 (Göttingen: Vandenhoeck & Ruprecht, 1990), pp. 35-51

Southwood, Charles H., 'The problematic *hᵃḏûrîm* of Isaiah XLV 2', *VT*, 25 (1975), 801-2

Steck, Odil Hannes, 'Der Kanon des hebräischen Alten Testaments: Historische Materialien für eine ökumenische Perspektive', in Jan Rohls and Gunther Wenz (eds), *Vernunft des Glaubens: Wissenschaftliche Theologie und kirchliche Lehre, Festschrift zum 60. Geburtstag von Pannenberg* (Göttingen: Vandenhoeck & Ruprecht, 1988), pp. 231-52

– *Studien zu Tritojesaja*, BZAW, 203 (Berlin: de Gruyter, 1991)

Stegemann, Hartmut, 'More identified Fragments of *4QDᵈ (4Q269)*', *RevQ*, 18 (1998), 497-509

– 'Towards Physical Reconstructions of the Qumran Damascus Document Scrolls', in Joseph M. Baumgarten, Esther G. Chazon, and Avital Pinnick (eds), *The Damascus Document: A Centennial of Discovery. Proceedings of the Third International Symposium of the Orion Center for the Study of the Dead Sea Scrolls and Associated Literature, 4-8 February 1998,* STDJ, 34 (Leiden: Brill, 2000), pp. 177-200

– 'Weitere Stücke von 4Q p Psalm 37, von 4Q Patriarchal Blessings und Hinweis auf eine unedierte Handschrift aus Höhle 4Q mit Exzerpten aus dem Deuteronomium', *RevQ*, 6 (1967), 193-227

– *Die Essener, Qumran, Johannes der Täufer und Jesus: Ein Sachbuch* (Freiburg: Herder, 1994)

– *Rekonstruktion der Hodajot: Ursprüngliche Gestalt und kritisch bearbeiteter Text der Hymnenrolle aus Höhle 1 von Qumran* (Diss., Heidelberg, 1963)

Stendahl, Krister, *The School of Matthew and its Use of the Old Testament*, Acta Seminarii Neotestamentici Upsaliensis, 20 (Lund: Gleerup, 1954)

Steudel, Annette, 'Testimonia', in *EDSS*, II, pp. 936-38

– *Der Midrasch zur Eschatologie aus der Qumrangemeinde (4QMidrEschatᵃ˙ᵇ)*, STDJ, 13 (Leiden: Brill, 1994)

Stipp, Hermann Josef, 'Das Verhältnis von Textkritik und Literarkritik in neueren alttestamentlichen Veröffentlichungen', *Biblische Zeitschrift*, Neue Folge, 34 (1990), 16-37

Strugnell, John, 'Notes en marge du volume V des "Discoveries in the Judaean Desert of Jordan"', *RevQ*, 7 (1970), 163-276

Stuckenbruck, Loren T., *The Book of Giants from Qumran* (Tübingen: Mohr-Siebeck, 1997)

Sukenik, E. L., (ed.), *The Dead Sea Scrolls of the Hebrew University* (Jerusalem: Magnes, 1955)

Sundberg, Albert C., Jr., *The Old Testament of the Early Church*, Harvard Theological Studies, 20 (Cambridge, MA: Harvard University Press; London: Oxford University Press, 1964)

Sutcliffe, Edmund F., 'The First Fifteen Members of the Qumran Community: A Note on 1QS 8:1ff.', *JSS*, 4 (1959), 134-38

Bibliography

Swete, Henry Barclay, *An Introduction to the Old Testament in Greek* (Cambridge: Cambridge University Press, 1914)

Talmon, Shemaryahu, 'Aspects of the Textual Transmission of the Bible in the Light of Qumran Manuscripts', *Textus*, 4 (1964), 95-132; repr. in *QHBT*, pp. 226-63

- 'Hebrew Fragments from Masada', in Shemaryahu Talmon and Yigael Yadin (eds), *Masada VI, The Yigael Yadin Excavations 1963–1965, Final Reports, Hebrew Fragments from Masada* (Jerusalem: IES, 1999), pp. 1-149

- 'Heiliges Schrifttum und Kanonische Bücher aus jüdischer Sicht—Überlegungen zur Ausbildung der Grösse "Die Schrift" im Judentum', in Martin Klopfenstein and others (eds), *Mitte der Schrift? Ein jüdisch-christliches Gespräch: Texte des Berner Symposions vom 6.-12. Januar 1985*, Judaica et Christiana, 11 (Bern: Peter Lang, 1987), pp. 45-79

- 'Oral Tradition and Written Transmission, or the Heard and the Seen Word in Judaism of the Second Temple Period', in Henry Wansbrough (ed.), *Jesus and the Oral Gospel Tradition*, JSNTSup, 64 (Sheffield: Sheffield Academic Press, 1991), pp. 121-58

- 'Pisqah Be'emṣaᶜ Pasuq and 11QPsᵃ', *Textus*, 5 (1966), 11-21

- 'Synonymous Readings in the Textual Traditions of the Old Testament', in Chaim Rabin (ed.), *Studies in the Bible*, Scripta Hierosolymitana, 8 (Jerusalem: Magnes, 1961), pp. 335-83

- 'Textual Criticism: The Ancient Versions', in Andrew D. H. Mayes, (ed.), *Text in Context: Essays by Members of the Society for Old Testament Study* (Oxford: Oxford University Press, 2000), pp. 141-70

- 'The Community of the Renewed Covenant: Between Judaism and Christianity', in *CRC*, pp. 3-24

- 'The Emergence of Institutionalized Prayer in Israel in the Light of the Qumrân Literature', in M. Delcor (ed.), *Qumrân: sa piété, sa théologie et son milieu*, Bibliotheca Ephemeridum Theologicarum Lovaniensium, 46 (Leuven: Leuven University Press, 1978), pp. 265-84; enlarged version repr. in S. Talmon (ed.), *The World of Qumran From Within*, (Jerusalem: Magnes, 1989), pp. 200-43

- 'The Old Testament Text', in P. R. Ackroyd and C. F. Evans (eds), *The Cambridge History of the Bible*. I: *From the Beginnings to Jerome*, (Cambridge: Cambridge University Press, 1970), pp. 159-99 (repr. in *QHBT*, pp. 1-41)

- 'The Textual Study of the Bible - A New Outlook', in *QHBT*, pp. 321-400

- 'Was the Book of Esther Known at Qumran?', *DSD*, 2 (1995), 249-67

- *King, Cult and Calendar in Ancient Israel: Collected Studies* (Jerusalem: Magnes, 1986)

- *Literary Studies in the Hebrew Bible: Form and Content: Collected Studies* (Jerusalem: Magnes; Leiden: Brill, 1993)

- *The World of Qumran from Within: Collected Studies* (Jerusalem: Magnes; Leiden: Brill, 1989)

Teicher, J. L., 'The Christian Interpretation of the Sign x in the Isaiah Scroll', *VT*, 5 (1955), 189-98

Tertel, H. Jürgen, *Text and Transmission: An Empirical Model for Literary Development of Old Testament Narratives*, BZAW, 221 (Berlin: de Gruyter, 1994)

Thackeray, H. St. J., 'The Greek Translators of the Four Books of Kings', *JTS*, 8 (1907), 262-78

Thenius, O., *Die Bücher Samuels* (Leipzig: Hirzel, 1842)

Thuesen, Peter, 'The Leather-Bound Shrine in Every Home', *Books and Culture*, March/April 2000, 20-22

Tov, Emanuel, 'Further Evidence for the Existence of a Qumran Scribal School', in Lawrence H. Schiffman, and others (eds), *The Dead Sea Scrolls: Fifty Years After Their Discovery: Proceedings of the Jerusalem Congress, July 20-25, 1997* (Jerusalem: IES, 2000), pp. 199-216

- 'The "Temple Scroll" and Old Testament Textual Criticism', *ErIsr*, 16 (Archaeological, Historical and Geographical Studies (Harry M. Orlinsky Volume, 1982; Jerusalem: IES, 1982), Heb. with Eng. Summary, 100-111

- 'A Modern Textual Outlook Based on the Qumran Scrolls', *HUCA*, 53 (1982), 11-27

Bibliography

- 'A Qumran Origin for the Masada Non-biblical Texts?', *DSD*, 7 (2000), 57-73
- 'Biblical Texts as Reworked in Some Qumran Manuscripts with Special Attention to 4QRP and 4QParaGen-Exod', in *CRC*, pp. 111-34
- 'Die biblischen Handschriften aus der Wüste Juda – Eine neue Synthese', in Ulrich Dahmen, Armin Lange and Hermann Lichtenberger (eds), *Die Textfunde vom Toten Meer und der Text der Hebräischen Bibel* (Neukirchen-Vluyn: Neukirchner Verlag, 2000), pp. 1-34
- 'Excerpted and Abbreviated Biblical Texts from Qumran', *RevQ*, 16 (1995), 581-600
- 'Groups of Biblical Texts Found at Qumran', in Devorah Dimant and Lawrence H. Schiffman (eds), *A Time to Prepare the Way in the Wilderness: Papers on the Qumran Scrolls by Fellows of the Institute for Advanced Studies of the Hebrew University, Jerusalem, 1989–1990*, STDJ, 16 (Leiden: Brill, 1995), pp. 85-102
- 'Hebrew Biblical Manuscripts from the Judaean Desert: Their Contribution to Textual Criticism', *JJS*, 39 (1988), 5-37
- 'Rewritten Bible Compositions and Biblical Manuscripts, with Special Attention to the Samaritan Pentateuch', *DSD*, 5 (1998), 334-54
- 'Scribal Markings in the Texts from the Judean Desert', in Donald W. Parry, and Stephen D. Ricks (eds), *Current Research and Technological Developments on the Dead Sea Scrolls: Conference on the Texts from the Judean Desert, Jerusalem, 30 April 1995*, STDJ, 20 (Leiden: Brill, 1996), pp. 41-77
- 'Scribal Practices Reflected in the Documents from the Judean Desert and in the Rabbinic Literature: A Comparative Study', in Michael V. Fox and others (eds), *Texts, Temples, and Traditions: A Tribute to Menahem Haran* (Winona Lake, IN: Eisenbrauns, 1996), pp. 383-403
- 'Scribal Practices Reflected in the Paleo-Hebrew Texts from the Judean Desert', *Scripta Classica Israelica*, 15 (1996), Studies in Memory of Abraham Wasserstein, vol. I, 268-73
- 'Some Notes on a Generation of Qumran Studies (by Frank M. Cross): Reply by Emanuel Tov', in *MQC*, I, pp. 15-21
- '*Tefillin* of Different Origin from Qumran?', in Yair Hoffman and Frank H. Polak, *A Light for Jacob, Studies in the Bible and the Dead Sea Scrolls in Memory of Jacob Shalom Licht* (Jerusalem: University of Tel Aviv, Bialik Institute, 1997), pp. 44*-54*
- 'Texts from the Judean Desert', in Patrick H. Alexander and others (eds), *The SBL Handbook of Style For Ancient Near Eastern, Biblical, and Early Christian Studies* (Peabody, MA: Hendrickson, 1999), pp. 176-233
- 'The Contribution of the Qumran Scrolls to the Understanding of the LXX', in *SSCW*, pp. 11-47
- 'The Orthography and Language of the Hebrew Scrolls Found at Qumran and the Origin of These Scrolls', *Textus*, 13 (1986), 31-57
- 'The Significance of the Texts from the Judean Desert for the History of the Text of the Hebrew Bible: A New Synthesis', in *QONT*, pp. 277-309
- 'The Socio-Religious Background of the Paleo-Hebrew Biblical Texts Found at Qumran', in Hubert Cancik, Hermann Lichtenberger and Peter Shäfer (eds), *Geschichte – Tradition – Reflexion, Festschrift für Martin Hengel zum 70. Geburtstag*, 2 vols (Tübingen: Mohr-Siebeck, 1996), I: *Judentum*, 353-74
- 'The Text of Isaiah at Qumran', in Craig C. Broyles and Craig A. Evans (eds), *Writing and Reading the Scroll of Isaiah: Studies of an Interpretative Tradition*, 2 vols, FIOTL, I, 1 and 2; VTSup, 70, 1 and 2 (Leiden: Brill, 1997), II, pp. 481-89
- 'The Textual Affiliations of 4QSam^a', *JSOT*, 14 (1979), 37-53
- 'The Textual Base of the Corrections in the Biblical Texts Found at Qumran', in D. Dimant and U. Rappaport (eds), *The Dead Sea Scrolls—Forty Years of Research*, STDJ, 10 (Jerusalem: Magnes; Leiden: Brill, 1992), pp. 299-314

Bibliography

- 'The Textual Basis of Modern Translations of the Hebrew Bible: The Argument against Eclecticism', *Textus*, 20 (2000), 193-211
- 'The Textual Status of 4Q364-367 (4QPP)', in *MQC*, I, pp. 43-82
- 'Three Manuscripts (Abbreviated Texts?) of Canticles from Qumran Cave 4', *JJS*, 46 (1995), 88-111
- , and Stephen J. Pfann (eds), *Companion Volume to the Dead Sea Scrolls Microfiche Edition*, 2nd edn (Leiden: Brill and IDC, 1995)
- , and Stephen J. Pfann (eds), *The Dead Sea Scrolls on Microfiche: A Comprehensive Facsimile Edition of the Texts from the Judean Desert* (Leiden: Brill and IDC, 1993)
- *Textual Criticism of the Hebrew Bible* (Assen/Maastricht: Van Gorcum; Minneapolis: Fortress Press, 1992); 2nd edn (Minneapolis: Augsburg Fortress, 2001) [=*TCHB*]
- *The Text-Critical Use of the Septuagint in Biblical Research*, 2nd edn, Jerusalem Biblical Studies, 8 (Jerusalem: Simor, 1997)

Trebolle Barrera, J., 'Textual Variants in 4QJudg^a and the Textual and Editorial History of the Book of Judges', in Florentino García Martínez (ed.), *RevQ*, 14 (1989; The Texts of Qumran and the History of the Community: Proceedings of the Groningen Congress on the Dead Sea Scrolls (20–23 August 1989), vol. 1: Biblical Texts), pp. 229-45

- , Julio C., and Luis Vegas Montaner (eds), *The Madrid Qumran Congress—Proceedings of the International Congress on the Dead Sea Scrolls—Madrid, 18–21 March, 1991*, STDJ, 11, 2 vols (Leiden: Brill, 1992) [=*MQC*]
- 'Qumran Evidence for a Biblical Standard Text and for Non-Standard and Parabiblical Texts', in *DSSTHC*, pp. 89-106

Troxel, Ronald L., 'Ἔσχατος and Eschatology in LXX-Isaiah', *BIOSCS*, 25 (1992), 18-27

Turner, E. G., *Greek Manuscripts of the Ancient World*, 2nd edn, revised and enlarged by P. J. Parsons; Institute of Classical Studies Bulletin Supplement, 46 (London: University of London, Institute of Classical Studies, 1987)

Ulrich, Eugene Charles, '4QSam^c: A Fragmentary Manuscript of 2 Samuel 14–15 from the Scribe of the *Serek Hay-yaḥad* (1QS)' BASOR, 235 (1979), 1-25

- *The Qumran Text of Samuel and Josephus*, HSM, 19 (Missoula, MT: Scholars Press, 1978)
- '4QJoshua^a and Joshua's First Altar in the Promised Land', in *NQTS*, pp. 89-104
- 'An Index of the Passages in the Biblical Manuscripts from the Judean Desert (Genesis–Kings)', *DSD*, 1 (1994), 113-29
- 'An Index of the Passages in the Biblical Manuscripts from the Judean Desert (Part 2: Isaiah–Chronicles)', *DSD*, 2 (1995), 86-107
- 'Appendix I: Index of Passages in the Biblical Scrolls', in *DSSAFY*, II, pp. 649-65
- 'Canon', in *EDSS*, I, pp. 117-20
- 'Isaiah, Book of', in *EDSS*, I, pp. 384-88
- 'Multiple Literary Editions: Reflections toward a Theory of the History of the Biblical Text', in Donald W. Parry, and Stephen D. Ricks (eds), *Current Research and Technological Developments on the Dead Sea Scrolls: Conference on the Texts from the Judean Desert, Jerusalem, 30 April 1995*, STDJ, 20 (Leiden: Brill, 1996), pp. 78-105
- 'Multiple Literary Editions: Reflections Toward a Theory of the History of the Biblical Text', in Eugene Ulrich, *The Dead Sea Scrolls and the Origins of the Bible* (Leiden: Brill; Grand Rapids: Eerdmans, 1999), pp. 99-120
- 'Pluriformity in the Biblical Text, Text Groups, and Questions of Canon', in *MQC*, I, pp. 23-41
- 'The Biblical Scrolls from Qumran Cave 4: An Overview and a Progress Report on Their Publication', *RevQ*, 14 (1989), 207-28
- 'The Canonical Process, Textual Criticism, and Latter Stages in the Composition of the Bible', in Michael

Bibliography

Fishbane, and Emanuel Tov with the assistance of Weston W. Fields (eds), *"Sha'arei Talmon": Studies in the Bible, Qumran, and the Ancient Near East Presented to Shemaryahu Talmon* (Winona Lake, IN: Eisenbrauns, 1992), pp. 267-91

– 'The Dead Sea Scrolls and the Biblical Text', in *DSSAFY*, I, pp. 79-100

– 'The Dead Sea Scrolls and the Hebrew Scriptural Texts', in James H. Charlesworth (ed.), *The Bible and the Dead Sea Scrolls: Proceedings of the Dead Sea Scrolls Jubilee Symposium Held at Princeton Theological Seminary, November 1997*, vol. 1: *The Hebrew Bible and Qumran* (North Richland, TX: Bibal Press, forthcoming), pp. 105-33

– 'The Qumran Biblical Scrolls–The Scriptures of Late Second Temple Judaism', in *DSSTHC*, pp. 67-87

– 'The Qumran Scrolls and the Biblical Text', in Lawrence H. Schiffman, and others (eds), *The Dead Sea Scrolls: Fifty Years After Their Discovery: Proceedings of the Jerusalem Congress, July 20-25, 1997* (Jerusalem: IES, 2000), pp. 51-59

– , and James VanderKam (eds), *The Community of the Renewed Covenant: The Notre Dame Symposium on the Dead Sea Scrolls*, Christianity and Judaism in Antiquity Series, 10 (Notre Dame, IN: University of Notre Dame Press, 1994) [= *CRC*]

– , and Patrick W. Skehan, 'An Edition of 4QIsa^e, Including the Former 4Qisa^b', *RevQ*, 17 (Milik Festschrift, 1996), 23-36

– *The Dead Sea Scrolls and the Origins of the Bible* (Grand Rapids: Eerdmans; Leiden: Brill, 1999)

Urbach, Ephraim E., *The Sages - Their Concepts and Beliefs*, trans. by Israel Abrahams, 2 vols (Jerusalem: Magnes, 1975)

van der Kooij, Arie, 'The Canonization of Ancient Books Kept in the Temple of Jerusalem', in A. van der Kooij and K. van der Toorn (eds), *Canonization and Decanonization: Papers presented to the International Conference of the Leiden Institute for the Study of Religions (LISOR) held at Leiden 9-10 January 1997*, Studies in the History of Religion, 82 (Leiden: Brill, 1998), pp. 17-40

– '1QIsa^a Col. VIII, 4-11 (Isa 8, 11-18): A Contextual Approach of Its Variants', *RevQ*, 13 (1988; Mémorial Jean Carmignac), 569-81

– 'Perspectives on the Study of the Septuagint: Who are the Translators?', in Florentino García Martínez and Ed Noort (eds), *Perspectives in the Study of the Old Testament and Early Judaism: A Symposium in Honour of Adam S. van der Woude on the Occasion of his 70th Birthday*, VTSup, 73 (Leiden: Brill, 1998), pp. 214-29

– 'Textual Witnesses to the Hebrew Bible and the History of Reception: The Case of Habakkuk 1:11-12', in Ulrich Dahmen, Armin Lange and Hermann Lichtenberger (eds), *Die Textfunde vom Toten Meer und der Text der Hebräischen Bibel* (Neukirchen-Vluyn: Neukirchener Verlag, 2000), pp. 91-108

– 'Zum Verhältnis von Textkritik und Literarkritik: Überlegungen anhand einiger Beispiele', in J. A. Emerton (ed.), *Congress Volume Cambridge 1995*, VTSup, 66 (Leiden: Brill, 1997), pp. 185-202

– *Die alten Textzeugen des Jesajabuches: Ein Beitrag zur Textgeschichte des Alten Testaments*, OBO, 35 (Freiburg: Universitätsverlag; Göttingen: Vandenhoeck & Ruprecht, 1981)

– *The Oracle of Tyre: The Septuagint of Isaiah XXIII as Version and Vision*, VTSup, 71 (Leiden: Brill, 1998)

Van der Ploeg, J., 'Le Rouleau d'Habacuc de la grotte de 'Ain Fešḫa', *BO*, 8 (1951), 2-11

van der Woude, Adam S., 'Fifty years of Qumran Research', in *DSSAFY*, I, pp. 1-45

– 'Fünfzehn Jahre Qumranforschung (1974–1988)', *Theologische Rundschau*, 55 (1990), 245-307; 57 (1992), 1-57

– 'Pluriformity and Uniformity: Reflections on the Transmission of the Text of the Old Testament', in J. N. Bremmer, and F. García Martínez (eds), *Sacred History and Sacred Texts in Early Judaism: A Symposium in Honour of A.S. van der Woude*, Contributions to Biblical Exegesis and Theology, 5 (Kampen: Kok Pharos, 1992), pp. 151-69

Bibliography

VanderKam, James C., 'Authoritative Literature in the Dead Sea Scrolls', *DSD*, 5 (1998), 382-402

- 'Jubilees and Hebrew Texts of Genesis-Exodus', *Textus*, 14 (1988), 71-85
- 'The Textual Affinities of the Biblical Citations in the Genesis Apocryphon', *JBL*, 97 (1978), 45-55
- *Calendars in the Dead Sea Scrolls: Measuring Time* (London: Routledge, 1998)
- *Textual and Historical Studies in the Book of Jubilees*, HSM, 14 (Missoula, MT: Scholars Press, 1977)
- *The Dead Sea Scrolls Today* (Grand Rapids, MI: Eerdmans, 1994)

Vegas Montaner, L., 'Computer-Assisted Study of the Relation between *1QpHab* and the Ancient (mainly Greek) Biblical Versions', *RevQ*, 14 (1989-1990), pp. 307-23

Vermes, Geza, 'Biblical Proof-Texts in Qumran Literature', *JSS*, 34 (1989), 493-508

- 'Preliminary Remarks on Unpublished Fragments of the Community Rule from Qumran Cave 4', *JJS*, 42 (1991), 250-55
- , and Martin D. Goodman, *The Essenes: According to the Classical Sources*, Oxford Centre Textbooks, 1 (Sheffield: JSOT Press, 1989)
- *Scripture and Tradition in Judaism: Haggadic Studies*, Studia Post-Biblica, 4, 2nd edn (Leiden: Brill, 1973)
- *The Complete Dead Sea Scrolls in English*, 5th edn (London: Penguin, 1998)

Waard, J. de, *A Comparative Study of the Old Testament Text in the Dead Sea Scrolls and in the New Testament*, STDJ, 4 (Leiden: Brill, 1965)

Watson, Wilfred G. E., *Classical Hebrew Poetry: A Guide to its Techniques*, JSOTSup, 26 (Sheffield: JSOT Press, 1984)

Wechsler, Michael G., 'Two Para-Biblical Novellae from Qumran Cave 4: A Reevaluation of 4Q550', *DSD*, 7 (2000), 130-72

Weinfeld, Moshe, *The Organizational Pattern and the Penal Code of the Qumran Sect: A Comparison with Guilds and Religious Associations of the Hellenistic-Roman Period*, Novum Testamentum et Orbis Antiquus, 2 (Fribourg: Universitätsverlag; Göttingen: Vandenhoeck & Ruprecht, 1986)

Weiss, Raphael, 'A Comparison between the Masoretic and the Qumran Texts of Nahum III, 1-11', *RevQ*, 4 (1963), 433-39

Weitzman, M. P., *The Syriac Version of the Old Testament: An Introduction*, University of Cambridge Oriental Publications, 56 (Cambridge: Cambridge University Press, 1999)

Wellhausen, Julius, *Der Text der Bücher Samuelis* (Göttingen: Vandenhoeck und Ruprecht, 1871)

Werline, Rodney Alan, *Penitential Prayer in Second Temple Judaism: The Development of a Religious Institution*, SBL Early Judaism and Its Literature, 13 (Atlanta, GA: Scholars Press, 1998)

West, M. L., *Early Greek Philosophy and the Orient* (Oxford: Clarendon Press, 1971)

Westermann, Claus, *Genesis 1-11: A Continental Commentary*, trans. by John J. Scullion (Minneapolis: Fortress Press, 1984)

White, Sidnie Ann, 'A Comparison of the "A" and "B" Manuscripts of the Damascus Document', *RevQ*, 12 (1987), 537-53

- 'Esther: A Feminine Model for Jewish Diaspora', in Peggy L. Day (ed.), *Gender and Difference in Ancient Israel* (Minneapolis, MN: Fortress Press, 1989), pp. 161-77

Wildeboer, G., *Die Entstehung des Alttestamentlichen Kanons: Historisch-Kritische Untersuchung* (Gotha: Perthes, 1891); = *The Origin of the Canon of the Old Testament: an Historico-Critical Enquiry*, trans. by F. Risch (London: Luzac, 1895)

Williams, James B. (ed.), *From the Mind of God to the Mind of Man* (Greenville, NC and Belfast: Ambassador-Emerald International, 1999)

Wills, Lawrence M., *The Jew in the Court of the Foreign King: Ancient Jewish Court Legends*, Harvard Dissertations in Religion, 26 (Minneapolis, MN: Fortress Press, 1990)

Bibliography

- *The Jewish Novel in the Ancient World* (Ithaca: Cornell University Press, 1995)

Wise, Michael Owen, *Thunder in Gemini: And Other Essays on the History, Language and Literature of Second Temple Palestine*, JSPSup, 15 (Sheffield: JSOT Press, 1994)

Würthwein, Ernst, *Der Text des Alten Testaments*. 4. Aufl. (Stuttgart: Württembergische Bibelanstalt, 1973)

Xeravits, Géza, 'Précisions sur le texte original et le concept messianique de CD 7:13-8:1 et 19:5-14', *RevQ*, 19 (1999), 47-59

Yadin, Yigael, (ed.), *The Temple Scroll*, 3 vols (Jerusalem: IES, The Institute of Archaeology of the Hebrew University of Jerusalem, The Shrine of the Book, 1983; Hebrew, 1977)

- *Tefillin from Qumran* (Jerusalem: IES and The Shrine of the Book, 1969)

Ziegler, Joseph, 'Die Vorlage der Isaias-Septuaginta (LXX) und die Erste Isaias-Rolle von Qumran (1QIs^a)', *JBL*, 78 (1959), 34-59

INDEX OF ANCIENT TEXTS

Index of Ancient Texts

Index of Ancient Texts

Index of Ancient Texts

Index of Ancient Texts

Index of Ancient Texts

Index of Ancient Texts

Index of Ancient Texts

Index of Ancient Texts

GENERAL INDEX

General Index

General Index

General Index

General Index